ACCA

STUDY TEXT

PAPER P2

CORPORATE REPORTING (INTERNATIONAL AND UNITED KINGDOM)

BPP Learning Media is an **ACCA Approved Content Provider**. This means we work closely with ACCA to ensure this Study Text contains the information you need to pass your exam.

- **Highlight** the **most important elements** in the syllabus and the **key skills** you need
- **Signpost** how each chapter links to the syllabus and the study guide
- **Provide** lots of **exam focus points** demonstrating what is expected of you in the exam
- **Emphasise key points** in regular **fast forward summaries**
- **Test your knowledge** in **quick quizzes**
- **Examine your understanding** in our **practice question bank**
- **Reference all the important topics** in our **full index**

BPP's **Practice & Revision Kit** also supports this paper.

FOR EXAMS IN SEPTEMBER 2017, DECEMBER 2017, MARCH 2018 AND JUNE 2018

BPP LEARNING MEDIA

First edition 2007
Tenth edition January 2017

ISBN 9781 5097 0844 4
(Previous ISBN 9781 4727 4428 9)

e-ISBN 9781 5097 0987 8

British Library Cataloguing-in-Publication Data
A catalogue record for this book
is available from the British Library

Published by

BPP Learning Media Ltd
BPP House, Aldine Place
London W12 8AA

www.bpp.com/learningmedia

Printed in the United Kingdom by

Wheatons Exeter Ltd
Hennock Road
Marsh Barton
Exeter
EX2 8RP

Your learning materials, published by BPP Learning Media Ltd, are printed on paper obtained from traceable sustainable sources.

We are grateful to the Association of Chartered Certified Accountants for permission to reproduce past examination questions. The suggested solutions in the practice answer bank have been prepared by BPP Learning Media Ltd, unless otherwise stated.

BPP Learning Media is grateful to the IASB for permission to reproduce extracts from the International Financial Reporting Standards including all International Accounting Standards, SIC and IFRIC Interpretations (the Standards). The Standards together with their accompanying documents are issued by:

The International Accounting Standards Board (IASB) 30 Cannon Street, London, EC4M 6XH, United Kingdom. Email: info@ifrs.org Web: www.ifrs.org

Contents

Helping you to pass

BPP Learning Media – ACCA Approved Content Provider

As an ACCA **Approved Content Provider**, BPP Learning Media gives you the **opportunity** to use study materials reviewed by the ACCA examination team. By incorporating the examination team's comments and suggestions regarding the depth and breadth of syllabus coverage, the BPP Learning Media Study Text provides excellent, **ACCA-approved** support for your studies.

The PER alert

Before you can qualify as an ACCA member, you not only have to pass all your exams but also fulfil a three year **practical experience requirement** (PER). To help you to recognise areas of the syllabus that you might be able to apply in the workplace to achieve different performance objectives, we have introduced the '**PER alert**' feature. You will find this feature throughout the Study Text to remind you that what you are **learning to pass** your ACCA exams is **equally useful to the fulfilment of the PER requirement**.

Your achievement of the PER should now be recorded in your on-line *My Experience* record.

Tackling studying

Studying can be a daunting prospect, particularly when you have lots of other commitments. The **different features** of the Study Text, the **purposes** of which are explained fully on the **Chapter features** page, will help you whilst studying and improve your chances of **exam success**.

Developing exam awareness

Our Texts are completely **focused** on helping you pass your exam.

Our advice on **Studying P2** outlines the **content** of the paper, the **necessary skills** you are expected to be able to demonstrate and any **brought forward knowledge** you are expected to have.

Exam focus points are included within the chapters to highlight when and how specific topics were examined, or how they might be examined in the future.

Testing what you can do

Testing yourself helps you develop the skills you need to pass the exam and also confirms that you can recall what you have learnt.

We include **Questions** – lots of them – both within chapters and in the **Practice Question Bank**, as well as **Quick Quizzes** at the end of each chapter to test your knowledge of the chapter content.

Chapter features

Each chapter contains a number of helpful features to guide you through each topic.

Topic list	What you will be studying in this chapter and the relevant section numbers, together with ACCA syllabus references.

Topic list	Syllabus reference

Introduction	Puts the chapter content in the context of the syllabus as a whole.
Study Guide	Links the chapter content with ACCA guidance.
Exam Guide	Highlights how examinable the chapter content is likely to be and the ways in which it could be examined.
Knowledge brought forward from earlier studies	What you are assumed to know from previous studies/exams.
FAST FORWARD	Summarises the content of main chapter headings, allowing you to preview and review each section easily.
Examples	Demonstrate how to apply key knowledge and techniques.
Key terms	Definitions of important concepts that can often earn you easy marks in exams.
Exam focus points	When and how specific topics were examined, or how they may be examined in the future.
Formula to learn	Formulae that are not given in the exam but which have to be learnt.
PER alert	Gives you a useful indication of syllabus areas that closely relate to performance objectives in your Practical Experience Requirement (PER).
Question	Gives you essential practice of techniques covered in the chapter.
Case Study	Real world examples of theories and techniques.
Chapter Roundup	A full list of the Fast Forwards included in the chapter, providing an easy source of review.
Quick Quiz	A quick test of your knowledge of the main topics in the chapter.
Exam Question Bank	Found at the back of the Study Text with more comprehensive chapter questions. Cross referenced for easy navigation.

Studying P2

Paper P2 Corporate Reporting is a tough paper, reflecting the demands that will be made upon the professional accountant in his or her working life. At the Fundamentals level, you will have studied the essentials of financial statement preparation and analysis, including those of group accounts. At the Professional level, these essentials will be assumed knowledge. You will be required to apply them, assuming the role of a professional adviser and analyst to the management as well as the shareholders and other stakeholders.

1 What P2 is about

The P2 syllabus comprises eight main areas:

A The professional and ethical duty of the accountant
B The financial reporting framework
C Reporting the financial performance of entities
D Financial statements of groups of entities
E Specialised entities
F Implications of changes in accounting regulation on financial reporting
G The appraisal of financial performance and position of entities
H Current developments

There is, of course, some overlap between these areas. For example, if you are discussing current developments (H), you might be talking about the proposed changes to accounting for business combinations (D) and considering the implications of changes in accounting regulation (F) and perhaps even the ethical duty of the accountant to report those changes fairly and accurately (A).

2 Skills you have to demonstrate

At the Fundamentals level, the questions would be more easily categorised into syllabus areas. However, at this level you may need to demonstrate knowledge, skills and thinking from outside the syllabus area that the question seems to be about on the surface. The examination team has stated:

> Students should be capable of relating professional issues to relevant concepts and practical situations. The evaluation of alternative accounting practices and the identification and prioritisation of issues will be a key element of the paper. Professional and ethical judgement will need to be exercised, together with the integration of technical knowledge when addressing corporate reporting issues in a business context.

So the paper is not predictable. That said, clear guidance has been given. The compulsory Section A question, worth 50 marks, will always be on group accounts. It will also deal with issues in financial reporting and will be case study based. In Section B, questions could be on any area of the syllabus, but we have been told that two questions will be scenario based and one question will be an essay. You have a choice of two from three.

Increasingly, questions are discursive rather than numerical, so it is vital that you get practice at answering this type of question.

Important note for UK students

If you are sitting the UK P2 paper you will be studying under International standards and up to 20 marks will be for comparisons between International and UK GAAP. The ACCA UK Syllabus and Study Guide gives the following advice:

> International Financial Reporting Standards (IFRS) are the main accounting standards examined in the preparation of financial information. The key differences between UK GAAP and International Financial Reporting Standards are looked at on a subject by subject basis. The comparison between IFRS and UK GAAP will be based on the new UK GAAP as set out in FRSs 100-102, so the standard by standard comparisons that appeared in previous editions of this study guide are now combined in outcome C11 (d): *Discuss the key differences between the IFRS for SMEs and UK GAAP.*

This Study Text covers all the topics you need to know under International Financial Reporting Standards. An online supplement will be available at www.bpp.com/learning-media, covering the additional UK issues.

Exam technique for P2

Do not be needlessly intimidated

There is no shortcut to passing this exam. It looks very difficult indeed, and many students wonder if they will ever pass. But many do. How do they do this?

Easy marks

All the questions are demanding, but there are many easy marks to be gained. Suppose, for example, you had a consolidated statement of cash flows with a disposal, some foreign exchange complications and an impairment calculation. There will be easy marks available simply for the basic cash flow aspects, setting out the proforma, setting up your workings, presenting your work neatly. If you recognise, as you should, that the disposal needs to be taken into account, of course you will get marks for that, even if you make a mistake in the arithmetic. If you get the foreign exchange right, so much the better, but you could pass the question comfortably omitting this altogether. If you're short of time, this is what you should do.

Be ruthless in ignoring the complications

Look at the question. Within reason, if there are complications – often only worth a few marks – that you know you will not have time or knowledge to do, cross them out. It will make you feel better. Then tackle the bits you can do. This is how people pass a seemingly impossible paper.

Answer all questions and all parts of questions

The examination team frequently comments that students don't do this, so they miss easy opportunities to gain marks.

Be ruthless in allocating your time

At BPP, we have seen how very intelligent students do one almost perfect question, one averagely good and one sketchy. For a fifty mark question, the first twenty marks are the easiest to get. Then you have to push it up to what you think is thirty to get yourself a clear pass. For a twenty-five mark question, the first eight to ten marks are the easiest to get, and then you must try to push it up to fifteen.

Do your best question either first or second, and the compulsory question either first or second. The compulsory question, being on groups, will always have some easy marks available for consolidation techniques.

The exam paper

The paper will comprise two sections.

		Number of marks
Section A:	1 compulsory case study	50
Section B:	Choice of 2 from 3 questions (25 marks each)	50
		100

Time allowed: 3 hours and 15 minutes

Section A will be a scenario-based question which will include:

- The preparation of consolidated financial statements (including consolidated statements of cash flows) with adjustments on other syllabus areas
- A written part normally covering a particular accounting treatment and ethical and social issues in financial reporting.

Section B will normally include:

- Two scenario or case study-based questions (covering a range of standards and syllabus topics, one usually in the context of a particular industry)
- An essay-style discussion question, often encompassing current developments in corporate reporting, which may also include some short calculations.

Analysis of past papers – by sitting

December 2016 Sample Exam

Note. This was not the actual exam sat in June 2016, but ACCA's selection of questions from the September and December 2016 exams.

Section A

1 Consolidated SPLOCI with disposal; employee benefits

Section B

2 Functional currency; trademark; related parties
3 Bonus issue to be settled as liability or equity; classification as held for sale; 'bargain purchase' not part of a business combination
4 Materiality and IR framework; ED on statement of cash flows

June 2016 Sample Exam

Note. This was not the actual exam sat in June 2016, but ACCA's selection of questions from the March and June 2016 exams.

Section A

1 Consolidated statement of cash flows; usefulness of SOCF; ethics and intragroup loan

Section B

2 Scenario question, mainly on IFRS 13 and also IFRS 9
3 Specialised industry question set in the context of a sports organisation, covering borrowing costs, intangibles and fair value measurement
4 Move to a new IFRS; IAS 8; IAS 36; IAS 38

December 2015 Sample Exam

Note. This was not the actual exam sat in December 2015, but ACCA's selection of questions from the September and December 2015 exams.

Section A

1 Consolidated statement of financial position with foreign subsidiary; IAS 21 explanation; ethics

Section B

2 Scenario question covering IAS 38, IAS 1 and IAS 12
3 Specialised industry question set in the natural gas industry, covering IFRS 9, IFRS 11 and IAS 10
4 IFRS 15: discussion and application

June 2015

Section A

1 Consolidated statement of financial position with two acquisitions and a disposal; debt/equity distinction; ethics

Section B

2 Fair value measurement in the context of various scenarios
3 Specialised industry question set in the pharmaceutical industry, covering segment reporting, purchase of intangible in exchange for shares and research and development
4 Recognition in profit or loss versus other comprehensive income (discussion and application); integrated reporting

December 2014

Section A

1 Business combination in stages with adjustments for non-current asset held for sale and joint venture; share-based payment; ethical issue

Section B

2 Related parties; financial guarantee contracts; interest rate swap; credit risk
3 IFRS 3 and control; IAS 16 application to a scenario
4 Impairment: factors to consider and application to a scenario

June 2014

Section A

1 Consolidated statement of profit or loss and other comprehensive income with two disposals and various adjustments; fair value in IFRS; ethical issue

Section B

2 Foreign transactions (functional currency, goodwill, deferred tax and a loan)
3 Specialised industry question set in the property industry, covering revenue, interim reporting, asset held for sale, provisions and intangibles
4 Distinction between debt and equity: discussion and scenario

Analysis of past papers – by syllabus topic

The table below provides details of when each element of the syllabus has been examined and the question number and section in which each element appeared. Further details can be found in the Exam Focus Points in the relevant chapters.

Covered in Text chapter		June 2014	Dec 2014	June 2015	ACCA Sep/Dec 2015	March/ June 2016	ACCA Sep/Dec 2016
A	**THE PROFESSIONAL AND ETHICAL DUTY OF THE ACCOUNTANT**						
2	Professional behaviour and compliance with accounting standards	Q1(c)	Q1(c)	Q1(c)		Q1(c)	
2	Ethical requirements of corporate reporting and the consequences of unethical behaviour	Q1(c)	Q1(c)		Q1(c)	Q1(c)	Q1(c)
18	Social responsibility						
B	**THE FINANCIAL REPORTING FRAMEWORK**						
1	The applications, strengths and weaknesses of an accounting framework						
1	Critical evaluation of principles and practices – Revenue recognition – Substance over form issues	Q3			Q4		
C	**REPORTING THE FINANCIAL PERFORMANCE OF ENTITIES**						
10	Performance reporting			Q4	Q2	Q1(b) Q4	
42	Non-current assets – Property, plant and equipment – Intangible assets – Impairment – Investment properties – Government grants – Borrowing costs	Q1(a)	Q3, Q6	Q3		Q3 Q4 Q3	Q3(c)
	– Fair value			Q2		Q2, Q3	
7	Financial instruments	Q1, Q2, Q4	Q1, Q2, Q4		Q1(a), Q3	Q2	Q3(a)

Covered in Text chapter		June 2014	Dec 2014	June 2015	ACCA Sep/Dec 2015	March/ June 2016	ACCA Sep/Dec 2016
8	Leases						
10	Segment reporting			Q3			
4	Employee benefits	Q1(a)				Q1(a)	Q1(b), (c)
6	Income taxes	Q2				Q2	
5	Provisions, contingencies and events after the reporting period – Provisions, contingency liabilities and contingent assets – Events after the reporting period	Q3				Q3	
11	Related parties		Q2				Q2(c)
9	Share-based payment	Q1(a)				Q1(a)	
21	Reporting requirements of small and medium-sized entities						
D	**FINANCIAL STATEMENTS OF GROUPS OF ENTITIES**						
12-17	Group accounting including statements of cash flow – Complex groups – Associates – Joint ventures – Group statements of cash flows	Q3 Q1(a)	Q3		Q2 Q3	Q1(a)	Q4(b)
15	Continuing and discontinued interests – Discontinued operations – Non-current assets held for sale	Q3				Q3	Q3(b)
14	Changes in group structure – Mid year acquisitions – Disposals – Business combinations achieved in stages	Q1(a)	Q1(a)	Q1(a) Q1(a) Q1(a)	Q1(a)	Q1(a)	Q1(a)
	– Group reorganisations						

Covered in Text chapter		June 2014	Dec 2014	June 2015	ACCA Sep/Dec 2015	March/ June 2016	ACCA Sep/Dec 2016
16	Foreign transactions and entities – Foreign currency transactions – Foreign subsidiaries	 Q2 Q2			 Q1(a) Q1(b)	 Q2 Q2	
E	**SPECIALISED ENTITIES**						
20	Financial reporting in specialised, not-for-profit and public sector entities	Q3			Q3	Q3	
E2	Entity reconstructions						
F	**IMPLICATIONS OF CHANGES IN ACCOUNTING REGULATION ON FINANCIAL REPORTING**						
Throughout	The effect of changes in accounting standards on accounting systems						
18	Proposed changes to accounting standards					Q4	
G	**THE APPRAISAL OF FINANCIAL PERFORMANCE AND POSITION ENTITIES**						
10	The creation of suitable accounting policies				Q1(c)		
10	Analysis and interpretation of financial information and measurement of performance						
H	**CURRENT DEVELOPMENTS**						
18	Environmental and social reporting						
19	Convergence between national and international reporting standards						

Covered in Text chapter		June 2014	Dec 2014	June 2015	ACCA Sep/Dec 2015	March/ June 2016	ACCA Sep/Dec 2016
	Current reporting issues						
	– Conceptual Framework						
	– Disclosures in financial statements						
	– Fair value measurement			Q2		Q2, Q3	
H3	– Financial instruments	Q4				Q2	
	– Revenue recognition				Q4		
	– Provisions and measurement of financial liabilities						
	– Integrated reporting			Q4		Q1(b)	Q4(a)

Syllabus and study guide

The complete P2 syllabus and study guide (International and UK) can be found by visiting the exam resource finder on the ACCA website: www.accaglobal.com/uk/en/student/exam-support-resources.html

PART A

Regulatory and ethical framework

Financial reporting framework

1

Topic list	Syllabus reference
1 International Financial Reporting Standards (IFRSs)	A1
2 Corporate governance	C1
3 Conceptual framework	B2
4 Revenue recognition	A2, B1
5 Professional skills: guidance from the ACCA	N/A

Introduction

Welcome to the Corporate Reporting paper using International Financial Reporting Standards (IFRS). This paper is about thinking and applying your knowledge of the IFRS. Most of the standards and topics have been covered in your earlier studies. However, at the Professional level, you need to think critically about them and show an understanding of topical issues. In the exam, you will need to put yourself in the role of an adviser to a business entity, using your knowledge to give practical advice.

In the exam, you will often be required to consider the impact of proposed changes to IFRS. Any such proposals are dealt with in this Study Text within the topic to which they relate.

Study guide

		Intellectual level
A1	**Professional behaviour and compliance with accounting standards**	
(a)	Appraise the ethical and professional issues in advising on corporate reporting	3
(b)	Assess the relevance and importance of ethical and professional issues in complying with accounting standards	3
A2	**Ethical requirements of corporate reporting and the consequences of unethical behaviour**	
(a)	Appraise the potential ethical implications of professional and managerial decisions in the preparation of corporate reports	3
B1	**The applications, strengths and weaknesses of an accounting framework**	
(a)	Evaluate the valuation models adopted by standard setters	
C1	**Performance reporting**	
(a)	Prepare reports relating to corporate performance for external stakeholders	3
(b)	Discuss and apply the criteria that must be met before an entity can apply the revenue recognition model to that contract	3
(c)	Discuss and apply the five-step model which relates to revenue earned from a contract with a customer	3
B2	**Critical evaluation of principles and practices**	
(a)	Evaluate the valuation models adopted by standard setters	3
(b)	Discuss the use of an accounting framework in underpinning the production of accounting standards	3
(c)	Assess the success of such a framework in introducing rigorous and consistent accounting standards	3

Exam guide

This chapter is partly background knowledge to set the scene about the reporting framework before you look at ethical issues. It also discusses the Management Commentary and the *Conceptual Framework*.

The examiner has stated that revenue recognition is important.

1 International Financial Reporting Standards (IFRSs)

PER alert

One of the competences you need to fulfil Objective 10 of the Practical Experience Requirement (PER) is to recognise and apply the external legal and professional framework and regulations to financial reporting. You can apply the knowledge you obtain from this section of the Text to demonstrate this competence.

To date the IASB has the following standards in issue.

1.1 Current accounting standards and documents examinable at P2

The documents listed as being examinable are the latest that were issued before 1 September 2016, and will be examinable in September 2017 to June 2018. **This Study Text is for exams in September and December 2017 and March and June 2018.**

The study guide offers more detail guidance on the depth and level at which the examinable documents will be examined. The study guide should be read in conjunction with the examinable documents list.

	Title	Date issued
	International Accounting Standards (IASs) / International Financial Reporting Standards (IFRSs)	
IAS 1	Presentation of financial statements	Dec 03, rev. Sept 07 and June 11 and (amended December 2014 per Disclosure Initiative)
IAS 2	Inventories	Dec 03
IAS 7	Statement of cash flows	Dec 92
IAS 8	Accounting policies, changes in accounting estimates and errors	Dec 03
IAS 10	Events after the reporting period	Dec 03
IAS 12	Income taxes	Nov 00
IAS 16	Property, plant and equipment	Dec 03
IAS 19	Employee benefits	Nov 00, revised 2011
IAS 20	Accounting for government grants and disclosure of government assistance	Jan 95
IAS 21	The effects of changes in foreign exchange rates	Dec 03
IAS 23	Borrowing costs	Dec 93
IAS 24	Related party disclosures	Dec 03
IAS 27	Separate financial statements	Dec 03, revised 2011 and 2014
IAS 28	Investments in associates and joint ventures	Dec 03, revised 2011
IAS 32	Financial Instruments: presentation	Dec 03
IAS 33	Earnings per share	Dec 03
IAS 34	Interim financial reporting	Feb 98
IAS 36	Impairment of assets	June 98
IAS 37	Provisions, contingent liabilities and contingent assets	Sept 98
IAS 38	Intangible assets	Sept 98
IAS 40	Investment property	Dec 03
IAS 41	Agriculture	Feb 01
IFRS 1	First-time adoption of International Financial Reporting Standards	June 03
IFRS 2	Share-based payment	Feb 04
IFRS 3	Business combinations	Mar 04, revised Jan 08
IFRS 5	Non-current assets held for sale and discontinued operations	Mar 04
IFRS 7	Financial instruments: disclosures	Aug 05
IFRS 8	Operating segments	Nov 06

	Title	Date issued
IFRS 9	Financial instruments	July 14
IFRS 10	Consolidated financial statements	May 11
IFRS 11	Joint arrangements	May 11
IFRS 12	Disclosure of interests in other entities	May 11
IFRS 13	Fair value measurement	May 11
IFRS 15	Revenue from contracts with customers	May 14
IFRS 16	Leases	Jan 16
IFRS	For Small and Medium-sized Entities	July 09, amended May 2015
	Other Statements	
	Conceptual Framework for Financial Reporting	
	Practice Statement: Management Commentary	
	The International <IR> Framework	
	EDs, Discussion Papers and Other Documents	
ED	Measuring quoted investments in subsidiaries, joint ventures and associates at fair value	
ED	Classification of liabilities – proposed amendments to IAS 1	
ED	Conceptual Framework for Financial Reporting	
ED	IFRS Practice Statement: Application of Materiality in Financial Statements	

2 Corporate governance

FAST FORWARD

Corporate governance has been important in recent years and in the current syllabus it is important in the context of ethical behaviour.

One of the major business debates recently is about corporate governance, particularly in the UK and the USA.

Key term

Corporate governance is the system by which companies are directed and controlled. *(Cadbury Report)*

The trigger for this debate was the **collapse** of major international companies during the 1980s, including Maxwell, BCCI and Polly Peck. These collapses were often unexpected, and dubious (or even fraudulent) activities were sometimes attributed to their owners and managers. These events represented a nasty shock for countries, such as the UK and the USA, that felt they had well-regulated markets and strong company legislation. It became obvious, however, that part of the problem was the way in which regulation was spread between **different national authorities** for these global conglomerates, so that no one national authority had the whole picture of the affairs of such companies, nor full powers over the whole of the business.

Individual countries began to develop **better guidelines** for corporate governance, and efforts have been made to produce an international standard on corporate governance.

Exam focus point

Corporate governance is covered in other papers, so is not examinable in P2. This is for background information only.

3 Conceptual framework 12/07

FAST FORWARD

The 1989 *Framework for the Preparation and Presentation of Financial Statements* was replaced in 2010 by the *Conceptual Framework for Financial Reporting*. This is the result of a joint project with the FASB. In 2015 an ED was issued with proposals for a revised *Conceptual Framework*.

3.1 The search for a conceptual framework

Key term

A **conceptual framework**, in the field we are concerned with, is a statement of generally accepted theoretical principles which form the frame of reference for financial reporting. These theoretical principles provide the basis for the development of new accounting standards and the evaluation of those already in existence.

The financial reporting process is concerned with providing information that is useful in the business and economic decision-making process. Therefore a conceptual framework will form the theoretical basis for determining which events should be accounted for, how they should be measured and how they should be communicated to the user.

Although it is theoretical in nature, a conceptual framework for financial reporting has highly practical final aims.

The **danger of not having a conceptual framework** is demonstrated in the way some countries' standards have developed over recent years; standards tend to be produced in a **haphazard and fire-fighting approach**. Where an agreed framework exists, the standard-setting body acts as an architect or designer, rather than a fire-fighter, building accounting rules on the foundation of sound, agreed basic principles.

The lack of a conceptual framework also means that fundamental principles are tackled more than once in different standards, thereby producing contradictions and inconsistencies in basic concepts, such as those of prudence and matching. This leads to ambiguity and it affects the true and fair concept of financial reporting.

Another problem with the lack of a conceptual framework has become apparent in the USA. The large number of highly detailed standards produced by the Financial Accounting Standards Board (FASB) has created a financial reporting environment governed by specific rules rather than general principles. This would be avoided if a cohesive set of principles were in place.

A conceptual framework can also bolster standard setters against political pressure from various 'lobby groups' and interested parties. Such pressure would only prevail if it was acceptable under the conceptual framework.

3.2 Advantages of a conceptual framework

The **advantages** arising from using a conceptual framework may be summarised as follows.

(a) The situation is **avoided** whereby standards are being developed on a **piecemeal** basis, where a particular accounting problem is recognised as having emerged, and resources were then channelled into standardising accounting practice in that area, without regard to whether that particular issue was necessarily the most important issue remaining at that time without standardisation.

(b) As stated above, the development of certain standards (particularly national standards) have been subject to considerable political interference from interested parties. Where there is a conflict of interest between user groups on which policies to choose, policies deriving from a conceptual framework will be **less open** to criticism that the standard-setter buckled to **external pressure**.

(c) Some standards may concentrate on the statement of profit or loss and other comprehensive income (formerly statement of comprehensive income, see Chapter 10 for the details of the change of name) whereas some may concentrate on the valuation of net assets (statement of financial position).

3.3 Counter-argument

A counter-argument might be as follows:

(a) Financial statements are intended for a variety of users, and it is not certain that a single conceptual framework can be devised which will suit all users.

(b) Given the diversity of user requirements, there may be a need for a variety of accounting standards, each produced for a different purpose (and with different concepts as a basis).

(c) It is not clear that a conceptual framework makes the task of preparing and then implementing standards any easier than without a framework.

Before we look at the IASB's attempt to produce a conceptual framework, we need to consider another term of importance to this debate: generally accepted accounting practice; or GAAP.

3.4 Generally Accepted Accounting Practice (GAAP)

This term has sprung up in recent years and it signifies all the rules, from whatever source, which govern accounting. In individual countries this is seen primarily as a combination of:

- National corporate law
- National accounting standards
- Local stock exchange requirements

Although those sources are the basis for the GAAP of individual countries, the concept also includes the effects of non-mandatory sources such as:

- International financial reporting standards
- Statutory requirements in other countries

In many countries, like the UK, GAAP does not have any statutory or regulatory authority or definition, unlike other countries, such as the USA. The term is mentioned rarely in legislation, and only then in fairly limited terms.

3.5 GAAP and a conceptual framework

A conceptual framework for financial reporting can be defined as an attempt to codify existing GAAP in order to reappraise current accounting standards and to produce new standards.

3.6 The IASB Conceptual Framework

The IASB *Framework for the Preparation and Presentation of Financial Statements* was produced in 1989 and is gradually being replaced by the new *Conceptual Framework for Financial Reporting.* This is the result of an IASB/FASB joint project and is being carried out in phases. The first phase, comprising Chapters 1 and 3, was published in September 2010. Chapter 2 entitled 'The reporting entity' has not yet been published. The current version of the *Conceptual Framework* includes the remaining chapters of the 1989 Framework as Chapter 4.

The *Conceptual Framework for Financial Reporting* is currently as follows:

Chapter 1: The objective of general purpose financial reporting

Chapter 2: The reporting entity (to be issued)

Chapter 3: Qualitative characteristics of useful financial information

Chapter 4: Remaining text of the 1989 *Framework*:

- Underlying assumption
- The elements of financial statements
- Recognition of the elements of financial statements
- Measurement of the elements of financial statements
- Concepts of capital and capital maintenance

You have studied the 1989 *Framework* in your earlier studies. We will now look at some of these sections in more detail.

3.7 Introduction to the *Conceptual Framework*

The Introduction provides a list of the purposes of the *Conceptual Framework*:

(a) To assist the Board in the **development of future IFRSs** and in its review of existing IFRSs.

(b) To assist the Board in **promoting harmonisation** of regulations, accounting standards and procedures relating to the presentation of financial statements by providing a basis for reducing the number of alternative accounting treatments permitted by IFRSs.

(c) To assist **national standard-setting bodies** in developing national standards.

(d) To assist **preparers of financial statements** in applying IFRSs and in dealing with topics that have yet to form the subject of an IFRS.

(e) To assist **auditors** in forming an opinion as to whether financial statements comply with IFRSs.

(f) To assist **users of financial statements** in interpreting the information contained in financial statements prepared in compliance with IFRSs.

(g) To provide those who are interested in the work of the IASB with **information** about its approach to the formulation of IFRSs.

The *Conceptual Framework* is not an IFRS and so does not overrule any individual IFRS. In the (rare) case of conflict between an IFRS and the *Conceptual Framework*, the **IFRS will prevail**. (*Conceptual Framework: Introduction* 2010)

3.8 Chapter 1: The Objective of General Purpose Financial Reporting

The *Conceptual Framework* states that:

'The objective of general purpose financial reporting is to provide information about the reporting entity that is useful to existing and potential investors, lenders and other creditors in making decisions about providing resources to the entity.' (*Conceptual Framework*, Chapter 1: para. 2)

These users need information about:

- The **economic resources of the entity**;
- The **claims against the entity**; and
- Changes in the entity's **economic resources and claims**

Information about the entity's **economic resources and the claims against it** helps users to assess the entity's liquidity and solvency and its likely needs for additional financing.

Information about a reporting entity's financial performance (the **changes in its economic resources and claims**) helps users to understand the return that the entity has produced on its economic resources. This is an indicator of how efficiently and effectively management has used the resources of the entity and is helpful in predicting future returns.

The *Conceptual Framework* makes it clear that this information should be prepared on an **accruals basis.** (*Conceptual Framework*, Chapter 1: para. 17)

Information about a reporting entity's cash flows during a period also helps users assess the entity's ability to generate future net cash inflows and gives users a better understanding of its operations.

3.9 Chapter 3: Qualitative Characteristics of Useful Financial Information

Qualitative characteristics are attributes that make financial information useful to users.

Chapter 3 distinguishes between **fundamental** and **enhancing** qualitative characteristics, for analysis purposes. Fundamental qualitative characteristics distinguish useful financial reporting information from information that is not useful or misleading. Enhancing qualitative characteristics distinguish more useful information from less useful information.

The two fundamental qualitative characteristics (*Conceptual Framework,* Chapter 3: QC 5–18) are:

(a) **Relevance**: Relevant information has predictive value or confirmatory value, or both. It is capable of making a difference in the decisions made by users.

The relevance of information is affected by its **nature** and its **materiality**.

(b) **Faithful representation**: Information must be **complete, neutral** and **free from error** (replacing 'reliability').

Financial reports represent **economic phenomena** in words and numbers. To be useful, financial information must not only represent relevant phenomena but must **faithfully represent** the phenomena that it purports to represent.

A **complete** depiction includes all information necessary for a user to understand the phenomenon being depicted, including all necessary descriptions and explanations.

A **neutral** depiction is without bias in the selection or presentation of financial information. This means that information must not be manipulated in any way in order to influence the decisions of users.

Free from error means there are no errors or omissions in the description of the phenomenon and no errors made in the process by which the financial information was produced. It does not mean that no inaccuracies can arise, particularly where estimates have to be made.

Substance over form

This is **not a separate qualitative characteristic** under the *Conceptual Framework.* The IASB says that to do so would be redundant because it is **implied in faithful representation.** Faithful representation of a transaction is only possible if it is accounted for according to its **substance and economic reality**.

3.9.1 Materiality

IFRS/IAS apply to material items.

Key term

Material. Information is material if omitting it or misstating it could influence decisions that users make on the basis of financial information about a specific reporting entity. (*Conceptual Framework,* Chapter 3: para. 11)

Materiality is an entity-specific aspect of relevance based on the nature or magnitude (or both) of the items to which the information relates in the context of an individual entity's financial report. Information may be judged relevant simply because of its nature (eg remuneration of management). In other cases, both the nature and materiality of the information are important. Materiality is not a qualitative characteristic itself (like relevance or faithful representation) because it is merely a threshold or cut-off point.

The IASB is working on materiality in a current project and in 2014 made amendments to IAS 1 *Presentation of financial statements.* These arose as part of the Disclosure Initiative are discussed in Chapter 10. The IASB is focusing on how materiality is applied in practice.

3.9.2 Enhancing qualitative characteristics

These are found in *Conceptual Framework,* Chapter 3: QC 9 – 32.

Comparability

Comparability is the qualitative characteristic that enables users to identify and understand similarities in, and differences among, items. Information about a reporting entity is more useful if it can be compared with similar information about other entities and with similar information about the same entity for another period or another date.

Consistency, although related to comparability, **is not the same**. It refers to the use of the same methods for the same items (ie consistency of treatment) either from period to period within a reporting entity or in a single period across entities.

The **disclosure of accounting policies** is particularly important here. Users must be able to distinguish between different accounting policies in order to be able to make a valid comparison of similar items in the accounts of different entities.

Comparability is **not the same as uniformity**. Entities should change accounting policies if those policies become inappropriate.

Corresponding information for preceding periods should be shown to enable comparison over time.

Verifiability

Verifiability helps assure users that information faithfully represents the economic phenomena it purports to represent. It means that different knowledgeable and independent observers could reach consensus that a particular depiction is a faithful representation.

Timeliness

Information may become less useful if there is a delay in reporting it. There is a **balance between timeliness and the provision of reliable information**.

If information is reported on a timely basis when not all aspects of the transaction are known, it may not be complete or free from error.

Conversely, if every detail of a transaction is known, it may be too late to publish the information because it has become irrelevant. The overriding consideration is how best to satisfy the economic decision-making needs of the users.

Understandability

Financial reports are prepared for users who have a **reasonable knowledge of business and economic activities** and who review and analyse the information diligently. Some phenomena are inherently complex and cannot be made easy to understand. Excluding information on those phenomena might make the information easier to understand, but without it those reports would be incomplete and therefore misleading. Therefore matters should not be left out of financial statements simply due to their difficulty as even well-informed and diligent users may sometimes need the aid of an adviser to understand information about complex economic phenomena.

The cost constraint on useful financial reporting

This is a pervasive constraint, not a qualitative characteristic. When information is provided, its benefits must exceed the costs of obtaining and presenting it. This is a **subjective area** and there are other difficulties: others, not the intended users, may gain a benefit; also the cost may be paid by someone other than the users. It is therefore difficult to apply a cost-benefit analysis, but preparers and users should be aware of the constraint.

3.9.3 Underlying assumption

The 1989 *Framework* identified two underlying assumptions – **accruals** and **going concern**.
The *Conceptual Framework* makes it clear that financial information should be prepared on an accruals basis but only identifies one underlying assumption – **going concern**. *(Conceptual Framework,* Chapter 4: para. 4.1)

3.10 Exposure Draft: Conceptual Framework for Financial Reporting

In May 2015, the IASB issued an exposure draft: *The Conceptual Framework for Financial Reporting.* The exposure draft is the latest document in a project that has been ongoing since 2004, although interrupted in 2010. The ED proposes comprehensive changes to the *Conceptual Framework,* notably:

- Revisions to the **definitions of elements** in the financial statements
- Guidance on **derecognition**
- Discussions on **measurement bases**
- Principles for including items in **other comprehensive income**
- High-level concepts for **presentation and disclosure**

The ED follows a 2013 discussion paper covering all aspects of the framework project, and was published at the same time as another ED covering references to the Conceptual Framework in other IASB pronouncements (not on your examinable documents list).

3.10.1 Background and approach

While the existing *Conceptual Framework* was found to be useful in helping the IASB with its stated mission to 'develop Standards that bring transparency, accountability and efficiency to financial markets around the world', it was also found to be lacking in the following respects *(ED Conceptual Framework for Financial Reporting, IN1)*.

Problem	Solution
Gaps in the current *Conceptual Framework,* such as insufficient guidance on presentation and disclosure.	**Fill gaps**
Parts of the existing *Conceptual Framework* are **out of date.** An example is the guidance on when assets and liabilities should be recognised.	**Update**
Some of the guidance is **unclear,** for example regarding the role of measurement uncertainty in deciding how to measure assets, liabilities, income or expenses.	**Clarify**

3.10.2 Structure

The ED is structured as follows:

Chapter	Topic
	Introduction
1	The objective of general purpose financial reporting
2	Qualitative characteristics of useful financial information
3	Financial statements and the reporting entity
4	The elements of financial statements
5	Recognition and derecognition
6	Measurement
7	Presentation and disclosure
8	Concepts of capital and capital maintenance
Appendix A	Cash-flow-based measurement techniques
Appendix B	Glossary

3.10.3 Introduction

The ED's introduction to the *Conceptual Framework* states (ED Conceptual Framework for Financial Reporting, IN1) that its purpose is:

(a) To **assist** the International Accounting Standards Board (IASB) to **develop Standards that are based on consistent concepts**

(b) To **assist preparers to develop consistent accounting policies when no Standard applies** to a particular transaction or event, or when a Standard allows a choice of accounting policy, and

(c) To **assist all parties to understand and interpret** the Standards

The *Conceptual Framework* is **not an IFRS, nor does it override any specific IFRS**. If the IASB decides to issue a new or revised pronouncement that is in conflict with the framework, the IASB will highlight the fact and explain the reasons for the departure.

3.10.4 Chapter 1: The Objective of General Purpose Financial Reporting

This Chapter (ED Conceptual Framework for Financial Reporting, Chapter 1: para. 1.2, 1.12*)*, together with Chapter 2, was finalised in the 2010 version of the *Conceptual Framework*, and so there are only limited changes from that version.

The main change is that more emphasis is placed on the importance of providing information needed to assess management's **stewardship** of an entity's resources.

3.10.5 Chapter 2: Qualitative characteristics of useful financial information

This Chapter, together with Chapter 1, was finalised in the 2010 version of the *Conceptual Framework*, and so there are generally only limited changes from that version. However, one change that could be regarded as important is the introduction of an **explicit reference to the idea of prudence.** Prudence is described as the **exercise of caution when making judgements under conditions of uncertainty.** It is explicitly stated that prudence is important in achieving **neutrality,** and therefore in achieving **faithful representation** (ED Conceptual Framework for Financial Reporting, Chapter 2: para. 2.18). Prudence had been removed from the *Conceptual Framework* in 2010.

The IASB has further clarified that prudence works both ways: assets and liabilities should be neither overstated nor understated.

Another key change is to the explanation of faithful representation (ED Conceptual Framework for Financial Reporting, Chapter 2: para. 2.19). The chapter contains a proposed addition that would clarify **that faithful representation means representation of the substance of an economic phenomenon instead of representation of merely its legal form.**

3.10.6 Chapter 3: Financial Statements and the reporting entity

This Chapter is not in the current version of the *Conceptual Framework*, and is based on the feedback received on a 2010 Exposure Draft on the topic.

The ED states the objective of financial statements as being to provide information about an entity's assets, liabilities, equity, income and expenses that is useful to financial statements users in assessing the prospects for future net cash inflows to the entity and in assessing management's stewardship of the entity's resources. It then sets out the going concern assumption, which is unchanged from the current version.

Definition of the reporting entity

A reporting entity is an entity that chooses, or is required, to present general purpose financial statements. It does not need to be a legal entity and can comprise only a portion of an entity or two or more entities. (ED Conceptual Framework for Financial Reporting, Chapter 3: para. 3.13).

Boundary of the reporting entity

The Exposure Draft proposes to determine the boundary of a reporting entity that has one or more subsidiaries on the basis of **control.** The boundary can be determined by either **direct control,** which results in **unconsolidated** or individual financial statements or by **direct and indirect control**, which results in **consolidated financial statements.** (ED Conceptual Framework for Financial Reporting, Chapter 3: para. 3.13 – 3.16).

The following diagram, taken from the IASB's 'Snapshot' *(ED Conceptual Framework for Financial Reporting: Snapshot, page 10)*, provides a summary of the approach:

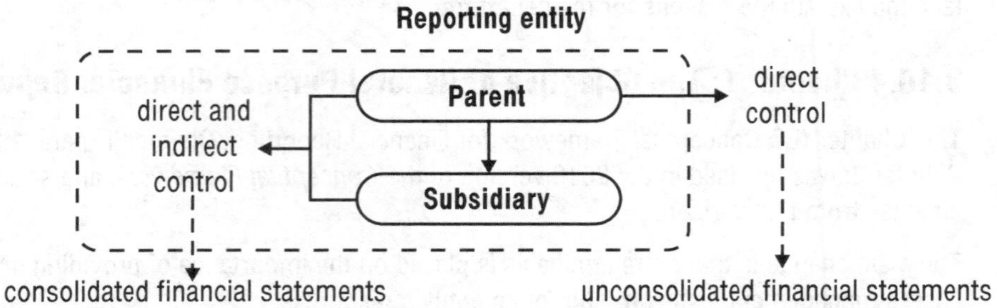

Consolidated financial statements, according to the ED, are generally more likely to provide useful information to users than unconsolidated financial statements. If an entity prepares both, the unconsolidated financial statements must disclose how users may obtain the consolidated financial statements.

3.10.7 Chapter 4: The elements of financial statements

The elements of financial statements are, as in the existing *Conceptual Framework,* assets, liabilities, equity, income and expense. However, the definitions have been modified (ED Conceptual Framework for Financial Reporting, Chapter 4: para. 4.4):

The current definitions of assets and liabilities require a probable expectation of future economic benefits or resource outflow. The IASB argues that the definitions of assets and liabilities should not require an expected or probable inflow or outflow as it should be sufficient that a resource or obligation can produce or result in a transfer of economic benefits. While the IASB believes that the current definitions have worked well in the past, it wishes to refine them in order to place more emphasis on the fact that an asset is a resource and a liability is an obligation. In addition, the notion of probability will be removed from the definitions. The proposed definitions are:

(a) An **asset** is a present economic resource controlled by the entity because of past events.

(b) A **liability** is a present obligation of the entity to transfer an economic resource because of past events.

An **economic resource** is a right that has the potential to produce economic benefits.

A **present obligation** is an obligation to transfer economic resources that:

(a) The entity has no practical ability to avoid, and

(b) Has arisen from a past event (ie economic benefits already received or activities already conducted).

For the definitions of both assets and liabilities, the IASB decided not to retain the notion of an 'expected inflow or outflow of resources' in acknowledgement of concerns about varied interpretations of the term 'expected' and the notion of a threshold level of probability.

Equity continues to be defined as 'the residual interest in the assets of the entity after deducting all its liabilities'. It should be noted that **while the 2013 Discussion Paper addressed problems that arise in classifying instruments with characteristics of both liabilities and equity, the ED does not do so.** Exploring those problems has been transferred to the IASB's research project on financial instruments with the characteristics of equity.

Income is increases in assets or decreases in liabilities that result in increases in equity, other than those relating to contributions from holders of equity claims.

Expenses are decreases in assets or increases in liabilities that result in decreases in equity, other than those relating to distributions to holders of equity claims.

3.10.8 Chapter 5: Recognition and derecognition

Recognition

Recognition is the **process of capturing an asset or a liability** for inclusion in the statement of financial position. The ED states that only items that meet the definition of an asset, a liability or equity are recognised in the statement of financial position, and only items that meet the definition of income or expenses are to be recognised in the statement(s) of financial performance. (ED Conceptual Framework for Financial Reporting, Chapter 5: para. 5.2).

The ED requires that **recognition criteria** (ED Conceptual Framework for Financial Reporting, Chapter 5: para. 5.9) , based on the qualitative characteristics of useful financial information, must be met. An entity recognises an asset or liability if such recognition provides users of the financial statements with:

(a) **Relevant information** about the asset or liability
(b) A **faithful representation** of the asset or liability and of any resulting income and expenses, and
(c) Information that results in **benefits exceeding the cost** of providing that information

Those criteria may not always be met in the following cases:

(a) It is uncertain whether an asset or liability exists.

(b) There is only a low probability of future inflows (outflows) of economic benefits from the asset (liability).

(c) The level of measurement uncertainty is so high that the resulting information has little relevance.

Whether the information provided is useful to users depends on the item and the specific facts and circumstances. Entities may also be required to **exercise judgement**, and recognition may vary, depending on the IFRS being applied.

Derecognition

Guidance on derecognition is new to this proposed version of the *Conceptual Framework*. The **guidance is driven by the requirement of faithful representation.** A faithful representation must be provided of:

(a) The **assets and liabilities retained after a transaction** or other event that led to derecognition, and
(b) The **change in the entity's assets and liabilities as a result of that transaction** or other event.

Decisions about derecognition are generally straightforward. However, in some cases the two aims described above conflict with each other, making the decisions more difficult. The discussion in the Exposure Draft focuses on these cases. (ED Conceptual Framework for Financial Reporting, Chapter 5: para. 5.25 to para. 5.36).

3.10.9 Chapter 6: Measurement

The guidance on measurement is an example of filling in gaps present in the existing *Conceptual Framework.* While developing the ED, the IASB considered whether the *Conceptual Framework* should advocate the use of a single measurement basis. Considering the different assets and liabilities being measured, relevance and the cost constraint, the Board eventually concluded that a **multiple measurement approach** is more appropriate.

The ED covers the following (ED Conceptual Framework for Financial Reporting, Chapter 6: paras. 6.4 to 6.47).:

(a) A **description of various measurement bases**, the information that these measurement bases provide and their advantages and disadvantages. The measurement bases are historical cost and current value measures (fair value and value in use/fulfilment value)

(b) **Factors to consider** when selecting a measurement basis (relevance, faithful representation, enhancing qualitative characteristics, and factors specific to initial measurement)

(c) Situations when **more than one measurement basis** provides relevant information. Consideration of the objective of financial reporting, the qualitative characteristics of useful financial information and the cost constraint are likely to result in the selection of different measurement bases for different assets, liabilities and items of income and expense

(d) Measurement of **equity**

Appendix A of the ED supplements this Chapter, and describes (ED Conceptual Framework for Financial Reporting, Appendix A: paras A1 to A10.) cash-flow-based measurement techniques for cases when a measure determined using a measurement basis cannot be observed.

3.10.10 Chapter 7: Presentation and disclosure

This Chapter discusses concepts that determine what information is included in the financial statements and how that information should be presented and disclosed. These concepts are intended to guide the IASB in setting presentation and disclosure requirements in individual standards and to guide entities in providing information in financial statements.

Disclosure initiative

The IASB is also undertaking a *Disclosure Initiative,* a collection of implementation and research projects aimed at improving disclosure in IFRS financial reporting. In the Disclosure Initiative, the IASB will seek to provide additional specific guidance to support the application of the concepts. This is discussed in more detail in Chapter 19.

Concepts and principles discussed in the ED

The ED discusses the following issues (ED Conceptual Framework for Financial Reporting, Chapter 7: paras. 7.2 to 7.7):

(a) The balance between entities' flexibility to provide relevant information that faithfully represents the entity's assets and liabilities and the transactions and other events of the period, and comparability among entities and across reporting periods.

(b) Entity-specific information is more useful than boilerplate language for efficient and effective communication.

(c) Duplication of information in various sections of the financial statements is unnecessary and makes financial statements less understandable.

Profit or loss and other comprehensive income

This part of the ED (ED Conceptual Framework for Financial Reporting, Chapter 7: paras. 7.19 to 7.27 5.2). discusses presentation disclosure in the statement of financial performance, and provides conceptual guidance on whether to present income and expenses in profit or loss or in other comprehensive income.

Both profit or loss and other comprehensive income would be retained and marked by subtotals or totals.

The purpose of the statement of profit or loss is to depict the return an entity has made on its economic resources during the period and to provide information that is helpful in assessing future cash flows and management's stewardship of the entity's resources. By default, therefore, **all income and expense will be shown in profit or loss unless relating to the remeasurement of assets and liabilities** - these would normally be shown in other comprehensive income. However, for an item recognised in other comprehensive income in one period, there is a presumption that it will be included in the statement of profit or loss in a future period, unless there is no clear basis for identifying the period in which reclassification would enhance the relevance of the information in the statement of profit or loss.

3.10.11 Chapter 8: Concepts of capital and capital maintenance

This Chapter comprises material carried forward from Chapter 4 of the existing *Conceptual Framework* with minor changes for consistency of terminology

3.11 Possible criticisms

3.11.1 EY

In a June 2015 overview (EYGM, 2015), EY commented:

> We support the IASB's proposal to update the Conceptual Framework. However, there are certain significant topics that are not addressed in the proposals, such as the distinction between equity and liability, the content of 'financial performance', the characteristics of income and expenses that should be presented in OCI, and the rationale for recycling of gains and losses in OCI to P/L. A framework that does not explore such topics in more detail may have gaps that will make its applicability less useful.

3.11.2 The Financial Reporting Council (FRC)

In a July 2015 meeting, the FRC's Accounting Council considered the ED and produced a draft response. While the proposals were broadly welcome, the FRC had tentative criticisms, of which the following are the most relevant to your exam.

(a) **Prudence.** The ED does not reflect the notion of 'asymmetric prudence'—the recognition of losses and liabilities at a lower level of likelihood (and hence often earlier) than gains and assets. This notion is mentioned in the Basis for Conclusions, but ought to be part of the *Conceptual Framework* itself.

(b) **Neutrality.** Prudence is a way of achieving 'neutrality', defined as 'without bias'. However, the FRC believe that 'unbiased' would be a clearer word.

(c) **Reliability.** The description of faithful representation given in the Exposure Draft does not include the idea, which was in the discussion of reliability in a previous version of the Conceptual Framework, that the information 'can be depended upon by users'. The idea of reliability needs to be reinstated.

(d) **Statement of profit or loss.** Terms such as 'profit', 'return' and 'performance' need to be defined, and the significance of recycling adjustments needs to be explained.

(e) **Elements.** The Exposure Draft does not propose to define elements for the statement of cash flows.

Exam focus point

> The examining team have flagged this topic as important. Keep an eye on future developments by reading *Student Accountant* and www.iasplus.com/agenda/framework.htm

4 Revenue recognition 6/08, 12/08, 6/11, 12/11, 6/13, 12/13, 6/14, 12/15

FAST FORWARD

> **Revenue recognition** is straightforward in most business transactions, but some situations are more complicated.

4.1 Introduction

Accruals accounting is based on the **matching of costs with the revenue they generate**. It is crucially important under this convention that we can establish the point at which revenue may be recognised so that the correct treatment can be applied to the related costs. For example, the costs of producing an item of finished goods should be carried as an asset in the statement of financial position until such time as it is sold; they should then be written off as a charge to the trading account. Which of these two treatments should be applied cannot be decided until it is clear at what moment the sale of the item takes place.

The decision has a **direct impact on profit** since under the prudence concept it would be unacceptable to recognise the profit on sale until a sale had taken place in accordance with the criteria of revenue recognition.

Revenue is generally recognised as **earned at the point of sale**, because at that point four criteria will generally have been met.

- The product or service has been **provided to the buyer**.
- The buyer has **recognised his liability** to pay for the goods or services provided. The converse of this is that the seller has recognised that ownership of goods has passed from himself to the buyer.
- The buyer has indicated his **willingness to hand over cash** or other assets in settlement of his liability.
- The **monetary value** of the goods or services has been established.

At earlier points in the business cycle there will not, in general, be **firm evidence** that the above criteria will be met. Until work on a product is complete, there is a risk that some flaw in the manufacturing process will necessitate its writing off; even when the product is complete there is no guarantee that it will find a buyer.

At later points in the business cycle, for example when cash is received for the sale, the recognition of revenue may occur in a period later than that in which the related costs were charged. Revenue recognition would then depend on fortuitous circumstances, such as the cash flow of a company's customers, and might fluctuate misleadingly from one period to another.

However, there are times when revenue is **recognised at other times than at the completion of a sale**. For example, in the recognition of profit on long-term construction contracts (performance obligations satisfied over time, see below). Contract revenue and contract costs associated with the construction contract are recognised as revenue and expenses respectively by reference to the stage of completion of the contract activity at the year end.

(a) Owing to the length of time taken to complete such contracts, to defer taking profit into account until completion may result in the statement of profit or loss and other comprehensive income reflecting, not so much a fair view of the activity of the company during the year, but rather the results relating to contracts which have been completed by the year end.

(b) Revenue in this case is recognised when production on, say, a section of the total contract is complete, even though no sale can be made until the whole is complete.

4.2 IFRS 15 *Revenue from contracts with customers*

FAST FORWARD

IFRS 15 *Revenue from contracts with customers* is concerned with the **recognition of revenues** arising from fairly common transactions.

- The sale of goods
- The rendering of services
- The use by others of entity assets yielding interest, royalties and dividends

Generally revenue is recognised when the entity has transferred promised goods or services to the customer. The standard sets out five steps for the recognition process.

Income, as defined by the IASB *Conceptual Framework (ED Conceptual Framework for Financial Reporting, Chapter 4: para. 4.4)* includes both revenues and gains. Revenue is income arising in the ordinary course of an entity's activities and it may be called different names, such as sales, fees, interest, dividends or royalties.

IFRS 15 *Revenue from contracts with customers* was issued in May 2014. It is the result of a joint IASB and FASB project on revenue recognition. It seeks to strike a balance between the IASB rules in IAS 18, which were felt to be too general, leading to a lot of diversity in practice, and the FASB regulations, which were too numerous.

IFRS 15 replaces both IAS 18 *Revenue* and IAS 11 *Construction contracts*. It is effective for reporting periods beginning on or after 1 January 2017. Its core principle is that revenue is recognised to depict the transfer of goods or services to a customer in an amount that reflects the consideration to which the entity expects to be entitled in exchange for those goods or services.

Under IFRS 15 the transfer of goods and services is based upon the transfer of **control**, rather than the transfer of risks and rewards as in IAS 18. **Control of an asset** is described in the standard as the ability to direct the use of, and obtain substantially all of the remaining benefits from, the asset.

For straightforward retail transactions IFRS 15 will have little, if any, effect on the amount and timing of revenue recognition. For contracts such as long-term service contracts and multi-element arrangements it could result in changes either to the amount or to the timing of revenue recognised.

4.3 Scope

IFRS 15 applies to all contracts with customers except:

- Leases within the scope of IFRS 16
- Insurance contracts within the scope of IAS 4
- Financial instruments and other contractual rights and obligations within the scope of IFRS 9, IFRS 10, IFRS 11, IAS 27 or IAS 28.
- Non-monetary exchanges between entities in the same line of business

(IFRS 15: para. 5)

4.4 Definitions

The following definitions are given in the standard.

Key terms

Income – Increases in economic benefits during the accounting period in the form of inflows or enhancements of assets or decreases of liabilities that result in an increase in equity, other than those relating to contributions from equity participants.

Revenue – Income arising in the course of an entity's ordinary activities.

Contract – An agreement between two or more parties that creates enforceable rights and obligations.

Contract asset – An entity's right to consideration in exchange for goods or services that the entity has transferred to a customer when that right is conditioned on something other than the passage of time (for example the entity's future performance).

Receivable – An entity's right to consideration that is unconditional – ie only the passage of time is required before payment is due.

Contract liability – An entity's obligation to transfer goods or services to a customer for which the entity has received consideration (or the amount is due) from the customer.

Customer – A party that has contracted with an entity to obtain goods or services that are an output of the entity's ordinary activities in exchange for consideration.

Performance obligation – A promise in a contract with a customer to transfer to the customer either:

(a) A good or service (or a bundle of goods or services) that is distinct; or

(b) A series of distinct goods or services that are substantially the same ad that have the same pattern of transfer to the customer.

Stand-alone selling price – The price at which an entity would sell a promised good or service separately to a customer.

Transaction price – The amount of consideration to which an entity expects to be entitled in exchange for transferring promised goods or services to a customer, excluding amounts collected on behalf of third parties. *(IFRS 15: Appendix A)*

Revenue **does not include** sales taxes, value added taxes or goods and service taxes which are only collected for third parties, because these do not represent an economic benefit flowing to the entity.

4.5 Recognition and measurement of revenue

Under IFRS 15 revenue is recognised and measured using a five step model.

Step 1 **Identify the contract with the customer**.

A contract with a customer is within the scope of IFRS 15 only when:

(a) The parties have approved the contract and are committed to carrying it out.
(b) Each party's rights regarding the goods and services to be transferred can be identified.
(c) The payment terms for the goods and services can be identified
(d) The contract has commercial substance
(e) It is probable that the entity will collect the consideration to which it will be entitled.

The contract can be written, verbal or implied. (IFRS 15: para. 9, 10, 17, 24)

Step 2 **Identify the separate performance obligations**. The key point is distinct goods or services. A contract includes promises to provide goods or services to a customer. Those promises are called performance obligations. A company would account for a performance obligation separately only if the promised good or service is distinct. A good or service is distinct if it is sold separately or if it could be sold separately because it has a distinct function and a distinct profit margin. Factors for consideration as to whether an entity's promise to transfer the good or service to the customer is separately identifiable include, but are not limited to:

(a) The entity does not provide a significant service of integrating the good or service with other goods or services promised in the contract.

(b) The good or service does not significantly modify or customize another good or service promised in the contract.

(c) The good or service is not highly dependent on or highly interrelated with other goods or services promised in the contract. (IFRS 15: paras. 22, 27, 29)

Step 3 **Determine the transaction price**. The transaction price is the amount of consideration a company expects to be entitled to from the customer in exchange for transferring goods or services. The transaction price would reflect the company's probability-weighted estimate of **variable consideration** (including reasonable estimates of contingent amounts) in addition to the effects of the customer's credit risk and the time value of money (if material). Variable contingent amounts are only included where it is highly probable that there will not be a reversal of revenue when any uncertainty associated with the variable consideration is resolved. Examples of where a variable consideration can arise include: discounts, rebates, refunds, price concessions, credits and penalties. (IFRS 15: paras. 47 to 72)

Step 4 **Allocate the transaction price to the performance obligations**. Where a contract contains more than one distinct performance obligation a company allocates the transaction price to all separate performance obligations in proportion to the stand-alone selling price of the good or service underlying each performance obligation. If the good or service is not sold separately, the company would estimate its stand-alone selling price.

So, if any entity sells a bundle of goods and/or services which it also supplies unbundled, the separate performance obligations in the contract should be priced in the same proportion as the unbundled prices. This would apply to mobile phone contracts where the handset is supplied 'free'. The entity must look at the stand-alone price of such a handset and some of the consideration for the contract should be allocated to the handset. (IFRS 15: paras. 73 to 74, 78 to 79)

Step 5 **Recognise revenue when (or as) a performance obligation is satisfied**. The entity satisfies a performance obligation by transferring **control** of a promised good or service to the customer. A performance obligation can be satisfied **at a point in time**, such as when goods are delivered to the customer, or **over time**. An obligation satisfied **over time** will meet one of the following criteria:

- The customer simultaneously receives and consumes the benefits as the performance takes place.
- The entity's performance creates or enhances an asset that the customer controls as the asset is created or enhanced.
- The entity's performance does not create an asset with an alternative use to the entity and the entity has an enforceable right to payment for performance completed to date.

The amount of revenue recognised is the amount allocated to that performance obligation in Step 4. (IFRS 15: paras. 25, 31, 32)

An entity must be able to **reasonably measure** the outcome of a performance obligation before the related revenue can be recognised. In some circumstances, such as in the early stages of a contract, it may not be possible to reasonably measure the outcome of a performance obligation, but the entity expects to recover the costs incurred. In these circumstances, revenue is recognised only to the extent of costs incurred.

4.5.1 Example: identifying the separate performance obligation

Office Solutions, a limited company, has developed a communications software package called CommSoft. Office Solutions has entered into a contract with Logisticity to supply the following:

(a) Licence to use CommSoft

(b) Installation service. This may require an upgrade to the computer operating system, but the software package does not need to be customized

(c) Technical support for three years

(d) Three years of updates for CommSoft

Office Solutions is not the only company able to install CommSoft, and the technical support can also be provided by other companies. The software can function without the updates and technical support.

Required

Explain whether the goods or services provided to Logisticity are distinct in accordance with IFRS 15 *Revenue from contracts with customers.*

Solution

CommSoft was delivered before the other goods or services and remains functional without the updates and the technical support. It may be concluded that Logisticity can benefit from each of the goods and services either on their own or together with the other goods and services that are readily available.

The promises to transfer each good and service to the customer are separately identifiable In particular, the installation service does not significantly modify the software itself and, as such, the software and the installation service are separate outputs promised by Office Solutions rather than inputs used to produce a combined output.

In conclusion, the goods and services are distinct and amount to four performance obligations in the contract under IFRS 15.

4.5.2 Example: determining the transaction price

Taplop supplies laptop computers to large businesses. On 1 July 20X5, Taplop entered into a contract with TrillCo, under which TrillCo was to purchase laptops at $500 per unit. The contract states that if TrillCo purchases more than 500 laptops in a year, the price per units is reduced retrospectively to $450 per unit. Taplop's year end is 30 June.

(a) As at 30 September 20X5, TrillCo had bought 70 laptops from Taplop. Taplop therefore estimated that TrillCo's purchases would not exceed 500 in the year to 30 June 20X6, and would therefore not be entitled to the volume discount.

(b) During the quarter ended 31 December 20X5, TrillCo expanded rapidly as a result of a substantial acquisition, and purchased an additional 250 laptops from Taplop. Taplop then estimated that TrillCo's purchases would exceed the threshold for the volume discount in the year to 30 June 20X6.

Required

Calculate the revenue Taplop would recognise in:

(a) The quarter ended 30 September 20X5
(b) The quarter ended 31 December 20X5

Your answer should apply the principles of IFRS 15 *Revenue from contracts with customers.*

Solution

(a) Applying the requirements of IFRS 15 to TrillCo's purchasing pattern at 30 September 20X5, Taplop should conclude that it was highly probable that a significant reversal in the cumulative amount of revenue recognised ($500 per laptop) would not occur when the uncertainty was resolved, that is when the total amount of purchases was known. Consequently, Taplop should recognise revenue of 70 x $500 = $35,000 for the first quarter ended 30 September 20X5.

(b) In the quarter ended 31 December 20X5, TrillCo's purchasing pattern changed such that it would be legitimate for Taplop to conclude that TrillCo's purchases would exceed the threshold for the volume discount in the year to 30 June 20X6, and therefore that it was appropriate to reduce the price to $450 per laptop. Taplop should therefore recognise revenue of $109,000 for the quarter ended 31 December 20X5. The amount is calculated as from $112,500 (250 laptops x $450) less the change in transaction price of $3,500 (70 laptops x $50 price reduction) for the reduction of the price of the laptops sold in the quarter ended 30 September 20X5.

4.6 Contract costs

The incremental costs of **obtaining** a contract (such as sales commission) are **recognised as an asset** if the entity expects to recover those costs.

Costs that would have been incurred regardless of whether the contract was obtained are recognised as an expense as incurred.

Costs incurred in **fulfilling** a contract, unless within the scope of another standard (such as IAS 2 *Inventories*, IAS 16 *Property, plant and equipment* or IAS 38 *Intangible assets*) are recognised as an asset if they meet the following criteria:

(a) The costs relate directly to an identifiable contract (costs such as labour, materials, management costs)
(b) The costs generate or enhance resources of the entity that will be used in satisfying (or continuing to satisfy) performance obligations in the future; and
(c) The costs are expected to be recovered

Costs recognised as assets are amortised on a systematic basis consistent with the transfer to the customer of the goods or services to which the asset relates. (IFRS 15: paras. 95 to 98)

4.7 Performance obligations satisfied over time

A performance obligation satisfied over time meets the criteria in Step 5 above and, if it entered into more than one accounting period, would previously have been described as a long-term contract.

In this type of contract an entity has an enforceable right to payment for performance completed to date. The standard describes this as an amount that approximates the selling price of the goods or services transferred to date (for example recovery of the costs incurred by the entity in satisfying the performance plus a reasonable profit margin).

Methods of measuring the amount of performance completed to date encompass **output methods** and **input methods**.

Output methods recognise revenue on the basis of the value to the **customer** of the goods or services transferred. They include surveys of performance completed, appraisal of units produced or delivered etc.

Input methods recognise revenue on the basis of the **entity's** inputs, such as labour hours, resources consumed, and costs incurred. If using a cost-based method, the costs incurred must contribute to the entity's progress in satisfying the performance obligation. (IFRS 15: para. 39 to 45)

4.8 Performance obligations satisfied at a point in time

A performance obligation not satisfied over time will be satisfied at a point in time. This will be the point in time at which the customer obtains control of the promised asset and the entity satisfies a performance obligation (IFRS 15: para. 38).

Some indicators of the transfer of control are:

(a) The entity has a present right to payment for the asset.
(b) The customer has legal title to the asset.
(c) The entity has transferred physical possession of the asset.
(d) The significant risks and rewards of ownership have been transferred to the customer.
(e) The customer has accepted the asset.

4.9 Sale with a right of return

Where goods are sold with a right of return, an entity should not recognise revenue for goods that it expects to be returned. It can calculate the level of returns using the expected value method (the probability-weighted sum of amounts) or simply estimate the most likely amount. This will be shown as a refund liability and a deduction from revenue.

The entity also recognises an asset (adjusted against cost of sales) for its right to recover products from customers on settlement of the refund liability. (IFRS 15: para. B20)

4.10 Warranties

If a customer has the option to purchase a warranty separately from the product to which it relates, it constitutes a distinct service and is accounted for as a separate performance obligation. This would apply to a warranty which provides the customer with a service in addition to the assurance that the product complies with agreed-upon specifications.

If the customer does not have the option to purchase the warranty separately, for instance if the warranty is required by law, that does not give rise to a performance obligation and the warranty is accounted for in accordance with IAS 37. (IFRS 15: para. B28)

4.11 Principal versus agent

An entity must establish in any transaction whether it is acting as principal or agent.

It is a principal if it controls the promised good or service before it is transferred to the customer. When the performance obligation is satisfied, the entity recognises revenue in the gross amount of the consideration for those goods or services.

It is acting as an agent if its performance obligation is to arrange for the provision of goods or services by another party. Satisfaction of this performance obligation will give rise to the recognition of revenue in the amount of any fee or commission to which it expects to be entitled in exchange for arranging for the other party to provide its goods or services.

Indicators that an entity is an agent rather than a principal include the following:

(a) Another party is primarily responsible for fulfilling the contract.

(b) The entity does not have inventory risk before or after the goods have been ordered by a customer, during shipping or on return.

(c) The entity does not have discretion in establishing prices for the other party's goods or services and, therefore, the benefit that the entity can receive from those goods or services is limited.

(d) The entity's consideration is in the form of a commission.

(e) The entity is not exposed to credit risk for the amount receivable from a customer in exchange for the other party's goods or services.

(IFRS 15: para. B34 to B28)

4.11.1 Example: principal versus agent

This example is taken from the standard.

An entity operates a website that enables customers to purchase goods from a range of suppliers. The suppliers deliver directly to the customers, who have paid in advance, and the entity receives a commission of 10% of the sales price.

The entity's website also processes payments from the customer to the supplier at prices set by the supplier. The entity has no further obligation to the customer after arranging for the products to be supplied.

Is the entity a principal or an agent?

Solution

The following points are relevant:

- Goods are supplied directly from the supplier to the customer, so the entity does not obtain control of the goods.
- The supplier is primarily responsible for fulfilling the contract.
- The entity's consideration is in the form of commission.
- The entity does not establish prices and bears no credit risk.

The entity would therefore conclude that it is acting as an agent and that the only revenue to be recognised is the amounts received as commission.

4.12 Options for additional goods or services

If an option in the contract grants the customer the right to acquire additional goods or services at a discount which can only be obtained by entering into the contract, that option gives rise to a performance obligation.

Revenue is recognised when the additional future goods or services are transferred, or when the option expires. Revenue will be based on the stand-alone selling price of the goods or services, taking account of the discount.

If the option granted to the customer does not offer a discount, it is treated as a marketing offer and no contract exists until the customer exercises the option to purchase.

(IFRS 15: paras. B39 to B43)

4.13 Customers' unexercised rights

When a customer pays in advance for goods or services the prepayment gives rise to a contract liability, which is derecognised when the performance obligation is satisfied.

If, having made a non-refundable prepayment, the customer does not exercise their right to receive the good or service, the unexercised right is often referred to as breakage. A breakage amount can be recognised as revenue if the pattern of rights exercised by the customer gives rise to the expectation that the entity will be entitled to a breakage amount. If this does not apply, it can be recognised as revenue when the likelihood of the customer exercising its rights becomes remote.

(IFRS 15: paras. B44 to B47)

4.14 Non-refundable upfront fees

A non-refundable upfront fee is often charged at the beginning of a contract, such as joining fees in health club membership contracts.

In many cases upfront fees do not relate to the transfer of any promised good or service but are simply advance payments for **future** goods or services. In this case revenue is recognised when the future goods or services are provided.

If the fee relates to a good or service the entity should evaluate whether or not it amounts to a separate performance obligation. This depends on whether it results in the transfer of an asset to the customer. The fee may relate to costs incurred in setting up a contract, but these setup activities may not result in the transfer of services to the customer. (IFRS 15: paras. B48 to B51)

4.15 Licensing

A licence establishes a customer's rights to the intellectual property of an entity. Intellectual property can include software, music, franchises, patents, trademarks and copyrights.

The promise to grant a licence may be accompanied by the promise to transfer other goods or services to the customer. If the promise to grant the licence is **not** distinct from the promised goods or services, this is treated as a single performance obligation.

If the promise to grant the licence **is** distinct, it will constitute a separate performance obligation. The entity must establish whether the performance obligation is satisfied 'at a point in time' or 'over time'.

In this respect the entity should consider whether the nature of the entity's promise in granting the licence to a customer is to provide the customer with either:

(a) A **right to access** the entity's intellectual property as it exists throughout the licence period; or

(b) A **right to use** the entity's intellectual property as it exists at the point in time at which the licence is granted.

A **right to access** exists where the entity can make changes to the intellectual property throughout the licence period, the customer is exposed to the effects of these changes and the changes do not constitute the transfer of a good or service to the customer. In this case the promise to grant a licence is treated as a performance obligation satisfied over time and the entity recognises revenue over time by measuring the progress towards complete satisfaction of that performance obligation.

Where this does not apply, the nature of the entity's promise is the **right to use** its intellectual property as it exists at the point in time at which the licence is granted. This means that the customer can direct the use of, and obtain substantially all of the remaining benefits from, the licence at the point at which it is transferred. The point at which revenue can be recognised may be later than the date on which the licence is granted if the customer does not have immediate access to the intellectual property, for instance if it has to wait to be granted an access code.

When **royalties**, based on sales or on usage, are promised by the customer in exchange for a licence of intellectual property, revenue can be recognised at the later of the following occurrences:

(a) The sale or usage occurs; and
(b) The performance obligation to which the royalty has been allocated has been satisfied.

(IFRS 15: paras. B39 to B43)

4.16 Repurchase agreements

Under a repurchase agreement an entity sells an asset and promises, or has the option, to repurchase it. Repurchase agreements generally come in three forms:

(a) An entity has an obligation to repurchase the asset (a forward contract)
(b) An entity has the right to repurchase the asset (a call option)
(c) An entity must repurchase the asset if requested to do so by the customer (a put option).

In the case of a forward or a call option the customer does not obtain control of the asset, even if it has physical possession. The entity will account for the contract in one of two ways:

(a) A lease in accordance with IFRS 16, if the repurchase price is below the original selling price, unless the contract is part of a sale and leaseback transaction. If the contract is part of a sale and leaseback transaction, the entity must continue to recognise the asset and recognise a financial liability for any consideration received from the customer. The liability must be accounted for in accordance with IFRS 9.

(b) A financing arrangement if the repurchase price is equal to or greater than the original selling price. In this case the entity will recognise both the asset and a corresponding liability.

If the entity is obliged to repurchase at the request of the customer (a put option), it must consider whether or not the customer is likely to exercise that option.

If the repurchase price is lower than the original selling price and it is considered that the customer does not therefore have significant economic incentive to exercise the option, the contract should be accounted for as an outright sale, with a right of return.

If the repurchase price is greater than or equal to the original selling price and is above the expected market value of the option, the contract is treated as a financing arrangement.

(IFRS 15: paras. B64 to B76)

4.16.1 Example: contract with a call option

This example is taken from the standard (IFRS 15: illustrative example 62).

An entity enters into a contract with a customer for the sale of a tangible asset on 1 January 20X7 for $1 million. The contract includes a call option that gives the entity the right to repurchase the asset for $1.1 million on or before 31 December 20X7.

This means that the customer does not obtain control of the asset, because the repurchase option means that it is limited in its ability to use and obtain benefit from the asset.

Solution

As control has not been transferred, the entity accounts for the transaction as a **financing arrangement**, because the exercise price is above the original selling price. The entity continues to recognise the asset and recognises the cash received as a financial liability. The difference of $0.1 million is recognised as interest expense.

If on 31 December 20X7 the option lapses unexercised, the customer now obtains control of the asset. The entity will derecognise the asset and recognise revenue of $1.1 million (the $1 million already received plus the $0.1 million charged to interest).

4.16.2 Example: contract with a put option

The same contract as above includes instead a put option that obliges the entity to repurchase the asset at the customer's request for $900,000 on or before 31 December 20X7, at which time the market value is expected to be $750,000.

Solution

In this case the customer has a significant economic incentive to exercise the put option because the repurchase price exceeds the market value at the repurchase date. This means that control does not pass to the customer. Since the customer will be exercising the put option, this limits its ability to use or obtain benefit from the asset.

In this situation the entity accounts for the transaction as a lease in accordance with IFRS 16 The asset has been leased to the customer for the period up to the repurchase and the difference of $100,000 will be accounted for as payments received under a lease.

4.17 Consignment arrangements

When a product is delivered to a customer under a consignment arrangement, the customer (dealer) does not obtain control of the product at that point in time, so no revenue is recognised upon delivery.

Indicators of a consignment arrangement include (IFRS 15: paras. B77 to B787):

(a) The product is controlled by the entity until a specified event occurs, such as the product is sold on, or a specified period expires.

(b) The entity can require the return of the product, or transfer it to another party.

(c) The customer (dealer) does not have an unconditional obligation to pay for the product

4.18 Bill-and-hold arrangements

Under a bill-and-hold arrangement goods are sold but remain in the possession of the seller for a specified period, perhaps because the customer lacks storage facilities.

An entity will need to determine at what point the customer obtains control of the product. For some contracts, control will not be transferred until the goods are delivered to the customer. For others, a customer may obtain control even though the goods remain in the entity's physical possession. In this case the entity would be providing custodial services to the customer over the customer's asset.

For a customer to have obtained control of a product in a bill and hold arrangement, the following criteria must all be met:

(a) The reason for the bill-and-hold must be substantive (for example, requested by the customer).
(b) The product must be separately identified as belonging to the customer.
(c) The product must be ready for physical transfer to the customer.
(d) The entity cannot have the ability to use the product or to transfer it to another customer.

(IFRS 15: paras. B79 to B82)

4.18.1 Example: bill and hold arrangement

This example is taken from the standard (IFRS 15: illustrative example 63).

An entity enters into a contract with a customer on 1 January 20X8 for sale of a machine and spare parts. It takes two years to manufacture these and on 31 December 20X9 the customer pays for both the machine and the spare parts but only takes physical possession of the machine. The customer inspects and accepts the spare parts but requests that they continue to be stored at the entity's warehouse.

Solution

There are now three performance obligations – transfer of the machine, transfer of the spare parts and the custodial services. The transaction price is allocated to the three performance obligations and revenue is recognised when (or as) control passes to the customer.

The machine and the spare parts are both performance obligations satisfied at a point in time, and for both of them that point in time is 31 December 20X9. In the case of the spare parts, the customer has paid for them, the customer has legal title to them and the customer as control of them as they can remove them from storage at any time.

The custodial services are a performance obligation satisfied over time, so revenue will be recognised over the period during which the spare parts are stored.

4.19 Example: applying the IFRS five-step model

On 1 January 20X4, Angelo enters into a twelve-month 'pay monthly' contract for a mobile phone. The contract is with TeleSouth, and terms of the plan are:

(a) Angelo receives a free handset on 1 January 20X4

(b) Angelo pays a monthly fee of $200, which includes unlimited free minutes. Angelo is billed on the last day of the month

Customers may purchase the same handset from TeleSouth for $500 without the payment plan. They may also enter into the payment plan without the handset, in which case the plan costs them $175 per month.

The company's year-end is 31 July 20X4.

Required

Show how TeleSouth should recognise revenue from this plan in accordance with IFRS 15 *Revenue from contracts with customers.* Your answer should give journal entries:

(a) On 1 January 20X4
(b) On 31 January 20X4

Solution

IFRS 15 requires application of its five-step process:

(i) **Identify the contract with a customer.** A contract can be written, oral or implied by customary business practices.

(ii) **Identify the separate performance obligations in the contract.** If a promised good or service is not distinct, it can be combined with others.

(iii) **Determine the transaction price.** This is the amount to which the entity expects to be **'entitled'**. For variable consideration, the probability – weighted expected amount is used. The effect of any credit losses shown as a separate line item (just below revenue).

(iv) **Allocate the transaction price to the separate performance obligations in the contract.** For multiple deliverables, the transaction price is allocated to each separate performance obligation in proportion to the **stand-alone selling price** at contract inception of each performance obligation.

(v) **Recognise revenue when (or as) the entity satisfies a performance obligation,** that is when the entity **transfers** a promised good or service to a customer. The good or service is only considered as transferred when the customer obtains **control** of it.

Application of the five-step process to TeleSouth

(i) **Identify the contract with a customer.** This is clear. TeleSouth has a twelve-month contract with Angelo.

(ii) **Identify the separate performance obligations in the contract.** In this case there are two distinct performance obligations:

  (1) The obligation to deliver a handset
  (2) The obligation to provide network services for twelve months

  (The obligation to deliver a handset would not be a distinct performance obligation if the handset could not be sold separately, but it is in this case because the handsets are sold separately.)

(iii) **Determine the transaction price.** This is straightforward: it is $2,400, that is 12 months × the monthly fee of $200.

(iv) **Allocate the transaction price to the separate performance obligations in the contract.** The transaction price is allocated to each separate performance obligation in proportion to the **stand-alone selling price** at contract inception of each performance obligation, that is the stand-alone price of the handset ($500 and the stand-alone price of the network services ($175 × 12 = $2,100.00):

Performance obligation	*Stand-alone selling price*	*% of total*	*Revenue (=relative selling price = $2,400 × %)*
	$		$
Handset	500.00	19.2%	460.80
Network services	2,100.00	80.8%	1,939.20
Total	2,600.00	100%	2,400.00

(v) **Recognise revenue when (or as) the entity satisfies a performance obligation,** that is when the entity **transfers** a promised good or service to a customer. This applies to each of the performance obligations:

(1) When TeleSouth gives a handset to Angelo, it needs to recognize the revenue of $460.80.

(2) When TeleSouth provides network services to Angelo, it needs to recognize the total revenue of $1,939.20. It's practical to do it once per month as the billing happens.

Journal entries

On 1 January 20X4

The entries in the books of TeleSouth will be:

DEBIT	Receivable (unbilled revenue)	$460.80	
CREDIT	Revenue		$460.80

Being recognition of revenue from the sale of the handset

On 31 January 20X4

The monthly payment from Angelo is split between amounts owing for network services and amounts owing for the handset.

DEBIT	Receivable (Angelo)	$200	
CREDIT	Revenue (1,939.20/12)		$161.60
CREDIT	Receivable (unbilled revenue)(460.80/12)		$38.40

Being recognition of revenue from monthly provision of network services and 'repayment' of handset

4.20 Presentation

Contracts with customers will be presented in an entity's statement of financial position as a contract liability, a contract asset or a receivable, depending on the relationship between the entity's performance and the customer's payment.

A **contract liability** is recognised and presented in the statement of financial position where a customer has paid an amount of consideration prior to the entity performing by transferring control of the related good or service to the customer.

When the entity has performed but the customer has not yet paid the related consideration, this will give rise to either a **contract asset** or a **receivable**. A contract asset is recognised when the entity's right to consideration is conditional on something other than the passage of time, for instance future performance. A receivable is recognised when the entity's right to consideration is unconditional except for the passage of time.

In practice, this aligns with the previous IAS 11 treatment. Where revenue has been invoiced a receivable is recognised. Where revenue has been earned but not invoiced, it is recognised as a contract asset.

(IFRS 15: para. 105).

4.21 Disclosure

The following amounts should be disclosed unless they have been presented separately in the financial statements in accordance with other standards (IFRS 15: para. 110:

(a) Revenue recognised from contracts with customers, disclosed separately from other sources of revenue.

(b) Any impairment losses recognised (in accordance with IFRS 9) on any receivables or contract assets arising from an entity's contracts with customers, disclosed separately from other impairment losses.

(c) The opening and closing balances of receivables, contract assets and contract liabilities from contracts with customers.

(d) Revenue recognised in the reporting period that was included in the contract liability balance at the beginning of the period; and

(e) Revenue recognised in the reporting period from performance obligations satisfied in previous periods (such as changes in transaction price).

Other information that should be provided;

(a) An explanation of significant changes in the contract asset and liability balances during the reporting period

(b) Information regarding the entity's performance obligations, including when they are typically satisfied (upon delivery, upon shipment, as services are rendered etc.), significant payment terms (such as when payment is typically due) and details of any agency transactions, obligations for returns or refunds and warranties granted.

(c) The aggregate amount of the transaction price allocated to the performance obligations that are not fully satisfied at the end of the reporting period and an explanation of when the entity expects to recognise these amounts as revenue.

(d) Judgements, and changes in judgements, made in applying the standard that significantly affect the determination of the amount and timing of revenue from contracts with customers.

(e) Assets recognised from the costs to obtain or fulfil a contract with a customer. This would include pre-contract costs and set-up costs. The method of amortisation should also be disclosed.

4.22 Contracts where performance obligations are satisfied over time

These contracts are generally construction contracts, and it is possible that you will see this term used as the old standard, IAS 11 used it.

A company is building a large tower block that will house offices, under a contract with an investment company. It will take three years to build the block and over that time it will obviously have to pay for building materials, wages of workers on the building, architects' fees and so on. It will receive periodic payments from the investment company at various predetermined stages of the construction. How does it decide, in each of the three years, **what to include as income and expenditure** for the contract in profit or loss?

Example: contract where performance obligations are satisfied over time

Suppose that a contract is started on 1 January 20X5, with an estimated completion date of 31 December 20X6. The final contract price is $1,500,000. In the first year, to 31 December 20X5:

(a) Costs incurred amounted to $600,000.
(b) Half the work on the contract was completed.
(c) Certificates of work completed have been issued, to the value of $750,000.
(d) It is estimated with reasonable certainty that further costs to completion in 20X6 will be $600,000.

What is the contract profit in 20X5, and what entries would be made for the contract at 31 December 20X5?

Solution

This is a contract in which the performance obligation is satisfied **over time**. The entity is carrying out the work for the benefit of the customer rather than creating an asset for its own use and it has an enforceable right to payment for work completed to date. We can see this from the fact that certificates of work completed have been issued.

IFRS 15 states that the amount of payment that the entity is entitled to corresponds to the amount of performance completed to date, which approximates to the costs incurred in satisfying the performance obligation plus a reasonable profit margin.

In this case the contract is certified as 50% complete. At 31 December 20X5 the entity will recognise revenue of $750,000 and cost of sales of $600,000, leaving profit of $150,000. The **contract asset** will be the costs to date plus the profit – $750,000. We are not told that any of this amount has yet been invoiced, so no amount is deducted for receivables.

Summary of accounting treatment

Statement of profit or loss

(a) **Revenue and costs**

(i) Sales revenue and associated costs should be recorded in profit or loss as the contract activity progresses.

(ii) Include an appropriate proportion of total contract value as sales revenue in profit or loss.

(iii) The costs incurred in completing that amount of the performance obligation are matched with this sales revenue, resulting in the reporting of results which can be attributed to the proportion of work completed.

(iv) Sales revenue is the value of work carried out to date.

(b) **Profit recognised in the contract**

(i) It must reflect the proportion of work carried out.

(ii) It should take into account any known inequalities in profitability in the various stages of a contract.

Statement of financial position

(a) **Contract asset** (presented separately under current assets)

	$
Costs to date	X
Plus recognised profits	(X)
	X
Less any recognised losses	(X)
	X
Less receivables (amounts invoiced)	(X)
Contract asset (amount due from the customer)	X

(b) **Receivables**

Unpaid invoices X

(c) **Contract liability**. Where (a) gives a net amount due **to** the customer this amount should be included as a contract liability, presented separately under current liabilities.

Example

P Co has the following construction contract (performance obligations satisfied over time) in progress:

	$m
Total contract price	750
Costs incurred to date	225
Estimated costs to completion	340
Progress payments invoiced and received	290

Now we will calculate the amounts to be recognised for the contract in the statement of profit or loss and statement of financial position assuming the amount of performance obligation satisfied is calculated using the proportion of costs incurred method.

1 *Estimated profit*

	$m
Total contract price	750
Less costs incurred to date	(225)
Less estimated costs to completion	(340)
Estimated profit	185

2 Percentage complete

Costs to date / total estimated costs: 225 / (225 + 340) = 40%

3 *Statement of profit or loss*

	$m
Revenue (40% x $750)	300
Cost of sales (40% × (225 + 340))	(226)
Profit (40% × 185)	74

4 *Statement of financial position*

	$m
Costs incurred to date	225
Recognised profits	74
Less receivable	(290)
Contract asset	9

How would we account for this if it was a loss-making contract? We will reduce P Co's contract price to $550m.

1 *Estimated loss*

	$m
Total contract price	550
Less costs incurred to date	(225)
Less estimated costs to completion	(340)
Estimated loss	(15)

2 *Percentage complete*

Costs to date / total estimated costs: 225 / (225 + 340) = 40%

3 *Statement of profit or loss*

	$m
Revenue (40% × $550)	220
Cost of sales (balancing figure)	(235)
Loss	(15)

4 *Statement of financial position*

	$m
Costs incurred to date	225
Recognised loss	(15)
Less receivable	(290)
Contract liability	(80)

4.23 Likely impact on companies

Revenue is generally an entity's most important financial performance indicator, and one extensively scrutinised by analysts and investors. IFRS 15 is likely to impact on **the timing, measurement, recognition and disclosure of revenue**. These impacts will require adjustments **in policies, procedures, internal controls and systems.**

4.23.1 Timing of revenue

By far the most significant change in IFRS 15 is to the **pattern of revenue reporting. Even if the total revenue reported does not change,** the timing will change in many cases.

The example of TeleSouth, our fictitious company in Section 4.19 above, illustrates this point. Under IAS 18 *Revenue,* the old standard, TeleSouth would **not recognise any revenue from the sale of handset,** on the grounds that TeleSouth has given it to Angelo free. TeleSouth would view the free handset as a cost of acquiring a new customer, and the cost would be recognised in profit or loss immediately.

Revenue from the provision of network services would be recognised on a monthly basis as follows:

DEBIT	Receivable/Cash	$200	
CREDIT	Revenue		$200

TeleSouth's year-end is 31 July 20X4, which means that the contract falls into more than one accounting period. The impact of changing from IAS 18 to IFRS 15 for TeleSouth, for the year ended 31 July 20X4 is as follows:

Performance obligation	*Under IAS 18*	*Under IFRS 15*
	$	$
Handset	00.00	460.80
Network services: (200 × 6)/ (161.60 × 6)	1,200.00	969.60
Total	1,200.00	1,430.40

The variation in timing has tax implications, and if the tax rate changes, may have an overall effect on profit.

4.23.2 Use of judgement

The standard will require entities to use more judgement and make more estimates than under IAS 18, which, as seen from the example above, is simpler, although less realistic.

4.23.3 Retrospective application

IFRS 15 must be applied retrospectively, that is as if it has always been in place. Companies will therefore need to re-perform any calculations performed under IAS 18 and adjust opening balances. This will be labour intensive for companies with a lot of long-term contracts, particularly in the construction industry.

4.23.4 Practical implications

As the firm EY pointed out (EYGM, 2014), it is not only accounting that is affected. EY stated that IFRS 15 will require changes to a large number of business functions, including:

(a) Project management
(b) Tax planning
(c) Business operations
(d) Training and communication

(e) Business operations
(f) Management information
(g) Investor relations
(h) Legal issues
(i) Human resources
(j) IT systems

4.24 Topical example

Case Study

In September 2014, supermarket giant, Tesco made headline news amid claims that it had overstated its first-half profits by some £250m. At the time of writing a full investigation has yet to take place, but it is possible that the issue of incorrect timing of revenue recognition could definitely have played a part. IAS 18's vagueness and inconsistency will not have helped in this respect, and has allowed scope for aggressive earnings management, although this has not yet been demonstrated in the case of Tesco. In particular, the timing of revenue has been a cause for criticism because of the lack of clear and comprehensive guidance.

On the website Wiley Global Insight, Steve Colling wrote:

> It appears that Tesco may have accelerated the recognition of revenue relating to suppliers' rebates (hence recognising revenue too early) and at the same time delayed the recognition of costs. The result of this accounting treatment is that accounting profits are brought into the first half of the year, with costs pushed into the second half of the year so that the profits look disproportionately healthy in the first-half of the year.
>
> [...]
>
> Whether this new standard [IFRS 15] will lessen the potential for companies to adopt aggressive earnings management in their revenue recognition policies remains to be seen. The steps in IFRS 15 *do* offer more clarity than IAS 18.

4.25 Recommended articles

Two *Student Accountant* articles, *Revenue Revisited* Parts 1 and 2, should be read, as they may give an indication of the examining team's focus. The first of the articles goes into detail on the five-step process for revenue recognition. The second explores the issues surrounding the definition and nature of a contract according to IFRS 15 in greater depth, as well as the scope of the standard and its interaction with other standards. Key points to take away from the second article are the five criteria that must be met before an entity can apply the revenue recognition model to a contract and these have been derived from previous revenue recognition and other standards:

Criterion 1 The parties should have approved the contract and are committed to perform their respective obligations.

Criterion 2 It is essential that each party's rights can be identified regarding the goods or services to be transferred.

Criterion 3 It is essential that the payment terms can be identified regarding the goods or services to be transferred.

Criterion 4 The contract must have commercial substance before revenue can be recognised

Criterion 5 It should be probable that the entity will collect the consideration due under the contract.

Links are as follows.

Part 1: http://www.accaglobal.com/an/en/student/exam-support-resources/professional-exams-study-resources/p2/technical-articles/revenue-revisited1.html

Part 2: http://www.accaglobal.com/uk/en/student/exam-support-resources/professional-exams-study-resources/p2/technical-articles/revenue-revisited2.html

4.26 Question practice

Exam focus point

A key member of the examining team recently emphasised that revenue recognition is an important topic, so have a go at the questions below.

Question

Recognition

Discuss under what circumstances, if any, revenue might be recognised at the following stages of a sale.

(a) Goods are acquired by the business which it confidently expects to resell very quickly.
(b) A customer places a firm order for goods.
(c) Goods are delivered to the customer.
(d) The customer is invoiced for goods.
(e) The customer pays for the goods.
(f) The customer's cheque in payment for the goods has been cleared by the bank.

Answer

(a) A sale must never be recognised before the goods have even been ordered by a customer. There is no certainty about the value of the sale, nor when it will take place, even if it is virtually certain that goods will be sold.

(b) A sale must never be recognised when the customer places an order. No performance obligation has been satisfied at that point. Even though the order will be for a specific quantity of goods at a specific price, control over the goods has not yet been transferred to the customer. The customer may cancel the order, the supplier might be unable to deliver the goods as ordered or it may be decided that the customer is not a good credit risk.

(c) A sale will be recognised when delivery of the goods is made only when:

  (i) The sale is for cash, and so the cash is received at the same time; or
  (ii) The sale is on credit and the customer accepts delivery (eg by signing a delivery note).

(d) The critical event for a credit sale is usually the despatch of an invoice to the customer. At that point the performance obligation has been satisfied. There is then a legally enforceable debt, payable on specified terms, for a completed sale transaction.

(e) The critical event for a cash sale is when delivery takes place and when cash is received; both take place at the same time.

It would be too cautious or 'prudent' to await cash payment for a credit sale transaction before recognising the sale, unless the customer is a high credit risk and there is a serious doubt about his ability or intention to pay.

(f) It would again be over-cautious to wait for clearance of the customer's cheques before recognising sales revenue. Such a precaution would only be justified in cases where there is a very high risk of the bank refusing to honour the cheque.

Question

Revenue recognition

Caravans Deluxe is a retailer of caravans, dormer vans and mobile homes, with a year end of 30 June 20X8. It is having trouble selling one model – the $30,000 Mini-Lux, and so is offering incentives for customers who buy this model before 31 May 20X7:

(a) Customers buying this model before 31 May 20X7 will receive a period of interest free credit, provided they pay a non-refundable deposit of $3,000, an instalment of $15,000 on 1 August 20X7 and the balance of $12,000 on 1 August 20X9.

(b) A three-year service plan, normally worth $1,500, is included free in the price of the caravan.

On 1 May 20X7, a customer agrees to buy a Mini-Lux caravan, paying the deposit of $3,000. Delivery is arranged for 1 August 20X7.

As the sale has now been made, the director of Caravans Deluxe wishes to recognise the full sale price of the caravan, $30,000, in the accounts for the year ended 30 June 20X7.

Required

Advise the director of the correct accounting treatment for this transaction. Assume a 10% discount rate. Show the journal entries for this treatment.

Answer

The director wishes to recognise the sale as early as possible. However, following IFRS 15 *Revenue from contracts with customers*, he cannot recognise revenue from this sale because control of the caravan has not been transferred, so the performance obligation has not been satisfied. This happens on the date of delivery, which is 1 August 20X7. Accordingly, no revenue can be recognised in the current period.

The receipt of cash in the form of the $3,000 deposit must be recognised. However, while the deposit is termed 'non-refundable', it does create an obligation to complete the contract. The other side of the entry is therefore to deferred income in the statement of financial position.

The journal entries would be as follows:

DEBIT	Cash	$3,000	
CREDIT	Liability (deferred income)		$3,000

Being deposit received in advance of the sale being recognised.

On 1 August 20X7, when the sale is recognised, this deferred income account will be cleared. In addition:

The revenue from the sale of the caravan will be recognised. Of this, $12,000 is receivable in two years' time, which, with a 10% discount rate, is: $\$12,000/1.1^2 = \$9,917$. $15,000 is receivable on 1 August 20X7.

The service plan is not really 'free' – nothing is. It is merely a deduction from the cost of the caravan. The service plan must be recognised separately at its stand-alone selling price of $1,500. It is deferred income and will be recognised over the three year period as the performance obligation of providing a service plan is satisfied.

The sales revenue recognised in respect of the caravan will be a balancing figure.

The journal entries are as follows:

DEBIT	Deferred income	$3,000	
DEBIT	Cash (1st instalment)	$15,000	
DEBIT	Receivable (balance discounted)	$9,917	
CREDIT	Deferred income (service plan monies received in advance)		$1,500
CREDIT	Revenue (balancing figure)		$26,417

BPP Note. This question is rather fiddly, so do not worry too much if you didn't get all of it right. Read through our solution carefully, going back to first principles where required.

5 Professional skills: guidance from the ACCA

FAST FORWARD

Marks are awarded for **professional skills**.

Ethics and professionalism are a key part of your ACCA qualification. Accordingly, the ACCA has stated that marks for professional skills will be awarded at the Professional Level. The examiner has provided specific guidance for P2 *Corporate Reporting.*

5.1 Professional Skills – Basis of the award of marks

Marks will be awarded for professional skills in this paper. These skills encompass the creation, analysis, evaluation and synthesis of information, problem solving, decision making and communication skills.

More specifically they will be awarded for:

(a) Developing information and ideas and forming an opinion.

(b) Developing an understanding of the implications for the entity of the information including the entity's operating environment.

(c) Analysing information and ideas by identifying:

The purpose of the analysis
The limitations of given information
Bias and underlying assumptions and their impact
Problems of liability and inconsistency

(d) Identifying the purpose of a computation and whether it meets its purpose.

(e) Analysing information, drawing conclusions and considering implications, and any further action required.

(f) Identifying appropriate action in response to the information/analysis including advice or amendments to the data.

(g) Considering, discussing and combining ideas and information from diverse sources to arrive at a solution or a broader understanding of the issues.

(h) Analysing the information in the context of the views and reactions of the stakeholders.

(i) Identifying solutions to problems or ranking potential solutions, or ways to manage the problem, or recommending a course of action.

(j) Exercising good judgement and an ethical approach to providing advice in line with:

Relevant standards
Stakeholders' interests
The stated objectives

(k) Communicating effectively and efficiently in producing required documents including:

The intended purpose of the document
Its intended users and their needs
The appropriate type of document
Logical and appropriate structure/format
Nature of background information and technical language
Detail required
Clear, concise and precise presentation

There will be **four marks awarded in each paper for the above professional skills. The marks will be awarded in Questions 2, 3 and 4, but not in Question 1.** Not all skills will be required in each paper.

Chapter Roundup

- **Corporate governance** has been important in recent years and in the current syllabus it is important in the context of ethical behaviour.
- The 1989 *Framework for the Preparation of Financial Statements* was replaced in 2010 by the *Conceptual Framework for Financial Reporting*. This is the result of a joint project with the FASB. In 2015 an ED was issued with proposals for a revised *Conceptual Framework*.
- **Revenue recognition** is straightforward in most business transactions, but some situations are more complicated.
- IFRS 15 *Revenue from contracts with customers* is concerned with the **recognition of revenues** arising from fairly common transactions.
  - The sale of goods
  - The rendering of services
  - The use by others of entity assets yielding interest, royalties and dividends
- Generally revenue is recognised when the entity has transferred promised goods or services to the customer. The standard sets out five steps for the recognition process.
- Marks are awarded for **professional skills**.

Quick Quiz

1 What is corporate governance?

2 Why is a conceptual framework necessary?

3 What are the disadvantages of a conceptual framework?

4 What are the seven sections of the IASB's *Framework*?

5 Which concept will be reintroduced in the *Conceptual Framework* under the proposals in the May 2015 Exposure Draft?

6 Revenue is generally recognised; under IFRS 15, as earned at the .... **(fill in the blanks)**.

7 How is revenue measured?

8 How should revenue be recognised when the transaction involves the rendering of services?

Answers to Quick Quiz

1 Corporate governance is the system by which companies are directed and controlled.

2 To provide a theoretical basis for financial reporting.

3 (a) A single conceptual framework may not suit all users
(b) Different standards, based on a different framework, may be needed to meet the needs of different users
(c) It is not clear that a conceptual framework does in fact facilitate the preparation of financial statements

4 (a) The objective of financial statements
(b) Underlying assumptions
(c) Qualitative characteristics of financial statements
(d) The elements of financial statements
(e) Recognition of the elements of financial statements
(f) Measurement of the elements of financial statements
(g) Concepts of capital and capital maintenance

5 Prudence

6 Time when the performance obligation is satisfied, which is when the customer obtains control of the promised good or service.

7 At the fair value of the consideration received.

8 By reference to the progress towards complete satisfaction of the performance obligation.

Now try the question below from the Practice Question Bank

Number	Level	Marks	Time
Q1	Introductory	n/a	n/a
Q3	Introductory	n/a	n/a

2

Professional and ethical duty of the accountant

Topic list	Syllabus reference
1 Ethical theories	A2
2 Influences on ethics	A2
3 The social and ethical environment	A2
4 Ethics in organisations	A2
5 Principles and guidance on professional ethics	A2
6 Practical situations	A2
7 Examination questions: an approach	A2

Introduction

Ethics are an important aspect of the ACCA qualification. They need to be applied in all aspects of managerial behaviour. An attempt to massage profit figures, or non-disclosure of a close relationship may amount to unethical behaviour. However, it is the nature of ethics to deny easy answers; furthermore, in the context of business, ethical prescriptions have to be practical to be of any use. This chapter focuses on the professional integrity of the accountant and director, but you will also consider ethics in the context of off balance sheet finance.

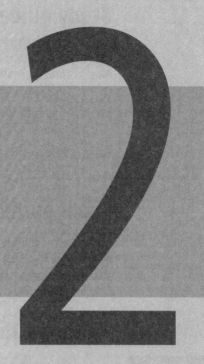

Study guide

		Intellectual level
A2	**Ethical requirements of corporate reporting and the consequences of unethical behaviour**	
(a)	Appraise the potential ethical implications of professional and managerial decisions in the preparation of corporate reports	3
(b)	Assess the consequences of not upholding ethical principles in the preparation of corporate reports	3

Exam guide

Ethics are most likely to be considered in the context of the accountant's role as adviser to the directors. A question on the Pilot Paper asked you to explain why a deliberate misrepresentation in the financial statements was unethical. A scenario question at the end of this Study Text asks for a discussion of why directors might have acted unethically in adopting accounting policies to boost earnings.

1 Ethical theories

FAST FORWARD

A key debate in ethical theory is whether ethics can be determined by **objective, universal principles**. How important the **consequences of actions** should be in determining an ethical position is also a significant issue.

1.1 An introduction to ethics

In this chapter you will encounter various philosophical, academic terms. We have to use this terminology as the examiner will use it in questions. However provided that you focus on certain basic issues, you will be able to negotiate this chapter successfully.

1.1.1 Do ethics change over time and place?

One viewpoint is that ethics do vary between time and place. Slavery for example is now regarded as wrong, whereas in Roman times slavery was acceptable. The view that ethics vary between different ages and different communities is known as **ethical relativism** and is discussed in Section 1.3.

The opposing view is that ethics are unchanging over time and place; some courses of action are always right, others are always wrong. A simple example would be saying that it is always wrong to steal. The view that there are certain unchanging ethical rules is known as **ethical absolutism** and is discussed in Section 1.4.

1.1.2 Should you consider the consequences of your actions when making ethical decisions?

One view is that society is best served by everyone following certain ethical rules, and obeying them no matter what the results are. The argument is that people will undermine society if they disobey the ethical rules, even if they do so with the intention of avoiding adverse consequences. This viewpoint, known as **deontological ethics**, was developed by Kant.

The opposing viewpoint is that you cannot divorce an action from its consequences, and when taking ethical decisions you must take account of what the consequences will be. This viewpoint is known as **teleological ethics**. If you take this viewpoint, that implies that you have to define what the best possible consequences are. The different variations of the teleological viewpoint try to do this.

1.1.3 What thought processes do people use when making ethical decisions?

What the theories are aiming to do is to complete the following sentence:

'You should act ethically because ...

In Section 2 we shall look at the work of Kohlberg who supplied various examples of thought processes, depending on the degree of ethical development of the individual.

- People who are less ethically developed may think: 'You should act ethically because you'll be punished if you don't.'
- People who have more advanced ethical development may think: 'You should act ethically because your country's laws say you should.'
- People at the highest level of ethical development may think: 'You should act ethically because it's always right to do so, no matter what the consequences and costs are to you personally.'

Question — **Ethical issues**

Briefly explain the main ethical issues that are involved in the following situations.

(a) Dealing with a repressive authoritarian government abroad
(b) An aggressive advertising campaign
(c) Employee redundancies
(d) Payments or gifts to officials who have the power to help or hinder the payees' operations

Answer

(a) Dealing with unpleasantly authoritarian governments can be supported on the grounds that it **contributes to economic growth and prosperity** and all the benefits they bring to society in both countries concerned. This is a consequentialist argument. It can also be opposed on consequentialist grounds as **contributing to the continuation of the regime**, and on deontological grounds as **fundamentally repugnant**.

(b) Honesty in advertising is an important problem. Many products are promoted exclusively on image. Deliberately creating the impression that purchasing a particular product will enhance the happiness, success and sex-appeal of the buyer can be attacked as **dishonest**. It can be defended on the grounds that the supplier is actually **selling a fantasy or dream** rather than a physical article.

(c) Dealings with employees are coloured by the **opposing views of corporate responsibility and individual rights**. The idea of a job as property to be defended has now disappeared from labour relations in many countries, but corporate decisions that lead to redundancies are still deplored. This is because of the obvious **impact of sudden unemployment on aspirations and living standards**, even when the employment market is buoyant. Nevertheless businesses have to consider the cost of employing labour as well as its productive capacity.

(d) The main problems with payments or gifts to officials are making distinction between those that should never be made, and those that can be made in certain cultural circumstances.

(i) **Extortion**. Foreign officials have been known to threaten companies with the complete closure of their local operations unless suitable payments are made.

(ii) **Bribery**. This is payments for services to which a company is not legally entitled. There are some fine distinctions to be drawn; for example, some managers regard political contributions as bribery.

(iii) **Grease money**. Multinational companies are sometimes unable to obtain services to which they are legally entitled because of deliberate stalling by local officials. Cash payments to the right people may then be enough to oil the machinery of bureaucracy.

(iv) **Gifts**. In some cultures (such as Japan) gifts are regarded as an essential part of civilised negotiation, even in circumstances where to Western eyes they might appear ethically dubious. Managers operating in such a culture may feel at liberty to adopt the local customs.

PER alert

One of the competences you need to fulfil Objective 1 of the Practical Experience Requirement (PER) is to demonstrate the application of professional ethics, values and judgement. So although you should read through the theory, the application is more important. You will be faced with ethical dilemmas in your working life.

1.2 Role of ethical theory

Ethics is concerned with right and wrong and how conduct should be judged to be good or bad. It is about how we should live our lives and, in particular, how we should **behave towards other people**. It is therefore relevant to all forms of human activity.

Business life is a fruitful source of ethical dilemmas because its whole purpose is **material gain**, the making of profit. Success in business requires a constant, avid search for potential advantage over others and business people are under pressure to do whatever yields such advantage.

It is important to understand that if ethics is applicable to corporate behaviour at all, it must therefore be a fundamental aspect of **mission**, since everything the organisation does flows from that. Managers responsible for strategic decision making cannot avoid responsibility for their organisation's ethical standing. They should consciously apply ethical rules to all of their decisions in order to filter out potentially undesirable developments. The question is however what ethical rules should be obeyed. Those that always apply or those that hold only in certain circumstances?

Ethical assumptions underpin all business activity as well as guiding behaviour. The continued existence of capitalism makes certain assumptions about the 'good life' and the desirability of private gain, for example. As we shall see in Chapter 10, accountancy is allegedly not a value-neutral profession. It establishes and follows rules for the protection of shareholder wealth and the reporting of the performance of capital investment. Accordingly accounting, especially in the private sector, can be seen as a servant of capital, making the implicit assumptions about morality that capitalism does.

1.3 Ethical relativism and non-cognitivism

Key term

Relativism is the view that a **wide variety of acceptable ethical beliefs and practices** exist. The ethics that are most appropriate in a given situation will depend on the conditions at that time.

The relativist approach suggests that all moral statements are essentially subjective and arise from the culture, belief or emotion of the speaker.

Non-cognitivism recognises the differences that exist between the rules of behaviour prevailing in different cultures. The view that right and wrong are culturally determined is called **ethical relativism** or **moral relativism**. Ethical rules will differ in different periods within the same society, and will differ between different societies. Acceptance of ethical relativism implies that a society should not impose moral imperatives strictly, since it accepts that different ethical and belief systems are acceptable.

This is clearly a matter of significance in the context of international business. Managers encountering cultural norms of behaviour that differ significantly from their own may be puzzled to know what rules to follow.

Question

What can be said about the morality of a society that allows abortion within certain time limits in certain circumstances, or which allows immigration if immigrants fulfil certain requirements (will benefit the local economy)?

Answer

The suggested treatment of these issues implies that the society is a non-cognitivist, ethically relative society. Banning abortion would be one sign of an ethically absolute society.

1.3.1 Strengths of relativism

(a) Relativism highlights our **cognitive bias** in observing with our senses (we see only what we know and understand) and our **notational bias** (what we measure without using our senses is subject to the bias of the measurement methods used).

(b) Relativism also highlights differences in **cultural beliefs**; for example all cultures may say that it is wrong to kill innocents, but different cultures may have different beliefs about who innocents actually are.

(c) The philosopher Bernard Crick argued that differing absolutist beliefs result in **moral conflict** between people; (relativist) ethics should act to resolve such conflicts.

(d) In the global economy, where companies conduct businesses in many different countries and cultures, adopting a relativist approach presumes **more flexibility** and therefore greater success.

1.3.2 Criticisms of relativism

(a) Put simply, strong relativism is based on a **fundamental contradiction**; the statement that 'All statements are relative' is itself an absolute, non-relative statement. However it is possible to argue that some universal truths (certain laws of physics) exist, but deny other supposedly objective truths.

(b) A common criticism of relativism, particularly by religious leaders, is that it leads to a **philosophy of 'anything goes'**, denying the existence of morality and permitting activities that are harmful to others.

(c) Alternatively, some critics have argued for the existence of **natural moral laws** (discussed below). These are not necessarily religious laws; the atheist scientist Richard Dawkins has argued in favour of natural laws.

(d) Ideas such as **objectivity and final truth** do have value – consider for example, the ethical principle that we shall discuss later for accountants to be objective.

(e) If it's valid to say that everyone's differing opinions are **right**, then it's equally valid to say that **everyone's differing opinions are wrong**.

1.4 Ethical absolutism and cognitivism

Key term

Absolutism is the view that there is an unchanging set of ethical principles that will apply in all situations, at all times and in all societies.

Absolutist approaches to ethics are built on the principle that **objective, universally applicable moral truths** exist and can be known. There is a set of moral rules that are always true. There are various methods of establishing these:

(a) **Religions** are based on the concept of universally applicable principles.

(b) **Law** can be a source of reference for establishing principles. However, ethics and law are not the same thing. Law must be free from ambiguity. However, unlike law, ethics can quite reasonably be an arena for debate, about both the principles involved and their application in specific rules.

(c) **Natural law** approaches to ethics are based on the idea that a set of objective or 'natural' moral rules exists and we can come to know what they are. In terms of business ethics, the natural law approach deals mostly with **rights and duties**. Where there is a right, there is also a duty to respect that right. For those concerned with business ethics there are undeniable implications for behaviour towards individuals. Unfortunately, the implications about duties can only be as clear as the rights themselves and there are wide areas in which disagreement about rights persists.

(d) **Deontological approaches** (see below).

Many absolutists would accept that some ethical truths may differ between different cultures. However they would also believe in certain basic truths that should be common to all cultures (for example, 'thou shall not kill').

1.5 Deontological ethics

Key term

Deontology is concerned with the application of absolute, universal ethical principles in order to arrive at rules of conduct, the word deontology being derived from the Greek for 'duty'.

Deontology lays down **criteria** by which actions may be judged in advance, the outcomes of the actions are not relevant. The definitive treatment of deontological ethics is found in the work of the eighteenth century German philosopher, *Immanuel Kant*.

Kant's approach to ethics is based on the idea that facts themselves are neutral: they are what they are; they do not give us any indication of what should be. If we make moral judgements about facts, the criteria by which we judge are separate from the facts themselves. Kant suggested that the criteria come from within ourselves and are based on a **sense of what is right**; an intuitive awareness of the nature of good.

Kant spoke of motivation to act in terms of 'imperatives'. A **hypothetical imperative** lays down a course of action to achieve a certain result. For instance, if I wish to pass an examination I must study the syllabus. A **categorical imperative**, however, defines a course of action in terms of acting in accordance with **moral duty** without reference to outcomes, desire or motive. For Kant, moral conduct is defined by categorical imperatives. We must act in certain ways because it is right to do so – right conduct is an **end in itself**.

Kant arrived at three formulations of the categorical imperative.

(a) 'So act that the maxim of your will could hold as a principle establishing universal law.'

This is close to the common sense maxim called the golden rule found in many religious teachings, for example the bible:

In everything do to others what you would have them do to you, for this sums up the Law and the Prophets (Matthew 7:12).

The difference between Kant's views and the golden rule is that under the golden rule, one could inflict harm on others if one was happy for the same harm to be inflicted on oneself. Kant however would argue that certain actions were universally right or wrong, irrespective of the personal, societal or cultural conditions.

Kant went on to suggest that this imperative meant that we have a duty not to act by maxims that result in logical contradictions. Theft of property for examples implies that it is permissible to steal, but also implies the existence of property; however if theft is allowed there can be no property, a logical contradiction. Kant also argued that we should act only by maxims that we believe should be universal maxims. Thus if we only helped others when there was advantage for ourselves, no-one would ever give help to others.

(b) 'Do not treat people simply as means to an end but as an end in themselves.'

The point of this rule is that it distinguishes between **people** and **objects**. We use objects as means to achieve an end: a chair is for sitting on, for instance. People are different.

We regard people differently from the way we regard objects, since they have unique intellects, feelings, motivations and so on of their own: treating them as objects denies their rationality and hence rational action.

Note, however, that this does not preclude us from using people as means to an end as long as we, at the same time, recognise their right to be treated as autonomous beings. Clearly, organisations and even society itself could not function if we could not make use of other people's services.

(c) 'So act as though you were through your maxims a law-making member of the kingdom of ends.'

Autonomous human beings are not subject to any particular interest and are therefore only subject to the universal laws which they make for themselves. However, they must regard those laws as binding on others, or they would not be universal and would not be laws at all.

1.5.1 Criticisms of Kant

(a) Critics have pointed out a dualism in Kant's views; he sees humans as part of nature whose actions can be explained in terms of natural causes. Yet Kant also argues that human beings are **capable of self-determination** with full freedom of action and in particular an ability to act in accordance with the principles of duty. Man is therefore capable in effect of rising above nature, which appears to conflict with the view that man is a natural animal.

(b) It is argued that you cannot take actions in a vacuum and must have regard for their **consequences**. The Swiss philosopher Benjamin Constant put forward the 'enquiring murderer' argument; if you agree with Kant and hold that Truth telling must be universal, then one must, if asked, tell a known murderer the location of his prey. Kant's response was that lying to a murderer denied the murderer's rationality, and hence denied the possibility of there being free rational action at all. In addition, Kant pointed out that we cannot always know what the consequences of our actions would be.

(c) Kierkegaard argued that, whatever their expectations of others, **people failed to apply Kant's duties** to themselves, either by not exercising moral laws or not punishing themselves if they morally transgressed.

1.6 Teleological or consequentialist ethics: utilitarianism

There are two versions of consequentialist ethics:

- Utilitarianism – what is best for the greatest number
- Egoism – what is best for me

The teleological approach to ethics is to make moral judgements about courses of action by reference to their **outcomes or consequences**. The prefix *telios* is derived from the Greek and refers to issues of ends or outcomes.

Right or wrong becomes a question of **benefit or harm** rather than observance of universal principles.

Utilitarianism is the best-known formulation of this approach and can be summed up in the '**greatest good**' principle – 'greatest happiness of the greatest number'. This says that when deciding on a course of action we should choose the one that is likely to result in the greatest good for the greatest number of people. It therefore contrasts sharply with any absolute or universal notion of morality. The 'right' or 'wrong' can **vary between situations and over time** according to the greatest happiness of the greatest number.

Utilitarianism underlies the assumption that the **operation of the free market** produces the **best possible consequences**. Free markets, it is argued, create wealth, this leads to higher tax revenue, this can pay for greater social welfare expenditures.

1.6.1 Problems with utilitarianism

There is an immediate problem here, which is how we are to define what is good for people. Bentham, a philosopher who wrote on utilitarianism, considered that **happiness** was the measure of good and that actions should therefore be judged in terms of their potential for promoting happiness or relieving unhappiness. Others have suggested that longer lists of harmful and beneficial things should be applied.

Case Study

A connected problem lies in outcomes that may in fact be beneficial but are not recognised as such. The **structural adjustment programmes** provided by the International Monetary Fund are a case in point. They are designed to align a country's economic incentives so that, by improving trade and public finances, to meet an objective, such as debt repayment. The IMF might argue, therefore, that the pain and dislocation suffered are short-term difficulties for long-term well-being. Critics of IMF structural adjustment programmes might suggest the opposite: that they are designed to remove money from the very poorest. The rights of the poor are more important than those of bondholders and to insist on repayment is unethical.

The utilitarian approach may also be questioned for its potential effect upon minorities. A situation in which a large majority achieved great happiness at the expense of creating misery among a small minority would satisfy the 'greatest good' principle. It could not, however, be regarded as ethically desirable.

However, utilitarianism can be a useful guide to conduct. It has been used to derive wide ranging rules and can be applied to help us make judgements about individual, unique problems.

Exam focus point

The Pilot Paper asked for the consequentialist and deontological approaches to ethics to be contrasted.

1.7 Teleological or consequentialist ethics: egoism

Key term

Egoism states that an act is ethically justified if decision-makers freely decide to pursue their own short-term desires or their long-term interests. The subject to all ethical decisions is the self.

Adam Smith argued that an egoistic pursuit of individual self-interest produced a desired outcome for society through **free competition and perfect information** operating in the marketplace. Producers of goods for example have to offer value-for-money, since competition means that customers will buy from competitors if they don't. Egoism can also link in with enlightened self-interest; a business investing in good facilities for its workforce to keep them content and hence maintain their loyalty.

1.7.1 Criticisms of egoism

One criticism of pure egoism is that it makes short-term selfish desires equivalent to longer-term, more beneficial, interests. A modified view would give most validity to exercising those short-term desires that were in long-term interests. A more serious criticism has been that the markets do not function perfectly, and that some participants can benefit themselves at the expense of others and also the wider environment – hence the debate on sustainability which we shall consider in Chapter 18. Most fundamentally egoism is argued to be the **ethics of the thief** as well as the short-termist.

1.8 Pluralism

Pluralism accepts that different views may exist on morality, but suggests a consensus may be able to be reached in certain situations. A pluralist viewpoint is helpful in business situations where a range of perspectives have to be understood in order to establish a **course of action**. It emphasises the importance of morality as a **social phenomenon**; that some rules and arrangements need to be established for us to live together and we therefore need a good understanding of the different moralities that we will encounter.

However a consensus may not always be possible, and this is a key message of this section of the Text. Irreconcilable ethical disputes tend to arise when absolutists argue with relativists, or if you have a deontological viewpoint opposed to a teleological viewpoint. For example, during the recent debate in the UK about embryology, deontological arguments on the sanctity of life were opposed to teleological arguments about the scientific benefits of experimentation on embryos.

2 Influences on ethics

FAST FORWARD

Ethical decision making is influenced by **individual and situational factors.**

Individual factors include **age and gender**, **beliefs**, **education and employment**, how much **control** individuals believe they have over their own situation and their **personal integrity**.

Kohlberg's framework relates to individuals' degree of **ethical maturity**, the extent to which they can take their own ethical decisions.

Situational factors include **the systems of reward**, **authority** and **bureaucracy**, **work roles**, **organisational factors**, and the **national and cultural contexts**.

2.1 The cultural context of ethics and corporate social responsibility

Models of ethical decision-making divide the cultural factors that influence decision-making into two categories:

- **Individual** – the characteristics of the individual making the decision.
- **Situational** – the features of the context which determine whether the individual will make an ethical or unethical decision.

The problem with identifying these factors is that it is difficult to break them down individually since many of them are interdependent. Also evidence on the importance of **individual factors** seems to be mainly from the **USA**, whereas information on **situational factors** seems mainly to be from **Europe**. This arguably reflects an American focus on individual economic participants, whereas European attention is more focused on the design of economic institutions and how they function morally and promote moral behaviour in others.

2.2 Individual influences

2.2.1 Age and gender

Although some evidence suggests that the ways in which men and women respond to ethical dilemmas may differ, empirical studies do not clearly show whether men or women can be considered as more ethical. Similarly, although different age groups have been influenced by different experiences, again empirical evidence does not suggest that certain age groups are more moral than others.

2.2.2 National and cultural beliefs

By contrast national and cultural beliefs seem to have a significant effect on ethical beliefs, shaping what individuals regard as acceptable business issues. Hofstede has indicated that significant differences lie in the following four areas:

(a) **Individualism/collectivism** – the extent to which the culture emphasises the autonomous individual as opposed to group and community goals.

(b) **Power distance** – how much acceptance there is in the society of the unequal distribution of power, and the perceived gap between juniors and seniors in a society or social structure (eg children/parents, students/teachers, citizens/legislators).

Hickson and Pugh describe power distance as 'how removed subordinates feel from superiors in a social meaning of the word distance. In a high power distance culture, inequality is accepted... in a low power distance culture inequalities and overt status symbols are minimised and subordinates expect to be consulted and to share decisions with approachable managers'.

(c) **Uncertainty avoidance** – individuals' preferences for certainties, rules and absolute truths.

(d) **Masculinity/femininity** – or the extent to which money and possessions are valued as against people and relationships.

These factors may influence how an individual tackles an ethical problem; alone (in an individualist culture) or in consultation (in a collectivist situation). Other influences might be on how individuals respond to ethically questionable directives from their superiors; in power distance cultures, where hierarchy is respected, commands are less likely to be questioned (I was only obeying orders). Globalisation may weaken the influence of national factors, although there is often a close connection between the local culture and a particular geographical region.

2.2.3 Education and employment

By contrast globalisation might be expected to strengthen the influence of education and employment. There do appear to be some differences in ethical decision-making between those with different educational and professional experiences.

2.2.4 Psychological factors

Psychological factors are concerned with the ways in which people think, and hence **decide what is the morally right or wrong course of action**. Discussion has centred on **cognitive moral development** and **locus of control**.

2.2.5 Locus of control

The locus of control is **how much influence individuals believe** they have over the course of their own lives. Individuals with a high internal locus believe that they can shape their own lives significantly, whereas those with external locus believe that their lives will be shaped by circumstances or luck. This distinction suggests that those with an internal locus will take more responsibility for their actions and are more likely to consider the moral consequences of what they do. Research however does not clearly indicate whether this is true in practice. This may also link into attitudes towards risk and what can be done to deal with risk.

2.2.6 Personal integrity

Integrity can be defined as adhering to moral principles or values. Its ethical consequences are potentially very significant, for example in deciding whether to **whistleblow** on questionable practice at work, despite pressure from colleagues or superiors or negative consequences of doing so. However, evidence of its importance is limited because strangely it has not been included in many ethical decision models.

2.2.7 Moral imagination

Moral imagination is the level of awareness individuals have about the variety of moral consequences of what they do, how creatively they reflect on ethical dilemmas. The consequences of having a wide moral imagination could be an ability to see beyond the conventional organisational responses to moral difficulties, and formulate different solutions. Again, there is little research on this subject, but differing levels of moral imagination would seem to be a plausible reason why individuals with the same work background view moral problems in different ways.

2.3 Situational influences

The reason for considering situational influences on moral decision-making is that individuals appear to have 'multiple ethical selves' – they make different decisions in different circumstances. These circumstances might include **issue-related factors** (the nature of the issue and how it is viewed in the organisation) and **context-related factors** (the expectations and demands that will be placed on people working in an organisation).

2.4 Issue-related factors

2.4.1 Moral intensity

Thomas Jones proposed a list of six criteria that decision-makers will use to decide how ethically significant an issue was, and hence what they should do:

- **Magnitude of consequences** – the harms or the benefits that will result
- **Social consequences** – the degree of general agreement about the problem
- **Probability of effect** – the probability of the harms or benefits actually happening
- **Temporal immediacy** – the speed with which the consequences are likely to occur; if they are likely to take years, the moral intensity may be lower
- **Proximity** – the feelings of nearness that the decision-maker has for those who will suffer the impacts of the ethical decision
- **Concentration of effect** – whether some persons will suffer greatly or many people will suffer lightly

Research suggests that moral intensity is significant but has to be seen in the context of how an issue is perceived in an organisation.

2.4.2 Moral framing

Moral framing sets the context for how issues are **perceived** in organisations. Language is very important. Using words such as fairness and honesty is likely to trigger moral thinking. However, evidence suggests that many managers are reluctant to frame issues in moral terms seeing it as promoting disharmony, distorting decision-making and suggesting that they are not practical. Instead issues are more likely to be discussed in terms of **rational corporate self-interest**.

2.5 Context-related factors

2.5.1 Systems of reward

Reward mechanisms have obvious potential consequences for ethical behaviour. This works both ways. Basing awards on sales values achieved may encourage questionable selling practices; failing to reward ethical behaviour (or worst still penalising whistleblowers or other staff who act ethically) will not encourage an ethical culture.

Sadly a majority of studies on this area seem to indicate that there is a significant link between the rewarding of unethical behaviour and its continuation.

2.5.2 Authority

There are various ways in which managers may encourage ethical behaviour; by **direct instructions** to subordinates, by setting subordinates **targets** that are so challenging that they can only be achieved through taking unethical shortcuts. Failing to act can be as bad as acting, for example failing to prevent bullying. Studies suggest that many employees perceive their managers as lacking ethical integrity.

2.5.3 Bureaucracy

Key term

Bureaucracy is a system characterised by detailed rules and procedures, impersonal hierarchical relations and a fixed division of tasks.

Bureaucracy underpins the authority and reward system, and may have a number of impacts on individual's reactions to ethical decision-making:

- **Suppression of moral autonomy** – individual ethical beliefs tend to be overridden by the rules and roles of the bureaucracy
- **Instrumental morality** – seeing morality in terms of following procedures rather than focusing on the moral substance of the goals themselves.
- **Distancing** individuals from the consequences of what they do.
- **Denial of moral status** – that ultimately individuals are resources for carrying out the organisation's will rather than autonomous moral beings.

2.5.4 Work roles

Education and experience build up expectations of how people in particular roles will act. Strong evidence suggests that the expectations staff have about the roles that they adopt in work will override the individual ethics that may influence their decisions in other contexts.

2.5.5 Organisational field

Key term

> An **organisational field** is a community of organisations with a common 'meaning system' and whose participants interact more frequently with one another than those outside the field.

Organisations within an organisational field tend to share a common business environment, such as a common system of training or regulation. This means that they tend to cohere round common norms and values.

Within an organisational field a **recipe** is a common set of assumptions about organisational purposes and how to manage organisations. If the recipe is followed, it means that organisations within the organisational field can provide consistent standards for consumers for example. However, it can also mean that managers within the field cannot appreciate the lessons that could be learnt from organisations outside the field, and therefore transition outside the field may be difficult.

Case Study

An example would be a private sector manager joining a public service organisation and having to get used to different traditions and mechanisms, for example having to build consensus into the decision-making process.

The result of being in an organisational field can be a desire to achieve **legitimacy** – meeting the **expectations** that those in the same organisational field have in terms of the assumptions, behaviours and strategies that will be pursued.

2.5.6 Organisational culture

Key term

> **Organisational culture** is the 'basic assumptions and beliefs that are shared by members of an organisation, that operate unconsciously and define in a basic taken-for-granted fashion an organisation's view of itself and its environment.'
> (Handy)

Organisational culture relates to ways of acting, talking, thinking and evaluating. It can include shared:

- **Values** that often have 'official' status being connected to the organisation's mission statement but which can be vague (acting in the interests of the community).

- **Beliefs** that are more specific than assumptions but represent aspects of an organisation that are talked about, for example using 'ethical suppliers'.
- **Behaviours**, the ways in which people within the organisation and the organisation itself operates, including work routines and symbolic gestures.
- **Taken** for **granted assumptions**, which are at the core of the organisation's culture which people find difficult to explain but are central to the organisation. The **paradigm** represents the common assumptions and collective experience that an organisation must have to function meaningfully

Organisational culture may be different to (may conflict with) the official rules of the bureaucracy. Unsurprisingly it has been identified as a key element in decisions of what is morally right or wrong, as employees become conditioned by it into particular attitudes to ethical decision making.

Case Study

In his memoirs the journalist Hunter Davies related that when he started working on a newspaper in London, he discovered that he was financially rather better off than he thought he would be because of being able to claim expenses. 'This was something that was explained to me on my very first day, not by the management, but by other reporters.' Staff would spend the first working morning of their week filling out their expenses 'for some the hardest part of their week'.

Davies was told what the normal expense claim for his role as a junior reporter was. All he had to do in order to claim that amount was submit bills for lunch or dinner with anyone; it didn't matter who they were so long as he had a piece of paper and could name them as a potential contact. Davies was informed that management knew, that it was an accepted part of national newspaper life and he would undermine the system if he didn't do what everyone else did.

This is a very good example of Level 2 Stage 3 of Kohlberg's framework, doing something because those close to you (colleagues) are doing it.

In addition to the main organisational culture, there may also be **distinct subcultures** often dependent upon the way the organisation is structured, for example function or division subcultures.

2.5.7 National and cultural context

In an organisational context, this is the **nation** in which the ethical decision is made rather than the nationality of the decision-maker. If someone spends a certain length of time working in another country, their views of ethical issues may be shaped by the norms of that other country, for example on sexual harassment. Globalisation may complicate the position on this.

3 The social and ethical environment 12/07 – 12/16

FAST FORWARD

Firms have to ensure they obey the law: but they also face **ethical concerns**, because their reputations depend on a good image.

Key term

Ethics: a set of moral principles to guide behaviour.

Whereas the political environment in which an organisation operates consists of laws, regulations and government agencies, the social environment consists of the customs, attitudes, beliefs and education of society as a whole, or of different groups in society; and the ethical environment consists of a set (or sets) of well-established rules of personal and organisational behaviour.

Social attitudes, such as a belief in the merits of education, progress through science and technology, and fair competition, are significant for the management of a business organisation. Other beliefs have either gained strength or been eroded in recent years:

(a) There is a growing belief in preserving and improving the quality of life by reducing working hours, reversing the spread of pollution, developing leisure activities and so on. Pressures on organisations to consider the environment are particularly strong because most environmental damage is irreversible and some is fatal to humans and wildlife.

(b) Many pressure groups have been organised in recent years to protect social minorities and under-privileged groups. Legislation has been passed in an attempt to prevent discrimination on grounds of race, sex, disability, age and sexual orientation.

(c) Issues relating to the environmental consequences of corporate activities are currently debated, and respect for the environment has come to be regarded as an unquestionable good.

The ethical environment refers to justice, respect for the law and a moral code. The conduct of an organisation, its management and employees will be measured against ethical standards by the customers, suppliers and other members of the public with whom they deal.

3.1 Ethical problems facing managers

Managers have a duty (in most entities) to aim for profit. At the same time, modern ethical standards impose a duty to guard, preserve and enhance the value of the entity for the good of all touched by it, including the general public. Large organisations tend to be more often held to account over this than small ones.

In the area of **products and production**, managers have responsibility to ensure that the public and their own employees are protected from danger. Attempts to increase profitability by cutting costs may lead to dangerous working conditions or to inadequate safety standards in products. In the United States, product liability litigation is so common that this legal threat may be a more effective deterrent than general ethical standards. The Consumer Protection Act 1987 and EU legislation generally is beginning to ensure that ethical standards are similarly enforced in the UK.

Another ethical problem concerns **payments by companies to government or municipal officials** who have power to help or hinder the payers' operations. In *The Ethics of Corporate Conduct, Clarence Walton* refers to the fine distinctions which exist in this area (Walton, 1977).

(a) **Extortion**. Foreign officials have been known to threaten companies with the complete closure of their local operations unless suitable payments are made.

(b) **Bribery**. This refers to payments for services to which a company is not legally entitled. There are some fine distinctions to be drawn; for example, some managers regard political contributions as bribery.

(c) **Grease money**. Multinational companies are sometimes unable to obtain services to which they are legally entitled because of deliberate stalling by local officials. Cash payments to the right people may then be enough to oil the machinery of bureaucracy.

(d) **Gifts**. In some cultures (such as Japan) gifts are regarded as an essential part of civilised negotiation, even in circumstances where to Western eyes they might appear ethically dubious. Managers operating in such a culture may feel at liberty to adopt the local customs.

Business ethics are also relevant to competitive behaviour. This is because a market can only be free if competition is, in some basic respects, fair. There is a distinction between competing aggressively and competing unethically.

3.2 Examples of social and ethical objectives

Companies are not passive in the social and ethical environment. Many organisations pursue a variety of social and ethical objectives.

Employees

(a) A minimum wage, perhaps with adequate differentials for skilled labour
(b) Job security (over and above the protection afforded to employees by government legislation)
(c) Good conditions of work (above the legal minima)
(d) Job satisfaction

Customers may be regarded as entitled to receive a produce of good quality at a reasonable price.

Suppliers may be offered regular orders and timely payment in return for reliable delivery and good service.

Society as a whole

(a) Control of pollution

(b) Provision of financial assistance to charities, sports and community activities

(c) Co-operation with government authorities in identifying and preventing health hazards in the products sold

As far as it is possible, social and ethical objectives should be expressed quantitatively, so that actual results can be monitored to ensure that the targets are achieved. This is often easier said than done – more often, they are expressed in the organisation's mission statement which can rarely be reduced to a quantified amount.

Many of the above objectives are commercial ones – for example, satisfying customers is necessary to stay in business. The question as to whether it is the business of businesses to be concerned about wider issues of social responsibility **at all** is discussed shortly.

3.3 Social responsibility and businesses

Arguably, institutions like hospitals, schools and so forth exist because health care and education are seen to be desirable social objectives by government at large, if they can be afforded.

However, where does this leave businesses? How far is it reasonable, or even appropriate, for businesses to exercise 'social responsibility' by giving to charities, voluntarily imposing strict environmental objectives on themselves and so forth?

One school of thought would argue that **the management of a business has only one social responsibility, which is to maximise wealth for its shareholders**. There are two reasons to support this argument.

(a) If the business is owned by the shareholders the assets of the company are, ultimately, the shareholders' property. Management has no moral right to dispose of business assets (like cash) on non-business objectives, as this has the effect of reducing the return available to shareholders. The shareholders might, for example, disagree with management's choice of beneficiary. Anyhow, it is for the shareholders to determine how their money should be spent.

(b) A second justification for this view is that management's job is to maximise wealth, as this is the best way that society can benefit from a business's activities.

   (i) Maximising wealth has the effect of increasing the tax revenues available to the State to disburse on socially desirable objectives.

   (ii) Maximising wealth for the few is sometimes held to have a 'trickle down' effect on the disadvantaged members of society.

   (iii) Many company shares are owned by pension funds, whose ultimate beneficiaries may not be the wealthy anyway.

This argument rests on certain assumptions.

(a) The first assumption is, in effect, the opposite of the stakeholder view. In other words, it is held that the **rights** of legal ownership are paramount over all other **interests** in a business: while other stakeholders have an interest, they have few legal or moral rights over the wealth created.

(b) The second assumption is that a business's **only** relationship with the wider social environment is an economic one. After all, that is what businesses exist for, and any other activities are the role of the State.

(c) The defining purpose of business organisations is the maximisation of the wealth of their owners.

4 Ethics in organisations

Ethics is a code of moral principles that people follow with respect to what is right or wrong. Ethical principles are not necessarily enforced by law, although the law incorporates moral judgements (murder is wrong ethically, and is also punishable legally).

Companies have to follow legal standards, or else they will be subject to fines and their officers might face similar charges. Ethics in organisations relates to **social responsibility** and **business practice**.

People that work for organisations bring their own values into work with them. Organisations contain a variety of ethical systems.

(a) **Personal ethics** (eg deriving from a person's upbringing, religious or non-religious beliefs, political opinions, personality). People have different ethical viewpoints at different stages in their lives. Some will judge situations on 'gut feel'. Some will consciously or unconsciously adopt a general approach to ethical dilemmas, such as 'the end justifies the means'.

(b) **Professional ethics** (eg ACCA's code of ethics, medical ethics).

(c) **Organisation cultures** (eg 'customer first'). Culture, in denoting what is normal behaviour, also denotes what is the right behaviour in many cases.

(d) **Organisation systems**. Ethics might be contained in a formal code, reinforced by the overall statement of values. A problem might be that ethics does not always save money, and there is a real cost to ethical decisions. Besides, the organisation has different ethical duties to different stakeholders. Who sets priorities?

Case Study

Organisation systems and targets do have ethical implications. The *Harvard Business Review* reported that the US retailer, Sears, Roebuck was deluged with complaints that customers of its car service centre were being charged for unnecessary work: apparently this was because mechanics had been given targets of the number of car spare parts they should sell.

4.1 Leadership practices and ethics

The role of culture in determining the ethical climate of an organisation can be further explored by a brief reflection on the role of leaders in setting the ethical standard. A culture is partly a collection of symbols and attitudes, embodying certain truths about the organisation. Senior managers are also symbolic managers; inevitably they decide priorities; they set an example, whether they like it or not. Remember, too, that one of the roles of managers, according to Mintzberg is the **ceremonial one**.

There are four types of cultural leadership in organisations. (Note that these should **not** be confused with leadership styles.)

(a) **Creative**. The culture of an organisation often reflects its founder, and it is therefore reasonable to expect that the founding visionary should set the ethical tone. Such leaders create the ethical style.

(b) **Protective**. Such leaders sustain, or exemplify, the organisation's culture: for example, a company which values customer service may have leaders who are 'heroic' in their efforts to achieve it.

(c) **Integrative**. Other leaders aim to create consensus through people, and perhaps flourish in an involvement culture. The danger is that this can turn to political manipulation; the 'consensus' created should work towards some valued cultural goal.

(d) **Adaptive**. These leaders change an existing culture or set of ethics. (When appointed to run *British Airways, Colin Marshall* changed the sign on his door from Chief Executive to his own name.) However, a leader has to send out the right signals, to ensure that competitive behaviour remains ethical, to avoid bad publicity if nothing else.

4.2 Two approaches to managing ethics

FAST FORWARD

Inside the organisation, a **compliance based approach** highlights conformity with the law. An **integrity based approach** suggests a wider remit, incorporating ethics in the organisation's values and culture.

Organisations sometimes issue **codes of conduct** to employees. Many employees are bound by professional codes of conduct.

Lynne Paine (*Harvard Business Review*, March-April 1994) suggests that ethical decisions are becoming more important as penalties, in the US at least, for companies which break the law become tougher. (This might be contrasted with UK, where a fraudster whose deception ran into millions received a sentence of community service.) Paine suggests that there are two approaches to the management of ethics in organisations.

- Compliance-based
- Integrity-based

4.2.1 Compliance-based approach

A compliance-based approach is primarily designed to ensure that the company acts within the letter of the law, and that violations are prevented, detected and punished. Some organisations, faced with the legal consequences of unethical behaviour take legal precautions such as those below.

- Compliance procedures
- Audits of contracts
- Systems for employees to inform superiors about criminal misconduct without fear of retribution
- Disciplinary procedures

Corporate compliance is limited in that it refers only to the law, but legal compliance is 'not an adequate means for addressing the full range of ethical issues that arise every day'. This is especially the case in the UK, where **voluntary** codes of conduct and self-regulation are perhaps more prevalent than in the US.

An example of the difference between the **legality** and **ethicality** of a practice is the sale in some countries of defective products without appropriate warnings. 'Companies engaged in international business often discover that conduct that infringes on recognised standards of human rights and decency is legally permissible in some jurisdictions.'

The compliance approach also overemphasises the threat of detection and punishment in order to channel appropriate behaviour. Arguably, some employers view compliance programmes as an insurance policy for senior management, who can cover the tracks of their arbitrary management practices. After all, some performance targets are impossible to achieve without cutting corners: managers can escape responsibility by blaming the employee for not following the compliance programme, when to do so would have meant a failure to reach target.

Furthermore, mere compliance with the law is no guide to **exemplary** behaviour.

4.2.2 Integrity-based programmes

'An integrity-based approach combines a concern for the law with an **emphasis on managerial responsibility** for ethical behaviour. Integrity strategies strive to define companies' guiding values, aspirations and patterns of thought and conduct. When integrated into the day-to-day operations of an organisation, such strategies can help prevent damaging ethical lapses, while tapping into powerful human impulses for moral thought and action.

It should be clear to you from this quotation that an integrity-based approach to ethics treats ethics as an issue of organisation culture.

Ethics management has several tasks:

- To define and give life to an organisation's defining values
- To create an environment that supports ethically sound behaviour
- To instil a sense of shared accountability amongst employees

The table below indicates some of the differences between the two main approaches.

	Compliance	Integrity
Ethos	Knuckle under to external standards	Choose ethical standards
Objective	Keep to the law	Enable legal and responsible conduct
Originators	Lawyers	Management, with lawyers, HR specialists etc
Methods (both includes education, and audits, controls, penalties)	Reduced employee discretion	Leadership, organisation systems
Behavioural assumptions	People are solitary self-interested beings	People are social beings with values
Standards	The law	Company values, aspirations (including law)
Staffing	Lawyers	Managers and lawyers
Education	The law, compliance system	Values, the law, compliance systems
Activities	Develop standards, train and communicate, handle reports of misconduct, investigate, enforce, oversee compliance	Integrate values *into* company systems, provide guidance and consultation, identify and resolve problems, oversee compliance

In other words, an integrity-based approach **incorporates** ethics into corporate culture and systems.

Case Study

Charles Hampden-Turner, 1990(in his book *Corporate Culture*) notes that attitudes to safety can be part of a corporate *culture*. He quotes the example of a firm called (for reasons of confidentiality) *Western Oil*.

Western Oil had a bad safety record. 'Initially, safety was totally at odds with the main cultural values of productivity (management's interests) and maintenance of a macho image (the worker's culture) ... Western Oil had a culture which put safety in conflict with other corporate values.' In particular, the problem was with its long-distance truck drivers (which in the US have a culture of solitary independence and self reliance) who drove sometimes recklessly with loads large enough to inundate a small town. The company instituted *Operation Integrity* to improve safety, in a lasting way, changing the policies and drawing on the existing features of the culture but using them in a different way.

The culture had five dilemmas.

- **Safety-first vs macho-individualism**. Truckers see themselves as 'fearless pioneers of the unconventional lifestyle ... "Be careful boys!" is hardly a plea likely to go down well with this particular group'. Instead of trying to control the drivers, the firm recommended that they become **road safety consultants** (or design consultants). Their advice was sought on improving the system. This had the advantage that 'by making drivers critics of the system their roles as outsiders were preserved and promoted'. It tried to tap their heroism as promoters of public safety.
- **Safety everywhere vs safety specialists**. Western Oil could have hired more specialist staff. However, instead, the company promoted cross functional safety teams from existing parts of the business, for example, to help in designing depots and thinking of ways to reduce hazards.
- **Safety as cost vs productivity as benefit**. 'If the drivers raced from station to station to win their bonus, accidents were bound to occur .... The safety engineers rarely spoke to the line manager in charge of the delivery schedules. The unreconciled dilemma between safety and productivity had been evaded at management level and passed down the hierarchy until drivers were subjected to two incompatible injunctions, work fast and work safely'. To deal with this problem, safety would be built into the reward system.

- **Long-term safety vs short-term steering.** The device of recording 'unsafe' acts in operations enabled them to be monitored by cross-functional teams, so that the causes of accidents could be identified and be reduced.
- **Personal responsibility vs collective protection.** It was felt that if 'safety' was seen as a form of management policing it would never be accepted. The habit of management 'blaming the victim' had to stop. Instead, if an employee reported another to the safety teams, the person who was reported would be free of **official** sanction. Peer presence was seen to be a better enforcer of safety than the management hierarchy.

It has also been suggested that the following institutions can be established.

- An **ethics committee** is a group of executives (perhaps including non-executive directors) appointed to oversee company ethics. It rules on misconduct. It may seek advice from specialists in business ethics.
- An **ethics ombudsperson** is a manager who acts as the corporate conscience.

Accountants can also appeal to their professional body for ethical guidance.

Whistle-blowing is the disclosure by an employee of illegal, immoral or illegitimate practices on the part of the organisation. In theory, the public ought to welcome the public trust: however, confidentiality is very important in the accountants' code of ethics. Whistle-blowing frequently involves **financial loss** for the whistle-blower.

- The whistle-blower may lose his or her job.
- If the whistle-blower is a member of a professional body, he or she cannot, sadly, rely on that body to take a significant interest, or even offer a sympathetic ear. Some professional bodies have narrow interpretations of what is meant by ethical conduct. For many the duties of **commercial confidentiality** are felt to be more important.

Exam focus point

The ethics codes described above can be related to mission, culture and control strategies. A compliance-based approach suggest that bureaucratic control is necessary; an integrity-based approach relies on cultural control.

5 Principles and guidance on professional ethics

FAST FORWARD

IFAC's and ACCA's guidance is very similar.

5.1 The public interest

FAST FORWARD

Organisations sometimes issue **codes of conduct** to employees. Many employees are bound by professional codes of conduct.

Accountants require an **ethical code** because they hold positions of trust, and people rely on them.

The International Federation of Accountants' (IFAC's) *Code of Ethics* gives the key reason why accountancy bodies produce ethical guidance: the public interest.

'A distinguishing mark of the accountancy profession is its acceptance of the responsibility to act in the public interest. Therefore, a professional accountant's responsibility is not exclusively to satisfy the needs of an individual client or employer.

The public interest is considered to be the collective well-being of the community of people and institutions the professional accountant serves, including clients, lenders, governments, employers, employees, investors, the business and financial community and others who rely on the work of professional accountants.'

The **key reason** that **accountants need** to have an **ethical code** is that **people rely on them and their expertise**.

Accountants deal with a range of issues on behalf of clients. They often have access to confidential and sensitive information. Auditors claim to give an independent view. It is therefore critical that accountants, and particularly auditors, are, and are seen to be, independent.

As the auditor is required to be, and seen to be, ethical in his dealings with clients, ACCA publishes guidance for its members, the *Code of Ethics and Conduct* (ACCA, 2016). This guidance is given in the form of fundamental principles, specific guidance and explanatory notes.

IFAC also lays down fundamental principles in its *Code of Ethics*. The fundamental principles of the two Associations are extremely similar.

5.2 The fundamental principles

ACCA
• **Integrity**. Members should be **straightforward** and **honest** in all professional and business relationships.
• **Objectivity**. Members **should not allow bias, conflict of interest or undue influence of others** to override professional or business judgements.
• **Professional Competence and Due Care**. Members have a continuing duty to maintain professional knowledge and skill at a level required to ensure that a client or employer receives the advantage of competent professional service based on current developments in practice, legislation and techniques. Members should act diligently and in accordance with applicable technical and professional standards when providing professional services.
• **Confidentiality**. Members should respect the confidentiality of information acquired as a result of professional or business relationships **and should not disclose** any such information to third parties without proper and specific authority **unless there is a legal or professional right or duty to disclose**. Confidential information acquired as a result of professional and business relationships should not be used for the personal advantage of the professional accountant or third parties.
• **Professional Behaviour**. Members should **comply with relevant laws and regulations and should avoid any action that discredits the profession.**

5.3 Ethical framework

The ethical guidance discussed above is in the form of a framework. It contains some rules, for example, ACCA prohibits making loans to clients, but in the main it is flexible guidance. It can be seen as being a **framework rather than a set of rules**. There are a number of advantages of a framework over a system of ethical rules. These are outlined in the table below.

Advantages of an ethical framework over a rules based system
A framework of guidance places the onus on the auditor to **actively consider** independence for every given situation, rather than just agreeing a checklist of forbidden items. It also requires him to **demonstrate** that a responsible conclusion has been reached about ethical issues.
The framework **prevents auditors interpreting legalistic requirements narrowly** to get around the ethical requirements. There is an extent to which rules engender deception, whereas principles encourage compliance.
A framework **allows for** the variations that are found in every **individual situation**. Each situation is likely to be different.
A framework can accommodate a **rapidly changing environment**, such as the one that auditors are constantly in.
However, a **framework can contain prohibitions** (as noted above) where these are necessary as safeguards are not feasible.

6 Practical situations 12/07 – 12/16

FAST FORWARD

Exam questions may ask you to think about what should be done if breaches of laws, regulations or ethical guidelines occur. **Close relationships** between the parties or other **conflicts of interest** are often a complication.

6.1 Examination questions

Examination questions will expect you to be able to apply your understanding of ethical issues to practical problems arising in organisations. Later in this chapter we are going to suggest an approach that you may find helpful in dealing with such questions, but first we are going to take the bare bones of a situation and see how it might be built up into the kind of scenario you will have to face.

6.2 The problem

The exam may present you with a scenario, typically containing an array of detail much of which is potentially relevant. The problem, however, will be one or other of two basic types.

(a) A wishes B to do C which is in breach of D

where

A	=	A situation, person, group of people, institution or the like
B	=	You/a management accountant, the person with the ethical dilemma
C	=	Acting, or refraining from acting, in a certain way
D	=	An ethical principle, quite possibly one of the ACCA's fundamental principles

(b) Alternatively, the problem may be that A has done C, B has become aware of it and D requires some kind of response from B.

6.3 Example: the problem

An accountant joined a manufacturing company as its Finance Director. The company had acquired land on which it built industrial units. The Finance Director discovered that, before he had started at the company, one of the units had been sold and the selling price was significantly larger than the amount which appeared in the company's records. The difference had been siphoned off to another company – one in which his boss, the Managing Director, was a major shareholder. Furthermore, the Managing Director had kept his relationship with the second company a secret from the rest of the board.

The Finance Director confronted the Managing Director and asked him to reveal his position to the board. However, the Managing Director refused to disclose his position to anyone else. The secret profits on the sale of the unit had been used, he said, to reward the people who had secured the sale. Without their help, he added, the company would be in a worse position financially.

The Finance Director then told the Managing Director that unless he reported to the board he would have to inform the board members himself. The Managing Director still refused. The Finance Director disclosed the full position to the board.

The problem is of the **second basic type. B** is of course the easiest party to identify. Here it is the **Finance Director**. **A** is clear, as well: it is the **Managing Director**. **C** is the **MD's breach of his directorial duties** regarding related party transactions not to obtain any personal advantage from his position of director without the consent of the company for whatever gain or profit he has obtained. **D** is the **principle that requires B not to be a party to an illegal act**. (Note that we distinguish between ethical and legal obligations. B has legal obligations as a director of the company. He has ethical obligations not to ignore his legal obligations. In **this** case the two amount to the same thing.)

6.4 Relationships

You may have a feeling that the resolution of the problem described above is just too easy, and you would be right. This is because A, B, C and D are either people, or else situations involving people, who stand in certain relationships to each other.

- A may be B's boss, B's subordinate, B's equal in the organisational hierarchy, B's husband, B's friend.
- B may be new to the organisation, or well-established and waiting for promotion, or ignorant of some knowledge relevant to the situation that A possesses or that the people affected by C possess.
- C or D, as already indicated, may involve some person(s) with whom B or A have a relationship – for example, the action may be to misrepresent something to a senior manager who controls the fate of B or A (or both) in the organisation.

Question — Relationships

Identify the relationships in the scenario above. What are the possible problems arising from these relationships?

Answer

The MD is the Finance Director's boss. He is also a member of the board and is longer established as such than B, the Finance Director.

In outline the problems arising are that **by acting ethically the Finance Director will alienate the MD**. Even if the problem were to be resolved the episode would sour all future dealings between these two parties. Also, **the board may not be sympathetic to the accusations of a newcomer**. The Finance Director may find that he is ignored or even dismissed.

Relationships should never be permitted to affect ethical judgement. If you knew that your best friend at work had committed a major fraud, for example, **integrity** would demand that **in the last resort** you would have to bring it to the attention of somebody in authority. But note that this is only in the last resort. Try to imagine what you would do in practice in this situation.

Surely your **first course** would be to try to **persuade your friend** that what they had done was wrong, and that they themselves had an ethical responsibility to own up. Your **second option**, if this failed, might be to try to get **somebody** (perhaps somebody outside the organisation) that you knew could **exert pressure** on your friend to persuade him or her to own up.

There is obviously a limit to how far you can take this. The important point is that just because you are dealing with a situation that involves ethical issues, this **does not mean that all the normal principles of good human relations and good management have to be suspended**. In fact, this is the time when such business principles are most important.

6.5 Consequences

Actions have consequences and the consequences themselves are quite likely to have their own ethical implications.

In the example given above, we can identify the following further issues:

(a) The MD's secret transaction appears to have been made in order to secure the sale of an asset the proceeds of which are helping to prop up the company financially. Disclosure of the truth behind the sale may mean that the company is pursued for compensation by the buyer of the site. The **survival of the company** as a whole may be jeopardised.

(b) If the truth behind the transaction becomes public knowledge this could be highly damaging for the company's **reputation**, even if it can show that only one black sheep was involved.

(c) The board may simply rubber stamp the MD's actions and so the Finance Director may still find that he is expected to be party to dishonesty. (This assumes that the **company as a whole is amoral** in its approach to ethical issues. In fact the MD's refusal to disclose the matter to the board suggests otherwise.)

In the last case we are back to square one. In the first two cases, the Finance Director has to consider the ethicality or otherwise of taking action that could lead to the collapse of the company, extensive redundancies, unpaid creditors and shareholders and so on.

6.6 Actions

In spite of the difficulties, your aim will usually be to reach a satisfactory resolution to the problem. **The actions that you recommend** will often include the following.

- **Informal discussions** with the parties involved.
- **Further investigation** to establish the full facts of the matter. What extra information is needed?
- The **tightening up of controls or the introduction of new ones**, if the situation arose due to laxity in this area. This will often be the case and the principles of professional competence and due care and of technical standards will usually be relevant.
- **Attention to organisational matters** such as changes in the management structure, improving communication channels, attempting to change attitudes.

Question **Cunning plan**

Your Finance Director has asked you to join a team planning a takeover of one of your company's suppliers. An old school friend works as an accountant for the company concerned, the Finance Director knows this, and has asked you to try and find out 'anything that might help the takeover succeed, but it must remain secret'.

Answer

There are three issues here. First, you have a **conflict of interest** as the Finance Director wants you to keep the takeover a secret, but you probably feel that you should tell your friend what is happening as it may affect their job.

Second, the finance director is asking you to deceive your friend. Deception is unprofessional behaviour and will break your ethical guidelines. Therefore the situation is presenting you with **two conflicting demands**. It is worth remembering that no employer can ask you to break your ethical rules.

Finally, the request to break your own ethical guidelines constitutes **unprofessional behaviour** by the Finance Director. You should consider reporting him to their relevant body.

7 Examination questions: an approach

7.1 Dealing with questions

FAST FORWARD

In a situation involving ethical issues, there are **practical steps** that should be taken.

- Establish the facts of the situation by further investigation and work.
- Consider the alternative options available for action.
- Consider whether any professional guidelines have been breached.
- State the best course of action based on the steps above.

An article in a student magazine contained the following advice for candidates who wish to achieve good marks in ethics questions. (The emphasis is BPP's.)

'The precise question requirements will vary, but in general marks will be awarded for:

- Analysis of the situation
- A recognition of ethical issues
- Explanation if appropriate of relevant part of ethical guidelines, and interpretation of its relevance to the question
- Making clear, logical, and appropriate recommendations for action. Making inconsistent recommendations does not impress examiners
- Justifying recommendations in practical business terms and in ethical terms

As with all scenario based questions there is likely to be **more than one acceptable answer**, and marks will depend on how well the case is argued, rather than for getting the 'right' answer.

However, questions based on ethical issues tend to produce a range of possible solutions which are, on the one hand, consistent with the ethical guidelines and acceptable, and on the other hand, a range of clearly inadmissible answers which are clearly in breach of the ethical guidelines and possibly the law.'

7.2 Step-by-step approach

We suggest, instead, that:

(a) You use the question format to structure your answer
(b) You bear in mind what marks are being awarded for (see above)
(c) You adhere to the following list of do's and don'ts. Be sure to read the notes following.

DO	Note	DON'T
Identify the key facts as briefly as possible (one sentence?)	1	Merely paraphrase the question
Identify the major principle(s) at issue	2	Regurgitate the entire contents of the *Ethical Guidelines*
Consider alternative actions and their consequences	3	List every single possible action and then explain how all the unsuitable ones can be eliminated
Make a decision and recommend action as appropriate	4	Fail to make a decision or recommend action. Propose actions in breach of the *Ethical Guidelines* or the law
Justify your decision	5	Be feeble. 'This should be done because it is ethical' is not terribly convincing

Notes

1 **One sentence** is an ideal to aim for.

2 (a) **Use the terminology of the ethical guidelines, but not *ad nauseam***. 'Integrity' is often more clearly described as 'honesty' (although the two words are not synonymous). Don't forget the words 'fairness', 'bias', and 'influence' when discussing 'objectivity'.

(b) **Don't torture the case study to make it fit a fundamental principle**: if, say, 'justice' is the most persuasive word for a situation don't be afraid of using it.

(c) If the law is involved, don't get carried away – this is **not a law exam**. 'The director has a statutory duty to ...' is sufficient: there is no need to go into legal detail.

3 Useful ways of generating alternatives are:

(a) To **consider the problem from the other side of the fence**: imagine you are the guilty party

(b) To **consider the problem from the point of view of the organisation** and its culture and environment

4 Making a decision is often very hard, but if you cannot do this you are simply not ready to take on the responsibilities of a qualified accountant. There are usually a number of decisions that could be justified, so **don't be afraid of choosing the 'wrong' answer.**

5 This is not actually as hard as you might think.

7.3 Regurgitating the question

Possibly the most **common fault** in students' answers to questions on ethics is that they include large **amounts of unanalysed detail copied out from the question** scenarios in their answers. This earns no marks.

You can very easily avoid the temptation to merely paraphrase the question. Simply **begin your answer by stating that you are referring to 'issues'** (by which you mean all the details contained in the question) **discussed at a previous meeting, or set out in full in 'appended documents'**. If you do this you will be writing your report to someone already in possession of the same facts as you have.

7.4 Justifying your decision

The article quoted above says that **marks will be awarded for 'justifying recommendations in practical business terms and in ethical terms'.** We shall conclude by examining a passage from a model solution to a question on ethics to see how this can be done.

> 'Perhaps the first thing to do is to **report** the whole matter, **in confidence** and **informally**, to the chief internal auditor with suggestions that a **tactful investigation** is undertaken to **verify as many of the facts** as possible. The fact that the sales manager has already been tackled (informally) about the matter may be a positive advantage as **he/she may be recruited** to assist in the investigation. It could however be a problem as the information needed for further **investigation** may already been removed. **Tact** is crucial as handling the matter the wrong way could adversely influence the whole situation. An understanding of who participants are and how they are implicated can be used positively to bring about change with the **minimum of disruption**.'

The key to this approach is **using the right language**, and to a large extent you cannot help doing so if you have sensible suggestions to make. The real problem that many students experience with questions of this type is lack of confidence in their own judgement. If you have sound business and managerial sense and you know the ethical guidelines there is every reason to suppose that an answer that you propose will be acceptable, so don't be shy of expressing an opinion.

Exam focus point

In an internal company role, ethical problems could be in the following forms:

- Conflict of duties to different staff superiors
- Discovering an illegal act or fraud perpetrated by the company (ie its directors)
- Discovering a fraud or illegal act perpetrated by another employee
- Pressure from superiors to take certain viewpoints, for example towards budgets (pessimistic/optimistic etc) or not to report unfavourable findings

Chapter Roundup

- A key debate in ethical theory is whether ethics can be determined by **objective, universal principles**. How important the **consequences of actions** should be in determining an ethical position is also a significant issue.
- Ethical decision-making is influenced by **individual and situational factors**.
- **Individual factors** include **age and gender, beliefs, education and employment**, how much **control** individuals believe they have over their own situation and their **personal integrity**.
- **Kohlberg's** framework relates to individuals' degree of **ethical maturity**, the extent to which they can take their own ethical decisions.
- **Situational factors** include **the systems of reward**, **authority** and **bureaucracy**, **work roles**, **organisational factors**, and the **national and cultural contexts**.
- Firms have to ensure they obey the law: but they also face **ethical concerns**, because their reputations depend on a good image.
- Inside the organisation, a **compliance based approach** highlights conformity with the law. An **integrity based approach** suggests a wider remit, incorporating ethics in the organisation's values and culture.
- Organisations sometimes issue **codes of conduct** to employees. Many employees are bound by professional codes of conduct.
- Accountants require an **ethical code** because they hold positions of trust, and people rely on them.
- IFAC's and ACCA's guidance is very similar.
- Organisations sometimes issue **codes of conduct** to employees. Many employees are bound by professional codes of conduct.
- Exam questions may ask you to think about what should be done if breaches of laws, regulations or ethical guidelines occur. **Close relationships** between the parties or other **conflicts of interest** are often a complication.
- In a situation involving ethical issues, there are **practical steps** that should be taken.
  - Establish the facts of the situation by further investigation and work.
  - Consider the alternative options available for action.
  - Consider whether any professional guidelines have been breached.
  - State the best course of action based on the steps above.

Quick Quiz

1 Which view of ethics states that right and wrong are culturally determined?

A Ethical relativism
B Cognitivism
C Teleological
D Deontological

2 Fill in the blank.

The .... approach to ethics is to make moral judgements about courses of action by reference to their outcomes or consequences.

3 In what areas of national and cultural beliefs has Hofstede identified significant differences?

4 What is the significance of the post-conventional stage of an individual's moral development according to Kohlberg?

5 What ethical problems face management?

6 What objectives might a company have in relation to wider society?

7 To whom might management have responsibilities, and what are some of these responsibilities?

8 Why does Mintzberg say that the profit motive is not enough?

9 Describe two approaches to the management of ethics in an organisation.

10 What systems of ethics might you find in an organisation?

11 What is whistle-blowing?

12 Match the fundamental principle to the characteristic.

(a) Integrity

(b) Objectivity

(i) Members should be straightforward and honest in all professional and business relationships.

(ii) Members should not allow bias, conflict or interest or undue influence of others to override professional or business judgements.

Answers to Quick Quiz

1 A Ethical relativism

2 Teleological or consequentialist

3
- Individualism vs collectivism
- Acceptance of unequal distribution of power and status
- How much individuals wish to avoid uncertainties
- Masculinity vs femininity, money and possessions vs people and relationships

4 The post-conventional stage is when individuals make their own ethical decisions in terms of what they believe to be right, not just acquiescing in what others believe to be right.

5 There is a constant tension between the need to achieve current profitability, the need to safeguard the stakeholders' long term investment and the expectations of wider society.

6 Protection of the environment, support for good causes, a responsible attitude to product safety.

7 Managers of businesses are responsible to the owners for economic performance and to wider society for the externalities related to their business operations.

8 Large businesses are rarely controlled by their shareholders; they receive a lot of support from public funds; and their activities have wider consequences.

9 A compliance-based approach aims to remain within the letter of the law by establishing systems of audit and review so that transgressions may be detected and punished. An integrity-based approach tries to promote an ethical culture in which individuals will do the right thing.

10 Personal ethics, professional ethics, organisation culture, organisation systems.

11 Informing outside regulatory agencies about transgressions by one's organisation.

12 (a) (i)

(b) (ii)

Now try the question below from the Practice Question Bank

Number	Level	Marks	Time
Q2	Introductory	n/a	n/a

PART B

Accounting standards

3

Non-current assets

Topic list	Syllabus reference
1 The definition of an asset	C2
2 Revision of IASs 16, 20 and 23	C2
3 IAS 36 *Impairment of assets*	C2
4 IAS 40 *Investment property*	C2
5 IAS 38 *Intangible assets*	C2
6 Goodwill	C2, D1

Introduction

We look again here at the **IASB definition of an asset**, as given in the *Framework* and compare it with the definitions given by other standard setters, particularly FASB in the USA and the ASB in the UK.

You have covered several of the relevant standards relating to non-current assets in your earlier studies. These are straightforward and are revised briefly in Section 2, with some questions for you to try. If you have any problems, **go back to your earlier study material**.

The IASB has a standard covering the **impairment of assets**. This is a controversial topic and you must understand the relevant standard. **IAS 36** is discussed in depth in Section 3.

IAS 40 on **investment property** is discussed in detail in Section 4. This standard has been amended by IFRS 16 *Leases* (see Chapter 8).

We begin our examination of intangible non-current assets with a discussion of **IAS 38**.

Goodwill and its treatment is a controversial area, as is the accounting for items similar to goodwill, such as brands. Goodwill is very important in **group accounts**.

Study guide

		Intellectual level
C2	**Non-current assets**	
(a)	Apply and discuss the timing of the recognition of non-current assets and the determination of their carrying amounts, including impairments and revaluations	3
(c)	Apply and discuss accounting treatment of investment properties including classification, recognition and measurement issues	3

Exam guide

The approach of Paper P2 to accounting standards is very different from your earlier studies. You will need to think critically and deal with controversial issues. Ensure that you visit the IASB website on a regular basis. However, the standards met at F7 are very examinable at P2, just in a different and more challenging way.

On intangibles, you may be given an unusual situation and asked to identify the issues. Is a football player an intangible asset?

1 The definition of an asset

FAST FORWARD

You must learn the IASB *Framework* **definition of an asset**: a resource controlled by the entity as a result of past events and from which future economic benefits are expected to flow to the entity.

This definition ties in closely with the definitions produced by **other standard-setters**, particularly FASB (USA) and ASB (UK).

Assets have been defined in many different ways and for many purposes. The definition of an asset is important because it directly affects the **treatment** of such items. A good definition will prevent abuse or error in the accounting treatment: otherwise some assets might be treated as expenses, and some expenses might be treated as assets.

Let us begin with a simple definition from the CIMA *Official Terminology*.

Key term

An **asset** is any tangible or intangible possession which has value.

This admirably succinct definition seems to cover the main points: **ownership** and **value**. An asset is so called because it is owned by someone who values it. However, this definition leaves several questions unanswered.

(a) What determines ownership?
(b) What determines value?

Such a simple definition is not adequate in the current accounting climate, where complex transactions are carried out daily.

1.1 IASB definition

Remember the definition of an asset in the IASB's *Conceptual Framework*.

Key term

Asset. A resource controlled by the entity as a result of past events and from which future economic benefits are expected to flow to the entity. *(Conceptual Framework, IASB, 2010: Chapter 4, para. 4(a))*

Let us also look at one or two other definitions from other standard-setters.

1.2 Accounting Standards Board (ASB): UK

In the ASB's *Statement of Principles,* Chapter 4, paragraph 4.6 *The Elements of Financial Statements* assets are defined as follows (ASB, 1999).

Key term

Assets are rights or other access to future economic benefits controlled by an entity as a result of past transactions or events.

The *Statement* goes on to discuss various aspects of this definition, and it is broadly consistent with the IASB's *Conceptual Framework*. The *Statement* then goes further in discussing the complementary nature of assets and liabilities.

1.3 Financial Accounting Standards Board (FASB): USA

The definition given by the FASB in its *Statement of Financial Accounting Concepts* (FASB, 1985) is very similar.

Key term

Assets are probable future economic benefits obtained or controlled by a particular entity as a result of past transactions or events.

'Probable' is given in its general meaning merely to reflect the fact that no future outcome can be predicted with total certainty.

1.4 Comparison of definitions

FAST FORWARD

The definition has three important characteristics:

- **Future economic benefit**
- **Control (ownership)**
- **Transaction to acquire control has taken place**

It is clear from what we have seen so far that a general consensus seems to exist in the standard setting bodies as to the definition of an asset. That definition encompasses the following:

- Future economic benefit
- Control (ownership)
- The transaction to acquire control has already taken place

1.5 Definition of a non-current asset

Non-current assets may be defined as follows.

Key term

A **non-current asset** is one intended for use on a continuing basis in the company's activities, ie it is not intended for resale.

2 Revision of IASs 16, 20 and 23 12/08, 12/12, 6/13, 6/14, 12/14, 12/15, 6/16

FAST FORWARD

You should already be familiar with many standards relating to **non-current assets** from earlier studies. If not, go back to your earlier study material.

- IAS 16 *Property, plant and equipment*
- IAS 20 *Accounting for government grants and disclosure of government assistance*
- IAS 23 *Borrowing costs*

You have studied these standards for earlier papers, but they are fairly straightforward. Read the summary of knowledge brought forward and try the relevant questions. If you have any difficulty, go back to your earlier study material and re-read it.

Exam focus point

IASs studied in earlier papers will probably not be examined in any depth in Paper 2, but you will be expected to know the principles of the standards. In particular, it would not look very good if you mentioned something in the exam which actually contradicted any of these standards.

2.1 IAS 16 Property, plant and equipment

Knowledge brought forward from earlier studies

IAS 16 ***Property, plant and equipment***

Definitions (IAS 16, para. 6)

- **Property, plant and equipment** are tangible assets with the following properties.
  - Held by an entity for use in the production or supply of goods or services, for rental to others, or for administrative purposes
  - Expected to be used during more than one period
- **Cost** is the amount of cash or cash equivalents paid or the fair value of the other consideration given to acquire an asset at the time of its acquisition or construction.
- **Residual value** is the estimated amount that an entity would currently obtain from disposal of the asset, after deducting the estimated costs of disposal, if the asset were already of the age and in the condition expected at the end of its useful life.
- **Fair value** is the price that would be received to sell an asset or paid to transfer a liability in an orderly transaction between market participants at the measurement date.
- **Carrying amount** is the amount at which an asset is recognised after deducting any accumulated depreciation and accumulated impairment losses.

Accounting treatment

- As with all assets, **recognition** depends on two criteria:
  - It is probable that **future economic benefits** associated with the item will flow to the entity
  - The cost of the item can be **measured reliably**
- These recognition criteria apply to **subsequent expenditure** as well as costs incurred initially (ie, there are no longer separate criteria for recognising subsequent expenditure).

(IAS 16, para. 7 to 10)

- Once recognised as an asset, items should **initially be measured at cost**. (IAS 16, para. 15)
  - **Purchase price**, less trade discount/rebate
  - **Directly attributable costs** of bringing the asset to working condition for intended use
  - **Initial estimate** of the **costs of dismantling and removing the item** and **restoring the site** on which it is located

The revised IAS 16 provides additional guidance (IAS 16: para. 16) on directly attributable costs included in the cost of an item of property, plant and equipment.

(a) These costs bring the asset to the location and working condition necessary for it to be capable of operating in the manner intended by management, including those costs to test whether the asset is functioning properly.

(b) These are determined after deducting the net proceeds from selling any items produced when bringing the asset to its location and condition.

Knowledge brought forward from earlier studies (continued)

The standard also states that income and related expenses of operations that are incidental to the construction or development of an item of property, plant and equipment should be recognised in the profit or loss.

IAS 16 specifies (IAS 16: para. 24) that exchanges of items of property, plant and equipment, regardless of whether the assets are similar, are measured at fair value, unless the exchange transaction lacks commercial substance or the fair value of neither of the assets exchanged can be measured reliably. If the acquired item is not measured at fair value, its cost is measured at the carrying amount of the asset given up.

- **Measurement subsequent to initial recognition**. (IAS 16: paras. 30, 31)
  - **Cost model:** carry asset at cost less depreciation and any accumulated impairment losses
  - **Revaluation model:** carry asset at revalued amount, ie fair value less subsequent accumulated depreciation and any accumulated impairment losses. (The revised IAS 16 makes clear that the revaluation model is available only if the fair value of the item can be measured reliably.)
- **Revaluations**. (IAS 16: para. 36)
  - Carry out regularly, depending on volatility
  - Fair value is usually market value, or depreciated replacement cost
  - If one asset is revalued, so must be the whole of the rest of the class at the same time
  - Increase in value is credited to a revaluation surplus (part of owners' equity)
  - Decrease is an expense in profit or loss after cancelling a previous revaluation surplus
  - Additional disclosure required
- **Depreciation and revaluations**. (IAS 16: para. 42)
  - Depreciation is based on the carrying value in the statement of financial position. It must be determined separately for each significant part of an item.
  - Excess over historical cost depreciation can be transferred to realised earnings through reserves.
  - The residual value and useful life of an asset, as well as the depreciation method must be reviewed at least at each financial year end, rather than periodically as per the previous version of IAS 16. Changes are changes in accounting estimates and are accounted for prospectively as adjustments to future depreciation.
  - Depreciation of an item does not cease when it becomes temporarily idle or is retired from active use and held for disposal.
- **Retirements and disposals:** gains or losses are calculated by comparing net proceeds with carrying amount of the asset and are recognised as income/expense in profit or loss. (IAS 16: para. 67)

A further point worth emphasising here is the relationship between the accounting treatment of **impairments and revaluations**.

(a) An **impairment loss** should be treated in the same way as a **revaluation decrease**, ie the decrease should be recognised as an expense. However, a revaluation decrease (or impairment loss) should be charged directly against any related revaluation surplus to the extent that the decrease does not exceed the amount held in the revaluation surplus in respect of that same asset.

(b) A **reversal of an impairment** loss should be treated in the same way as a **revaluation increase**, ie a revaluation increase should be recognised as income to the extent that it reverses a revaluation decrease or an impairment loss of the same asset previously recognised as an expense.

Question **Depreciation**

What are the purposes of providing for depreciation?

Answer

The accounts of a business try to recognise that the cost of a non-current asset is gradually consumed as the asset wears out. This is done by gradually writing off the asset's cost in profit or loss over several accounting periods. This process is known as depreciation, and is an example of the accrual assumption. Depreciation should be allocated on a systematic basis to each accounting period during the useful life of the asset.

With regard to the accrual principle, it is fair that the profits should be reduced by the depreciation charge, this is not an arbitrary exercise. Depreciation is not, as is sometimes supposed, an attempt to set aside funds to purchase new long-term assets when required. Depreciation is not generally provided on freehold land because it does not 'wear out' (unless it is held for mining).

2.1.1 Acceptable methods

In 2014, the IASB published amendments to IAS 16 and IAS 38 in a document *Clarification of acceptable methods of depreciation and amortisation.*

Technical or commercial obsolescence

The first of these amendments concerned technical or commercial obsolescence, clarifying that **expected future reductions in the selling price of an item that was produced using an asset could indicate the expectation of technical or commercial obsolescence of the asset**, which, in turn, might reflect a reduction of the future economic benefits embodied in the asset. (IAS 16: para. 56)

Depreciation method

The second amendment to IAS 16 concerned the depreciation method, which must reflect the pattern in which the asset's future economic benefits are expected to be consumed by the entity. The 2014 amendment **disallows depreciation methods that are based on revenue generated by an activity that includes the use of an asset**. The revenue generated by an activity that includes the use of an asset generally **reflects factors other than the consumption of the economic benefits of the asset.** For example, revenue is affected by other inputs and processes, selling activities and changes in sales volumes and prices. The price component of revenue may be affected by inflation, which has no bearing upon the way in which an asset is consumed. (IAS 16: para. 62A)

2.1.2 Measurement subsequent to initial recognition

The standard offers two possible treatments here, essentially a choice between keeping an asset recorded at **cost** or revaluing it to **fair value**.

(a) **Cost model.** Carry the asset at its cost less depreciation and any accumulated impairment loss.

(b) **Revaluation model.** Carry the asset at a revalued amount, being its fair value at the date of the revaluation less any subsequent accumulated depreciation and subsequent accumulated impairment losses. The revised IAS 16 makes clear that the **revaluation model is available only if the fair value of the item can be measured reliably**. (IAS 16: paras. 30, 31)

2.1.3 Revaluations

The **market value** of land and buildings usually represents fair value, assuming existing use and line of business. Such valuations are usually carried out by professionally qualified valuers.

In the case of **plant and equipment**, fair value can also be taken as **market value**. Where a market value is not available, however, depreciated replacement cost should be used. There may be no market value where types of plant and equipment are sold only rarely or because of their specialised nature (ie they would normally only be sold as part of an ongoing business).

The frequency of valuation depends on the **volatility of the fair values** of individual items of property, plant and equipment. The more volatile the fair value, the more frequently revaluations should be carried out. Where the current fair value is very different from the carrying value then a revaluation should be carried out.

Most importantly, when an item of property, plant and equipment is revalued, **the whole class of assets to which it belongs should be revalued**.

All the items within a class should be **revalued at the same time**, to prevent selective revaluation of certain assets and to avoid disclosing a mixture of costs and values from different dates in the financial statements. A rolling basis of revaluation is allowed if the revaluations are kept up to date and the revaluation of the whole class is completed in a short period of time.

How should any **increase in value** be treated when a revaluation takes place? The debit will be the increase in value in the statement of financial position, but what about the credit? IAS 16 requires the increase to be credited to a **revaluation surplus** (ie part of owners' equity), **unless** the increase is reversing a previous decrease which was recognised as an expense. To the extent that this offset is made, the increase is recognised as income; any excess is then taken to the revaluation reserve.

(IAS 16: para. 36)

2.1.4 Example: revaluation surplus

Binkie Co has an item of land carried in its books at $13,000. Two years ago a slump in land values led the company to reduce the carrying value from $15,000. This was taken as an expense in profit or loss for the year. There has been a surge in land prices in the current year, however, and the land is now worth $20,000.

Account for the revaluation in the current year.

Solution

The double entry is:

DEBIT	Asset value (statement of financial position)	$7,000	
CREDIT	Profit or loss for the year		$2,000
	Revaluation surplus		$5,000

The case is similar for a **decrease in value** on revaluation. Any decrease should be recognised as an expense, except where it offsets a previous increase taken as a revaluation surplus in owners' equity. Any decrease greater than the previous upwards increase in value must be taken as an expense in profit or loss for the year.

2.1.5 Example: revaluation decrease

Let us simply swap round the example given above. The original cost was $15,000, revalued upwards to $20,000 two years ago. The value has now fallen to $13,000.

Account for the decrease in value.

Solution

The double entry is:

DEBIT	Revaluation surplus	$5,000	
DEBIT	Profit or loss for the year	$2,000	
CREDIT	Asset value (statement of financial position)		$7,000

There is a further complication when a **revalued asset is being depreciated**. As we have seen, an upward revaluation means that the depreciation charge will increase. Normally, a revaluation surplus is only realised when the asset is sold, but when it is being depreciated, part of that surplus is being realised as the asset is used. The amount of the surplus realised is the difference between depreciation charged on the revalued amount and the (lower) depreciation which would have been charged on the asset's original cost. **This amount can be transferred to retained (ie realised) earnings but *not* through profit or loss.**

2.1.6 Example: revaluation and depreciation

Crinckle Co bought an asset for $10,000 at the beginning of 20X6. It had a useful life of five years. On 1 January 20X8 the asset was revalued to $12,000. The expected useful life has remained unchanged (ie three years remain).

Account for the revaluation and state the treatment for depreciation from 20X8 onwards.

Solution

On 1 January 20X8 the carrying value of the asset is $10,000 – (2 × $10,000 ÷ 5) = $6,000. For the revaluation:

DEBIT	Asset value (statement of financial position)	$6,000	
CREDIT	Revaluation surplus		$6,000

The depreciation for the next three years will be $12,000 ÷ 3 = $4,000, compared to depreciation on cost of $10,000 ÷ 5 = $2,000. So each year, the extra $2,000 can be treated as part of the surplus which has become realised:

DEBIT	Revaluation surplus	$2,000	
CREDIT	Retained earnings		$2,000

This is a movement on owners' equity only, not through profit or loss.

2.1.7 On disposal

When a revalued asset is **disposed** of, any revaluation surplus may be **transferred directly to retained earnings**.

Alternatively, it may be **left in equity** under the heading revaluation surplus.

The transfer to retained earnings **should not be made through profit or loss for the year**. In other words it must not be made as a reclassification adjustment ('recycling').

2.1.8 Bearer biological assets

An amendment has been issued to IAS 41 regarding plant-based bearer biological assets, which would include trees grown in plantations, such as grape vines, rubber trees and oil palms.

These plants are used solely to grow produce crops over several periods and are not in themselves consumed. When no longer productive they are usually scrapped.

It was decided that fair value was not an appropriate measurement for these assets as, once they reach maturity, the only economic benefit they produce comes from the agricultural produce they create. In this respect, they are similar to assets in a manufacturing activity.

Consequently, these assets have been removed from the scope of IAS 41 and should be accounted for under IAS 16 *Property, Plant and Equipment* (IAS 16: paras. 80A to 80C). They are measured at accumulated costs until maturity and are then subject to depreciation and impairment charges. The IAS 16 revaluation model could also be applied. Agricultural produce from these plants continues to be recognised under IAS 41.

2.2 IAS 20: Government grants

IAS 20 is very straightforward. The question after the following summary covers the accounting problem it tackled.

Knowledge brought forward from earlier studies

IAS 20 *Accounting for government grants and disclosure of government assistance*

Definitions (IAS 20: para. 3)

- **Government assistance**. Action by government designed to provide an economic benefit specific to an entity or range of entities qualifying under certain criteria.
- **Government grants**. Assistance by government in the form of transfers of resources to an entity in return for past or future compliance with certain conditions relating to the operating activities of the entity. They exclude those forms of government assistance which cannot reasonably have a value placed upon them and transactions with government which cannot be distinguished from the normal trading transactions of the entity.
- **Grants related to assets**. Government grants whose primary condition is that an entity qualifying for them should purchase, construct or otherwise acquire long-term assets. Subsidiary conditions may also be attached restricting the type or location of the assets or the periods during which they are to be acquired or held.
- **Grants related to income**. Government grants other than those related to assets.
- **Forgivable loans**. Loans which the lender undertakes to waive repayment of under certain prescribed conditions.

Knowledge brought forward from earlier studies (continued)

Accounting treatment

- **Recognise government grants and forgivable loans** once conditions complied with and receipt/waiver is assured. (IAS 20: para. 7)
- Grants are recognised under the **income approach**: recognise grants as income to match them with related costs that they have been received to compensate. (IAS 20: para. 12)
- Use a **systematic basis** of matching over the relevant periods. (IAS 20: para. 12)
- Grants for **depreciable assets** should be recognised as income on the same basis as the asset is depreciated. (IAS 20: para. 24)
- Grants for **non-depreciable assets** should be recognised as income over the periods in which the cost of meeting the obligation is incurred. (IAS 20: para. 24)
- A grant may be **split into parts** and allocated on different bases where there are a series of conditions attached. (IAS 20: para. 24)
- Where **related costs have already been incurred**, the grant may be recognised as income in full immediately.
- A grant in the form of a **non-monetary asset** may be valued at fair value or a nominal value.

- **Grants related to assets** may be presented in the statement of financial position *either* as **deferred income** *or* deducted in arriving at the carrying value of the asset. (IAS 20: para. 25)
- **Grants related to income** may be presented in profit or loss for the year *either* as a **separate credit** *or* **deducted** from the related expense. (IAS 20: para. 29)
- Repayment of government grants should be accounted for as a **revision of an accounting estimate**. (IAS 20: para. 32)

Disclosure (IAS 20: para. 39)

- **Accounting policy** note
- **Nature and extent** of government grants and other forms of assistance received
- **Unfulfilled conditions** and other contingencies attached to recognised government assistance

Question — Government grants

IAS 20 suggests that there are two approaches to recognising government grants: a capital approach (credit directly to shareholders' interests) and an income approach. IAS 20 requires the use of the income approach, but what are the arguments in support of each method?

Answer

IAS 20 gives the following arguments in support of each method.

Capital approach

(a) The grants are a **financing device**, so should go through profit or loss for the year they would simply offset the expenses which they are financing. No repayment is expected by the Government, so the grants should be credited directly to shareholders' interests.

(b) Grants are **not earned**, they are incentives without related costs, so it would be wrong to take them to profit or loss.

Income approach

(a) The grants are **not received from shareholders** so should not be credited directly to shareholders' interests.

(b) Grants are **not given or received for nothing**. They are earned by compliance with conditions and by meeting obligations. There are therefore associated costs with which the grant can be matched in profit or loss for the year as these costs are being compensated by the grant.

(c) Grants are an extension of **fiscal policies** and so as income and other taxes are charged against income, so grants should be credited to income.

2.3 IAS 23 Borrowing costs — 6/16

This is another straightforward standard. This time there are two calculation questions to remind you of how IAS 23 is applied.

Knowledge brought forward from earlier studies

IAS 23 *Borrowing costs*

- IAS 23 deals with the treatment of borrowing costs, often associated with the construction of **self-constructed assets**, but which can also be applied to an asset purchased that takes time to get ready for use/sale.

Definitions (IAS 23: para. 5)

- **Borrowing costs**. Interest and other costs incurred by an entity in connection with the borrowing of funds.
- **Qualifying asset**. An asset that necessarily takes a substantial period of time to get ready for its intended use or sale.

Accounting treatment

- **Borrowing costs must** be **capitalised** as part of the cost of the asset if they are directly attributable to acquisition/construction/production. **Other borrowing costs must be expensed.** (IAS 23: para. 26)
- **Borrowing costs eligible for capitalisation** are those that would have been avoided otherwise. Use judgement where a range of debt instruments is held for general finance. (IAS 23: para. 10)
- **Amount of borrowing costs available for capitalisation** is actual borrowing costs incurred less any investment income from temporary investment of those borrowings. (IAS 23: para. 12)
- For borrowings obtained generally, apply the **capitalisation rate** to the expenditure on the asset (weighted average borrowing cost). It must not exceed actual borrowing costs. (IAS 23: para. 14)
- **Capitalisation is suspended** if active development is interrupted for extended periods (IAS 23: para. 20). (Temporary delays or technical/administrative work will not cause suspension.)
- **Capitalisation ceases** (normally) when physical construction of the asset is completed, capitalisation should cease when each stage or part is completed. (IAS 23: para. 22)
- Where the carrying amount of the asset falls below cost, it must be **written down/off**. (IAS 23: para. 16)

Disclosure (IAS 23: para. 26)

- **Accounting policy** note.
- Amount of **borrowing costs capitalised** during the period.
- **Capitalisation rate** used to determine borrowing costs eligible for capitalisation.

Question — Borrowing costs 1

On 1 January 20X6 Rechno Co borrowed $15m to finance the production of two assets, both of which were expected to take a year to build. Production started during 20X8. The loan facility was drawn down on 1 January 20X8, and was utilised as follows, with the remaining funds invested temporarily.

	Asset X	*Asset Y*
	$m	$m
1 January 20X8	2.5	5.0
1 July 20X8	2.5	5.0

The loan rate was 10% and Rechno Co can invest surplus funds at 8%.

Required

Ignoring compound interest, calculate the borrowing costs which may be capitalised for each of the assets and consequently the cost of each asset as at 31 December 20X8.

Answer

		Asset X $'000	Asset Y $'000
Borrowing costs			
To 31 December 20X8	$5.0m/$10m × 10%	500	1000
Less investment income			
To 30 June 20X8	$2.5m/$5.0m × 8% × 6/12	(100)	(200)
		400	800
Cost of assets			
Expenditure incurred		5,000	10,000
Borrowing costs		400	800
		5,400	10,800

Question

Borrowing costs 2

Zenzi Co had the following loans in place at the beginning and end of 20X8.

	1 January 20X8 $m	*31 December 20X8* $m
10.0% Bank loan repayable 20Y3	120	120
9.5% Bank loan repayable 20Y1	80	80
8.9% debenture repayable 20Y8	–	150

The 8.9% debenture was issued to fund the construction of a qualifying asset (a piece of mining equipment), construction of which began on 1 July 20X8.

On 1 January 20X8, Zenzi Co began construction of a qualifying asset, a piece of machinery for a hydro-electric plant, using existing borrowings. Expenditure drawn down for the construction was: $30m on 1 January 20X8, $20m on 1 October 20X8.

Required

Calculate the borrowing costs to be capitalised for the hydro-electric plant machine.

Answer

Capitalisation rate = weighted average rate = $(10\% \times \frac{120}{120+80}) + (9.5\% \times \frac{80}{120+80}) = 9.8\%$

Borrowing costs = ($30m × 9.8%) + ($20m × 9.8% × 3/12)
= $3.43m

3 IAS 36 *Impairment of assets* 12/07, 12/11, 12/12, 12/13, 12/14, 6/16

FAST FORWARD

IAS 36 ***Impairment of assets*** covers a controversial topic and it affects goodwill as well as tangible long-term assets.

There is an established principle that assets should not be carried at above their recoverable amount. An entity should write down the carrying value of an asset to its recoverable amount if the carrying value of an asset is not recoverable in full. It puts in place a detailed methodology for carrying out impairment reviews and related accounting treatments and disclosures.

3.1 Scope

IAS 36 applies to all tangible, intangible and financial assets except inventories, assets arising from construction contracts, deferred tax assets, assets arising under IAS 19 *Employee benefits* and financial assets within the scope of IAS 32 *Financial instruments: presentation*. This is because those IASs already have rules for recognising and measuring impairment. Note also that IAS 36 does not apply to non-current assets held for sale, which are dealt with under IFRS 5 *Non-current assets held for sale and discontinued operations*. (IAS 36: para. 2)

Key terms

Impairment: a fall in the value of an asset, so that its 'recoverable amount' is now less than its carrying value in the statement of financial position.

Carrying amount: is the net value at which the asset is included in the statement of financial position (ie after deducting accumulated depreciation and any impairment losses). *(IAS 36: para. 6)*

The basic principle underlying IAS 36 is relatively straightforward. If an asset's value in the accounts is higher than its realistic value, measured as its 'recoverable amount', the asset is judged to have suffered an impairment loss. It should therefore be reduced in value, by the amount of the **impairment loss**. The amount of the impairment loss should be **written off against profit** immediately.

The main accounting issues to consider are therefore as follows:

(a) How is it possible to **identify when** an impairment loss may have occurred?
(b) How should the **recoverable amount** of the asset be measured?
(c) How should an 'impairment loss' be **reported in the accounts**?

3.2 Identifying a potentially impaired asset

An entity should carry out a **review of its assets at each year end**, to assess whether there are any indications of impairment to any assets. The concept of **materiality** applies, and only material impairment needs to be identified.

If there are indications of possible impairment, the entity is required to make a formal estimate of the **recoverable amount** of the assets concerned. (IAS 36: para. 9)

IAS 36 suggests (IAS 36: para. 12) how **indications of a possible impairment** of assets might be recognised. The suggestions are based largely on common sense.

(a) **External sources of information**

 (i) A fall in the asset's market value that is more significant than would normally be expected from passage of time over normal use.

 (ii) A significant change in the technological, market, legal or economic environment of the business in which the assets are employed.

 (iii) An increase in market interest rates or market rates of return on investments likely to affect the discount rate used in calculating value in use.

 (iv) The carrying amount of the entity's net assets being more than its market capitalisation.

(b) **Internal sources of information**: evidence of obsolescence or physical damage, adverse changes in the use to which the asset is put, or the asset's economic performance

Even if there are no indications of impairment, the following assets must **always** be tested for impairment annually.

(a) An intangible asset with an **indefinite useful life**
(b) **Goodwill** acquired in a business combination

3.3 Measuring the recoverable amount of the asset

FAST FORWARD

Impairment is determined by comparing the carrying amount of the asset with its **recoverable amount**.

The recoverable amount of an asset is the higher of the asset's **fair value less costs of disposal** and **its value in use**.

What is an asset's recoverable amount?

Key term

> The **recoverable amount of an asset** should be measured as the *higher value* of:
>
> (a) The asset's fair value less costs of disposal
>
> (b) Its value in use *(IAS 36: para. 6)*

An asset's fair value less costs of disposal is the amount net of selling costs that could be obtained from the sale of the asset. Selling costs include sales transaction costs, such as legal expenses.

(a) If there is **an active market** in the asset, the net selling price should be based on the **market value**, or on the price of recent transactions in similar assets.

(b) If there is **no active market** in the assets it might be possible to **estimate** a net selling price using best estimates of what market participants might pay in an orderly transaction at the measurementdate.

Net selling price **cannot** be reduced, however, by including within selling costs any **restructuring or reorganisation expenses**, or any costs that have already been recognised in the accounts as liabilities.

The concept of 'value in use' is very important.

Key term

> The **value in use** of an asset is measured as the present value of estimated future cash flows (inflows minus outflows) generated by the asset, including its estimated net disposal value (if any) at the end of its expected useful life. *(IAS 36: para. 6)*

The cash flows used in the calculation should be **pre-tax cash flows** and a **pre-tax discount rate** should be applied to calculate the present value.

The calculation of **value in use** must reflect the following:

(a) An estimate of the **future cash flows** the entity expects to derive from the asset
(b) Expectations about **possible variations** in the amount and timing of future cash flows
(c) The **time value of money**
(d) The price for bearing the **uncertainty** inherent in the asset, and
(e) **Other factors** that would be reflected in pricing future cash flows from the asset

Calculating a value in use therefore calls for estimates of future cash flows, and the possibility exists that an entity might come up with **over-optimistic estimates** of cash flows. The IAS therefore states the following (IAS 36: paras. 33 to 35):

(a) Cash flow projections should be based on **'reasonable and supportable' assumptions**.

(b) Projections of cash flows, normally up to a maximum period of five years, should be based on the most **recent budgets or financial forecasts**.

(c) Cash flow projections beyond this period should be obtained by extrapolating short-term projections, using either a **steady or declining growth rate** for each subsequent year (unless a rising growth rate can be justified). The long-term growth rate applied should not exceed the average long term growth rate for the product, market, industry or country, unless a higher growth rate can be justified.

3.3.1 Composition of estimates of future cash flows

These should include the following (IAS 36: para. 50):

(a) Projections of **cash inflows** from **continuing use** of the asset

(b) Projections of **cash outflows** necessarily incurred to **generate the cash inflows** from continuing use of the asset

(c) **Net cash flows** received/paid on **disposal** of the asset at the end of its useful life

There is an underlying principle that future cash flows should be estimated for the asset in its current condition. Future cash flows relating to restructurings to which the entity is not yet committed, or to future costs to add to, replace part of, or service the asset are excluded.

Estimates of future cash flows should **exclude** the following:

(a) Cash inflows/ outflows from financing activities
(b) Income tax receipts/payments

The amount of net cash inflow/outflow on **disposal** of an asset should in an orderly transaction between market participants.

Foreign currency future cash flows should be forecast in the currency in which they will arise and will be discounted using a rule appropriate for that currency. The resulting figure should then be translated into the reporting currency at the spot rate at the year end.

The **discount rate** should be a current pre-tax rate (or rates) that reflects the current assessment of the time value of money and the risks specific to the asset. The discount should not include a risk weighting if the underlying cash flows have already been adjusted for risk.

3.4 Recognition and measurement of an impairment loss

FAST FORWARD

When it is not possible to calculate the recoverable amount of a single asset, then that of its **cash generating unit** should be measured instead.

The rule for assets at historical cost is:

Rule to learn

If the recoverable amount of an asset is lower than the carrying amount, the carrying amount should be reduced by the difference (ie the impairment loss) which should be charged as an expense in profit or loss for the year. (IAS 36: para. 59)

The rule for assets held at a revalued amount (such as property revalued under IAS 16) is:

Rule to learn

The impairment loss is to be treated as a revaluation decrease under the relevant IFRS/IAS. (IAS 36: para. 60)

In practice this means:

- To the extent that there is a revaluation surplus held in respect of the asset, the impairment loss should be charged to revaluation surplus.
- Any excess should be charged to profit or loss.

The IAS goes into quite a large amount of detail about the important concept of cash generating units. As a basic rule, the recoverable amount of an asset should be calculated for the **asset individually**. However, there will be occasions when it is not possible to estimate such a value for an individual asset, particularly in the calculation of value in use. This is because cash inflows and outflows cannot be attributed to the individual asset.

If it is not possible to calculate the recoverable amount for an individual asset, the recoverable amount of the asset's cash generating unit should be measured instead.

Key term

A **cash generating unit** is the smallest identifiable group of assets for which independent cash flows can be identified and measured. *(IAS 36: para. 6)*

Question — Cash generating unit 1

Can you think of some examples of how a cash generating unit would be identified?

Answer

Here are two possibilities:

(a) A mining company owns a private railway that it uses to transport output from one of its mines. The railway now has no market value other than as scrap, and it is impossible to identify any separate cash inflows with the use of the railway itself. Consequently, if the mining company suspects an impairment in the value of the railway, it should treat the mine as a whole as a cash generating unit, and measure the recoverable amount of the mine as a whole.

(b) A bus company has an arrangement with a town's authorities to run a bus service on four routes in the town. Separately identifiable assets are allocated to each of the bus routes, and cash inflows and outflows can be attributed to each individual route. Three routes are running at a profit and one is running at a loss. The bus company suspects that there is an impairment of assets on the loss-making route. However, the company will be unable to close the loss-making route, because it is under an obligation to operate all four routes, as part of its contract with the local authority. Consequently, the company should treat all four bus routes together as a cash generating unit, and calculate the recoverable amount for the unit as a whole.

Question — Cash generating unit 2

Minimart belongs to a retail store chain Maximart. Minimart makes all its retail purchases through Maximart's purchasing centre. Pricing, marketing, advertising and human resources policies (except for hiring Minimart's cashiers and salesmen) are decided by Maximart. Maximart also owns five other stores in the same city as Minimart (although in different neighbourhoods) and 20 other stores in other cities. All stores are managed in the same way as Minimart. Minimart and four other stores were purchased five years ago and goodwill was recognised.

What is the cash-generating unit for Minimart?

Answer

In identifying Minimart's cash-generating unit, an entity considers whether, for example:

(a) Internal management reporting is organised to measure performance on a store-by-store basis.
(b) The business is run on a store-by-store profit basis or on a region/city basis.

All Maximart's stores are in different neighbourhoods and probably have different customer bases. So, although Minimart is managed at a corporate level, Minimart generates cash inflows that are largely independent from those of Maximart's other stores. Therefore, it is likely that Minimart is a cash-generating unit.

Question — Cash generating unit 3

Mighty Mag Publishing Co owns 150 magazine titles of which 70 were purchased and 80 were self-created. The price paid for a purchased magazine title is recognised as an intangible asset. The costs of creating magazine titles and maintaining the existing titles are recognised as an expense when incurred. Cash inflows from direct sales and advertising are identifiable for each magazine title. Titles are managed by customer segments. The level of advertising income for a magazine title depends on the range of titles in the customer segment to which the magazine title relates. Management has a policy to abandon old titles before the end of their economic lives and replace them immediately with new titles for the same customer segment.

What is the cash-generating unit for an individual magazine title?

Answer

It is likely that the recoverable amount of an individual magazine title can be assessed. Even though the level of advertising income for a title is influenced, to a certain extent, by the other titles in the customer segment, cash inflows from direct sales and advertising are identifiable for each title. In addition, although titles are managed by customer segments, decisions to abandon titles are made on an individual title basis.

Therefore, it is likely that individual magazine titles generate cash inflows that are largely independent one from another and that each magazine title is a separate cash-generating unit.

If an active market exists for the output produced by the asset or a group of assets, this asset or group should be identified as a cash generating unit, even if some or all of the output is used internally.

Cash generating units should be identified consistently from period to period for the same type of asset unless a change is justified.

The group of net assets less liabilities that are considered for impairment should be the same as those considered in the calculation of the recoverable amount. (For the treatment of goodwill and corporate assets see below.)

3.5 Example: Recoverable amount and carrying amount

Fourways Co is made up of four cash generating units. All four units are being tested for impairment.

(a) Property, plant and equipment and separate intangibles would be allocated to be cash generating units as far as possible.

(b) Current assets such as inventories, receivables and prepayments would be allocated to the relevant cash generating units.

(c) Liabilities (eg payables) would be deducted from the net assets of the relevant cash generating units.

(d) The net figure for each cash generating unit resulting from this exercise would be compared to the relevant recoverable amount, computed on the same basis.

3.6 Goodwill and the impairment of assets

3.6.1 Allocating goodwill to cash-generating units

Goodwill acquired in a business combination does not generate cash flows independently of other assets. It must be **allocated** to each of the acquirer's **cash-generating units** (or groups of cash-generating units) that are expected to benefit from the synergies of the combination. Each unit to which the goodwill is so allocated should (IAS 36: para. 90):

(a) Represent the **lowest level** within the entity at which the goodwill is monitored for internal management purposes

(b) Not be **larger than a reporting segment** determined in accordance with IFRS 8 *Operating segments*

It may be impractical to complete the allocation of goodwill before the first reporting date after a business combination, particularly if the acquirer is accounting for the combination for the first time using provisional values. The initial allocation of goodwill must be completed before the end of the first reporting period after the acquisition date.

3.6.2 Testing cash-generating units with goodwill for impairment

There are two situations to consider:

(a) Where goodwill has been allocated to a cash-generating unit

(b) Where it has not been possible to allocate goodwill to a specific cash-generating unit, but only to a group of units

A cash-generating unit to which goodwill has been allocated is tested for impairment annually. The **carrying amount** of the unit, including goodwill, is **compared with the recoverable amount**. If the carrying amount of the unit exceeds the recoverable amount, the entity must recognise an impairment loss.

(IAS 36: para. 9)

If there is a **non-controlling (minority) interest** in a cash-generating unit to which goodwill has been allocated, the carrying amount of the goodwill allocated to that unit must be **grossed up** to include the goodwill attributable to the non-controlling interest. This is because the goodwill recognised in a business combination represents only the goodwill owned by the parent, not the amount of goodwill actually controlled by the parent. Part of the recoverable amount of the cash-generating unit is attributable to the non-controlling interest in goodwill.

Where goodwill relates to a cash-generating unit but has not been allocated to that unit, the unit is tested for impairment by **comparing its carrying amount** (excluding goodwill) **with its recoverable amount**. The entity must recognise an impairment loss if the carrying amount exceeds the recoverable amount.

The annual impairment test may be performed at any time during an accounting period, but must be performed at the **same time every year**.

3.7 Example: Non-controlling interest

On 1 January 20X4 a parent acquires an 80% interest in a subsidiary for $1,600,000, when the identifiable net assets of the subsidiary are $1,500,000. The subsidiary is a cash-generating unit.

At 31 December 20X4, the recoverable amount of the subsidiary is $1,000,000. The carrying amount of the subsidiary's identifiable assets is $1,350,000.

Calculate the impairment loss at 31 December 20X4.

Solution

At 31 December 20X4 the cash-generating unit consists of the subsidiary's identifiable net assets (carrying amount $1,350,000) and goodwill of $400,000 (1,600,000 –80% × $1,500,000)). Goodwill is grossed up to reflect the 20% non-controlling interest.

	Goodwill	*Net assets*	*Total*
	$	$	$
Carrying amount	400	1,350	1,750
Unrecognised non-controlling interest	100		100
	500	1,350	1,850
Recoverable amount			(1,000)
Impairment loss			850

3.8 Corporate assets

Corporate assets are group or divisional assets such as a head office building, EDP equipment or a research centre. Essentially, corporate assets are assets that do not generate cash inflows independently from other assets, hence their carrying amount cannot be fully attributed to a cash-generating unit under review.

In testing a cash generating unit for impairment, an entity should identify all the corporate assets that relate to the cash-generating unit. (IAS 36: para. 100)

(a) If a portion of the carrying amount of a corporate asset **can be allocated** to the unit on a reasonable and consistent basis, the entity compares the carrying amount of the unit (including the portion of the asset) with its recoverable amount.

(b) If a portion of the carrying amount of a corporate asset **cannot be allocated** to the unit on a reasonable and consistent basis, the entity:

    (i) Compares the carrying amount of the unit (excluding the asset) with its recoverable amount and recognises any impairment loss.

    (ii) Identifies the smallest group of cash-generating units that includes the cash-generating unit to which the asset belongs and to which a portion of the carrying amount of the asset can be allocated on a reasonable and consistent basis.

    (iii) Compares the carrying amount of that group of cash-generating units, (including the portion of the asset allocated to the group of units) with the recoverable amount of the group of units and recognises any impairment loss.

3.9 Accounting treatment of an impairment loss

If, and only if, the recoverable amount of an asset is less than its carrying amount in the statement of financial position, an impairment loss has occurred. This loss should be **recognised immediately**.

(a) The asset's **carrying amount** should be reduced to its recoverable amount in the statement of financial position.

(b) The **impairment loss** should be recognised immediately in profit or loss (unless the asset has been revalued in which case the loss is treated as a revaluation decrease; see Paragraph 3.4).

After reducing an asset to its recoverable amount, the **depreciation charge** on the asset should then be based on its new carrying amount, its estimated residual value (if any) and its estimated remaining useful life.

An impairment loss should be recognised for a **cash generating unit** if (and only if) the recoverable amount for the cash generating unit is less than the carrying amount in the statement of financial position for all the assets in the unit. When an impairment loss is recognised for a cash generating unit, the loss should be allocated between the assets in the unit in the following order.

(a) First, to the **goodwill** allocated to the cash generating unit
(b) Then to all other assets in the cash-generating unit, on a **pro rata basis**

In allocating an impairment loss, the carrying amount of an asset should not be reduced below the highest of:

(a) Its fair value less costs of disposal
(b) Its value in use (if determinable)
(c) Zero

Any remaining amount of an impairment loss should be recognised as a liability if required by other IASs.
(IAS 36: para. 59 to 63)

3.10 Example 1: Impairment loss

A company that extracts natural gas and oil has a drilling platform in the Caspian Sea. It is required by legislation of the country concerned to remove and dismantle the platform at the end of its useful life. Accordingly, the company has included an amount in its accounts for removal and dismantling costs, and is depreciating this amount over the platform's expected life.

The company is carrying out an exercise to establish whether there has been an impairment of the platform.

(a) Its carrying amount in the statement of financial position is \$3m.

(b) The company has received an offer of \$2.8m for the platform from another oil company. The bidder would take over the responsibility (and costs) for dismantling and removing the platform at the end of its life.

(c) The present value of the estimated cash flows from the platform's continued use is \$3.3m.

(d) The carrying amount in the statement of financial position for the provision for dismantling and removal is currently \$0.6m.

What should be the value of the drilling platform in the statement of financial position, and what, if anything, is the impairment loss?

Solution

Fair value less costs of disposal	=	\$2.8m
Value in use	=	PV of cash flows from use less the carrying amount of the provision/liability = \$3.3m – \$0.6m = \$2.7m
Recoverable amount	=	Higher of these two amounts, ie \$2.8m
Carrying value	=	\$3m
Impairment loss	=	\$0.2m

The carrying value should be reduced to $2.8m

3.11 Example 2: Impairment loss

A company has acquired another business for $4.5m: tangible assets are valued at $4.0m and goodwill at $0.5m.

An asset with a carrying value of $1m is destroyed in a terrorist attack. The asset was not insured. The loss of the asset, without insurance, has prompted the company to estimate whether there has been an impairment of assets in the acquired business and what the amount of any such loss is. The recoverable amount of the business is measured at $3.1m.

Solution

The recoverable amount of the business (a single cash generating unit) is measured as $3.1m. There has consequently been an impairment loss of $1.4m ($4.5m – $3.1m).

The impairment loss will be recognised in profit or loss. The loss will be allocated between the assets in the cash generating unit as follows:

(a) A loss of $1m can be attributed directly to the uninsured asset that has been destroyed.
(b) The remaining loss of $0.4m should be allocated to goodwill.

The carrying value of the assets will now be $3m for tangible assets and $0.1m for goodwill.

3.12 Example: Impairment loss and revaluation

The Antimony Company acquired its head office on 1 January 20W8 at a cost of $5.0 million (excluding land). Antimony's policy is to depreciate property on a straight-line basis over 50 years with a zero residual value.

On 31 December 20X2 (after five years of ownership) Antinomy revalued the non-land element of its head office to $8.0 million. Antinomy does not transfer annual amounts out of revaluation reserves as assets are used: this is in accordance with the permitted treatment in IAS 16 *Property, plant and equipment.*

In January 20X8 localised flooding occurred and the recoverable amount of the non-land element of the head office property fell to $2.9 million.

Required

What impairment charge should be recognised in the profit or loss of Antimony arising from the impairment review in January 20X8 according to IAS 36 *Impairment of assets*?

Solution

$0.7 million

IAS 36.60 and 61 (also IAS 16.40) require that an impairment that reverses a previous revaluation should be recognised through other comprehensive income to the extent of the amount in the revaluation surplus for that same asset. Any remaining amount is recognised through profit or loss. Thus:

(a) The carrying amount at 31 December 20X2 is 45/50 × $5.0m = $4.5m

(b) The revaluation reserve created is $3.5m (ie $8.0m – $4.5m)

(c) The carrying amount at 31 December 20X7 is 40/45 × $8.0m = $7.1m

(d) The recoverable amount at 31 December 20X7 is $2.9m

(e) The total impairment charge is $4.2m (ie $7.1m – $2.9m)

(f) Of this, $3.5m is a reversal of the revaluation reserve, so only $0.7 million is recognised through profit or loss.

3.13 Reversal of an impairment loss

The annual review of assets to determine whether there may have been some impairment should be **applied to all assets**, including assets that have already been impaired in the past.

In some cases, the recoverable amount of an asset that has previously been impaired might turn out to be **higher** than the asset's current carrying value. In other words, there might have been a reversal of some of the previous impairment loss.

(a) The reversal of the impairment loss should be **recognised immediately** as income in profit or loss for the year.

(b) The carrying amount of the asset should be increased to its **new recoverable amount**.

(IAS 36: para. 119)

Rule to learn

An impairment loss recognised for an asset in prior years should be recovered if, and only if, there has been a change in the estimates used to determine the asset's recoverable amount since the last impairment loss was recognised. (IAS 36: para. 114)

The asset cannot be revalued to a carrying amount that is higher than its value would have been if the asset had not been impaired originally, ie its **depreciated carrying value** had the impairment not taken place. Depreciation of the asset should now be based on its new revalued amount, its estimated residual value (if any) and its estimated remaining useful life.

An exception to the rule above is for **goodwill**. An impairment loss for goodwill should not be reversed in a subsequent period. (IAS 36: para. 124)

Question — Reversal of impairment loss

A cash generating unit comprising a factory, plant and equipment etc and associated purchased goodwill becomes impaired because the product it makes is overtaken by a technologically more advanced model produced by a competitor. The recoverable amount of the cash generating unit falls to $60m, resulting in an impairment loss of $80m, allocated as follows:

	Carrying amounts before impairment	*Carrying amounts after impairment*
	$m	$m
Goodwill	40	
Patent (with no market value)	20	
Tangible long-term assets	80	60
Total	140	60

After three years, the entity makes a technological breakthrough of its own, and the recoverable amount of the cash generating unit increases to $90m. The carrying amount of the tangible long-term assets had the impairment not occurred would have been $70m.

Required

Calculate the reversal of the impairment loss.

Answer

The reversal of the impairment loss is recognised to the extent that it increases the carrying amount of the tangible non-current assets to what it would have been had the impairment not taken place, ie a reversal of the impairment loss of $10m is recognised and the tangible non-current assets written back to $70m. Reversal of the impairment is not recognised in relation to the goodwill and patent because the effect of the external event that caused the original impairment has not reversed – the original product is still overtaken by a more advanced model.

3.14 Impairment loss and goodwill

IFRS 3 (para. 19) allows two methods of initially valuing the non-controlling interest in an entity:

- As a share of the net assets of the entity at the acquisition date, or
- At fair value

The non-controlling interest is then taken into account in the goodwill calculation per the revised standard:

	$
Purchase consideration	X
Non-controlling interest	X
	X
Total fair value of net assets of acquiree	(X)
Goodwill	X

This means that the resulting goodwill will represent:

(a) Only the parent's share of total goodwill when valuing the non-controlling interest using the proportion of net assets method.

(b) Full goodwill (ie the parent's share plus the non-controlling interest share) when using the fair value method.

Where the proportionate share of net assets method is used to value the non-controlling interest, the carrying amount of a cash generating unit therefore comprises:

- The parent and non-controlling share of the identifiable net assets of the unit
- Only the parent's share of the goodwill

Part of the calculation of the recoverable amount of the cash generating unit relates to the unrecognised share in the goodwill.

For the purpose of calculating the impairment loss, the carrying amount of the cash generating unit is therefore notionally adjusted to include the non-controlling share in the goodwill by grossing it up.

The consequent impairment loss calculated is only recognised to the extent of the parent's share.

Where the fair value method is used to value the non-controlling interest, no adjustment is required.

3.15 Example: Impairment loss and goodwill: partial goodwill

Note. If you are unsure what is meant by the terms 'partial' and 'full' goodwill, work through the revision of basic groups in Chapter 12, or look back to your F7 studies.

The Acetone Company is testing for impairment two subsidiaries which have been identified as separate cash-generating units.

Some years ago Acetone acquired 80% of The Dushanbe Company for $600,000 when the fair value of Dushanbe's identifiable assets was $400,000. As Dushanbe's policy is to distribute all profits by way of dividend, the fair value of its identifiable net assets remained at $400,000 on 31 December 20X7. The impairment review indicated Dushanbe's recoverable amount at 31 December 20X7 to be $520,000.

Some years ago Acetone acquired 85% of The Maclulich Company for $800,000 when the fair value of Maclulich's identifiable net assets was $700,000. Goodwill of $205,000 ($800,000 – ($700,000 × 85%)) was recognised. As Maclulich's policy is to distribute all profits by way of dividend, the fair value of its identifiable net assets remained at $700,000 on 31 December 20X7. The impairment review indicated Maclulich's recoverable amount at 31 December 20X7 to be $660,000.

It is Acetone group policy to value the non-controlling interest using the proportion of net assets method.

Required

Determine the following amounts in respect of Acetone's consolidated financial statements at 31 December 20X7 according to IAS 36 *Impairment of assets*.

(a) The carrying amount of Dushanbe's assets to be compared with its recoverable amount for impairment testing purposes

(b) The carrying amount of goodwill in respect of Dushanbe after the recognition of any impairment loss

(c) The carrying amount of the non-controlling interest in Maclulich after recognition of any impairment loss

Solution

(a) $750,000
(b) $96,000
(c) $99,000

Workings

(a)

	$
Book value of Dushanbe's net assets	400,000
Goodwill recognised on acquisition	
$600,000 – (80% × $400,000)	280,000
Notional goodwill ($280,000 × 20/80)	70,000
	750,000

(b) The impairment loss is the total $750,000 less the recoverable amount of $520,000 = $230,000. Under IAS 36 this is firstly allocated against the $350,000 goodwill. (As the impairment loss is less than the goodwill, none is allocated against identifiable net assets.) As only the goodwill relating to Acetone is recognised, only its 80% share of the impairment loss is recognised:

	$
Carrying value of goodwill	280,000
Impairment (80% × 230,000)	(184,000)
Revised carrying amount of goodwill	96,000

(c)

	$
Carrying amount of Maclulich's net assets	700,000
Recognised goodwill	205,000
Notional goodwill (15/85 × $205,000)	36,176
	941,176
Recoverable amount	(660,000)
Impairment loss	281,176
Allocated to:	
Recognised and notional goodwill	241,176
Other net assets	40,000

Therefore the non-controlling interest is ($700,000 – $40,000) × 15% = $99,000.

As the non-controlling interests does not include goodwill, only the impairment allocated to other net assets is included here.

3.16 Example: Impairment loss and goodwill: full goodwill

Assume that the facts relating to the acquisition of Dushanbe are the same as above, except that it is Acetone group's policy to value the non-controlling interest on the acquisition of Dushanbe at fair value. The fair value of the non-controlling interest in Dushanbe at acquisition was $100,000.

Required

Determine the following amounts in respect of Acetone's consolidated financial statements at 31 December 20X7 according to IAS 36 *Impairment of assets.*

(a) The carrying amount of Dushanbe's assets to be compared with its recoverable amount for impairment testing purposes

(b) The carrying amount of goodwill in respect of Dushanbe after the recognition of any impairment loss

Solution

(a) $700,000
(b) $120,000

Workings

(a)

	$
Consideration transferred	600,000
Fair value of NCI	100,000
	700,000
Fair value of net assets acquired	400,000
Goodwill	300,000

	$
Book value of Dushanbe's net assets	400,000
Goodwill recognised on acquisition	300,000
	700,000

(b) The impairment loss is the total $700,000 less the recoverable amount of $520,000 = $180,000. Under IAS 36 this is first allocated against the $300,000 goodwill. (As the impairment loss is less than the goodwill, none is allocated against identifiable net assets.)

	$
Carrying value of goodwill	300,000
Impairment	(180,000)
Revised carrying amount of goodwill	120,000

In the equity of the group statement of financial position, the retained earnings will be reduced by the parent's share of the impairment loss on the full goodwill, ie $144,000 (80% × $180,000) and the NCI reduced by the NCI's share, ie $36,000 (20% × $180,000).

In the statement of profit or loss and other comprehensive income, the impairment loss of $180,000 will be charged as an extra operating expense. As the impairment loss relates to the full goodwill of the subsidiary, so it will reduce the NCI in the subsidiary's profit for the year by $36,000 (20% × $180,000).

3.17 Disclosure

IAS 36 calls for substantial disclosure about impairment of assets (IAS 36: para. 126).

The information to be disclosed includes the following:

(a) For each class of assets, the amount of **impairment losses recognised** and the amount of any **impairment losses recovered** (ie reversals of impairment losses).

(b) For each individual asset or cash generating unit that has suffered a **significant impairment loss**, details of the nature of the asset, the amount of the loss, the events that led to recognition of the loss, whether the recoverable amount is fair value price less costs of disposal or value in use, and if the recoverable amount is value in use, the basis on which this value was estimated (eg the discount rate applied).

3.18 Section summary

The main aspects of IAS 36 to consider are:

- **Indications** of impairment of assets
- **Measuring recoverable amount**, as net selling price or value in use
- **Measuring value in use**
- **Cash generating units**

- **Accounting treatment** of an impairment loss, for individual assets and cash generating units
- **Reversal** of an impairment loss

4 IAS 40 Investment property 12/12, 6/13

FAST FORWARD

IAS 40 *Investment property* defines investment property as property **held to earn rentals or for capital appreciation** or both, rather than for:

- Use in production or supply of goods or services
- Sale in the ordinary course of business

An entity may own land or a building **as an investment** rather than for use in the business. It may therefore generate cash flows largely independently of other assets which the entity holds.

Consider the following definitions.

Key terms

Investment property is property (land or a building – or part of a building – or both) held (by the owner or by the lessee as a right-of-use asset) to earn rentals or for capital appreciation or both, rather than for:

(a) Use in the production or supply of goods or services or for administrative purposes, or
(b) Sale in the ordinary course of business

Owner-occupied property is property held by the owner (or by the lessee as a right-of-use asset) for use in the production or supply of goods or services or for administrative purposes.

Fair value is the price that would be received to sell an asset or paid to transfer a liability in an orderly transaction between market participants at the measurement date.

Cost is the amount of cash or cash equivalents paid or the fair value of other consideration given to acquire an asset at the time of its acquisition or construction.

Carrying amount is the amount at which an asset is recognised in the statement of financial position.

IAS 16 applies to owned owner-occupied property and IFRS 16 applies to owner-occupied property held by a lessee as a **right-of-use asset.**

(IAS 40: Para. 5)

Examples of investment property include:

(a) **Land held for long-term capital appreciation** rather than for short-term sale in the ordinary course of business

(b) A **building** owned by the reporting entity (or held by the entity as a right-of-use asset) and **leased out under an operating lease**

(c) **Property being constructed** or developed for future use as investment property

Question — Investment property

Rich Co owns a piece of land. The directors have not yet decided whether to build a factory on it for use in its business or to keep it and sell it when its value has risen.

Would this be classified as an investment property under IAS 40?

Answer

Yes. If an entity has not determined that it will use the land either as an owner-occupied property or for short-term sale in the ordinary course of business, the land is considered to be held for capital appreciation.

4.1 IAS 40

The objective of IAS 40 *Investment property* is to prescribe the accounting treatment for investment property and related disclosure requirements. (IAS 40: para. 1)

You now know what **is** an investment property under IAS 40. Below are examples of items that are **not investment property.** (IAS 40: para. 9)

Type of non-investment property	Applicable IAS
Property held for sale in the ordinary course of business	IAS 2 *Inventories*
Property being constructed or developed on behalf of third parties	IAS 11 *Construction contracts*
Owner-occupied property	IAS 16 *Property, plant and equipment*

4.2 Recognition

Investment property should be recognised as an asset when **two conditions** are met.

(a) It is **probable** that the **future economic benefits** that are associated with the investment property will **flow to the entity**.

(b) The **cost** of the investment property can be **measured reliably**.

An investment property held by a lessee as a right-of-use asset must be recognised in accordance with IFRS 16 *Leases* (IFRS 40: Para. 29A)'. IFRS 16 is covered in Chapter 8.

4.3 Initial measurement

An owned investment property should be measured initially at its **cost,** including transaction costs.

An investment property held by a lessee as a right-of-use asset must be measured initially in accordance with IFRS 16 *Leases.* (IAS 40: Para. 29A)

4.4 Measurement subsequent to initial recognition

FAST FORWARD

Entities can choose between:

- A **fair value model**, with changes in fair value being measured
- A **cost model** – the treatment most commonly used under IAS 16

IAS 40 requires an entity to **choose between two models:**

- The fair value model
- The cost model

Whatever policy it chooses should be applied to **all of its investment property**. (IAS 40: para. 30)

4.4.1 Fair value model 6/15, 6/16

Key point

(a) After initial recognition, an entity that chooses the **fair value model** should measure all of its investment property at fair value, except in the extremely rare cases where this cannot be measured reliably. In such cases it should apply the IAS 16 cost model. (IAS 40: para. 33)

(b) A gain or loss arising from a change in the fair value of an investment property should be recognised in net profit or loss for the period in which it arises. (IAS 40: para. 35)

Unusually, the IASB allows a fair value model for non-financial assets. This is not the same as a revaluation, where increases in carrying amount above a cost-based measure are recognised as revaluation surplus. Under the fair-value model all changes in fair value are recognised in profit or loss.

When a lessee uses the fair value model to measure an investment property that is held as a right-of-use asset, it must measure the right of use asset, not the underlying property, at fair value. (IFRS 40: Para. 40A)

IFRS 13 *Fair value measurement,* issued in 2011, deleted much of the guidance provided in IAS 40 in respect of the determination of fair value. Instead the requirements of IFRS 13 (see Chapter 7) apply in measuring the fair value of investment properties. This standard requires that the following are considered in determining fair value (IAS 13: para. 72 to 89):

The asset being measured:

(a) The principal market (ie that where the most activity takes place) or where there is no principal market, the most advantageous market (ie that in which the best price could be achieved) in which an orderly transaction would take place for the asset

(b) The highest and best use of the asset and whether it is used on a stand-alone basis or in conjunction with other assets

(c) Assumptions that market participants would use when pricing the asset

Having considered these factors, IFRS 13 provides a hierarchy of inputs for arriving at fair value. It requires that level 1 inputs are used where possible:

Level 1 Quoted prices in active markets for identical assets that the entity can access at the measurement date.

Level 2 Inputs other than quoted prices that are directly or indirectly observable for the asset.

Level 3 Unobservable inputs for the asset.

More detail

Level 1 inputs are prices quoted in active markets for items identical to the asset (in this case investment property) being measured. Active markets are ones where transactions take place with sufficient frequency and volume for pricing information to be provided.

In general, IFRS 13 requires in respect of non-financial assets that fair value is decided on the basis of the **highest and best use of the asset as determined by a market participant**. Highest and best use is determined from the perspective of market participants, even if the reporting entity intends a different use. For example, an entity may intend to use assets acquired in a business combination differently from how other market participants might use them. If, however, there is no evidence to suggest that the current use of an asset is not its highest and best use an entity does not need to carry out an exhaustive search for other potential uses.

The 'highest and best use' requirement would appear not to contradict point (b) below, because it requires a market participant rather than solely the knowledge of the entity. The real estate sector frequently dealso with alternative use values, for example an existing commercial property which could generate additional value through conversion into a residential development would be valued based on the higher amount if there is reasonable certainty over the planning being gained.

More detail on IFRS 13 is given in Chapters 7 and 12.

The guidance which remains in IAS 40 is as follows (IFRS 40: Para. 50):

(a) Double counting should be prevented in deciding on the fair value of the assets. For example, elevators or air conditioning, which form an integral part of a building should be incorporated in the investment property rather than recognised separately.

(b) According to the definition in **IAS 36** ***Impairment of assets,*** fair value is not the same as 'value in use'. The latter reflects factors and knowledge as relating solely to the entity, while the former reflects factors and knowledge applicable to the market.

(c) In those uncommon cases in which the **fair value of an investment property cannot be measured reliably** by an entity, the cost model in **IAS 16** must be employed until the investment property is disposed of. **The residual value must be assumed to be zero**.

4.4.2 Cost model

After initial recognition, an entity that chooses the **cost model** must measure investment property (IFRS 40: para. 56):

(a) In accordance with **IFRS 5** *Non-current assets held for sale and discontinued operations* if it **meets the IFRS 5 criteria**

(b) In accordance with **IFRS 16** *Leases* if it is held by a lessee as a **right-of-use asset** and not held for sale in accordance with IFRS 5

(c) **In all other cases in accordance with IAS 16**

Investment property should be measured at **depreciated cost, less any accumulated impairment losses.** An entity that chooses the cost model should **disclose the fair value of its investment property**.

4.4.3 Changing models

Once the entity has chosen the fair value or cost model, it should apply it to all its investment property. It **should not change from one model to the other unless the change will result in a more appropriate presentation**. IAS 40 states (IFRS 40: Para. 31)that it is highly unlikely that a change from the fair value model to the cost model will result in a more appropriate presentation.

4.5 Transfers

Transfers to or from investment property should **only** be made **when there is a change in use** (IFRS 40: Para. 57). For example, owner occupation commences so the investment property will be treated under IAS 16 as an owner-occupied property.

When there is a transfer from investment property carried at fair value to owner-occupied property or inventories, the property's cost for subsequent accounting under IAS 16 or IAS 2 should be its fair value at the date of change of use.

Conversely, an owner-occupied property may become an investment property and need to be carried at fair value. Up to the date of change of use, an entity should apply IAS 16 for owned property and IFRS 16 for property held by a lessee as a right-of-use asset. It should treat any difference at that date between the carrying amount of the property under IAS 16 or IFRS 16 and its fair value as a revaluation under IAS 16.

4.6 Disposals

Derecognise (eliminate from the statement of financial position) an investment property on disposal or when it is permanently withdrawn from use and no future economic benefits are expected from its disposal.

Any **gain or loss** on disposal is the difference between the net disposal proceeds and the carrying amount of the asset. It should generally be **recognised as income or expense in profit or loss.**

Compensation from third parties for investment property that was impaired, lost or given up shall be recognised in profit or loss when the compensation becomes receivable. (IFRS 40: Para. 66)

4.7 Disclosure requirements

These relate to (IFRS 40: paras. 74 to 76):

- Choice of fair value model or cost model
- Criteria for classification as investment property
- Use of independent professional valuer (encouraged but not required)
- Rental income and expenses
- Any restrictions or obligations

4.7.1 Fair value model – additional disclosures

An entity that adopts this must also disclose a **reconciliation** of the carrying amount of the investment property at the beginning and end of the period.

4.7.2 Cost model – additional disclosures

These relate mainly to the depreciation method. In addition, an entity which adopts the cost model **must disclose the fair value** of the investment property.

4.8 Decision tree

The decision tree below summarises which IAS apply to various kinds of property.

Exam focus point

Learn this decision tree – it will help you tackle most of the problems you are likely to meet in the exam!

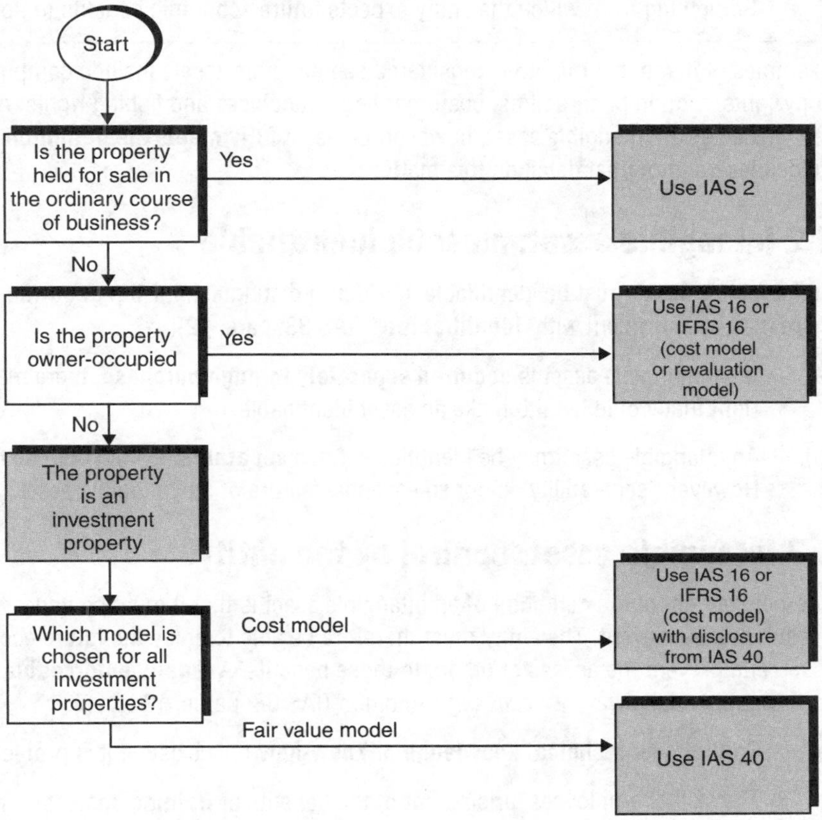

5 IAS 38 Intangible assets 12/08, 6/11, 12/11, 12/14, 6/15, 12/15, 6/16

FAST FORWARD

Intangible assets are defined by **IAS 38** as non-monetary assets without physical substance. They must be:

- **Identifiable**
- **Controlled** as a result of a past event
- Able to provide **future economic benefits**

The objectives of the standard are (IAS 38: para. 1):

(a) To establish the criteria for when an intangible assets may or should be **recognised**
(b) To specify how intangible assets should be **measured**
(c) To specify the **disclosure requirements** for intangible assets

It applies to all intangible assets with certain **exceptions**: deferred tax assets (IAS 12), intangible assets accounted for in accordance with IFRS 16 *Leases*, financial assets, insurance contracts, assets arising from employee benefits (IAS 19), non-current assets held for sale and mineral rights and exploration and extraction costs for minerals etc (although intangible assets used to develop or maintain these rights are covered by the standard). It does *not* apply to goodwill acquired in a business combination, which is dealt with under IFRS 3 *Business combinations.*

5.1 Definition of an intangible asset

The definition of an intangible assets is a key aspect of the proposed standard, because the rules for deciding whether or not an intangible asset may be **recognised** in the accounts of an entity are based on the definition of what an intangible asset is.

Key term

An **intangible asset** is an identifiable non-monetary asset without physical substance The asset must be:

(a) Controlled by the entity as a result of events in the past, and

(b) Something from which the entity expects future economic benefits to flow. (IAS 38: Para. 8)

Examples of items that might be considered as intangible assets include computer software, patents, copyrights, motion picture films, customer lists, franchises and fishing rights. An item should not be recognised as an intangible asset, however, unless it **fully meets the definition** in the standard. The guidelines go into great detail on this matter.

5.2 Intangible asset: must be identifiable

An intangible asset must be identifiable in order to distinguish it from goodwill. With non-physical items, there may be a problem with '**identifiability**' (IAS 38: para. 12):

(a) If an intangible asset is **acquired separately through purchase**, there may be a transfer of a legal right that would help to make an asset identifiable.

(b) An intangible asset may be identifiable if it is **separable**, ie if it could be rented or sold separately. However, 'separability' is not an essential feature of an intangible asset.

5.3 Intangible asset: control by the entity

Another element of the definition of an intangible asset is that it must be under the control of the entity as a result of a past event. The entity must therefore be able to enjoy the future economic benefits from the asset, and prevent the access of others to those benefits. A **legally enforceable right** is evidence of such control, but is not always a *necessary* condition (IAS 38: paras. 13 to 19).

(a) Control over **technical knowledge or know-how** only exists if it is protected by a **legal right**.

(b) The skill of employees, arising out of the benefits of **training costs**, are most unlikely to be recognisable as an intangible asset, because an entity does not control the future actions of its staff.

(c) Similarly, **market share and customer loyalty** cannot normally be intangible assets, since an entity cannot control the actions of its customers.

5.4 Intangible asset: expected future economic benefits

An item can only be recognised as an intangible asset if economic benefits are expected to flow in the future from ownership of the asset. Economic benefits may come from the **sale** of products or services, or from a **reduction in expenditures** (cost savings).

An intangible asset, when recognised initially, must be measured at **cost**. It should be recognised if, and only if **both** the following occur (IAS 38: para. 21).

(a) It is probable that the **future economic benefits** that are attributable to the asset will **flow to the entity**.

(b) The **cost can be measured reliably**.

Management has to exercise its judgement in assessing the degree of certainty attached to the flow of economic benefits to the entity. External evidence is best (IAS 38: para. 23).

(a) If an intangible asset is **acquired separately**, its cost can usually be measured reliably as its purchase price (including incidental costs of purchase such as legal fees, and any costs incurred in getting the asset ready for use).

(b) When an intangible asset is acquired as **part of a business combination** (ie an acquisition or takeover), the cost of the intangible asset is its fair value at the date of the acquisition.

IFRS 3 explains that the fair value of intangible assets acquired in business combinations can normally be measured with sufficient reliability to be **recognised separately** from goodwill.

Quoted market prices in an active market provide the most reliable measurement of the fair value of an intangible asset. If no active market exists for an intangible asset, its fair value is the amount that the entity would have paid for the asset, at the acquisition date, in an orderly transaction between market participants, on the basis of the best information available. In determining this amount, an entity should consider the outcome of recent transactions for similar assets. There are techniques for estimating the fair values of unique intangible assets (such as brand names) and these may be used to measure an intangible asset acquired in a business combination.

In accordance with IAS 20, intangible assets acquired by way of government grant and the grant itself may be recorded initially either at cost (which may be zero) or fair value.

5.5 Exchanges of assets

If one intangible asset is exchanged for another, the cost of the intangible asset is measured at fair value unless:

(a) The exchange transaction lacks commercial substance, or
(b) The fair value of neither the asset received nor the asset given up can be measured reliably.

Otherwise, its cost is measured at the carrying amount of the asset given up (IAS 38: paras. 45, 46).

5.6 Internally generated goodwill

Rule to learn

Internally generated goodwill may **not** be recognised as an **asset**. (IAS 38: para. 48)

The standard deliberately precludes recognition of internally generated goodwill because it requires that, for initial recognition, the cost of the asset rather than its fair value should be capable of being measured reliably and that it should be identifiable and controlled. Therefore, you do not recognise an asset which is subjective and cannot be measured reliably.

5.7 Research and development costs

5.7.1 Research

Research activities (IAS 38: para. 54), by definition do not meet the criteria for recognition under IAS 38. This is because, at the research stage of a project, it cannot be certain that future economic benefits will probably flow to the entity from the project. There is too much uncertainty about the likely success or otherwise of the project. **Research costs should therefore be written off as an expense as they are incurred**.

Examples of research costs

(a) Activities aimed at obtaining new knowledge

(b) The search for, evaluation and final selection of, applications of research findings or other knowledge

(c) The search for alternatives for materials, devices, products, processes, systems or services

(d) The formulation, design evaluation and final selection of possible alternatives for new or improved materials, devices, products, systems or services

5.7.2 Development

Development costs **may qualify** for recognition as intangible assets provided that the following **strict criteria** are met (IAS 38: para. 57).

(a) The technical feasibility of completing the intangible asset so that it will be available for use or sale.

(b) Its intention to complete the intangible asset and use or sell it.

(c) Its ability to use or sell the intangible asset.

(d) How the intangible asset will generate probable future economic benefits. Among other things, the entity should demonstrate the existence of a market for the output of the intangible asset or the intangible asset itself or, if it is to be used internally, the usefulness of the intangible asset.

(e) Its ability to measure the expenditure attributable to the intangible asset during its development reliably.

In contrast with research costs development costs are incurred at a later stage in a project, and the probability of success should be more apparent. Examples of development costs include the following:

(a) The design, construction and testing of pre-production or pre-use prototypes and models

(b) The design of tools, jigs, moulds and dies involving new technology

(c) The design, construction and operation of a pilot plant that is not of a scale economically feasible for commercial production

(d) The design, construction and testing of a chosen alternative for new or improved materials, devices, products, processes, systems or services

5.7.3 Other internally generated intangible assets

The standard **prohibits** the recognition of **internally generated brands, mastheads, publishing titles and customer lists** and similar items as intangible assets. These all fail to meet one or more (in some cases all) the definition and recognition criteria and in some cases are probably indistinguishable from internally generated goodwill. (IAS 38: para. 63)

5.7.4 Cost of an internally generated intangible asset

The costs allocated to an internally generated intangible asset should be only costs that can be **directly attributed** or allocated on a reasonable and consistent basis to creating, producing or preparing the asset for its intended use. The principles underlying the costs which may or may not be included are similar to those for other than non-current assets and inventory.

The cost of an internally operated intangible asset is the sum of the **expenditure incurred from the date when** the intangible asset first **meets the recognition criteria**. If, as often happens, considerable costs have already been recognised as expenses before management could demonstrate that the criteria have been met, this earlier expenditure should not be retrospectively recognised at a later date as part of the cost of an intangible asset (IAS 38: para. 66).

5.7.5 Example: Computer software and hardware

The treatments can be illustrated by reference to computer software and hardware. The treatment depends on the nature of the asset and its origin.

Asset	Origin	Treatment
Computer software	Purchased	Capitalise
Operating system for hardware	Purchased	Include in hardware cost
Computer software Operating system for hardware (For use or sale)	} Internally developed	Charge to expense until 'Development criteria' (Para 5.7.2) are met. Amortise over useful life, based on pattern of benefits. Straight line is default).

Question — **Recognition criteria**

Doug Co is developing a new production process. During 20X3, expenditure incurred was $100,000, of which $90,000 was incurred before 1 December 20X3 and $10,000 between 1 December 20X3 and 31 December 20X3. Doug Co can demonstrate that, at 1 December 20X3, the production process met the criteria for recognition as an intangible asset. The recoverable amount of the know-how embodied in the process is estimated to be $50,000.

How should the expenditure be treated?

Answer

At the end of 20X3, the production process is recognised as an intangible asset at a cost of $10,000. This is the expenditure incurred since the date when the recognition criteria were met, that is 1 December 20X3. The $90,000 expenditure incurred before 1 December 20X3 is expensed, because the recognition criteria were not met. It will never form part of the cost of the production process recognised in the statement of financial position.

5.8 Recognition of an expense

All expenditure related to an intangible which does not meet the criteria for recognition either as an identifiable intangible asset or as goodwill arising on an acquisition should be **expensed as incurred** (IAS 38: para. 68). The IAS gives examples of such expenditure.

- Start up costs
- Training costs
- Advertising costs
- Business relocation costs

Prepaid costs for services, for example advertising or marketing costs for campaigns that have been prepared but not launched, can still be recognised as a **prepayment**.

If tangible asset costs have been expensed in previous financial statements, they may not be recognised as part of the cost of the asset.

5.9 Measurement of intangible assets subsequent to initial recognition

FAST FORWARD

Intangible assets should initially be measured at cost, but subsequently they can be carried at **cost or at a fair value**. (IAS 38: para. 72)

The standard allows two methods of valuation for intangible assets after they have been first recognised.

Applying the **cost model**, an intangible asset should be **carried at its cost**, less any accumulated depreciation and less any accumulated impairment losses. (IAS 38: para. 74)

The **revaluation model** allows an intangible asset to be carried at a revalued amount, which is its **fair value** at the date of revaluation, less any subsequent accumulated amortisation and any subsequent accumulated impairment losses. (IAS 38: para. 75)

(a) The fair value must be able to be measured reliably with reference to an **active market** in that type of asset.

(b) The **entire class** of intangible assets of that type must be revalued at the same time (to prevent selective revaluations).

(c) If an intangible asset in a class of revalued intangible assets cannot be revalued because there is **no active market** for this asset, the asset should be carried at its **cost less any accumulated amortisation and impairment losses**.

(d) Revaluations should be made with such **regularity** that the carrying amount does not differ from that which would be determined using fair value at the year end.

Point to note

This treatment is **not** available for the **initial recognition** of intangible assets. This is because the cost of the asset must be reliably measured.

The guidelines state (IAS 38: para. 78). that there **will not usually be an active market** in an intangible asset; therefore the revaluation model will usually not be available. For example, although copyrights, publishing rights and film rights can be sold, each has a unique sale value. In such cases, revaluation to fair value would be inappropriate. A fair value might be obtainable however for assets such as fishing rights or quotas or taxi cab licences.

Where an intangible asset is revalued upwards to a fair value, the amount of the revaluation should be credited directly to equity under the heading of a **revaluation surplus.** (IAS 38: para. 85)

However, if a revaluation surplus is a **reversal of a revaluation decrease** that was previously charged against income, the increase can be recognised as income.

Where the carrying amount of an intangible asset is revalued downwards, the amount of the **downward revaluation** should be charged as an expense against income, unless the asset has previously been revalued upwards. A revaluation decrease should be first charged against any previous revaluation surplus in respect of that asset. (IAS 38: para. 86)

Question — Downward valuation

An intangible asset is measured by a company at fair value. The asset was revalued by $400 in 20X3, and there is a revaluation surplus of $400 in the statement of financial position. At the end of 20X4, the asset is valued again, and a downward valuation of $500 is required.

Required

State the accounting treatment for the downward revaluation.

Answer

In this example, the downward valuation of $500 can first be set against the revaluation surplus of $400. The revaluation surplus will be reduced to 0 and a charge of $100 made as an expense in 20X4.

When the revaluation model is used, and an intangible asset is revalued upwards, the cumulative revaluation **surplus may be transferred to retained earnings** when the surplus is eventually realised. The surplus would be realised when the asset is disposed of. However, the surplus may also be realised over time as the **asset is used** by the entity. The amount of the surplus realised each year is the difference between the amortisation charge for the asset based on the revalued amount of the asset, and the amortisation that would be charged on the basis of the asset's historical cost. The realised surplus in such case should be transferred from revaluation surplus directly to retained earnings, and should not be taken through profit or loss for the year.

5.10 Useful life

An entity should **assess** the useful life of an intangible asset, which may be **finite or infinite**. An intangible asset has an indefinite useful life when there is **no foreseeable limit** to the period over which the asset is expected to generate net cash inflows for the entity. (IAS 38: para. 88)

Many factors are considered in determining the useful life of an intangible asset, including: expected usage; typical product life cycles; technical, technological, commercial or other types of obsolescence; the stability of the industry; expected actions by competitors; the level of maintenance expenditure required; and legal or similar limits on the use of the asset, such as the expiry dates of related leases. Computer software and many other intangible assets normally have short lives because they are susceptible to technological obsolescence. However, uncertainty does not justify choosing a life that is unrealistically short.

The useful life of an intangible asset that arises from **contractual or other legal rights** should not exceed the period of the rights, but may be shorter depending on the period over which the entity expects to use the asset.

5.10.1 Acceptable methods of depreciation and amortisation

In 2014, the IASB published amendments to IAS 16 and IAS 38 in a document *Clarification of acceptable methods of depreciation and amortisation* (IAS 38: para. 130J).

Technical or commercial obsolescence

The first of these amendments concerned technical or commercial obsolescence, clarifying that **expected future reductions in the selling price of an item that was produced using an asset could indicate the expectation of technical or commercial obsolescence of the asset**, which, in turn, might reflect a reduction of the future economic benefits embodied in the asset.

Amortisation method

The second amendment to IAS 38 concerned the depreciation method, which must reflect the pattern in which the asset's future economic benefits are expected to be consumed by the entity. The 2014 amendment states that there is a **rebuttable presumption** that **amortisation methods that are based on revenue generated by an activity that includes the use of an intangible asset are inappropriate**. The revenue generated by an activity that includes the use of an asset generally **reflects factors other than the consumption of the economic benefits of the intangible asset.** For example, revenue is affected by other inputs and processes, selling activities and changes in sales volumes and prices. The price component of revenue may be affected by inflation, which has no bearing upon the way in which an asset is consumed.

The presumption may be rebutted under the following conditions.

(a) Where the **intangible asset is expressed as a measure of revenue**, that is the predominant limiting factor that is inherent in an intangible asset is the achievement of a revenue threshold, or

(b) When it can be demonstrated that **revenue and the consumption of the economic benefits** of the intangible asset are **highly correlated.**

An example of (a) might be the right to operate a toll road, if this right were based on a fixed total amount of revenue to be generated from cumulative tolls charged. A contract could, for example allow operation of the toll road until the cumulative amount of tolls generated from operating the road reaches $100 million. Revenue would in this case be established as the predominant limiting factor in the contract for the use of the intangible asset, so the revenue that is to be generated might be an appropriate basis for amortising the intangible asset, provided that the contract specifies a fixed total amount of revenue to be generated on which amortisation is to be determined.

5.11 Amortisation period and amortisation method

An intangible asset with a finite useful life should be amortised over its **expected useful life**.

(a) Amortisation should start when the asset is **available for use**.

(b) Amortisation should cease at the earlier of the date that the asset is classified **as held for sale** in accordance with IFRS 5 *Non-current assets held for sale and discontinued operations* and the date that the asset is **derecognised**.

(c) The amortisation method used should reflect the **pattern in which the asset's future economic benefits are consumed**. If such a pattern cannot be predicted reliably, the straight-line method should be used.

(d) The amortisation charge for each period should normally be recognised **in profit or loss**.

The **residual value** of an intangible asset with a finite useful life is **assumed to be zero** unless a third party is committed to buying the intangible asset at the end of its useful life or unless there is an active market for that type of asset (so that its expected residual value can be measured) and it is probable that there will be a market for the asset at the end of its useful life.

The amortisation period and the amortisation method used for an intangible asset with a finite useful life should be **reviewed at each financial year-end**. (IAS 38: para. 97)

5.12 Intangible assets with indefinite useful lives

An intangible asset with an indefinite useful life **should not be amortised**. (IAS 36 requires that such an asset is tested for impairment at least annually.)

The useful life of an intangible asset that is not being amortised should be **reviewed each year** to determine whether it is still appropriate to assess its useful life as indefinite. Reassessing the useful life of an intangible asset as finite rather than indefinite is an indicator that the asset may be impaired and therefore it should be tested for impairment. (IAS 38: para. 107)

Question — Useful life

It may be difficult to establish the useful life of an intangible asset, and judgement will be needed. Consider how to determine the useful life of a *purchased* brand name and how to provide evidence that its useful life might in fact exceed 20 years.

Answer

Factors to consider would include the following:

(a) Legal protection of the brand name and the control of the entity over the (illegal) use by others of the brand name (ie control over pirating)

(b) Age of the brand name

(c) Status or position of the brand in its particular market

(d) Ability of the management of the entity to manage the brand name and to measure activities that support the brand name (eg advertising and PR activities)

(e) Stability and geographical spread of the market in which the branded products are sold

(f) Pattern of benefits that the brand name is expected to generate over time

(g) Intention of the entity to use and promote the brand name over time (as evidenced perhaps by a business plan in which there will be substantial expenditure to promote the brand name)

5.13 Disposals/retirements of intangible assets

An intangible asset should be eliminated from the statement of financial position when it is disposed of or when there is no further expected economic benefit from its future use. On disposal the gain or loss arising from the **difference between the net disposal proceeds and the carrying amount** of the asset should be taken to the profit or loss for the year as a gain or loss on disposal (ie treated as income or expense). (IAS 38: para. 110)

5.14 Disclosure requirements

The standard has fairly extensive disclosure requirements for intangible assets. The financial statements should disclose the **accounting policies** for intangible assets that have been adopted.

(IAS 38: paras. 118 to 128)

For **each class of intangible assets**, disclosure is required of the following:

- The method of amortisation used
- The useful life of the assets or the amortisation rate used
- The gross carrying amount, the accumulated amortisation and the accumulated impairment losses as at the beginning and the end of the period
- A reconciliation of the carrying amount as at the beginning and at the end of the period (additions, retirements/disposals, revaluations, impairment losses, impairment losses reversed, amortisation charge for the period, net exchange differences, other movements)
- The carrying amount of internally-generated intangible assets

The financial statements should also disclose the following:

- In the case of intangible assets that are assessed as having a indefinite useful life, the carrying amounts and the reasons supporting that assessment
- For intangible assets acquired by way of a **government grant** and initially recognised at fair value, the **fair value initially recognised**, the **carrying amount**, and whether they are carried under the **benchmark or** the **allowed alternative** treatment for subsequent remeasurements
- The carrying amount, nature and remaining amortisation period of any intangible asset that is **material to the financial statements of the entity as a whole**
- The existence (if any) and amounts of intangible assets whose **title is restricted** and of intangible assets that have been **pledged as security** for liabilities
- The amount of any **commitments for the future acquisition of intangible assets**

Where intangible assets are accounted for at revalued amounts, disclosure is required of the following:

- The **effective date of the revaluation** (by class of intangible assets)
- The **carrying amount** of revalued intangible assets
- The carrying amount that would have been shown (by class of assets) **if the cost model had been used**, and the amount of amortisation that would have been charged
- The amount of any **revaluation surplus** on intangible assets, as at the beginning and end of the period, and movements in the surplus during the year (and any restrictions on the distribution of the balance to shareholders)

The financial statements should also disclose the amount of research and development expenditure that have been charged as expenses of the period.

5.15 Section summary

- An intangible asset should be recognised if, and only if, it is probable that future economic benefits will flow to the entity and the cost of the asset can be measured reliably.
- An asset is initially recognised at cost and subsequently carried either at cost or revalued amount.
- Costs that do not meet the recognition criteria should be expensed as incurred.
- An intangible asset with a finite useful life should be amortised over its useful life. An intangible asset with an indefinite useful life should not be amortised.

Question — List

As an aid to your revision, list the examples given in IAS 38 of activities that might be included in either research or development.

Answer

IAS 38 gives these examples.

Research

- Activities aimed at obtaining new knowledge
- The search for applications of research findings or other knowledge
- The search for product or process alternatives
- The formulation and design of possible new or improved product or process alternatives

Development

- The evaluation of product or process alternatives
- The design, construction and testing of pre-production prototypes and models
- The design of tools, jigs, moulds and dies involving new technology
- The design, construction and operation of a pilot plant that is not of a scale economically feasible for commercial production

Question — Project

Forkbender Co develops and manufactures exotic cutlery and has the following projects in hand.

	Project			
	1	*2*	*3*	*4*
	$'000	$'000	$'000	$'000
Deferred development				
Expenditure b/f 1.1.X2	280	450	–	–
Development expenditure				
Incurred during the year				
Salaries, wages and so on	35	–	60	20
Overhead costs	2	–	–	3
Materials and services	3	–	11	4
Patents and licences	1	–	–	–
Market research	–	–	2	–

Project 1: was originally expected to be highly profitable but this is now in doubt, since the scientist in charge of the project is now behind schedule, with the result that competitors are gaining ground.

Project 2: commercial production started during the year. Sales were 20,000 units in 20X1 and future sales are expected to be: 20X2 30,000 units; 20X3 60,000 units; 20X4 40,000 units; 20X5 30,000 units. There are no sales expected after 20X5.

Project 3: these costs relate to a new project, which meets the criteria for deferral of expenditure and which is expected to last for three years.

Project 4: is another new project, involving the development of a 'loss leader', expected to raise the level of future sales.

The company's policy is to defer development costs, where permitted by IAS 38. Expenditure carried forward is written off evenly over the expected sales life of projects, starting in the first year of sale.

Required

Show how the above projects should be treated in the accounting statements of Forkbender Co for the year ended 31 December 20X2 in accordance with best accounting practice. Justify your treatment of each project.

Answer

Project 1 expenditure, including that relating to previous years, should all be written off in 20X2, as there is now considerable doubt as to the profitability of the project.

Since commercial production has started under project 2 the expenditure previously deferred should now be amortised. This will be done over the estimated life of the product, as stated in the question.

Project 3: the development costs may be deferred.

Since project 4 is not expected to be profitable its development costs should not be deferred.

STATEMENT OF FINANCIAL POSITION AS AT 31 DECEMBER 20X2 (extract)

	$'000
NON-CURRENT ASSETS	
Intangible assets	
Development costs (Note 2)	431

NOTES TO THE ACCOUNTS

1 *Accounting policies*

Research and development

Research and development expenditure is written off as incurred, except that development costs incurred on an individual project are carried forward when their future recoverability can be foreseen with reasonable assurance. Any expenditure carried forward is amortised over the period of sales from the related project.

2 *Development costs*

	$'000	$'000
Balance brought forward 1 January 20X2		730
Development expenditure incurred during 20X2	139	
Development expenditure amortised during 20X2 (321 + 90 + 27)	438	
		(299)
Balance carried forward 31 December 20X2		431

Note. IAS 38 would not permit the inclusion of market research in deferred development costs. Market research costs might, however, be carried forward separately under the accruals principle.

Workings

	1	*2*	*3*	*4*	*Total*
	$'000	$'000	$'000	$'000	$'000
B/F	280	450			730
Salaries etc	35		60	20	115
Overheads	2			3	5
Materials etc	3		11	4	18
Patents etc	1				1
C/F		(360)	(71)		(431)
Written off	321	90	–	27	438

***Note.** An alternative basis for amortisation would be:

$$\frac{20}{180} \times 450 = 50$$

The above basis is more prudent, however, in this case.

6 Goodwill

FAST FORWARD

Impairment rules follow **IAS 36**. There are substantial disclosure requirements.

Goodwill is **created by good relationships** between a business and its customers.

(a) By building up a **reputation** (by word of mouth perhaps) for high quality products or high standards of service

(b) By **responding promptly and helpfully** to queries and complaints from customers

(c) Through the **personality of the staff** and their attitudes to customers

The value of goodwill to a business might be **extremely significant**. However, goodwill is not usually valued in the accounts of a business at all, and we should not normally expect to find an amount for goodwill in its statement of financial position. For example, the welcoming smile of the bar staff may contribute more to a bar's profits than the fact that a new electronic cash register has recently been acquired. Even so, whereas the cash register will be recorded in the accounts as a non-current asset, the value of staff would be ignored for accounting purposes.

On reflection, we might agree with this omission of goodwill from the accounts of a business.

(a) The goodwill is **inherent** in the business but it has not been paid for, and it does not have an 'objective' value. We can guess at what such goodwill is worth, but such guesswork would be a matter of individual opinion, and not based on hard facts.

(b) Goodwill **changes** from day to day. One act of bad customer relations might damage goodwill and one act of good relations might improve it. Staff with a favourable personality might retire or leave to find another job, to be replaced by staff who need time to find their feet in the job. Since goodwill is continually changing in value, it cannot realistically be recorded in the accounts of the business.

6.1 Purchased goodwill

FAST FORWARD

If a business has **goodwill**, it means that the value of the business as a going concern is greater than the value of its separate tangible assets. The valuation of goodwill is extremely subjective and fluctuates constantly. For this reason, non-purchased goodwill is **not** shown as an asset in the statement of financial position.

There is one exception to the general rule that goodwill has no objective valuation. This is **when a business is sold**. People wishing to set up in business have a choice of how to do it – they can either buy their own non-current assets and inventory and set up their business from scratch, or they can buy up an existing business from a proprietor willing to sell it. When a buyer purchases an existing business, he will have to purchase not only its long-term assets and inventory (and perhaps take over its accounts payable and receivable too) but also the goodwill of the business.

Purchased goodwill is shown in the statement of financial position because it has been paid for. It has no tangible substance, and so it is an **intangible non-current asset**.

6.2 How is the value of purchased goodwill decided?

FAST FORWARD

When someone **purchases a business** as a going concern the purchaser and vendor will fix an agreed price which includes an element in respect of goodwill. The way in which goodwill is then valued is not an accounting problem, but a matter of agreement between the two parties.

When a business is sold, there is likely to be some purchased goodwill in the selling price. But **how is the amount of this purchased goodwill decided**?

This is not really a problem for accountants, who must simply record the goodwill in the accounts of the new business. The value of the goodwill is a **matter for the purchaser and seller to agree upon in fixing the purchase/sale price**. However, two methods of valuation are worth mentioning here.

(a) The seller and buyer agree on a price **without specifically quantifying the Goodwill**. The purchased goodwill will then be the difference between the price agreed and the value of the tangible assets in the books of the new business.

(b) However, the calculation of goodwill often precedes the fixing of the purchase price and becomes a **central element of negotiation**. There are many ways of arriving at a value for goodwill and most of them are related to the profit record of the business in question.

No matter how goodwill is calculated within the total agreed purchase price, the goodwill shown by the purchaser in his accounts will be **the difference between the purchase consideration and his own valuation of the tangible net assets acquired**. If A values his tangible net assets at $40,000, goodwill is agreed at $21,000 and B agrees to pay $61,000 for the business but values the tangible net assets at only $38,000, then the goodwill in B's books will be $61,000 – $38,000 = $23,000.

6.3 IFRS 3 (Revised) *Business combinations*

FAST FORWARD

Purchased goodwill is retained in the statement of financial position as an intangible asset under the requirements of **IFRS 3**. It must then be reviewed for impairment annually.

IFRS 3 covers the accounting treatment of goodwill acquired in a business combination.

It is possible to define goodwill in different ways. The IFRS 3 definition of goodwill is different from the more traditional definition and emphasises benefits, rather than the method of calculation.

Key terms

Goodwill. An asset representing the future economic benefits arising from other assets acquired in a **business combination** that are not individually identified and separately recognised. *(IFRS 3)*

Goodwill recognised in a business combination is **an asset** and is initially measured at **cost**. Cost is the excess of the cost of the combination over the acquirer's interest in the net fair value of the acquiree's identifiable assets, liabilities and contingent liabilities.

After initial recognition goodwill acquired in a business combination is measured **at cost less any accumulated impairment losses**. It is **not amortised**. Instead, it is tested for impairment at least annually, in accordance with IAS 36 *Impairment of assets*.

6.3.1 Goodwill and non-controlling interests

The old IFRS 3 looked at goodwill from the point of view of the parent company, ie comparing, consideration transferred with the parent's share of net assets acquired.

IMPORTANT!

The revised IFRS 3 views the **group as an economic entity**. This means that it treats **all provides of equity including non-controlling interests as shareholders in the group**, even if they are not shareholders in the parent.

Therefore, goodwill attributed to the non-controlling interest needs to be recognised.

We will come back to this point in Chapter 12.

6.3.2 Bargain purchase

A **bargain purchase** arises when the net of the acquisition-date amounts of the identifiable assets acquired and the liabilities assumed exceeds the consideration transferred (see Chapter 12).

A bargain purchase might happen, for example, in a business combination that is a forced sale in which the seller is acting under compulsion. However, the recognition or measurement exceptions for particular items may also result in recognising a gain (or change the amount of a recognised gain) on a bargain purchase.

Before recognising a gain on a bargain purchase, the acquirer must reassess whether it has correctly identified all of the assets acquired and all of the liabilities assumed and must recognise any additional assets or liabilities that are identified in that review. The acquirer must then review the procedures used to measure the amounts this IFRS requires to be recognised at the acquisition date for all of the following:

(a) The identifiable assets acquired and liabilities assumed

(b) The non-controlling (formerly minority) interest in the acquiree, if any

(c) For a business combination achieved in stages, the acquirer's previously held interest in the acquiree

(d) The consideration transferred

The purpose of this review is to ensure that the measurements appropriately reflect all the available information as at the acquisition date.

Question — **Characteristics of goodwill**

What are the main characteristics of goodwill which distinguish it from other intangible non-current assets? To what extent do you consider that these characteristics should affect the accounting treatment of goodwill? State your reasons.

Answer

Goodwill may be distinguished from other intangible non-current assets by reference to the following characteristics.

(a) It is incapable of realisation separately from the business as a whole.

(b) Its value has no reliable or predictable relationship to any costs which may have been incurred.

(c) Its value arises from various intangible factors such as skilled employees, effective advertising or a strategic location. These indirect factors cannot be valued.

(d) The value of goodwill may fluctuate widely according to internal and external circumstances over relatively short periods of time.

(e) The assessment of the value of goodwill is highly subjective.

It could be argued that, because goodwill is so different from other intangible non-current assets it does not make sense to account for it in the same way. Therefore, the capitalisation and amortisation treatment would not be acceptable. Furthermore, because goodwill is so difficult to value, any valuation may be misleading, and it is best eliminated from the statement of financial position altogether. However, there are strong arguments for treating it like any other intangible non-current asset. This issue remains controversial.

Chapter Roundup

- You must learn the IASB *Framework* **definition of an asset**: a resource controlled by the entity as a result of past events and from which future economic benefits are expected to flow to the entity.
- This definition ties in closely with the definitions produced by **other standard-setters**, particularly FASB (USA) and ASB (UK).
- The definition has three important characteristics:
  - **Future economic benefit**
  - **Control (ownership)**
  - **Transaction to acquire control has taken place**
- You should already be familiar with many standards relating to **non-current assets** from earlier studies. If not, go back to your earlier study material.
  - IAS 16 *Property, plant and equipment*
  - IAS 20 *Accounting for government grants and disclosure of government assistance*
  - IAS 23 *Borrowing costs*
- **IAS 36 *Impairment of assets*** covers a controversial topic and it affects goodwill as well as tangible long-term assets.
- Impairment is determined by comparing the carrying amount of the asset with its **recoverable amount**.
- The recoverable amount of an asset is the higher of the asset's **fair value less costs of disposal** and **its value in use**.
- When it is not possible to calculate the recoverable amount of a single asset, then that of its **cash generating unit** should be measured instead.
- IAS 40 *Investment property* defines investment property as property **held to earn rentals or for capital appreciation** or both, rather than for:
  - Use in production or supply of goods or services
  - Sale in the ordinary course of business
- Entities can choose between:
  - A **fair value model**, with changes in fair value being measured
  - A **cost model** – the treatment most commonly used under IAS 16
- **Intangible assets** are defined by **IAS 38** as non-monetary assets without physical substance. They must be:
  - **Identifiable**
  - **Controlled** as a result of a past event
  - Able to provide **future economic benefits**
- Intangible assets should initially be measured at cost, but subsequently they can be carried at **cost or at a fair value**.
- **Impairment** rules follow **IAS 36**. There are substantial disclosure requirements.
- If a business has **goodwill**, it means that the value of the business as a going concern is greater than the value of its separate tangible assets. The valuation of goodwill is extremely subjective and fluctuates constantly. For this reason, non-purchased goodwill is **not** shown as an asset in the statement of financial position.

Chapter Roundup (continued)

- When someone **purchases a business** as a going concern the purchaser and vendor will fix an agreed price which includes an element in respect of goodwill. The way in which goodwill is then valued is not an accounting problem, but a matter of agreement between the two parties.
- **Purchased goodwill** is retained in the statement of financial position as an intangible asset under the requirements of **IFRS 3**. It must then be reviewed for impairment annually.

Quick Quiz

1 How does the IASB *Framework* define an asset?

2 How might a non-current asset be defined?

3 Define an impairment.

4 How is value in use calculated?

5 What is a cash generating unit?

6 What is the correct treatment for property being constructed for future use as investment property?

7 Investment property **must** be valued at fair value. *True or false*?

8 Internally generated goodwill can be recognised. *True or false*?

9 How should research and development costs be treated under IAS 38?

10 When can a revaluation surplus on intangible assets be transferred to retained earnings?

11 Over what period should an intangible asset normally be amortised?

12 How should the gain or loss on the disposal of an intangible asset be calculated?

13 Why is it unusual to record goodwill as an asset in the accounts?

14 What is purchased goodwill?

15 Over what period should goodwill be amortised?

16 What treatment does IFRS 3 prescribe for a gain on a bargain purchase?

Answers to Quick Quiz

1 A resource controlled by the entity as a result of past events and from which future economic benefits are expected to flow to the entity.

2 One intended for use on a continuing basis in the company's activities.

3 A fall in the value of an asset, so that its recoverable amount is now less than its carrying value.

4 The present value of estimated future cash flows generated by the asset, including its estimated net disposal value (if any).

5 The smallest identifiable group of assets for which independent cash flows can be identified and measured.

6 Use IAS 16 until the construction is complete, then IAS 40.

7 False, it can be valued at cost or fair value.

8 False

9
- Research costs are written off as an expense as they are incurred
- Development costs may qualify as intangible assets if the criteria in Paragraph 5.7.2 are met.

10 When the surplus is eventually realised.

11 Over its useful life, which may be finite or indefinite

12 The difference between the net disposal proceeds and the carrying value.

13 The value of goodwill is usually inherent in the business but does not have an 'objective' value.

14 The aggregate of the difference between the fair value of the consideration transferred and any non-controlling interest, and the fair value of any non-controlling interest, and the fair value of the net assets.

15 Goodwill should not be amortised.

16 Before recognising a gain, measurement procedures for assets and liabilities and for consideration must be reviewed.

Now try the questions below from the Practice Question Bank

Number	Level	Marks	Time
Q4	Examination	25	49 mins
Q5	Examination	25	49 mins
Q6	Examination	25	49 mins

4

Employee benefits

Topic list	Syllabus reference
1 IAS 19 *Employee benefits*	C6
2 Short-term employee benefits	C6
3 Post-employment benefits	C6
4 Defined contribution plans	C6
5 Defined benefit plans: recognition and measurement	C6
6 Defined benefit plans: other matters	C6
7 Other long-term benefits	C6, F2
8 Disclosures	C6

Introduction

An increasing number of companies and other entities now provide a **pension and other employee benefits** as part of their employees' remuneration package. In view of this trend, it is important that there is standard best practice for the way in which employee benefit costs are **recognised, measured, presented and disclosed** in the sponsoring entities' accounts.

Study guide

		Intellectual level
C6	**Employee benefits**	
(a)	Apply and discuss the accounting treatment of short term and long term employee benefits and defined contribution and defined benefit plans.	3
(b)	Account for gains and losses on settlements and curtailments	2
(c)	Account for the 'asset ceiling test' and the reporting of actuarial gains and losses	2
F2	**Proposed changes to accounting standards**	
(a)	Identify the issues and deficiencies which have led to a proposed change to an accounting standard	2

Exam guide

This topic will be new to you at this level. It may be examined as part of a multi-standard scenario question, or perhaps you will be asked to outline the changes proposed in the ED.

1 IAS 19 *Employee benefits* 12/07, 6/08, 6/12, 12/13, 6/14, 6/15

FAST FORWARD

IAS 19 *Employee benefits* is a long and complex standard covering both short-term and long-term (post-employment) benefits. The complications arise when dealing with **post-employment benefits**.

Exam focus point

This is a very difficult topic – employee benefit costs are inherently complex and their accounting is both **problematic and controversial**. As such this is a ripe topic for Paper P2 and is highlighted as a key topic by the examining team.

IAS 19 *Employee benefits* has been revised several times. The latest version was issued in 2011. The reason for the revision was to address some of the main criticisms of the previous methods of accounting for pensions. Before we look at IAS 19, we should consider the nature of employee benefit costs and why there is an accounting problem which must be addressed by a standard.

1.1 The conceptual nature of employee benefit costs

When a company or other entity employs a new worker, that worker will be offered a **package of pay and benefits**. Some of these will be short-term and the employee will receive the benefit at about the same time as he or she earns it, for example basic pay, overtime and so on. Other employee benefits are **deferred**, however, the main example being retirement benefits (ie a pension).

The cost of these deferred employee benefits to the employer can be viewed in various ways. They could be described as **deferred salary** to the employee. Alternatively, they are a **deduction** from the employee's true gross salary, used as a tax-efficient means of saving. In some countries, tax efficiency arises on retirement benefit contributions because they are not taxed on the employee, but they are allowed as a deduction from taxable profits of the employer.

1.2 Accounting for employee benefit costs

Accounting for **short-term employee benefit costs** tends to be quite straightforward, because they are simply recognised as an expense in the employer's financial statements of the current period.

Accounting for the cost of **deferred employee benefits** is much more difficult. This is because of the large amounts involved, as well as the long time scale, complicated estimates and uncertainties. In the past, entities accounted for these benefits simply by charging profit or loss (the income statements) of the employing entity on the basis of actual payments made. This led to substantial variations in reported profits of these entities and disclosure of information on these costs was usually sparse.

1.3 IAS 19 *Employee benefits*

IAS 19 is intended to prescribe the following.

(a) When the cost of employee benefits should be **recognised as a liability or an expense**
(b) The **amount** of the liability or expense that should be recognised

As a basic rule, the standard states the following (IAS 19: para. 1).

(a) A **liability** should be recognised when an employee has provided a service in exchange for benefits to be received by the employee at some time in the future.

(b) An **expense** should be recognised when the entity consumes the economic benefits from a service provided by an employee in exchange for employee benefits.

The basic problem is therefore fairly straightforward. An entity will often enjoy the **economic benefits** from the services provided by its employees in advance of the employees receiving all the employment benefits from the work they have done, for example they will not receive pension benefits until after they retire.

1.4 Categories of employee benefits

The standard recognises four categories of employee benefits, and proposes a different accounting treatment for each. These four categories are as follows (IAS 19: para. 8).

(a) **Short-term benefits** including, if expected to be settled wholly before twelve months after the end of the annual reporting period in which the employees render the related services:
- Wages and salaries
- Social security contributions
- Paid annual leave
- Paid sick leave
- Paid maternity/paternity leave
- Profit shares and bonuses
- Paid jury service
- Paid military service
- Non-monetary benefits, eg medical care, housing, cars, free or subsidised goods

(b) **Post-employment benefits**, eg pensions and post-employment medical care and post-employment insurance

(c) **Other long-term benefits**, eg profit shares, bonuses or deferred compensation payable later than 12 months after the year end, sabbatical leave, long-service benefits and long-term disability benefits

(d) **Termination benefits**, eg early retirement payments and redundancy payments

Benefits may be paid to the employees themselves, to their dependants (spouses, children, etc) or to third parties.

1.5 Definitions

IAS 19 uses a great many important definitions. This section lists those that relate to the different categories of employee benefits (IAS 19: para. 8).

Key terms

Employee benefits are all forms of consideration given by an entity in exchange for service rendered by employees or for the termination of employment.

Short-term employee benefits are employee benefits (other than termination benefits) that are expected to be settled wholly before twelve months after the end of the annual reporting period in which the employees render the related service.

Post-employment benefits are employee benefits (other than termination benefits and short-term employee benefits) that are payable after the completion of employment.

Other long-term employee benefits are all employee benefits other than short-term employee benefits, post-employment benefits and termination benefits.

Termination benefits are employee benefits provided in exchange for the termination of an employee's employment as a result of either:

(a) An entity's decision to terminate an employee's employment before the normal retirement date, or

(b) An employee's decision to accept an offer of benefits in exchange for the termination of employment.

2 Short-term employee benefits

FAST FORWARD

The accounting for **short term employee benefits** is simple. The principles are the same as for any expense that is accrued over a period.

Accounting for short-term employee benefits is fairly straightforward, because there are **no actuarial assumptions** to be made, and there is **no requirement to discount** future benefits (because they are all, by definition, payable no later than 12 months after the end of the accounting period).

2.1 Recognition and measurement

The rules for short-term benefits (IAS 19: para. 11) are essentially an application of **basic accounting principles and practice**.

(a) **Unpaid short-term employee benefits** as at the end of an accounting period should be recognised as an accrued expense. Any short-term benefits **paid in advance** should be recognised as a prepayment (to the extent that it will lead to, eg a reduction in future payments or a cash refund).

(b) The **cost of short-term employee benefits** should be recognised as an **expense** in the period when the economic benefit is given, as employment costs (except insofar as employment costs may be included within the cost of an asset, eg property, plant and equipment).

2.2 Short-term paid absences

There may be **short-term accumulating paid absences** (IAS 19: para. 13 to 18). These are absences for which an employee is paid, and if the employee's entitlement has not been used up at the end of the period, they are carried forward to the next period. An example is paid holiday leave, where any unused holidays in one year are carried forward to the next year. The cost of the benefits of such absences should be **charged as an expense** as the employees render service that increases their entitlement to future compensated absences.

There may be **short-term non-accumulating paid absences**. These are absences for which an employee is paid when they occur, but an **entitlement to the absences does not accumulate**. The employee can be absent, and be paid, but only if and when the circumstances arise. Examples are maternity/paternity pay, (in most cases) sick pay, and paid absence for jury service.

2.3 Measurement

The cost of accumulating paid absences should be measured as the additional amount that the entity expects to pay as a result of the unused entitlement that has accumulated at the end of the reporting period.

2.4 Example: Unused holiday leave

A company gives its employees an annual entitlement to paid holiday leave. If there is any unused leave at the end of the year, employees are entitled to carry forward the unused leave for up to 12 months. At the end of 20X9, the company's employees carried forward in total 50 days of unused holiday leave. Employees are paid $100 per day.

Required

State the required accounting for the unused holiday carried forward.

Solution

The short-term accumulating paid absences should be recognised as a cost in the year when the entitlement arises, ie in 20X9.

Question — Sick leave

Plyman Co has 100 employees. Each is entitled to five working days of paid sick leave for each year, and unused sick leave can be carried forward for one year. Sick leave is taken on a LIFO basis (ie first out of the current year's entitlement and then out of any balance brought forward).

As at 31 December 20X8, the average unused entitlement is two days per employee. Plyman Co expects (based on past experience which is expected to continue) that 92 employees will take five days or less sick leave in 20X9, the remaining eight employees will take an average of 6½ days each.

Required

State the required accounting for sick leave.

Answer

Plyman Co expects to pay an additional 12 days of sick pay as a result of the unused entitlement that has accumulated at 31 December 20X8, ie 1½ days × 8 employees. Plyman Co should recognise a liability equal to 12 days of sick pay.

2.5 Profit sharing or bonus plans

Profit shares or bonuses payable within 12 months after the end of the accounting period should be recognised as an expected cost when the entity has a **present obligation to pay it**, ie when the employer has no real option but to pay it. This will usually be when the employer recognises the profit or other performance achievement to which the profit share or bonus relates. The measurement of the constructive obligation reflects the possibility that some employees may leave without receiving a bonus (IAS 19: para. 19 to 24).

2.6 Example: Profit sharing plan

Mooro Co runs a profit sharing plan under which it pays 3% of its net profit for the year to its employees if none have left during the year. Mooro Co estimates that this will be reduced by staff turnover to 2.5% in 20X9.

Required

Which costs should be recognised by Mooro Co for the profit share?

Solution

Mooro Co should recognise a liability and an expense of 2.5% of net profit.

2.7 Disclosure

There are **no specific disclosure requirements for short-term employee benefits** in the standard.

3 Post-employment benefits

FAST FORWARD

There are **two types of post-employment benefit plan**:

- Defined contribution plans
- Defined benefit plans

Defined contribution plans are simple to account for as the benefits are defined by the contributions made.

Defined benefit plans are much more difficult to deal with as the benefits are promised, they define the contributions to be made.

Many employers provide post-employment benefits for their employees after they have stopped working. **Pension schemes** are the most obvious example, but an employer might provide post-employment death benefits to the dependants of former employees, or post-employment medical care.

Post-employment benefit schemes are often referred to as '**plans**'. The 'plan' receives regular contributions from the employer (and sometimes from current employees as well) and the money is invested in assets, such as stocks and shares and other investments. The post-employment benefits are paid out of the income from the plan assets (dividends, interest) or from money from the sale of some plan assets.

3.1 Definitions

IAS 19 para. 8 sets out the following definitions relating to classification of plans.

Key terms

Defined contribution plans are post-employment benefit plans under which an entity pays fixed contributions into a separate entity (a fund) and will have no legal or constructive obligation to pay further contributions if the fund does not hold sufficient assets to pay all employee benefits relating to employee service in the current and prior periods.

Defined benefit plans are post-employment benefit plans other than defined contribution plans.

Multi-employer plans are defined contribution plans (other than State plans) or defined benefit plans (other than State plans) that:

(a) Pool the assets contributed by various entities that are not under common control, and

(b) Use those assets to provide benefits to employees of more than one entity, on the basis that contribution and benefit levels are determined without regard to the identity of the entity that employs the employees concerned.

There are two types or categories of post-employment benefit plan, as given in the definitions above (IAS 19: paras. 26 to 30).

(a) **Defined contribution plans**. With such plans, the employer (and possibly current employees too) pay regular contributions into the plan of a given or 'defined' amount each year. The contributions are invested, and the size of the post-employment benefits paid to former employees depends on how well or how badly the plan's investments perform. If the investments perform well, the plan will be able to afford higher benefits than if the investments performed less well.

(b) **Defined benefit plans**. With these plans, the size of the post-employment benefits is determined in advance, ie the benefits are 'defined'. The employer (and possibly current employees too) pay contributions into the plan, and the contributions are invested. The size of the contributions is set at an amount that is expected to earn enough investment returns to meet the obligation to pay the post-employment benefits. If, however, it becomes apparent that the assets in the fund are insufficient, the employer will be required to make additional contributions into the plan to make up the expected shortfall. On the other hand, if the fund's assets appear to be larger than they need to be, and in excess of what is required to pay the post-employment benefits, the employer may be allowed to take a 'contribution holiday' (ie stop paying in contributions for a while).

It is important to make a clear distinction between the following.

- **Funding** a defined benefit plan, ie paying contributions into the plan
- **Accounting for** the cost of funding a defined benefit plan

The key difference between the two types of plan is the nature of the 'promise' made by the entity to the employees in the scheme:

(a) Under a **defined contribution** plan, the 'promise' is to pay the agreed amount of contributions. Once this is done, the entity has no further liability and no exposure to risks related to the performance of the assets held in the plan.

(b) Under a **defined benefit** plan, the 'promise' is to pay the amount of benefits agreed under the plan. The entity is taking on a far more uncertain liability that may change in future as a result of many variables and has continuing exposure to risks related to the performance of assets held in the plan. In simple terms, of the plan assets are insufficient to meet the plan liabilities to pay pensions in future, the entity will have to make up any deficit.

3.2 Multi-employer plans

These were defined above. IAS 19 (IAS 19: paras. 32 to 39) requires an entity to **classify** such a plan as a defined contribution plan or a defined benefit plan, depending on its terms (including any constructive obligation beyond those terms).

For a multi-employer plan that is a **defined benefit plan**, the entity should account for its proportionate share of the defined benefit obligation, plan assets and cost associated with the plan in the same way as for any other defined benefit plan and make full disclosure.

When there is **insufficient information** to use defined benefit accounting, then the multi-employer plan should be accounted for as a defined contribution plan and additional disclosures made (that the plan is in fact a defined benefit plan and information about any known surplus or deficit).

3.3 Section summary

- There are two categories of **post-retirement benefits**:
  - Defined contribution schemes
  - Defined benefit schemes
- **Defined contribution schemes** provide benefits commensurate with the fund available to produce them.
- **Defined benefit schemes** provide promised benefits and so contributions are based on estimates of how the fund will perform.
- **Defined contribution scheme costs** are easy to account for and this is covered in the next section.

4 Defined contribution plans

A typical defined contribution plan would be where the employing company agreed to contribute an amount of, say, 5% of employees' salaries into a post-employment plan.

Accounting for payments into defined contribution plans is straightforward.

(a) The **obligation** is measured by the amounts to be contributed for that period.

(b) There are no actuarial assumptions to make.

(c) If the obligation is settled in the current period (or at least no later than 12 months after the end of the current period) there is **no requirement for discounting**.

IAS 19 (IAS 19: paras. 51 and 52) requires the following.

(a) **Contributions** to a defined contribution plan should be recognised as an **expense** in the period they are payable (except to the extent that labour costs may be included within the cost of assets).

(b) Any liability for **unpaid contributions** that are due as at the end of the period should be recognised as a **liability** (accrued expense).

(c) Any **excess contributions** paid should be recognised as an asset (prepaid expense), but only to the extent that the prepayment will lead to, eg a reduction in future payments or a cash refund.

In the (unusual) situation where contributions to a defined contribution plan do not fall due entirely within 12 months after the end of the period in which the employees performed the related service, then these should be **discounted**. The discount rate to be used is discussed below in Paragraphs 5.10.2.

Disclosure requirements

(a) A **description** of the plan
(b) The amount recognised as an **expense** in the period

5 Defined benefit plans: recognition and measurement

6/11, 6/12, 6/15

Accounting for defined benefit plans is much more complex. The complexity of accounting for defined benefit plans stems largely from the following factors.

(a) The future benefits (arising from employee service in the current or prior years) **cannot be measured exactly**, but whatever they are, the employer will have to pay them, and the liability should therefore be recognised now. To measure these future obligations, it is necessary to use **actuarial assumptions**.

(b) The obligations payable in future years should be valued, by discounting, on a **present value** basis. This is because the obligations may be settled in many years' time.

(c) If actuarial assumptions change, the amount of required contributions to the fund will change, and there may be **actuarial gains or losses**. A contribution into a fund in any period will not equal the expense for that period, due to actuarial gains or losses.

IAS 19 para. 8 defines the following key terms to do with defined benefit plans.

Key terms

The **net defined benefit liability (asset)** is the deficit or surplus, adjusted for any effect of limiting a net defined benefit asset to the asset ceiling.

The **deficit or surplus** is:

(a) The present value of the defined benefit obligation less
(b) The fair value of plan assets (if any).

The **asset ceiling** is the present value of any economic benefits available in the form of refunds from the plan or reductions in future contributions to the plan.

The **present value of a defined benefit** obligation is the present value, without deducting any plan assets, of expected future payments required to settle the obligation resulting from employee service in the current and prior periods.

Key terms cont'd

Plan assets comprise:

(a) Assets held by a long-term employee benefit fund; and
(b) Qualifying insurance policies

Assets held by a long-term employee benefit fund are assets (other than non-transferable financial instruments issued by the reporting entity) that:

(a) Are held by an entity (a fund) that is legally separate from the reporting entity and exists solely to pay or fund employee benefits; and

(b) Are available to be used only to pay or fund employee benefits, are not available to the reporting entity's own creditors (even in bankruptcy), and cannot be returned to the reporting entity, unless either:

 (i) The remaining assets of the fund are sufficient to meet all the related employee benefit obligations of the plan or the reporting entity; or

 (ii) The assets are returned to the reporting entity to reimburse it for employee benefits already paid.

A **qualifying insurance policy** is an insurance policy issued by an insurer that is not a related party (as defined in IAS 24 *Related party disclosures*) of the reporting entity, if the proceeds of the policy:

(a) Can be used only to pay or fund employee benefits under a defined benefit plan; and

(b) Are not available to the reporting entity's own creditors (even in bankruptcy) and cannot be paid to the reporting entity, unless either:

 (i) The proceeds represent surplus assets that are not needed for the policy to meet all the related employee benefit obligations; or

 (ii) The proceeds are returned to the reporting entity to reimburse it for employee benefits already paid.

Fair value is the price that would be received to sell an asset in an orderly transaction between market participants at the measurement date.

5.1 Outline of the method

FAST FORWARD

There is a **four-step method** for recognising and measuring the expenses and liability of a defined benefit pension plan.

An outline of the method used by an employer to account for the expenses and obligation of a defined benefit plan is given below. The stages will be explained in more detail later.

Step 1 **Measure the deficit or surplus**:

(a) An **actuarial technique** (the **Projected Unit Credit Method**), should be used to make a reliable estimate of the amount of future benefits employees have earned from service in relation to the current and prior years. The entity must determine how much benefit should be attributed to service performed by employees in the current period, and in prior periods. Assumptions include, for example, assumptions about employee turnover, mortality rates, future increases in salaries (if these will affect the eventual size of future benefits such as pension payments).

(b) The benefit should be **discounted** to arrive at the present value of the defined benefit obligation and the current service cost.

(c) The **fair value** of any **plan assets** should be deducted from the present value of the defined benefit obligation.

Step 2 The surplus or deficit measured in Step 1 may have to be adjusted if a net benefit asset has to be restricted by the **asset ceiling**.

Step 3 Determine the amounts to be recognised in **profit or loss**:

(a) **Current service cost**
(b) Any **past service cost** and **gain or loss on settlement**
(c) **Net interest** on the **net defined benefit liability (asset)**

Step 4 Determine the **re-measurements** of the **net defined benefit liability (asset)**, to be recognised in **other comprehensive income** (items that will **not be reclassified to profit or loss**):

(a) **Actuarial gains and losses**
(b) **Return on plan assets** (excluding amounts included in net interest on the net defined benefit liability (asset))
(c) Any change in the effect of the **asset ceiling** (excluding amounts included in net interest on the net defined benefit liability (asset))

5.2 Constructive obligation

IAS 19 (IAS 19: para. 61) makes it very clear that it is not only its legal obligation under the formal terms of a defined benefit plan that an entity must account for, but also for any **constructive obligation** that it may have. A constructive obligation, which will arise from the entity's informal practices, exists when the entity has no realistic alternative but to pay employee benefits, for example if any change in the informal practices would cause unacceptable damage to employee relationships.

5.3 The Projected Unit Credit Method

With this method, it is assumed that each period of service by an employee gives rise to an **additional unit of future benefits**. The present value of that unit of future benefits can be calculated, and attributed to the period in which the service is given. The units, each measured separately, build up to the overall obligation. The accumulated present value of (discounted) future benefits will incur interest over time, and an interest expense should be recognised.

These calculations are complex and would normally be carried out by an actuary. In the exam, you will be given the figures but the following example (from IAS 19 para. 68) is included to explain the method.

5.4 Example: Defined benefit obligations and current service cost

A lump sum benefit is payable on termination of service and equal to 1% of final salary for each year of service. The salary in year 1 is $10,000 and is assumed to increase at 7% (compound) each year. The discount rate used is 10% per year. The following table shows how the obligation builds up for an employee who is expected to leave at the end of year 5, assuming that there are no changes in actuarial assumptions. For simplicity, this example ignores the additional adjustment needed to reflect the probability that the employee may leave the entity at an earlier or later date.

Year	*1*	*2*	*3*	*4*	*5*
	$	$	$	$	$
Benefit attributed to:					
Prior years	0	131	262	393	524
Current year (1% × final salary)	131	131	131	131	131
Current and prior years	131	262	393	524	655
Opening obligation	–	89	196	324	476
Interest at 10%	–	9	20	33	48
Current service cost	89	98	108	119	131
Closing obligation	89	196	324	476	655

Notes

1 The opening obligation is the present value of the benefit attributed to prior years.
2 The current service cost is the present value of the benefit attributed to the current year.
3 The closing obligation is the present value of the benefit attributed to current and prior years.

5.5 Actuarial assumptions

FAST FORWARD

Actuarial assumptions made should be unbiased and based on market expectations.

Discount rates used should be determined by reference to market yields on high-quality fixed-rate corporate bonds.

Actuarial assumptions are needed **to estimate the size of the future (post-employment) benefits** that will be payable under a defined benefits scheme. The main categories of actuarial assumptions are as follows (IAS 19: paras. 67, 68):

(a) **Demographic assumptions** are about mortality rates before and after retirement, the rate of employee turnover, early retirement, claim rates under medical plans for former employees, and so on.

(b) **Financial assumptions** include future salary levels (allowing for seniority and promotion as well as inflation) and the future rate of increase in medical costs (not just inflationary cost rises, but also cost rises specific to medical treatments and to medical treatments required given the expectations of longer average life expectancy).

The standard requires actuarial assumptions to be neither too cautious nor too imprudent: they should be **'unbiased'**. They should also be based on **'market expectations'** at the year end, over the period during which the obligations will be settled.

5.6 The statement of financial position

In the statement of financial position, the amount recognised as a **defined benefit liability** (which may be a negative amount, ie an asset) should be the following:

(a) The **present value of the defined obligation** at the year end, **minus**

(b) The **fair value of the assets of the plan** as at the year end (if there are any) out of which the future obligations to current and past employees will be directly settled

The earlier parts of this section have looked at the recognition and measurement of the defined benefit obligation. Now we will look at issues relating to the assets held in the plan.

5.7 Plan assets

Plan assets are (IAS 19: paras. 113 to 115):

(a) Assets such as stocks and shares, held by a fund that is legally separate from the reporting entity, which exists solely to pay employee benefits.

(b) Insurance policies, issued by an insurer that is not a related party, the proceeds of which can only be used to pay employee benefits.

Investments which may be used for purposes other than to pay employee benefits are not plan assets.

The standard requires that the plan assets are measured at fair value, as 'the price that would be received to sell an asset in an orderly transaction between market participants at the measurement date'. You may spot that this definition is slightly different to the revised definition in accordance with IFRS 13 *Fair value measurement* (see Chapter 7). The two standards were being updated around the same time so the definitions are currently out of step but this should make no difference to the practicalities you will have to deal with in questions, where the fair value is normally stated in the scenario information.

IAS 19 includes the following **specific requirements**:

(a) The plan assets should exclude any contributions due from the employer but not yet paid.

(b) Plan assets are reduced by any liabilities of the fund that do not relate to employee benefits, such as trade and other payables.

5.8 The statement of profit or loss and other comprehensive income

All of the gains and losses that affect the plan obligation and plan asset must be recognised. The **components of defined benefit cost must be recognised as follows** in the statement of profit or loss and other comprehensive income (IAS 19: paras. 120, 122):

	Component	*Recognised in*
(a)	**Service cost**	Profit or loss
(b)	**Net interest on the net defined benefit liability**	Profit or loss
(c)	**Re-measurements of the net defined benefit liability**	Other comprehensive income (not reclassified to P/L)

5.9 Service costs

These comprise (IAS 19: para. 120):

(a) **Current service cost**, this is the increase in the present value of the defined benefit obligation resulting from employee services during the period. The measurement and recognition of this cost was introduced in Section 5.1.

(b) **Past service cost**, which is the change in the obligation relating to service in **prior periods**. This results from amendments or curtailments to the pension plan, and

(c) Any **gain or loss on settlement**.

The detail relating to points (b) and (c) above will be covered in a later section. First, we will continue with the basic elements of accounting for defined benefit pension costs.

5.10 Net interest on the defined benefit liability (asset)

In Section 5.1 we looked at the recognition and measurement of the defined benefit obligation. This figure is the discounted **present value** of the future benefits payable. Every year the discount must be 'unwound', increasing the present value of the obligation as time passes through an interest charge.

5.10.1 Interest calculation

IAS 19 para. 83 requires that the interest should be calculated on the **net defined benefit liability (asset)**. This means that the amount recognised in profit or loss is the net of the interest charge on the obligation and the interest income recognised on the assets.

The calculation is as follows:

Net defined benefit liability/ (asset) × **Discount rate**

The **net defined benefit liability/ (asset)** should be measured as at the **start** of the accounting period, taking account of changes during the period as a result of contributions paid into the scheme and benefits paid out.

Many exam questions include the assumption that all payments into and out of the scheme take place at the end of the year, so that the interest calculations can be based on the opening balances.

5.10.2 Discount rate

The **discount rate** adopted should be determined by reference to **market yields** on high quality fixed-rate corporate bonds (IAS 19: para. 83). The bonds should be denominated in the same currency as the benefits to be paid. In the absence of a 'deep' market in such bonds, the yields on comparable government bonds should be used as reference instead. The maturity of the corporate bonds that are used to determine a discount rate should have a term to maturity that is consistent with the expected maturity of the post-employment benefit obligations, although a single weighted average discount rate is sufficient.

The guidelines comment that there may be some difficulty in obtaining a **reliable yield for long-term maturities**, say 30 or 40 years from now. This should not, however, be a significant problem: the present value of obligations payable in many years time will be relatively small and unlikely to be a significant proportion of the total defined benefit obligation. The total obligation is therefore unlikely to be sensitive to errors in the assumption about the discount rate for long-term maturities (beyond the maturities of long-term corporate or government bonds).

5.11 Re-measurements of the net defined benefit liability

Re-measurements of the net defined benefit liability/(asset) comprise (IAS 19: para. 127):

(a) Actuarial gains and losses;

(b) The return on plan assets, (excluding amounts included in net interest on the net defined benefit liability/(asset)); and

(c) Any change in the effect of the asset ceiling, (excluding amounts included in net interest on the net defined benefit liability/(asset)).

The gains and losses relating to points (a) and (b) above will arise in every defined benefit scheme so we will look at these in this section. The asset ceiling is a complication that is not relevant in every case, so it is dealt with separately, later in the chapter.

5.11.1 Actuarial gains and losses

FAST FORWARD

Actuarial gains and losses arise for several reasons, and IAS 19 requires these to be recognised, in full in other comprehensive income.

At the end of each accounting period, a new valuation, using updated assumptions, should be carried out on the obligation. Actuarial gains or losses arise because of the following.

- **Actual events** (eg employee turnover, salary increases) differ from the actuarial assumptions that were made to estimate the defined benefit obligations
- The effect of **changes to assumptions** concerning benefit payment options
- **Estimates are revised** (eg different assumptions are made about future employee turnover, salary rises, mortality rates, and so on)
- The effect of changes to the **discount rate**

Actuarial gains and losses are recognised in **other comprehensive income**. They are **not reclassified to profit or loss** under the 2011 revision to IAS 1 (see Chapter 10).

5.11.2 Return on plan assets

FAST FORWARD

The **return on plan assets** must be calculated.

A new valuation of the plan assets is carried out at each period end, using current fair values. Any difference between the new value, and what has been recognised up to that date (normally the opening balance, interest, and any cash payments into or out of the plan) is treated as a 're-measurement' and recognised in other comprehensive income.

5.12 Example

At 1 January 20X2 the fair value of the assets of a defined benefit plan were valued at $1,100,000 and the present value of the defined benefit obligation was $1,250,000. On 31 December 20X2, the plan received contributions from the employer of $490,000 and paid out benefits of $190,000.

The current service cost for the year was $360,000 and a discount rate of 6% is to be applied to the net liability/ (asset).

After these transactions, the fair value of the plan's assets at 31 December 20X2 was $1.5m. The present value of the defined benefit obligation was $1,553,600.

Required

Calculate the gains or losses on remeasurement through OCI and the return on plan assets and illustrate how this pension plan will be treated in the statement of profit or loss and other comprehensive income and statement of financial position for the year ended 31 December 20X2.

Solution

It is always useful to set up a working reconciling the assets and obligation:

	Assets	*Obligation*
	$	$
Fair value/present value at 1/1/X2	1,100,000	1,250,000
Interest (1,100,000 × 6%)/ (1,250,000 × 6%)	66,000	75,000
Current service cost		360,000
Contributions received	490,000	
Benefits paid	(190,000)	(190,000)
Return on plan assets excluding amounts in net interest (balancing figure) (OCI)	34,000	–
Loss on re-measurement (balancing figure) (OCI)	–	58,600
	1,500,000	1,553,600

The following accounting treatment is required.

(a) In the **statement of profit or loss and other comprehensive income**, the following amounts will be recognised

In **profit or loss**:

	$
Current service cost	360,000
Net interest on net defined benefit liability (75,000 – 66,000)	9,000

In **other comprehensive income** (34,000 – 58,600) 24,600

(b) In the **statement of financial position**, the net defined benefit liability of $53,600 (1,553,600 – 1,500,000) will be recognised.

5.13 Section summary

The recognition and measurement of defined benefit plan costs are complex issues.

- Learn and understand the definitions of the various elements of a defined benefit pension plan
- Learn the **outline of the method of accounting** (see Paragraph 5.1)
- Learn the recognition method for the:
  - Statement of financial position
  - Statement of profit or loss and other comprehensive income

6 Defined benefit plans: other matters

We have now covered the basics of accounting for defined benefit plans. This section looks at the special circumstances of past service costs, curtailments and settlements.

6.1 Past service cost and gains and losses on settlement

FAST FORWARD

You should know how to deal with **past service costs and curtailments and settlements.**

In Paragraph 5.9 we identified that the total service cost may comprise not only the current service costs but other items, past service cost and gains and losses on settlement. This section explain these issues and their accounting treatment.

6.1.1 Past service cost

Past service cost (IAS 19: paras. 102 to 106) is the change in the present value of the defined benefit obligation resulting from a plan **amendment** or **curtailment**.

A plan **amendment** arises when an entity either introduces a defined benefits plan or **changes the benefits payable** under an existing plan. As a result, the entity has taken on additional obligations that it has not hitherto provided for. For example, an employer might decide to introduce a medical benefits scheme for former employees. This will create a new defined benefit obligation, that has not yet been provided for.

A **curtailment occurs when an entity significantly reduces the number of employees covered by a plan**. This could result from an isolated event, such as closing a plant, discontinuing an operation or the termination or suspension of a plan.

Past service costs can be either **positive** (if the changes increase the obligation) or **negative** (if the change reduces the obligation).

6.1.2 Gains and losses on settlement

A **settlement** occurs either when an employer enters into a transaction to eliminate part or all of its post-employment benefit obligations (other than a payment of benefits to or on behalf of employees under the terms of the plan and included in the actuarial assumptions).

A curtailment and settlement might **happen together**, for example when an employer brings a defined benefit plan to an end by settling the obligation with a one-off lump sum payment and then scrapping the plan.

The gain or losses on a settlement is the difference between:

(a) The **present value of the defined benefit obligation** being settled, as valued on the date of the settlement; and

(b) The **settlement price**, including any plan assets transferred and any payments made by the entity directly in connection with the settlement. (IAS 19: paras. 109, 111)

6.1.3 Accounting for past service cost and gains and losses on settlement

An entity should **re-measure the obligation** (and the related plan assets, if any) using current actuarial assumptions, before determining past service cost or a gain or loss on settlement (IAS 19: paras. 109, 111).

The rules for recognition for these items are as follows:

Past service costs are recognised at the earlier of the following dates:

(a) When the plan amendment or curtailment occurs, and

(b) When the entity recognises related restructuring costs (in accordance with IAS 37, see Chapter 5) or termination benefits.

6.2 Asset ceiling test

When we looked at the recognition of the net defined benefit liability/(asset) in the statement of financial position at the beginning of Section 5 the term 'asset ceiling' was mentioned. This term relates to a threshold established by IAS 19 to ensure that any defined benefit asset (ie a pension surplus) is carried at **no more than its recoverable amount**. In simple terms, this means that any net asset is restricted to the amount of cash savings that will be available to the entity in future (IAS 19: paras. 64 and 65).

6.3 Net defined benefit assets

A net defined benefit asset may arise if the plan has been overfunded or if actuarial gains have arisen. This meets the definition of an asset (as stated in the *Conceptual Framework* Chapter 4: para. 4) because **all** of the following apply.

(a) The entity **controls a resource** (the ability to use the surplus to generate future benefits).

(b) That control is the **result of past events** (contributions paid by the entity and service rendered by the employee).

(c) **Future benefits** are available to the entity in the form of a reduction in future contributions or a cash refund, either directly or indirectly to another plan in deficit.

The **asset ceiling** is the **present value** of those future benefits. The **discount rate used is the same** as that used to calculate the net interest on the net defined benefit liability/(asset). The net defined benefit asset would be reduced to the asset ceiling threshold. Any related write down would be treated as a **re-measurement** and recognised in **other comprehensive income**.

If the asset ceiling adjustment was needed in a subsequent year, the changes in its value would be treated as follows:

(a) **Interest** (as it is a discounted amount) recognised in profit or loss as part of the net interest amount

(b) **Other changes** recognised in profit or loss

6.4 Suggested approach and question

The suggested approach to defined benefit schemes is to deal with the change in the obligation and asset in the following order.

Step	Item	Recognition
1	**Record opening figures:** • Asset • Obligation	
2	**Interest cost on obligation** • Based on discount rate and PV obligation at start of period. • Should also reflect any changes in obligation during period.	DEBIT *Interest cost (P/L)* *(x% × b/d obligation)* CREDIT *PV defined benefit obligation (SOFP)*
3	**Interest on plan assets** • Based on discount rate and asset value at start of period. • Technically, this interest is also time apportioned on contributions less benefits paid in the period.	DEBIT *Plan assets (SOFP)* CREDIT *Interest cost (P/L)* *(x% × b/d assets)*

Step	Item	Recognition
4	**Current service cost** • Increase in the present value of the obligation resulting from employee service in the current period.	DEBIT *Current service cost (P/L)* CREDIT *PV defined benefit obligation (SOFP)*
5	**Contributions** • As advised by actuary.	DEBIT *Plan assets (SOFP)* CREDIT *Company cash*
6	**Benefits** • Actual pension payments made.	DEBIT *PV defined benefit obligation (SOFP)* CREDIT *Plan assets (SOFP)*
7	**Past service cost** • Increase/decrease in PV obligation as a result of introduction or improvement of benefits.	**Positive (increase in obligation):** DEBIT *Past service cost (P/L)* CREDIT *PV defined benefit obligation (SOFP)* **Negative (decrease in obligation):** DEBIT *PV defined benefit obligation (SOFP)* CREDIT *Past service cost (P/L)*
8	**Gains and losses on settlement** • Difference between the value of the obligation being settled and the settlement price.	**Gain** DEBIT *PV defined benefit obligation (SOFP)* CREDIT *Service cost (P/L)* **Loss** DEBIT *Service cost (P/L)* CREDIT *PV defined benefit obligation (SOFP)*
9	**Re-measurements: actuarial gains and losses** • Arising from annual valuations of obligation. • On obligation, differences between actuarial assumptions and actual experience during the period, or changes in actuarial assumptions.	**Gain** DEBIT *PV defined benefit obligation (SOFP)* CREDIT *Other comprehensive income* **Loss** DEBIT *Other comprehensive income* CREDIT *PV defined benefit obligation (SOFP)*
10	**Re-measurements: return on assets (excluding amounts in net-interest)** • Arising from annual valuations of plan assets	**Gain** DEBIT *FV plan assets (SOFP)* CREDIT *Other comprehensive income* **Loss** DEBIT *Other comprehensive income* CREDIT *FV plan assets (SOFP)*
11	**Disclose in accordance with the standard**	See comprehensive question.

Exam focus point

It would be useful for you to do one last question on accounting for post-employment defined benefit schemes. Questions on these are likely in the exam.

Question

Comprehensive

For the sake of simplicity and clarity, all transactions are assumed to occur at the year end.

The following data applies to the post employment defined benefit compensation scheme of BCD Co.
Discount rate: 10% (each year)
Present value of obligation at start of 20X2: $1m
Market value of plan assets at start of 20X2: $1m

The following figures are relevant.

	20X2	*20X3*	*20X4*
	$'000	$'000	$'000
Current service cost	140	150	150
Benefits paid out	120	140	150
Contributions paid by entity	110	120	120
Present value of obligation at year end	1,200	1,650	1,700
Fair value of plan assets at year end	1,250	1,450	1,610

Additional information:

(1) At the end of 20X3, a division of the company was sold. As a result of this, a large number of the employees of that division opted to transfer their accumulated pension entitlement to their new employer's plan. Assets with a fair value of $48,000 were transferred to the other company's plan and the actuary has calculated that the reduction in BCD's defined benefit liability is $50,000. The year end valuations in the table above were carried out **before** this transfer was recorded.

(2) At the end of 20X4, a decision was taken to make a one-off additional payment to former employees currently receiving pensions from the plan. This was announced to the former employees before the year end. This payment was not allowed for in the original terms of the scheme. The actuarial valuation of the obligation in the table above **includes** the additional liability of $40,000 relating to this additional payment.

Required

Show how the reporting entity should account for this defined benefit plan in each of years 20X2, 20X3 and 20X4.

Answer

The actuarial gain or loss is established as a balancing figure in the calculations, as follows.

Present value of obligation

	20X2	*20X3*	*20X4*
	$'000	$'000	$'000
PV of obligation at start of year	1,000	1,200	1,600
Interest cost (10%)	100	120	160
Current service cost	140	150	150
Past service cost			40
Benefits paid	(120)	(140)	(150)
Settlements		(50)	
Actuarial (gain)/loss on obligation: balancing figure	80	320	(100)
PV of obligation at end of year	1,200	1,600 *	1,700

**(1,650 – 50)*

Market value of plan assets

	20X2	*20X3*	*20X4*
	$'000	$'000	$'000
Market value of plan assets at start of year	1,000	1,250	1,402
Interest on plan assets (10%)	100	125	140
Contributions	110	120	120
Benefits paid	(120)	(140)	(150)
Settlements	–	(48)	–
Gain on remeasurement through OCI: balancing figure	160	95	98
Market value of plan assets at year end	1,250	1,402*	1,610

**(1,450 – 48)*

In the statement of financial position, the liability that is recognised is calculated as follows.

	20X2	*20X3*	*20X4*
	$'000	$'000	$'000
Present value of obligation	1,200	1,600	1,700
Market value of plan assets	1,250	1,402	1,610
Liability/(asset) in statement of financial position	(50)	198	90

The following will be recognised in profit or loss for the year:

	20X2	*20X3*	*20X4*
	$'000	$'000	$'000
Current service cost	140	150	150
Past service cost	–	–	40
Net interest on defined benefit liability (asset)	–	(5)	20
Gain on settlement of defined benefit liability	–	(2)	–
Expense recognised in profit or loss	140	143	210

The following re-measurements will be recognised in other comprehensive income for the year:

	20X2	*20X3*	*20X4*
	$'000	$'000	$'000
Actuarial (gain)/loss on obligation	80	320	(100)
Return on plan assets (excluding amounts in net-interest)	(160)	(95)	(98)

7 Other long-term benefits

7.1 Definition

IAS 19 para. 8 defines **other long-term employee benefits** as all employee benefits other than short-term employee benefits, post-employment benefits and termination benefits if not expected to be settled wholly before twelve months after the end of the annual reporting period in which the employees render the related service.

The types of benefits that might fall into this category include:

(a) Long-term paid absences such as long-service or sabbatical leave
(b) Jubilee or other long-service benefits
(c) Long-term disability benefits; profit-sharing and bonuses
(d) Deferred remuneration

7.2 Accounting treatment for other long-term benefits

There are many similarities between these types of benefits and defined benefit pensions. For example, in a long-term bonus scheme, the employees may provide service over a number of periods to earn their entitlement to a payment at a later date. In some case, the entity may put cash aside, or invest it in some way (perhaps by taking out an insurance policy) to meet the liabilities when they arise.

As there is normally far less uncertainty relating to the measurement of these benefits, IAS 19 requires a simpler method of accounting for them (IAS 19: para. 153. Unlike the accounting method for post-employment benefits, this method does **not recognise re-measurements in other comprehensive income**.

The entity should recognise all of the following in **profit or loss**.

(a) **Service cost**
(b) **Net interest** on the defined benefit liability (asset)
(c) **Re-measurement** of the defined benefit liability (asset)

8 Disclosures

8.1 Principles of disclosures required by IAS 19

The outline requirements are for the entity to disclose information that (IAS 19: para. 139):

(a) Explains the characteristics of its defined benefit plans and risks associated with them;

(b) Identifies and explains the amounts in its financial statements arising from its defined benefit plans; and

(c) Describes how its defined benefit plans may affect the amount, timing and uncertainty of the entity's future cash flows.

Chapter Roundup

- **IAS 19 *Employee benefits*** is a long and complex standard covering both short-term and long-term (post-employment) benefits. The complications arise when dealing with **post-employment benefits**.
- The accounting for **short-term employee benefits** is simple. The principles are the same as for any expense that is accrued over a period.
- There are **two types of post-employment benefit plan**:
  - Defined contribution plans
  - Defined benefit plans
- **Defined contribution plans** are simple to account for as the benefits are defined by the contributions made.
- **Defined benefit plans** are much more difficult to deal with as the benefits are promised, they define the contributions to be made.
- There is a **four-step method** for recognising and measuring the expenses and liability of a defined benefit pension plan.
- **Actuarial assumptions** made should be unbiased and based on market expectations.
- **Discount rates** used should be determined by reference to market yields on high-quality fixed-rate corporate bonds.
- **Actuarial gains and losses** arise for several reasons, and IAS 19 requires these to be recognised, in full in other comprehensive income.
- The **return on plan assets** must be calculated.
- You should know how to deal with **past service costs** and **curtailments** and **settlements**.

Quick Quiz

1. What are the four categories of employee benefits given by IAS 19?
2. What is the difference between defined contribution and defined benefit plans?
3. What is a 'constructive obligation' compared to a legal obligation?
4. How should a defined benefit expense be recognised in profit or loss for the year?
5. What causes actuarial gains or losses?

Answers to Quick Quiz

1
- Short-term
- Post-employment
- Other long-term
- Termination

2 See Paragraph 3.1.

3 A constructive obligation exists when the entity has no realistic alternative than to pay employee benefits.

4 Current service cost + interest + expected return + recognised actuarial gains/losses + past service cost + curtailments or settlements.

5 Gains or losses due to changes in actuarial assumptions.

Now try the question below from the Practice Question Bank

Number	Level	Marks	Time
Q7	Introductory	12	23 mins

Provisions, contingencies and events after the reporting period

5

Topic list	Syllabus reference
1 Revision of IAS 10 *Events after the reporting period*	C8
2 IAS 37 *Provisions, contingent liabilities and contingent assets*	C8

Introduction

You should be very familiar with IAS 10 from your earlier studies, but in the light of the Study Guide, you should concentrate on the issue of window dressing.

Provisions are an important area. Expect more complex IAS 37 scenarios at P2.

Study guide

		Intellectual level
C8	**Provisions, contingencies, events after the reporting period**	
(a)	Apply and discuss the recognition, derecognition and measurement of provisions, contingent liabilities and contingent assets, including environmental provisions	3
(b)	Calculate and discuss restructuring provisions	3
(c)	Apply and discuss accounting for events after the reporting date	3
(d)	Determine going concern issues arising after the reporting date	3

Exam guide

These standards are likely to be tested as part of a scenario question. You may also be asked to advise the directors on the implications for the financial statements of the changes proposed in the ED.

1 Revision of IAS 10 *Events after the reporting period*

FAST FORWARD

IAS 10 should be familiar from your earlier studies, but it still could come up in part of a question.

You have already studied IAS 10 *Events after the reporting period* extensively. Note, that the parts of IAS 10 that cover contingencies have been superseded by IAS 37, covered in the next section.

Knowledge brought forward from earlier studies

IAS 10: Events after the reporting period

Definition

Events after the reporting period are those events, both favourable and unfavourable, that occur between the year end and the date on which the financial statements are authorised for issue. Two types of events can be identified (IAS 10: para. 3):

- Those that provide further evidence of conditions that existed at the year end, and
- Those that are indicative of conditions that arose subsequent to the year end.

Accounting treatment

- **Adjust** assets and liabilities where events after the end of the reporting period provide further evidence of conditions existing at the end of the reporting period (IAS 10: para. 8).
- **Do not adjust**, but instead disclose, important events after the end of the reporting period that do not affect condition of assets/liabilities at the year-end date (IAS 10: para. 10).
- **Dividends** for period proposed/declared after the end of the reporting period but before FS are approved should not be recognised as a liability at the end of the reporting period. Dividends do not need the criteria of a present obligation in IAS 37 (see below). They should be disclosed as required by IAS 1 (IAS 10: para. 12).

Disclosure (IAS 10: para. 21)

- Nature of event
- Estimate of financial effect (or statement that estimate cannot be made)

Window dressing is the arranging of transactions, the substance of which is primarily to alter the appearance of the SOFP: it is **not** falsification of accounts. IAS 10 does allow window dressing but **disclosure** should be made of such transactions.

2 IAS 37 *Provisions, contingent liabilities and contingent assets* 12/07, 6/11, 6/12, 12/12, 6/13, 6/14

As we have seen with regard to events after the reporting period events, financial statements must include **all the information necessary for an understanding of the company's financial position**. Provisions, contingent liabilities and contingent assets are 'uncertainties' that must be accounted for consistently if we are to achieve this understanding.

2.1 Objective

IAS 37 *Provisions, contingent liabilities and contingent assets* aims to ensure that appropriate **recognition criteria** and **measurement bases** are applied to provisions, contingent liabilities and contingent assets and that **sufficient information** is disclosed in the **notes** to the financial statements to enable users to understand their nature, timing and amount (IAS 37: obj).

2.2 Provisions

FAST FORWARD

Under IAS 37, a **provision** should be recognised:

- When an entity has a **present obligation**, legal or constructive
- It is probable that a **transfer of economic benefits** will be required to settle it
- A reliable estimate can be made of its amount

You will be familiar with provisions for depreciation and doubtful debts from your earlier studies. The sorts of provisions addressed by IAS 37 are, however, rather different.

Before IAS 37, there was no accounting standard dealing with provisions. Companies wanting to show their results in the most favourable light used to make large 'one off' provisions in years where a high level of underlying profits was generated. These provisions, often known as 'big bath' provisions, were then available to shield expenditure in future years when perhaps the underlying profits were not as good.

In other words, provisions were used for profit smoothing. Profit smoothing is misleading.

Important

The key aim of IAS 37 is to ensure that provisions are made only where there are valid grounds for them.

IAS 37 views a provision as a liability.

Key terms

A **provision** is a **liability** of uncertain timing or amount.

A **liability** is an obligation of an entity to transfer economic benefits as a result of past transactions or events. *(IAS 37: para. 10)*

The IAS distinguishes provisions from other liabilities such as trade payables and accruals. This is on the basis that for a provision there is **uncertainty** about the timing or amount of the future expenditure. While uncertainty is clearly present in the case of certain accruals the uncertainty is generally much less than for provisions.

2.3 Recognition

IAS 37 states that a provision should be **recognised** as a liability in the financial statements when (IAS 37: para. 14):

- An entity has a **present obligation** (legal or constructive) as a result of a past event
- It is probable that a **transfer of economic benefits** will be required to settle the obligation
- A **reliable estimate** can be made of the obligation

2.4 Meaning of obligation

It is fairly clear what a legal obligation is. However, you may not know what a **constructive obligation** is.

Key term

IAS 37 para. 10 defines a **constructive obligation** as:

'An obligation that derives from an entity's actions where:

- by an established pattern of past practice, published policies or a sufficiently specific current statement the entity has indicated to other parties that it will accept certain responsibilities, and
- as a result, the entity has created a valid expectation on the part of those other parties that it will discharge those responsibilities.'

Question **Recognise a provision**

In which of the following circumstances might a provision be recognised?

(a) On 13 December 20X9 the board of an entity decided to close down a division. The accounting date of the company is 31 December. Before 31 December 20X9 the decision was not communicated to any of those affected and no other steps were taken to implement the decision.

(b) The board agreed a detailed closure plan on 20 December 20X9 and details were given to customers and employees.

(c) A company is obliged to incur clean up costs for environmental damage (that has already been caused).

(d) A company intends to carry out future expenditure to operate in a particular way in the future.

Answer

(a) No provision would be recognised as the decision has not been communicated.

(b) A provision would be made in the 20X9 financial statements.

(c) A provision for such costs is appropriate.

(d) No present obligation exists and under IAS 37 no provision would be appropriate. This is because the entity could avoid the future expenditure by its future actions, maybe by changing its method of operation.

2.4.1 Probable transfer of economic benefits

For the purpose of the IAS, a transfer of economic benefits is regarded as '**probable**' if the event is **more likely than not** to occur (IAS 37: para. 23 to 24). This appears to indicate a probability of more than 50%. However, the standard makes it clear that where there is a number of similar obligations the probability should be based on considering the population as a whole, rather than one single item.

2.5 Example: Transfer of economic benefits

If a company has entered into a warranty obligation then the probability of an outflow of resources embodying economic benefits (transfer of economic benefits) may well be extremely small in respect of one specific item. However, when considering the population as a whole the probability of some transfer of economic benefits is quite likely to be much higher. If there is a **greater than 50% probability** of some transfer of economic benefits then a **provision** should be made for the **expected amount**.

2.5.1 Measurement of provisions

Important

> The amount recognised as a provision should be the best estimate of the expenditure required to settle the present obligation at the year end (IAS 37: para. 36).

The estimates will be determined by the **judgement** of the entity's management supplemented by the experience of similar transactions.

Allowance is made for **uncertainty**. Where the provision being measured involves a large population of items, the obligation is estimated by weighting all possible outcomes by their discounted probabilities, ie **expected value** (IAS 37: para. 39 to 40).

Question — **Warranty**

Parker Co sells goods with a warranty under which customers are covered for the cost of repairs of any manufacturing defect that becomes apparent within the first six months of purchase. The company's past experience and future expectations indicate the following pattern of likely repairs.

% of goods sold	*Defects*	*Cost of repairs* $m
75	None	–
20	Minor	1.0
5	Major	4.0

What is the expected cost of repairs?

Answer

The cost is found using 'expected values' (75% × $nil) + (20% × $1.0m) + (5% × $4.0m) = $400,000.

Where the effect of the **time value of money** is material, the amount of a provision should be the **present value** of the expenditure required to settle the obligation. An appropriate **discount** rate should be used (IAS 37: para. 45).

The discount rate should be a **pre-tax rate** that reflects current market assessments of the time value of money. **The discount rate(s) should not reflect risks for which future cash flow estimates have been adjusted.**

2.5.2 Future events

Future events which are reasonably expected to occur (eg new legislation, changes in technology) may affect the amount required to settle the entity's obligation and should be taken into account (IAS 37: para. 48).

2.5.3 Expected disposal of assets

Gains from the expected disposal of assets should not be taken into account in measuring a provision (IAS 37: para. 51).

2.5.4 Reimbursements

Some or all of the expenditure needed to settle a provision may be expected to be recovered from a third party. If so, the **reimbursement should be recognised only when it is virtually certain that reimbursement will be received if the entity settles the obligation** (IAS 37: para. 53).

- The reimbursement should be treated as a separate asset, and the amount recognised should not be greater than the provision itself.
- The provision and the amount recognised for reimbursement may be netted off in profit or loss for the year.

2.5.5 Changes in provisions

Provisions should be renewed at each year end and adjusted to reflect the current best estimate. If it is no longer probable that a transfer of economic benefits will be required to settle the obligation, the provision should be reversed (IAS 37: para. 59).

2.5.6 Use of provisions

A provision should be used only for expenditures for which the provision was originally recognised. Setting expenditures against a provision that was originally recognised for another purpose would conceal the impact of two different events (IAS 37: para. 61).

2.5.7 Future operating losses

Provisions should not be recognised for future operating losses. They do not meet the definition of a liability and the general recognition criteria set out in the standard (IAS 37: para. 63).

2.5.8 Onerous contracts

If an entity has a contract that is onerous, the present obligation under the contract **should be recognised and measured** as a provision (IAS 37: para. 66). An example might be vacant leasehold property.

Key term

An **onerous contract** is a contract entered into with another party under which the unavoidable costs of fulfilling the terms of the contract exceed any revenues expected to be received from the goods or services supplied or purchased directly or indirectly under the contract and where the entity would have to compensate the other party if it did not fulfil the terms of the contract (IAS 37: para. 10).

2.6 Examples of possible provisions

It is easier to see what IAS 37 is driving at if you look at examples of those items which are possible provisions under this standard. Some of these we have already touched on.

(a) **Warranties**. These are argued to be genuine provisions as on past experience it is probable, ie more likely than not, that some claims will emerge. The provision must be estimated, however, on the basis of the class as a whole and not on individual claims. There is a clear legal obligation in this case.

(b) **Major repairs**. In the past it has been quite popular for companies to provide for expenditure on a major overhaul to be accrued gradually over the intervening years between overhauls. Under IAS 37 this will no longer be possible as IAS 37 would argue that this is a mere intention to carry out repairs, not an obligation. The entity can always sell the asset in the meantime. The only solution is to treat major assets such as aircraft, ships, furnaces and so on as a series of smaller assets where each part is depreciated over shorter lives. Thus, any major overhaul may be argued to be replacement and therefore capital rather than revenue expenditure.

(c) **Self insurance**. A number of companies have created a provision for self insurance based on the expected cost of making good fire damage and so on instead of paying premiums to an insurance company. Under IAS 37 this provision would no longer be justifiable as the entity has no obligation until a fire or accident occurs. No obligation exists until that time.

(d) **Environmental contamination**. If the company has an environment policy such that other parties would expect the company to clean up any contamination or if the company has broken current environmental legislation then a provision for environmental damage must be made.

(e) **Decommissioning or abandonment costs**. When an oil company initially purchases an oilfield it is put under a legal obligation to decommission the site at the end of its life. Prior to IAS 37 most oil companies up the provision gradually over the field so that no one year would be unduly burdened with the cost.

IAS 37, however, insists that a legal obligation exists on the initial expenditure on the field and therefore a liability exists immediately. This would appear to result in a large charge to profit or loss in the first year of operation of the field. However, the IAS takes the view that the cost of purchasing the field in the first place is not only the cost of the field itself but also the costs of putting it right again. Thus all the costs of abandonment may be capitalised.

(f) **Restructuring**. This is considered in detail below.

2.6.1 Provisions for restructuring

One of the main purposes of IAS 37 was to target abuses of provisions for restructuring. Accordingly, IAS 37 lays down **strict criteria** to determine when such a provision can be made.

Key term

IAS 37 defines a **restructuring** as:

A programme that is planned and is controlled by management and materially changes either:

- The scope of a business undertaken by an entity, or
- The manner in which that business is conducted.

(IAS 37: para.10)

The IAS gives the following **examples** of events that may fall under the definition of restructuring (IAS 37: para. 70).

- The **sale or termination** of a line of business
- The **closure of business locations** in a country or region or the **relocation** of business activities from one country region to another
- **Changes in management structure**, for example, the elimination of a layer of management
- **Fundamental reorganisations** that have a material effect on the **nature and focus** of the entity's operations

The question is whether or not an entity has an obligation – legal or constructive – at the year end.

- An entity must have a **detailed formal plan** for the restructuring.
- It must have **raised a valid expectation** in those affected that it will carry out the restructuring by starting to implement that plan or announcing its main features to those affected by it.

Important

A mere management decision is not normally sufficient. Management decisions may sometimes trigger off recognition, but only if earlier events such as negotiations with employee representatives and other interested parties have been concluded subject only to management approval.

Where the restructuring involves the **sale of an operation** then IAS 37 states that no obligation arises until the entity has entered into a **binding sale agreement**. This is because until this has occurred the entity will be able to change its mind and withdraw from the sale even if its intentions have been announced publicly.

2.6.2 Costs to be included within a restructuring provision

The IAS states that a restructuring provision should include only the **direct expenditures** arising from the restructuring (IAS 37: para. 80).

- **Necessarily entailed** by the restructuring
- Not associated with the **ongoing activities** of the entity

The following costs should specifically **not** be included within a restructuring provision (IAS 37: para. 81).

- **Retraining** or relocating continuing staff

- **Marketing**
- **Investment in new systems** and distribution networks

2.6.3 Disclosure

Disclosures for provisions fall into two parts (IAS 37: paras. 84 to 86):

- Disclosure of details of the **change in carrying value** of a provision from the beginning to the end of the year
- Disclosure of the **background** to the making of the provision and the uncertainties affecting its outcome

2.7 Contingent liabilities

FAST FORWARD

An entity **should not recognise a contingent asset or liability**, but they **should be disclosed.**

Now you understand provisions it will be easier to understand contingent assets and liabilities.

Key term

IAS 37 defines a **contingent liability** as:

- A possible obligation that arises from past events and whose existence will be confirmed only by the occurrence or non-occurrence of one or more uncertain future events not wholly within the entity's control, or
- A present obligation that arises from past events but is not recognised because:
  - It is not probable that a transfer of economic benefits will be required to settle the obligation, or
  - The amount of the obligation cannot be measured with sufficient reliability.

(IAS 37: para. 10)

As a rule of thumb, probable means more than 50% likely. **If an obligation is probable, it is not a contingent liability** – instead, a **provision is needed**.

2.7.1 Treatment of contingent liabilities

Contingent liabilities **should not be recognised in financial statements** but they **should be disclosed** (IAS 37: paras. 27 and 28). The required disclosures are (IAS 37: para. 86):

- A brief description of the nature of the contingent liability
- An estimate of its financial effect
- An indication of the uncertainties that exist
- The possibility of any reimbursement

2.8 Contingent assets

Key term

IAS 37 para. 10 defines a **contingent asset** as:

- A possible asset that arises from past events and whose existence will be confirmed by the occurrence of one or more uncertain future events not wholly within the entity's control.

A contingent asset must not be recognised. Only when the realisation of the related economic benefits is **virtually certain** should recognition take place. At that point, **the asset is no longer a contingent asset**! (IAS 37: paras. 31, 33)

2.8.1 Disclosure: contingent liabilities

A **brief description** must be provided of all material contingent liabilities unless they are likely to be remote. In addition, provide (IAS 37: para. 64):

- An estimate of their **financial effect**
- Details of **any uncertainties**

2.8.2 Disclosure: contingent assets

Contingent assets must only be disclosed in the notes if they are **probable**. In that case a brief description of the contingent asset should be provided along with an estimate of its likely financial effect (IAS 37: para. 34).

2.8.3 'Let out'

IAS 37 permits reporting entities to avoid disclosure requirements relating to provisions, contingent liabilities and contingent assets if they would be expected to **seriously prejudice** the position of the entity in dispute with other parties (IAS 37: para. 92). However, this should only be employed in **extremely rare** cases. Details of the general nature of the provision/contingencies must still be provided, together with an explanation of why it has not been disclosed.

You must practise the questions below to get the hang of IAS 37. But first, study the flow chart, taken from IAS 37, which is a good summary of its requirements.

Exam focus point

If you learn this decision tree (IAS 32 IG: B) you should be able to deal with most tasks you are likely to meet on exam.

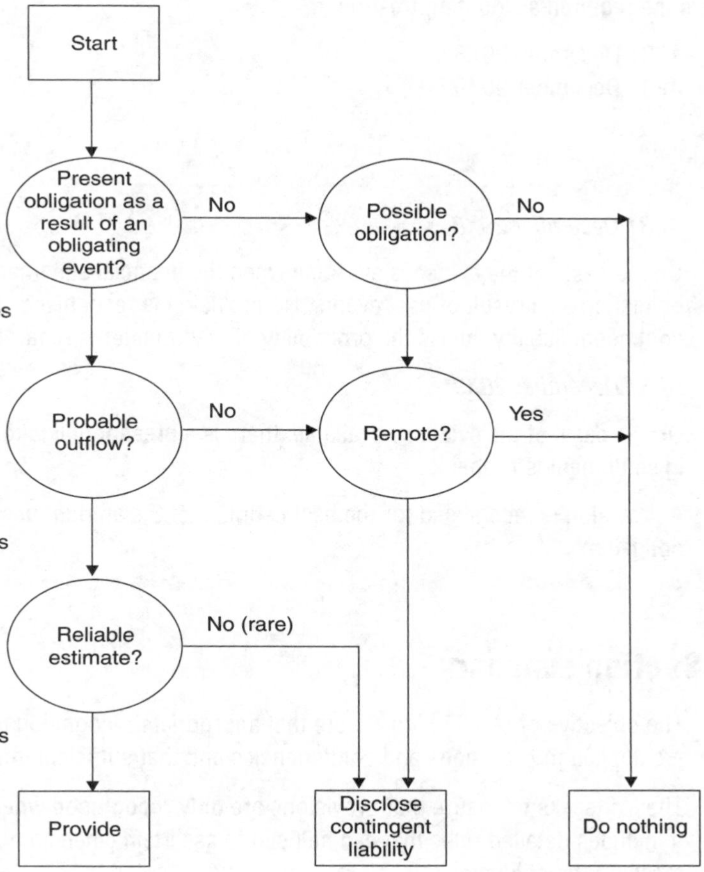

Question

Recognise or not 1?

Warren Co gives warranties at the time of sale to purchasers of its products. Under the terms of the warranty the manufacturer undertakes to make good, by repair or replacement, manufacturing defects that become apparent within a period of three years from the year end. Should a provision be recognised?

Answer

Warren Co **cannot avoid** the cost of repairing or replacing all items of product that manifest manufacturing defects in respect of which warranties are given before the end of the reporting period, and a provision for the cost of this should therefore be made.

Warren Co is obliged to repair or replace items that fail within the entire warranty period. Therefore, in respect of **this year's sales**, the obligation provided for at the year end should be the cost of making good items for which defects have been notified but not yet processed, **plus** an estimate of costs in respect of the other items sold for which there is sufficient evidence that manufacturing defects **will** manifest themselves during their remaining periods of warranty cover.

Question

Recognise or not 2?

After a wedding in 20X8 ten people died, possibly as a result of food poisoning from products sold by Callow Co. Legal proceedings are started seeking damages from Callow but it disputes liability. Up to the date of approval of the financial statements for the year to 31 December 20X8, Callow's lawyers advise that it is probable that it will not be found liable. However, when Callow prepares the financial statements for the year to 31 December 20X9 its lawyers advise that, owing to developments in the case, it is probable that it will be found liable.

What is the required accounting treatment:

(a) At 31 December 20X8?
(b) At 31 December 20X9?

Answer

(a) *At 31 December 20X8*

On the basis of the evidence available when the financial statements were approved, there is no obligation as a result of past events. No provision is recognised. The matter is disclosed as a contingent liability unless the probability of any transfer is regarded as remote.

(b) *At 31 December 20X9*

On the basis of the evidence available, there is a present obligation. A transfer of economic benefits in settlement is probable.

A provision is recognised for the best estimate of the amount needed to settle the present obligation.

2.9 Section summary

- The objective of IAS 37 is to ensure that appropriate recognition criteria and measurement bases are applied to provisions and contingencies and that sufficient information is disclosed.
- The IAS seeks to ensure that provisions are **only recognised** when a **measurable obligation** exists. It includes detailed rules that can be used to ascertain when an obligation exists and how to measure the obligation.
- The standard attempts to **eliminate** the '**profit smoothing**' which has gone on before it was issued.

Chapter Roundup

- **IAS 10** should be familiar from your earlier studies, but it still could come up in part of a question.
- Under IAS 37, a **provision** should be recognised:
  - When an entity has a **present obligation**, legal or constructive
  - It is probable that a **transfer of economic benefits** will be required to settle it
  - A reliable estimate can be made of its amount
- An entity **should not recognise a contingent asset or liability**, but they **should be disclosed**.

Quick Quiz

1 According to IAS 37 when, and only when, can a provision be recognised?

2 A provision can be made for future operating losses. *True or false*?

3 When should a contingent liability be recognised?

Answers to Quick Quiz

1
- Present obligation
- Probable transfer of economic benefits
- Reliable estimate of value

2 False

3 Never. However, they should be disclosed in a note to the accounts.

Now try the question below from the Practice Question Bank

Number	Level	Marks	Time
Q8	Examination	25	49 mins

6 Income taxes

Topic list	Syllabus reference
1 Current tax revised	C7
2 Deferred tax	C7
3 Taxable temporary differences	C7
4 Deductible temporary differences	C7
5 Measurement and recognition of deferred tax	C7
6 Deferred taxation and business combinations	C7

Introduction

In almost all countries entities are taxed on the basis of their trading income. In some countries this may be called corporation or corporate tax, but we will follow the terminology of IAS 12 *Income taxes* and call it **income tax**.

There are two main systems for taxing corporate income: the **classical system** and the **imputation system**: go back to your earlier study material if necessary. For this chapter we will assume a classical system. Of course, each country will be different in its tax legislation and its method of accounting for taxation may reflect this.

There are two aspects of income tax which must be accounted for: **current tax** and **deferred tax**. Current tax is revised briefly in Section 1. The rest of this chapter is concerned with deferred tax, which students invariably find difficult.

Section 6 introduces a new aspect of deferred tax, relating to **business combinations**. This represents one of the most complex areas of deferred tax.

Note. Throughout this chapter we will assume a current corporate income tax rate of 30% and a current personal income tax rate of 20%, unless otherwise stated.

Study guide

		Intellectual level
C7	**Income taxes**	
(a)	Apply and discuss the recognition and measurement of deferred tax liabilities and deferred tax assets	3
(b)	Determine the recognition of tax expenses or income and its inclusion in the financial statements	3

Exam guide

Be prepared for a whole question on deferred tax, as happened on the Pilot Paper, when you were asked to discuss the conceptual basis for its accounting treatment and to calculate the deferred tax provision after making adjustments.

1 Current tax revised

FAST FORWARD

Taxation consists of **two components**:

- Current tax
- Deferred tax

Current tax is ordinarily straightforward. Complexities arise, however, when we consider the future tax consequences of what is going on in the accounts now. This is an aspect of tax called deferred tax, which we will look at in the next section. IAS 12 *Income taxes* covers both current and deferred tax. The parts relating to current tax are fairly brief, because this is the simple and uncontroversial area of tax.

1.1 Definitions

These are some of the definitions given in IAS 12. We will look at the rest later.

Key terms

Accounting profit. Net profit or loss for a period before deducting tax expense.

Taxable profit (tax loss). The profit (loss) for a period, determined in accordance with the rules established by the taxation authorities, upon which income taxes are payable (recoverable).

Tax expense (tax income). The aggregate amount included in the determination of net profit or loss for the period in respect of current tax and deferred tax.

Current tax. The amount of income taxes payable (recoverable) in respect of the taxable profit (tax loss) for a period. *(IAS 12: para. 5)*

Remember the difference between current and deferred tax.

(a) **Current tax** is the amount **actually payable** to the tax authorities in relation to the trading activities of the entity during the period.

(b) **Deferred tax** is an **accounting measure**, used to match the tax effects of transactions with their accounting impact and thereby produce less distorted results.

1.2 Recognition of current tax liabilities and assets

FAST FORWARD

Current tax is the amount payable to the tax authorities in relation to the trading activities during the period. It is generally straightforward.

IAS 12 requires any **unpaid tax** in respect of the current or prior periods to be recognised as a **liability** (IAS 12: para. 12)

Conversely, any **excess tax** paid in respect of current or prior periods over what is due should be recognised as an asset (IAS 12: para. 13).

Question

Current tax

In 20X8 Darton Co had taxable profits of $120,000. In the previous year (20X7) income tax on 20X7 profits had been estimated as $30,000. The tax rate is 33%.

Required

Calculate tax payable and the charge for 20X8 if the tax due on 20X7 profits was subsequently agreed with the tax authorities as:

(a) $35,000
(b) $25,000

Any under- or over-payments are not settled until the following year's tax payment is due.

Answer

(a)

	$
Tax due on 20X8 profits ($120,000 × 33%)	40,000
Underpayment for 20X7	5,000
Tax charge and liability	45,000

(b)

	$
Tax due on 20X8 profits (as above)	40,000
Overpayment for 20X7	(5,000)
Tax charge and liability	35,000

Alternatively, the rebate due could be shown separately as income in the statement of profit or loss and other comprehensive income and as an asset in the statement of financial position. An offset approach like this is, however, most likely.

Taking this a stage further, IAS 12 also requires recognition as an asset of the benefit relating to any tax loss that can be **carried back** to recover current tax of a previous period. This is acceptable because it is probable that the benefit will flow to the entity **and** it can be reliably measured (IAS 12: para. 13).

1.3 Example: Tax losses carried back

In 20X7 Eramu Co paid $50,000 in tax on its profits. In 20X8 the company made tax losses of $24,000. The local tax authority rules allow losses to be carried back to offset against current tax of prior years.

Required

Show the tax charge and tax liability for 20X8.

Solution

Tax repayment due on tax losses = 30% × $24,000 = $7,200.

The double entry will be:

DEBIT	Tax receivable (statement of financial position)	$7,200	
CREDIT	Tax repayment (statement of profit or loss and other comprehensive income)		$7,200

The tax receivable will be shown as an asset until the repayment is received from the tax authorities.

1.4 Measurement

Measurement of current tax liabilities (assets) for the current and prior periods is very simple. They are measured at the **amount expected to be paid to (recovered from) the tax authorities**. The tax rates (and tax laws) used should be those enacted (or substantively enacted) by the year end.

1.5 Recognition of current tax

Normally, current tax is recognised as income or expense and included in the net profit or loss for the period, except in two cases (IAS 12: paras. 58, 61A).

(a) Tax arising from a **business combination** which is an acquisition is treated differently (see Section 6 of this chapter).

(b) Tax arising from a transaction or event recognised in **other comprehensive income**.

(c) Tax arising from a transaction or event which is recognised **directly in equity** (in the same or a different period).

The rule in (b) is logical. If a transaction or event is charged or credited directly to equity, rather than to profit or loss, then the related tax should be also. An example of such a situation is where, under IAS 8, an adjustment is made to the **opening balance of retained earnings** due to either a change in accounting policy that is applied retrospectively, or to the correction of a fundamental error.

1.6 Presentation

In the statement of financial position, **tax assets and liabilities** should be shown separately from other assets and liabilities (IAS 12: para. 77).

Current tax assets and liabilities can be **offset**, but this should happen only when certain conditions apply (IAS 12: para. 71).

(a) The entity has a **legally enforceable right** to set off the recognised amounts.

(b) The entity intends to settle the amounts on a **net basis**, or to realise the asset and settle the liability at the same time.

The **tax expense (income)** related to the profit or loss for the year should be shown in the profit or loss section of the statement of profit or loss and other comprehensive income.

2 Deferred tax 12/07, 6/10, 6/12, 12/12, 6/14, 12/15

FAST FORWARD

Deferred tax is an accounting measure, used to match the tax effects of transactions with their accounting impact. It is quite complex.

Exam focus point

Students invariably find deferred tax very confusing. It is an inherently difficult topic and as such is likely to appear frequently in its most complicated forms in Paper P2. You *must* understand the contents of the rest of this chapter.

2.1 What is deferred tax?

When a company recognises an asset or liability, it expects to **recover or settle the carrying amount** of that asset or liability. In other words, it expects to sell or use up assets, and to pay off liabilities. What happens if that recovery or settlement is likely to make future tax payments larger (or smaller) than they would otherwise have been if the recovery or settlement had no tax consequences? In these circumstances, IAS 12 requires companies to recognise a **deferred tax liability** (or **deferred tax asset**) (IAS 12: paras. 12, 13).

2.2 Definitions

Here are the definitions relating to deferred tax given in IAS 12: para. 5.

Key terms

Deferred tax liabilities are the amounts of income taxes payable in future periods in respect of taxable temporary differences.

Deferred tax assets are the amounts of income taxes recoverable in future periods in respect of:

- Deductible temporary differences
- The carryforward of unused tax losses
- The carryforward of unused tax credits

Temporary differences are differences between the carrying amount of an asset or liability in the statement of financial position and its tax base. Temporary differences may be either:

- **Taxable temporary differences**, which are temporary differences that will result in taxable amounts in determining taxable profit (tax loss) of future periods when the carrying amount of the asset or liability is recovered or settled.
- **Deductible temporary differences**, which are temporary differences that will result in amounts that are deductible in determining taxable profit (tax loss) of future periods when the carrying amount of the asset or liability is recovered or settled.

The **tax base** of an asset or liability is the amount attributed to that asset or liability for tax purposes.

(IAS 12: para. 5)

2.3 Tax base

We can expand on the definition given above by stating that the **tax base of an asset** is the amount that will be deductible for tax purposes against any taxable economic benefits that will flow to the entity when it recovers the carrying value of the asset. Where those economic benefits are not taxable, the tax base of the asset is the same as its carrying amount.

Question — Tax base 1

State the tax base of each of the following assets:

(a) A machine cost $10,000. For tax purposes, depreciation of $3,000 has already been deducted in the current and prior periods and the remaining cost will be deductible in future periods, either as depreciation or through a deduction on disposal. Revenue generated by using the machine is taxable, any gain on disposal of the machine will be taxable and any loss on disposal will be deductible for tax purposes.

(b) Interest receivable has a carrying amount of $1,000. The related interest revenue will be taxed on a cash basis.

(c) Trade receivables have a carrying amount of $10,000. The related revenue has already been included in taxable profit (tax loss).

(d) A loan receivable has a carrying amount of $1m. The repayment of the loan will have no tax consequences.

(e) Dividends receivable from a subsidiary have a carrying amount of $5,000. The dividends are not taxable.

Answer

(a) The tax base of the machine is $7,000.
(b) The tax base of the interest receivable is nil.
(c) The tax base of the trade receivables is $10,000.
(d) The tax base of the loan is $1m.
(e) The tax base of the dividend is $5,000.

In the case of (e), in substance the entire carrying amount of the asset is deductible against the economic benefits. There is no taxable temporary difference. An alternative analysis is that the accrued dividends receivable have a tax base of nil and a tax rate of nil is applied to the resulting taxable temporary difference ($5,000). Under both analyses, there is no deferred tax liability.

In the case of a **liability**, the tax base will be its carrying amount, less any amount that will be deducted for tax purposes in relation to the liability in future periods. For revenue received in advance, the tax base of the resulting liability is its carrying amount, less any amount of the revenue that will **not** be taxable in future periods.

Question

Tax base 2

State the tax base of each of the following liabilities.

(a) Current liabilities include accrued expenses with a carrying amount of $1,000. The related expense will be deducted for tax purposes on a cash basis.

(b) Current liabilities include interest revenue received in advance, with a carrying amount of $10,000. The related interest revenue was taxed on a cash basis.

(c) Current assets include prepaid expenses with a carrying amount of $2,000. The related expense has already been deducted for tax purposes.

(d) Current liabilities include accrued fines and penalties with a carrying amount of $100. Fines and penalties are not deductible for tax purposes.

(e) A loan payable has a carrying amount of $1m. The repayment of the loan will have no tax consequences.

Answer

(a) The tax base of the accrued expenses is nil.
(b) The tax base of the interest received in advance is nil.
(c) The tax base of the accrued expenses is $2,000.
(d) The tax base of the accrued fines and penalties is $100.
(e) The tax base of the loan is $1m.

IAS 12 gives the following examples of circumstances in which the carrying amount of an asset or liability will be **equal to its tax base** (IAS 12: IE, C).

- **Pre-paid expenses** have already been deducted in determining an entity's current tax liability for the current or earlier periods.
- A **loan payable** is measured at the amount originally received and this amount is the same as the amount repayable on final maturity of the loan.
- **Accrued expenses** will never be deductible for tax purposes.
- **Accrued income** will never be taxable.

2.4 Temporary differences

You may have found the definition of temporary differences somewhat confusing. Remember that accounting profits form the basis for computing **taxable profits**, on which the tax liability for the year is calculated. However, accounting profits and taxable profits are different. There are two reasons for the differences.

(a) **Permanent differences**. These occur when certain items of revenue or expense are excluded from the computation of taxable profits (for example, entertainment expenses may not be allowable for tax purposes).

(b) **Temporary differences**. These occur when items of revenue or expense are included in both accounting profits and taxable profits, but not for the same accounting period. For example, an expense which is allowable as a deduction in arriving at taxable profits for 20X7 might not be included in the financial accounts until 20X8 or later. In the long run, the total taxable profits and total accounting profits will be the same (except for permanent differences) so that timing differences originate in one period and are capable of reversal in one or more subsequent periods. Deferred tax is the tax attributable to **temporary differences**.

The distinction made in the definition between **taxable temporary differences** and **deductible temporary differences** can be made clearer by looking at the explanations and examples given in the standard and its appendices.

2.5 Section summary

- Deferred tax is an **accounting device**. It does *not* represent tax payable to the tax authorities.
- The **tax base** of an asset or liability is the value of that asset or liability for tax purposes.
- You should understand the difference between **permanent and temporary differences**.
- Deferred tax is the tax attributable to **temporary differences**.

3 Taxable temporary differences

FAST FORWARD

Deferred tax assets and liabilities arise from taxable and deductible temporary differences.

Exam focus point

The rule to remember here is that:

'All taxable temporary differences give rise to a deferred tax liability.'

The following are examples of circumstances that give rise to taxable temporary differences.

3.1 Transactions that affect the statement of profit or loss and other comprehensive income

- **Interest revenue** received in arrears and included in accounting profit on the basis of time apportionment. It is included in taxable profit, however, on a cash basis.
- **Sale of goods revenue** is included in accounting profit when the goods are delivered, but only included in taxable profit when cash is received.
- **Depreciation** of an asset may be accelerated for tax purposes. When new assets are purchased, allowances may be available against taxable profits which exceed the amount of depreciation chargeable on the assets in the financial accounts for the year of purchase.
- **Development costs** which have been capitalised will be amortised in profit or loss, but they were deducted in full from taxable profit in the period in which they were incurred.
- **Prepaid expenses** have already been deducted on a cash basis in determining the taxable profit of the current or previous periods.

(IAS 12: IE, paras. 1 to 5)

3.2 Transactions that affect the statement of financial position

- **Depreciation of an asset** is not deductible for tax purposes. No deduction will be available for tax purposes when the asset is sold/scrapped.

- A borrower records a **loan** at proceeds received (amount due at maturity) less transaction costs. The carrying amount of the loan is subsequently increased by amortisation of the transaction costs against accounting profit. The transaction costs were, however, deducted for tax purposes in the period when the loan was first recognised.
- A **loan** payable is measured on initial recognition at net proceeds (net of transaction costs). The transaction costs are amortised to accounting profit over the life of the loan. Those transaction costs are not deductible in determining the taxable profit of future, current or prior periods.
- The liability component of a **compound financial instrument** (eg a convertible bond) is measured at a discount to the amount repayable on maturity, after assigning a portion of the cash proceeds to the equity component (see IAS 32). The discount is not deductible in determining taxable profit.

(IAS 12: IE, paras. 6 to *)

3.3 Fair value adjustments and revaluations

- **Current investments** or financial instruments are carried at fair value. This exceeds cost, but no equivalent adjustment is made for tax purposes.
- Property, plant and equipment is **revalued** by an entity (under IAS 16), but no equivalent adjustment is made for tax purposes. This also applies to long-term investments.

(IAS 12: para. 20)

The standard also looks at the deferred tax implications of business combinations and consolidations. We will look at these in Section 6.

Remember the rule we gave you above, that all taxable temporary differences give rise to a deferred tax liability? There are **two circumstances** given in the standards where this does **not** apply.

(a) The deferred tax liability arises from the initial recognition of goodwill.

(b) The deferred tax liability arises from the initial recognition of an asset or liability in a transaction which:

  (i) Is **not** a business combination (see Section 6), **and**
  (ii) At the time of the transaction affects neither accounting profit nor taxable profit.

Try to **understand the reasoning** behind the recognition of deferred tax liabilities on taxable temporary differences.

(a) When an **asset is recognised**, it is expected that its carrying amount will be recovered in the form of economic benefits that flow to the entity in future periods.

(b) If the carrying amount of the asset is **greater than** its tax base, then taxable economic benefits will also be greater than the amount that will be allowed as a deduction for tax purposes.

(c) The difference is therefore a **taxable temporary difference** and the obligation to pay the resulting income taxes in future periods is a **deferred tax liability**.

(d) As the entity recovers the carrying amount of the asset, the taxable temporary difference will **reverse** and the entity will have taxable profit.

(e) It is then probable that economic benefits will flow from the entity in the form of **tax payments**, and so the recognition of all deferred tax liabilities (except those excluded above) is required by IAS 12.

3.3.1 Example: Taxable temporary differences

A company purchased an asset costing $1,500. At the end of 20X8 the carrying amount is $1,000. The cumulative depreciation for tax purposes is $900 and the current tax rate is 25%.

Required

Calculate the deferred tax liability for the asset.

Solution

First, what is the tax base of the asset? It is $1,500 – $900 = $600.

In order to recover the carrying value of $1,000, the entity must earn taxable income of $1,000, but it will only be able to deduct $600 as a taxable expense. The entity must therefore pay income tax of $400 × 25% = $100 when the carrying value of the asset is recovered.

The entity must therefore recognise a deferred tax liability of $400 × 25% = $100, recognising the difference between the carrying amount of $1,000 and the tax base of $600 as a taxable temporary difference.

3.4 Revalued assets

Under IAS 16 assets may be revalued. If this affects the taxable profit for the current period, the tax base of the asset changes and **no temporary difference** arises.

If, however (as in some countries), the revaluation does **not** affect current taxable profits, the tax base of the asset is not adjusted. Consequently, the taxable flow of economic benefits to the entity as the carrying value of the asset is recovered will differ from the amount that will be deductible for tax purposes. The difference between the carrying amount of a revalued asset and its tax base is a temporary difference and gives rise to a **deferred tax liability or asset**.

(IAS 12: para. 20)

3.5 Initial recognition of an asset or liability

A temporary difference can arise on initial recognition of an asset or liability, eg if part or all of the cost of an asset will not be deductible for tax purposes. The **nature of the transaction** which led to the initial recognition of the asset is important in determining the method of accounting for such temporary differences.

If the transaction affects **either** accounting profit or taxable profit, an entity will **recognise any deferred tax liability** or asset. The resulting deferred tax expense or income will be recognised in profit or loss.

Where a transaction affects **neither accounting profit nor taxable profit** it would be normal for an entity to recognise a deferred tax liability or asset and adjust the carrying amount of the asset or liability by the same amount (unless exempted by IAS 12 as under Paragraph 3.3 above). However, IAS 12 does **not** permit this recognition of a deferred tax asset or liability as it would make the financial statements less transparent. This will be the case both on initial recognition and subsequently, nor should any subsequent changes in the unrecognised deferred tax liability or asset as the asset is depreciated be made (IAS 20: para. 22).

3.6 Example: Initial recognition

As an example of the last paragraph, suppose Petros Co intends to use an asset which cost $10,000 in 20X7 through its useful life of five years. Its residual value will then be nil. The tax rate is 40%. Any capital gain on disposal would not be taxable (and any capital loss not deductible). Depreciation of the asset is not deductible for tax purposes.

Required

State the deferred tax consequences in each of years 20X7 and 20X8.

Solution

As at 20X7, as it recovers the carrying amount of the asset, Petros Co will earn taxable income of $10,000 and pay tax of $4,000. The resulting deferred tax liability of $4,000 would not be recognised because it results from the initial recognition of the asset.

As at 20X8, the carrying value of the asset is now $8,000. In earning taxable income of $8,000, the entity will pay tax of $3,200. Again, the resulting deferred tax liability of $3,200 is not recognised, because it results from the initial recognition of the asset.

The following question on accelerated depreciation should clarify some of the issues and introduce you to the calculations which may be necessary in the exam.

Question

Deferred tax

Jonquil Co buys equipment for $50,000 and depreciates it on a straight line basis over its expected useful life of five years. For tax purposes, the equipment is depreciated at 25% per annum on a straight line basis. Tax losses may be carried back against taxable profit of the previous five years. In year 20X0, the entity's taxable profit was $25,000. The tax rate is 40%.

Required

Assuming nil profits/losses after depreciation in years 20X1 to 20X5 show the current and deferred tax impact in years 20X1 to 20X5 of the acquisition of the equipment.

Answer

Jonquil Co will recover the carrying amount of the equipment by using it to manufacture goods for resale. Therefore, the entity's current tax computation is as follows.

			Year		
	20X1	*20X2*	*20X3*	*20X4*	*20X5*
	$	$	$	$	$
Taxable income*	10,000	10,000	10,000	10,000	10,000
Depreciation for tax purposes	12,500	12,500	12,500	12,500	0
Taxable profit (tax loss)	(2,500)	(2,500)	(2,500)	(2,500)	10,000
Current tax expense (income) at 40%	(1,000)	(1,000)	(1,000)	(1,000)	4,000

* ie nil profit plus ($50,000 ÷ 5) depreciation add-back.

The entity recognises a current tax asset at the end of years 20X1 to 20X4 because it recovers the benefit of the tax loss against the taxable profit of year 20X0.

The temporary differences associated with the equipment and the resulting deferred tax asset and liability and deferred tax expense and income are as follows.

			Year		
	20X1	*20X2*	*20X3*	*20X4*	*20X5*
	$	$	$	$	$
Carrying amount	40,000	30,000	20,000	10,000	0
Tax base	37,500	25,000	12,500	0	0
Taxable temporary difference	2,500	5,000	7,500	10,000	0
Opening deferred tax liability	0	1,000	2,000	3,000	4,000
Deferred tax expense (income): bal fig	1,000	1,000	1,000	1,000	(4,000)
Closing deferred tax liability @ 40%	1,000	2,000	3,000	4,000	0

The entity recognises the deferred tax liability in years 20X1 to 20X4 because the reversal of the taxable temporary difference will create taxable income in subsequent years. The entity's statement of profit or loss and other comprehensive income is as follows.

			Year		
	20X1	*20X2*	*20X3*	*20X4*	*20X5*
	$	$	$	$	$
Income	10,000	10,000	10,000	10,000	10,000
Depreciation	10,000	10,000	10,000	10,000	10,000
Profit before tax	0	0	0	0	0
Current tax expense (income)	(1,000)	(1,000)	(1,000)	(1,000)	4,000
Deferred tax expense (income)	1,000	1,000	1,000	1,000	(4,000)
Total tax expense (income)	0	0	0	0	0
Net profit for the year	0	0	0	0	0

4 Deductible temporary differences

Refer again to the definition given in Section 2 above.

Exam focus point

> The rule to remember here is that:
>
> 'All deductible temporary differences give rise to a deferred tax asset.'

There is a proviso, however. The deferred tax asset must also satisfy the **recognition criteria** given in IAS 12. This is that a deferred tax asset should be recognised for all deductible temporary differences to the extent that it is **probable that taxable profit will be available** against which it can be utilised. This is an application of prudence. Before we look at this issue in more detail, let us consider the examples of deductible temporary differences given in the standard.

4.1 Transactions that affect the statement of profit or loss and other comprehensive income

- **Retirement benefit costs** (pension costs) are deducted from accounting profit as service is provided by the employee. They are not deducted in determining taxable profit until the entity pays either retirement benefits or contributions to a fund. (This may also apply to similar expenses.)
- **Accumulated depreciation** of an asset in the financial statements is greater than the accumulated depreciation allowed for tax purposes up to the year end.
- The **cost of inventories** sold before the year end is deducted from accounting profit when goods/services are delivered, but is deducted from taxable profit when the cash is received. (**Note.** There is also a taxable temporary difference associated with the related trade receivable, as noted in Section 3 above.)
- The **NRV** of inventory, or the **recoverable amount** of an item of property, plant and equipment falls and the carrying value is therefore **reduced**, but that reduction is ignored for tax purposes until the asset is sold.
- **Research costs** (or organisation/other start-up costs) are recognised as an expense for accounting purposes but are not deductible against taxable profits until a later period.
- Income is **deferred** in the statement of financial position, but has already been included in taxable profit in current/prior periods.
- A **government grant** is included in the statement of financial position as deferred income, but it will not be taxable in future periods. (**Note.** A deferred tax asset may **not** be recognised here according to the standard.)

(IAS 12: IE, B, paras. 1 to 7)

4.2 Fair value adjustments and revaluations

Current investments or **financial instruments** may be carried at fair value which is less than cost, but no equivalent adjustment is made for tax purposes.

Other situations discussed by the standard relate to **business combinations** and consolidation (see Section 6).

4.3 Recognition of deductible temporary differences

We looked earlier at the important recognition criteria above. As with temporary taxable differences, there are also circumstances where the overall rule for recognition of deferred tax asset is **not** allowed. This applies where the deferred tax asset arises from **initial recognition** of an asset or liability in a transaction which is not a business combination, **and** at the time of the transaction, affects neither accounting nor taxable profit/tax loss.

Let us lay out the reasoning behind the recognition of deferred tax assets arising from deductible temporary differences.

(a) When a **liability is recognised**, it is assumed that its carrying amount will be settled in the form of outflows of economic benefits from the entity in future periods.

(b) When these resources flow from the entity, part or all may be deductible in determining taxable profits of a **period later** than that in which the liability is recognised.

(c) A **temporary tax difference** then exists between the carrying amount of the liability and its tax base.

(d) A **deferred tax asset** therefore arises, representing the income taxes that will be recoverable in future periods when that part of the liability is allowed as a deduction from taxable profit.

(e) Similarly, when the carrying amount of an asset is **less than its tax base**, the difference gives rise to a deferred tax asset in respect of the income taxes that will be recoverable in future periods.

(IAS 12: paras 27 to 30)

4.3.1 Example: Deductible temporary differences

Pargatha Co recognises a liability of $10,000 for accrued product warranty costs on 31 December 20X7. These product warranty costs will not be deductible for tax purposes until the entity pays claims. The tax rate is 25%.

Required

State the deferred tax implications of this situation.

Solution

What is the tax base of the liability? It is nil (carrying amount of $10,000 less the amount that will be deductible for tax purposes in respect of the liability in future periods).

When the liability is settled for its carrying amount, the entity's future taxable profit will be reduced by $10,000 and so its future tax payments by $10,000 × 25% = $2,500.

The difference of $10,000 between the carrying amount ($10,000) and the tax base (nil) is a deductible temporary difference. The entity should therefore recognise a deferred tax asset of $10,000 × 25% = $2,500 **provided that** it is probable that the entity will earn sufficient taxable profits in future periods to benefit from a reduction in tax payments.

4.4 Taxable profits in future periods

When can we be sure that sufficient taxable profit will be available against which a deductible temporary difference can be utilised? IAS 12 states that this will be assumed when sufficient **taxable temporary differences** exist which relate to the same taxation authority and the same taxable entity. These should be expected to reverse as follows:

(a) In the same period as the expected reversal of the deductible temporary difference.

(b) In periods into which a tax loss arising from the deferred tax asset can be carried back or forward.

Only in these circumstances is the deferred tax asset **recognised**, in the period in which the deductible temporary differences arise.

What happens when there are **insufficient taxable temporary differences** (relating to the same taxation authority and the same taxable entity)? It may still be possible to recognise the deferred tax asset, but only to the following extent.

(a) **Taxable profits** are sufficient in the same period as the reversal of the deductible temporary difference (or in the periods into which a tax loss arising from the deferred tax asset can be carried forward or backward), ignoring taxable amounts arising from deductible temporary differences arising in future periods.

(b) **Tax planning opportunities** exist that will allow the entity to create taxable profit in the appropriate periods.

With reference to (b), **tax planning opportunities** are actions that an entity would take in order to create or increase taxable income in a particular period before the expiry of a tax loss or tax credit carryforward. For example, in some countries it may be possible to increase or create taxable profit by electing to have interest income taxed on either a received or receivable basis, or deferring the claim for certain deductions from taxable profit.

In any case, where tax planning opportunities **advance taxable profit** from a later period to an earlier period, the utilisation of a tax loss or a tax credit carryforward will still depend on the existence of future taxable profit from sources other than future originating temporary differences.

If an entity has a **history of recent losses**, then this is evidence that future taxable profit may not be available (see below).

4.5 Initial recognition of an asset or liability

Consider Paragraph 3.5 on **initial recognition of an asset or liability**. The example given by the standard is of a non-taxable government grant related to an asset, deducted in arriving at the carrying amount of the asset. For tax purposes, however, it is **not** deducted from the asset's depreciable amount (ie its tax base). The carrying amount of the asset is less than its tax base and this gives rise to a deductible temporary difference. Paragraph 3.5 applies to this type of transaction.

4.6 Unused tax losses and unused tax credits

An entity may have unused tax losses or credits (ie which it can offset against taxable profits) at the end of a period. Should a deferred tax asset be recognised in relation to such amounts? IAS 12 states that a deferred tax asset may be recognised in such circumstances **to the extent that it is probable future taxable profit will be available against which the unused tax losses/credits can be utilised**.

The **criteria for recognition** of deferred tax assets here is the same as for recognising deferred tax assets arising from deductible differences. The existence of **unused tax losses** is strong evidence, however, that future taxable profit may not be available. So where an entity has a history of recent tax losses, a deferred tax asset arising from unused tax losses or credits should be recognised only to the extent that the entity has sufficient taxable temporary differences or there is other convincing evidence that sufficient taxable profit will be available against which the unused losses/credits can be utilised by the entity.

In these circumstances, the following criteria should be considered when assessing the probability that taxable profit will be available against which unused tax losses/credits can be utilised.

- Existence of **sufficient taxable temporary differences** (same tax authority/taxable entity) against which unused tax losses/credits can be utilised before they expire
- Probability that the entity will have **taxable profits** before the unused tax losses/credits expire
- Whether the unused tax losses result from **identifiable causes**, unlikely to recur
- Availability of **tax planning opportunities** (see above)

To the extent that it is **not probable** that taxable profit will be available, the deferred tax asset is **not** recognised.

(IAS 12: paras. 34 to 36)

4.7 Reassessment of unrecognised deferred tax assets

For **all** unrecognised deferred tax assets, at each year end an entity should **reassess the availability of future taxable profits** and whether part or all of any unrecognised deferred tax assets should now be recognised. This may be due to an improvement in trading conditions which is expected to continue (IAS 12: para. 37).

4.8 Section summary

- Deductible temporary differences give rise to a **deferred tax asset**.
- **Prudence** dictates that deferred tax assets can only be recognised when **sufficient future taxable profits** exist against which they can be utilised.

5 Measurement and recognition of deferred tax

FAST FORWARD

IAS 12 *Income taxes* covers both current and deferred tax. It has substantial presentation and disclosure requirements.

5.1 Basis of provision of deferred tax

IAS 12 adopts the full provision method of providing for deferred tax.

The **full provision method** has the **advantage** that it recognises that each timing difference at the year end has an effect on future tax payments. If a company claims an accelerated tax allowance on an item of plant, future tax assessments will be bigger than they would have been otherwise. Future transactions may well affect those assessments still further, but that is not relevant in assessing the position at the year end. The **disadvantage** of full provision is that, under certain types of tax system, it gives rise to large liabilities that may fall due only far in the future.

5.2 Example: Full provision

Suppose that Girdo Co begins trading on 1 January 20X7. In its first year it makes profits of $5m, the depreciation charge is $1m and the tax allowances on those assets is $1.5m. The rate of corporation tax is 30%.

Solution: Full provision

The tax liability is $1.35m, but the debit to profit or loss is increased by the deferred tax liability of 30% × $0.5m = $150,000. The total charge to profit or loss is therefore $1.5m which is an effective tax rate of 30% on accounting profits (ie 30% × $5.0m). No judgement is involved in using this method.

5.3 Deferral/liability methods: changes in tax rates

Where the corporate rate of income tax **fluctuates from one year to another**, a problem arises in respect of the amount of deferred tax to be credited (debited) to profit or loss in later years. The amount could be calculated using either of two methods.

(a) The **deferral method** assumes that the deferred tax account is an item of 'deferred tax relief' which is credited to profits in the years in which the timing differences are reversed. Therefore the tax effects of timing differences are calculated using tax rates current when the differences **arise**.

(b) The **liability method** assumes that the tax effects of timing differences should be regarded as amounts of tax ultimately due by or to the company. Therefore deferred tax provisions are calculated at the rate at which it is estimated that tax will be paid (or recovered) when the timing differences **reverse**.

The deferral method involves **extensive record keeping** because the timing differences on each individual capital asset must be held. In contrast, under the liability method, the total originating or reversing timing difference for the year is converted into a deferred tax amount at the current rate of tax (and if any change in the rate of tax has occurred in the year, only a single adjustment to the opening balance on the deferred tax account is required).

IAS 12 requires deferred tax assets and liabilities to be measured at the tax rates expected to apply in the period **when the asset is realised or liability settled**, based on tax rates and laws enacted (or substantively enacted) at the year end. In other words, IAS 12 requires the **liability method** to be used.

(IAS 12: para. 47)

5.4 Different rates of tax

In addition, in some countries different tax rates apply to different levels of taxable income. In such cases, deferred tax assets and liabilities should be measured using the **average rates** that are expected to apply to the taxable profit (loss) of the periods in which the temporary differences are expected to reverse

(IAS 12: para. 49).

5.5 Manner of recovery or settlement

In some countries, the way in which an entity **recovers or settles** the carrying amount of an asset or liability may affect the following:

(a) The tax rate applying when the entity recovers/settles the carrying amount of the asset/liability
(b) The tax base of the asset/liability

In such cases, the entity must consider the expected manner of recovery or settlement. Deferred tax liabilities and assets must be measured accordingly, using an **appropriate tax rate and tax base**.

(IAS 12: para. 51, 51A)

5.6 Example: Manner of recovery/settlement

Richcard Co has an asset with a carrying amount of \$10,000 and a tax base of \$6,000. If the asset were sold, a tax rate of 20% would apply. A tax rate of 30% would apply to other income.

Required

State the deferred tax consequences if the entity:

(a) Sells the asset without further use.
(b) Expects to return the asset and recover its carrying amount through use.

Solution

(a) A deferred tax liability is recognised of \$(10,000 – 6,000) × 20% = \$800.
(b) A deferred tax liability is recognised of \$(10,000 – 6,000) × 30% = \$1,200.

Question — Recovery 1

Emida Co has an asset which cost \$100,000. In 20X9 the carrying value was \$80,000 and the asset was revalued to \$150,000. No equivalent adjustment was made for tax purposes. Cumulative depreciation for tax purposes is \$30,000 and the tax rate is 30%. If the asset is sold for more than cost, the cumulative tax depreciation of \$30,000 will be included in taxable income but sale proceeds in excess of cost will not be taxable.

Required

State the deferred tax consequences of the above. (**Hint**. Assume first that the entity expects to recover the carrying value through use, and secondly that it will not and therefore will sell the asset instead.)

Answer

The tax base of the asset is \$70,000 (\$100,000 – \$30,000).

If the entity expects to recover the carrying amount by using the asset it must generate taxable income of $150,000, but will only be able to deduct depreciation of $70,000. On this basis there is a deferred tax liability of $24,000 ($80,000 × 30%).

If the entity expects to recover the carrying amount by selling the asset immediately for proceeds of $150,000, the deferred tax liability will be computed as follows.

	Taxable temporary difference	*Tax rate*	*Deferred tax liability*
	$		$
Cumulative tax depreciation	30,000	30%	9,000
Proceeds in excess of cost	50,000	Nil	–
Total	80,000		9,000

Note. The additional deferred tax that arises on the revaluation is charged directly to equity: see below.

Question

Recovery 2

The facts are as in Recovery 1 above, except that if the asset is sold for more than cost, the cumulative tax depreciation will be included in taxable income (taxed at 30%) and the sale proceeds will be taxed at 40% after deducting an inflation-adjusted cost of $110,000.

Required

State the deferred tax consequences of the above (use the same hint as in Recovery 1).

Answer

If the entity expects to recover the carrying amount by using the asset, the situation is as in Recovery 1 above in the same circumstances.

If the entity expects to recover the carrying amount by selling the asset immediately for proceeds of $150,000, the entity will be able to deduct the indexed costs of $110,000. The net profit of $40,000 will be taxed at 40%. In addition, the cumulative tax depreciation of $30,000 will be included in taxable income and taxed at 30%. On this basis, the tax base is $80,000 ($110,000 – $30,000), there is a taxable temporary difference of $70,000 and there is a deferred tax liability of $25,000 ($40,000 × 40% plus $30,000 × 30%).

Exam focus point

If the tax base is not immediately apparent in Recovery 2 above, it may be helpful to consider the fundamental principle of IAS 12: that an entity should recognise a deferred tax liability (asset) whenever recovery or settlement of the carrying amount of an asset or liability would make future tax payments larger (smaller) than they would be if such recovery or settlement would have no consequences.

5.7 Discounting

IAS 12 states that deferred tax assets and liabilities **should not be discounted** because the complexities and difficulties involved will affect reliability (IAS 12: paras. 53, 54). Discounting would require detailed scheduling of the timing of the reversal of each temporary difference, but this is often impracticable. If discounting were permitted, this would affect comparability, so it is barred completely. However, carrying amounts determine temporary differences even when such carrying amounts are discounted (eg retirement benefit obligations: see Chapter 4).

5.8 Carrying amount of deferred tax assets

The carrying amount of deferred tax assets should be **reviewed at each year end** and reduced where appropriate (insufficient future taxable profits). Such a reduction may be reversed in future years.

5.9 Recognition

As with current tax, deferred tax should normally be recognised as income or an expense and included in the net profit or loss for the period (IAS 12: paras. 58, 61A). The exceptions are where the tax arises from the events below.

(a) A transaction or event which is recognised (in the same or a different period) **directly in equity.**
(b) A business combination that is an **acquisition** (see Part C).

The figures shown for deferred tax in profit or loss will consist of **two components.**

(a) Deferred tax relating to **timing differences.**

(b) Adjustments relating to **changes in the carrying amount of deferred tax assets/liabilities** (where there is no change in timing differences), eg changes in tax rates/laws, reassessment of the recoverability of deferred tax assets, or a change in the expected recovery of an asset.

Items in (b) will be recognised in the profit or loss, **unless** they relate to items previously charged/credited to equity.

Deferred tax (and current tax) should be **charged/credited directly to equity** if the tax relates to items also charged/credited directly to equity (in the same or a different period).

The following show examples of IFRSs which allow certain items to be credited/charged directly to equity.

(a) **Revaluations** of property, plant and equipment (IAS 16)

(b) The effect of a **change in accounting policy** (applied retrospectively) or correction of an **error** (IAS 8)

Where it is not possible to determine the amount of current/deferred tax that relates to items credited/charged to equity, such tax amounts should be based on a reasonable **prorata allocation** of the entity's current/deferred tax.

5.10 Section summary

- You should understand and be able to explain the different **bases for provision** of deferred tax.
  - **Flow-through method** (no tax provided)
  - **Full provision method** (tax provided in full, as per IAS 12)
  - **Partial provision method** (tax provided to the extent it is expected to be paid)
- There are two methods of calculating deferred tax when **tax rates change.**
  - **Deferral method** (use tax rates current when differences **arise**)
  - **Liability method** (use tax rate expected when differences **reverse**: per IAS 12)
- Where different rates of tax apply to different rates of income, the **manner of recovery/settlement** of assets/liabilities is important.

6 Deferred taxation and business combinations

FAST FORWARD

You must appreciate the deferred tax aspects of **business combinations**: this is the aspect of deferred tax most likely to appear in the Paper P2 exam.

Much of the above will be familiar to you from your earlier studies. In Paper P2 you are likely to be asked about the **group aspects of deferred taxation**. Everything that IAS 12 states in relation to deferred tax and business combinations is brought together in this section.

6.1 Tax bases

Remember the definition of the tax base of an asset or liability given in Section 2 above? In relation to business combinations and consolidations, IAS 12 gives (IAS 12: IE, paras. 12 to 17) examples of circumstances that give rise to taxable temporary differences and to deductible temporary differences.

6.1.1 Circumstances that give rise to taxable temporary differences

- The carrying amount of an asset is increased to **fair value** in a business combination that is an acquisition and no equivalent adjustment is made for tax purposes.
- **Unrealised losses resulting from intragroup transactions** are eliminated by inclusion in the carrying amount of inventory or property, plant and equipment.
- **Retained earnings** of subsidiaries, branches, associates and joint ventures are included in consolidated retained earnings, but income taxes will be payable if the profits are distributed to the reporting parent.
- Investments in foreign subsidiaries, branches or associates or interests in foreign joint ventures are affected by **changes in foreign exchange rates**.
- An entity accounts in its own currency for the cost of the non-monetary assets of a foreign operation that is **integral to the reporting entity's operations** but the taxable profit or tax loss of the foreign operation is determined in the foreign currency.

Question — **Deferred tax and business combinations 1**

What are the consequences of the above situations?

Note. You may want to read through to the end of this section before you attempt this question.

Answer

(a) *Fair value adjustment*
On initial recognition, the resulting deferred tax liability increases goodwill or decreases negative goodwill.

(b) *Unrealised losses*
The tax bases of the assets are unaltered.

(c) *Consolidated earnings*
IAS 12 does not allow recognition of the resulting deferred tax liability if the parent, investor or venturer is able to control the timing of the reversal of the temporary difference and it is probable that the temporary difference will not reverse in the foreseeable future.

(d) *Changes in exchange rates: investments*
There may be either a taxable temporary difference or a deductible temporary difference in this situation. IAS 12 does not allow recognition of the resulting deferred tax liability if the parent, investor or venturer is able to control the timing of the reversal of the temporary difference and it is probable that the temporary difference will not reverse in the foreseeable future.

(e) *Changes in exchange rates: use of own currency*
Again, there may be either a taxable temporary difference or a deductible temporary difference. Where there is a taxable temporary difference, the resulting deferred tax liability is recognised, because it relates to the foreign operation's own assets and liabilities, rather than to the reporting **entity's** investment in that foreign operation. The deferred tax is charged to profit or loss.

6.1.2 Circumstances that give rise to deductible temporary differences

- A **liability is recognised at its fair value** in a business combination that is an acquisition, but none of the related expense is deducted in determining taxable profit until a later period
- **Unrealised profits resulting from intragroup transactions** are eliminated from the carrying amount of assets, such as inventory or property, plant or equipment, but no equivalent adjustment is made for tax purposes
- Investments in foreign subsidiaries, branches or associates or interests in foreign joint ventures are affected by **changes in foreign exchange rates**
- A foreign operation accounts for its non-monetary assets in its own (functional) currency. If its taxable profit or loss is determined in a different currency (under the presentation currency method) changes in the exchange rate result in temporary differences. The resulting deferred tax is charged or credited to profit or loss.

(IAS 12: IE paras. 9 to 13)

Question — **Deferred tax and business combinations 2**

What are the consequences of the above situations?

Note. Again, you should read to the end of this section before you answer this question.

Answer

(a) *Fair value of liabilities*

The resulting deferred tax asset decreases goodwill or increases negative goodwill.

(b) *Unrealised profits*

As in above.

(c) *Changes in exchange rates: investments*

As noted in the question before this, there may be a taxable temporary difference or a deductible temporary difference. IAS 12 requires recognition of the resulting deferred tax asset to the extent, and only to the extent, that it is probable that:

(i) The temporary difference will reverse in the foreseeable future; and
(ii) Taxable profit will be available against which the temporary difference can be utilised.

(d) *Changes in exchange rates: use of own currency*

As noted in the question before this, there may be either a taxable temporary difference or a deductible temporary difference. Where there is a deductible temporary difference, the resulting deferred tax asset is recognised to the extent that it is probable that sufficient taxable profit will be available, because the deferred tax asset relates to the foreign operation's own assets and liabilities, rather than to the reporting **entity**'s investment in that foreign operation. The deferred tax is charged to profit or loss.

6.2 Taxable temporary differences

In a business combination, the cost of the acquisition must be allocated to the fair values of the identifiable assets and liabilities acquired as at the date of the transaction. Temporary differences will arise when the tax bases of the identifiable assets and liabilities acquired are not affected by the business combination or are affected differently. For example, the carrying amount of an asset is increased to fair value but the tax base of the asset remains at cost to the previous owner; a taxable temporary difference arises which results in a deferred tax liability and this will also affect goodwill.

6.3 Deductible temporary differences

In a business combination that is an acquisition, as in Paragraph 6.2 above, when a **liability** is recognised on acquisition but the related costs are not deducted in determining taxable profits until a later period, a deductible temporary difference arises resulting in a deferred tax asset. A deferred tax asset will also arise when the fair value of an identifiable asset acquired is less than its tax base. In both these cases goodwill is affected (see below).

6.4 Investments in subsidiaries, branches and associates and interests in joint arrangements

When such investments are held, **temporary differences** arise because the carrying amount of the investment (ie the parent's share of the net assets including goodwill) becomes different from the tax base (often the cost) of the investment. Why do these differences arise? These are some examples.

- There are **undistributable profits** held by subsidiaries, branches, associates and joint ventures.
- There are **changes in foreign exchange rates** when a parent and its subsidiary are based in different countries.
- There is a **reduction in the carrying amount** of an investment in an associate to its recoverable amount.

The **temporary difference in the consolidated financial statements** may be different from the temporary difference associated with that investment in the parent's separate financial statements when the parent carries the investment in its separate financial statements at cost or revalued amount.

IAS 12 requires entities to **recognise a deferred tax liability** for all taxable temporary differences associated with investments in subsidiaries, branches and associates, and interests in joint ventures, *except* to the extent that both of these conditions are satisfied (IAS 12: para. 39):

(a) The parent/investor/venturer is able to **control the timing of the reversal** of the temporary difference

(b) It is probable that the temporary difference **will not reverse** in the foreseeable future.

As well as the fact of parent control over reversal of temporary differences, it would often be **impracticable** to determine the amount of income taxes payable when the temporary differences reverses. So when the parent has determined that those profits will not be distributed in the foreseeable future, the parent does not recognise a deferred tax liability. The same applies to investments in branches.

Where a foreign operation's taxable profit or tax loss (and therefore the tax base of its non-monetary assets and liabilities) is determined in a **foreign currency**, changes in the exchange rate give rise to temporary differences. These relate to the foreign entity's own assets and liabilities, rather than to the reporting entity's investment in that foreign operation, and so the reporting entity should recognise the resulting deferred tax liability or asset. The resulting deferred tax is charged or credited to profit or loss.

An investor in an **associate** does not control that entity and so cannot determine its dividend policy. Without an agreement requiring that the profits of the associate should not be distributed in the foreseeable future, therefore, an investor should recognise a deferred tax liability arising from taxable temporary differences associated with its investment in the associate. Where an investor cannot determine the exact amount of tax, but only a minimum amount, then the deferred tax liability should be that amount.

In a **joint venture**, the agreement between the parties usually deals with profit sharing. When a venturer can control the sharing of profits and it is probable that the profits will not be distributed in the foreseeable future, a deferred liability is not recognised.

IAS 12 then states that a **deferred tax asset** should be recognised for all deductible temporary differences arising from investments in subsidiaries, branches and associates, and interests in joint ventures, to the extent that (and **only** to the extent that) both these are probable (IAS 12: para. 44):

(a) That the temporary difference will **reverse** in the foreseeable future, **and**
(b) That **taxable profit** will be available against which the temporary difference can be utilised.

The **prudence principle** discussed above for the recognition of deferred tax assets should be considered.

6.5 Deferred tax assets of an acquired subsidiary

Deferred tax assets of a subsidiary may not satisfy the criteria for recognition when a business combination is initially accounted for but may be realised subsequently (IAS 12: para. 87).

These should be recognised as follows:

- If recognised within 12 months of the acquisition date and resulting from new information about circumstances existing at the acquisition date, the credit entry should be made to goodwill. If the carrying amount of goodwill is reduced to zero, any further amounts should be recognised in profit or loss.
- If recognised outside the 12 months 'measurement period' or not resulting from new information about circumstances existing at the acquisition date, the credit entry should be made to profit or loss.

Question — Recognition

In 20X2 Jacko Co acquired a subsidiary, Jilly Co, which had deductible temporary differences of $3m. The tax rate at the date of acquisition was 30%. The resulting deferred tax asset of $0.9m was not recognised as an identifiable asset in determining the goodwill of $5m resulting from the business combination. Two years after the acquisition, Jacko Co decided that future taxable profit would probably be sufficient for the entity to recover the benefit of all the deductible temporary differences.

Required

(a) Consider the accounting treatment of the subsequent recognition of the deferred tax asset in 20X4.
(b) What would happen if the tax rate had risen to 40% by 20X4 or decreased to 20%?

Answer

(a) The entity recognises a deferred tax asset of £0.9m (£3m × 30%) and, in profit or loss, deferred tax income of £0.9m. Goodwill is not adjusted as the recognition does not arise within the measurement period (ie within the 12 months following the acquisition).

(b) If the tax rate rises to 40%, the entity should recognise a deferred tax asset of $1.2m ($3m × 40%) and, in profit or loss, deferred tax income of $1.2m.

If the tax rate falls to 20%, the entity should recognise a deferred tax asset of $0.6m ($3m × 20%) and deferred tax income of $0.6m.

In both cases, the entity will also reduce the cost of goodwill by $0.9m and recognise an expense for that amount in profit or loss.

6.6 Example: Deferred tax adjustments 1

Red is a private limited liability company and has two 100% owned subsidiaries, Blue and Green, both themselves private limited liability companies. Red acquired Green on 1 January 20X2 for $5 million when the fair value of the net assets was $4 million, and the tax base of the net assets was $3.5 million. The acquisition of Green and Blue was part of a business strategy whereby Red would build up the 'value' of the group over a three-year period and then list its existing share capital on the stock exchange.

(a) The following details relate to the acquisition of Green, which manufactures electronic goods.

(i) Part of the purchase price has been allocated to intangible assets because it relates to the acquisition of a database of key customers from Green. The recognition and measurement criteria for an intangible asset under IFRS 3 *Business combinations*/IAS 38 *Intangible assets* do not appear to have been met but the directors feel that the intangible asset of

$0.5 million will be allowed for tax purposes and have computed the tax provision accordingly. However, the tax authorities could possibly challenge this opinion.

(ii) Green has sold goods worth $3 million to Red since acquisition and made a profit of $1 million on the transaction. The inventory of these goods recorded in Red's statement of financial position at the year end of 31 May 20X2 was $1.8 million.

(iii) The balance on the retained earnings of Green at acquisition was $2 million. The directors of Red have decided that, during the three years to the date that they intend to list the shares of the company, they will realise earnings through future dividend payments from the subsidiary amounting to $500,000 per year. Tax is payable on any remittance or dividends and no dividends have been declared for the current year.

(b) Blue was acquired on 1 June 20X1 and is a company which undertakes various projects ranging from debt factoring to investing in property and commodities. The following details relate to Blue for the year ending 31 May 20X2.

(i) Blue has a portfolio of readily marketable government securities which are held as current assets. These investments are stated at market value in the statement of financial position with any gain or loss taken to profit or loss for the year. These gains and losses are taxed when the investments are sold. Currently the accumulated unrealised gains are $4 million.

(ii) Blue has calculated that it requires a specific allowance of $2 million against loans in its portfolio. Tax relief is available when the specific loan is written off.

(iii) When Red acquired Blue it had unused tax losses brought forward. At 1 June 20X1, it appeared that Blue would have sufficient taxable profit to realise the deferred tax asset created by these losses but subsequent events have proven that the future taxable profit will not be sufficient to realise all of the unused tax loss.

The current tax rate for Red is 30% and for public companies is 35%.

Required

Write a note suitable for presentation to the partner of an accounting firm setting out the deferred tax implications of the above information for the Red Group of companies.

Solution: Deferred tax adjustments 1

Acquisition of the subsidiaries – general

Fair value adjustments have been made for consolidation purposes in both cases and these will **affect** the **deferred tax charge for the year**. This is because the deferred tax position is viewed **from the perspective of the group as a whole**. For example, it may be possible to recognise deferred tax assets which previously could not be recognised by individual companies, because there are now sufficient tax profits available within the group to utilise unused tax losses. Therefore a **provision** should be made for **temporary differences between fair values of the identifiable net assets acquired and their carrying values** ($4 million less $3.5 million in respect of Green). **No provision should be made for the temporary difference** of $1 million arising on goodwill recognised as a result of the combination with Green.

Future listing

Red plans to seek a listing in three years' time. Therefore it will become a **public company** and will be subject to a **higher rate of tax**. IAS 12 states that deferred tax should be measured at the **average tax rates expected to apply in the periods in which the timing differences are expected to reverse**, based on current enacted tax rates and laws. This means that Red may be paying tax at the higher rate when some of its timing differences reverse and this should be taken into account in the calculation.

Acquisition of Green

(a) The directors have calculated the tax provision on the assumption that the intangible asset of $0.5 million will be allowed for tax purposes. However, this is not certain and the directors **may eventually have to pay the additional tax**. If the directors cannot be persuaded to adjust their calculations a **liability for the additional tax should be recognised**.

(b) The intra-group transaction has resulted in an **unrealised profit** of $0.6 million in the group accounts and this will be **eliminated on consolidation**. The tax charge in the group statement of profit or loss and other comprehensive income includes the tax on this profit, for which **the group will not become liable to tax until the following period. From the perspective of the group, there is a temporary difference**. Because the temporary difference arises in the financial statements of Red, **deferred tax should be provided** on this difference (an asset) using the rate of tax payable by Red.

(c) **Deferred tax should be recognised on the unremitted earnings of subsidiaries** unless the parent is able to **control the timing of dividend payments** or it is **unlikely that dividends will be paid for the foreseeable future**. Red controls the dividend policy of Green and this means that there would normally be no need to make a provision in respect of unremitted profits. However, the profits of Green **will be distributed** to Red over the next few years and **tax will be payable** on the dividends received. Therefore a **deferred tax liability should be shown**.

Acquisition of Blue

(a) A **temporary difference arises** where non-monetary assets are **revalued upwards** and the **tax treatment of the surplus is different from the accounting treatment**. In this case, the revaluation surplus has been **recognised in profit or loss** for the current period, rather than in equity but no corresponding adjustment has been made to the tax base of the investments because the gains will be taxed in future periods. Therefore the company **should recognise a deferred tax liability on the temporary difference of $4 million**.

(b) A temporary difference arises when the provision for the loss on the loan portfolio is first recognised. The general allowance is expected to increase and therefore it is unlikely that the temporary difference will reverse in the near future. However, a **deferred tax liability should still be recognised**. The temporary difference gives rise to a **deferred tax asset**. IAS 12 states that **deferred tax assets should not be recognised unless it is probable that taxable profits will be available** against which the taxable profits can be utilised. **This is affected by the situation in point (c) below**.

(c) In theory, unused tax losses give rise to a deferred tax asset. However, IAS 12 states that **deferred tax assets should only be recognised to the extent that they are regarded as recoverable**. They should be regarded as recoverable to the extent that on the basis of all the evidence available it is **probable that there will be suitable taxable profits against which the losses can be recovered**. The future taxable profit of Blue **will not be sufficient to realise all the unused tax loss. Therefore the deferred tax asset is reduced to the amount that is expected to be recovered**.

This reduction in the deferred tax asset implies that it was **overstated at 1 June 20X1**, when it was acquired by the group. As these are the first post-acquisition financial statements, **goodwill should also be adjusted**.

6.7 Example: Deferred tax adjustments 2

You are the accountant of Payit. Your assistant is preparing the consolidated financial statements of the year ended 31 March 20X2. However, he is unsure how to account for the deferred tax effects of certain transactions as he has not studied IAS 12. These transactions are given below.

Transaction 1

During the year, Payit sold goods to a subsidiary for $10 million, making a profit of 20% on selling price. 25% of these goods were still in the inventories of the subsidiary at 31 March 20X2. The subsidiary and Pay it are in the same tax jurisdiction and pay tax on profits at 30%.

Transaction 2

An overseas subsidiary made a loss adjusted for tax purposes of $8 million ($ equivalent). The only relief available for this tax loss is to carry it forward for offset against future taxable profits of the overseas subsidiary. Taxable profits of the oversees subsidiary suffer tax at a rate of 25%.

Required

Compute the effect of both the above transactions on the deferred tax amounts in the consolidated statement of financial position of Payit at 31 March 20X2. You should provide a full explanation for your calculations and indicate any assumptions you make in formulating your answer.

Solution: Deferred tax adjustments 2

Transaction 1

This intra-group sale will give rise to a **provision for unrealised profit** on the unsold inventory of $10,000,000 × 20% × 25% = $500,000. This provision must be made in the consolidated accounts. However, this profit has already been taxed in the financial statements of Payit. In other words there is a **timing difference**. In the following year when the stock is sold outside the group, the provision will be released, but the profit will not be taxed. The timing difference therefore gives rise to a **deferred tax asset**. The asset is 30% × $500,000 = $150,000.

Deferred tax assets are recognised to the extent that they are **recoverable**. This will be the case if **it is more likely than not** that **suitable tax profits** will exist from which the reversal of the timing difference giving rise to the asset can be deducted. The asset is carried forward on this assumption.

Transaction 2

An unrelieved tax loss gives rise to a **timing difference** because the loss is recognised in the financial statements but not yet allowed for tax purposes. When the overseas subsidiary generates sufficient taxable profits, the loss will be offset against these in arriving at taxable profits.

The amount of the deferred tax asset to be carried forward is 25% × $8m = $2m.

As with Transaction 1, deferred tax assets are recognised to the extent that they are **recoverable**. This will be the case if **it is more likely than not** that **suitable tax profits** will exist from which the reversal of the timing difference giving rise to the asset can be deducted.

6.8 Amendment: Recognition of deferred tax assets for unrealised losses

6.8.1 The issue

This amendment was issued in January 2016 in order to clarify when a deferred tax asset should be recognised for unrealised losses. For example, an entity holds a debt instrument that is falling in value, without a corresponding tax deduction, but the entity knows that it will receive the full nominal amount on the due date, and there will be no tax consequences of that repayment. The question arises of whether to recognise a deferred tax asset on this unrealised loss.

6.8.2 2016 change

The IASB clarified **that unrealised losses on debt instruments measured at fair value and measured at cost for tax purposes give rise to a deductible temporary difference** regardless of whether the debt instrument's holder expects to recover the carrying amount of the debt instrument by sale or by use.

This may seem to contradict the key requirement that an entity recognises deferred tax assets only if it is probable that it will have future taxable profits. However, the amendment also addresses the issue of what constitutes future taxable profits, and clarifies that:

(a) Unrealised losses on debt instruments measured at fair value and measured at cost for tax purposes give rise to a deductible temporary difference regardless of whether the debt instrument's holder expects to recover the carrying amount of the debt instrument by sale or by use

(b) The carrying amount of an asset does not limit the estimation of probable future taxable profits

(c) Estimates for future taxable profits exclude tax deductions resulting from the reversal of deductible temporary differences.

(d) An entity assesses a deferred tax asset in combination with other deferred tax assets. Where tax law restricts the utilisation of tax losses, an entity would assess a deferred tax asset in combination with other deferred tax assets of the same type.

IAS 12: para. 29, 29A

6.8.3 Example: deferred tax asset and unrealised loss

(Adapted from IAS 12, Illustrative Example 7)

Humbert has a debt instrument with a nominal value of $2,000,000. The fair value of the financial instrument at the company's year end of 30 June 20X4 is $1,800,000. Humbert has determined that there is a deductible temporary difference of $200,000. Humbert intends to hold the instrument until maturity on 30 June 20X5, and expects that the $2,000,000 will be paid in full. This means that the deductible temporary difference will reverse in full.

Humbert has, in addition, $60,000 of taxable temporary differences that will also reverse in full in 20X5. The company expects the bottom line of its tax return to show a tax loss of $40,000.

Assume a tax rate of 20%.

Required

Discuss, with calculations, whether Humbert can recognise a deferred tax asset under IAS 12 *Income taxes*.

Solution

The first stage is to use the reversal of the taxable temporary difference to arrive at the amount to be tested for recognition.

Under the current requirements of IAS 12 Humbert will consider whether it has a tax liability from a taxable temporary difference that will support the recognition of the tax asset:

	$'000
Deductible temporary difference	200
Reversing taxable temporary difference	(60)
Remaining amount (recognition to be determined)	140

At least $60,000 may be recognised as a deferred tax asset.

The next stage is to calculate the future taxable profit. Following the amendment, this is done using a formula, the aim of which is to derive the amount of tax profit or loss before the reversal of any temporary difference:

	$'000
Expected tax loss (per bottom line of tax return)	(40)
Less reversing taxable temporary difference	(60)
Add reversing deductible temporary difference	200
Taxable profit for recognition test	100

Finally, the results of the above two steps should be added, and the tax calculated:

Humbert would recognise a deferred tax asset of ($60,000 + $100,000) × 20% = $32,000. This deferred tax asset would be recognised even though the company has an expected loss on its tax return.

6.9 Section summary

In relation to deferred tax and business combinations you should be familiar with:

- Circumstances that give rise to **taxable temporary differences**
- Circumstances that give rise to **deductible temporary differences**
- Their **treatment** once an acquisition takes place
- Reasons **why deferred tax arises** when investments are held
- **Recognition** of deferred tax on business combinations

Chapter Roundup

- Taxation consists of **two components**.
  - Current tax
  - Deferred tax
- **Current tax** is the amount payable to the tax authorities in relation to the trading activities during the period. It is generally straightforward.
- **Deferred tax** is an accounting measure, used to match the tax effects of transactions with their accounting impact. It is quite complex.
- **Deferred tax assets and liabilities** arise from taxable and deductible temporary differences.
- **IAS 12 *Income taxes*** covers both current and deferred tax. It has substantial presentation and disclosure requirements.
- You must appreciate the deferred tax aspects of **business combinations**: this is the aspect of deferred tax most likely to appear in the Paper P2 exam.

Quick Quiz

1. What is the difference between 'current tax' and 'deferred tax'?
2. How should current tax be measured?

   A The total liability, including deferred tax
   B The amount expected to be paid to (or recovered from) the tax authorities
   C The amount calculated on profit at current tax rates
   D The amount calculated on profit at future tax rates
3. A taxable temporary difference gives rise to a deferred tax liability. *True or false*?
4. What is the basis of provision for deferred tax required by IAS 12?
5. What two methods can be used for calculating deferred tax when the tax rate changes?
6. Current tax assets and liabilities cannot be offset. *True or false*?
7. How do temporary differences arise when investments are held in subsidiaries, associates and so on?

Answers to Quick Quiz

1 (a) Current tax is the amount actually payable to the tax authorities.
(b) Deferred tax is used to match the tax effects of transactions with their accounting impact.

2 B The amount expected to be paid to (or recovered from) the tax authorities.

3 True.

4 Full provision

5
- Deferral method
- Liability method

6 False. They can be offset only if the entity has a legally enforceable right to offset *and* it intends to actually carry out the offset.

7 When the carrying amounts of the investment become different to the tax base of the investment.

Now try the question below from the Practice Question Bank

Number	Level	Marks	Time
Q9	Examination	25	49 mins

Financial instruments

7

Topic list	Syllabus reference
1 Financial instruments	C3
2 Presentation of financial instruments	C3
3 Recognition of financial instruments	C3
4 Measurement of financial instruments	C3
5 Embedded derivatives	C3
6 Hedging	C3
7 Disclosure of financial instruments	C3
8 Fair value measurement	F2

Introduction

Financial instruments sounds like a daunting subject, and indeed this is a complex and controversial area. The numbers involved in financial instruments are often huge, but don't let this put you off. In this chapter we aim to simplify the topic as much as possible and to focus on the important issues.

IFRS 9 *Financial instruments* was issued in final form in 2014, replacing IAS 39.

Study guide

		Intellectual level
C3	**Financial instruments**	
(a)	Apply and discuss the recognition and derecognition of financial assets and financial liabilities	2
(b)	Apply and discuss the classification of financial assets and financial liabilities and their measurement	2
(c)	Apply and discuss the treatment of gains and losses arising on financial assets or financial liabilities	2
(d)	Apply and discuss the treatment of the expected loss impairment model	2
(e)	Account for derivative financial instruments and simple embedded derivatives	2
(f)	Outline the principle of hedge accounting and account for fair value hedges and cash flow hedges, including hedge effectiveness	2

Exam guide

This is a highly controversial topic and therefore, likely to be examined, probably in Section B.

Exam focus point

Although the very complexity of this topic makes it a highly likely subject for an exam question in Paper P2, there are limits as to how complicated and detailed a question the examiner can set with any realistic expectation of students being able to answer it. You should therefore concentrate on the essential points. To date, financial instruments have mainly been examined within a larger scenario based question. However, the expected loss impairment model in particular could be tested using a numerical example.

1 Financial instruments 6/12 – 12/16

FAST FORWARD

Financial instruments can be very complex, particularly **derivative instruments**, although **primary instruments** are more straightforward.

1.1 Background

If you read the financial press you will probably be aware of **rapid international expansion** in the use of financial instruments. These vary from straightforward, traditional instruments, eg bonds, through to various forms of so-called 'derivative instruments'.

We can perhaps summarise the reasons why a project on the accounting for financial instruments was considered necessary as follows:

(a) The **significant growth of financial instruments** over recent years has outstripped the development of guidance for their accounting.

(b) The topic is of **international concern**, other national standard-setters are involved as well as the IASB.

(c) There have been recent **high-profile disasters** involving derivatives (eg Barings) which, while not caused by accounting failures, have raised questions about accounting and disclosure practices.

There are three accounting standards on financial instruments:

(a) IAS 32 *Financial instruments: Presentation*, which deals with:

  (i) The classification of financial instruments between liabilities and equity
  (ii) Presentation of certain compound instruments

(b) IFRS 7 *Financial instruments: Disclosures*, which revised, simplified and incorporated disclosure requirements previously in IAS 32.

(c) IFRS 9 *Financial instruments*, issued in final form in July 2014, replaces IAS 39 *Financial instruments: Recognition and measurement*. The standard covers:

  (i) Recognition and derecognition

  (ii) The measurement of financial instruments

  (iii) Impairment

  (iv) General hedge accounting (not macro hedge accounting, which is a separate IASB project, currently at the discussion paper stage)

1.2 Definitions

The most important definitions are common to all three standards.

FAST FORWARD

The important definitions to learn are:

- **Financial asset**
- **Financial liability**
- **Equity instrument**

Key terms

Financial instrument. Any contract that gives rise to both a financial asset of one entity and a financial liability or equity instrument of another entity.

Financial asset. Any asset that is:

(a) Cash

(b) An equity instrument of another entity

(c) A contractual right to receive cash or another financial asset from another entity; or to exchange financial instruments with another entity under conditions that are potentially favourable to the entity, or

(d) A contract that will or may be settled in the entity's own equity instruments and is:

  (i) A non-derivative for which the entity is or may be obliged to receive a variable number of the entity's own equity instruments; or

  (ii) A derivative that will or may be settled other than by the exchange of a fixed amount of cash or another financial asset for a fixed number of the entity's own equity instruments.

Financial liability. Any liability that is:

(a) A contractual obligation:

  (i) To deliver cash or another financial asset to another entity, or

  (ii) To exchange financial instruments with another entity under conditions that are potentially unfavourable; or

(b) A contract that will or may be settled in the entity's own equity instruments and is:

  (i) A non-derivative for which the entity is or may be obliged to deliver a variable number of the entity's own equity instruments; or

  (ii) A derivative that will or may be settled other than by the exchange of a fixed amount of cash or another financial asset for a fixed number of the entity's own equity instruments.

Equity instrument. Any contract that evidences a residual interest in the assets of an entity after deducting all of its liabilities.

Fair value is the price that would be received to sell an asset or paid to transfer a liability in an orderly transaction between market participants at the measurement date.

Derivative. A financial instrument or other contract with all three of the following characteristics:

(a) Its value changes in response to the change in a specified interest rate, financial instrument price, commodity price, foreign exchange rate, index of prices or rates, credit rating or credit index, or other variable (sometimes called the 'underlying');

(b) It requires no initial net investment or an initial net investment that is smaller than would be required for other types of contracts that would be expected to have a similar response to changes in market factors; and

(c) It is settled at a future date.

(IAS 32: para. 11, AG3 to 23), IFRS 9, Appendix A and IFRS 13 Appendix A)

Exam focus point

These definitions are very important so learn them.

We should clarify some points arising from these definitions. First, one or two terms above should be themselves defined.

(a) A '**contract**' need not be in writing, but it must comprise an agreement that has 'clear economic consequences' and which the parties to it cannot avoid, usually because the agreement is enforceable in law.

(b) An '**entity**' here could be an individual, partnership, incorporated body or government agency.

The definitions of **financial assets and financial liabilities** may seem rather circular, referring as they do to the terms financial asset and financial instrument. The point is that there may be a chain of contractual rights and obligations, but it will lead ultimately to the receipt or payment of cash **or** the acquisition or issue of an equity instrument.

Examples of **financial assets** include:

(a) Trade receivables
(b) Options
(c) Shares (when used as an investment)

Examples of **financial liabilities** include:

(a) Trade payables
(b) Debenture loans payable
(c) Redeemable preference (non-equity) shares
(d) Forward contracts standing at a loss

As we have already noted, financial instruments include both of the following.

(a) **Primary instruments**: eg receivables, payables and equity securities

(b) **Derivative instruments**: eg financial options, futures and forwards, interest rate swaps and currency swaps, **whether recognised or unrecognised**

IAS 32 AG 8 makes it clear that the following items are **not** financial instruments.

(a) **Physical assets**, eg inventories, property, plant and equipment, leased assets and intangible assets (patents, trademarks etc)

(b) **Prepaid expenses**, deferred revenue and most warranty obligations

(c) Liabilities or assets that are **not contractual** in nature

(d) Contractual rights/obligations that **do not involve transfer of a financial asset**, eg commodity futures contracts, operating leases for lessors

Question

Why not?

Can you give the reasons why the first two items listed above do not qualify as financial instruments?

Answer

Refer to the definitions of financial assets and liabilities given above.

(a) **Physical assets**: control of these creates an opportunity to generate an inflow of cash or other assets, but it does not give rise to a present right to receive cash or other financial assets.

(b) **Prepaid expenses, etc**: the future economic benefit is the receipt of goods/services rather than the right to receive cash or other financial assets.

(c) **Deferred revenue, warranty obligations**: the probable outflow of economic benefits is the delivery of goods/services rather than cash or another financial asset.

Contingent rights and obligations meet the definition of financial assets and financial liabilities respectively (IAS 32: AG 20, 21), even though many do not qualify for recognition in financial statements. This is because the contractual rights or obligations exist because of a past transaction or event (eg assumption of a guarantee).

1.3 Derivatives

A **derivative** is a financial instrument that **derives** its value from the price or rate of an underlying item. Common **examples** of derivatives include:

(a) **Forward contracts**: agreements to buy or sell an asset at a fixed price at a fixed future date

(b) **Futures contracts**: similar to forward contracts except that contracts are standardised and traded on an exchange

(c) **Options**: rights (but not obligations) for the option holder to exercise at a pre-determined price; the option writer loses out if the option is exercised

(d) **Swaps**: agreements to swap one set of cash flows for another (normally interest rate or currency swaps)

IAS 32: AG 15

The nature of derivatives often gives rise to **particular problems**. The **value** of a derivative (and the amount at which it is eventually settled) depends on **movements** in an underlying item (such as an exchange rate). This means that settlement of a derivative can lead to a very different result from the one originally envisaged. A company which has derivatives is exposed to **uncertainty and risk** (potential for gain or loss) and this can have a very material effect on its financial performance, financial position and cash flows.

Yet because a derivative contract normally has **little or no initial cost**, under traditional accounting it **may not be recognised** in the financial statements at all. Alternatively, it may be recognised at an amount which bears no relation to its current value. This is clearly **misleading** and leaves users of the financial statements unaware of the **level of risk** that the company faces. IASs 32 and 39 were developed in order to correct this situation.

1.4 Section summary

- Three accounting standards are relevant:
  - **IFRS 9** *Financial instruments* , now complete with the final version published in July 2014
  - **IAS 32**: *Financial instruments: Presentation*
  - **IFRS 7**: *Financial instruments: Disclosures*

- The definitions of **financial asset, financial liability** and **equity instrument** are fundamental to the standards.
- Financial instruments include:
  - **Primary** instruments
  - **Derivative** instruments

2 Presentation of financial instruments

2.1 Objective

The objective of IAS 32 is:

> 'to establish principles for presenting financial instruments as liabilities or equity and for offsetting financial assets and financial liabilities.' (IAS 32: para. 2)

2.2 Scope

IAS 32 should be applied in the presentation of **all types of financial instruments**, whether recognised or unrecognised (IAS 32: para. 4).

Certain items are **excluded**.

- Interests in subsidiaries (IAS 27: Chapter 12)
- Interests in associates (IAS 28: Chapter 12)
- Interests in joint ventures (IFRS 11: Chapter 13)
- Pensions and other post-retirement benefits (IAS 19: Chapter 4)
- Insurance contracts
- Contracts for contingent consideration in a business combination
- Contracts that require a payment based on climatic, geological or other physical variables
- Financial instruments, contracts and obligations under share-based payment transactions (IFRS 2: Chapter 9)

2.3 Liabilities and equity

FAST FORWARD

Financial instruments must be classified as **liabilities** or **equity** according to their **substance**.

The critical feature of a financial liability is the **contractual obligation to deliver cash** or another financial asset.

The main thrust of IAS 32 here is that financial instruments should be presented according to their **substance, not merely their legal form**. In particular, entities which issue financial instruments should classify them (or their component parts) as **either financial liabilities, or equity** (IAS 32: para. 16).

The classification of a financial instrument as a liability or as equity depends on the following.

- The substance of the contractual arrangement on initial recognition
- The definitions of a financial liability and an equity instrument

How should a **financial liability be distinguished from an equity instrument**? The critical feature of a **liability** is an **obligation** to transfer economic benefit. Therefore, a financial instrument is a financial liability if there is a **contractual obligation** on the issuer either to deliver cash or another financial asset to the holder or to exchange another financial instrument with the holder under potentially unfavourable conditions to the issuer.

The financial liability exists **regardless of the way in which the contractual obligation will be settled**. The issuer's ability to satisfy an obligation may be restricted, eg by lack of access to foreign currency, but this is irrelevant as it does not remove the issuer's obligation or the holder's right under the instrument.

Where the above critical feature is **not** met, then the financial instrument is an **equity instrument**. IAS 32 explains that although the holder of an equity instrument may be entitled to a *pro rata* share of any distributions out of equity, the issuer does **not** have a contractual obligation to make such a distribution.

Although substance and legal form are often **consistent with each other**, this is not always the case. In particular, a financial instrument may have the legal form of equity, but in substance it is in fact a liability. Other instruments may combine features of both equity instruments and financial liabilities.

For example, many entities issue **preference shares** which must be **redeemed** by the issuer for a fixed (or determinable) amount at a fixed (or determinable) future date. In such cases, the issuer has an **obligation**. Therefore the instrument is a **financial liability** and should be classified as such.

Another example is **cumulative irredeemable preference shares**. While the issuer does not redeem the preference shares, there is an obligation on the issuer to pay fixed dividends. If the entity has insufficient retained earnings in a given year, the dividends still must be paid in future years. Again, because the issuer has an obligation, the instrument should be classified as a financial liability.

The classification of the financial instrument is made when it is **first recognised** and this classification will continue until the financial instrument is removed from the entity's statement of financial position.

2.4 Contingent settlement provisions

An entity may issue a financial instrument where the way in which it is settled depends on:

(a) The occurrence or non-occurrence of uncertain future events, or
(b) The outcome of uncertain circumstances

that are beyond the control of both the holder and the issuer of the instrument. For example, an entity might have to deliver cash instead of issuing equity shares. In this situation it is not immediately clear whether the entity has an equity instrument or a financial liability.

Such financial instruments should be classified as **financial liabilities** unless the possibility of settlement is remote. (IAS 32: para. 25)

2.5 Settlement options

When a derivative financial instrument gives one party a **choice** over how it is settled (eg, the issuer can choose whether to settle in cash or by issuing shares) the instrument is a **financial asset** or a **financial liability** unless **all the alternative choices** would result in it being an equity instrument (IAS 32: para. 26).

2.6 Compound financial instruments

FAST FORWARD

Compound instruments are split into **equity** and **liability** components and presented accordingly in the statement of financial position.

Some financial instruments contain both a liability and an equity element. In such cases, IAS 32 requires the component parts of the instrument to be **classified separately**, according to the substance of the contractual arrangement and the definitions of a financial liability and an equity instrument (IAS 32: paras. 28 to 32).

One of the most common types of compound instrument is **convertible debt**. This creates a primary financial liability of the issuer and grants an option to the holder of the instrument to convert it into an equity instrument (usually ordinary shares) of the issuer. This is the economic equivalent of the issue of conventional debt plus a warrant to acquire shares in the future.

Although in theory there are several possible ways of calculating the split, the following method is recommended:

(a) Calculate the value for the liability component.
(b) Deduct this from the instrument as a whole to leave a residual value for the equity component.

The reasoning behind this approach is that an entity's equity is its residual interest in its assets amount after deducting all its liabilities.

The **sum of the carrying amounts** assigned to liability and equity will always be equal to the carrying amount that would be ascribed to the instrument **as a whole**.

2.7 Example: Valuation of compound instruments

Rathbone Co issues 2,000 convertible bonds at the start of 20X2. The bonds have a three-year term, and are issued at par with a face value of $1,000 per bond, giving total proceeds of $2,000,000. Interest is payable annually in arrears at a nominal annual interest rate of 6%. Each bond is convertible at any time up to maturity into 250 common shares.

When the bonds are issued, the prevailing market interest rate for similar debt without conversion options is 9%. At the issue date, the market price of one common share is $3. The dividends expected over the three-year term of the bonds amount to 14c per share at the end of each year. The risk-free annual interest rate for a three-year term is 5%.

Required

What is the value of the equity component in the bond?

Solution

The liability component is valued first, and the difference between the proceeds of the bond issue and the fair value of the liability is assigned to the equity component. The present value of the liability component is calculated using a discount rate of 9%, the market interest rate for similar bonds having no conversion rights, as shown.

	$
Present value of the principal: $2,000,000 payable at the end of three years ($2m × 0.772)*	1,544,000
Present value of the interest: $120,000 payable annually in arrears for three years ($120,000 × 2.531)*	303,720
Total liability component	1,847,720
Equity component (balancing figure)	152,280
Proceeds of the bond issue	2,000,000

* These figures can be obtained from discount and annuity tables.

The split between the liability and equity components remains the same throughout the term of the instrument, even if there are changes in the **likelihood of the option being exercised**. This is because it is not always possible to predict how a holder will behave. The issuer continues to have an obligation to make future payments until conversion, maturity of the instrument or some other relevant transaction takes place.

2.8 Treasury shares

If an entity **reacquires its own equity instruments**, those instruments ('treasury shares') shall be **deducted from equity**. No gain or loss shall be recognised in profit or loss on the purchase, sale, issue or cancellation of an entity's own equity instruments. Consideration paid or received shall be recognised directly in equity (IAS 32: para. 33).

2.9 Interest, dividends, losses and gains

As well as looking at statement of financial position presentation, IAS 32 considers how financial instruments affect the profit or loss (and movements in equity). The treatment varies according to whether interest, dividends, losses or gains relate to a financial liability or an equity instrument (IAS 32: para. 35, 36, 40, 41).

(a) Interest, dividends, losses and gains relating to a financial instrument (or component part) classified as a **financial liability** should be recognised as **income or expense** in profit or loss.

(b) Distributions to holders of a financial instrument classified as an **equity instrument** should be **debited directly to equity** by the issuer.

(c) **Transaction costs** of an equity transaction shall be accounted for as a **deduction from equity** (unless they are directly attributable to the acquisition of a business, in which case they are accounted for under IFRS 3).

You should look at the requirements of IAS 1 *Presentation of financial statements* for further details of disclosure, and IAS 12 *Income taxes* for disclosure of tax effects.

2.10 Offsetting a financial asset and a financial liability

A financial asset and financial liability should **only** be **offset**, with the net amount reported in the statement of financial position, when an entity:

(a) Has a legally enforceable right of set off, and

(b) Intends to settle on a net basis, or to realise the asset and settle the liability simultaneously, ie at the same moment.

This will reflect the expected **future cash flows** of the entity in these specific circumstances. In all other cases, financial assets and financial liabilities are presented separately.

(IAS 32: para. 42, AG 38 A to F)

2.11 Puttable financial instruments and obligations arising on liquidation

IAS 32 requires that if the holder of a financial instrument can require the issuer to redeem it for cash it should be classified as a liability. Some ordinary shares and partnership interests allow the holder to 'put' the instrument (that is to require the issuer to redeem it in cash). Such shares might more usually be considered as equity, but application of IAS 32 results in their being classified as liabilities.

IAS 32 requires entities to classify such instruments as equity, so long as they meet certain conditions. The standard further requires that instruments imposing an obligation on an entity to deliver to another party a pro rata share of the net assets only on liquidation should be classified as equity.

(IAS 32: para. 96A)

2.12 Section summary

- Financial instruments issued to raise capital must be classified as **liabilities** or **equity.**
- The **substance** of the financial instrument is more important than its **legal form.**
- The **critical feature of a financial liability** is the contractual obligation to deliver cash or another financial instrument.
- **Compound instruments** are split into equity and liability parts and presented accordingly.
- **Interest, dividends, losses and gains** are treated according to whether they relate to an equity instrument or a financial liability.

3 Recognition of financial instruments

FAST FORWARD

IFRS 9 issued in final form in 2014, replaced ***IAS 39 Financial instruments: recognition and measurement.*** It will come into force on 1 January 2018.

IFRS 9 *Financial instruments* establishes principles for recognising and measuring financial assets and financial liabilities.

3.1 Background

It had been the IASB's intention to replace IAS 39 with a principles-based standard for some time, due to criticism of the complexity of IAS 39, which is difficult to understand, apply and interpret.

The replacement of IAS 39 became more urgent after the financial crisis. The IASB and US FASB set up a Financial Crisis Advisory Group (FCAG) to advise on how improvements in financial reporting could help enhance investor confidence in financial markets.

IFRS 9 was published in stages: new classification and measurement models (2009 and 2010) and a new hedge accounting model (2013). The version of IFRS 9 issued in 2014 supersedes all previous versions and completes the IASB's project to replace IAS 39. It covers recognition and measurement, impairment, derecognition and general hedge accounting. It does not cover portfolio fair value hedge accounting for interest rate risk ('macro hedge accounting'), which is a separate IASB project, currently at the discussion paper stage.

3.1.1 Effective date

IFRS 9 is mandatorily effective for periods beginning on or after 1 January 2018 with early adoption permitted. For a limited period, previous versions of IFRS 9 may be adopted early if not already done so provided the relevant date of initial application is before 1 February 2015 (IFRS 9: Chapter 7, para. 7.1.1).

3.2 Scope

IFRS 9 applies to **all entities** and to **all types of financial instruments except** those specifically excluded, as listed below (IFRS 9: Chapter 2, para. 2.1).

(a) Investments in **subsidiaries, associates, and joint ventures** that are accounted for under IFRS 10, IAS 27 or IAS 28

(b) **Leases** covered in IFRS 16

(c) **Employee benefit plans** covered in IAS 19

(d) **Equity instruments issued by the entity** eg ordinary shares issued, or options and warrants

(e) **Insurance contracts** and **financial guarantee contracts**

(f) **Contracts for contingent consideration** in a business combination, covered in IFRS 3

(g) **Loan commitments** that cannot be settled net in cash or another financial instrument

(h) Financial instruments, contracts and obligations under **share based payment transactions**, covered in IFRS 2.

(i) Rights to **reimbursement** under IAS 37

(j) Rights and obligations within the scope of **IFRS 15** *Revenue from contracts with customers*

3.2.1 Financial contracts and executory contracts

IFRS 9 applies to those contracts to buy or sell a **non-financial item** that can be **settled net in cash** or another financial instrument, or by exchanging financial instruments, as if the contracts were financial instruments. However, contracts that allow net settlement in cash can be entered into for satisfying the normal sales and purchases requirements of the two parties. Such contracts would be **executory contracts** (IFRS 9: Chapter 2, para. 2.4).

In the legal sense, an executory contract is a contract in which something remains to be done by one or both parties. Executory contracts are contracts under which neither party has performed any of its obligations or both parties have partially performed their obligations to an equal extent. For example, an unfulfilled order for the purchase of goods, where at the end of the reporting period, the goods have neither been delivered nor paid for. In the context of whether such a contract is outside the scope of IFRS 9, the issue of 'own use' comes into play. If an entity **takes delivery of a commodity in accordance with its own sales or usage requirements**, then the contract will generally be regarded as an **executory contract** and **outside the scope** of IFRS 9.

3.2.2 Example: executory contract

This example is adapted from IFRS 9, IG: para. A1.

Ferro enters into a fixed price forward contract to buy 2 million kilograms of iron in accordance with its expected usage requirements. The contract permits Ferro to take physical delivery of the iron at the end of twelve months or to pay or receive a net settlement in cash, based on the change in fair value of iron. Is the contract accounted for as a derivative?

While such a contract meets the definition of a derivative, it is not necessarily accounted for as a derivative. The contract is a derivative instrument because there is no initial net investment, the contract is based on the price of iron, and it is to be settled at a future date. However, if Ferro intends to settle the contract by taking delivery and has no history for similar contracts of settling net in cash or of taking delivery of the iron and selling it within a short period after delivery for the purpose of generating a profit from short-term fluctuations in price or dealer's margin, the contract is not accounted for as a derivative under IFRS 9. Instead, it is accounted for as an executory contract (unless the entity irrevocably designates it as measured at fair value through profit or loss in accordance with IFRS 9: para. 2.5).

3.3 Initial recognition

Financial instruments should be recognised in the statement of financial position when the entity becomes a party to the **contractual provisions of the instrument** (IFRS 9: Chapter 3, para. 3.1.1).

Point to note

An important consequence of this is that all derivatives should be in the statement of financial position.

Notice that this is **different** from the recognition criteria in the *Conceptual Framework* and in most other standards. Items are normally recognised when there is a probable inflow or outflow of resources and the item has a cost or value that can be measured reliably.

3.4 Example: initial recognition

An entity has entered into two separate contracts:

(a) A firm commitment (an order) to buy a specific quantity of iron.

(b) A forward contract to buy a specific quantity of iron at a specified price on a specified date, provided delivery of the iron is not taken.

Contract (a) is a **normal trading contract**. The entity does not recognise a liability for the iron until the goods have actually been delivered. (Note that this contract is not a financial instrument because it involves a physical asset, rather than a financial asset.)

Contract (b) is a **financial instrument**. Under IFRS 9, the entity recognises a financial liability (an obligation to deliver cash) on the **commitment date**, rather than waiting for the closing date on which the exchange takes place.

Note that planned future transactions, no matter how likely, are not assets and liabilities of an entity – the entity has not yet become a party to the contract.

3.5 Derecognition of financial assets 6/12

Derecognition is the removal of a previously recognised financial instrument from an entity's statement of financial position (IFRS 9: Chapter 3, paras. 3.2.3 to 3.2.6).

An entity should derecognise a **financial asset** when:

(a) The **contractual rights** to the cash flows from the financial asset **expire**, or

(b) The entity **transfers the financial asset or substantially all the risks and rewards of ownership** of the financial asset to another party.

IFRS 9 gives **examples of where an entity has transferred substantially all the risks and rewards of ownership**. These include:

(a) An unconditional sale of a financial asset

(b) A sale of a financial asset together with an option to repurchase the financial asset at its fair value at the time of repurchase

The standard also **provides examples of situations where the risks and rewards of ownership have not been transferred**:

(a) A sale and repurchase transaction where the repurchase price is a fixed price or the sale price plus a lender's return

(b) A sale of a financial asset together with a total return swap that transfers the market risk exposure back to the entity

(c) A sale of short-term receivables in which the entity guarantees to compensate the transferee for credit losses that are likely to occur

It is possible for only **part** of a financial asset or liability to be derecognised. This is allowed if the part comprises:

(a) Only specifically identified cash flows; or
(b) Only a fully proportionate (pro rata) share of the total cash flows.

For example, if an entity holds a bond it has the right to two separate sets of cash inflows: those relating to the principal and those relating to the interest. It could sell the right to receive the interest to another party while retaining the right to receive the principal.

On derecognition, the amount to be included in net profit or loss for the period is calculated as follows.

Formula to learn

	$	$
Carrying amount (measured at the date of derecognition) allocated to the part derecognised		X
Less consideration received for the part derecognised (including any new asset obtained less any new liability assumed)	X	
		(X)
Difference to profit or loss		X

The following flowchart, taken from the appendix to the standard (IFRS 9: AG, Appendix B, para. 3.2.1), will help you decide whether, and to what extent, a financial asset is derecognised.

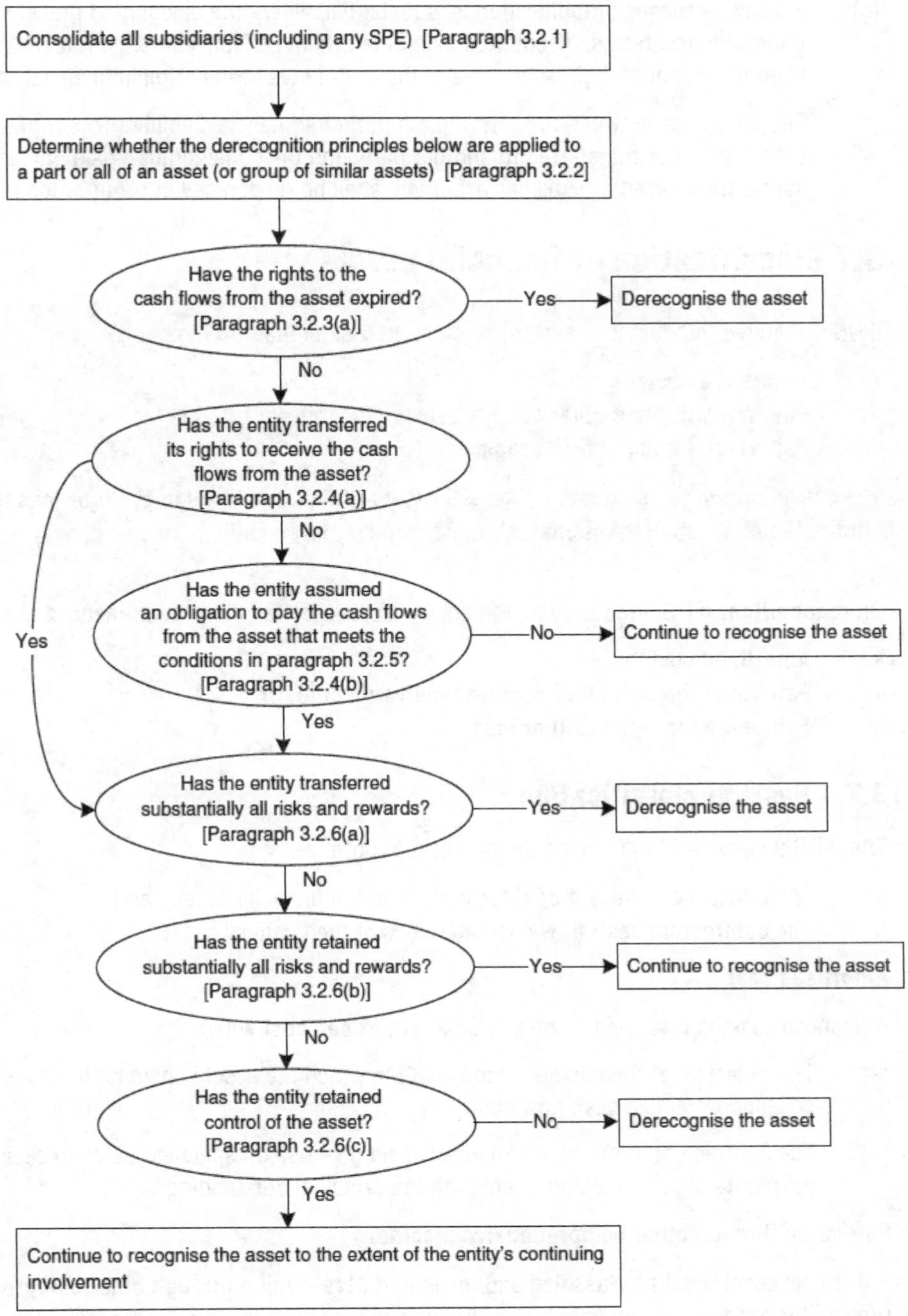

Source: IFRS 9 Application Guidance

3.6 Derecognition of financial liabilities

A financial liability is derecognised **when it is extinguished** – ie when the obligation specified in the contract is discharged or cancelled or expires (IFRS 9: Chapter 3, para. 3.3.1).

(a) Where an existing borrower and lender of debt instruments exchange one financial instrument for another with substantially different terms, this is accounted for as an extinguishment of the original financial liability and the recognition of a new financial liability.

(b) Similarly, a substantial modification of the terms of an existing financial liability or a part of it should be accounted for as an extinguishment of the original financial liability and the recognition of a new financial liability.

(c) For this purpose, a modification is 'substantial' where the discounted present value of cash flows under the new terms, discounted using the original effective interest rate, is at least 10% different from the discounted present value of the cash flows of the original financial liability.

(d) The difference between the carrying amount of a financial liability (or part of a financial liability) extinguished or transferred to another party and the consideration paid, including any non-cash assets transferred or liabilities assumed, shall be recognised in profit or loss.

3.7 Classification of financial assets 6/12

FAST FORWARD

IFRS 9 requires that financial assets are **classified as measured** at either:

- **Amortised cost**, or
- **Fair value through other comprehensive income,** or
- **Fair value through profit or loss**

There is an **option to designate** a financial asset **at fair value through profit or loss** to **reduce or eliminate an 'accounting mismatch'** (measurement or recognition inconsistency).

On **recognition,** IFRS 9 requires that financial assets are **classified as measured** at either:

- **Amortised cost**, or
- **Fair value through other comprehensive income,** or
- **Fair value through profit or loss**

3.7.1 Basis of classification

The IFRS 9 classification is made on the basis of both:

(a) The **entity's business model** for managing the financial assets, and
(b) The **contractual cash flow** characteristics of the financial asset.

Amortised cost

A financial asset is classified as measured at **amortised cost** where:

(a) The objective of the business model within which the asset is held is to hold assets in order to collect contractual cash flows and

(b) The contractual terms of the financial asset give rise on specified dates to cash flows that are solely payments of principal and interest on the principal outstanding.

Fair value through other comprehensive income

A financial asset **must** be classified and measured **at fair value through other comprehensive income** (unless the asset is designated at fair value through profit or loss under the fair value option) if it meets both the following criteria:

(a) The financial asset is held within a business model whose objective is achieved by both collecting contractual cash flows and selling financial assets.

(b) The contractual terms of the financial asset give rise on specified dates to cash flows that are solely payments of principal and interest on the principal amount outstanding.

Fair value through profit or loss

All other debt instruments must be measured at **fair value through profit or loss.**

Fair value through profit or loss option to avoid an 'accounting mismatch'

Even if an instrument meets the above criteria for measurement at amortised cost or fair value through other comprehensive income, IFRS 9 allows such financial assets to be **designated, at initial recognition, as being measured at fair value through profit or loss if a recognition or measurement inconsistency** (an 'accounting mismatch') would **otherwise arise** from measuring assets or liabilities or recognising the gains and losses on them on different bases.

Equity instruments

Equity instruments may not be classified as measured at amortised cost and must be measured at fair value. This is because contractual cash flows on specified dates are not a characteristic of equity instruments. However, if an equity instrument is **not held for trading**, an entity can make an **irrevocable election** at initial recognition to measure it at **fair value through other comprehensive income** with only dividend income recognised in profit or loss.

This is **different from the treatment of debt instruments**, where the **fair value through other comprehensive income classification is mandatory** for assets meeting the criteria, unless the fair value option through profit or loss option is chosen.

(IFRS 9: Chapter 4, paras. 4.1.1 and 4.1.2)

3.7.2 Business model test in more detail (IFRS 9: AG, paras. B4.1.1 to B4.1.26)

IFRS 9 introduces a business model test that requires an entity to assess whether its **business objective for a debt instrument is to collect the contractual cash flows of the instrument as opposed to realising its fair value change from sale prior to its contractual maturity**. Note the following key points:

(a) The assessment of a 'business model' is not made at an individual financial instrument level.

(b) The assessment is based on how key management personnel actually manage the business, rather than management's intentions for specific financial assets.

(c) An entity may have more than one business model for managing its financial assets and the classification need not be determined at the reporting entity level. For example, it may have one portfolio of investments that it manages with the objective of collecting contractual cash flows and another portfolio of investments held with the objective of trading to realise changes in fair value. It would be appropriate for entities like these to carry out the assessment for classification purposes at portfolio level, rather than at entity level.

(d) Although the objective of an entity's business model may be to hold financial assets in order to collect contractual cash flows, the entity need not hold all of those assets until maturity. Thus an entity's business model can be to hold financial assets to collect contractual cash flows even when sales of financial assets occur.

3.7.3 Business model test examples: collecting contractual cash flows

(IFRS 9: AG, paras. B4.1.1 to B4.1.26)

The following examples, from the Application Guidance to IFRS 9, are of situations where the objective of an entity's business model may be to hold financial assets to collect the contractual cash flows.

Example 1

A Co holds investments to collect their contractual cash flows but would sell an investment in particular circumstances, perhaps to fund capital expenditure, or because the credit rating of the instrument falls below that required by A Co's investment policy.

Analysis

Although A Co may consider, among other information, the financial assets' fair values from a liquidity perspective (ie the cash amount that would be realised if A Co needs to sell assets), A Co's objective is to hold the financial assets and collect the contractual cash flows. Some sales would not contradict that objective. If sales became frequent, A Co might be required to reconsider whether the sales were consistent with an objective of collecting contractual cash flows.

Example 2

B Co has a business model with the objective of originating loans to customers and subsequently to sell those loans to a securitisation vehicle. The securitisation vehicle issues instruments to investors.

B Co, the originating entity, controls the securitisation vehicle and thus consolidates it. The securitisation vehicle collects the contractual cash flows from the loans and passes them on to its investors in the vehicle.

It is assumed for the purposes of this example that the loans continue to be recognised in the consolidated statement of financial position because they are not derecognised by the securitisation vehicle.

Analysis

The consolidated group originated the loans with the objective of holding them to collect the contractual cash flows.

However, B Co has an objective of realising cash flows on the loan portfolio by selling the loans to the securitisation vehicle, so for the purposes of its separate financial statements it would not be considered to be managing this portfolio in order to collect the contractual cash flows.

Example 3

C Co's business model is to purchase portfolios of financial assets, such as loans. Those portfolios may or may not include financial assets that are credit impaired. If payment on the loans is not made on a timely basis, C Co attempts to extract the contractual cash flows through various means – for example, by contacting the debtor through mail, telephone, and so on.

In some cases, C Co enters into interest rate swaps to change the interest rate on particular financial assets in a portfolio from a floating interest rate to a fixed interest rate.

Analysis

The objective of C Co's business model is to hold the financial assets and collect the contractual cash flows. The entity does not purchase the portfolio to make a profit by selling them.

The same analysis would apply even if C Co does not expect to receive all of the contractual cash flows (eg some of the financial assets are credit impaired at initial recognition).

Moreover, the fact that C Co has entered into derivatives to modify the cash flows of the portfolio does not in itself change C Co's business model.

3.7.4 Contractual cash flow test in more detail

The requirement in IFRS 9 to assess the contractual cash flow characteristics of a financial asset is based on the concept that **only instruments with contractual cash flows of principal and interest on principal may qualify for amortised cost measurement**. By interest, IFRS 9 means consideration for the time value of money and the credit risk associated with the principal outstanding during a particular period of time.

Question — **Contractual cash flows**

Would an investment in a convertible loan qualify to be measured at amortised cost under IFRS 9?

Answer

No, because of the inclusion of the conversion option which is not deemed to represent payments of principal and interest

Measurement at amortised cost is permitted when the cash flows on a loan are entirely fixed (eg a fixed interest rate loan or zero coupon bond), or where interest is floating (eg a GBP loan where interest is contractually linked to GBP LIBOR), or combination of fixed and floating (eg where interest is LIBOR plus a fixed spread).

3.7.5 Examples of instruments that pass the contractual cash flows test

The following instruments satisfy the IFRS 9 criteria.

(a) A variable rate instrument with a stated maturity date that permits the borrower to choose to pay three-month LIBOR for a three-month term or one-month LIBOR for a one-month term

(b) A fixed term variable market interest rate bond where the variable interest rate is capped

(c) A fixed term bond where the payments of principal and interest are linked to an unleveraged inflation index of the currency in which the instrument is issued

3.7.6 Examples of instruments that do not pass the contractual cash flows test

The following instruments do not satisfy the IFRS 9 criteria.

(a) A bond that is convertible into equity instruments of the issuer (see question above)
(b) A loan that pays an inverse floating interest rate (eg 8% minus LIBOR)

3.7.7 Business model test examples: both collecting contractual cash flows and selling financial assets

The following examples, from the Application Guidance to IFRS 9, are of situations where the objective of an entity's business model is achieved by both collecting contractual cash flows and selling financial assets.

Example 4

D Co expects to incur capital expenditure in a few years' time. D Co invests its excess cash in short and long-term financial assets so that it can fund the expenditure when the need arises. Many of the financial assets have contractual lives that exceed D Co's anticipated investment period.

D Co will hold financial assets to collect the contractual cash flows and, when an opportunity arises, it will sell financial assets to re-invest the cash in financial assets with a higher return.

The remuneration of the managers responsible for the portfolio is based on the overall return generated by the portfolio.

Analysis

The objective of the business model is achieved by **both collecting contractual cash flows and selling financial assets.** D Co decides on an ongoing basis whether collecting contractual cash flows or selling financial assets will maximise the return on the portfolio until the need arises for the invested cash.

Question

Business model objective

E Co expects to pay a cash outflow in ten years to fund capital expenditure and invests excess cash in short-term financial assets. When the investments mature, E Co reinvests the cash in new short-term financial assets. E Co maintains this strategy until the funds are needed, at which time E Co uses the proceeds from the maturing financial assets to fund the capital expenditure. Only sales that are insignificant in value occur before maturity (unless there is an increase in credit risk).

Required

How is the business model of E Co achieved under IFRS 9?

Answer

The objective of E Co's business model is to hold financial assets to collect contractual cash flows. Selling financial assets is only incidental to E Co's business model.

Example 5

F Bank holds financial assets to meet its everyday liquidity needs. The bank actively manages the return on the portfolio in order to minimise the costs of managing those liquidity needs. That return consists of collecting contractual payments as well as gains and losses from the sale of financial assets.

To this end, F Bank holds financial assets to collect contractual cash flows and sells financial assets to reinvest in higher yielding financial assets or to better match the duration of its liabilities. In the past, this strategy has resulted in frequent sales activity and such sales have been significant in value. This activity is expected to continue in the future.

Analysis

The objective of the business model is to maximise the return on the portfolio to meet everyday liquidity needs and F Bank achieves that objective by **both collecting contractual cash flows and selling financial assets.** In other words, **both collecting contractual cash flows and selling financial assets are integral** to achieving the business model's objective.

(IFRS 9: AG, paras. B4.1.1 to B4.1.26)

3.8 Classification of financial liabilities

On **recognition**, IFRS 9 requires that financial assets are **classified as measured** at either:

(a) At **fair value through profit or loss**, or
(b) Financial liabilities at **amortised cost**.

A financial liability is classified at fair value through profit or loss if:

(a) It is **held for trading**, or

(b) Upon initial recognition it is **designated at fair value through profit or loss**. This is permitted when it results in more relevant information because:

 (i) It eliminates or significantly reduces a measurement or recognition inconsistency ('accounting mismatch'), or

 (ii) It is a group of financial liabilities or financial assets and liabilities and its performance is evaluated on a fair value basis, in accordance with a documented risk management or investment strategy.

Derivatives are **always measured at fair value through profit or loss.**

(IFRS 9: Chapter 4, paras. 4.4.1 and 4.4.2)

3.9 Re-classification of financial assets

Although on initial recognition financial instruments must be classified in accordance with the requirements of IFRS 9, in some cases they may be subsequently reclassified. IFRS 9 requires that **when an entity changes its business model for managing financial assets, it should reclassify all affected financial assets.** This reclassification applies only to debt instruments, as equity instruments must be classified as measured at fair value (IFRS 9: Chapter 4, paras. 4.4.1 and 4.4.2).

The application guidance to IFRS 9 includes examples of circumstances when a reclassification is required or is not permitted (IFRS 9: AG, paras. B4.4.1 to 4.4.3).

3.9.1 Examples: Reclassification permitted

Reclassification is permitted in the following circumstances, because a **change in the business model** has taken place:

(a) An entity has a portfolio of commercial loans that it holds to sell in the short term. The entity acquires a company that manages commercial loans and has a business model that holds the loans in order to collect the contractual cash flows. The portfolio of commercial loans is no longer for sale, and the portfolio is now managed together with the acquired commercial loans and all are held to collect the contractual cash flows.

(b) A financial services firm decides to shut down its retail mortgage business. That business no longer accepts new business and the financial services firm is actively marketing its mortgage loan portfolio for sale.

3.9.2 Examples: Reclassification not permitted

Reclassification is **not permitted** in the following circumstances, because a **change in the business model has not taken place**.

(a) A change in intention related to particular financial assets (even in circumstances of significant changes in market conditions)

(b) A temporary disappearance of a particular market for financial assets

(c) A transfer of financial assets between parts of the entity with different business models.

- Reclassification of financial liabilities is not permitted.
- Reclassification of equity instruments is not permitted. Investments in equity instruments are always held at fair value and any election to measure them at fair value through other comprehensive income is an irrevocable one.

3.9.3 Gains and losses on reclassification of financial assets

If a financial asset is reclassified **from amortised cost to fair value**, any **gain or loss** arising from a difference between the previous carrying amount and fair value is **recognised in profit or loss.**

If a financial asset is reclassified **from fair value to amortised cost, fair value** at the date of reclassification becomes the **new carrying amount.**

3.10 Section summary

- **All financial assets** and **liabilities** should be **recognised in the statement of financial position**, including derivatives.
- Financial assets should be derecognised when the **rights to the cash flows** from the asset **expire** or where **substantially all the risks and rewards of ownership are transferred** to another party.
- Financial liabilities should be derecognised when they are **extinguished.**
- On **recognition,** IFRS 9 requires that financial assets are **classified as measured** at either:
  - **Amortised cost**, or
  - **Fair value through other comprehensive income,** or
  - **Fair value through profit or loss**

4 Measurement of financial instruments 6/11 – 12/16

Exam focus point

IFRS 9 has been examined in part for several years now, but the sections on impairment and hedging are relatively recent, so these areas are likely to be tested.

FAST FORWARD

Financial assets should initially be measured at **cost = fair value**.

Transaction costs increase this amount for financial assets classified as measured at amortised cost, or where an irrevocable election has been made to take all gains and losses through other comprehensive income and **decrease this amount for financial liabilities** classified as measured at amortised cost.

Subsequent measurement of both financial assets and financial liabilities depends on how the instrument is classified: at amortised cost or fair value.

4.1 Initial measurement: financial assets

Financial instruments are initially measured at the transaction price, that is the **fair value** of the consideration given (IFRS 9: Chapter 5, para. 5.1.1).

An **exception** is where part of the consideration given is for something other than the financial asset. In this case the financial asset is initially measured at fair value evidenced by a quoted price in an active market for an identical asset (ie an IFRS 13 level 1 input) or based on a valuation technique that uses only data from observable markets. The difference between the fair value at initial recognition and the transaction price is recognised as a gain or loss.

In the case of financial assets classified as measured at **amortised cost**, **transaction costs** directly attributable to the acquisition of the financial asset are **added** to this amount.

4.2 Initial measurement: financial liabilities

IFRS 9 requires that financial liabilities are initially measured at transaction price, ie the fair value of consideration received except where part of the consideration received is for something other than the financial liability. In this case the financial liability is initially measured at fair value measured as for financial assets (see above). Transaction costs are deducted from this amount for financial liabilities classified as measured at amortised cost (IFRS 9: Chapter 5, para. 5.5.1).

4.3 Subsequent measurement of financial assets

Under IFRS 9, financial assets are measured subsequent to recognition either at:

- At **amortised cost,** using the **effective interest method**, or
- At **fair value through other comprehensive income,** or
- At **fair value through profit or loss**

(IFRS 9: Chapter 5, para. 5.2.1)

4.4 Financial assets measured at amortised cost

Key terms

Amortised cost of a financial asset or financial liability is the amount at which the financial asset or liability is measured at initial recognition minus principal repayments, plus or minus the cumulative amortisation using the **effective interest method** of any difference between that initial amount and the maturity amount and, for financial assets, adjusted for any **loss allowance**.

The **effective interest method** is a method of calculating the amortised cost of a financial instrument and of allocating the interest income or interest expense over the relevant period.

The **effective interest rate** is the rate that exactly discounts estimated future cash payments or receipts through the expected life of the financial instrument to the net carrying amount of the financial asset or liability. *(IFRS 9)*

4.5 Example: Financial asset at amortised cost

On 1 January 20X1 Abacus Co purchases a debt instrument for its fair value of $1,000. The debt instrument is due to mature on 31 December 20X5. The instrument has a principal amount of $1,250 and the instrument carries fixed interest at 4.72% that is paid annually. (The effective interest rate is 10%.)

How should Abacus Co account for the debt instrument over its five year term?

Solution

Abacus Co will receive interest of $59 (1,250 × 4.72%) each year and $1,250 when the instrument matures.

Abacus must allocate the discount of $250 and the interest receivable over the five year term at a constant rate on the carrying amount of the debt. To do this, it must apply the effective interest rate of 10%.

The following table shows the allocation over the years:

Year	Amortised cost at beginning of year	Profit or loss: Interest income for year (@10%)	Interest received during year (cash inflow)	Amortised cost at end of year
	$	$	$	$
20X1	1,000	100	(59)	1,041
20X2	1,041	104	(59)	1,086
20X3	1,086	109	(59)	1,136
20X4	1,136	113	(59)	1,190
20X5	1,190	119	(1,250 + 59)	–

Each year the carrying amount of the financial asset is increased by the interest income for the year and reduced by the interest actually received during the year.

Investments whose **fair value cannot be reliably measured** should be measured at **cost**.

4.6 Financial assets measured at fair value

Where a financial asset is classified as measured at fair value, fair value is established at each period end in accordance with IFRS 13 *Fair value measurement.* That standard requires that a fair value hierarchy is applied with three levels of input (IFRS 13: paras. 76, 81, 86):

Level 1 inputs. Unadjusted quoted prices in active markets for identical assets or liabilities that the entity can access at the measurement date.

Level 2 inputs. Inputs other than quoted prices included within Level 1 that are observable for the asset or liability, either directly or indirectly. These may include quoted prices for similar assets or liabilities in active markets or quoted prices for identical or similar assets and liabilities in markets that are not active.

Level 3 inputs. Unobservable inputs for the asset or liability.

Any changes in fair value are normally recognised in profit or loss.

There are three **exceptions** to this rule:

(a) The asset is **part of a hedging relationship** (see Section 6).

(b) The financial asset is an investment in an **equity instrument not held for trading.** In this case the entity can make an **irrevocable election** to recognise changes in the fair value in **other comprehensive income**.

(c) It is a **financial asset measured at fair value through other comprehensive income** because it meets the criteria in 3.7.1 above, that is the financial asset is held within a business model whose objective is achieved by both collecting contractual cash flows and selling financial assets.

Note that direct costs of acquisition are capitalised only in the case of a financial asset or financial liability **not** held at fair value through profit or loss If the asset or liability is held at fair value through profit or loss, the costs of acquisition are expensed. This means that in the case of **financial assets held at amortised cost, costs of acquisition are capitalised.** They would be added to the asset and deducted from the liability amount. Similarly, if an **irrevocable election** has been made to take **gains and losses** on the financial asset **to other comprehensive income,** costs of acquisition should be **added to the purchase cost.**

4.7 Example: Asset measurement

On 8 February 20X8 Orange Co acquires a quoted investment in the shares of Lemon Co with the intention of holding it in the long term. The investment cost $850,000. At Orange Co's year end of 31 March 20X8, the market price of an identical investment is $900,000. How is the asset initially and subsequently measured?

Orange Co has elected to recognise changes in the fair value of the equity investment in other comprehensive income.

Solution

- The asset is initially recognised at the fair value of the consideration, being $850,000
- At the period end it is re-measured to $900,000
- This results in the recognition of $50,000 in other comprehensive income

Question — **Equity instrument and transaction costs**

In January 20X6 Wolf purchased 10 million $1 listed equity shares in Hall at a price of $5 per share. Transaction costs were $3m. Wolf's year end is 30 November.

At 30 November 20X6, the shares in Hall were trading at $6.50. On 31 October 20X6 Wolf received a dividend from Hall of 20c per share.

Show the financial statement extracts of Wolf at 30 November 20X6 relating to the investment in Hall on the basis that:

(i) The shares were bought for trading.

(ii) The shares were bought as a source of dividend income and were the subject of an irrevocable election at initial recognition to recognise them at fair value through other comprehensive income.

Answer

(i)

STATEMENT OF PROFIT OR LOSS AND OTHER COMPREHENSIVE INCOME (EXTRACT)

	$m
Profit or loss for the year	
Investment income (10m × (6.5 – 5.0))	15
Dividend income (10m × 20c)	2
Transaction costs	(3)

STATEMENT OF FINANCIAL POSITION (EXTRACT)

Investments in equity instruments (10m × 6.5)	65

(ii)

STATEMENT OF PROFIT OR LOSS AND OTHER COMPREHENSIVE INCOME (EXTRACT)

	$m
Profit or loss for the year	
Dividend income	2
Other comprehensive income	
Gain on investment in equity instruments	15

STATEMENT OF FINANCIAL POSITION (EXTRACT)

Investments in equity instruments (10m × 6.5)	65

4.7.1 Subsequent measurement of financial liabilities

After initial recognition, all financial liabilities should be measured at **amortised cost**, with the exception of financial liabilities at fair value through profit or loss (including most derivatives). These should be measured at **fair value**, but where the fair value **is not capable of reliable measurement**, they should be measured at **cost** (IFRS 9: Chapter 5, para. 5.3.1).

4.8 Financial liabilities measured at amortised cost

The definitions of amortised cost, effective interest method and effective interest rate that are used for measurement of financial assets are also used for financial liabilities.

4.9 Example: Financial liability at amortised cost

Galaxy Co issues a bond for $503,778 on 1 January 20X2. No interest is payable on the bond, but it will be redeemed on 31 December 20X4 for $600,000. The effective interest rate of the bond is 6%.

Required

Calculate the charge to profit or loss of Galaxy Co for the year ended 31 December 20X2 and the balance outstanding at 31 December 20X2.

Solution

The bond is a 'deep discount' bond and is a financial liability of Galaxy Co. It is measured at amortised cost. Although there is no interest as such, the difference between the initial cost of the bond and the price at which it will be redeemed is a finance cost. This must be allocated over the term of the bond at a constant rate on the carrying amount.

The effective interest rate is 6%.

The charge to profit or loss for the year is $30,226 (503,778 × 6%)

The balance outstanding at 31 December 20X2 is $534,004 (503,778 + 30,226)

Question — **Finance cost 1**

On 1 January 20X3 Deferred issued $600,000 loan notes. Issue costs were $200. The loan notes do not carry interest, but are redeemable at a premium of $152,389 on 31 December 20X4. The effective finance cost of the debentures is 12%.

What is the finance cost in respect of the loan notes for the year ended 31 December 20X4?

A $72,000
B $76,194
C $80,613
D $80,640

Answer

C The premium on redemption of the preferred shares represents a finance cost. The effective rate of interest must be applied so that the debt is measured at amortised cost.

At the time of issue, the loan notes are recognised at their net proceeds of $599,800 (600,000 – 200).

The finance cost for the year ended 31 December 20X4 is calculated as follows:

	B/f	*Interest @ 12%*	*C/f*
	$	$	$
20X3	599,800	71,976	671,776
20X4	671,776	80,613	752,389

Question — Finance cost 2

On 1 January 20X1, an entity issued a debt instrument with a coupon rate of 3.5% at a par value of $6,000,000. The directly attributable costs of issue were $120,000. The debt instrument is repayable on 31 December 20X7 at a premium of $1,100,000.

What is the total amount of the finance cost associated with the debt instrument?

A $1,470,000
B $1,590,000
C $2,570,000
D $2,660,600

Answer

D

	$
Issue costs	120,000
Interest ($6,000,000 - 120) × 3.5% × 7	1,440,600
Premium on redemption	1,100,000
Total finance cost	2,660,600

Question — Classification

During the financial year ended 28 February 20X5, MN issued the two financial instruments described below. For *each* of the instruments, identify whether it should be classified as debt or equity, **explaining in not more than 40 words each** the reason for your choice. In each case you should refer to the relevant International Financial Reporting Standard.

(i) Redeemable preference shares with a coupon rate 8%. The shares are redeemable on 28 February 20X9 at premium of 10%.

(ii) A grant of share options to senior executives. The options may be exercised from 28 February 20X8.

Answer

(i) **Debt.** The preference shares require regular distributions to the holders but more importantly have the debt characteristic of being redeemable. Therefore, according to IAS 32 *Financial instruments: Presentation* they must be classified as debt.

(ii) **Equity.** According to IFRS 2 *Share based payment* the grant of share options must be recorded as equity in the statement of financial position. It is an alternative method of payment to cash for the provision of the services of the directors.

Question — Hybrid financial instrument

On 1 January 20X1, EFG issued 10,000 5% convertible bonds at their par value of $50 each. The bonds will be redeemed on 1 January 20X6. Each bond is convertible at the option of the holder at any time during the five-year period. Interest on the bond will be paid annually in arrears.

The prevailing market interest rate for similar debt without conversion options at the date of issue was 6%.

At what value should the equity element of the hybrid financial instrument be recognised in the financial statements of EFG at the date of issue?

Answer

Top tip. The method to use here is to find the present value of the principal value of the bond, $500,000 (10,000 × $50) and the interest payments of $25,000 annually (5% × $500,000) at the market rate for non-convertible bonds of 6%, using the discount factor tables. The difference between this total and the principal amount of $500,000 is the equity element.

	$
Present value of principal $500,000 × 0.747	373,500
Present value of interest $25,000 × 4.212	105,300
Liability value	478,800
Principal amount	500,000
Equity element	21,200

Question

Subsequent measurement

After initial recognition, all financial liabilities should be measured at amortised cost.

True ☐ False ☐

Answer

False. Some may be measured at fair value through profit or loss.

4.10 Financial liabilities at fair value through profit or loss

Financial liabilities which are held for trading are re-measured to fair value each year in accordance with IFRS 13 *Fair value measurement* (see Section 4.6) with any gain or loss recognised in profit or loss (IFRS 9: Chapter 5, para. 5.7.1).

4.10.1 Exceptions

The exceptions to the above treatment of financial liabilities are:

(a) It is part of a hedging arrangement (see Section 6).

(b) It is a financial liability designated as at fair value through profit or loss and the entity is required to present the effects of changes in the liability's **credit risk** in other comprehensive income (see 4.10. 2 below).

4.10.2 Credit risk

IFRS 9 requires that financial liabilities which are **designated as measured at fair value through profit or loss are treated differently**. In this case the gain or loss in a period must be classified into:

- Gain or loss **resulting from credit risk**, and
- **Other** gain or loss.

This provision of IFRS 9 was in response to an anomaly regarding changes in the credit risk of a financial liability.

Changes in a financial liability's credit risk affect the fair value of that financial liability. This means that when an entity's creditworthiness deteriorates, the fair value of its issued debt will decrease (and *vice versa*). For financial liabilities measured using the fair value option, this causes **a gain (or loss) to be recognised in profit or loss for the year**. For example:

STATEMENT OF PROFIT OR LOSS AND OTHER COMPREHENSIVE INCOME (EXTRACT)
PROFIT OR LOSS FOR THE YEAR

Liabilities at fair value (except derivatives and liabilities held for trading)	$'000
Change in fair value	100
Profit (loss) for the year	100

Many users of financial statements found this result to be **counter-intuitive** and confusing. Accordingly, IFRS 9 requires the gain or loss as a result of credit risk to be recognised in other comprehensive income, unless it creates or enlarges an **accounting mismatch** (see 4.10.4), in which case it is recognised in profit or loss. The other gain or loss (not the result of credit risk) is recognised in profit or loss.

On derecognition any gains or losses recognised in other comprehensive income are **not** transferred to **profit or loss**, although the cumulative gain or loss may be transferred within equity.

4.10.3 Example of IFRS 9 presentation

STATEMENT OF PROFIT OR LOSS AND OTHER COMPREHENSIVE INCOME (EXTRACT)
PROFIT OR LOSS FOR THE YEAR

Liabilities at fair value (except derivatives and liabilities held for trading)	$'000
Change in fair value not attributable to credit risk	90
Profit (loss) for the year	90
OTHER COMPREHENSIVE INCOME (NOT RECLASSIFIED TO PROFIT OR LOSS)	
Fair value loss on financial liability attributable to change in credit risk	10
Total comprehensive income	100

4.10.4 Accounting mismatch

The new guidance allows the recognition of the full amount of change in the fair value in the profit or loss only if the recognition of changes in the liability's **credit risk** in other comprehensive income would **create** or **enlarge** an **accounting mismatch** in profit or loss. That determination is made at initial recognition and is not reassessed (IFRS 9: Chapter 4, para. 4.1.5).

An accounting mismatch is a measurement or recognition **inconsistency** arising from measuring assets or liabilities or recognising the gains or losses on them on different bases.

4.11 Impairment of financial assets

FAST FORWARD

The impairment model in IFRS 9 is based on the premise of providing for **expected losses.**

Key term

Credit-impaired financial asset. A financial asset is credit impaired when one or more events have occurred that have a detrimental impact on the estimated future cash flows of that financial asset. *(IFRS 9: Appendix A)*

The following are indications that a financial asset or group of assets may be impaired (IFRS 9: Appendix A).

(a) Significant financial difficulty of the issuer

(b) A breach of contract, such as a default in interest or principal payments

(c) The lender granting a concession to the borrower that the lender would not otherwise consider, for reasons relating to the borrower's financial difficulty

(d) It becomes probable that the borrower will enter bankruptcy

(e) The disappearance of an active market for that financial asset because of financial difficulties

(f) The purchase or origination of a financial asset at a deep discount that reflects the incurred credit losses

It is not always possible to single out one particular event; rather, several events may combine to cause an asset to become credit-impaired.

4.12 Expected credit loss model

The impairment model in IFRS 9 is based on the premise of providing for **expected losses.** The financial statements should reflect the general pattern of deterioration or improvement in the credit quality of financial instruments within the scope of IFRS 9. This is a **forward-looking** impairment model (IFRS 9: Chapter 5, para. 5.5.2).

4.12.1 Background

IAS 39, the forerunner of IFRS 9, used **an 'incurred loss' model** for the impairment of financial assets. This model assumed that all loans would be repaid there was until evidence to the contrary, that is until the occurrence of an event that triggers an impairment indicator. Only at this point was the impaired loan written down to a lower value. The global financial crisis led to criticism of this approach for many reasons, including that it leads to an **overstatement of interest revenue** in the periods prior to the occurrence of a loss event, and produces deficient information.

In a 2009 ED *Amortised cost and impairment*, the IASB proposed to remedy this by measuring expected credit losses through adjusting the effective interest rate of a financial instrument. The IASB issued an Exposure Draft Supplement with revised proposals in January 2011, both based on recognition of 'expected' rather than 'incurred' credit losses. Feedback on both Exposure Drafts was that the proposed methodologies would be difficult to apply in practice.

In March 2013 the IASB issued a third set of proposals for impairment of financial assets following feedback on the earlier Exposure Draft and Exposure Draft Supplement. The proposals in this Exposure Draft formed the basis of the IFRS 9 impairment model.

4.12.2 Objective of the IFRS 9 impairment model

The objective of the IFRS 9 impairment model is to recognise expected credit losses for all financial instruments within the scope of the requirements. Expected credit losses are defined (IFRS 9 Appendix A) as the expected shortfall in contractual cash flows. An entity should estimate expected credit losses considering past events, current conditions and reasonable and supportable forecasts.

The IASB believes that this will provide users of financial statements with **more useful and timely information.**

4.12.3 Key definitions

The following definitions are important in understanding this section, and you should refer back to them when studying this material.

Key terms

Credit loss. The expected shortfall in contractual cash flows.

Expected credit losses. The weighted average of credit losses with the respective risks of a default occurring as the weights.

Lifetime expected credit losses. The expected credit losses that result from all possible default events over the expected life of a financial instrument.

Past due. A financial asset is past due when a counterparty has failed to make a payment when that payment was contractually due. *(IFRS 9: Appendix A)*

Purchased or originated credit-impaired financial asset. Purchased or originated financial asset(s) that are credit impaired on initial recognition. *(IFRS 9: Appendix A)*

4.12.4 Scope

IAS 39 was criticised for treating the impairment of different items in different ways. Under IFRS 9, the same impairment model applies to the following (IFRS 9: Chapter 2, para. 2.2).

(a) Financial assets measured at amortised cost

(b) Financial assets mandatorily measured at fair value through other comprehensive income

(c) Loan commitments when there is a present obligation to extend credit (except where these are measured at fair value through profit or loss)

(d) Financial guarantee contracts to which IFRS 9 is applied (except those measured at fair value through profit or loss)

(e) Lease receivables within the scope of IFRS 16 *Leases*; and

(f) Contract assets within the scope of IFRS 15 *Revenue from contracts with customers* (ie rights to consideration following transfer of goods or services)

4.12.5 Basic principle behind the model

The **financial statements should reflect the general pattern of deterioration or improvement in the credit quality of financial instruments** within the scope of the model.

IFRS 9 requires entities to base their measurement of expected credit losses on **reasonable and supportable information** that is available **without undue cost or effort.** This will include **historical, current and forecast information.**

Expected credit losses are **updated at each reporting date** for new information and changes in expectations, even if there has not been a significant increase in credit risk.

4.12.6 On initial recognition

The entity must **create a credit loss allowance/provision equal to twelve months' expected credit losses.** This is calculated by **multiplying the probability of a default occurring in the next twelve months by the total lifetime expected credit losses that would result from that default** (IFRS 9: Chapter 5, para. 5.5.1). (This is not the same as the expected cash shortfalls over the next twelve months.)

The intention is that the amount recognised on initial recognition acts as a proxy for the initial expectation of credit losses that are factored into the pricing of the instrument, which do not represent an economic loss to an entity because they are expected when pricing the instrument.

4.12.7 Subsequent years

If the **credit risk increases** significantly since initial recognition this amount will be replaced **by lifetime expected credit losses** (IFRS 9: Chapter 5, para. 5.5.2). If the credit quality subsequently improves and the lifetime expected credit losses criterion is no longer met, the twelve-month expected credit loss basis is reinstated (IFRS 9: Chapter 5, para. 5.5.3).

4.12.8 Rebuttable presumption: provide if 30 days past due

There is a rebuttable presumption that lifetime expected losses should be provided for if contractual cash flows are 30 days past due (overdue) (IFRS 9: Chapter 5, para. 5.5.11).

4.12.9 Financial instruments with low credit risk

Certain financial instruments have a low credit risk and would not, therefore, meet the lifetime expected credit losses criterion. Entities do not recognise lifetime expected credit losses for financial instruments that are equivalent to 'investment grade', which means that the asset has a low risk of default (IFRS 9: AG, para. B5.5.22).

4.12.10 Amount of impairment

The amount of the impairment to be recognised on these financial instruments **depends on whether or not they have significantly deteriorated** since their initial recognition (IFRS 9: Chapter 5, para. 5.5.3 and 5.5.10).

Stage 1 Financial instruments whose credit quality has not significantly deteriorated since their initial recognition

Stage 2 Financial instruments whose credit quality has significantly deteriorated since their initial recognition

Stage 3 Financial instruments for which there is objective evidence of an impairment as at the reporting date

For stage 1 financial instruments, the impairment represents the present value of expected credit losses that will result if a default occurs in the 12 months after the reporting date **(12 months expected credit losses).**

For financial instruments classified as stage 2 or 3, an impairment is recognised at the present value of expected credit shortfalls over their remaining life **(lifetime expected credit loss).** Entities are required to reduce the gross carrying amount of a financial asset in the period in which they no longer have a reasonable expectation of recovery.

4.12.11 Interest

For **stage 1 and 2** instruments interest revenue would be calculated on their **gross carrying amounts** (IFRS 9: Chapter 5, para. 5.4.1).

Interest revenue for **stage 3** financial instruments would be recognised on a **net basis** (ie after deducting expected credit losses from their carrying amount) (IFRS 9: Chapter 5, para. 5.4.1).

4.12.12 Summary

The following table gives a useful summary of the process.

	Stage 1 ⇨	Stage 2 ⇨	Stage 3
When?	Initial recognition (and subsequently if no significant deterioration in credit risk)	Credit risk increases significantly (rebuttable presumption if > 30 days past due)	Objective evidence of impairment exists at the reporting date
Credit losses recognised	12-month expected credit losses	Lifetime expected credit losses	Lifetime expected credit losses
Calculation of effective interest	On gross carrying amount	On gross carrying amount	On carrying amount net of allowance for credit losses after date evidence exists

4.12.13 Measuring expected credit losses

Credit losses are the present value of all cash shortfalls. Expected credit losses are an estimate of credit losses over the life of the financial instrument. An entity should consider the following when measuring expected credit losses (IFRS 9: Chapter 5, para. 5.5.17).

(a) The **probability-weighted outcome.** Expected credit losses should not be a best or worst-case scenario, but should reflect the possibility that a credit loss will occur, and the possibility that it will not.

(b) The **time value of money:** they should be discounted at the reporting date.

(c) **Reasonable and supportable information** that is available without undue cost or effort, including information about past events, current conditions and forecasts of future conditions. A 'crystal ball' is not required.

4.12.14 Example: portfolio of mortgages and personal loans

Credito Bank operates in South Zone, a region in which clothing manufacture is a significant industry. The bank provides personal loans and mortgages in the region. The average loan to value ratio for all its mortgage loans is 75%.

All loan applicants are required to provide information regarding the industry in which they are employed. If the application is for a mortgage, the customer must provide the postcode of the property which is to serve as collateral for the mortgage loan.

Credito Bank applies the expected credit loss impairment model in IFRS 9 *Financial instruments.* The bank tracks the probability of customer default by reference to overdue status records. In addition, it is required to consider forward-looking information as far as that information is available.

Credito Bank has become aware that a number of clothing manufacturers are losing revenue and profits as a result of competition from abroad, and that several are expected to close.

Required

How should Credito Bank apply IFRS 9 to its portfolio of mortgages in the light of the changing situation in the clothing industry?

Solution

Credito Bank should segment the mortgage portfolio to identify borrowers who are employed by suppliers and service providers to the clothing manufacturers. This segment of the portfolio may be regarded as being 'in Stage 2', that is having a significant increase in credit risk. Lifetime credit losses must be recognised.

In estimating lifetime credit losses for the mortgage loans portfolio, Credito Bank will take into account amounts that will be recovered from the sale of the property used as collateral. This may mean that the lifetime credit losses on the mortgages are very small even though the loans are in Stage 2.

Question **Particular defaults identified**

Later in the year, more information emerged, and Credito Bank was able to identify the particular loans that defaulted or were about to default.

Required

How should Credito Bank treat these loans?

Answer

The loans are now in Stage 3. Lifetime credit losses should continue to be recognised, and interest revenue should switch to a net interest basis, that is on the carrying amount net of allowance for credit losses.

4.12.15 Undrawn facilities

Under IFRS 9, the 'three stage' expected credit loss model also applies to the undrawn portions of overdraft, credit card and other approved but undrawn facilities.

Stage	Apply to	Recognise
Stage 1 – No significant increase in credit risk	Expected portion to be drawn down within the next 12 months	12 months expected credit losses
Stage 2 – Significant increase in credit risk	Expected portion to be drawn down over the remaining life of the facility	Lifetime credit losses

Question — **Undrawn overdraft facilities**

Debita Bank applies the expected credit loss impairment model of IFRS 9. At 30 September 20X4, the bank approved a total of $10 million overdraft facilities which have not yet been drawn.

Debita Bank considers that $8 million is in Stage 1 (ie, no significant increase in credit risk). Of that $8 million in Stage 1, $4 million is expected to be drawn down within the next 12 months, with a 3% probability of default over the next 12 months.

Debita Bank considers that $2 million is in Stage 2 and $2 million is expected be drawn down over the remaining life of the facilities, with a probability of default of 10%.

Required

Calculate the additional allowance required in respect of the undrawn overdraft facilities, taking account of the above information.

Answer

Stage		*Expected credit loss*
		$
Stage 1	$4 million × 3%	120,000
Stage 2	$2 million × 10%	200,000
		320,000

Under the IFRS 9 model, Debita bank would recognise an additional allowance of $320,000 for the undrawn portion of its overdraft facilities.

4.12.16 Recognition of impairment

In all three cases credit losses would be recognised in **profit or loss** and held in a **separate allowance account** (although this would not be required to be shown separately on the face of the statement of financial position). Where the expected credit losses relate to a **loan commitment or financial guarantee contract** a **provision** rather than allowance would be made (IFRS 9: Chapter 5, para. 5.5.5).

4.12.17 Adjustment of loss allowance

Entities must recognise in profit or loss, as an impairment gain or loss, the amount of expected credit losses (or reversal) that is required to adjust the loss allowance at the reporting date to the amount that is required to be recognised in accordance with IFRS 9 (IFRS 9: Chapter 5, para. 5.5.8).

4.12.18 Presentation

(a) With the exception of investments in debt measured at fair value through OCI, for all three stages, credit losses are recognised in **profit or loss** and held in a **separate allowance account** which is **offset against the carrying amount of the asset**.

(b) For investments in debt measured at fair value through OCI, the **portion** in the fall in fair value relating to **credit losses** should be recognised in **profit or loss** with the **remainder** being recognised in **other comprehensive income**. No allowance account is needed because the financial asset is already carried at fair value (automatically reduced for any fall in value including credit losses).

(IFRS 9: Chapter 5, para. 5.5.8)

4.12.19 Simplified approach for trade and lease receivables

For trade receivables that **do not have an IFRS 15 financing element**, the loss allowance is measured at the **lifetime expected credit losses**, from initial recognition.

For **other** trade receivables and for lease receivables, the entity can **choose** (as a separate accounting policy for trade receivables and for lease receivables) to apply the 3 Stage approach or to recognise an allowance for lifetime expected credit losses from initial recognition.

(IFRS 9: Chapter 5, para. 5.5.15)

4.12.20 Example: trade receivable provision matrix

On 1 June 20X4, Kredco sold goods on credit to Detco for $200,000. Detco has a credit limit with Kredco of 60 days. Kredco applies IFRS 9, and uses a pre-determined matrix for the calculation of allowances for receivables as follows.

Days overdue	*Expected loss provision*
Nil	1%
1 to 30	5%
31 to 60	15%
61 to 90	20%
90 +	25%

Detco had not paid by 31 July 20X4, and so failed to comply with its credit term, and Kredco learned that Detco was having serious cash flow difficulties due to a loss of a key customer. The finance controller of Detco has informed Kredco that they will receive payment.

Ignore sales tax.

Required

Show the accounting entries on 1 June 20X4 and 31 July 20X4 to record the above, in accordance with the expected credit loss model in IFRS 9.

Solution

On 1 June 20X4

The entries in the books of Kredco will be:

DEBIT Trade receivables	$200,000	
CREDIT Revenue		$200,000

Being initial recognition of sales

An expected credit loss allowance, based on the matrix above, would be calculated as follows:

DEBIT	Expected credit losses	$2,000	
CREDIT	Allowance for receivables		$2,000

Being expected credit loss: $200,000 × 1%
On 31 July 20X4

Applying Kredco's matrix, Detco has moved into the 5% bracket, because it has exhausted its 60-day credit limit. (Note that this does not equate to being 60 days overdue!) Despite assurances that Kredco will receive payment, the company should still increase its credit loss allowance to reflect the increased credit risk. Kredco will therefore record the following entries on 31 July 20X4

DEBIT	Expected credit losses	$8,000	
CREDIT	Allowance for receivables		$8,000

Being expected credit loss: $200,000 × 5% – $2,000

Question — Trade receivables provision matrix

Redblack Co has a customer base consisting of a large number of small clients. At 30 June 20X4, it has a portfolio of trade receivables of $60 million. Redblack applies IFRS 9, using a provision matrix to determine the expected credit losses for the portfolio. The provision matrix is based on its historical observed default rates, adjusted for forward looking estimates. The historical observed default rates are updated at every reporting date.

At 30 June 20X4, Redblack estimates the following provision matrix.

	Expected default rate	*Gross carrying amount*	*Credit loss allowance Default rate × gross carrying amount*
		$'000	$'000
Current	0.3%	30,000	90
1 to 30 days overdue	1.6%	15,000	240
31 to 60 days overdue	3.6%	8,000	288
61 to 90 days overdue	6.6%	5,000	330
More than 90 days overdue	10.6%	2,000	212
		60,000	1,160

At 30 June 20X5, Redblack has a portfolio of trade receivables of $68 million. The company revises its forward looking estimates and the general economic conditions are deemed to be less favourable than previously thought. The partially competed provision matrix is as follows.

	Expected default rate	*Gross carrying amount*
		$'000
Current	0.5%	32,000
1 to 30 days overdue	1.8%	16,000
31 to 60 days overdue	3.8%	10,000
61 to 90 days overdue	7%	7,000
More than 90 days overdue	11%	3,000
		68,000

Required

Complete the provision matrix for Redblack at 30 June 20X5 and show the journal entries to record the credit loss allowance.

Answer

	Expected default rate	Gross carrying amount	Credit loss allowance Default rate × gross carrying amount
		$'000	$'000
Current	0.5%	32,000	160
1 to 30 days overdue	1.8%	16,000	288
31 to 60 days overdue	3.8%	10,000	380
61 to 90 days overdue	7%	7,000	490
More than 90 days overdue	11%	3,000	330
		68,000	1,648

The credit loss allowance has increased by $488,000 to $1,648,000 as at 30 June 20X5. The journal entry at 30 June 20X5 would be:

DEBIT	Expected credit losses	$488,000	
CREDIT	Allowance for receivables		$488,000

Being expected credit loss

4.12.21 Purchased or originated credit-impaired financial assets

IFRS 9 requires that purchased or originated credit-impaired financial assets are treated differently because the asset is credit-impaired at initial recognition. For these assets, an entity **must recognise changes in lifetime expected losses since initial recognition as a loss allowance with any changes recognised in profit or loss**. Under the requirements**, any favourable changes** for such assets are an impairment gain even if the resulting expected cash flows of a financial asset exceed the estimated cash flows on initial recognition (IFRS 9: Chapter 5, para. 5.5.13).

4.12.22 Disclosures

IFRS 9 requires (by way of amendments to IFRS 7) **extensive disclosures** with emphasis on **information that identifies and explains the amounts in the financial statements that arise from expected losses** and the **effect of deterioration and improvement in the credit risk** of financial instruments.

The disclosures must be provided either in the financial statements or by way of a cross reference to other statements, such as a risk report, available to users at the same time as the financial statements.

Disclosures include a reconciliation, a description of inputs and assumptions used to measure expected credit losses, and information about the effects of the deterioration and improvement in the credit risk of financial instruments.

4.12.23 Possible effects

Possible effects of the new model include the following.

(a) It is likely that this model will result in **earlier recognition of credit losses** than under the current incurred loss model because it requires the recognition not only of credit losses that have already occurred, but also losses that are expected in the future. However, in the case of shorter term and higher-quality financial instruments the effects may not be significant.

(b) The new model will require significantly **more judgment** when considering information related to the past, present and future. It relies on more forward-looking information, which means that any losses would be accounted for earlier than happens under the current rules.

(c) **Costs** of implementing the new model are likely to be material.

(d) There are differences between the IASB and the FASB approach which may lead to significant **differences** in the figures reported

4.13 Section summary

- On initial recognition, **financial assets** are measured at **the fair value of the consideration given. Financial liabilities** are measured at the **fair value of the consideration received.** *(IFRS 9)*
- Subsequent measurement depends on how a financial asset is **classified. Financial assets and financial liabilities** are classified at **amortised cost** or at **fair value.**
- Financial instruments at **fair value through profit or loss** are measured at **fair value**; gains and losses are recognised in **profit or loss.**
- Financial assets held within a business model whose objective is achieved by **both collecting contractual cash flows** and selling financial assets **must** be measured at **fair value** with gains and losses recognised in **other comprehensive income.**
- If an **investment in equity instruments is not held for trading**, the entity **may** make an **irrevocable election** to recognise changes in the fair value in **other comprehensive income.**
- Financial instruments at **amortised cost** are measured using the **effective interest method.**
- **Impairment of financial assets** is governed by an **expected loss model, which recognises expected credit losses for all financial instruments subject to impairment accounting.**

5 Embedded derivatives

FAST FORWARD

An **embedded derivative** is a derivative instrument that is combined with a non-derivate **host contract** to form a single hybrid instrument.

Certain contracts that are not themselves derivatives (and may not be financial instruments) include derivative contracts that are 'embedded' within them. These non-derivatives are called **host contracts.**

Key term

An **embedded derivative** is a derivative instrument that is combined with a non-derivative host contract to form a single hybrid instrument. *(IFRS 9: Appendix A)*

5.1 Examples of host contracts

Possible examples include:

(a) A lease
(b) A debt or equity instrument
(c) An insurance contract
(d) A sale or purchase contract
(e) A construction contract

5.2 Examples of embedded derivatives

Possible examples include:

(a) A bond which is redeemable in five years' time with part of the redemption price being based on the increase in the FTSE 100 Index.

'Host' contract	Bond	⇨	Accounted for as normal (amortised cost)
Embedded derivative	Option on equities	⇨	Treat as derivative, ie remeasured to FV with changes recognised in P/L

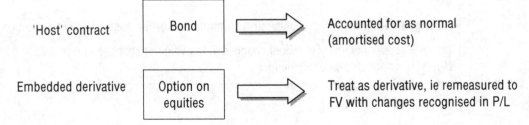

(b) A construction contract priced in a foreign currency. The construction contract is a non-derivative contract, but the changes in foreign exchange rate is the embedded derivative.

5.3 Accounting treatment of embedded derivatives

5.3.1 Financial asset host contract

Where the host contract is a financial asset within the scope of the standard, the classification and **measurement rules of the standard are applied to the entire hybrid contract**.

This is a simplification of the IAS 39 rules, and different from the treatment of financial liability host contracts (see below).

(IFRS 9: Chapter 4, paras. 4.3.2 to 4.3.4)

5.3.2 Other host contracts

Where the host contract is not a financial asset within the scope of IFRS 9, the standard requires that an embedded derivative be **separated from its host contract** and accounted for as a derivative when the following conditions are met.

(a) The economic characteristics and risks of the embedded derivative are not closely related to the economic characteristics and risks of the host contract.

(b) A separate instrument with the same terms as the embedded derivative would meet the definition of a derivative.

(c) The hybrid (combined) instrument is not measured at fair value with changes in fair value recognised in the profit or loss (a derivative embedded in a financial liability need not be separated out if the entity holds the combined instrument at fair value through profit or loss).

5.4 Section summary

- Where the host contract is **an asset within the scope of IFRS 9** the hybrid contract is accounted for as **one instrument**.
- **Otherwise**, IFRS 9 requires that the embedded derivative is **separated from the host contract** where certain conditions are met and accounted for separately.

6 Hedging

FAST FORWARD

Hedging is allowed in certain strictly defined circumstances.

6.1 Introduction

IFRS 9 **requires hedge accounting** where there is a **designated hedging relationship** between a hedging instrument and a hedged item. It is **prohibited otherwise**.

Key terms

Hedging, for accounting purposes, means designating one or more hedging instruments so that their change in fair value is an offset, in whole or in part, to the change in fair value or cash flows of a hedged item.

A **hedged item** is an asset, liability, firm commitment, or forecasted future transaction that:

(a) Exposes the entity to risk of changes in fair value or changes in future cash flows, and that
(b) Is designated as being hedged.

Key terms cont'd

A **hedging instrument** is a designated derivative or (in limited circumstances) another financial asset or liability whose fair value or cash flows are expected to offset changes in the fair value or cash flows of a designated hedged item. (A non-derivative financial asset or liability may be designated as a hedging instrument for hedge accounting purposes only if it hedges the risk of changes in foreign currency exchange rates.)

Hedge effectiveness is the degree to which changes in the fair value or cash flows of the hedged item attributable to a hedged risk are offset by changes in the fair value or cash flows of the hedging instrument. *(IFRS 9: Appendix 5)*

In simple terms, entities hedge to reduce their exposure to risk and uncertainty, such as changes in prices, interest rates or foreign exchange rates. Hedge accounting recognises hedging relationships by allowing (for example) losses on a hedged item to be offset against gains on a hedging instrument.

Generally only assets, liabilities etc that involve external parties can be designated as hedged items. The foreign currency risk of an intragroup monetary item (eg payable/receivable between two subsidiaries) may qualify as a hedged item in the group financial statements if it results in an exposure to foreign exchange rate gains or losses that are not fully eliminated on consolidation. This can happen (per IAS 21) when the transaction is between entities with different functional currencies.

In addition, the foreign currency risk of a highly probable group transaction may qualify as a hedged item if it is in a currency other than the functional currency of the entity and the foreign currency risk will affect profit or loss.

6.2 IFRS 9's new model for hedge accounting

The hedge accounting rules in IFRS 9's predecessor, IAS 39 *Financial instruments: recognition and measurement,* were criticised as being complex and not reflecting the entity's risk management activities, nor the extent to which they are successful. The IASB addressed these issues in IFRS 9 and the revised rules appear in the 2014 version of the standard.

6.2.1 Why change the hedge accounting requirements?

(a) **The IAS 39 provisions were not based on consistent principles.** The provisions were rules-based, which led to inconsistency and arbitrariness.

(b) **The IAS 39 rules did not provide sufficient information on risk management.** Increasingly users of financial statements have said that they wish to understand the risks that an entity faces, and the entity's strategy in managing those risks. Many believed that the IAS 39 requirements did not provide such an understanding.

(c) **The IAS 39 rules on hedging did not reflect risk management practice.** For example:

(i) **There were instances where hedge accounting cannot be applied to groups of items, whereas for risk management purposes, items are often hedged on a group basis**. One example of this is equities making up an index such as the FTSE 100. These have an apparent economic link, but under the IAS 39 rules they could not be grouped together for hedging purposes, because they did not have similar risk characteristics.

(ii) IAS 39 did not allow components of non-financial items to be hedged but entities usually hedge components of such items. For instance, an entity may wish to hedge the oil price component of the jet fuel price exposure by entering into a forward contract for crude oil. Under the IAS 39 rules, the entity could only hedge the price of jet fuel itself or the foreign currency risk.

(iii) IAS 39 did not allow net positions to be hedged. However, companies often hedge net positions. For example, they may hedge a net foreign exchange position of $60m that is made up of an asset of $200m and a liability of $140m.

(d) IAS 39's rules **were confusing and complex.**

(e) IAS 39's rules provided **insufficient disclosures** in the financial statements about an entity's risk management activities.

(f) IAS 39 permitted hedge accounting only if a hedge is highly effective, both prospectively and retrospectively. IAS 39 regarded a hedge as highly effective if the offset is within the range of 80 to 125%. This was a **purely quantitative test** and has been felt to be narrow and arbitrary.

6.2.2 Principles-based model

IFRS 9 contains a new, **principles based model** for hedge accounting that aims to **align accounting with risk management activities**. This will combine the following.

(a) A **management view**, that aims to use information produced internally for risk management purposes,

(b) An **accounting view** that seeks to address the risk management issue of the timing of recognition of gains and losses.

(c) An **objective-based assessment** for hedge effectiveness, replacing the somewhat arbitrary 80%-125% 'bright line' test of IAS 39.

6.3 Conditions for hedge accounting

Before a hedging relationship qualifies for hedge accounting, **all** of the following **conditions** must be met (IFRS 9: Chapter 6, para. 6.4.1).

(a) The hedging relationship consists **only of eligible hedging instruments and eligible hedged items**.

(b) There must be **formal documentation** (including identification of the hedged item, the hedging instrument, the nature of the risk that is to be hedged and how the entity will assess the hedging instrument's effectiveness in offsetting the exposure to changes in the hedged item's fair value or cash flows attributable to the hedged risk).

(c) The hedging relationship meets all of the following hedge effectiveness criteria

  (i) There is an **economic relationship** between the hedged item and the hedging instrument, ie the hedging instrument and the hedged item have values that generally move in the opposite direction because of the same risk, which is the hedged risk;

  (ii) The **effect of credit risk does not dominate the value** changes that result from that economic relationship, ie the gain or loss from credit risk does not frustrate the effect of changes in the underlyings on the value of the hedging instrument or the hedged item, even if those changes were significant; and

  (iii) The **hedge ratio of the hedging relationship** (quantity of hedging instrument vs quantity of hedged item) is the same as that resulting from the quantity of the hedged item that the entity **actually hedges** and the quantity of the hedging instrument that the entity **actually uses** to hedge that quantity of hedged item.

6.4 Example: Hedging

A company owns inventories of 20,000 gallons of oil which cost $400,000 on 1 December 20X3.

In order to hedge the fluctuation in the market value of the oil the company signs a futures contract to deliver 20,000 gallons of oil on 31 March 20X4 at the futures price of $22 per gallon.

The market price of oil on 31 December 20X3 is $23 per gallon and the futures price for delivery on 31 March 20X4 is $24 per gallon.

Required

Explain the impact of the transactions on the financial statements of the company:

(a) Without hedge accounting
(b) With hedge accounting

Solution

The futures contract was intended to protect the company from a fall in oil prices (which would have reduced the profit when the oil was eventually sold). However, oil prices have actually risen, so that the company has made a loss on the contract.

Without hedge accounting:

The futures contract is a derivative and therefore must be re-measured to fair value under IFRS 9. The loss on the futures contract is recognised in profit or loss:

DEBIT	Profit or loss (20,000 × 24 – 22)	$40,000	
CREDIT	Financial liability		$40,000

With hedge accounting:

The loss on the futures contract is recognised in the profit or loss as before.

The inventories are revalued to fair value:

	$
Fair value at 31 December 20X3 (20,000 × 23)	460,000
Cost	(400,000)
Gain	60,000

The gain is also recognised in profit or loss:

DEBIT	Inventory	$60,000	
CREDIT	Profit or loss		$60,000

The net effect on the profit or loss is a gain of $20,000 compared with a loss of $40,000 without hedging.

The **standard** identifies three types of **hedging relationship**.

Key terms

Fair value hedge: a hedge of the exposure to changes in fair value of a recognised asset or liability or an unrecognised firm commitment, or a component of any such item, that is attributable to a particular risk and could affect profit or loss.

Cash flow hedge: a hedge of the exposure to variability in cash flows that

(a) is attributable to a particular risk associated with all, or a component of, a recognised asset or liability (such as all or some future interest payments on variable-rate debt) or a highly probable forecast transaction, and

(b) Could affect profit or loss.

Hedge of a net investment in a foreign operation: IAS 21 defines a net investment in a foreign operation as the amount of the reporting entity's interest in the net assets of that operation. (*IFRS 9: Appendix A*)

The hedge in the example above is a **fair value hedge** (it hedges exposure to changes in the fair value of a recognised asset: the oil).

This is a highly controversial topic and therefore, likely to be examined, probably in Section B.

Exam focus point

Only **cash flow hedges** and **fair value hedges** are examinable at P2.

6.5 Accounting treatment

6.5.1 Fair value hedges

Hedging instrument

The **gain or loss** resulting from **re-measuring** the hedging instrument at fair value is **recognised in profit or loss**. However, **if** the hedging instrument hedges **an equity instrument** for which an entity has **elected** to present **changes in fair value in other comprehensive income**, then the **gain or loss** on the hedging instrument must be recognised in **other comprehensive income.**

Hedged item

The gain or loss on the hedged item attributable to the **hedged risk** should **adjust the carrying amount** of the hedged item and be **recognised in profit or loss**. If the hedged item is a **financial asset through other comprehensive income** (mandatory), the **gain or loss** on the hedged item is also **recognised through profit or loss.**

However, if the hedged item is an **investment in an equity instrument held at fair value through other comprehensive income**, the **gains and losses on both** the hedged investment and the hedging instrument will be **recognised in other comprehensive income**.

This ensures that hedges of investments of equity instruments held at fair value through other comprehensive income can be accounted for as hedges.

(IFRS 9: Chapter 6, para. 6.5.8)

6.5.2 Example: fair value hedge

On 1 July 20X6 Joules acquired 10,000 ounces of a material which it held in its inventory. This cost $200 per ounce, so a total of $2 million. Joules was concerned that the price of this inventory would fall, so on 1 July 20X6 he sold 10,000 ounces in the futures market for $210 per ounce for delivery on 30 June 20X7. On 1 July 20X6 the conditions for hedge accounting were all met.

At 31 December 20X6, the end of Joules' reporting period, the fair value of the inventory was $220 per ounce while the futures price for 30 June 20X7 delivery was $227 per ounce. On 30 June 20X7 the trader sold the inventory and closed out the futures position at the then spot price of $230 per ounce.

The IFRS 9 hedging criteria have been met.

Required

Set out the accounting entries in respect of the above transactions.

Solution

At 31 December 20X6 the increase in the fair value of the inventory was $200,000 (10,000 × ($220 – $200)) and the increase in the forward contract liability was $170,000 (10,000 × ($227 – $210)). The IFRS 9 hedge accounting criteria have been met, so hedge accounting was permitted.

	Debit	*Credit*
31 December 20X6	$	$
Profit or loss	170,000	
Financial liability		170,000
(To record the loss on the forward contract)		
Inventories	200,000	
Profit or loss		200,000
(To record the increase in the fair value of the inventories)		

At 30 June 20X7 the increase in the fair value of the inventory was another $100,000 (10,000 × ($230 – $220)) and the increase in the forward contract liability was another $30,000 (10,000 × ($230 – $227)).

	Debit	*Credit*
	$	$
30 June 20X7		
Profit or loss	30,000	
Financial liability		30,000
(To record the loss on the forward contract)		
Inventories	100,000	
Profit or loss		100,000

	Debit $	Credit $
(To record the increase in the fair value of the inventories)		
Profit or loss	2,300,000	
Inventories		2,300,000
(To record the inventories now sold)		
Cash	2,300,000	
Profit or loss – revenue		2,300,000
(To record the revenue from the sale of inventories)		
Financial liability	200,000	
Cash		200,000
(To record the settlement of the net balance due on closing the financial liability)		

Note that because the fair value of the material rose, Joules made a profit of only £100,000 on the sale of inventories. Without the forward contract, the profit would have been £300,000 (2,300,000 – 2,000,000). In the light of the rising fair value the trader might in practice have closed out the futures position earlier, rather than waiting until the settlement date.

6.5.3 Cash flow hedges

These hedge the risk of change in value of future cash flows from a recognised asset or liability (or highly probable forecast transaction) that could affect profit or loss, e.g. hedging a variable rate interest income stream. The hedging instrument is accounted for as follows:

(a) The portion of the gain or loss on the hedging instrument that is effective (i.e. up to the value of the loss or gain on cash flow hedged) is recognised in other comprehensive income ('items that may be reclassified subsequently to profit or loss') and the cash flow hedge reserve.

(b) Any excess is recognised immediately in profit or loss.

The amount that has been accumulated in the cash flow hedge reserve is then accounted for as follows:

(a) if a hedged forecast transaction subsequently results in the recognition of a non-financial asset or non-financial liability, the amount shall be removed from the cash flow reserve and be included directly in the initial cost or carrying amount of the asset or liability;

(b) for all other cash flow hedges, the amount shall be reclassified from other comprehensive income to profit or loss in the same period(s) that the hedged expected future cash flows affect profit or loss.

(IFRS 9: Chapter 6, para. 6.5.11)

6.5.4 Example: Cash flow hedge

Bets Co signs a contract on 1 November 20X1 to purchase an asset on 1 November 20X2 for €60,000,000. Bets reports in US$ and hedges this transaction by entering into a forward contract to buy €60,000,000 on 1 November 20X2 at US$1: €1.5.

Spot and forward exchange rates at the following dates are:

	Spot	*Forward (for delivery on 1.11.X2)*
1.11.X1	US$1: €1.45	US$1: €1.5
31.12.X1	US$1: €1.20	US$1: €1.24
1.11.X2	US$1: €1.0	US$1: €1.0 (actual)

The IFRS 9 hedging criteria have been met.

Required

Show the double entries relating to these transactions at 1 November 20X1, 31 December 20X1 and 1 November 20X2.

Solution

Entries at 1 November 20X1

The value of the forward contract at inception is zero so no entries recorded (other than any transaction costs), but risk disclosures will be made.

The contractual commitment to buy the asset would be disclosed if material (IAS 16).

Entries at 31 December 20X1

Gain on forward contract:

	$
Value of contract at 31.12.X1 (€60,000,000/1.24)	48,387,096
Value of contract at 1.11.X1 (€60,000,000/1.5)	40,000,000
Gain on contract	8,387,096

Compare to movement in value of asset (unrecognised):

Increase in $ cost of asset

(€60,000,000/1.20 – €60,000,000/1.45) $8,620,690

As this is higher, the hedge is deemed fully effective at this point:

DEBIT Financial asset (Forward a/c)	$8,387,096	
CREDIT Equity		$8,387,096

Entries at 1 November 20X2

Additional gain on forward contract

	$
Value of contract at 1.11.X2 (€60,000,000/1.0)	60,000,000
Value of contract at 31.12.X1 (€60,000,000/1.24)	48,387,096
Gain on contract	11,612,904

Compare to movement in value of asset (unrecognised):

Increase in $ cost of asset

(€60,000,000/1.0 – €60,000,000/1.2) $10,000,000

Therefore, the hedge is not fully effective during this period, but it still meets the IFRS 9 hedging criteria (and hence hedge accounting can be used):

DEBIT Financial asset (Forward a/c)	$11,612,904	
CREDIT Equity		$10,000,000
CREDIT Profit or loss		$1,612,904

Purchase of asset at market price

DEBIT Asset (€60,000,000/1.0)	$60,000,000	
CREDIT Cash		$60,000,000

Settlement of forward contract

DEBIT Cash	$20,000,000	
CREDIT Financial asset (Forward a/c)		$20,000,000

Realisation of gain on hedging instrument

The cumulative gain of $18,387,096 recognised in equity is removed from equity (the cash flow hedge reserve) and included directly in the initial cost of the asset.

6.5.5 Rebalancing hedging relationships

Rebalancing denotes adjustments to the designated quantities of the hedged item or the hedging instrument of an already existing hedging relationship for the purpose of maintaining a hedge ratio that complies with the hedge.

IFRS 9 requires rebalancing to be undertaken if the risk management objective remains the same, but the hedge effectiveness requirements are no longer met. Where the risk management objective for a hedging relationship has changed, rebalancing does not apply and the hedging relationship must be discontinued.

(IFRS 9: AG, paras. 6.5.7 to 6.5.21)

6.5.6 Discontinuing

An entity cannot voluntarily discontinue hedge accounting as it could under the old IAS 39. Under IFRS 9, an entity is **not allowed to discontinue hedge accounting where the hedging relationship still meets the risk management objective and continues to meet all other qualifying criteria.**

Hedge accounting should be discontinued only when the hedging relationship ceases to meet the qualifying criteria. This includes instances when the hedging instrument expires or is sold, terminated or exercised. Discontinuing hedge accounting can either affect a hedging relationship in its entirety, or only a part of it. If only part of the hedging relationship is affected, hedge accounting continues for the remainder of the hedging relationship.

(IFRS 9: Chapter 6, para. 6.5.6)

6.5.7 Premium paid for options

Under IFRS 9, **the part of an option that reflects time value premium should be treated as a cost of hedging**, which will be presented in other comprehensive income. This is intended to decrease inappropriate volatility in profit or loss and it should be more consistent with risk management practices.

Under IAS 39 the time value premium was treated as if it was a derivative held for trading purposes. This created volatility in profit or loss for the year. It did not reflect the way risk managers saw it: when hedging, risk managers viewed the time value premium paid as a cost of hedging rather than a speculative trading position.

(IFRS 9: Chapter 6, para. 6.5.15)

6.5.8 Forward element of forward contracts and foreign currency basis spreads

When an entity separates the forward element and the spot element of a forward contract and designates as the hedging instrument only the change in the value of the spot element, or when an entity excludes the foreign currency basis spread from a hedge the entity may recognise the change in value of the excluded portion in other comprehensive income. The change in value of the excluded portion will later be removed or reclassified from equity as a single amount or on an amortised cost basis (depending on the nature of the hedged item) and ultimately **recognised in profit or loss.**

(IFRS 9: Chapter 5, para. 6.5.16)

6.5.9 Hedges of a group of items

IFRS 9 **permits** the designation of a group of assets as a hedged item provided that the following **three conditions** are met.

(a) It consist of items that are eligible individually for hedging.

(b) The items in the group are managed together on a group basis for the purposes of risk management.

(c) In the case of a cash flow hedge of a group of items whose variabilities in cash flows are not expected to be approximately proportional to the overall variability in cash flows of the group so that offsetting risk positions arise:

   (i) It is a hedge of foreign currency risk, and

   (ii) The designation of that net position specifies the reporting period in which the forecast transactions are expected to affect profit or loss, as well as their nature and volume.

(IFRS 9: Chapter 6, para. 6.6.1)

6.5.10 Accounting for hedges of credit risk using credit derivatives

IFRS 9 **permits certain credit exposures to be designated at fair value through profit or loss** if a credit derivative that is measured at fair value through profit or loss is used to manage the credit risk of all, or a part of, the exposure on a fair value basis.

A credit exposure may be a financial instrument within or outside the scope of IFRS 9, for example, loan commitments, that is managed for credit risk. The designation would be permitted if both of the following apply.

(a) The name of the credit exposure matches the reference entity of the credit derivative.

(b) The seniority of the financial instrument matches that of the instruments that can be delivered in accordance with the credit derivative.

If the qualifying criteria are no longer met and the instrument is not otherwise required to be measured at fair value through profit or loss, the entity must discontinue measuring the financial instrument that gave rise to the credit risk at fair value through profit or loss.

(IFRS 9: Chapter 6, para. 6.7.1)

6.5.11 Option to use IAS 39 rules

The IASB will allow an accounting policy choice to apply either the IFRS 9 hedging model or the IAS 39 model, with an additional option to use IAS 39 for macro hedging (currently a separate project) if using IFRS 9 for general hedge accounting (IFRS 9: Chapter 7, para. 7.2.21).

6.5.12 Disclosures

IFRS 7 *Financial Instruments: Disclosures* is revised by IFRS 9.

Disclosures relating to hedging must be presented in a **single note** (or alternatively a **separate section**) of the financial statements. In that way, all the effects of hedging are seen together in detail in this note.

6.6 Section summary

- **Hedge accounting** means designating one or more instruments so that their change in fair value is **offset** by the change in fair value or cash flows of another item.
- **Hedge accounting** is permitted in certain circumstances, provided **the qualifying criteria are met.**
- There are three types of hedge: **fair value** hedge; **cash flow** hedge; hedge of a **net investment in a foreign operation**. Only the first two are examinable.
- The accounting treatment of a hedge **depends on its type**.

7 Disclosure of financial instruments 6/13

Exam focus point

Skim through for background only – disclosures will not be tested in detail.

FAST FORWARD

IFRS 7 specifies the **disclosures** required for financial instruments. The standard requires qualitative and quantitative disclosures about exposure to risks arising from financial instruments and specifies minimum disclosures about credit risk, liquidity risk and market risk.

The IASB maintains that users of financial instruments need information about an entity's exposures to risks and how those risks are managed, as this information can **influence a user's assessment of the financial position and financial performance of an entity** or of the amount, timing and uncertainty of its **future cash flows**.

There have been new techniques and approaches to measuring risk management, which highlighted the need for guidance.

Accordingly, IFRS 7 *Financial instruments: Disclosures* was issued in 2005.

7.1 General requirements

The extent of disclosure required depends on the extent of the entity's use of financial instruments and of its exposure to risk. It **adds to the requirements previously in IAS 32** by requiring:

(a) Enhanced statement of financial position and statement of profit or loss and other comprehensive income disclosures

(b) Disclosures about an allowance account when one is used to reduce the carrying amount of impaired financial instruments.

The standard requires **qualitative and quantitative disclosures about exposure to risks** arising from financial instruments, and specifies minimum disclosures about **credit risk**, **liquidity risk** and **market risk**.

7.2 Objective

The objective of the IFRS is to require entities to provide disclosures in their financial statements that enable users to evaluate:

(a) The significance of financial instruments for the entity's financial position and performance

(b) The nature and extent of risks arising from financial instruments to which the entity is exposed during the period and at the reporting date, and how the entity manages those risks.

The principles in IFRS 7 complement the principles for recognising, measuring and presenting financial assets and financial liabilities in IAS 32 *Financial instruments: Presentation* and IFRS 9 *Financial instruments.*

(IFRS 7: para. 1)

7.3 Classes of financial instruments and levels of disclosure

The entity must group financial instruments into classes **appropriate to the nature of the information disclosed**. An entity must decide in the light of its circumstances how much detail it provides. Sufficient information must be provided to permit reconciliation to the line items presented in the statement of financial position (IFRS 7: para. 6).

7.3.1 Statement of financial position

The following must be disclosed (IFRS 7: paras. 7 to 19).

(a) **Carrying amount** of financial assets and liabilities by IFRS 9 category.

(b) **Reason for any reclassification** between fair value and amortised cost (and *vice versa*).

(c) **Details** of the assets and exposure to risk where the entity has made a **transfer** such that part or all of the financial assets do not qualify for derecognition.

(d) The **carrying amount** of financial assets the entity has **pledged as collateral** for liabilities or contingent liabilities and the associated terms and conditions.

(e) When financial assets are impaired by credit losses and the entity records the impairment in a separate account (eg an **allowance account** used to record individual impairments or a similar account used to record a collective impairment of assets) rather than directly reducing the carrying amount of the asset, it must disclose a **reconciliation** of changes in that account during the period for each class of financial assets.

(f) The **existence of multiple embedded derivatives**, where compound instruments contain these.

(g) Defaults and breaches.

7.3.2 Statement of comprehensive income

The entity must disclose the following **items of income, expense, gains or losses**, either on the face of the financial statements or in the notes (IFRS 7: para. 20).

(a) Net gains/losses by IFRS 9 category (broken down as appropriate: eg interest, fair value changes, dividend income)

(b) Interest income/expense

(c) Impairments losses by class of financial asset

7.3.3 Other disclosures

Entities must disclose in the summary of **significant accounting policies** the measurement basis used in preparing the financial statements and the other accounting policies that are relevant to an understanding of the financial statements.

Hedge accounting

The following disclosures are required in respect of hedge accounting (IFRS 7: paras. 22 to 24).

(a) A **description** of each hedge, hedging instrument, and fair values of those instruments, and nature of risks being hedged

(b) For **cash flow hedges:**

   (i) The periods in which the cash flows are expected to occur, when they are expected to enter into the determination of profit or loss, and a description of any forecast transaction for which hedge accounting had previously been used but which is no longer expected to occur.

   (ii) If a gain or loss on a hedging instrument in a cash flow hedge has been recognised in other comprehensive income, an entity should disclose the following: [IAS 7.23].

   (iii) The amount that was so recognised in other comprehensive income during the period.

   (iv) The amount that was removed from equity and included in profit or loss for the period.

   (v) The amount that was removed from equity during the period and included in the initial measurement of the acquisition cost or other carrying amount of a non-financial asset or non- financial liability in a hedged highly probable forecast transaction.

(c) For **fair value hedges**, information about the fair value changes of the hedging instrument and the hedged item.

(d) **Hedge ineffectiveness recognised in profit and loss** (separately for cash flow hedges and hedges of a net investment in a foreign operation).

Fair value

IFRS 7 retains the following general requirements in relation to the disclosure of fair value for those financial instruments **measured at amortised cost** (IFRS 7: paras. 25 and 26):

(a) For each class of financial assets and financial liabilities an entity should disclose the **fair value of that class of assets and liabilities** in a way that permits it to be compared with its carrying amount.

(b) In disclosing fair values, an entity should group financial assets and financial liabilities into classes, but should **offset them only to the extent that their carrying amounts are offset in the statement of financial position.**

It also states that **disclosure of fair value is not required** where:

- Carrying amount is a reasonable approximation of fair value
- For investments in equity instruments that do not have a quoted market price in an active market for an identical instrument, or derivatives linked to such equity instruments

IFRS 13 (see Section 8) provides disclosure requirements in respect of the fair value of financial instruments **measured at fair values** (IFRS 13: para. 21, 23, 25 and 27). It requires that information is disclosed to help users assess:

(a) For assets and liabilities measured at **fair value after initial recognition, the valuation techniques and inputs used to develop those measurements**.

(b) For **recurring fair value measurements** (ie those measured at each period end) using significant unobservable (Level 3) inputs, the **effect of the measurements on profit or loss** or other comprehensive income for the period.

In order to achieve this, the following should be **disclosed as a minimum** for each class of financial assets and liabilities measured at fair value (asterisked disclosures are also required for financial assets and liabilities measured at amortised cost but for which fair value is disclosed).

(a) The fair value measurement at the end of the period.

(b) The level of the fair value hierarchy within which the fair value measurements are categorised in their entirety.

(c) For assets and liabilities measured at fair value at each reporting date (recurring fair value measurements), the amounts of any transfers between Level 1 and Level 2 of the fair value hierarchy and reasons for the transfers.

(d) For fair value measurements categorised within Levels 2 and 3 of the hierarchy, a description of the valuation techniques and inputs used in the fair value measurement, plus details of any changes in valuation techniques.

(e) For recurring fair value measurements categorised within Level 3 of the fair value hierarchy:

    (i) A reconciliation from the opening to closing balances.

    (ii) The amount of unrealised gains or losses recognised in profit or loss in the period and the line item in which they are recognised.

    (iii) A narrative description of the sensitivity of the fair value measurement to changes in unobservable inputs.

(f) For recurring and non-recurring fair value measurements categorised within Level 3 of the fair value hierarchy, a description of the valuation processes used by the entity.

(g) If the highest and best use of a non-financial asset differs from its current use, an entity shall disclose that fact and why the non-financial asset is being used in a manner that differs from its highest and best use.

An entity should also disclose its policy for determining when transfers between levels of the fair value hierarchy are deemed to have occurred.

7.3.4 Example: Fair value disclosures

For assets and liabilities measured at fair value at the end of the reporting period, the IFRS requires quantitative disclosures about the fair value measurements for each class of assets and liabilities. An entity might disclose the following for assets (adapted from IFRS 13: paras. 91 to 99):

	$'000	*Fair value measurements at the end of the reporting period using*		
Description	*31.12.X9*	*Level 1 inputs*	*Level 2 inputs*	*Level 3 inputs*
Trading equity securities	45	45		
Non-trading equity securities	32			32
Corporate securities	90	9	81	
Derivatives – interest rate contracts	78		78	
Total recurring fair value measurements	245	54	159	32

7.4 Nature and extent of risks arising from financial instruments

In undertaking transactions in financial instruments, an entity may assume or transfer to another party one or more of **different types of financial risk** as defined below. The disclosures required by the standard show the extent to which an entity is exposed to these different types of risk, relating to both recognised and unrecognised financial instruments (IFRS 7: paras. 36 to 39).

Credit risk	The risk that one party to a financial instrument will cause a financial loss for the other party by failing to discharge an obligation.
Currency risk	The risk that the fair value or future cash flows of a financial instrument will fluctuate because of changes in foreign exchange rates.
Interest rate risk	The risk that the fair value or future cash flows of a financial instrument will fluctuate because of changes in market interest rates.
Liquidity risk	The risk that an entity will encounter difficulty in meeting obligations associated with financial liabilities.
Loans payable	Loans payable are financial liabilities, other than short-term trade payables on normal credit terms.
Market risk	The risk that the fair value or future cash flows of a financial instrument will fluctuate because of changes in market prices. Market risk comprises three types of risk: **currency risk**, **interest rate risk** and **other price risk**.
Other price risk	The risk that the fair value or future cash flows of a financial instrument will fluctuate because of changes in market prices (other than those arising from **interest rate risk** or **currency risk**), whether those changes are caused by factors specific to the individual financial instrument or its issuer, or factors affecting all similar financial instruments traded in the market.
Past due	A financial asset is past due when a counterparty has failed to make a payment when contractually due.

7.4.1 Qualitative disclosures

For each type of risk arising from financial instruments, an entity must disclose (IFRS 7: para. 33):

(a) The **exposures to risk** and how they arise

(b) Its objectives, policies and processes for managing the risk and the methods used to measure the risk

(c) Any **changes** in (a) or (b) from the previous period

7.4.2 Quantitative disclosures

For each financial instrument risk, **summary quantitative data** about risk exposure must be disclosed. This should be based on the information provided internally to key management personnel. More information should be provided if this is unrepresentative (IFRS 7: paras. 34 to 38).

Information about **credit risk** must be disclosed by class of financial instrument:

(a) Maximum exposure at the year end

(b) Any collateral pledged as security

(c) In respect of the amount disclosed in (b), a description of collateral held as security and other credit enhancements

(d) Information about the credit quality of financial assets that are neither **past due** nor impaired

(e) Financial assets that are past due or impaired, giving an age analysis and a description of collateral held by the entity as security

(f) Collateral and other credit enhancements obtained, including the nature and carrying amount of the assets and policy for disposing of assets not readily convertible into cash

For **liquidity risk** entities must disclose:

(a) A maturity analysis of financial liabilities
(b) A description of the way risk is managed

Disclosures required in connection with **market risk** are:

(a) Sensitivity analysis, showing the effects on profit or loss of changes in each market risk

(b) If the sensitivity analysis reflects interdependencies between risk variables, such as interest rates and exchange rates the method, **assumptions and limitations** must be disclosed

7.5 Capital disclosures

Certain disclosures about **capital** are required. An entity's capital does not relate solely to financial instruments, but has more general relevance. Accordingly, those disclosures are included in IAS 1, rather than in IFRS 7.

8 Fair value measurement 6/12, 12/12, 6/15, 6/16

FAST FORWARD

IFRS 13 *Fair value measurement* gives extensive guidance on how the fair value of assets and liabilities should be established.

In 2011 the IASB published IFRS 13 *Fair value measurement.* The project arose as a result of the Memorandum of Understanding between the IASB and FASB (2006) reaffirming their commitment to the convergence of IFRSs and US GAAP. With the publication of IFRS 13, IFRS and US GAAP now have the same definition of fair value and the measurement and disclosure requirements are now aligned.

8.1 Objective

IFRS 13 sets out to:

(a) Define fair value
(b) Set out in a single IFRS a framework for measuring fair value
(c) Require disclosure about fair value measurements

(IFRS 13: para. 1)

8.2 Definitions

IFRS 13 defines fair value as '**the price that would be received to sell an asset or paid to transfer a liability in an orderly transaction between market participants at the measurement date**' (IFRS 3: Appendix A).

The previous definition used in IFRS was 'the amount for which an asset could be exchanged, or a liability settled, between knowledgeable, willing parties in an arm's length transaction'.

The price which would be received to sell the asset or paid to transfer (not settle) the liability is described as the 'exit price' and this is the definition used in US GAAP. Although the concept of the 'arm's length transaction' has now gone, the market-based current exit price retains the notion of an exchange between unrelated, knowledgeable and willing parties.

8.3 Scope

IFRS 13 applies when another IFRS requires or permits fair value measurements or disclosures. The measurement and disclosure requirements do not apply in the case of:

(a) Share-based payment transactions within the scope of IFRS 2 *Share-based payment*
(b) Leasing transactions within the scope of IFRS 16 *Leases*; and
(c) Net realisable value as in IAS 2 *Inventories* or value in use as in IAS 36 *Impairment of assets.*

Disclosures are not required for:

(a) Plan assets measured at fair value in accordance with IAS 19 *Employee benefits*

(b) Plan investments measured at fair value in accordance with IAS 26 *Accounting and reporting by retirement benefit plans*; and

(c) Assets for which the recoverable amount is fair value less disposal costs under IAS 36 *Impairment of assets*

(IFRS 13: paras. 5 to 7)

8.4 Measurement

Fair value is a market-based measurement, not an entity-specific measurement. It focuses on assets and liabilities and on exit (selling) prices. It also takes into account market conditions at the measurement date. In other words, it looks at the amount for which the holder of an asset could sell it and the amount which the holder of a liability would have to pay to transfer it. It can also be used to value an entity's own equity instruments.

Because it is a market-based measurement, fair value is measured using the assumptions that market participants would use when pricing the asset, taking into account any relevant characteristics of the asset.

It is assumed that the transaction to sell the asset or transfer the liability takes place either:

(a) In the **principal market** for the asset or liability; or
(b) In the absence of a principle market, in the **most advantageous** market for the asset or liability.

The principal market is the market which is the most liquid (has the greatest volume and level of activity) for that asset or liability. In most cases the principal market and the most advantageous market will be the same.

IFRS 13 acknowledges that when market activity declines an entity must use a valuation technique to measure fair value. In this case the emphasis must be on whether a transaction price is based on an **orderly transaction**, rather than a forced sale.

Fair value is **not adjusted for transaction costs.** Under IFRS 13, these are **not a feature of the asset or liability,** but may be taken into account when **determining the most advantageous market.**

Fair value measurements are based on an asset or a liability's **unit of account**, which is specified by each IFRS where a fair value measurement is required. For most assets and liabilities, the unit of account is the individual asset or liability, but in some instances may be a group of assets or liabilities.

(IFRS 13: para. B2)

8.4.1 Example: unit of account

A premium or discount on a large holding of the same shares (because the market's normal daily trading volume is not sufficient to absorb the quantity held by the entity) is not considered when measuring fair value: the quoted price per share in an active market is used.

However, a control premium is considered when measuring the fair value of a controlling interest, because the unit of account is the controlling interest. Similarly, any non-controlling interest discount is considered where measuring a non-controlling interest.

8.4.2 Example: principal or most advantageous market

An asset is sold in two active markets, Market X and Market Y, at $58 and $57, respectively. Valor Co does business in both markets and can access the price in those markets for the asset at the measurement date as follows.

	Market X	*Market Y*
	$	$
Price	58	57
Transaction costs	(4)	(3)
Transport costs (to transport the asset to that market)	(4)	(2)
	50	52

Remember that fair value is not adjusted for transaction costs. Under IFRS 13, these are not a feature of the asset or liability, but may be taken into account when determining the most advantageous market.

If Market X is the principal market for the asset (ie the market with the greatest volume and level of activity for the asset), the fair value of the asset would be $54, measured as the price that would be received in that market ($58) less transport costs ($4) and ignoring transaction costs.

If neither Market X nor Market Y is the principal market for the asset, Valor must measure the fair value of the asset using the price in the most advantageous market. The most advantageous market is the market that maximises the amount that would be received to sell the asset, after taking into account both transaction costs and transport costs (ie the net amount that would be received in the respective markets).

The maximum net amount (after deducting both transaction and transport costs) is obtainable in Market Y ($52, as opposed to $50). But this is not the fair value of the asset. The fair value of the asset is obtained by deducting transport costs but not transaction costs from the price received for the asset in Market Y: $57 less $2 = $55.

8.4.3 Non-financial assets

For non-**financial assets** the fair value measurement looks at the use to which the asset can be put. It takes into account the ability of a market participant to generate economic benefits by using the asset in its **highest and best** use (IFRS 13: paras. 27 to 29).

8.5 Valuation techniques

IFRS 13 states that valuation techniques must be those which are appropriate and for which sufficient data are available. Entities should maximise the use of relevant **observable inputs** and minimise the use of **unobservable inputs**.

The standard establishes a three-level hierarchy for the inputs that valuation techniques use to measure fair value:

Level 1 Quoted prices (unadjusted) in active markets for identical assets or liabilities that the reporting entity can access at the measurement date.

Level 2 Inputs other than quoted prices included within Level 1 that are observable for the asset or liability, either directly or indirectly, eg quoted prices for similar assets in active markets or for identical or similar assets in non active markets or use of quoted interest rates for valuation purposes.

Level 3 Unobservable inputs for the asset or liability, ie using the entity's own assumptions about market exit value.

(IFRS 13: paras. 61 to 66)

8.5.1 Valuation approaches

The IFRS identifies **three valuation approaches:**

(a) **Income approach.** Valuation techniques that convert future amounts (eg cash flows or income and expenses) to a single current (ie discounted) amount. The fair value measurement is determined on the basis of the value indicated by current market expectations about those future amounts.

(b) **Market approach.** A valuation technique that uses prices and other relevant information generated by market transactions involving identical or comparable (ie similar) assets, liabilities or a group of assets and liabilities, such as a business.

(c) **Cost approach.** A valuation technique that reflects the amount that would be required currently to replace the service capacity of an asset (often referred to as current replacement cost).

Entities may use more than one valuation technique to measure fair value in a given situation. A change of valuation technique is considered to be a change of accounting estimate in accordance with IAS 8, and must be disclosed in the financial statements.

(IFRS 13: paras. B5 to B11)

8.5.2 Examples of inputs used to measure fair value

	Asset or liability	Input
Level 1	Equity shares in a listed company	Unadjusted quoted prices in an active market
Level 2	Licencing arrangement arising from a business combination	Royalty rate in the contract with the unrelated party at inception of the arrangement
	Cash generating unit	Valuation multiple (eg a multiple of earnings or revenue or a similar performance measure) derived from observable market data, eg from prices in observed transactions involving comparable businesses
	Finished goods inventory at a retail outlet	Price to customers adjusted for differences between the condition and location of the inventory item and the comparable (ie similar) inventory items

	Asset or liability	Input
	Building held and used	Price per square metre for the derived from observable market data, eg prices in observed transactions involving comparable buildings in similar locations
Level 3	Cash generating unit	Financial forecast (eg of cash flows or profit or loss) developed using the entity's own data
	Three-year option on exchange-traded shares	Historical volatility, ie the volatility for the shares derived from the shares' historical prices
		Adjustment to a mid-market consensus (non-binding) price for the swap developed using data not directly observable or otherwise corroborated by observable market data

8.6 Measuring liabilities

Fair value measurement of a liability assumes that that liability is transferred at the measurement date to a market participant, who is then obliged to fulfill the obligation. The obligation is not settled or otherwise extinguished on the measurement date (IFRS 13: paras. 34, 42).

8.6.1 Entity's own credit risk

The fair value of a liability reflects the effect of **non-performance risk,** which includes but is not limited to **the entity's own credit risk.** This may be different for different types of liabilities.

8.6.2 Example: Entity's own credit risk

Black Co and Blue Co both enter into a legal obligation to pay $20,000 cash to Green Go in seven years.

Black Co has a top credit rating and can borrow at 4%. Blue Co's credit rating is lower and it can borrow at 8%.

Black Co will receive approximately $15,200 in exchange for its promise. This is the present value of $20,000 in seven years at 4%.

Blue Co will receive approximately $11,660in exchange for its promise. This is the present value of $20,000 in seven years at 8%.

8.7 IFRS 13 and business combinations

Fair value generally applies on a business combination. This topic is covered in Chapter 12, together with some further examples.

8.8 Disclosure

An entity must disclose information that helps users of its financial statements assess both of the following (IFRS 13: paras. 91 to 99):

(a) For assets and liabilities that are measured at fair value on a recurring or non-recurring basis, the valuation techniques and inputs used to develop those measurements.

(b) For recurring fair value measurements using significant **unobservable inputs** (Level 3), the effect of the measurements on profit or loss or other comprehensive income for the period. Disclosure requirements will include:

(i) Reconciliation from opening to closing balances
(ii) Quantitative information regarding the inputs used
(iii) Valuation processes used by the entity
(iv) Sensitivity to changes in inputs

Exam focus point

IFRS 13 is likely to be tested in the context of IFRS 9, but it has been tested in connection with other assets/scenarios, as in June 2015 and June 2016.

8.9 Was the project necessary?

The IASB is already considering the matter of the measurement basis for assets and liabilities in financial reporting as part of its *Conceptual Framework* project. It could therefore be argued that it was not necessary to have a separate project on fair value. The *Conceptual Framework* might have been the more appropriate forum for discussing **when** fair value should be used **as well as how to define and measure it.**

However, it has been argued that a concise definition and clear measurement framework is needed because there is so much inconsistency in this area, and this may form the basis for discussions in the *Conceptual Framework* project.

The IASB has also pointed out that the global financial crisis has highlighted the need for:

- Clarifying how to measure fair value when the market for an asset becomes less active; and
- Improving the transparency of fair value measurements through disclosures about measurement uncertainty.

8.9.1 Advantages and disadvantages of fair value (v historical cost)

Fair value

Advantages

- Relevant to users' decisions
- Consistency between companies
- Predicts future cash flows

Disadvantages

- Subjective (not reliable)
- Hard to calculate if no active market
- Time and cost
- Lack of practical experience/familiarity
- Less useful for ratio analysis (bias)
- Misleading in a volatile market

Historical cost

Advantages

- Reliable
- Less open to manipulation
- Quick and easy to ascertain
- Matching (cost and revenue)
- Practical experience & familiarity

Disadvantages

- Less relevant to users' decisions
- Need for additional measure of recoverable amounts (impairment test)
- Does not predict future cash flows

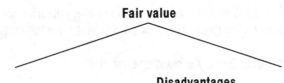

Chapter Roundup

- Financial instruments can be very complex, particularly **derivative instruments**, although **primary instruments** are more straightforward.
- The important definitions to learn are:
  - **Financial asset**
  - **Financial liability**
  - **Equity instrument**
- Financial instruments must be classified as **liabilities** or **equity** according to their **substance**.
- The critical feature of a financial liability is the **contractual obligation to deliver cash** or another financial asset.
- **Compound instruments** are split into **equity** and **liability** components and presented accordingly in the statement of financial position.
- **IFRS 9** ***Financial Instruments,*** issued in final form in July 2014, replaced ***IAS 39 Financial instruments: recognition and measurement.*** It will come into force on 1 January 2018.
- IFRS 9 requires that financial assets are **classified as measured** at either:
  - **Amortised cost**, or
  - **Fair value through other comprehensive income**, or
  - **Fair value through profit or loss**

  There is an **option to designate** a financial asset **at fair value through profit or loss** to **reduce or eliminate an 'accounting mismatch'** (measurement or recognition inconsistency).
- Financial assets should initially be measured at **cost** = **fair value**.

  Transaction costs increase this amount for financial assets classified as measured at amortised cost, or where an irrevocable election has been made to take all gains and losses through other comprehensive income and **decrease this amount for financial liabilities** classified as measured at amortised cost.

  Subsequent measurement of both financial assets and financial liabilities depends on how the instrument is classified: at amortised cost or fair value.
- The impairment model in IFRS 9 is based on the premise of providing for **expected losses.**
- An **embedded derivative** is a derivative instrument that is combined with a non-derivative **host contract** to form a single hybrid instrument.
- **Hedging** is allowed in certain strictly defined circumstances.
- **IFRS 7** specifies the **disclosures** required for financial instruments. The standard requires quantitative and qualitative disclosures about exposure to risks arising from financial instruments and specifies minimum disclosures about credit risk, liquidity risk and market risk.
- **IFRS 13** *Fair value measurement* gives extensive guidance on how the fair value of assets and liabilities should be established.

Quick Quiz

1 Which issues are dealt with by IAS 32?

2 What items are not financial instruments according to IAS 32?

3 What is the critical feature used to identify a financial liability?

4 How should compound instruments be presented in the statement of financial position?

5 When should a financial asset be de-recognised?

6 How are financial instruments initially measured?

7 How are financial assets measured under IFRS 9, subsequent to initial recognition?

8 When measuring expected credit losses under the IFRS 9 impairment model, entities should always consider the worst-case scenario? True or false?

9 How are embedded derivatives treated under IFRS 9?

10 What is hedging?

11 Name the three types of hedging relationship identified by IFRS 9.

12 Fill in the blanks:

In applying IFRS 13 *Fair value measurement*, entities should maximise the use of ________________ and minimise the use of ________________.

Answers to Quick Quiz

1 Classification and disclosure

2 Physical assets; prepaid expenses; non-contractual assets or liabilities; contractual rights not involving transfer of assets

3 The contractual obligation to deliver cash or another financial asset to the holder

4 By calculating the present value of the liability component and then deducting this from the instrument as a whole to leave a residual value for the equity component

5 An entity should derecognise a financial asset when:

(a) The contractual rights to the cash flows from the financial asset expire, or

(b) The entity transfers substantially all the risks and rewards of ownership of the financial asset to another party.

6 At cost = fair value

7 At amortised cost or at fair value through other comprehensive income or at fair value through profit or loss.

8 False. The probability-weighted outcome should reflect the possibility that a credit loss occurs and a possibility that it does not occur.

9 Where the host contract is a financial asset within the scope of IFRS 9, the classification and measurement rules of the standard are applied to the entire hybrid contract. Where the host contract is not a financial asset within the scope of IFRS 9, the standard requires that an embedded derivative be separated from its host contract and accounted for as a derivative when certain conditions are met.

10 Hedging, for accounting purposes, means designating one or more hedging instruments so that their change in fair value is an offset, in whole or in part, to the change in fair value or cash flows of a hedged item.

11 Fair value hedge; cash flow hedge; hedge of a net investment in a foreign operation

12 Entities should maximise the use of relevant *observable inputs* and minimise the use of *unobservable inputs.*

Now try the questions below from the Practice Question Bank

Number	Level	Marks	Time
Q10	Examination	10	20 mins
Q11	Introductory	n/a	n/a
Q12	Examination	25	49 mins

8

Leases

Topic list	Syllabus reference
1 IFRS 16	C4
2 Lessee accounting	C4
3 Lessor accounting	C4
4 Sale and leaseback	C4
5 Implications of the changes	C4

Introduction

Leasing transactions are extremely common in business and you will often come across them in both your business and personal capacity. Lease accounting is regulated by IFRS 16, which replaces IAS 17.

IFRS 16 represents the completion of the IASB's project to end off balance sheet accounting for leases.

Study guide

		Intellectual level
C4	**Leases**	
(a)	Apply and discuss the accounting for leases by lessees including the measurement of the right of use asset and liability	3
(b)	Apply and discuss the accounting for leases by lessors	3
(c)	Apply and discuss the circumstances where there may be re-measurement of the lease liability	3
(d)	Apply and discuss the reasons behind the separation of the components of a lease contract into lease and no lease elements	3
(e)	Discuss the recognition exemptions under the current leasing standard	3
(f)	Account for and discuss sale and leaseback transactions	3

Exam guide

This topic has been tested as a current issue for some time. Now that the new standard is out, the topic is ripe for examination.

1 IFRS 16

FAST FORWARD

IFRS 16 was brought in to remedy the non-recognition of liabilities for assets held under operating leases.

1.1 Objective

IFRS 16 *Leases* was published in January 2016, following many years of debate, a Discussion Paper and two Exposure Drafts. It is effective from 1 January 2019. Companies can choose to apply IFRS 16 before that date but only if they also apply IFRS 15 *Revenue from contracts with customers*.

IFRS 16 sets out the principles for the recognition, measurement, presentation and disclosure of leases. The objective is to ensure that lessees and lessors provide relevant information in a manner that faithfully represents those transactions (IFRS 16: para.IN1).

It replaces IAS 17, which required lessees and lessors to classify their leases as either finance leases or operating leases and account for these two types of lease differently. IAS 17 did not require lessees to recognise assets and liabilities arising from operating leases (IFRS 16: para. IN5). The IASB estimated that global leasing liabilities were $3.3 trillion of which 85% were off balance sheet (Hoogervorst, 2016). IFRS 16 was brought in to remedy this.

1.2 Main features

IFRS 16 introduces a single lessee accounting model and requires a lessee to recognise assets and liabilities for all leases with a term of more than twelve months, unless the underlying asset is of low value. For short-term leases or low value assets, the lease payments are simply charged to profit or loss as an expense (see below).

For all other leases, the lessee recognises a right-of-use asset, representing its right to use the underlying asset and a lease liability representing its obligation to make lease payments (IFRS 16: para.IN10). For lessors, there is little change from the IAS 17 requirements. Lessors will continue to recognise the distinction between finance and operating leases.

1.3 Identifying a lease

FAST FORWARD

A **lease** is a contract, or part of a contract, that conveys the right to use an asset, the underlying asset, for a period of time in exchange for consideration. (IFRS 16, Appendix A)

A contract is, or contains, a lease if the contract conveys the right to control the use of an identified asset for a period of time in exchange for consideration (IFRS 16: para.9). The contract may contain other elements which are not leases, such as a service contract. These other components must be separated out from the lease and separately accounted for, allocating the consideration on the basis of the stand-alone prices of the lease and non-lease components (IFRS 16: para.13).

The right to control the use of an identified asset depends on the lessee having:

(a) The right to obtain substantially all of the economic benefits from use of the identified asset; and

(b) The right to direct the use of the identified asset (IFRS 16: para. B9). This arises if either:

(i) The customer has the right to direct how and for what purpose the asset is used during the whole of its period of use, or

(ii) The relevant decisions about use are pre-determined and the customer can operate the asset without the supplier having the right to change those operating instructions.

A lessee does not control the use of an identified asset if the lessor can substitute the underlying asset for another asset during the lease term and would benefit economically from doing so. (IFRS 16: para B14)

Key terms

Lease. A contract, or part of a contract, that conveys the right to use an asset, **the underlying asset**, for a period of time in exchange for consideration.

Underlying asset. An asset that is the subject of a lease, for which the right to use that asset has been provided by a **lessor** to a **lessee**.

Right-of-use asset. An asset that represents a lessee's right to use an **underlying asset** for the **lease term**.

- **Lease payments**. Payments made by a **lessee** to a **lessor** relating to the right to use an **underlying asset** during the **lease term**, comprising:

  (a) Fixed payments, less any **lease incentives**

  (b) **Variable lease payments** that depend on an index or rate

  (c) The exercise price of a purchase option if the lessee is reasonably certain to exercise that option

  (d) Payment of lease termination penalties if applicable

- **Interest rate implicit in the lease.**

  The discount rate that, at the inception of the lease, causes the aggregate present value of:

  (a) The lease payments, and
  (b) The **unguaranteed residual value**

  to be equal to the sum of:

  (a) The fair value of the **underlying asset**, and
  (b) Any initial direct costs.

- **Lessee's incremental borrowing rate**. The rate of interest that a **lessee** would have to pay to borrow over a similar term, and with a similar security, the funds necessary to obtain an asset of similar value to the **right of use asset** in a similar economic environment.

- **Unguaranteed residual value**. That portion of the residual value of the underlying asset, the realisation of which by the lessor is not assured.

- **Variable lease payments**. The portion of payments made by a **lessee** to a **lessor** for the right to use an **underlying asset** during the **lease term** that varies because of changes in facts or circumstances occurring after the commencement date, other than the passage of time.
- **Lease term.** The non-cancellable period for which the lessee has contracted to lease the asset together with any further terms for which the lessee has the option to continue to lease the asset, with or without further payment, when at the inception of the lease it is reasonably certain that the lessee will exercise the option and any periods covered by an option to terminate the lease if the lessee is reasonably certain not to exercise that option *(IFRS 16: para.18).*
- **Short-term lease**. A lease that at the commencement date has a term of 12 months or less and does not contain a purchase option.
- **Lease incentives.** Payments made by the **lessor** to the **lessee**, or the reimbursement or assumption by the lessor of costs of the lessee. *(IFRS 16: Appendix A)*

Note. In an exam question you will be given the interest rate implicit in the lease.

1.4 Identifying a lease: examples

The following flowchart, taken from IFRS 16, Appendix B, paragraph B31, may assist you in determining whether a lease may be identified in the examples that follow:

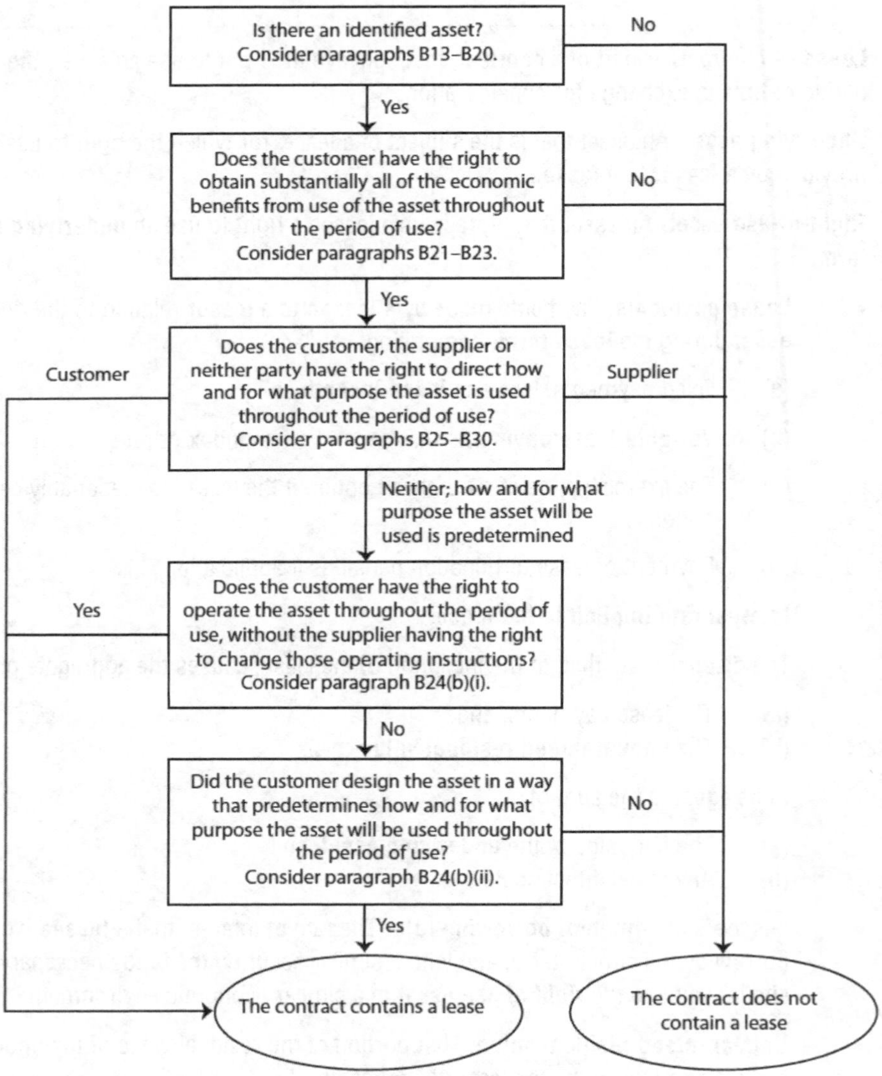

1.4.1 Is it a lease (1)?

Coketown Council has entered into a five-year contract with Carefleet Co, under which Carefleet Co supplies the council with ten vehicles to for the purposes of community transport. Carefleet Co owns the relevant vehicles, all ten of which are specified in the contract. Coketown Council determines the routes taken for community transport and the charges and eligibility for discounts. The council can choose to use the vehicles for purposes other than community transport. When the vehicles are not being used, they are kept at the council's offices and cannot be retrieved by Carefleet unless Coketown Council defaults on payment. If a vehicle needs to be serviced or repaired, Carefleet is obliged to provide a temporary replacement vehicle of the same type.

Conclusion: this is a lease. There is an identifiable asset, the ten vehicles specified in the contract. The council has a right to use the vehicles for the period of the contract. Carefleet Co does not have the right to substitute any of the vehicles unless they are being serviced or repaired. Therefore Coketown Council would need to recognise an asset and liability in its statement of financial position.

1.4.2 Is it a lease (2)?

Broketown Council has recently made substantial cuts to its community transport service. It will now provide such services only in cases of great need, assessed on a case by case basis. It has entered into a two-year contract with Fleetcar Co for the use of one of its minibuses for this purpose. The minibus must seat ten people, but Fleetcar Co can use any of its ten-seater minibuses when required.

Conclusion: this is not a lease. There is no identifiable asset. Fleetcar can exchange one minibus for another. Therefore Broketown council should account for the rental payments as an expense in profit or loss.

1.4.3 Is it a lease (3)?

This example is taken from IFRS 16 illustrative example 3.

Kabal enters into a ten -year contract with a utilities company (Telenew) for the right to use three specified, physically distinct dark fibres within a larger cable connecting North Town to South Town. Kabal makes the decisions about the use of the fibres by connecting each end of the fibres to its electronic equipment (ie Kabal 'lights' the fibres and decides what data, and how much data, those fibres will transport). If the fibres are damaged, Telenew is responsible for the repairs and maintenance. Telenew owns extra fibres, but can substitute those for Kabal's fibres only for reasons of repairs, maintenance or malfunction (and is obliged to substitute the fibres in these cases).

Conclusion: this is a lease. The contract contains a lease of dark fibres. Kabal has the right to use the three dark fibres for ten years.

There are three identified fibres. The fibres are explicitly specified in the contract and are physically distinct from other fibres within the cable. Telenew cannot substitute the fibres other than for reasons of repairs, maintenance or malfunction (IFRS 16: Para B18).

Kabal has the right to control the use of the fibres throughout the ten-year period of use because:

(a) Kabal has the right to obtain substantially all of the economic benefits from use of the fibres over the ten-year period of use and Kabal has exclusive use of the fibres throughout the period of use.

(b) Kabal has the right to direct the use of the fibres because IFRS 16: Para B24 applies:

 (i) The customer has the right to direct how and for what purpose the asset is used during the whole of its period of use, or

 (ii) The relevant decisions about use are pre-determined and the customer can operate the asset without the supplier having the right to change those operating instructions.

Kabal makes the relevant decisions about how and for what purpose the fibres are used by deciding (i) when and whether to light the fibres and (ii) when and how much output the fibres will produce (ie what data, and how much data, those fibres will transport). Kabal has the right to change these decisions during the ten-year period of use.

Although Telenew's decisions about repairing and maintaining the fibres are essential to their efficient use, those decisions do not give Telenew the right to direct how and for what purpose the fibres are used. Consequently, Telenew does not control the use of the fibres during the period of use.

1.5 Recognition exemptions

FAST FORWARD

In the case of **short-term leases** and **leases of low-value assets,** lessees may elect to account for lease payments as an expense on a straight-line basis over the lease term instead of applying IFRS 16. (IFRS 16: para 5, 6 and 8)

Instead of applying the recognition requirements of IFRS 16 described below, a lessee may elect to account for lease payments as an expense on a straight-line basis over the lease term or another systematic basis for the following two types of leases (IFRS 16: para 5, 6 and 8).

(a) **Short-term leases.** These are leases with a lease term of twelve months or less. This election is made by class of underlying asset. A lease that contains a purchase option cannot be a short-term lease.

(b) **Leases of low-value assets.** These are leases where the underlying asset has a low value when new (such as tablet and personal computers or small items of office furniture and telephones.). This election can be made on a lease-by-lease basis. An underlying asset qualifies as low value only if two conditions apply:

(i) The lessee can benefit from using the underlying asset.

(ii) The underlying asset is not highly dependent on, or highly interrelated with, other assets. (IFRS 16: Para B5)

Leases of low-value assets are leases of assets with a value when new of $5,000 or less (IFRS 16, Basis for Conclusions, Para 100).

Example: leases of low-value assets and portfolio application

IFRS 16 Illustrative Example 11 is of a lessee in the pharmaceutical manufacturing and distribution industry, with leases including the following:

(a) Leases of IT equipment for use by individual employees (such as laptop computers, desktop computers, hand held computer devices, desktop printers and mobile phones)

(b) Leases of servers, including many individual modules that increase the storage capacity of those servers. The modules have been added to the mainframe servers over time as the lessee has needed to increase the storage capacity of the servers

(c) Leases of office equipment:

(i) Office furniture such as desks, chairs and partitions
(ii) Water dispensers

The company determines that the leases of IT equipment to individual employees and the office furniture and water dispensers qualify as leases of low-value assets on the basis that the underlying assets, when new, are individually of low value.

However, although each module within the servers, if considered individually, might be an asset of low value, the leases of modules within the servers do not qualify as leases of low-value assets. This is because each module is highly interrelated with other parts of the servers. The lessee would not lease the modules without also leasing the servers. Accordingly, the company would apply the recognition and measurement requirements of IFRS 16 to the servers.

1.6 Separating components of a contract

FAST FORWARD

In the case of **contracts with both a lease component and a non-lease component,** entities must account for the lease component of the contract **separately** from the non-lease component. (IFRS 16: Para 12)

A contract may contain both a lease component and a non-lease component. In other words it may include an amount payable by the lessee for activities and costs that do not transfer goods or services to the lessee (IFRS 16: Para B33). These activities and costs might, for example, include maintenance, repairs or cleaning.

IFRS 16 requires entities to **account for the lease component of the contract separately from the non-lease component.** The entity must split the rental or lease payment and:

- Account for the lease component under IFRS 16, and
- Account for the service element separately, generally as an expense in profit or loss

The consideration in the contract is **allocated on the basis of the stand-alone prices** of the lease component(s) and the non-lease component(s).

Example: separating components of a contract

Livery Co leases a delivery van from Bettalease Co for three years at $12,000 per year. This payment includes servicing costs.

Livery could lease the same make and model of van for $11,000 per year and would need to pay $2,000 a year for servicing.

Solution

Livery Co would allocate $10,154 ($12,000 × $11,000 ÷ $(11,000 + 2,000) to the lease component and account for that as a lease under IFRS 16.

Livery Co would allocate $1,846 ($12,000 × $2,000 ÷ $(11,000 + 2,000) to the servicing component and recognise it in profit or loss as an expense.

1.7 Initial measurement of the right-of-use asset

At the commencement date the right-of-use asset is measured at cost. This comprises:

(a) The amount of the initial measurement of the lease liability

(b) Any lease payments made before the commencement date, less any lease incentives received

(c) Any initial direct costs incurred by the lessee

(d) Any costs which the lessee will incur for dismantling and removing the underlying asset or restoring the site at the end of the lease term

1.8 Initial measurement of the lease liability

At the commencement date the lease liability is measured at the present value of future lease payments, including any expected payments at the end of the lease, discounted at the interest rate implicit in the lease (IFRS 16: para. 24). If that rate cannot be readily determined, the lessee's incremental borrowing rate should be used (IFRS 16: para. 26)

1.9 Subsequent measurement of the right-of-use asset

After the commencement date the right-of-use asset should be measured should be measured using the cost model in IAS 16, unless it is an investment property or belongs to a class of assets to which the revaluation model applies (IFRS 16: para. 29).

If the lease transfers ownership of the underlying asset at the end of the lease term or if the cost reflects a purchase option which the lessee is expected to exercise, the right-of-use asset should be depreciated over the useful life of the underlying asset.

If there is no transfer of ownership and no purchase option, the right-of-use asset should be depreciated from the commencement date to the earlier of the end of the useful life and the end of the lease term (IFRS 16: paras 31,32).

1.10 Subsequent measurement of lease liability

After the commencement date the carrying amount of the lease liability is increased by interest charges on the outstanding liability and reduced by lease payments made (IFRS 16: para. 36).

2 Lessee accounting

FAST FORWARD

For lessees, IFRS 16 removes the distinction between finance leases and operating leases which was a feature of IAS 17.

All leases result in a company, the lessee, obtaining:

- The **right to use an asset** at the start of the lease, and
- **Financing**, if lease payments are made over time

2.1 Presentation

In the statement of financial position right-of use assets can be presented on a separate line under non-current assets or they can be included in the total of corresponding underlying assets and disclosed in the notes.

Lease liabilities should be either presented separately from other liabilities or disclosed in the notes (IFRS 16: para. 47).

IFRS 16 does not specify that lease liabilities should be split between non-current and current liabilities, but this should be done as best practice.

2.2 Apportionment of rental payments

When the lessee makes a rental payment it will comprise two elements.

(a) An **interest charge** on the finance provided by the lessor. This proportion of each payment is interest payable in the statement of profit or loss of the lessee.

(b) A repayment of part of the **capital cost** of the asset. In the lessee's books this proportion of each rental payment must be debited to the lessor's account to reduce the outstanding liability.

The accounting problem is to decide what proportion of each instalment paid by the lessee represents interest, and what proportion represents a repayment of the capital advanced by the lessor. This is done by the actuarial method, using the interest rate implicit in the lease.

2.3 Example: apportionment of rental payments

[This is based on IFRS 16 Illustrative example 13.]

A lessee enters into a five-year lease of a building which has a remaining useful life of 10 years. Lease payments are $50,000 per annum, payable at the beginning of each year.

The lessee incurs initial direct costs of $20,000 and receives lease incentives of $5,000. There is no transfer of the asset at the end of the lease and no purchase option.

The interest rate implicit in the lease is not immediately determinable but the lessee's incremental borrowing rate is 5%.

At the commencement date the lessee pays the initial $50,000, incurs the direct costs and receives the lease incentives.

The lease liability is measured at the present value of the remaining four payments:

	$
$50,000/1.05	47,619
$50,000/1.05^2	45,351
$50,000/1.05^3	43,192
$50,000/1.05^4	41,135
	177,297

Assets and liabilities will initially be recognised as follows:

		Debit $	*Credit* $
Right-of-use asset:			
Initial payment	50,000		
Discounted liability	177,297		
Initial direct costs	20,000		
Incentives received	(5,000)		
		242,297	
Lease liability			177,297
Cash	(50,000 + 20,000 – 5,000)		65,000
		242,297	242,297

At the end of year 1 the liability will be measured as:

	$
Opening balance	177,297
Interest 5%	8,865
	186,162
Current liability	50,000
Non-current liability	136,162
	186,162

The right of use asset will be depreciated over five years, being the shorter of the lease term and the useful life of the underlying asset.

Now we will see how this would work out if the lease payments were made **in arrears**.

At the commencement date the lessee would incur the direct costs and receive the lease incentives.

The lease would be measured at the present value of **five** payments:

	$
$50,000/1.05	47,619
$50,000/1.05^2	45,351
$50,000/1.05^3	43,192
$50,000/1.05^4	41,135
$50,000/1.05^5	39,176
	216,473

Assets and liabilities would be recognised as follows:

		Debit	*Credit*
		$	$
Right-of-use asset:			
Discounted liability	216,473		
Direct costs	20,000		
Lease incentives	(5,000)		
		231,473	
Lease liability			216,473
Cash (20,000 – 5,000)			15,000
		231,473	231,473

At the end of year 1 the liability will be measured as:

	$
Opening balance	216,473
Interest 5%	10,824
Lease payment year 1	(50,000)
Year-end balance	177,297

In order to ascertain the split between non-current and current liabilities, we work out the balance at the end of year 2:

	$
Opening balance	177,297
Interest 5%	8,865
Lease payment year 2	(50,000)
Year-end balance	136,162

The statement of financial position will show:

	$
Non-current liability	136,162
Current liability (177,297 – 136,162)	41,135
	177,297

Note that when payments are made in arrears the next instalment due will contain interest, so this is effectively deducted to arrive at the capital repayment.

2.4 Remeasurement of lease liability

There are a number of circumstances where the lease liability might be remeasured, with a corresponding adjustment to the right of use asset:

(a) The lease term is revised
(b) Variable lease payments (future lease payments based on an index or rate) are revised
(c) The lease is modified
(d) There is a change in the amount expected to be paid under residual value guarantees.

2.4.1 Revision of lease term

Here is a reminder of the IFRS 16 definition of lease term:

Key term

Lease term. The non-cancellable period for which the lessee has contracted to lease the asset together with any further terms for which the lessee has the option to continue to lease the asset, with or without further payment, when at the inception of the lease it is reasonably certain that the lessee will exercise the option and any periods covered by an option to terminate the lease if the lessee is reasonably certain not to exercise that option *(IFRS 16: para.18).*

A change in the assessment of whether an extension or termination option will be exercise gives rise to a **remeasurement of the lease liability.** To account for this, the lessee must:

(a) Adjust the lease liability by:

 (i) Including the lease payments over the revised term
 (ii) Applying a revised discount rate

(b) Make a corresponding adjustment to the right of use asset.

Example: revision of lease term

(Adapted from Illustrative Example 13 of IFRS 16)

Lester enters into a ten-year lease of a floor of a building, with an option to extend for five years. Lease payments are $50,000 per year during the initial term and $55,000 per year during the optional period, all payable at the beginning of each year. The interest rate implicit in the lease was not readily determinable. Lester's incremental borrowing rate was 5 per cent per annum.

Lester is now in the sixth year of the ten-year lease, with its option to renew for another five years. The optional period has not been included in the initial assessment of the lease term. Lester acquires Wester, which has been leasing a floor in another building. The lease entered into by Wester contains a termination option that is exercisable by Wester. Following the acquisition of Wester, Lester needs two floors in a building suitable for the increased workforce of the combined companies. To minimise costs, Lester (a) enters into a separate eight-year lease of another floor in the building it currently occupies that will be available for use at the end of Year 7 and (b) terminates early the lease entered into by Wester with effect from the beginning of Year 8. Wester will then move into the new floor leased by Lester.

Lester's incremental borrowing rate at the end of Year 6 is 6 per cent per annum.

Solution

Moving Wester's staff to the same building occupied by Lester creates an economic incentive for Lester to extend its original lease at the end of the non-cancellable period of ten years. The acquisition of Wester and the relocation of Wester's staff is a significant event that is within the control of Lester and affects whether Lester is reasonably certain to exercise the extension option not previously included in its determination of the lease term. This is because the original floor has greater utility (and thus provides greater benefits) to Lester than alternative assets that could be leased for a similar amount to the lease payments for the optional period – Lester would incur additional costs if it were to lease a similar floor in a different building because the workforce would be located in different buildings. Consequently, at the end of Year 6, Lester concludes that it is now reasonably certain to exercise the option to extend its original lease as a result of its acquisition and planned relocation of Wester.

Lester remeasures the lease liability at the present value of four payments of $50,000 followed by five payments of $55,000, all discounted at the revised discount rate of 6 per cent per annum.

2.4.2 Variable lease payments

The treatment of variable lease payments (called 'contingent rentals' under IAS 17) depends on the type of variable payment.

(a) Payments that **vary according to an index** or rate are included in the lease liability and asset based on the index or rate at the measurement date. The **lease liability is remeasured when the index or rate changes** and the lease payments are revised.

(b) Payments that **vary based on future usage** of the leased asset are **not included in the lease liability or asset.** They are **recognised as an expense in the period** in which the event or condition that triggers the payment takes place.

(c) However, variable payments that are **in-substance fixed payments are included** in the lease payments. They are treated as fixed payments.

In-substance fixed payments are lease payments that are variable in legal form but should be treated as fixed payments. Examples include (IFRS 16: Para B42):

- Payments that are initially variable but may become fixed in the future if the variability is 'resolved'
- Arrangements where there is more than one set of payments that could be made but only one set is realistic
- Payments that must be made if an asset is incapable of operating during the period

2.4.3 Lease modifications

Lease modifications may result in a number of outcomes, depending on the nature of the modification:

(a) A separate lease

(b) A remeasurement of the lease liability using a discount rate determined at that date (and corresponding adjustment to the right of use asset)

(c) A remeasurement of the lease liability using a discount rate determined at that date and partial termination of the lease.

The requirements of IFRS 16 may be summarised in the following diagram:

Types of lease modification

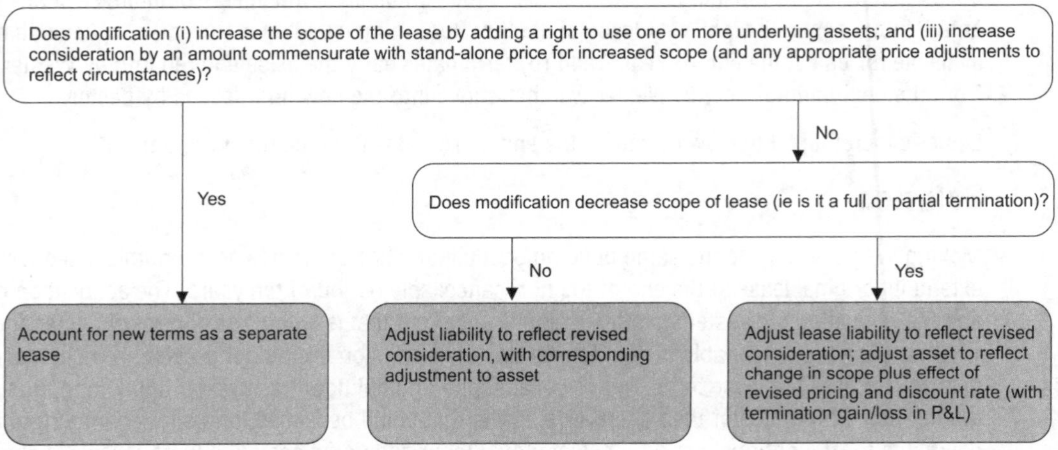

[Source: Grant Thornton, February 2016, IFRS News Special Edition, February 2016]

2.5 Disclosure requirements for lessees

The objective of the disclosure requirements is to allow users to assess the effect that leases have on the financial position, financial performance and cash flows of the lessee (IFRS 16: para.51)

Amounts to be disclosed include:

- Depreciation charge for right-of-use assets
- Interest expense on lease liabilities
- Expenses relating to short-term and leases of low-value assets
- Details of sale and leaseback transactions
- The carrying amount of right-of-use assets at the end of the reporting period, by class of underlying asset
- Additions to right-of-use asset

2.6 Other disclosure requirements relating to leasing

Amounts to be disclosed include (IFRS 16: Para. 92) additional qualitative and quantitative information about leasing activities as necessary to meet disclosure objectives, including but not limited to:

- Nature of leasing activities
- How the risk associated with any rights retained in the underlying asset is managed

3 Lessor accounting

FAST FORWARD

- For **lessor accounting** IFRS 16 **retains the** IAS 17 **distinction between finance leases and operating leases.**
- **Finance leases:** record the amount due from the lessor in the statement of financial position at the net investment in the lease, recognise finance income to give a constant periodic rate of return.
- **Operating leases:** record as long-term asset and depreciate over useful life, record income on a straight-line basis over the lease term.

Several **definitions** are relevant to lessor accounting in particular.

Key terms

Finance lease. A lease that transfers substantially all the risks and rewards incidental to ownership of an underlying asset.
Operating lease. A lease that does not transfer substantially all the risks and rewards incidental to ownership of an underlying asset.

Guaranteed residual value is:

(a) For a lessee, that part of the residual value which is guaranteed by the lessee or by a party related to the lessee (the amount of the guarantee being the maximum amount that could, in any event, become payable)

(b) For a lessor, that part of the residual value which is guaranteed by the lessee or by a third party unrelated to the lessor who is financially capable of discharging the obligations under the guarantee.

Unguaranteed residual value is that portion of the residual value of the underlying asset, the realisation of which by the lessor is not assured or is guaranteed solely by a party related to the lessor.

Gross investment in the lease is the sum of:

(a) The lease payments receivable by the lessor under a finance lease, and
(b) Any unguaranteed residual value accruing to the lessor.

Net investment in the lease is the gross investment in the lease discounted at the interest rate implicit in the lease.

Unearned finance income is the difference between:

(a) The gross investment in the lease, and
(b) The net investment in the lease.

(IFRS 16, Appendix A)

3.1 Finance leases

A **finance lease** is a lease that lease that transfers substantially all the risks and rewards incidental to ownership of an underlying asset. It can be considered, to be, like hire purchase, a form of instalment credit.

When we talk of **risks** here, we specifically mean the risks of ownership, not other types of risk. Risks of **ownership** include the possibility of losses from idle capacity or technological obsolescence, or variations in return due to changing economic conditions. The **rewards** are represented by the expectation of profitable operation over the asset's economic life, and also any gain from appreciation in value or realisation of a residual value. (IFRS 16: Para B53).

For lessors, but not lessees, finance leases are distinguished from operating leases.

3.2 Accounting treatment

IFRS 16 requires the **amount due from the lessee** under a finance lease to be recorded in the statement of financial position of a lessor as a receivable at the amount of the **net investment in the lease**.

The **recognition of finance income** under a finance lease should normally be based on a pattern to give a **constant periodic rate of return** on the lessor's net investment outstanding in respect of the finance lease in each period. In arriving at the constant periodic rate of return, a reasonable approximation may be made.

The lease payments (excluding costs for services) relating to the accounting period should be applied against the gross investment in the lease, so as to **reduce both the principal and the unearned finance income**.

The **estimated unguaranteed residual values** used to calculate the lessor's gross investment in a lease should be reviewed regularly. If there has been a reduction in the value, then the income allocation over the lease term must be revised. Any reduction in respect of amounts already accrued should be recognised immediately.

Initial direct costs incurred by lessors (eg commissions, legal fees and other costs that are directly attributable to negotiating and arranging a lease) are included in the initial measurement of the finance lease receivable.

FAST FORWARD

You should also know how to deal with:

- **Manufacturer/dealer lessors**
- **Sale and leaseback transactions**

3.3 Manufacturer/dealer lessors

IFRS 16 looks at the situation where manufacturers or dealers offer customers the choice of either buying or leasing an asset. There will be two types of income under such a lease.

(a) Profit/loss equal to that from an **outright sale** (normal selling price less any discount)
(b) **Finance income** over the lease term

IFRS 16 requires the following treatment.

(a) Recognise the **selling profit/loss** in income for the period as if it was an outright sale.

(b) If **interest rates are artificially low**, restrict the selling profit to that which would apply had a commercial rate been applied.

(c) Recognise **costs** incurred in connection with negotiating and arranging a lease as an **expense** when the **selling profit** is recognised (at the start of the lease term).

3.4 Lessors' disclosures for finance leases

The objective of the disclosures is to provide users of financial statements with a basis to The objective of the disclosure requirements is to allow users to assess the effect that leases have on the financial position, financial performance and cash flows of the lessee (IFRS 16: para.89).

The following should be disclosed.

- Selling profit or loss
- Finance income on the net investment in the lease

- Income relating to variable lease payments not included in the measurement of the net investment in the lease
- Qualitative and quantitative explanation of significant changes in net investment in the lease
- Maturity analysis of lease receivable

3.5 Operating leases

3.5.1 Definition

An **operating lease** is a lease that does not transfer substantially all the risks and rewards incidental to ownership of an underlying asset. its useful life. The distinction between finance and operating leases applies only to lessors, not lessees.

3.5.2 Accounting treatment

An **asset** held for use in operating leases by a lessor should be recorded as a long-term asset and depreciated over its useful life. The basis for depreciation should be consistent with the lessor's policy on similar non-lease assets and follow the guidance in IAS 16.

Income from an operating lease, excluding charges for services such as insurance and maintenance, should be recognised on **a straight-line basis** over the period of the lease (even if the receipts are not on such a basis), unless another systematic and rational basis is more representative of the time pattern in which the benefit from the leased asset is receivable.

Initial direct costs incurred by lessors in negotiating and arranging an operating lease should be **added to the carrying amount** of the leased asset and recognised as an expense over the lease term on the same basis as lease income, ie capitalised and amortised over the lease term.

Lessors should refer to IAS 36 in order to determine whether a leased asset has become impaired.

A lessor who is a **manufacturer or dealer** should not recognise any selling profit on entering into an operating lease because it is not the equivalent of a sale.

3.5.3 Lessors' disclosures for operating leases

The following should be disclosed (IFRS 16: para.89).

- Lease income, separately disclosing income for variable lease payments that do not depend on an index or rate
- As applicable for underlying asset, relevant disclosures in:
  – IAS 16 for leases of property, plant and equipment, disaggregated by class
  – IAS 36 'Impairment', IAS 38, IAS 40 and IAS 41
- Maturity analysis of lease payments

3.6 Subleases

A lessee, L, may sublease an asset which it in turn leases from another lessor, H. In this situation, H is the 'head lessor' who ultimately owns the asset from a legal perspective. L then becomes an 'intermediate lessor' An intermediate lessor must assess whether the sublease is a finance or operating lease in the context of the right-of-use asset being leased, not the actual underlying asset (IFRS 16: Para: B 57).

Example: sublease

[This example is adapted from Illustrative Example 18 of IFRS 16.]

Interliss, enters into a ten-year lease for 6,000 square metres of office space (the head lease) with Headliss, (the head lessor). At the beginning of year 5, Interliss subleases the 6,000 square metres of office space for the remaining six years of the head lease to a Subliss.

Solution

In this situation, Headliss is the head lessor, Interliss is the intermediate lessor, and Subliss is the sublessee. From the perspective of the intermediate lessor, at the time the sub-lease is entered into, the right-of-use asset has a six-year remaining life, and it is being sub-leased for the entirety of that remaining period of time. As such, the sub-lease is for a major part of the useful life of the right-of-use asset and the lease is classified as a finance lease.

4 Sale and leaseback 6/12, 12/13

FAST FORWARD

A sale and leaseback transaction involves the sale of an asset and the leasing back of the same asset.

IFRS 16 requires an initial assessment to be made regarding whether or not the transfer constitutes a sale. This is done by determining when the performance obligation is satisfied in accordance with IFRS 15 *Revenue from Contracts with Customers* (IFRS 16: para.98).

4.1 Transfer is a sale

If the transfer satisfies the IFRS 15 requirement to be accounted for as a sale:

- The seller/lessee measures the right-of-use asset arising from the leaseback at the proportion of the previous carrying amount of the asset that relates to the **right-of use retained** by the seller/lessee.
- The seller/lessee only recognises the amount of any gain or loss on the sale that relates to the **rights transferred** to the buyer (IFRS 16: para. 100)

If the fair value of the consideration for the sale does not equal the fair value of the asset, or if the lease payments are not at market rates, the following adjustments should be made:

- Any below-market terms should be accounted for as a prepayment of lease payments (the shortfall in consideration received from the lessor is treated as a lease payment made by the lessee)
- Any above-market terms are accounted for as additional financing provided by the buyer/lessor (the additional amount paid by the lessor is treated as additional liability, **not** as gain on the sale) (IFRS 16: para.101).

4.2 Transfer is not a sale

If the transfer does not satisfy the IFRS 15 requirements to be accounted for as a sale, the seller continues to recognise the transferred asset and the transfer proceeds are treated as a financial liability, accounted for in accordance with IFRS 9. The transaction is more in the nature of a secured loan.

4.3 Example: sale and leaseback

[Adapted from IFRS 16 Illustrated example 24]

Selleasy Co sells a building to Buylesser for $800,000 cash. The carrying amount of the building prior to the sale was $600,000. Selleasy arranges to lease the building back for five years at $120,000 per annum, payable in arrears. The remaining useful life is 15 years.

The transaction satisfies the performance obligations in IFRS 15, so will be accounted for as a sale and leaseback.

At the date of sale the fair value of the building was $750,000, so the excess $50,000 paid by the buyer is recognised as additional financing provided by Buylesser.

The interest rate implicit in the lease is 4.5% and the present value of the annual payments is:

	$
$120,000/1.045$	114,833
$120,000/1.045^2$	109,888
$120,000/1.045^3$	105,155
$120,000/1.045^4$	100,627
$120,000/1.045^5$	96,294
	526,797

Of this, $476,797 relates to the lease and $50,000 relates to the additional financing.

At the commencement date, the seller/lessee measures the right-of-use asset arising from the leaseback of the building at the proportion of the previous carrying amount of the building that relates to the right-of-use retained. This is calculated as carrying amount × discounted lease payments/fair value.

In our example: $600,000 × 476,797/750,000 = $381,437

Selleasy only recognises the amount of gain that relates to the rights transferred. The gain on sale of the building is $150,000 (750,000 – 600,000), of which:

(a) 150,000 × 476,797/750,000 = $95,360 – relates to the rights retained
(b) The balance -150,000 – 95,360 = $54,640 – relates to the rights transferred to the buyer.

At the commencement date the lessee accounts for the transaction as follows:

	Debit	*Credit*
	$	$
Cash	800,000	
Right-of-use asset	381,437	
Building		600,000
Financial liability		526,797
Gain on rights transferred		54,640
	1,181,437	1,181,437

The right-of-use asset will be depreciated over five years, the gain will be recognised in profit or loss and the financial liability will be increased each year by the interest charge and reduced by the lease payments.

Question

Sale and leaseback

Magna Co entered into a sale and leaseback on 1 April 20X7. It sold a lathe with a carrying amount of $300,00 for $400,00 (equivalent to fair value) and leased it back over a five-year period, equivalent to its remaining useful life. The transaction constitutes a sale in accordance with IFRS 15.

The lease provided for five annual payments in arrears of $90,000. The rate of interest implicit in the lease is 5%.

Required

What are the amounts to be recognised in the financial statements at 31 March 20X8 in respect of this transaction?

Answer

The lease liability at commencement will be:

	$
$90,000/1.05$	85,714
$90,000/1.05^2$	81,633
$90,000/1.05^3$	77,745
$90,000/1.05^4$	74,043
$90,000/1.05^5$	70,517
	389,652

The right-of-use asset = 300,000 × 389,652/400,000 = $292,239

The gain on the sale is $100,000. Of this, the amount relating to rights retained is:

100,000 × 389,652/400,000 = 97,413. The balance ($2,587) is the gain on rights transferred.

The initial posting will be:

	Debit	*Credit*
	$	$
Cash	400,000	
Right of use asset	292,239	
Underlying asset		300,000
Liability		389,652
Gain on transfer		2,587
	692,239	692,239

STATEMENT OF PROFIT OR LOSS

	$
Gain on transfer	2,587
Depreciation (292,239/5)	(38,448)
Interest (W)	(19,483)

STATEMENT OF FINANCIAL POSITION

Non-current asset	
Right-of-use asset	292,239
Non-current liabilities	
Lease liability (W)	245,092
Current liabilities	
Lease liability (319,135 – 245,092) (W)	74,043

Working – lease liability

	$
1 April 20X7	389,652
Interest 5%	19,483
Instalment paid	(90,000)
Balance 31 March 20X8	319,135
Interest 5%	15,957
Instalment paid	(90,000)
Balance 31 March 20X9	245,092

Current liabilities reflect the amount of the lease liability that will become due within 12 months.

5 Implications of the changes

FAST FORWARD

IFRS 16 comes after much discussion and debate. The new standard will:

- Increase lease assets and financial liabilities in the statement of financial position.
- Change the pattern and timing of expenses in the statement of profit or loss
- Reduce operating cash outflows but increase financing cash outflows

5.1 Why was a new standard needed?

The different accounting treatment of finance and operating leases was **criticised** for a number of reasons.

(a) Many users of financial statements believed that **all lease contracts give rise to assets and liabilities that should be recognised in the financial statements of lessees.** Therefore, these users routinely adjusted the recognised amounts in the statement of financial position in an attempt to assess the effect of the assets and liabilities resulting from operating lease contracts.

(b) The split between finance leases and operating leases could result in **similar transactions being accounted for very differently**, reducing comparability for users of financial statements.

(c) The difference in the accounting treatment of finance leases and operating leases also provided **opportunities to structure transactions so as to achieve a particular lease classification**.

It was also argued that the current accounting treatment of operating leases was **inconsistent with** the definition of assets and liabilities in the **IASB's *Conceptual Framework***. An operating lease contract conferred a valuable right to use a leased item. This right met the *Conceptual Framework's* definition of an asset, and the liability of the lessee to pay rentals met the *Conceptual Framework's* definition of a liability. However, the right and obligation were not recognised for operating leases.

5.2 Basic principle – recognition of all leases in the statement of financial position

Leasing is the subject of a wider IASB project. Many believed that the current lease accounting was too reliant on bright lines and subjective judgements that may result in economically similar transactions being accounted for differently. A 2009 Discussion Paper and two Exposure Drafts (2010 and 2013) established the basic principle that all leases (with limited exceptions for low-value and short-term leases) should be recognised in the statement of financial position.

5.3 Impact

The new standard will have an impact on the statement of financial position, statement of profit or loss and statement of cash flows.

5.3.1 Impact on statement of financial position

Companies will be required to report larger amounts of assets and liabilities in their statements of financial position. This will particularly affect companies that currently have much of their leasing commitments off balance sheet in the form of operating leases. For example, many airlines lease their planes and show no assets or liabilities for their future commitments. Under IFRS 16, an airline entering into a lease for an aircraft would show an asset for the 'right to use' the aircraft and an equal liability based on the current value of the lease payments it has promised to make. Possibly, as a result, loan covenants may be breached and have to be renegotiated.

The diagram below, taken from the IASB's IFRS 16 Project Summary and Feedback Statement, illustrates the impact:

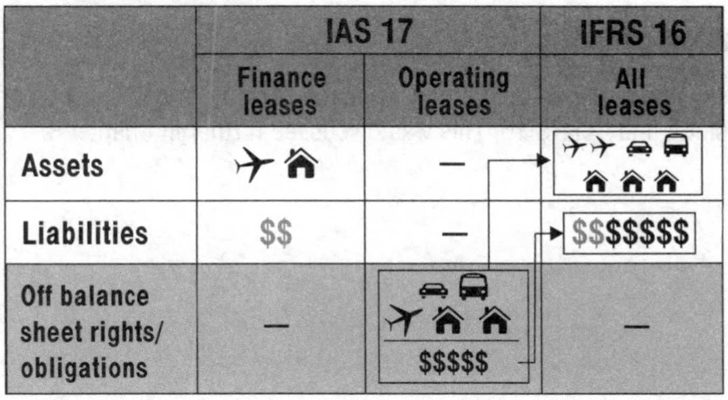
IAS 17
IFRS 16
Finance leases
Operating leases
All leases
Assets
Liabilities
Off balance sheet rights/ obligations
$$
$$$$$$
$$$$$
—

5.3.2 Impact on statement of profit or loss

For companies that currently hold material operating leases, the pattern of expenses will change. Specifically, the lease expense will be 'front-loaded'. This is because IFRS 16 replaces the usual straight-line operating lease expense for those applying IAS 17 with a depreciation charge for leased assets, included within operating costs and an interest expense on lease liabilities included within financing costs. While the depreciation charge is usually even, the interest expense is higher in the early years of the lease but reduces over the life of the asset. The total expense will generally be the same but there will be a **difference in expense profile** between IFRS 16 and IAS 17, with a consequent effect on EBITDA and operating profit, as seen in the diagram below, also taken from the IASB's IFRS 16 *Project Summary and Feedback Statement:*

	IAS 17		IFRS 16
	Finance leases	Operating leases	All leases
Revenue	X	X	X
Operating costs (*excluding depreciation and amortisation*)	–	*Single expense*	–
EBITDA			⇧⇧
Depreciation and amortisation	*Depreciation*	–	*Depreciation*
Operating profit			⇧
Finance costs	*Interest*	–	*Interest*
Profit before tax			⇔

5.3.3 Impact on cash flows

While IFRS 16 does not change the amount of cash paid by the lessee to the lessor, or the total amount of cash flows reported, it will generally change the **presentation of cash flows** in respect of leases previously accounted for as operating leases.

Operating cash outflows, which is where operating lease payments are reported under IAS 17, will **reduce**. However, there will be a corresponding **increase in financing cash outflows**. This is because repayments of the capital component of a lease liability are included within financing activities.

5.3.4 Impact on investment property

Investment property previously held under an operating lease as defined by IAS 17 must be brought into the statement of financial position under IFRS 16. This was discussed further in Chapter 3.

Chapter Roundup

- IFRS 16 was brought in to remedy the non-recognition of liabilities for assets held under operating leases.
- For lessees, IFRS 16 removes the distinction between finance and operating leases which was a feature of IAS 17.
- All leases result in a company, the lessee, obtaining:
  - The **right to use an asset** at the start of the lease, and
  - **Financing, if** lease payments are made over time
- A **lease** is a contract, or part of a contract, that conveys the right to use an asset, the underlying asset, for a period of time in exchange for consideration. (IFRS 16, Appendix A)
- In the case of **short-term leases** and **leases of low-value assets,** lessees may elect to account for lease payments as an expense on a straight-line basis over the lease term instead of applying IFRS 16. (IFRS 16: para 5, 6 and 8)
- In the case of **contracts with both a lease component and a non-lease component,** entities must account for the lease component of the contract **separately** from the non-lease component. (IFRS 16: Para 12)
- For **lessor accounting** IFRS 16 **retains the** IAS 17 **distinction between finance leases and operating leases.**
- **Finance leases:** record the amount due from the lessor in the statement of financial position at the net investment in the lease, recognise finance income to give a constant periodic rate of return.
- **Operating leases:** record as long-term asset and depreciate over useful life, record income on a straight-line basis over the lease term.
- You should also know how to deal with:
  - **Manufacturer/dealer lessors**
  - **Sale and leaseback transactions**
- A **sale and leaseback transaction** involves the sale of an asset and the **leasing back** of the same asset
- IFRS 16 comes after much discussion and debate. The new standard will:
  - **Increase lease assets and financial liabilities** in the statement of financial position.
  - **Change the pattern and timing of expenses** in the statement of profit or loss
  - **Reduce operating cash outflows** but **increase financing cash outflows**

Quick Quiz

1 A contract is, or contains, a lease if the contract conveys the right to …. an identified asset for a period of time in exchange for ….

2 A business acquires an asset under a high-value, five-year lease. What is the double entry?

3 List the disclosures required under IFRS 16 for lessees.

4 A lorry has an expected useful life of six years. It is acquired under a four year lease with no purchase options. Over which period should it be depreciated?

5 A company leases a tablet computer. What how should this lease be treated in its financial statements?

6 In a sale and leaseback transaction, the sale price is above fair value. How should this excess be treated under IFRS 16?

Answers to Quick Quiz

1 A contract is, or contains, a lease if the contract conveys the right to **control the use of** an identified asset for a period of time in exchange for **consideration** (IFRS 16: para.9).

2 DEBIT Right of use asset account
CREDIT Lease liability

3 See Section 2.4.

4 The four-year term, being the shorter of the lease term and the useful life.

5 This is a low-value lease, so the company should recognise the lease rentals as an expense over the lease term.

6 Any above-market terms are accounted for as additional financing provided by the buyer/lessor. The additional amount paid by the lessor is treated as additional liability, **not** as gain on the sale (IFRS 16: Para. 101).

Now try the question below from the Practice Question Bank

Number	Level	Marks	Time
Q13	Introductory	n/a	n/a

Share-based payment

9

Topic list	Syllabus reference
1 IFRS 2 *Share-based payment*	C10
2 Deferred tax implications	C10

Introduction

This chapter deals with IFRS 2 on share based payment, a favourite P2 topic.

Study guide

		Intellectual level
C10	**Share-based payment**	
(a)	Apply and discuss the recognition and measurement criteria for share-based payment transactions	3
(b)	Account for modifications, cancellations and settlements of share-based payment transactions	2

Exam guide

This examiner is fond of testing share-based payment as part of a scenario question.

PER alert

One of the competences you need to fulfil Objective 10 of the Practical Experience Requirement (PER) is to compile financial statements and accounts in line with appropriate standards and guidelines. You can apply the knowledge you obtain from this chapter, on share-based payment, to demonstrate this competence.

1 IFRS 2 *Share-based payment* Pilot paper, 12/08, 12/10, 6/12, 12/13, 6/14

FAST FORWARD

Share-based payment transactions should be recognised in the financial statements. You need to understand and be able to advise on:

- Recognition
- Measurement
- Disclosure

of both equity settled and cash settled transactions.

1.1 Background

Transactions whereby entities purchase goods or services from other parties, such as suppliers and employees, by **issuing shares or share options** to those other parties are **increasingly common**. Share schemes are a common feature of director and executive remuneration and in some countries the authorities may offer tax incentives to encourage more companies to offer shares to employees. Companies whose shares or share options are regarded as a valuable 'currency' commonly use share-based payment to obtain employee and professional services.

The increasing use of share-based payment has raised questions about the accounting treatment of such transactions in company financial statements.

Share options are often granted to employees at an exercise price that is equal to or higher than the market price of the shares at the date the option is granted. Consequently, the options have no intrinsic value and so **no transaction is recorded in the financial statements**.

This leads to an **anomaly:** if a company pays its employees in cash, an expense is recognised in profit or loss, but if the payment is in share options, no expense is recognised.

1.1.1 Arguments against recognition of share-based payment in the financial statements

There are a number of arguments against recognition. The IASB has considered and rejected the arguments below.

(a) **No cost therefore no charge**

There is no cost to the entity because the granting of shares or options does not require the entity to sacrifice cash or other assets. Therefore, a charge should not be recognised.

This argument is unsound because it ignores the fact that a transaction has occurred. The employees have provided valuable services to the entity in return for valuable shares or options.

(b) **Earnings per share is hit twice**

It is argued that the charge to profit or loss for the employee services consumed reduces the entity's earnings, while at the same time there is an increase in the number of shares issued.

However, the dual impact on earnings per share simply reflects the two economic events that have occurred.

(i) The entity has issued shares or options, thus increasing the denominator of the earnings per share calculation.

(ii) It has also consumed the resources it received for those shares or options, thus reducing the numerator.

(c) **Adverse economic consequences**

It could be argued that entities might be discouraged from introducing or continuing employee share plans if they were required to recognise them on the financial statements. However, if this happened, it might be because the requirement for entities to account properly for employee share plans had revealed the economic consequences of such plans.

A situation where entities are able to obtain and consume resources by issuing valuable shares or options without having to account for such transactions could be perceived as a distortion.

1.2 Objective and scope

IFRS 2 requires an entity to **reflect the effects of share-based payment transactions** in its profit or loss and financial position.

IFRS 2 applies to all share-based payment transactions. There are three types:

(a) **Equity-settled share-based payment transactions**, in which the entity receives goods or services in exchange for equity instruments of the entity (including shares or share options).

(b) **Cash-settled share-based payment transactions**, in which the entity receives goods or services in exchange for amounts of cash that are based on the price (or value) of the entity's shares or other equity instruments of the entity.

(c) Transactions in which the entity receives or acquires goods or services and either the entity or the supplier has a **choice** as to whether the entity settles the transaction in cash (or other assets) or by issuing equity instruments.

IFRS 2 was amended in June 2009 to address situations in those parts of the world where, for public policy or other reasons, companies give their shares or rights to shares to individuals, organisations or groups that have not provided goods or services to the company. An example is the issue of shares to a charitable organisation for less than fair value, where the benefits are more intangible than usual goods or services.

(IFRS 2: paras. 1 to 6)

1.2.1 Share-based payment among group entities

Payment for goods or services received by an entity within a group may be made in the form of granting equity instruments of the parent company, or equity instruments of another group company.

IFRS 2 states that this type of transaction qualifies as a share-based payment transaction within the scope of IFRS 2.

In 2009, the standard was amended to clarify that it applies to the following arrangements:

(a) Where the entity's suppliers (including employees) will receive cash payments that are linked to the price of the equity instruments of the entity.

(b) Where the entity's suppliers (including employees) will receive cash payments that are linked to the price of the equity instruments of the entity's parent.

Under either arrangement, the entity's parent had an obligation to make the required cash payments to the entity's suppliers. The entity itself did not have any obligation to make such payments. IFRS 2 applies to arrangements such as those described above even if the entity that receives goods or services from its suppliers has no obligation to make the required share-based cash payments.

1.2.2 Transactions outside the scope of IFRS 2

Certain transactions are **outside the scope** of the IFRS:

(a) Transactions with employees and others in their capacity as a holder of equity instruments of the entity (for example, where an employee receives additional shares in a rights issue to all shareholders)

(b) The issue of equity instruments in exchange for control of another entity in a business combination

Key terms

Share-based payment transaction: A transaction in which the entity receives goods or services as consideration for equity instruments of the entity (including shares or share options), or acquires goods or services by incurring liabilities to the supplier of those goods or services for amounts that are based on the price of the entity's shares or other equity instruments of the entity.

Share-based payment arrangement. An agreement between the entity and another party (including an employee) to enter into a share-based payment transaction, which thereby entitles the other party to receive cash or other assets of the entity for amounts that are based on the price of the entity's shares or other equity instruments of the entity, or to receive equity instruments of the entity, provided the specified vesting conditions, if any, are met.

Equity instrument. A contract that evidences a residual interest in the assets of an entity after deducting all of its liabilities.

Equity instrument granted. The right (conditional or unconditional) to an equity instrument of the entity conferred by the entity on another party, under a share-based payment arrangement.

Share option. A contract that gives the holder the right, but not the obligation, to subscribe to the entity's shares at a fixed or determinable price for a specified period of time.

Fair value. The amount for which an asset could be exchanged, a liability settled, or an equity instrument granted could be exchanged, between knowledgeable, willing parties in an arm's length transaction. (Note that this definition is different from that in IFRS 13 *Fair value measurement*, but the IFRS 2 definition applies.)

Grant date. The date at which the entity and another party (including an employee) agree to a share-based payment arrangement, being when the entity and the other party have a shared understanding of the terms and conditions of the arrangement. At grant date the entity confers on the other party (the counterparty) the right to cash, other assets, or equity instruments of the entity, provided the specified vesting conditions, if any, are met. If that agreement is subject to an approval process (for example, by shareholders), grant date is the date when that approval is obtained.

Intrinsic value. The difference between the fair value of the shares to which the counterparty has the (conditional or unconditional) right to subscribe or which it has the right to receive, and the price (if any) the other party is (or will be) required to pay for those shares. For example, a share option with an exercise price of $15 on a share with a fair value of $20, has an intrinsic value of $5.

Measurement date. The date at which the fair value of the equity instruments granted is measured. For transactions with employees and others providing similar services, the measurement date is the grant date. For transactions with parties other than employees (and those providing similar services), the measurement date is the date the entity obtains the goods or the counterparty renders service.

Key terms (cont'd)

Vest. To become an entitlement. Under a share-based payment arrangement, a counterparty's right to receive cash, other assets, or equity instruments of the entity vests upon satisfaction of any specified vesting conditions.

Vesting conditions. The conditions that must be satisfied for the counterparty to become entitled to receive cash, other assets or equity instruments of the entity, under a share-based payment arrangement. Vesting conditions include service conditions, which require the other party to complete a specified period of service, and performance conditions, which require specified performance targets to be met (such as a specified increase in the entity's profit over a specified period of time).

Vesting period. The period during which all the specified vesting conditions of a share-based payment arrangement are to be satisfied.

(IFRS 2: Appendix A)

1.3 Vesting conditions

IFRS 2 recognises two types of vesting conditions (IFRS 2: para. 15):

Non-market based vesting conditions

These are conditions other than those relating to the market value of the entity's shares. Examples include vesting dependent on:

- The employee completing a minimum period of service (also referred to as a service condition)
- Achievement of minimum sales or earnings target
- Achievement of a specific increase in profit or earnings per share
- Successful completion of a flotation
- Completion of a particular project

Market based vesting conditions

Market-based performance or vesting conditions are conditions linked to the market price of the shares in some way. Examples include vesting dependent on achieving:

- A minimum increase in the share price of the entity
- A minimum increase in shareholder return
- A specified target share price relative to an index of market prices

The definition of vesting conditions is:

- Restricted to service conditions and performance conditions, and
- Excludes other features such as a requirement for employees to make regular contributions into a savings scheme.

1.4 Recognition: the basic principle

An entity should **recognise goods or services received or acquired in a share-based payment transaction when it obtains the goods or as the services are received**. Goods or services received or acquired in a share-based payment transaction **should be recognised as expenses unless they qualify for recognition as assets.** For example, services are normally recognised as expenses (because they are normally rendered immediately), while goods are recognised as assets.

If the goods or services were received or acquired in an **equity-settled** share-based payment transaction the entity should recognise **a corresponding increase in equity** (reserves).

If the goods or services were received or acquired in a **cash-settled** share-based payment transaction the entity should recognise a **liability**.

(IFRS 2: paras. 7 and 8)

1.5 Equity-settled share-based payment transactions

1.5.1 Measurement

The issue here is how to measure the 'cost' of the goods and services received and the equity instruments (eg the share options) granted in return.

The general principle in IFRS 2 is that when an entity recognises the goods or services received and the corresponding increase in equity, it should measure these at the **fair value of the goods or services received**. Where the transaction is with **parties other than employees**, there is a rebuttable presumption that the fair value of the goods or services received can be estimated reliably.

If the fair value of the goods or services received cannot be measured reliably, the entity should measure their value by reference to the **fair value of the equity instruments granted**.

Where the transaction is with a party other than an employee fair value should be measured at the date the entity obtains the goods or the counterparty renders service.

Where shares, share options or other equity instruments are granted to **employees** as part of their remuneration package, it is not normally possible to measure directly the services received. For this reason, the entity should measure the fair value of the employee services received by reference to the **fair value of the equity instruments granted**. The fair value of those equity instruments should be measured at the **grant date**.

(IFRS 2: paras. 11 to 13)

1.5.2 Determining the fair value of equity instruments granted

Where a transaction is measured by reference to the fair value of the equity instruments granted, fair value is based on **market prices** if available, taking into account the terms and conditions upon which those equity instruments were granted (IFRS 2: para. 16).

If market prices are not available, the entity should estimate the fair value of the equity instruments granted using a **valuation technique**. (These are beyond the scope of this exam.)

1.5.3 Transactions in which services are received

The issue here is **when** to recognise the transaction. When equity instruments are granted they may vest immediately, but often the counterparty has to meet specified conditions first. For example, an employee may have to complete a specified period of service. This means that the effect of the transaction normally has to be allocated over more than one accounting period.

If the equity instruments granted **vest immediately**, (ie the counterparty is not required to complete a specified period of service before becoming unconditionally entitled to the equity instruments) it is presumed that the services have already been received (in the absence of evidence to the contrary). The entity should **recognise the services received in full**, with a corresponding increase in equity, **on the grant date**.

If the equity instruments granted do not vest until the counterparty completes a specified period of service, the entity should account for those services **as they are rendered** by the counterparty during the vesting period. For example if an employee is granted share options on condition that he or she completes three years' service, then the services to be rendered by the employee as consideration for the share options will be received in the future, over that three-year vesting period.

The entity should recognise an amount for the goods or services received during the vesting period based on the **best available estimate** of the **number of equity instruments expected to vest**. It should **revise** that estimate if subsequent information indicates that the number of equity instruments expected to vest differs from previous estimates. On **vesting date**, the entity should revise the estimate to **equal the number of equity instruments that actually vest**.

Once the goods and services received and the corresponding increase in equity have been recognised, the entity should make no subsequent adjustment to total equity after vesting date.

(IFRS 2: paras. 14 and 15)

1.6 Example: Equity-settled share-based payment transaction

On 1 January 20X1 an entity grants 100 share options to each of its 400 employees. Each grant is conditional upon the employee working for the entity until 31 December 20X3. The fair value of each share option is $20.

During 20X1 20 employees leave and the entity estimates that 20% of the employees will leave during the three-year period.

During 20X2 a further 25 employees leave and the entity now estimates that 25% of its employees will leave during the three-year period.

During 20X3 a further 10 employees leave.

Required

Calculate the remuneration expense that will be recognised in respect of the share-based payment transaction for each of the three years ended 31 December 20X3.

Solution

IFRS 2 requires the entity to recognise the remuneration expense, based on the fair value of the share options granted, as the services are received during the three-year vesting period.

In 20X1 and 20X2 the entity estimates the number of options expected to vest (by estimating the number of employees likely to leave) and bases the amount that it recognises for the year on this estimate.

In 20X3 it recognises an amount based on the number of options that actually vest. A total of 55 employees left during the three-year period and therefore 34,500 options ((400 – 55) × 100) vested. The amount recognised as an expense for each of the three years is calculated as follows:

		Cumulative expense at year-end	*Expense for year*
		$	$
20X1	40,000 × 80% × 20 × 1/3	213,333	213,333
20X2	40,000 × 75% × 20 × 2/3	400,000	186,667
20X3	34,500 × 20	690,000	290,000

Question — Share options

During its financial year ended 31 January 20X6, TSQ issued share options to several of its senior employees. The options vest immediately upon issue.

Which **one** of the following describes the accounting entry that is required to recognise the options?

A	DEBIT the statement of changes in equity	CREDIT liabilities
B	DEBIT the statement of changes in equity	CREDIT equity
C	DEBIT profit or loss	CREDIT liabilities
D	DEBIT profit or loss	CREDIT equity

Answer

D Under IFRS 2 a charge must be made to the profit or loss.

Question — Share based payment 1

On 1 January 20X3 an entity grants 250 share options to each of its 200 employees. The only condition attached to the grant is that the employees should continue to work for the entity until 31 December 20X6. Five employees leave during the year.

The market price of each option was $12 at 1 January 20X3 and $15 at 31 December 20X3.

Required

Show how this transaction will be reflected in the financial statements for the year ended 31 December 20X3.

Answer

The remuneration expense for the year is based on the fair value of the options granted at the grant date (1 January 20X3). As five of the 200 employees left during the year it is reasonable to assume that 20 employees will leave during the four-year vesting period and that therefore 45,000 options (250 × 180) will actually vest.

Therefore, the entity recognises a remuneration expense of \$135,000 (45,000 × 12 × ¼) in profit or loss and a corresponding increase in equity of the same amount.

Question — Share based payment 2

J&B granted 200 options on its \$1 ordinary shares to each of its 800 employees on 1 January 20X1. Each grant is conditional upon the employee being employed by J&B until 31 December 20X3.

J&B estimated at 1 January 20X1 that:

(i) The fair value of each option was \$4 (before adjustment for the possibility of forfeiture).

(ii) Approximately 50 employees would leave during 20X1, 40 during 20X2 and 30 during 20X3 thereby forfeiting their rights to receive the options. The departures were expected to be evenly spread within each year.

The exercise price of the options was \$1.50 and the market value of a J&B share on 1 January 20X1 was \$3.

In the event, only 40 employees left during 20X1 (and the estimate of total departures was revised down to 95 at 31 December 20X1), 20 during 20X2 (and the estimate of total departures was revised to 70 at 31 December 20X2) and none during 20X3, spread evenly during each year.

Required

The directors of J&B have asked you to illustrate how the scheme is accounted for under IFRS 2 *Share-based payment.*

(a) Show the double entries for the charge to profit or loss for employee services over the three years and for the share issue, assuming all employees entitled to benefit from the scheme exercised their rights and the shares were issued on 31 December 20X3.

(b) Explain how your solution would differ had J&B offered its employees cash based on the share value rather than share options.

Answer

(a) **Accounting entries**

		\$	\$
31.12.X1			
DEBIT	Profit or loss (Staff costs)	188,000	
CREDIT	Equity reserve ((800 – 95) × 200 × \$4 × 1/3)		188,000
31.12.X2			
DEBIT	Profit or loss (Staff costs) (W1)	201,333	
CREDIT	Equity reserve		201,333
31.12.X3			
DEBIT	Profit or loss (Staff costs) (W2)	202,667	
CREDIT	Equity reserve		202,667
Issue of shares:			
DEBIT	Cash (740 × 200 × \$1.50)	222,000	
DEBIT	Equity reserve	592,000	
CREDIT	Share capital (740 × 200 × \$1)		148,000
CREDIT	Share premium (balancing figure)		666,000

Workings

1 *Equity reserve at 31.12.X2*

	$
Equity b/d	188,000
∴ P/L charge	201,333
Equity c/d ((800 – 70) × 200 × $4 × 2/3)	389,333

2 *Equity reserve at 31.12.X3*

Equity b/d	389,333
∴ P/L charge	202,667
Equity c/d ((800 – 40 – 20) × 200 × $4 × 3/3)	592,000

(b) **Cash-settled share-based payment**

If J&B had offered cash payments based on the value of the shares at vesting date rather than options, in each of the three years an accrual would be shown in the statement of financial position representing the expected amount payable based on the following:

No of employees estimated at the year end to be entitled to rights at the vesting date	×	Number of rights each	×	Fair value of each right at year end	×	Cumulative proportion of vesting period elapsed

The movement in the accrual would be charged to profit or loss representing further entitlements received during the year and adjustments to expectations accrued in previous years.

The accrual would continue to be adjusted (resulting in a profit or loss charge) for changes in the fair value of the right over the period between when the rights become fully vested and are subsequently exercised. It would then be reduced for cash payments as the rights are exercised.

1.7 Cancellation and reissuance

Where an entity has been through a capital restructuring or there has been a significant downturn in the equity market through external factors, an alternative to **repricing** the **share options** is to **cancel** them and issue new options based on revised terms. The end result is essentially the same as an entity modifying the original options and therefore should be recognised in the same way.

As well as the entity, two other parties may cancel an equity instrument:

- Cancellations by the counterparty (eg the employee)
- Cancellations by a third party (eg a shareholder)

Cancellations by the employee must be treated in the same way as cancellations by the employer, resulting in an **accelerated charge to profit or loss of the unamortised balance of the options granted**.

(IFRS 2: para. 26)

1.8 Cash-settled share-based payment transactions

Examples of this type of transaction include:

(a) **Share appreciation rights** granted to employees: the employees become entitled to a future cash payment (rather than an equity instrument), based on the increase in the entity's share price from a specified level over a specified period of time, or

(b) An entity might grant to its employees a right to receive a future cash payment by granting to them a **right to shares that are redeemable**.

The basic principle is that the entity measures the goods or services acquired and the liability incurred at the **fair value of the liability**.

The entity should **remeasure** the fair value of the liability **at each reporting date** until the liability is settled **and at the date of settlement**. Any **changes** in fair value are recognised in **profit or loss** for the period.

The entity should recognise the services received, and a liability to pay for those services, **as the employees render service.** For example, if share appreciation rights do not vest until the employees have completed a specified period of service, the entity should recognise the services received and the related liability, over that period.

(IFRS 2: paras. 31 to 32)

1.9 Example: Cash-settled share-based payment transaction

On 1 January 20X1 an entity grants 100 cash share appreciation rights (SARS) to each of its 500 employees, on condition that the employees continue to work for the entity until 31 December 20X3.

During 20X1 35 employees leave. The entity estimates that a further 60 will leave during 20X2 and 20X3.

During 20X2 40 employees leave and the entity estimates that a further 25 will leave during 20X3.

During 20X3 22 employees leave.

At 31 December 20X3 150 employees exercise their SARs. Another 140 employees exercise their SARs at 31 December 20X4 and the remaining 113 employees exercise their SARs at the end of 20X5.

The fair values of the SARs for each year in which a liability exists are shown below, together with the intrinsic values at the dates of exercise.

	Fair value	*Intrinsic value*
	$	$
20X1	14.40	
20X2	15.50	
20X3	18.20	15.00
20X4	21.40	20.00
20X5		25.00

Required

Calculate the amount to be recognised in the profit or loss for each of the five years ended 31 December 20X5 and the liability to be recognised in the statement of financial position at 31 December for each of the five years.

Solution

For the three years to the vesting date of 31 December 20X3 the expense is based on the entity's estimate of the number of SARs that will actually vest (as for an equity-settled transaction). However, the fair value of the liability is **re-measured** at each year-end.

The intrinsic value of the SARs at the date of exercise is the amount of cash actually paid.

		Liability at year-end		*Expense for year*
		$	$	$
20X1	Expected to vest (500 – 95):			
	405 × 100 × 14.40 × 1/3	194,400		194,400
20X2	Expected to vest (500 – 100):			
	400 × 100 × 15.50 × 2/3	413,333		218,933
20X3	Exercised:			
	150 ×100 × 15.00		225,000	
	Not yet exercised (500 – 97 – 150):			
	253 × 100 × 18.20	460,460	47,127	
				272,127

	Liability at year-end		*Expense for year*
20X4 Exercised:			
140 × 100 × 20.00			280,000
Not yet exercised (253 – 140):			
113 × 100 × 21.40	241,820		(218,640)
			61,360
	$	$	$
20X5 Exercised:			
113 × 100 × 25.00		282,500	
	Nil	(241,820)	
			40,680
			787,500

1.10 Transactions which either the entity or the other party has a choice of settling in cash or by issuing equity instruments

If the entity has incurred a liability to settle in cash or other assets it should account for the transaction as a cash-settled share-based payment transaction (IFRS 2: para. 41).

If no such liability has been incurred the entity should account for the transaction as an equity-settled share-based payment transaction (IFRS 2: paras. 43).

1.11 Amendment to IFRS 2 *Classification and measurement of share-based payment transactions*

This amendment was issued in June 2016. It addresses the following three issues (IFRS 2: paras 33A to 33D.

(a) Accounting for cash-settled **share-based payment transactions that include a performance condition (vesting condition)**. The amendment clarifies that the accounting in the case of **cash-settled** share-based payments should follow the **same approach as used for equity-settled** share-based payments.

(b) **Classification of share-based payment transactions with net settlement features**, for example, where an employer settles a share based payment transaction by issuing a net number of shares to the employee and paying cash to the tax authority. An exception is added to IFRS 2 so that a share-based payment where the entity settles the share-based payment arrangement net would be **classified as equity-settled in its entirety provided the share-based payment would have been classified as equity-settled had it not included the net settlement feature**.

(c) **Accounting for modifications of share-based payment transactions from cash-settled to equity-settled.** The amendment requires the following approach.

   (i) The **original liability** recognised in respect of the cash-settled share-based payment should be **derecognised** and the **equity-settled share-based payment should be recognised at the modification date fair value to the extent services have been rendered** up to the modification date.

   (ii) The **difference**, if any, between the carrying amount of the liability as at the modification date and the amount recognised in equity at the same date would **be recognised in profit or loss immediately**.

1.12 Section summary

IFRS 2 requires entities to **recognise** the goods or services received as a result of **share based payment transactions**.

- Equity settled transactions: DEBIT Asset/Expense, CREDIT Equity
- Cash settled transactions: DEBIT Asset/Expense, CREDIT Liability
- Transactions are **recognised when goods/services are obtained/received** (usually over the performance period)
- Transactions are measured at fair value

2 Deferred tax implications

FAST FORWARD

An entity may receive a tax deduction that is different in timing or amount from the related expense.

2.1 Issue

An entity may receive a tax deduction that differs from related cumulative remuneration expense, and may arise in a later accounting period.

For example, an entity recognises an expense for share options granted under IFRS 2, but does not receive a tax deduction until the options are exercised and receives the tax deduction at the share price on the exercise date.

2.2 Measurement

The deferred tax asset temporary difference is measured as:

Carrying amount of share-based payment expense	0
Less: tax base of share-based payment expense (estimated amount tax authorities will permit as a deduction in future periods, based on year end information)	(X)
Temporary difference	(X)
Deferred tax asset at X%	X

If the amount of the tax deduction (or estimated future tax deduction) exceeds the amount of the related cumulative remuneration expense, this indicates that the tax deduction relates also to an equity item.

The excess is therefore recognised directly in equity (IAS 12: paras. 68A to 68C).

2.3 Example: Deferred tax implications of share-based payment

On 1 January 20X2, Bruce granted 5,000 share options to an employee vesting two years later on 31 December 20X3. The fair value of each option measured at the grant date was $3.

Tax law in the jurisdiction in which the entity operates allows a tax deduction of the intrinsic value of the options on exercise. The intrinsic value of the share options was $1.20 at 31 December 20X2 and $3.40 at 31 December 20X3 on which date the options were exercised.

Assume a tax rate of 30%.

Required

Show the deferred tax accounting treatment of the above transaction at 31 December 20X2, 31 December 20X3 (before exercise), and on exercise.

Solution

	31/12/20X2	31/12/20X3 before exercise
Carrying amount of share-based payment expense	0	0
Less: Tax base of share-based payment expense (5,000 × $1.2 × ½)/(5,000 × $3.40)	(3,000)	(17,000)
Temporary difference	(3,000)	(17,000)
Deferred tax asset @ 30%	900	5,100
Deferred tax (Cr P/L) (5,100 – 900 – (Working) 600)	900	3,600
Deferred tax (Cr Equity) (Working)	0	600

On exercise, the deferred tax asset is replaced by a current tax one. The double entry is:

DEBIT Deferred tax (I/S)	4,500		reversal
DEBIT Deferred tax (equity)	600		
CREDIT Deferred tax asset		5,100	

DEBIT Current tax asset	5,100	
CREDIT Current tax (I/S)		4,500
CREDIT Current tax (equity)		600

Working

Accounting expense recognised (5,000 × $3 × ½)/(5,000 × $3)	7,500	15,000
Tax deduction	(3,000)	(17,000)
Excess temporary difference	0	(2,000)
Excess deferred tax asset to equity @ 30%	0	600

Chapter Roundup

- **Share-based payment** transactions should be recognised in the financial statements. You need to understand and be able to advise on:

  – Recognition
  – Measurement
  – Disclosure

  of both equity settled and cash settled transactions.

- An entity may receive a tax deduction that differs in timing or amount from the related expense.

Quick Quiz

1 What is a cash-settled share based payment transaction?

2 What is the grant date?

3 If an entity has entered into an equity settled share-based payment transaction, what should it recognise in its financial statements?

4 Where an entity has granted share options to its employees in return for services, how is the transaction measured?

Answers to Quick Quiz

1 A transaction in which the entity receives goods or services in exchange for amounts of cash that are based on the price (or value) of the entity's shares or other equity instruments of the entity.

2 The date at which the entity and another party (including an employee) agree to a share-based payment arrangement, being when the entity and the other party have a shared understanding of the terms and conditions of the arrangement.

3 The goods or services received and a corresponding increase in equity.

4 By reference to the fair value of the equity instruments granted, measured at grant date.

Now try the question below from the Practice Question Bank

Number	Level	Marks	Time
Q14	Examination	25	49 mins

10

Performance reporting

Topic list	Syllabus reference
1 Reporting financial performance	C1
2 Segment reporting	C1
3 IAS 33 *Earnings per share*	C1
4 IAS 34 *Interim financial reporting*	C1
5 Ratio analysis	G2
6 Impact of changes in accounting standards and policies	F2
7 Accounting theory and practice	B2
8 Management Commentary – a global Operating and Financial Review?	F2

Introduction

This chapter covers a great many standards, but you are very familiar with some of them. **IAS 1** was revised in 2007 and again in 2011.

Earnings per share is important: it is used internationally as a comparative performance figure.

Ratio analysis at P2 is likely to come up in the category of changing accounting policies.

Study guide

		Intellectual level
C1	**Performance reporting**	
(a)	Prepare reports relating to corporate performance for external stakeholders	3
C5	**Segment reporting**	
(a)	Determine business and geographical segments and reportable segments	3
(b)	Specify and discuss the nature of information to be disclosed	
G2	**Analysis and interpretation of financial information and measurement of performance**	
(a)	Select and calculate relevant indicators of financial and non-financial performance	3
(b)	Identify and evaluate significant features and issues in financial statements	3
(c)	Highlight inconsistencies in financial information through analysis and application of knowledge	3
(d)	Make inferences from the analysis of the information, taking into account the limitation of the information, the analytical methods used and the business environment in which the entity operates.	3
F1	**The effect of changes in accounting standards on accounting systems**	
(a)	Apply and discuss the accounting implications of the first time adoption of a body of new accounting standards	3
F2	**Proposed changes to accounting standards**	
(a)	Identify the issues and deficiencies which have led to a proposed change to an accounting standard	2
B2	**Critical evaluation of principles and practices**	
(a)	Identify the relationship between accounting theory and practice	2
(b)	Critically evaluate accounting principles and practices used in corporate reporting	3

Exam guide

EPS is covered at an earlier level, so the details are not covered here. However, you may need to know how the earnings figure can be manipulated.

1 Reporting financial performance 6/11

FAST FORWARD

Go back to your earlier studies and revise **IAS 1** and **IAS 8. IAS 1 was revised in 2007 and 2011.** The changes and new formats are given in this section.

1.1 Revision of IAS 1 Presentation of Financial Statements

1.1.1 Format of statement of financial position and statement of changes in equity

Below are current IAS 1 formats for the statement of financial position and statement of changes in equity (IAS 1: IG).

XYZ GROUP – STATEMENT OF FINANCIAL POSITION AT 31 DECEMBER

	20X7	20X6
Assets	$'000	$'000
Non-current assets		
Property, plant and equipment	350,700	360,020
Goodwill	80,800	91,200
Other intangible assets	227,470	227,470
Investments in associates	100,150	110,770
Investments in equity instruments	142,500	156,000
	901,620	945,460
Current assets		
Inventories	135,230	132,500
Trade receivables	91,600	110,800
Other current assets	25,650	12,540
Cash and cash equivalents	312,400	322,900
	564,880	578,740
Total assets	1,466,500	1,524,200
Equity and liabilities		
Equity attributable to owners of the parent		
Share capital	650,000	600,000
Retained earnings	243,500	161,700
Other components of equity	10,200	21,200
	903,700	782,900
Non-controlling interest*	70,050	48,600
Total equity	973,750	831,500
Non-current liabilities		
Long-term borrowings	120,000	160,000
Deferred tax	28,800	26,040
Long-term provisions	28,850	52,240
Total non-current liabilities	177,650	238,280
Current liabilities		
Trade and other payables	115,100	187,620
Short-term borrowings	150,000	200,000
Current portion of long-term borrowings	10,000	20,000
Current tax payable	35,000	42,000
Short-term provisions	5,000	4,800
Total current liabilities	315,100	454,420
Total liabilities	492,750	692,700
Total equity and liabilities	1,466,500	1,524,200

XYZ GROUP – STATEMENT OF CHANGES IN EQUITY FOR THE YEAR ENDED 31 DECEMBER 20X7

	Share capital	*Retained earnings*	*Translation of foreign operations*	*Available for-sale financial assets*	*Cash flow hedges*	*Revaluation surplus*	*Total*	*NCI*	*Total equity*
	$'000	$'000	$'000	$'000	$'000	$'000	$'000	$'000	$'000
Balance at 1 January 20X6	600,000	118,100	(4,000)	1,600	2,000	–	717,700	29,800	747,500
Changes in accounting policy	–	400	–	–	–	–	400	100	500
Restated balance	600,000	118,500	(4,000)	1,600	2,000	–	718,100	29,900	748,000
Changes in equity for 20X6									
Dividends	–	(10,000)	–	–	–	–	(10,000)	–	(10,000)
Total comprehensive income for the year	–	53,200	6,400	16,000	(2,400)	1,600	74,800	18,700	93,500
Balance at 31 December 20X6	600,000	161,700	2,400	17,600	(400)	1,600	782,900	48,600	831,500
Changes in equity for 20X7									
Issue of share capital	50,000	–	–	–	–	–	50,000	–	50,000
Dividends	–	(15,000)	–	–	–	–	(15,000)	–	(15,000)
Total comprehensive income for the year	–	96,600	3,200	(14,400)	(400)	800	85,800	21,450	107,250
Transfer to retained earnings	–	200	–	–	–	(200)	–	–	–
Balance at 31 December 20X7	650,000	243,500	5,600	3,200	(800)	2,200	903,700	70,050	973,750

PER alert

One of the competences you need to fulfil Objective 11 of the Practical Experience Requirement (PER) is to draw valid conclusions from the information contained within financial statements or financial data. You can apply the knowledge you obtain from this chapter, on performance reporting, to demonstrate this competence.

Exam focus point

IAS 1 is very straightforward, but it is important. If necessary, go back to your previous study material. In particular you need to be aware of the **current/non-current distinction**, which is not discussed above. You should also be aware of the recent revisions to IAS 1.

1.2 Presentation of items of other comprehensive income

FAST FORWARD

IAS 1 requires the presentation of items of other comprehensive income.

IAS 1 para. 82A deals with the presentation of items contained in Other Comprehensive Income (OCI) and their classification within OCI.

1.2.1 Issue

The **blurring of distinctions** between different items in OCI is the result of an underlying **general lack of agreement** among users and preparers about **which items should be presented in OCI** and which should be part of the profit or loss section. For instance, a common misunderstanding is that the split between profit or loss and OCI is on the basis of realised versus unrealised gains. This is not, and has never been, the case.

This lack of a consistent basis for determining how items should be presented led to the somewhat inconsistent use of OCI in financial statements.

1.2.2 Current rules

Entities are required to group items presented in other comprehensive income (OCI) on the basis of **whether they would be reclassified** to (recycled through) profit or loss at a later date, when specified conditions are met.

1.2.3 Illustrative example

Note. This example illustrates the classification of expenses within profit or loss by function. The important aspect to focus on is the treatment of other comprehensive income (IAS 1: IG).

XYZ GROUP – STATEMENT OF PROFIT OR LOSS AND OTHER COMPREHENSIVE INCOME
FOR THE YEAR ENDED 31 DECEMBER 20X7

	$'000	$'000
Revenue	390,000	355,000
Cost of sales	(245,000)	(230,000)
Gross profit	145,000	125,000
Other income	20,667	11,300
Distribution costs	(9,000)	(8,700)
Administrative expenses	(20,000)	(21,000)
Other expenses	(2,100)	(1,200)
Finance costs	(8,000)	(7,500)
Share of profit of associates	35,100	30,100
Profit before tax	161,667	128,000
Income tax expense	(40,417)	(32,000)
Profit for the year from continuing operations	121,250	96,000
Loss for the year from discontinued operations	–	(30,500)
PROFIT FOR THE YEAR	121,250	65,500

	$'000	$'000
Other comprehensive income:		
Items that will not be reclassified to profit or loss:		
Gains on property revaluation	933	3,367
Investment in equity instruments	(24,000)	26,667
Actuarial gains (losses) on defined benefit pension plans	(667)	1,333
Share of gain (loss) on property revaluation of associates	400	(700)
Income tax relating to items that will not be reclassifed	5,834	(7,667)
	(17,500)	23,000
Items that may be reclassified subsequently to profit or loss:		
Exchange differences on translating foreign operations	5,334	10,667
Cash flow hedges	(667)	(4,000)
Income tax relating to items that may be reclassified	(1,167)	(1,667)
	3,500	5,000
Other comprehensive income for the year, net of tax	(14,000)	28,000
TOTAL COMPREHENSIVE INCOME FOR THE YEAR	107,250	93,500
Profit attributable to:		
Owners of the parent	97,000	52,400
Non-controlling interests	24,250	13,100
	121,250	65,500
Total comprehensive income attributable to:		
Owners of the parent	85,800	74,800
Non-controlling interests	21,450	18,700
	107,250	93,500
Earnings per share ($)		
Basic and diluted	0.46	0.30

Alternatively, items could be presented in the statement of profit or loss and other comprehensive income net of tax.

Note that gains or losses on financial assets held within a business model whose objective is achieved by both collecting contractual cash flows and selling financial assets, and which must be classified at fair value through other comprehensive income, must be re-classified to profit or loss when the asset is sold.

1.3 Disclosure initiative: Amendments to IAS 1

An overview of the IASB's disclosure initiative is given in Chapter 19 on current developments. Of the various projects being undertaken, only one, the amendments to IAS 1 is complete. The amendments were published in 2014 and took effect from January 2016. Their purpose is to address perceived obstacles that prevent preparers from exercising their judgement in presenting financial reports

1.3.1 Materiality

Entities should avoid aggregating or disaggregating information in a manner that obscures useful information, for example, by aggregating items that have different characteristics or disclosing a large amount of immaterial detail. This reduces understandability.

When management determines an item is material, IAS 1 requires assessment of which specific disclosures (set out in the relevant standard) should be presented. An assessment is also required of whether additional information is necessary to meet the needs of users or the disclosure objectives of the standard in question.

(IAS 1: paras. 35, 55A)

1.3.2 Draft Practice Statement: Application of Materiality to Financial Statements

This Draft Practice Statement was issued as part of the Disclosure Initiative in October 2015. The Statement was developed in response to concerns with the level of uncertainty over the application of the concept of materiality, which can result in excessive disclosure of immaterial information while important information can be obscured or even missed out of the financial statements. It provides non-mandatory guidance to assist with the application of the concept of materiality to financial statements prepared in accordance with IFRS. The statement is divided into the following three key areas (ED/2015/8: Para. IN4):

(a) **Characteristics of materiality**, including:

 (i) The pervasiveness of the concept in IFRS

 (ii) The importance of management's use of judgement

 (iii) Who the primary users of the financial statements are and what decisions they make based on those financial statements

 (iv) The need for a quantitative and qualitative assessment when applying the concept and

 (v) The need to assess whether information is material, both individually and collectively

(b) How to apply the concept of materiality when making decisions about **presenting and disclosing information** in the financial statements, in particular:

 (i) The objective of the financial statements and how it relates to materiality decisions

 (ii) How to deal with immaterial information

 (iii) When to aggregate and disaggregate information

 (iv) Making judgements about materiality in the context of the face of the financial statements, the notes to the financial statements, the complete set of financial statements (ie considering the financial statements as a whole) and interim reports

(c) How to assess **whether omissions and misstatements of information are material** to the financial statements. Guidance is given on:

 (i) Assessing whether misstatements are material

 (ii) Current period misstatements versus prior period misstatements

 (iii) Dealing with misstatements that are made intentionally to mislead

It also includes a short section on applying materiality when applying recognition and measurement requirements and includes illustrative examples throughout.

1.3.3 Disaggregation and subtotals

IAS 1 allows subtotals additional to the ones required by IAS 1 in the statement of financial position or the statement of profit or loss and other comprehensive income. The amendments to IAS 1 specify what additional subtotals are acceptable and how they are presented.

Additional subtotals should meet the following requirements (IAS 1: para. 55).

(a) They must be comprised of items recognised and measured in accordance with IFRS.

(b) They must be presented and labelled in a manner that makes the components of the subtotal clear and understandable.

(c) They must be consistent from period to period.

(d) They must not be displayed with more prominence than the subtotals and totals specified in IAS 1.

(e) Any additional subtotals must be reconciled to the subtotals and totals required by IAS 1.

1.3.4 Notes

IAS 1 does not require entities to present the notes to the financial statements in a particular order. There is scope, therefore, for management to consider understandability and comparability when it determines the order of the notes. For example, an entity might present more significant notes first, or present linked areas sequentially. IAS 1 already permits this flexibility, which may enable management to provide further insight about the entity.

1.3.5 Disclosure of accounting policies

These amendments remove guidance and examples with regard to the identification of significant accounting policies that were perceived as being potentially unhelpful.

1.3.6 Other comprehensive income arising from investments accounted for under the equity method

The amendments clarify that the share of other comprehensive income arising from investments accounted for under the equity method is grouped based on whether the items will or will not subsequently be reclassified as profit or loss. Each group should then be presented as a single line item in the statement of other comprehensive income.

1.4 Other aspects of IAS 1

You should note the following further aspects of IAS 1.

(a) The standard includes various definitions.

Key terms

- **Material.** Omissions or misstatements of items are material if they could, individually or collectively, influence the economic decisions of users taken on the basis of the financial statements. Materiality depends on the size and nature of the omission or misstatement judged in the surrounding circumstances. The size or nature of the item, or a combination of both, could be the determining factor.
- **Impracticable.** Applying a requirement is impracticable when the entity cannot apply it after making every reasonable effort to do so.

(b) Guidance is provided on the meaning of **present fairly**, ie represent **faithfully** the effects of transactions and other events in accordance with the **definitions** and recognition criteria for assets, liabilities, income and expenses as set out in the ***Conceptual Framework***.

(c) The application of **IFRSs** with **additional disclosure** where necessary, is presumed to result in financial statements that achieve a **fair presentation**.

(d) In extremely rare circumstances, **compliance** with a requirement of an IFRS or IFRIC may be so **misleading** that it would conflict with the objective of financial statements set out in the *Framework*, the entity shall **depart from that specific requirement**.

  (i) Where the relevant regulatory framework requires or does not prohibit such a departure, the entity must disclose:

    (1) That management has concluded that the financial statements present fairly the entity's financial position, financial performance and cash flows

    (2) That it has complied with applicable IFRSs except that it has departed from a particular requirement to achieve a fair presentation

    (3) Full details of the departure

    (4) The impact on the financial statements for each item affected and for each period presented

  (ii) Where the relevant regulatory framework prohibits departure from the requirement, the entity shall, to the **maximum extent possible**, **reduce** the perceived **misleading aspects** of compliance by **disclosing**:

    (1) The relevant IFRS, the nature of the requirement and the reason why complying with the requirement is misleading

(2) For each period presented, the adjustments to each item in the financial statements that would be necessary to achieve a fair presentation

(e) An entity must present **current** and **non-current assets**, and **current** and **non-current liabilities**, as **separate classifications** in the statement of financial position. A presentation based on liquidity should only be used where it provides more relevant and reliable information, in which cases, all assets and liabilities shall be presented broadly in order of liquidity (IAS 1: paras. 60, 66, 68).

(f) A **long-term financial liability** due to be **settled within twelve months** of the year end date should be classified as a **current liability**, even if an agreement to refinance, or to reschedule payments, on a long-term basis is completed after the reporting period and before the financial statements are authorised for issue (IAS 1: paras. 60, 66, 68).

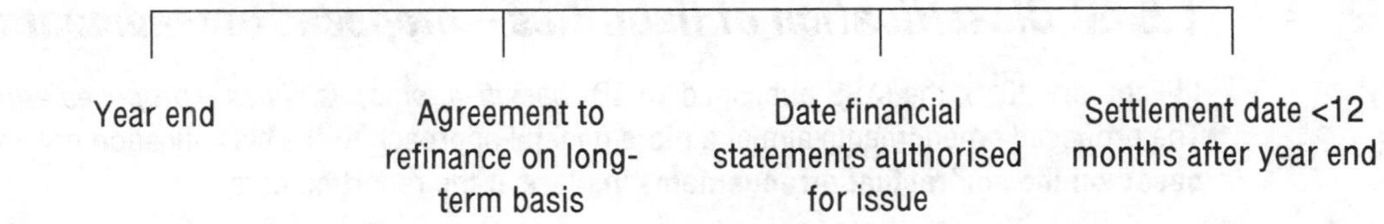

(g) A **long-term financial liability** that is payable on **demand** because the entity **breached** a **condition** of its loan agreement should be classified as **current** at the year end even if the **lender** has agreed **after the year end**, and **before** the financial statements are **authorised for issue**, **not** to **demand payment** as a consequence of the breach (IAS 1: paras. 60, 66, 68).

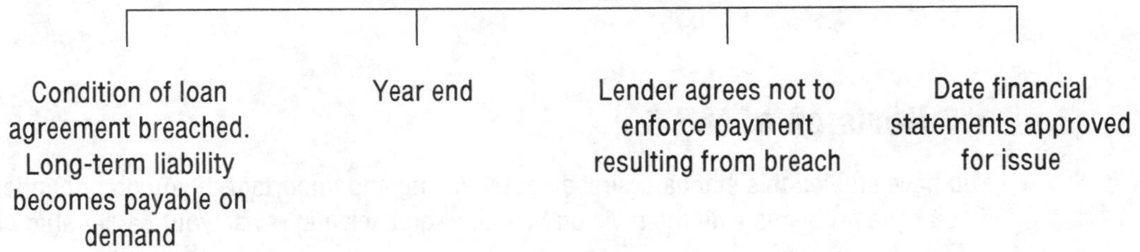

However, if the **lender** has **agreed** by the **year end** to provide a **period of grace** ending **at least twelve months after the year end** within which the entity can rectify the breach and during that time the lender cannot demand immediate repayment, the liability is classified as **non-current**.

(h) All requirements previously set out in other standards for the presentation of particular line items in the statement of financial position and statement of profit or loss and other comprehensive income are now dealt with in IAS 1. These line items are: biological assets; liabilities and assets for current tax and deferred tax; and pre-tax gain or loss recognised on the disposal of assets or settlement of liabilities attributable to discontinuing operations (IAS 1: paras. 54, 55).

(i) The section that set out the **presentation requirements** for the **net profit or loss** for the period in **IAS 8** has now been **transferred** to **IAS 1** instead (IAS 1: IG).

(j) The following disclosures are no longer required:

(i) The results of operating activities, as a line item on the face of the statement of profit or loss and other comprehensive income. '**Operating activities**' are **not defined in IAS 1**

(ii) **Extraordinary items**, as a line item on the face of the statement of profit or loss and other comprehensive income (note that the disclosure of 'extraordinary items' is now **prohibited**)

(iii) The **number** of an **entity's employees**

(k) An entity must disclose, in the summary of significant accounting policies and/or other notes, the **judgements** made by management in **applying** the **accounting policies** that have the **most significant effect** on the amounts of items recognised in the financial statements (IAS 1: para. 117).

(l) An entity must disclose in the notes information regarding **key assumptions** about the **future**, and other sources of **measurement uncertainty**, that have a significant **risk of** causing a **material**

adjustment to the carrying amounts of assets and liabilities within the **next financial year**. (IAS 1: para. 125).

(m) The following items must be disclosed on the **face of the statement of profit or loss and other comprehensive income** (IAS 1: para. 81B).

(i) Profit or loss attributable to **non-controlling interest**
(ii) Profit or loss attributable to **equity** holders of the parent

The allocated amounts must not be presented as items of income or expense. There is a similar requirement for the statement of changes in equity or statement of recognised income and expense. (See the example formats above.)

1.5 ED *Classification of liabilities – proposed amendments to IAS 1.*

In February 2015, the IASB published an ED *Classification of liabilities – proposed amendments to IAS 1.* The proposed amendments aim at a more general approach to the classification of liabilities under IAS 1 **based on the contractual arrangements** in place at the reporting date.

The amendment seeks to clarify the principles for **classifying liabilities as current or non-current**. It proposes that classification should be based only on the entity's rights in place at the end of the reporting period and in particular, rights to 'roll over' a loan facility. The amendment also clarifies the term 'settlement' to include the 'transfer to the counterparty of cash, equity instruments, other assets and services'.

(IAS 1: para. 72R).

1.6 Revision of IAS 8 12/13

You have studied this standard already but it is long and important. If you do not understand any of this or if you have problems with the revision question, go back and revise your earlier study material.

There have been extensive revisions to the standard, which is now called IAS 8 *Accounting policies, changes in accounting estimates and errors.* The new title reflects the fact that the material on determining net profit and loss for the period has been transferred to IAS 1.

Knowledge brought forward from earlier studies

IAS 8 *Accounting policies, changes in accounting estimates and errors*

Definitions

- **Accounting policies** are the specific principles, bases, conventions, rules and practices adopted by an entity in preparing and presenting financial statements.

The remaining definitions are either new or heavily amended.

- A **change in accounting estimate** is an adjustment of the carrying amount of an asset or a liability or the amount of the periodic consumption of an asset, that results from the assessment of the present status of, and expected future benefits and obligations associated with, assets and liabilities. Changes in accounting estimates result from new information or new developments and, accordingly, are not corrections of errors.
- **Material**: as defined in IAS 1 (see above)
- **Prior period errors** are omissions from, and misstatements in, the entity's financial statements for one or more prior periods arising from a failure to use, or misuse of, reliable information that:

  (a) Was available when financial statements for those periods were authorised for issue, and

  (b) Could reasonably be expected to have been obtained and taken into account in the preparation and presentation of those financial statements.

Such errors include the effects of mathematical mistakes, mistakes in applying accounting policies, oversights or misinterpretations of facts, and fraud.

- **Retrospective application** is applying a new accounting policy to transactions, other events and conditions as if that policy had always been applied.
- **Retrospective restatement** is correcting the recognition, measurement and disclosure of amounts of elements of financial statements as if a prior period error had never occurred.
- **Prospective application** of a change in accounting policy and of recognising the effect of a change in an accounting estimate, respectively, are:
  - (a) Applying the new accounting policy to transactions, other events and conditions occurring after the date as at which the policy is changes; and
  - (b) Recognising the effect of the change in the accounting estimate in the current and future periods affected by the change.
- **Impracticable.** Applying a requirement is impracticable when the entity cannot apply it after making every reasonable effort to do so. It is impracticable to apply a change in an accounting policy retrospectively or to make a retrospective restatement to correct an error if one of the following apply.
  - (a) The effects or the retrospective application or retrospective restatement are not determinable.
  - (b) The retrospective application or retrospective restatement requires assumptions about what management's intent would have been in that period.
  - (c) The retrospective application or retrospective restatement requires significant estimates of amounts and it is impossible to distinguish objectively information about those estimates that: provides evidence of circumstances that existed on the date(s) at which those amounts are to be recognised, measured or disclosed; and would have been available when the financial statements for that prior period were authorised for issue from other information.

(IAS 8: para. 5)

Accounting policies (IAS 8: paras. 7 to 13)

- Accounting policies are determined by **applying the relevant IFRS or IFRIC** and considering any relevant Implementation Guidance issued by the IASB for that IFRS/IFRIC.
- Where there is no applicable IFRS or IFRIC management should use its **judgement** in developing and applying an accounting policy that results in information that is **relevant** and **reliable**. Management should refer to:
  - (a) The requirements and guidance in IFRSs and IFRICs dealing with **similar** and **related issues**
  - (b) The definitions, recognition criteria and measurement concepts for assets, liabilities and expenses in the ***Conceptual Framework***

  Management may also consider the most recent pronouncements of other standard setting bodies that use a similar conceptual framework to develop standards, other accounting literature and accepted industry practices if these do not conflict with the sources above.
- An entity shall select and apply its accounting policies for a period **consistently** for similar transactions, other events and conditions, unless an IFRS or an IFRIC specifically requires or permits categorisation of items for which different policies may be appropriate. If an IFRS or an IFRIC requires or permits categorisation of items, an appropriate accounting policy shall be selected and applied consistently to each category.

Knowledge brought forward from earlier studies (continued)

Changes in accounting policies (IAS 8: paras. 14 to 22)

- These are **rare**: only required by statute/standard-setting body/results in reliable and more relevant information.
- **Adoption of new IAS**: follow transitional provisions of IAS. If no transitional provisions: **retrospective** application.
- **Other changes in policy**: **retrospective** application. Adjust opening balance of each affected component of equity, ie as if new policy has always been applied.
- **Prospective** application is **no longer allowed** unless it is **impracticable** to determine the cumulative effect of the change. (See definition of impracticable above.)
- An entity should **disclose** information relevant to assessing the **impact of new IFRSs/IFRICs** on the financial statements where these have been **issued but have not yet come into force**.

Changes in accounting estimates (IAS 8: paras. 32 to 38)

- Estimates arise because of **uncertainties inherent within them**, judgement is required but this does not undermine reliability.
- Effect of a change in accounting estimate should be included in net profit/loss in:
  - Period of change, if change affects only current period, or
  - Period of change and future periods, if change affects both

Errors (IAS 8: paras. 41 to 48)

- **Prior period errors**: correct **retrospectively**.
- This involves:
  (a) Either restating the comparative amounts for the prior period(s) in which the error occurred,
  (b) Or when the error occurred before the earliest prior period presented, restating the opening balances of assets, liabilities and equity for that period so that the financial statements are presented as if the error had never occurred.
- Only where it is **impracticable** to determine the cumulative effect of an error on prior periods can an entity correct an error **prospectively**.

The following question will allow you to revise IAS 8.

Question — Prior period error

During 20X7 Lubi Co discovered that certain items had been included in inventory at 31 December 20X6, valued at $4.2m, which had in fact been sold before the year end. The following figures for 20X6 (as reported) and 20X7 (draft) are available.

	20X6	*20X7 (draft)*
	$'000	$'000
Sales	47,400	67,200
Cost of goods sold	(34,570)	(55,800)
Profit before taxation	12,830	11,400
Income taxes	(3,880)	(3,400)
Net profit	8,950	8,000

Reserves at 1 January 20X6 were $13m. The cost of goods sold for 20X7 includes the $4.2m error in opening inventory. The income tax rate was 30% for 20X6 and 20X7.

Required

Show the statement of profit or loss and other comprehensive income for 20X7, with the 20X6 comparative, and retained earnings.

Answer

STATEMENT OF PROFIT OR LOSS AND OTHER COMPREHENSIVE INCOME

	20X6	20X7
	$'000	$'000
Sales	47,400	67,200
Cost of goods sold (W1)	(38,770)	(51,600)
Profit before tax	8,630	15,600
Income tax (W2)	(2,620)	(4,660)
Net profit	6,010	10,940
RETAINED EARNINGS		
Opening retained earnings		
As previously reported	13,000	21,950
Correction of prior period error (4,200 – 1,260)	–	(2,940)
As restated	13,000	19,010
Net profit for year	6,010	10,940
Closing retained earnings	19,010	29,950

Workings

1 *Cost of goods sold*

	20X6	20X7
	$'000	$'000
As stated in question	34,570	55,800
inventory adjustment	4,200	(4,200)
	38,770	51,600

2 *Income tax*

	20X6	20X7
	$'000	$'000
As stated in question	3,880	3,400
Inventory adjustment (4,200 × 30%)	(1,260)	1,260
	2,620	4,660

2 Segment reporting 6/08, 12/11, 6/13, 6/15

FAST FORWARD

An important aspect of reporting financial performance is **segment reporting**. This is covered by IFRS 8 *Operating segments*, which replaced IAS 14 *Segment reporting* in 2006.

2.1 Introduction

Large entities produce a wide range of products and services, often in several different countries. Further information on how the overall results of entities are made up from each of these product or geographical areas will help the users of the financial statements. This is the reason for **segment reporting**.

- The entity's **past performance** will be better understood
- The entity's **risks and returns** may be better assessed
- More **informed judgements** may be made about the entity as a whole

Risks and returns of a **diversified, multi-national company** can only be assessed by looking at the individual risks and rewards attached to groups of products or services or in different groups of products or services or in different geographical areas. These are subject to differing rates of profitability, opportunities for growth, future prospects and risks.

Segment reporting is covered by IFRS 8 *Operating segments*, which replaced IAS 14 *Segment reporting* in November 2006.

2.2 Objective

An entity must disclose information to enable users of its financial statements to evaluate the nature and financial effects of the business activities in which it engages and the economic environments in which it operates (IFRS 8: para. 1).

2.3 Scope

Only entities whose **equity or debt securities are publicly traded** (ie on a stock exchange) need disclose segment information. In group accounts, only **consolidated** segmental information needs to be shown. (The statement also applies to entities filing or in the process of filing financial statements for the purpose of issuing instruments.)

(IFRS 8: para. 2)

2.4 Definition of operating segment

FAST FORWARD

Reportable segments are operating segments or aggregation of operating segments that meet specified criteria.

You need to learn this definition, as it is crucial to the standard.

Key term

Operating segment: This is a component of an entity:

(a) That engages in business activities from which it may earn revenues and incur expenses (including revenues and expenses relating to transactions with other items of the same entity)

(b) Whose operating results are regularly reviewed by the entity's chief operating decision maker to make decisions about resources to be allocated to the segment and assess its performance, and

(c) For which discrete financial information is available. *(IFRS 8: para. 5)*

The term 'chief operating decision maker' identifies a function, not necessarily a manager with a specific title. That function is to allocate resources and to assess the performance of the entity's operating segments

2.5 Aggregation

Two or more operating segments may be **aggregated** if the segments have **similar economic characteristics**, and the segments are similar in **each** of the following respects (IFRS 8: para. 12):

- The **nature of the products or services**
- The **nature of the production process**
- The **type or class of customer for their products or services**
- The **methods used to distribute their products or provide their services**, and
- If applicable, the **nature of the regulatory environment**

2.6 Determining reportable segments

An entity must report separate information about **each operating segment** that (IFRS 8: para. 13):

(a) Has been identified as meeting the **definition of an operating segment**; and

(b) Segment total is **10% or more of total**:

(i) **Revenue** (internal and external), or
(ii) All **segments not reporting a loss** (or all segments in loss if greater), or
(iii) **Assets**

At least **75% of total external revenue** must be reported by operating segments. Where this is not the case, additional segments must be identified (even if they do not meet the 10% thresholds) (IFRS 8: para. 15).

Two or more operating segments **below** the thresholds may be aggregated to produce a reportable segment if the segments have similar economic characteristics, and the segments are similar in a **majority** of the aggregation criteria above.

Operating segments that do not meet **any of the quantitative thresholds** may be reported separately if management believes that information about the segment would be useful to users of the financial statements (IFRS 8: para. 19).

2.6.1 Decision tree to assist in identifying reportable segments

The following decision tree will assist in identifying reportable segments (IFRS 8: IG 7).

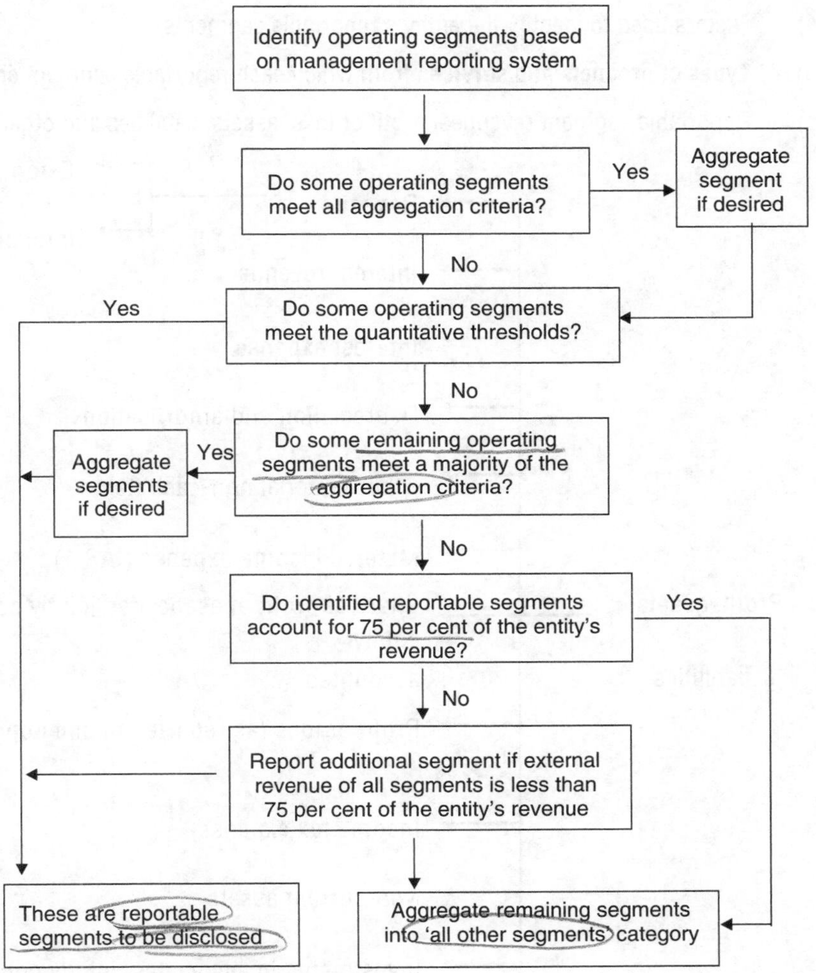

Exam focus point

> As this is a financial analysis paper, you may well be given a segment report and asked to interpret it, or to comment generally on the need for this kind of report.

2.7 Disclosures

FAST FORWARD

- IFRS 8 disclosures are of:
  - Operating segment profit or loss
  - Segment assets
  - Segment liabilities
  - Certain income and expense items
- Disclosures are also required about the **revenues derived from products or services** and about the countries in which revenues are earned or assets held, even if that information is not used by management in making decisions.

Disclosures required by the IFRS are extensive, and best learned by looking at the example and proforma, which follow the list (IFRS 8: paras. 20 to 24, 28):

(a) Factors used to identify the entity's reportable segments

(b) **Types of products and services** from which each reportable segment derives its revenues

(c) Reportable segment revenues, profit or loss, assets, liabilities and other material items:

Profit, assets & liabilities →
- Revenue → External / inter segment
- Interest revenue
- Interest expense
- Depreciation and amortisation
- Other material non-cash items
- Material income/expense (IAS 1)
- Share of profit of associates/jointly controlled entities equity accounted
- Profit or loss (as reported to chief operating decision
- Income tax expense
- Non-current assets
- Investments in associates/ jointly controlled entities
- Expenditures for reportable assets
- Segment liabilities

A **reconciliation** of each of the above material items to the entity's reported figures is required.

Reporting of a measure of **profit or loss** and **total assets** by segment is compulsory. Other items are disclosed if included in the figures reviewed by or regularly provided to the chief operating decision maker.

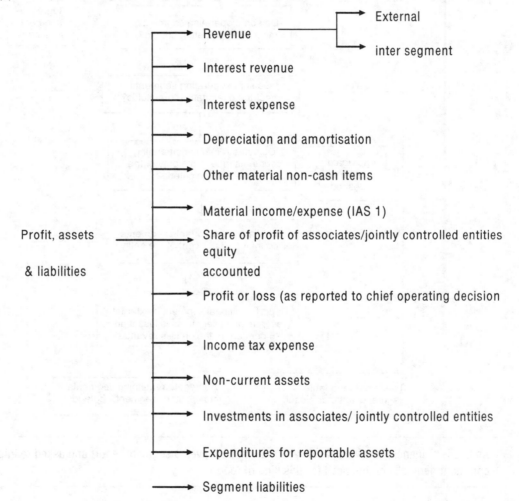

(d) **External revenue** by each product and service (if reported basis is not products and services)

(e) Geographical information:

Geographical areas → External revenue[(1)] / Non current assets[(2)]

by:

- Entity's country of domicile, and
- All foreign countries (subdivided if material)

Notes

(1) External revenue is allocated based on the customer's location.

(2) Non-current assets excludes financial instruments, deferred tax assets, post-employment benefit assets, and rights under insurance contracts.

(f) Information about **reliance on major customers** (ie those who represent more than 10% of external revenue)

(g) Segment asset disclosure is no longer compulsory if it is not reported internally.

2.7.1 Disclosure example from IFRS 8

The following example is adapted from the IFRS 8 *Implementation Guidance* (para. IG3), which emphasises that this is for illustrative purposes only and that the information must be presented in the most understandable manner in the specific circumstances.

The hypothetical company does not allocate tax expense (tax income) or non-recurring gains and losses to reportable segments. In addition, not all reportable segments have material non-cash items other than depreciation and amortisation in profit or loss. The amounts in this illustration, denominated as dollars, are assumed to be the amounts in reports used by the chief operating decision maker.

	Car parts $	*Motor vessel* $	*Software* $	*Electronics* $	*Finance* $	*All other* $	*Totals* $
Revenues from external customers	3,000	5,000	9,500	12,000	5,000	1,000[(a)]	35,500
Intersegment revenues	–	–	3,000	1,500	–	–	4,500
Interest revenue	450	800	1,000	1,500	–	–	3,750
Interest expense	350	600	700	1,100	–	–	2,750
Net interest revenue[(b)]	–	–	–	–	1,000	–	1,000
Depreciation and amortisation	200	100	50	1,500	1,100	–	2,950
Reportable segment profit	200	70	900	2,300	500	100	4,070
Other material non-cash items:							
Impairment of assets	–	200	–	–	–	–	200
Reportable segment assets	2,000	5,000	3,000	12,000	57,000	2,000	81,000
Expenditure for reportable segment non-current assets	300	700	500	800	600	–	2,900
Reportable segment liabilities	1,050	3,000	1,800	8,000	30,000	–	43,850

(a) Revenues from segments below the quantitative thresholds are attributable to four operating segments of the company. Those segments include a small property business, an electronics equipment rental business, a software consulting practice and a warehouse leasing operation. None of those segments has ever met any of the quantitative thresholds for determining reportable segments.

(b) The finance segment derives a majority of its revenue from interest. Management primarily relies on net interest revenue, not the gross revenue and expense amounts, in managing that segment. Therefore, as permitted by IFRS 8, only the net amount is disclosed.

2.7.2 Suggested proforma

Information about profit or loss, assets and liabilities

	Segment A	*Segment B*	*Segment C*	*All other segments*	*Inter segment*	*Entity total*
Revenue – external customers	X	X	X	X	–	X
Revenue – inter segment	X	X	X	X	X	–
	X	X	X	X	(X)	X
Interest revenue	X	X	X	X	(X)	X
Interest expense	(X)	(X)	(X)	(X)	X	(X)
Depreciation and amortisation	(X)	(X)	(X)	(X)	–	(X)
Other material non-cash items	X/(X)	X/(X)	X/(X)	X/(X)	X/(X)	X/(X)
Material income/expense (IAS 1)	X/(X)	X/(X)	X/(X)	X/(X)	X/(X)	X/(X)
Share of profit of associate/JVs	X	X	X	X	–	X
Segment profit before tax	X	X	X	X	(X)	X
Income tax expense	(X)	(X)	(X)	(X)	–	(X)
Unallocated items						X/(X)
Profit for the year						X
Segment assets	X	X	X	X	(X)	X
Investments in associate/JVs	X	X	X	X	–	X
Unallocated assets						X
Entity's assets						X
Expenditures for reportable assets	X	X	X	X	(X)	X
Segment liabilities	X	X	X	X	(X)	X
Unallocated liabilities						X
Entity's liabilities						X

Information about geographical areas

	Country of domicile	*Foreign countries*	*Total*
Revenue – external customers	X	X	X
Non-current assets	X	X	X

2.8 Advantages and disadvantages of the IFRS 8 segment definition approaches

IFRS 8 uses the 'managerial' approach, unlike its predecessor, IAS 14, which used the 'risks and returns' approach. The following table summarises the advantages and disadvantages of each.

	Advantages	**Disadvantages**
'Risks and returns' approach (IAS 14)	• The information can be reconciled to the financial statements • It is a consistent method • The method helps to highlight the profitability, risks and returns of an identifiable segment	• The information may be commercially sensitive • The segments may include operations with different risks and returns
'Managerial' approach *(IFRS 8)*	• It is cost effective because the marginal cost of reporting segmental data will be low • Users can be sure that the segment data reflects the operational strategy of the business	• Segment determination is the responsibility of directors and is subjective • Management may report segments which are not consistent for internal reporting and control purposes making its usefulness questionable

2.9 Criticisms of IFRS 8

(a) Some commentators have criticised the 'management approach' as leaving segment identification **too much to the discretion of the entity**.

(b) The management approach may mean that financial statements of different entities are **not comparable**.

(c) Segment determination is the responsibility of directors and is **subjective**.

(d) Management may report segments which are **not consistent** for internal reporting and control purposes, making its usefulness questionable.

(e) For accounting periods beginning on or after 1 January 2005 listed entities within the EU are required to use adopted international standards in their consolidated financial statements. The **EU has not yet adopted IFRS 8** and until it does IAS 14 will continue to apply here. Some stakeholders believe the standard to be flawed due to the amount of discretion it gives to management.

(f) **Geographical information** has been **downgraded**. It could be argued that this **breaks the link between a company and its stakeholders**.

(g) There is **no defined measure** of segment profit or loss.

2.10 Example: Determining operating segments

Jesmond, a retail and leisure group, has three businesses operating in different parts of the world. Jesmond reports to management on the basis of region. The results of the regional segments for the year ended 31 December 20X9 are as follows.

	Revenue		*Segment results*	*Segment*	*Segment*
Region	*External*	*Internal*	*profit/(loss)*	*assets*	*liabilities*
	$m	$m	$m	$m	$m
European	200	3	(10)	300	200
North America	300	2	60	800	300
Other regions	500	5	105	2,000	1,400

segments not reporting a loss

There were no significant intra-group balances in the segment assets and liabilities. The retail outlets and leisure centres are located in capital cities in the various regions, and the company sets individual performance indicators for each hotel based on its city location.

Required

Discuss the principles in IFRS 8 *Operating segments* for the determination of a company's reportable operating segments and how these principles would be applied for Jesmond plc using the information given above.

Solution

IFRS 8 *Operating segments* states that an operating segment is reported **separately** if:

(i) It **meets the definition of an operating segment**, ie:

  (1) It engages in business activities from which it may **earn revenues** and **incur expenses**

  (2) Its operating results are **regularly reviewed by the entity's chief operating decision maker** to make decisions about resources to be allocated to the segment and assess its performance

  (3) **Discrete financial information** is available for the segment,

and

(ii) It exceeds **at least one** of the following quantitative thresholds:

  (1) Reported revenue is **10% or more the combined revenue** of all operating segments (external and intersegment), or

  (2) The absolute amount of its reported profit or loss is **10% or more of the greater of,** in absolute amount, **all operating segments not reporting a loss, and all operating segments reporting a loss,** or

  (3) Its assets are **10% or more of the total assets** of all operating segments.

At least **75% of total external revenue** must be reported by operating segments. Where this is not the case, additional segments must be identified (even if they do not meet the 10% thresholds).

Two or more operating segments **below** the thresholds may be aggregated to produce a reportable segment if the segments have similar economic characteristics, and the segments are similar in a **majority** of the following aggregation criteria:

(1) The nature of the products and services
(2) The nature of the production process
(3) The type or class of customer for their products or services
(4) The methods used to distribute their products or provide their services
(5) If applicable, the nature of the regulatory environment

Operating segments that do not meet **any of the quantitative thresholds** may be reported separately if management believes that information about the segment would be useful to users of the financial statements.

For Jesmond, **the thresholds are as follows.**

(i) Combined revenue is $1,010 million, so 10% is $101 million.
(ii) Combined reported profit is $165 million, so 10% is $16.5 million.
(iii) Combined reported loss is $10 million, so 10% is $1 million.
(iv) Total assets are $3,100 million, so 10% is $310 million.

The **North America segment** meets the criteria, passing all three tests. Its combined revenue is $302 million; its reported profit is $60 million, and its assets are $800 million.

The **European segment** also meets the criteria, but only marginally. Its reported revenue, at $203 million is greater than 10% of combined revenue, and only one of the tests must be satisfied. However, its loss of

$10 million is less than the greater of 10% of combined profit and 10% of combined loss, so it fails this test. It also fails the assets test, as its assets, at $300 million are less than 10% of combined assets ($310 million).

IFRS 8 requires further that at least 75% of total external revenue must be reported by operating segments. Currently, only 50% is so reported. Additional operating segments (the 'other regions') must be identified until this 75% threshold is reached.

IFRS 8 may result in a **change** to the way Jesmond's operating segments are reported, depending on how segments were previously identified.

2.11 Section summary

IFRS 8 is a **disclosure standard D**:

- **Segment reporting** is necessary for a better understanding and assessment of:
  - Past performance
  - Risks and returns
  - Informed judgements
- IFRS 8 adopts the **managerial approach** to identifying segments
- The standard gives guidance on how segments should be **identified** and **what information should be disclosed** for each

It also sets out **requirements for related disclosures** about products and services, geographical areas and major customers.

3 IAS 33 *Earnings per share*

FAST FORWARD

Earnings per share is a measure of the amount of profits earned by a company for each ordinary share. Earnings are profits after tax and preferred dividends.

Exam focus point

You studied the bulk of IAS 33 for earlier papers. The examining team have stated that it is not going to form the basis of a full question. However, you may have to talk about the potential for manipulation.

Remember that the objective of IAS 33 is to improve the **comparison** of the performance of different entities in the same period and of the same entity in different accounting periods.

3.1 Definitions

The following definitions are given in IAS 33 (IAS 33: paras. 5 to 7).

Key terms

Ordinary share: an equity instrument that is subordinate to all other classes of equity instruments.

Potential ordinary share: a financial instrument or other contract that may entitle its holder to ordinary shares.

Options, warrants and their equivalents: financial instrum
ordinary shares.

Contingently issuable ordinary shares are ordinary shares
consideration upon the satisfaction of certain conditions in a

Contingent share agreement: an agreement to issue shares
specified conditions.

Dilution is a reduction in earnings per share or an increase i
assumption that convertible instruments are converted, that
ordinary shares are issued upon the satisfaction of certain co

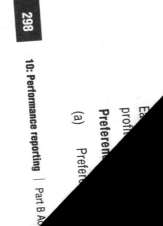

Key terms cont'd

> **Antidilution** is an increase in earnings per share or a reduction in loss per share resulting from the assumption that convertible instruments are converted, that options or warrants are exercised, or that ordinary shares are issued upon the satisfaction of certain conditions. *(IAS 33: paras. 5 to 7)*

3.1.1 Ordinary shares

There may be more than one class of ordinary shares, but ordinary shares of the same class will have the same rights to receive dividends. Ordinary shares participate in the net profit for the period **only after other types of shares**, eg preference shares (IAS 33: para. 6).

3.1.2 Potential ordinary shares

IAS 33 identifies the following examples of financial instrument and other contracts generating potential ordinary shares (IAS 33: para. 7).

(a) **Debts** (financial liabilities) **or equity instruments**, including preference shares, that are convertible into ordinary shares

(b) **Share warrants and options**

(c) Shares that would be issued upon the satisfaction of **certain conditions** resulting from contractual arrangements, such as the purchase of a business or other assets

3.2 Scope

IAS 33 has the following **scope restrictions** (IAS 33: para. 2):

(a) Only companies with (potential) ordinary shares which are **publicly traded** need to present EPS (including companies in the process of being listed).

(b) EPS need only be presented on the basis of **consolidated results** where the parent's results are shown as well.

(c) Where companies **choose** to present EPS, even when they have no (potential) ordinary shares which are traded, they must do so according to IAS 33.

3.3 Basic EPS

FAST FORWARD

> **Basic EPS** is calculated by dividing the net profit or loss for the period attributable to ordinary shareholders by the weighted average number of ordinary shares outstanding during the period.
>
> You should know how to calculate **basic EPS** and how to deal with related complications (issue of shares for cash, bonus issue, share splits/reverse share splits, rights issues).

Basic EPS should be calculated for **profit or loss attributable to ordinary equity holders** of the parent entity and **profit or loss from continuing operations** attributable to those equity holders (if this is presented).

Basic EPS should be calculated by dividing the **net profit** or loss for the period attributable to ordinary equity holders by the **weighted average number of ordinary shares** outstanding during the period (IAS 33: para. 10).

$$\frac{\text{Net profit/(loss) attributable to ordinary shareholders}}{\text{Weighted average number of ordinary shares outstanding during the period}}$$

3.3.1 Earnings

...rnings includes **all items of income and expense** (including tax and non-controlling interest) *less* net ...t attributable to **preference shareholders**, including preference dividends.

...**ce dividends** deducted from net profit consist of the following:

...ence dividends on non-cumulative preference shares declared in respect of the period.

(b) Preference dividends for cumulative preference shares required for the period, **whether** *or not* they have been declared (**excluding** those paid/declared during the period in respect of previous periods).

If an entity purchases its own preference shares for more than their carrying amount the excess should be treated as a return to the preference shareholders and deducted from profit or loss attributable to ordinary equity holders.
(IAS 33: para. 12)

3.3.2 Per share

The number of ordinary shares used should be the weighted average number of ordinary shares during the period. This figure (for all periods presented) should be **adjusted for events**, other than the conversion of potential ordinary shares, that have changed the number of shares outstanding without a corresponding change in resources (IAS 33: para. 19).

The **time-weighting factor** is the number of days the shares were outstanding compared with the total number of days in the period. A reasonable approximation is usually adequate.

Shares are usually included in the weighted average number of shares from the **date consideration is receivable** which is usually the date of issue. In other cases consider the specific terms attached to their issue (consider the substance of any contract). The treatment for the issue of ordinary shares in different circumstances is as follows (IAS 33: para. 21).

Consideration	Start date for inclusion
In exchange for cash	When cash is receivable
On the voluntary reinvestment of dividends on ordinary or preferred shares	The dividend payment date
As a result of the conversion of a debt instrument to ordinary shares	Date interest ceases accruing
In place of interest or principal on other financial instruments	Date interest ceases accruing
In exchange for the settlement of a liability of the entity	The settlement date
As consideration for the acquisition of an asset other than cash	The date on which the acquisition is recognised
For the rendering of services to the entity	As services are rendered

Ordinary shares issued as **purchase consideration** in an acquisition should be included as of the date of acquisition because the acquired entity's results will also be included from that date.

Where a **uniting of interests** takes place the number of ordinary shares used for the calculation is the aggregate of the weighted average number of shares of the combined entities, adjusted to equivalent shares of the entity whose shares are outstanding after the combination.

Ordinary shares that will be issued on the **conversion** of a mandatorily convertible instrument are included in the calculation from the **date the contract is entered into**.

If ordinary shares are **partly paid**, they are treated as a fraction of an ordinary share to the extent they are entitled to dividends relative to fully paid ordinary shares.

Contingently issuable shares (including those subject to recall) are included in the computation when all necessary conditions for issue have been satisfied.

3.4 Diluted EPS

FAST FORWARD

Diluted EPS is calculated by adjusting the net profit attributable to ordinary shareholders and the weighted average number of shares outstanding for the effects of all dilutive potential ordinary shares.

At the end of an accounting period, a company may have in issue some **securities** which do not (at present) have any 'claim' to a share of equity earnings, but **may give rise to such a claim in the future**.

(a) A **separate class of equity shares** which at present is not entitled to any dividend, but will be entitled after some future date

(b) **Convertible loan stock** or **convertible preferred shares** which give their holders the right at some future date to exchange their securities for ordinary shares of the company, at a pre-determined conversion rate

(c) **Options** or **warrants**

In such circumstances, the future number of shares ranking for dividend might increase, which in turn results in a fall in the EPS. In other words, a **future increase** in the **number of equity shares will cause a dilution or 'watering down' of equity**, and it is possible to calculate a **diluted earnings per share** (ie the EPS that would have been obtained during the financial period if the dilution had already taken place). This will indicate to investors the possible effects of a future dilution.

3.4.1 Earnings

The earnings calculated for basic EPS should be adjusted by the **post-tax** (including deferred tax) effect of the following (IAS 33: para. 31 to 33):

(a) Any **dividends** on dilutive potential ordinary shares that were deducted to arrive at earnings for basic EPS

(b) **Interest recognised** in the period for the dilutive potential ordinary shares

(c) Any **other changes in income or expenses** (fees and discount, premium accounted for as yield adjustments) that would result from the conversion of the dilutive potential ordinary shares

The conversion of some potential ordinary shares may lead to changes in **other income or expenses**. For example, the reduction of interest expense related to potential ordinary shares and the resulting increase in net profit for the period may lead to an increase in the expense relating to a non-discretionary employee profit-sharing plan. When calculating diluted EPS, the net profit or loss for the period is adjusted for any such consequential changes in income or expense.

3.4.2 Per share

The number of ordinary shares is the weighted average number of ordinary shares calculated for basic EPS plus the weighted average number of ordinary shares that would be issued on the conversion of all the **dilutive potential ordinary shares** into ordinary shares (IAS 33: para. 36).

It should be assumed that dilutive ordinary shares were converted into ordinary shares at the **beginning of the period** or, if later, at the actual date of issue. There are two other points.

(a) The computation assumes the most **advantageous conversion rate** or exercise rate from the standpoint of the holder of the potential ordinary shares.

(b) A **subsidiary, joint venture or associate** may issue potential ordinary shares that are convertible into either ordinary shares of the subsidiary, joint venture or associate, or ordinary shares of the reporting entity. If these potential ordinary shares have a dilutive effect on the consolidated basic EPS of the reporting entity, they are included in the calculation of diluted EPS.

Exam focus point

Read through the example for background only – you won't need to calculate a dilutive EPS in the exam.

3.5 Example: Diluted EPS

In 20X7 Farrah Co had a basic EPS of 105c based on earnings of $105,000 and 100,000 ordinary $1 shares. It also had in issue $40,000 15% Convertible Loan Stock which is convertible in two years' time at the rate of four ordinary shares for every $5 of stock. The rate of tax is 30%. In 20X7 gross profit of $150,000 was recorded.

Required

Calculate the diluted EPS.

Solution

Diluted EPS is calculated as follows.

Step 1 **Number of shares**: the additional equity on conversion of the loan stock will be 40,000 × 4/5 = 32,000 shares

Step 2 **Earnings**: Farrah Co will save interest payments of $6,000 but this increase in profits will be taxed

Hence the earnings figure may be recalculated:

	$
Gross profit $(150,000 + 6,000)	156,000
Tax (30%)	46,800
Profit after taxation	109,200

Step 3 **Calculation**: Diluted EPS = $\frac{\$109{,}200}{132{,}000}$ = 82.7c

Step 4 **Dilution**: the dilution in earnings would be 105c – 82.7c = 22.3c per share.

Question

EPS 1

Ardent Co has 5,000,000 ordinary shares of 25 cents each in issue, and also had in issue in 20X4:

(a) $1,000,000 of 14% convertible loan stock, convertible in three years' time at the rate of 2 shares per $10 of stock.

(b) $2,000,000 of 10% convertible loan stock, convertible in one year's time at the rate of 3 shares per $5 of stock.

The total earnings in 20X4 were $1,750,000.

The rate of income tax is 35%.

Required

Calculate the EPS and diluted EPS.

Answer

(a) EPS = $\frac{\$1{,}750{,}000}{5 \text{ million}}$ = 35 cents

(b) On dilution, the (maximum) number of shares in issue would be:

	Shares
Current	5,000,000
On conversion of 14% stock	200,000
On conversion of 10% stock	1,200,000
	6,400,000

	$	$
Current earnings		1,750,000
Add interest saved (140,000 + 200,000)	340,000	
Less tax thereon at 35%	119,000	
		221,000
Revised earnings		1,971,000

Fully diluted EPS = $\frac{\$1{,}971{,}000}{6.4 \text{ million}}$ = 30.8 cents

3.6 Presentation

An entity should present in the **statement of profit or loss and other comprehensive income** basic and diluted EPS for:

(a) Profit or loss from continuing operations; and
(b) Profit or loss for the period

for each class of ordinary share that has a different right to share in the net profit for the period.

The basic and diluted EPS should be presented with **equal prominence** for all periods presented.

Basic and diluted EPS for any **discontinuing operations** must also be presented.

Disclosure must still be made where the EPS figures (basic and/or diluted) are **negative** (ie a loss per share).

(IAS 33: paras. 64 to 68)

3.7 Alternative EPS figures

An entity may present **alternative EPS figures if it wishes**. However, IAS 33 lays out certain rules where this takes place (IAS 33: para. 73).

(a) The weighted average number of shares as calculated under IAS 33 **must** be used.

(b) A **reconciliation** must be given between the component of profit used in the alternative EPS (if it is not a line item in the statement of profit or loss and other comprehensive income) and the line item for profit reported in profit or loss

(c) The entity must indicate the basis on which the **numerator** is determined.

(d) Basic and diluted EPS must be shown with **equal prominence**.

3.8 Significance of earnings per share

Earnings per share (EPS) is one of the most frequently quoted statistics in financial analysis. Because of the widespread use of the price earnings **(P/E) ratio** as a yardstick for investment decisions, it became increasingly important.

It seems that reported and therefore, EPS can, through the P/E ratio, have a **significant effect on a company's share price**. Therefore, a share price might fall if it looks as if EPS is going to be low. This is not very rational, as EPS can depend on many, often subjective, assumptions used in preparing a historical statement, namely the statement of profit or loss and other comprehensive income. It does not necessarily bear any relation to the value of a company, and of its shares. Nevertheless, the market is sensitive to EPS.

3.9 The P2 exam

Be aware EPS was covered at an earlier level, it is assumed knowledge. You are unlikely to have to deal with the complications, except as they relate to **manipulation by the directors**, particularly of the earnings figure. Have a go at the Case Study question Wingit, at the end of the Text.

EPS has also served as a means of assessing the **stewardship and management** role performed by company directors and managers. Remuneration packages might be linked to EPS growth, thereby increasing the pressure on management to improve EPS. The danger of this, however, is that management effort may go into distorting results to produce a favourable EPS.

3.10 Section summary

EPS is an important measure for investors.

- **Basic EPS** is straightforward, although it may require adjustments for **changes in capital structure**

- **Diluted EPS** is more complex
- **In an exam**, you may have to deal with ways in which EPS can be **manipulated**

4 IAS 34 *Interim financial reporting*

IAS 34 recommends that **entities should produce interim financial reports**, and for entities that do publish such reports, it lays down principles and guidelines for their production.

The following definitions are used (IAS 34: para. 4).

Key terms

- **Interim period** is a financial reporting period shorter than a full financial year.
- **Interim financial report** means a financial report containing either a complete set of financial statements (as described in IAS 1) or a set of condensed financial statements (as described in this standard) for an interim period. *(IAS 34: para. 4)*

4.1 Scope

The standard does not make the preparation of interim financial reports **mandatory**, taking the view that this is a matter for governments, securities regulators, stock exchanges or professional accountancy bodies to decide within each country. The IASB does, however, strongly recommend to governments, etc, that interim financial reporting should be a requirement for companies whose equity or debt securities are **publicly traded**.

(a) An interim financial report should be produced by such companies for **at least the first six months of their financial year** (ie a half year financial report).

(b) The report should be **available no later than 60 days** after the end of the interim period.

Therefore, a company with a year ending 31 December would be required as a minimum to prepare an interim report for the half year to 30 June and this report should be available before the end of August.

(IAS 34: paras. 1 to 3)

4.2 Minimum components

The proposed standard specifies the **minimum component elements** of an interim financial report (IAS 34: paras. 6 and 8).

- Condensed statement of financial position
- Condensed statement of profit or loss and other comprehensive income
- Condensed statement of changes in equity
- Condensed statement of cash flows
- Selected note disclosures

The rationale for requiring only condensed statements and selected note disclosures is that entities need not duplicate information in their interim report that is contained in their report for the previous financial year. Interim statements should **focus more on new events, activities and circumstances**.

4.3 Form and content

Where **full financial statements** are given as interim financial statements, IAS 1 should be used as a guide, otherwise IAS 34 specifies minimum contents (IAS 34: para. 8).

The **condensed statement of financial position** should include, as a minimum, each of the major components of assets, liabilities and equity as were in the statement of financial position at the end of the previous financial year, thus providing a summary of the economic resources of the entity and its financial structure.

The **condensed statement of profit or loss and other comprehensive income** should include, as a minimum, each of the component items of income and expense as are shown in profit or loss for the previous financial year, together with the earnings per share and diluted earnings per share.

The **condensed statement of cash flows** should show, as a minimum, the three major sub-totals of cash flow as required in statements of cash flows by IAS 7, namely: cash flows from operating activities, cash flows from investing activities and cash flow from financing activities.

The **condensed statement of changes in equity** should include, as a minimum, each of the major components of equity as were contained in the statement of changes in equity for the previous financial year of the entity.

4.3.1 Selected explanatory notes

IAS 34 states that **relatively minor changes** from the most recent annual financial statements need not be included in an interim report. However, the notes to interim report should include the following, unless the information is contained elsewhere in the report (IAS 34: para. 16A).

(a) A statement that the **same accounting policies and methods of computation** have been used for the interim statements as were used for the most recent annual financial statements. If not, the nature of the differences and their effect should be described. (The accounting policies for preparing the interim report should only differ from those used for the previous annual accounts in a situation where there has been a change in accounting policy since the end of the previous financial year, and the new policy will be applied for the annual accounts of the current financial period.)

(b) Explanatory comments on the **seasonality or 'cyclicality'** of operations in the interim period. For example, if a company earns most of its annual profits in the first half of the year, because sales are much higher in the first six months, the interim report for the first half of the year should explain this fact.

(c) The **nature and amount** of items during the interim period affecting assets, liabilities, capital, net income or cash flows, that are unusual, due to their nature, incidence or size.

(d) The **issue or repurchase** of equity or debt securities

(e) Nature and amount of any **changes in estimates** of amounts reported in an earlier interim report during the financial year, or in prior financial years if these affect the current interim period

(f) **Dividends paid** on ordinary shares and the dividends paid on other shares

(g) **Segmental results** for the business segments or geographical segments of the entity (see IFRS 8)

(h) Any **significant events since the end of the interim period**

(i) Effect of the acquisition or disposal of subsidiaries during the interim period

(j) Any significant change in a **contingent liability or a contingent asset** since the date of the last annual statement of financial position

The entity should also disclose the fact that the interim report has been produced **in compliance with** IAS 34 on interim financial reporting.

Question **Disclosures**

Give some examples of the type of disclosures required according to the above list of explanatory notes.

Answer

The following are examples:

(a) Write-down of inventories to net realisable value and the reversal of such a write-down

(b) Recognition of a loss from the impairment of property, plant and equipment, intangible assets, or other assets, and the reversal of such an impairment loss

(c) Reversal of any provisions for the costs of restructuring

(d) Acquisitions and disposals of items of property, plant and equipment

(e) Commitments for the purchase of property, plant and equipment

(f) Litigation settlements

(g) Corrections of fundamental errors in previously reported financial data

(h) Any debt default or any breach of a debt covenant that has not been corrected subsequently

(i) Related party transactions

4.4 Periods covered

The standard requires that interim financial reports should provide financial information for the following periods or as at the following dates (IAS 34: para. 20).

(a) **Statement of financial position data** as at the end of the current interim period, and comparative data as at the end of the most recent financial year

(b) **Statement of comprehensive income data** for the current interim period and cumulative data for the current year to date, together with comparative data for the corresponding interim period and cumulative figures for the previous financial year

(c) **Statement of cash flows data** should be **cumulative** for the current year to date, with comparative cumulative data for the corresponding interim period in the previous financial year

(d) **Data for the statement of changes in equity** should be for both the current interim period and for the year to date, together with comparative data for the corresponding interim period, and cumulative figures, for the previous financial year

4.5 Materiality

Materiality should be assessed in relation to the interim period financial data. It should be recognised that interim measurements **rely to a greater extent on estimates** than annual financial data (IAS 34: para. 23).

4.6 Recognition and measurement principles

A large part of IAS 34 deals with recognition and measurement principles, and guidelines as to their practical application. The **guiding principle** is that an entity should use the **same recognition and measurement principles in its interim statements as it does in its annual financial statements**.

This means, for example, that a cost that would not be regarded as an asset in the year-end statement of financial position should not be regarded as an asset in the statement of financial position for an interim period. Similarly, an accrual for an item of income or expense for a transaction that has not yet occurred (or a deferral of an item of income or expense for a transaction that has already occurred) is inappropriate for interim reporting, just as it is for year-end reporting.

Applying this principle of recognition and measurement may result, in a subsequent interim period or at the year-end, in a **remeasurement** of amounts that were reported in a financial statement for a previous interim period. **The nature and amount of any significant remeasurements should be disclosed.**

(IAS 34: para. 28)

4.6.1 Revenues received occasionally, seasonally or cyclically

Revenue that is received as an occasional item, or within a seasonal or cyclical pattern, should not be anticipated or deferred in interim financial statements, if it would be inappropriate to anticipate or defer the revenue for the annual financial statements. In other words, the principles of revenue recognition should be applied consistently to the interim reports and year-end reports (IAS 34: para. 37).

4.6.2 Costs incurred unevenly during the financial year

These should only be anticipated or deferred (ie treated as accruals or prepayments) if it would be appropriate to anticipate or defer the expense in the annual financial statements. For example, it would be appropriate to anticipate a cost for property rental where the rental is paid in arrears, but it would be inappropriate to anticipate part of the cost of a major advertising campaign later in the year, for which no expenses have yet been incurred (IAS 34: para. 39).

The standard goes on, in an appendix, to deal with **specific applications** of the recognition and measurement principle. Some of these examples are explained below, by way of explanation and illustration (IAS 34: IE B).

4.6.3 Payroll taxes or insurance contributions paid by employers

In some countries these are assessed on an annual basis, but paid at an uneven rate during the course of the year, with a large proportion of the taxes being paid in the early part of the year, and a much smaller proportion paid later on in the year. In this situation, it would be appropriate to use an estimated average annual tax rate for the year in an interim statement, not the actual tax paid. This treatment is appropriate because it reflects the fact that the taxes are assessed on an annual basis, even though the payment pattern is uneven.

4.6.4 Cost of a planned major periodic maintenance or overhaul

The cost of such an event later in the year must not be anticipated in an interim financial statement **unless** there is a legal or constructive obligation to carry out this work. The fact that a maintenance or overhaul is planned and is carried out annually is not of itself sufficient to justify anticipating the cost in an interim financial report.

4.6.5 Other planned but irregularly-occurring costs

Similarly, these costs such as charitable donations or employee training costs, should not be accrued in an interim report. These costs, even if they occur regularly and are planned, are nevertheless discretionary.

4.6.6 Year-end bonus

A year-end bonus should not be provided for in an interim financial statement **unless** there is a constructive obligation to pay a year-end bonus (eg a contractual obligation, or a regular past practice) and the size of the bonus can be reliably measured.

4.6.7 Holiday pay

The same principle applies here. If holiday pay is an enforceable obligation on the employer, then any unpaid accumulated holiday pay may be accrued in the interim financial report.

4.6.8 Non-mandatory intangible assets

The entity might incur expenses during an interim period on items that might or will generate non-monetary intangible assets. IAS 38 *Intangible assets* requires that costs to generate non-monetary intangible assets (eg development expenses) should be recognised as an expense when incurred **unless** the costs form part of an identifiable intangible asset. Costs that were initially recognised as an expense cannot subsequently be treated instead as part of the cost of an intangible asset. IAS 34 states that interim financial statements should adopt the same approach. This means that it would be inappropriate in an interim financial statement to 'defer' a cost in the expectation that it will eventually be part of a non-monetary intangible asset that has not yet been recognised: such costs should be treated as an expense in the interim statement.

4.6.9 Depreciation

Depreciation should only be charged in an interim statement on non-current assets that have been acquired, not on non-current assets that will be acquired later in the financial year.

4.7 Foreign currency translation gains and losses

These should be calculated by the same principles as at the financial year end, in accordance with IAS 21.

4.7.1 Tax on income

An entity will include an expense for income tax (tax on profits) in its interim statements. The **tax rate** to use should be the estimated average annual tax rate for the year. For example, suppose that in a particular jurisdiction, the rate of tax on company profits is 30% on the first $200,000 of profit and 40% on profits above $200,000. Now suppose that a company makes a profit of $200,000 in its first half year, and expects to make $200,000 in the second half year. The rate of tax to be applied in the interim financial report should be 35%, not 30%, ie the expected average rate of tax for the year as a whole. This approach is appropriate because income tax on company profits is charged on an annual basis, and an effective annual rate should therefore be applied to each interim period.

As another illustration, suppose a company earns pre-tax income in the first quarter of the year of $30,000, but expects to make a loss of $10,000 in each of the next three quarters, so that net income before tax for the year is zero. Suppose also that the rate of tax is 30%. In this case, it would be inappropriate to anticipate the losses, and the tax charge should be $9,000 for the first quarter of the year (30% of $30,000) and a negative tax charge of $3,000 for each of the next three quarters, if actual losses are the same as anticipated.

Where the tax year for a company does not coincide with its financial year, a separate estimated weighted average tax rate should be applied for each tax year, to the interim periods that fall within that tax year.

Some countries give entities tax credits against the tax payable, based on amounts of capital expenditure or research and development, and so on. Under most tax regimes, these credits are calculated and granted on an annual basis; therefore it is appropriate to include anticipated tax credits within the calculation of the estimated average tax rate for the year, and apply this rate to calculate the tax on income for interim periods. However, if a tax benefit relates to a specific one-time event, it should be recognised within the tax expense for the interim period in which the event occurs.

4.7.2 Inventory valuations

Within interim reports, inventories should be valued in the same way as for year-end accounts. It is recognised, however, that it will be necessary to rely more heavily on estimates for interim reporting than for year-end reporting.

In addition, it will normally be the case that the net realisable value of inventories should be estimated from selling prices and related costs to complete and dispose at interim dates.

4.8 Use of estimates

Although accounting information must be reliable and free from material error, it may be necessary to sacrifice some accuracy and reliability for the sake of timeliness and cost-benefits. This is particularly the case with interim financial reporting, where there will be much less time to produce reports than at the financial year end. The proposed standard therefore recognises that estimates will have to be used to a greater extent in interim reporting, to assess values or even some costs, than in year-end reporting (IAS 34: para. 41).

An appendix to IAS 34 (IAS 34: Appendix B) gives some examples of the use of estimates.

(a) **Inventories**. An entity might not need to carry out a full inventory count at the end of each interim period. Instead, it may be sufficient to estimate inventory values using sales margins.

(b) **Provisions**. An entity might employ outside experts or consultants to advise on the appropriate amount of a provision, as at the year end. It will probably be inappropriate to employ an expert to make a similar assessment at each interim date. Similarly, an entity might employ a professional valuer to revalue non-current assets at the year end, whereas at the interim date(s) the entity will not rely on such experts.

(c) **Income taxes**. The rate of income tax (tax on profits) will be calculated at the year end by applying the tax rate in each country/jurisdiction to the profits earned there. At the interim stage, it may be sufficient to estimate the rate of income tax by applying the same 'blended' estimated weighted average tax rate to the income earned in all countries/jurisdictions.

The principle of **materiality** applies to interim financial reporting, as it does to year-end reporting. In assessing materiality, it needs to be recognised that interim financial reports will rely more heavily on estimates than year-end reports. Materiality should be assessed in relation to the interim financial statements themselves, and should be independent of 'annual materiality' considerations.

4.9 Section summary

- IAS 34 in concept makes **straightforward proposals** for the production of interim financial reports by entities.
- It is essential to apply **principles of recognition and measurement** that will prevent entities from 'massaging' the interim figures.
- The **detail** in the guidelines is therefore very important, and the application of the recognition and measurement principles to particular valuations and measurements needs to be understood.

5 Ratio analysis

FAST FORWARD

Keep the various **sources of financial information** in mind and the effects of insider dealing, the efficient market hypothesis and Stock Exchange regulations.

The accounts of a business are designed to provide users with information about its performance and financial position. The bare figures, however, are not particularly useful and it is only through **comparisons** (usually of ratios) that their significance can be established. Comparisons may be made with previous financial periods, with other similar businesses or with averages for the particular industry. The choice will depend on the purpose for which the comparison is being made and the information that is available.

Various groups are interested in the performance and financial position of a company.

(a) **Management** will use comparisons to ensure that the business is performing efficiently and according to plan

(b) **Employees**, trade unions and so on

(c) **Government**

(d) Present and potential **investors** will assess the company with a view to judging whether it is a sound investment

(e) **Lenders** and **suppliers** will want to judge its creditworthiness

This Text is concerned with financial rather than management accounting and the ratios discussed here are therefore likely to be calculated by external users. The following sources of information are readily available to external users.

- Published accounts and interim statements
- Documents filed as required by company legislation
- Statistics published by the government
- Other published sources eg *Investors Chronicle, The Economist, Wall Street Journal*

5.1 Financial analysis

The **lack of detailed information** available to the outsider is a considerable disadvantage in undertaking ratio analysis. The first difficulty is that there may simply be insufficient data to calculate all of the required ratios. A second concerns the availability of a suitable 'yardstick' with which the calculated ratios may be compared.

5.1.1 Inter-temporal analysis

Looking first at inter-temporal or trend analysis (comparisons for the same business over time), some of the **problems** include the following:

- Changes in the nature of the business
- Unrealistic depreciation rates under historical cost accounting
- The changing value of the pound
- Changes in accounting policies

Other factors will include changes in government incentive packages, changes from purchasing equipment to leasing and so on.

5.1.2 Cross-sectional analysis

When undertaking 'cross-sectional' analysis (making comparisons with other companies) the position is even more difficult because of the problem of identifying companies that are comparable. **Comparability** between companies may be impaired due to the following reasons.

(a) Different degrees of diversification

(b) Different production and purchasing policies (if an investor was analysing the smaller car manufacturers, he would find that some of them buy in engines from one of the 'majors' while others develop and manufacture their own)

(c) Different financing policies (eg leasing as opposed to buying)

(d) Different accounting policies (one of the most serious problems particularly in relation to non-current assets and inventory valuation)

(e) Different effects of government incentives

The major **intragroup comparison organisations** (whose results are intended for the use of participating companies and are not generally available) go to considerable length to adjust accounts to comparable bases. The external user will rarely be in a position to make such adjustments. Although the position is improved by increases in disclosure requirements direct comparisons between companies will inevitably, on occasion, continue to give rise to misleading results.

5.2 Social and political considerations

Social considerations tend to be **short-lived** or 'fashionable' and therefore each set of statements can be affected by a different movement or fad. In recent years, the social aspect much in evidence has been that of environmental issues. Companies have gone for a 'green' image, although this has been more in evidence in glossy pictures than in the accounts themselves.

Political considerations may be more far reaching. The regulatory regime may be instituted by statutes, but often self-regulation is encouraged through bodies such as the stock exchange.

5.3 Multinational companies

Multinational companies have great difficulties sometimes because of the need to comply with **legislation** in a large number of countries. As well as different reporting requirements, different rules of incorporation exist, as well as different directors' rules, tax legislation and so on. Sometimes the local rules can be so harsh that companies will avoid them altogether. In California, for example, multinational companies with operations there are taxed on their **world wide** profits, not just their US profits. Local tax regimes may also require information about the group as a whole because of the impact of internal transfer pricing on tax.

Different local reporting requirements will also make **consolidation** more difficult. The results of subsidiaries must be translated, not only to the company's base currency, but also using the accounting rules used by head office. This is a requirement of IASs as 'uniform accounting policies' are called for.

5.4 The efficient market hypothesis and stock exchanges

It has been argued that stock markets in the most sophisticated economies, eg the USA, are **efficient capital markets**.

(a) The prices of securities bought and sold reflect all the relevant information which is available to the buyers and sellers. In other words, share prices change quickly to reflect all new information about future prospects.

(b) No individual dominates the market.

(c) Transaction costs are not so high as to discourage trading significantly.

If the stock market is efficient, share prices should vary in a **rational way**, ie reflecting the known profits or losses of a company and the state of return required based on interest rates.

Research in both Britain and the USA has suggested that market prices anticipate mergers several months before they are formally announced, and the conclusion drawn is that the stock market in these countries **do** exhibit **semi-strong efficiency**. It has also been argued that the market displays sufficient efficiency for investors to see through 'window dressing' of accounts by companies which use accounting conventions to overstate profits (ie creative accounting).

Evidence suggests that stock markets show efficiency that is **at least weak form**, but tending more towards a semi-strong form. In other words, current share prices reflect all or most publicly available information about companies and their securities. However, it is very difficult to assess the market's efficiency in relation to shares which are not usually actively traded.

Fundamental analysis and **technical analysis** carried out by analysts and investment managers play an important role in creating an efficient stock market. This is because an efficient market depends on the widespread availability of cheap information about companies, their shares and market conditions, and this is what the firms of market makers and other financial institutions **do** provide for their clients and for the general investing public. In a market which demonstrates strong-form efficiency, such analysis would not identify profitable opportunities, ie where shares are undervalued, because such information would already be known and reflected in the share price.

On the other hand stock market crashes raise serious questions about the validity of the **fundamental theory of share values** and the efficient market hypothesis. If these theories are correct, how can shares that were valued at one level on one day suddenly be worth 40% less the next day, without any change in expectations of corporate profits and dividends? On the other hand, a widely feared crash may fail to happen, suggesting that stock markets may not be altogether out of touch with the underlying values of companies.

5.5 Insider dealing

In theory, the rules of various countries on **insider dealing** should limit the efficiency of the capital markets to semi-strong form.

Key term

> **Insider dealing** is dealing in securities while in possession of insider information as an insider, the securities being price-affected by the information. Off-market transactions between or involving 'professional intermediaries' may be included, not just transactions on a designated exchange.

There are various possible anti-avoidance measures, including disclosure of information to other parties.

Examples of securities

(a) Shares or stock in the share capital of a company

(b) Debt securities (eg gilts)

(c) All forms of warrants, depository receipts, options, futures, contracts for differences based on individual securities or an index

Insider information is 'price-sensitive information' relating to a particular issue of securities that are price-affected and not to securities generally; it must be specific or precise and, if made public, be likely to have a significant effect on price.

General defences may be available where the individual concerned can show that:

(a) He did not expect there to be a profit or avoidance of loss,

(b) He had reasonable grounds to believe that the information had been disclosed widely, or

(c) He would have done what he did even if he had not had the information, for example where securities are sold to pay a pressing debt.

In order to avoid false markets in shares and to keep investors and their advisors properly informed, listed companies should notify the relevant stock exchange of any **necessary information**. This is then public knowledge. More specific requirements may include the following.

- Preliminary announcements of profits and losses
- Major acquisitions
- Redemption of debt capital
- Changes in nature of business
- Proposals to purchase own shares
- Declaration of dividends

To publish information quickly is an effective way of reducing the opportunity for insider dealing.

The evil of insider dealing is obvious enough. On the other hand some **reasonable limits** have to be set on the prohibition on insider dealing. There are practical problems in applying rules on insider dealing. In particular, it is doubtful whether a director of a public company, who receives confidential information (say management accounts) at each board meeting, is ever in a position to deal in securities of his company without technical infringement of insider dealing rules.

5.6 The broad categories of ratios

FAST FORWARD

> Much of the material here on **ratios** should be revision for you. The next few chapters will cover much more complicated aspects of financial analysis.
>
> Make sure that you can **define** all the ratios. Look out for variations in definitions of ratios which might appear in questions.

Ratio analysis involves **comparing one figure against another** to produce a ratio, and assessing whether the ratio indicates a weakness or strength in the company's affairs.

Exam focus point

> You are unlikely to be asked to calculate many ratios in the P2 exam, or not directly at any rate. If, say, you were asked to comment on a company's past or potential future performance, you would be expected to select your own ratios in order to do so. The skill here is picking the key ratios in the context of the question and not calculating a lot of useless ratios.

Broadly speaking, basic ratios can be grouped into five categories.

- Profitability and return
- Long-term solvency and stability
- Short-term solvency and liquidity
- Efficiency (turnover ratios)
- Shareholders' investment ratios

Ratio analysis on its own is **not sufficient** for interpreting company accounts, and that there are other items of information which should be looked at.

(a) The content of any **accompanying commentary** on the accounts and other statements

(b) The age and nature of the **company's assets**

(c) Current and future **developments** in the company's markets, at home and overseas, recent acquisitions or disposals of a subsidiary by the company

(d) Any other **noticeable features** of the report and accounts, such as events after the reporting period, contingent liabilities, a qualified auditors' report, the company's taxation position

The following sections summarise what you already know about ratio analysis from your earlier studies. You should then perform the comprehensive questions given in this chapter.

5.7 Profitability and return on capital

One profit figure that should be calculated and compared over time is **PBIT, profit before interest and tax**, the amount of profit which the company earned before having to pay interest to the providers of loan capital. By providers of loan capital, we usually mean longer-term loan capital, such as debentures and medium-term bank loans, which will be shown in the statement of financial position as 'non-current liabilities'. Also, tax is affected by unusual variations which have a distorting effect.

Profit before interest and tax is therefore:

(a) The profit on operating activities before taxation, plus
(b) Interest charges on long-term loan capital

Published accounts do not always give sufficient detail on interest payable to determine how much is interest on long-term finance.

5.7.1 A warning about comments on profit margin and asset turnover

It might be tempting to think that a high profit margin is good, and a low asset turnover means sluggish trading. In broad terms, this is so. But there is **a trade-off** between profit margin and asset turnover, and you cannot look at one without allowing for the other.

(a) A high profit margin means a high profit per $1 of sales, but if this also means that sales prices are high, there is a strong possibility that sales revenue will be depressed, and so asset turnover lower.

(b) A high asset turnover means that the company is generating a lot of sales, but to do this it might have to keep its prices down and so accept a low profit margin per $1 of sales.

Knowledge brought forward from earlier studies

Profitability

Return on capital employed

$$\text{ROCE} = \frac{\text{PBIT}}{\text{Capital employed}} = \frac{\text{PBIT}}{\text{Total assets less current liabilities}}$$

When **interpreting** ROCE look for the following.

- How risky is the business?
- How capital intensive is it?
- What ROCE do similar businesses have?

Knowledge brought forward from earlier studies

Problems: which items to consider to achieve comparability:

- Revaluation reserves
- Policies, eg, R & D
- Bank overdraft: short/long-term liability
- Investments and related income: exclude

The following **considerations** are important.

- Change year to year
- Comparison to similar companies
- Comparison with current market borrowing rates

Return on equity

$$ROE = \frac{\text{Profit after tax and pref div}}{\text{Ordinary share capital + reserves}} \%$$

This gives a more **restricted view** of capital than ROCE, but the same principles apply.

Secondary ratios

Profit margin × Asset turnover = ROCE

Profit margin

$$\text{Profit margin} = \frac{\text{PBIT}}{\text{Revenue}} \% \quad \text{Gross profit margin} = \frac{\text{Gross profit}}{\text{Revenue}} \%$$

It is useful to compare profit margin to gross profit % to investigate movements which do not match. Take into account:

- Gross profit margin
  - Sales prices, sales volume and sales mix
  - Purchase prices and related costs (discount, carriage etc)
  - Production costs, both direct (materials, labour) and indirect (overheads both fixed and variable)
  - Inventory levels and inventory valuation, including errors, cut-off and stock-out costs
- Net profit margin
  - Sales expenses in relation to sales levels
  - Administrative expenses, including salary levels
  - Distribution expenses in relation to sales levels

  Depreciation should be considered as a separate item for each expense category.

Asset turnover

$$\text{Asset turnover} = \frac{\text{Revenue}}{\text{Total assets less current liabilities}}$$

This measures the **efficiency** of the use of assets. Amend to just non-current assets for capital intensive businesses.

5.8 Liquidity and working capital

Profitability is of course an important aspect of a company's performance and debt or gearing is another. Neither, however, addresses directly the key issue of liquidity in the **short term**.

Liquidity is the amount of cash a company can put its hands on quickly to settle its debts (and possibly to meet other unforeseen demands for cash payments too). Liquid funds consist of the following.

- Cash
- Short-term investments for which there is a ready market (as distinct from shares held in subsidiaries or associated companies)
- Fixed-term deposits with a bank (eg a six month high-interest deposit)
- Trade receivables (because they will pay what they owe within a short period of time)
- Bills of exchange receivable (because these represent cash due to be received within a relatively short period of time)

A company can obtain liquid assets from sources other than sales, such as the issue of shares for cash, a new loan or the sale of long-term assets. But a company cannot rely on these at all times, and in general obtaining liquid funds depends on making sales and profits. Even so, **profits do not always lead to increases in liquidity**. This is mainly because funds generated from trading may be immediately invested in long-term assets or paid out as dividends.

Efficiency ratios indicate how well a business is controlling aspects of its working capital.

Knowledge brought forward from earlier studies

Liquidity and working capital

This was very topical in the late 1980s as interest rates were high, and there was a recession. Can a company meet its short-term debts?

Current ratio

$$\text{Current ratio} = \frac{\text{Current assets}}{\text{Current liabilities}}$$

Assume assets realised at book value ∴ theoretical. 2:1 acceptable? 1.5:1? It depends on the industry.

Quick ratio

$$\text{Quick ratio (acid test)} = \frac{\text{Current assets} - \text{Inventory}}{\text{Current liabilities}}$$

Eliminates illiquid and subjectively valued inventory. Care is needed: it could be high if **overtrading** with receivables, but no cash. Is 1:1 OK? Many supermarkets operate on 0.3.

Collection period

$$\text{Average collection period} = \frac{\text{Trade receivables}}{\text{Credit turnover}} \times 365$$

Is it **consistent** with quick/current ratio? If not, investigate.

Inventory turnover period

$$\text{Inventory turnover} = \frac{\text{Cost of sales}}{\text{Inventory}} \quad \text{Inventory turnover period} = \frac{\text{Inventory}}{\text{Cost of sales}} \times 365$$

Higher the better? But remember:

- Lead times
- Seasonal fluctuations in orders
- Alternative uses of warehouse space
- Bulk buying discounts
- Likelihood of inventory perishing or becoming obsolete

Accounts payable payment period

$$\text{Accounts payable payment period} = \frac{\text{Trade payables}}{\text{Purchases}} \times 365$$

Use **cost of sales** if purchases are not disclosed.

Knowledge brought forward from earlier studies

Cash cycle

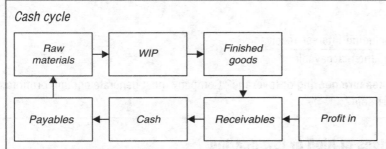

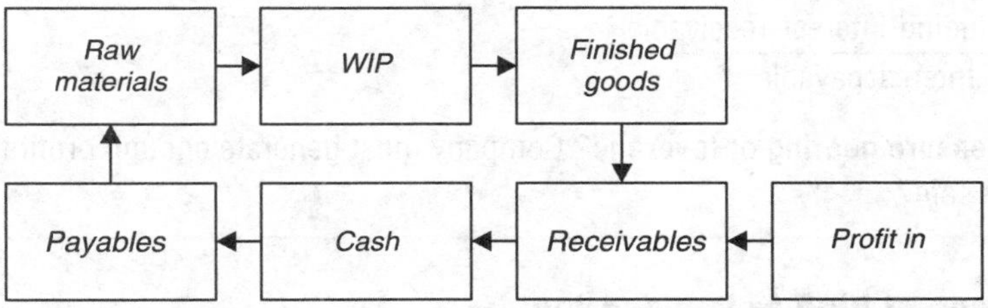

- Cash flow timing does not match sales/cost of sales timing as credit is taken
- Holding stock delays the time between payments for goods and sales receipts

Reasons for changes in liquidity

- **Credit control** efficiency altered
- Altering **payment period** of creditors as a source of funding
- Reduce **stock holdings** to maintain liquidity

5.9 Long-term solvency: Debt and gearing/leverage

Debt and gearing ratios are concerned with a company's **long-term stability**: how much the company owes in relation to its size, whether it is getting into heavier debt or improving its situation, and whether its debt burden seems heavy or light.

(a) When a company is heavily in debt, banks and other potential lenders may be unwilling to advance further funds.

(b) When a company is earning only a modest profit before interest and tax, and has a heavy debt burden, there will be very little profit left (if any) over for shareholders after the interest charges have been paid. And so if interest rates were to go up (on bank overdrafts and so on) or the company were to borrow even more, it might soon be incurring interest charges in excess of PBIT. This might eventually lead to the liquidation of the company.

Knowledge brought forward from earlier studies

Debt and gearing/leverage

Debt/equity

$$\text{Debt/equity ratio} = \frac{\text{Interest bearing net debt}}{\text{Shareholders' funds}}\%(>100\%=\text{high})$$

Or

$$\frac{\text{Interest bearing net debt}}{\text{Shareholders' funds} + \text{interest bearing net debt}}\%(>50\%=\text{high})$$

There is **no definitive answer**; elements included are subjective. The following could have an impact.

- Convertible loan stock
- Preferred shares
- Deferred tax
- Goodwill and development expenditure capitalisation
- Revaluation reserve

Gearing/leverage

$$\text{Gearing ratio} = \frac{\text{Prior charge capital}}{\text{Total capital}} \qquad \text{Leverage} = \frac{\text{Total capital}}{\text{Prior charge capital}}$$

Knowledge brought forward from earlier studies

Interest cover

$$\text{Interest cover} = \frac{\text{PBIT (including interest receivable)}}{\text{Interest payable}}$$

Is this a better way to **measure gearing** or **leverage**? Company must generate enough profit to cover interest. Is a figure of 3+ safe?

5.9.1 The implications of high or low gearing

Gearing or leverage is, amongst other things, an attempt to quantify the **degree of risk** involved in holding equity shares in a company, both in terms of the company's ability to remain in business and in terms of expected ordinary dividends from the company. The problem with a highly geared company is that, by definition, there is a lot of debt. Debt generally carries a fixed rate of interest (or fixed rate of dividend if in the form of preferred shares), hence there is a given (and large) amount to be paid out from profits to holders of debt before arriving at a residue available for distribution to the holders of equity.

The more highly geared the company, the greater the risk that little (if anything) will be available to distribute by way of dividend to the ordinary shareholders. The more highly geared the company, the greater the percentage change in profit available for ordinary shareholders for any given percentage change in profit before interest and tax. The relationship similarly holds when profits increase. This means that there will be greater **volatility** of amounts available for ordinary shareholders, and presumably therefore greater volatility in dividends paid to those shareholders, where a company is highly geared. That is the risk. You may do extremely well or extremely badly without a particularly large movement in the PBIT of the company.

The risk of a company's ability to remain in business was referred to earlier. Gearing is relevant to this. A highly geared company has a large amount of interest to pay annually. If those borrowings are 'secured' in any way (and debentures in particular are secured), then the holders of the debt are perfectly entitled to force the company to realise assets to pay their interest if funds are not available from other sources. Clearly, the more highly geared a company, the more likely this is to occur when and if profits fall. Note that problems related to **off balance sheet finance** hiding the level of gearing have gradually become rarer, due to standards such as IFRS 16 (on leasing).

Companies will only be able to increase their gearing if they have **suitable assets** to offer for security. Companies with assets which are depreciated rapidly or which are at high risk of obsolescence will be unable to offer sufficient security, eg computer software companies. On the other hand, a property company will have plenty of assets to offer as security whose value is fairly stable (but note the effect of a property slump).

Ideally, the following **gearing profiles** would apply, so that only certain types of company could have higher gearing.

Type of company	Assets	Profits
Highly geared companies	Holding value, long-term	Stable, steady trends
Low geared companies	Rapid depreciation/change	Erratic, volatile

5.9.2 The effect of GAAP on gearing/leverage

Variations in accounting policy can have a significant impact on gearing and it will be necessary to consider the individual policies of companies. The main areas which are likely to require consideration are as follows.

(a) Revaluation of non-current assets will have an impact on equity and it will be necessary to consider the frequency of such revaluations.

(b) The structure of group accounts and methods of consolidation will also have a substantial impact on gearing.

5.10 Shareholders' investment ratios

These are the ratios which help equity shareholders and other investors to assess the value and quality of an investment in the **ordinary shares** of a company.

The value of an investment in ordinary shares in a **listed company** is its market value, and so investment ratios must have regard not only to information in the company's published accounts, but also to the current price.

Earnings per share is a valuable indicator of an ordinary share's performance and you should refer to Section 3 of this Chapter to revise its calculation.

Knowledge brought forward from earlier studies

Investors' ratios

Dividend yield

$$\text{Dividend yield} = \frac{\text{Div per share}}{\text{Mid} - \text{market price}}\%$$

- **Low yield**: the company retains a large proportion of profits to reinvest
- **High yield**: this is a risky company or slow-growing

Dividend cover

$$\text{Dividend cover} = \frac{\text{EPS}}{\text{Net div per share}}$$

$$\text{Or} \quad \frac{\text{Profit after tax and pref div}}{\text{Div on ordinary shares}}$$

This shows **how safe the dividend is**, or the extent of profit retention. Variations are due to maintaining dividend when profits are declining.

P/E ratio

$$\text{P/E ratio} = \frac{\text{Mid} - \text{market price}}{\text{EPS}}$$

The **higher the better** here: it reflects the confidence of the market. A rise in EPS will cause an increase in P/E ratio, but maybe not to same extent: look at the context of the market and industry norms.

Earnings yield

$$\text{Earnings yield} = \frac{\text{EPS}}{\text{Mid} - \text{market price}}$$

This shows the dividend yield if there is no retention of profit. It allows you to compare companies with **different dividend policies**, showing growth rather than earnings.

Net assets per share

$$\text{Net assets per share} = \frac{\text{Net assets}}{\text{No of shares}}$$

This is a **crude measure** of value of a company, liable to distortion.

See also **EPS** and **dividend per share**.

FAST FORWARD

Always remember that 'profit' and 'net assets' are fairly **arbitrary figures**, affected by different accounting policies and manipulation.

Financial analysis is a vital tool for **auditors**.

Question

Ratio analysis report

RST Co is considering purchasing an interest in its competitor XYZ Co. The managing director of RST Co has obtained the three most recent statements of comprehensive income and statements of financial position of XYZ Co as shown below.

XYZ CO
STATEMENTS OF PROFIT OR LOSS AND OTHER COMPREHENSIVE INCOME
FOR YEARS ENDED 31 DECEMBER

	20X6	*20X7*	*20X8*
	$'000	$'000	$'000
Revenue	18,000	18,900	19,845
Cost of sales	10,440	10,340	11,890
Gross profit	7,560	8,560	7,955
Distribution costs	1,565	1,670	1,405
Administrative expenses	1,409	1,503	1,591
Operating profit	4,586	5,387	4,959
Interest payable on bank overdraft	104	215	450
Interest payable on 12% debentures	600	600	600
Profit before taxation	3,882	4,572	3,909
Income tax	1,380	2,000	1,838
Profit after taxation	2,502	2,572	2,071

XYZ CO
STATEMENTS OF FINANCIAL POSITION AS AT 31 DECEMBER

	20X6		*20X7*		*20X8*	
	$'000	$'000	$'000	$'000	$'000	$'000
Assets						
Non-current assets						
Land and buildings	11,460		12,121		11,081	
Plant and machinery	8,896		9,020		9,130	
		20,356		21,141		20,211
Current assets						
Inventory	1,775		2,663		3,995	
Trade receivables	1,440		2,260		3,164	
Cash	50		53		55	
		3,265		4,976		7,214
		23,621		26,117		27,425
Equity and liabilities						
Equity						
Share capital	8,000		8,000		8,000	
Retained earnings	6,434		7,313		7,584	
		14,434		15,313		15,584
Non-current liabilities						
12% debentures 20Y1 – 20Y4		5,000		5,000		5,000
Current liabilities						
Trade payables	390		388		446	
Bank	1,300		2,300		3,400	
Taxation	897		1,420		1,195	
Dividend payable	1,600		1,696		1,800	
		4,187		5,804		6,841
		23,621		26,117		27,425

Required

Prepare a report for the managing director of RST Co commenting on the financial position of XYZ Co and highlighting any areas that require further investigation.

(Marks will be awarded for ratios and other financial statistics where appropriate.)

Answer

To: MD of RST Co
From: An Accountant
Date: XX.XX.XX
Subject: *The financial position of XYZ* Co

Introduction

This report has been prepared on the basis of the three most recent statements of comprehensive income and statement of financial position of XYZ Co covering the years 20X6 to 20X8 inclusive. Ratio analysis used in this report is based on the calculations shown in the appendix attached.

Performance

Sales have increased at a steady 5% per annum over the three-year period.

In contrast, the gross profit percentage has increased from 42% in 20X6 to 45% in 20X7 before dropping back to 40% in 20X8. Similarly, operating profit as a percentage of sales was 26% in 20X6, 28.5% in 20X7 and 25% in 20X8. This may indicate some misallocation of costs between 20X7 and 20X8 and should be investigated or it may be indicative of a longer downward trend in profitability.

Return on capital employed, as one would expect, has shown a similar pattern with an increase in 20X7 with a subsequent fall in 20X8 to a level below that of 20X6.

Debt and liquidity

The debt ratio measures the ratio of a company's total debt to its total assets. Although we have no information as to the norm for the industry as a whole, the debt ratios appear reasonable. However, it should be noted that it has risen steadily over the three year period.

When reviewing XYZ Co's liquidity the situation has improved over the period. The current ratio measures a company's ability to meet its current liabilities out of current assets. A ratio of at least 1 should therefore be expected. XYZ Co did not meet this expectation in 20X6 and 20X7.

This ratio can be misleading as inventory is included in current assets. Because inventory can take some time to convert into liquid assets a second ratio, the quick ratio, is calculated which excludes inventory. As can be seen, the quick ratio, although improving, is low and this shows that current liabilities cannot be met from current assets if inventory is excluded. As a major part of current liabilities is the bank overdraft, the company is obviously relying on the bank's continuing support with short-term funding. It would be useful to find out the terms of the bank funding and the projected cash flow requirements for future funding.

Efficiency ratios

The efficiency ratios, receivables ratio and inventory turnover, give a useful indication of how the company is managing its current assets.

As can be seen from the appendix the debtors collection period has increased over the three years from 29 days to 58 days. This may indicate that the company is failing to follow up its debts efficiently or that it has given increased credit terms to some or all of its customers.

Looking at inventory turnover, this has also risen from 62 days to 122 days. This may be an indication of over-stocking, stocking up on the expectation of a substantial sales increase or the holding of obsolete or slow-moving inventory items which should be written down. More investigation needs to be done on both receivables and inventory.

The financing of additional receivables and inventory has been achieved in the main through the bank overdraft as the trade payables figure has not increased significantly.

Conclusion

The review of the three-year financial statements for XYZ Co has given rise to a number of queries which need to be resolved before a useful conclusion can be reached on the financial position of XYZ Co. It may also be useful to compare XYZ Co's ratios to those of other companies in the same industry in order to obtain some idea of the industry norms.

APPENDIX TO MEMORANDUM

	20X6	*20X7*	*20X8*
% sales increase		5%	5%
Gross profit %	42%	45%	40%
Operating profit %	25.5%	28.5%	25%

Return on capital employed

	20X6	*20X7*	*20X8*
$= \dfrac{\text{Profit before interest and tax}}{\text{Capital employed}}$	$\dfrac{4{,}586 - 104}{14{,}434 + 5{,}000}$	$\dfrac{5{,}387 - 215}{15{,}313 + 5{,}000}$	$\dfrac{4{,}959 - 450}{15{,}584 + 5{,}000}$
× 100%	= 23%	= 25.5%	= 21.9%

Debt ratio

	20X6	*20X7*	*20X8*
$= \dfrac{\text{Total debt}}{\text{Total assets}}$	$\dfrac{4{,}187 + 5{,}000}{20{,}356 + 3{,}265}$	$\dfrac{5{,}804 + 5{,}000}{21{,}114 + 4{,}976}$	$\dfrac{6{,}841 + 5{,}000}{20{,}211 + 7{,}214}$
× 100%	= 38.9%	= 41.4%	= 43.2%

Current ratio

	20X6	*20X7*	*20X8*
$= \dfrac{\text{Current assets}}{\text{Current liabilities}}$	$\dfrac{3{,}265}{4{,}187}$	$\dfrac{4{,}976}{5{,}804}$	$\dfrac{7{,}214}{6{,}814}$
	= 0.78	= 0.86	= 1.06

Quick ratio

	20X6	*20X7*	*20X8*
$= \dfrac{\text{Current assets} - \text{inventory}}{\text{Current liabilities}}$	$\dfrac{3{,}265 - 1{,}775}{4{,}187}$	$\dfrac{4{,}976 - 2{,}663}{5{,}804}$	$\dfrac{7{,}214 - 3{,}995}{6{,}814}$
	= 0.36	= 0.40	= 0.47

Receivables ratio

	20X6	*20X7*	*20X8*
$= \dfrac{\text{Trade receivables}}{\text{Sales}}$	$\dfrac{1{,}440}{18{,}000}$	$\dfrac{2{,}260}{18{,}900}$	$\dfrac{3{,}164}{19{,}845}$
× 365 days	= 29.2 days	= 43.6 days	= 58.2 days

Inventory turnover

	20X6	*20X7*	*20X8*
$= \dfrac{\text{Inventory}}{\text{Cost of sales}}$	$\dfrac{1{,}775}{10{,}440}$	$\dfrac{2{,}663}{10{,}340}$	$\dfrac{3{,}995}{11{,}890}$
× 365 days	= 62 days	= 94 days	= 122.6 days

Question — Ratio analysis report 2

You are the management accountant of Fry Co. Laurie Co is a competitor in the same industry and it has been operating for 20 years. Summaries of Laurie Co's statements of comprehensive income and financial position for the previous three years are given below.

SUMMARISED STATEMENTS OF PROFIT OR LOSS AND OTHER COMPREHENSIVE INCOME FOR THE YEAR ENDED 31 DECEMBER

	20X6	*20X7*	*20X8*
	$m	$m	$m
Revenue	840	981	913
Cost of sales	554	645	590
Gross profit	286	336	323
Selling, distribution and administration expenses	186	214	219
Profit before interest	100	122	104
Interest	6	15	19
Profit before taxation	94	107	85
Taxation	45	52	45
Profit after taxation	49	55	40
Dividends	24	24	24

SUMMARISED STATEMENTS OF FINANCIAL POSITION AS AT 31 DECEMBER

	20X6	*20X7*	*20X8*
	$m	$m	$m
Assets			
Non-current assets			
Intangible assets	36	40	48
Tangible assets at net book value	176	206	216
	212	246	264
Current assets			
Inventories	237	303	294
Receivables	105	141	160
Bank	52	58	52
	606	748	770
Equity and liabilities			
Equity			
Ordinary share capital	100	100	100
Retained earnings	299	330	346
	399	430	446
Non-current liabilities			
Long-term loans	74	138	138
Current liabilities			
Trade payables	53	75	75
Other payables	80	105	111
	606	748	770

You may assume that the index of retail prices has remained constant between 20X6 and 20X8.

Required

Write a report to the finance director of Fry Co:

(a) Analysing the performance of Laurie Co and showing any calculations in an appendix to this report.

(b) Summarising five areas which require further investigation, including reference to other pieces of information which would complement your analysis of the performance of Laurie Co.

Answer

(a) To: Finance Director
From: Management accountant
Subject: *Performance of Laurie Co 20X6 to 20X8*

An appendix is attached to this report which shows the ratios calculated as part of the performance review.

Profitability

The gross profit margin has remained relatively static over the three year period, although it has risen by approximately 1% in 20X8. ROCE, while improving very slightly in 20X7 to 21.5% has dropped dramatically in 20X8 to 17.8%. The net profit margin has also fallen in 20X8, in spite of the improvement in the gross profit margin. This marks a rise in expenses which suggests that they are not being well controlled. The utilisation of assets compared to the turnover generated has also declined reflecting the drop in trading activity between 20X7 and 20X8.

Trading levels

It is apparent that there was a dramatic increase in trading activity between 20X7 and 20X8, but then a significant fall in 20X8. Revenue rose by 17% in 20X7 but fell by 7% in 20X8. The reasons for this fluctuation are unclear. It may be the effect of some kind of one-off event, or it may be the effect of a change in product mix. Whatever the reason, it appears that improved credit terms granted to customers (receivables payment period up from 46 to 64 days) has not stopped the drop in sales.

Working capital

Both the current ratio and quick ratio demonstrate an adequate working capital situation, although the quick ratio has shown a slight decline. There has been an increased investment over the period in inventories and receivables which has been only partly financed by longer payment periods to trade payables and a rise in other payables (mainly between 20X6 and 20X7).

Capital structure

The level of gearing of the company increased when a further $64m was raised in long-term loans in 20X7 to add to the $74m already in the statement of financial position. Although this does not seem to be a particularly high level of gearing, the debt/equity ratio did rise from 18.5% to 32.0% in 20X7. The interest charge has risen to $19m from $6m in 20X6. The 20X7 charge was $15m, suggesting that either the interest rate on the loan is flexible, or that the full interest charge was not incurred in 20X7. The new long-term loan appears to have funded the expansion in both fixed and current assets in 20X7.

APPENDIX

Ratio	*Working*	*20X6*	*20X7*	*20X8*
Gross profit margin	(1)	34.0%	34.3%	35.4%
ROCE	(2)	21.1%	21.5%	17.8%
Profit margin	(3)	11.9%	12.4%	11.4%
Assets turnover	(4)	1.78	1.73	1.56
Gearing ratio	(5)	15.6%	24.3%	23.6%
Debt/equity ratio	(6)	18.5%	32.0%	30.9%
Interest cover	(7)	16.7	8.1	5.5
Current ratio	(8)	3.0	2.8	2.7
Quick ratio	(9)	1.2	1.1	1.1
Receivables payment period (days)	(10)	46	52	64
Inventory turnover period (days)	(11)	156	171	182
Payables turnover period	(12)	35	42	46

Workings (all in $m)

		20X6	20X7	20X8
1	Gross profit margin	$\frac{286}{840}$	$\frac{336}{981}$	$\frac{323}{913}$
2	ROCE *	$\frac{100}{473}$	$\frac{122}{568}$	$\frac{104}{584}$
3	Profit margin	$\frac{100}{840}$	$\frac{122}{981}$	$\frac{104}{913}$
4	Assets turnover	$\frac{840}{473}$	$\frac{981}{568}$	$\frac{913}{584}$
5	Gearing ratio	$\frac{74}{74 + 399}$	$\frac{138}{138 + 430}$	$\frac{138}{138 + 446}$

		20X6	20X7	20X8
6	Debt/equity ratio	$\frac{74}{399}$	$\frac{138}{430}$	$\frac{138}{446}$
7	Interest cover	$\frac{100}{6}$	$\frac{122}{15}$	$\frac{104}{19}$
8	Current ratio	$\frac{394}{133}$	$\frac{502}{180}$	$\frac{506}{186}$
9	Quick ratio	$\frac{157}{133}$	$\frac{199}{180}$	$\frac{212}{186}$
10	Receivables payment period	$\frac{105}{840} \times 365$	$\frac{141}{981} \times 365$	$\frac{160}{913} \times 365$
11	Inventory turnover period	$\frac{237}{554} \times 365$	$\frac{303}{645} \times 365$	$\frac{294}{590} \times 365$
12	Payables payment period	$\frac{53}{554} \times 365$	$\frac{75}{645} \times 365$	$\frac{75}{590} \times 365$

* ROCE has been calculated here as:

$$\frac{\text{Profit on ordinary activities before interest and taxation (PBIT)}}{\text{Capital employed}}$$

where capital employed = shareholders' funds plus payables falling due after one year and any long-term provision for liabilities and charges. It is possible to calculate ROCE using net profit after taxation and interest, but this admits variations and distortions into the ratio which are not affected by **trading** activity.

(b) Areas for further investigation include the following:

(i) *Long-term loan*

There is no indication as to why this loan was raised and how it was used to finance the business. Further details are needed of interest rate(s), security given and repayment dates.

(ii) *Trading activity*

The level of sales has fluctuated in quite a strange way and this requires further investigation and explanation. Factors to consider would include pricing policies, product mix, market share and any unique occurrence which would affect sales.

(iii) *Further breakdown*

It would be useful to break down some of the information in the financial statements, perhaps into a management accounting format. Examples would include the following.

(1) Sales by segment, market or geographical area
(2) Cost of sales split, into raw materials, labour and overheads
(3) Inventory broken down into raw materials, work in progress and finished goods
(4) Expenses analysed between administrative expenses, sales and distribution costs

(iv) *Accounting policies*

Accounting policies may have a significant effect on certain items. In particular, it would be useful to know what the accounting policies are in relation to intangible assets (and what these assets consist of), and whether there has been any change in accounting policies.

(v) *Dividend policy*

The company has maintained the level of dividend paid to shareholders (although it has not been raised during the three year period). Presumably the company would have been able to reduce the amount of long-term debt taken on if it had retained part or all of the dividend during this period. It would be interesting to examine the share price movement during the period and calculate the dividend cover.

Tutorial note. Other matters raised could have included:

(1) Working capital problems, particularly inventory turnover and control over receivables

(2) EPS (which cannot be calculated here as the number of shares is not given) and other related investor statistics, such as the P/E ratio.

6 Impact of changes in accounting standards and policies 12/08

FAST FORWARD

Accounting policies may be adopted for the purpose of **manipulation**.

Changes in accounting standards can have a significant impact on the financial statements.

We discussed the disclosure of accounting policies in your earlier studies. The choice of accounting policy and the effect of its implementation are almost as important as its disclosure in that the results of a company can be altered significantly by the choice of accounting policy.

6.1 The effect of choice of accounting policies

Where accounting standards allow alternative treatment of items in the accounts, then the accounting policy note should declare which policy has been chosen. It should then be applied consistently.

Consider, though, the **radically different effects produced by the different treatment of some items**. An example is the treatment of joint ventures, which may be proportionally consolidated or equity accounted.

You should be able to think of other examples of how the choice of accounting policy can affect the financial statements.

6.2 Changes in accounting policy

The effect of a change of accounting policy is treated as a retrospective adjustment to the opening balance of each affected component of equity, as if the accounting policy had always applied.

IAS 8 (revised) states that changes in accounting policies are rare, and only allowed if **required by statute** or if the change results in **more reliable and relevant information.**

There is still some scope for directors to **manipulate the results** through change(s) of accounting policies. This would be done to avoid the effect of an old accounting policy or gain the effect of a new one. It is likely to be done in a sensitive period, perhaps when the company's profits are low or the company is about to announce a rights issue. The management would have to convince the auditors that the new policy was much better, but it is not difficult to produce reasons in such cases.

The effect of such a change is **very short-term**. Most analysts and sophisticated users will discount its effect immediately, except to the extent that it will affect any dividend (because of the effect on distributable profits). It may help to avoid breaches of banking covenants because of the effect on certain ratios.

Obviously, the accounting policy for any item in the accounts could only be changed once in quite a long period of time. No auditors would allow another change, even back to the old policy, unless there was a wholly exceptional reason.

The managers of a company can choose accounting policies **initially** to suit the company or the type of results they want to get. Any changes in accounting policy must be justified, but some managers might try to change accounting policies just to manipulate the results.

6.3 Changes in accounting standards

FAST FORWARD

You will probably be asked to **advise the directors** on the implication of a change in accounting standards, or on the effect of using the correct accounting treatment.

The effect of a change of accounting standard can be far reaching. For example when IFRS 3 *Business combinations* was brought in, goodwill arising on consolidation could no longer be amortised, but had to be reviewed annually for impairment. Impairment tests are more subjective than amortisation, although both methods have their drawbacks. Further significant amendments in the area of business combinations are proposed.

6.4 The impact of change and the P2 examination

This topic has been examined regularly as the 'ethical' part of the longer case study question in Section A. Usually you will be in the position of advising the directors. The directors may have adopted an accounting treatment that is incorrect. You will need to advise them of the correct accounting treatment and show, usually with supporting calculations, the effect on the financial statements of adopting the correct treatment.

Ethics are an important aspect of the ACCA's qualification. If the directors, in adopting certain accounting treatments, are acting unethically, you may need to discuss this. This happened in Question 1 of the Pilot paper.

Alternatively the treatment may not be wrong, but a matter of accounting policy which the directors wish to change. As before, you will be asked to explain, with supporting calculations, the effect of the change.

You are very likely to be asked to explain the significance of a proposed change in accounting standards in Question 4, which may include a numerical element.

6.5 Practise case study questions

The impact of change in standards, policies or treatment is unlikely to comprise a whole question. It is more likely to come up as part of a longer question. For example, it may come up as part of the compulsory 50-mark case study question, the first part of which will always be on groups. You should therefore practise this type of question. Have a go at the question Wingit in the Exam Question Bank. Further questions of this type can be found in BPP's Practice & Revision Kit for this Paper.

Exam focus point

Case study questions to try: Planet, Wingit and the case study questions in the Practice and Revision Kit. The December 2008 paper had a question on accounting standards and disclosures, which required students to think broadly.

7 Accounting theory and practice

7.1 The nature of profit

We have seen throughout this Text that accounting 'profit' is an arbitrary figure, subject to the whims and biases of accountants and the variety of treatments in accounting standards. Go back to the contents page and pick out all the topics which demonstrate or indicate how company results are manipulated. Isn't it nearly all of them? Let us briefly mention some of them again.

7.1.1 IAS 2 Inventories

Companies are allowed to use different methods of valuing inventory under IAS 2, which means that the final inventory figure in the statement of financial position will be different under each method. Profit will be affected by the closing inventory valuation, particularly where the level of inventory fluctuates to a great extent.

7.1.2 IAS 16 Property, plant and equipment

As with IAS 2, IAS 16 allows different accounting bases for depreciation. Choosing to use the reducing balance method rather than the straight line method can front-load the depreciation charge for assets. It is also the case that the subjectivity surrounding the estimated economic lives of assets can lead to manipulation of profits. (Note. Remember that some companies refuse to depreciate some assets at all – mainly freehold property.)

7.2 Other problems with financial analysis

Two frequent problems affecting financial analysis are discussed here.

- Seasonal fluctuations
- Window dressing

7.2.1 Seasonal fluctuations

Many companies are located in industries where trade is seasonal. For example:

- Firework manufacturers
- Swimwear manufacturers
- Ice cream makers
- Umbrella manufacturers
- Gas companies
- Travel agents
- Flower suppliers and deliverers
- Football clubs

Year on year the seasonal fluctuations affecting such companies does not matter; a year end has to be chosen and as long as the fluctuations are at roughly the same time every year, then there should be no problem. Occasionally a perverse sense of humour will cause a company to choose an accounting period ending in the middle of the busy season: this may affect the cut off because the busy season might be slightly early or late.

A major difficulty can arise if companies affected by seasonal fluctuations change their accounting date. A shorter period (normally) may encompass part, all or none of the busy season. Whatever happens, the figures will be distorted and the comparatives will be meaningless. Analysts would not know how to extrapolate the figures from the shorter period to produce a comparison for the previous year. Weightings could be used, but these are likely to be inaccurate.

Case Study

An example of the problems this can cause occurred when the UK company British Gas plc changed its accounting period to 31 December from 31 March. The company published two reports and accounts.

- For the year to 31 March 1991
- For the year to 31 December 1991

thus including the first three months of the calendar year in both reports. As a note to the later accounts, the company produced a profit and loss account for the last nine months of the calendar year.

Although the British Gas auditors did not qualify the audit report, the Review Panel was not very happy about this double counting of results. The nine month profit and loss account did not meet the provisions of CA 1985 'either as to its location or its contents, nor did it contain the relevant earnings per share figure'. British Gas had to promise that, in their 1992 results, the 1991 comparative would be for the nine months period only.

The effect here is obvious. The first three months of the calendar year are when British Gas earns a high proportion of its profits (winter!). If the 1991 results had covered the period from 1 April only, then the profits would have been reduced by more than an average loss of three months' profit. By using a 12 month period, British Gas avoided the risk of the period's results looking too bad.

7.2.2 Window dressing

Window dressing transactions were made largely redundant by IAS 10 *Events after the reporting period*. Note that window dressing transactions were not outlawed, but full disclosure would render such transactions useless.

One example of window dressing is a situation where a large cheque is written against one group company's positive bank balance in favour of another group company with a large overdraft. The cheque is put through at the year end and then cancelled at the beginning of the next year, thus concealing the overdraft in the consolidated statement of financial position (where positive and negative bank balances cannot be netted off).

You may be able to think of other examples of window dressing and you should look for any potential examples which come up in examination questions.

Summary of limitations of financial analysis

(a) Information problems:

- (i) The base information is often out of date, so timeliness of information leads to problems of interpretation.
- (ii) Historic cost information may not be the most appropriate information for the decision for which the analysis is being undertaken.
- (iii) Information in published accounts is generally summarised information and detailed information may be needed.
- (iv) Analysis of accounting information only identifies symptoms not causes and thus is of limited use.

(b) Comparison problems: inter-temporal

- (i) Effects of price changes make comparisons difficult unless adjustments are made.
- (ii) Impacts of changes in technology on the price of assets, the likely return and the future markets.
- (iii) Impacts of a changing environment on the results reflected in the accounting information.
- (iv) Potential effects of changes in accounting policies on the reported results.
- (v) Problems associated with establishing a normal base year to compare other years with.

(c) Comparison problems: inter-firm

- (i) Selection of industry norms and the usefulness of norms based on averages.
- (ii) Different firms having different financial and business risk profiles and the impact on analysis.
- (iii) Different firms using different accounting policies.
- (iv) Impacts of the size of the business and its comparators on risk, structure and returns.
- (v) Impacts of different environments on results, for example different countries or home-based versus multinational firms.

You should use this summary as a type of checklist.

7.3 Is accounting theory too remote?

Even the IASB, which consults and co-operates extensively with practitioners, has been criticised for being an 'ivory tower'. 'Pure' accounting theory or research in a university may seem even more remote to the financial controller, let alone the bookkeeper, working at the 'coal face'.

As far back as 2002, Sauders, Fulkerson, Chau and Welch at the University of Texas wrote (our emphasis):

> [S]tudies of practicing accountants' perceptions of accounting journals are limited. Academic peers make tenure, promotion and program standing determinations based upon colleagues' frequency and quality of publication. Hence, academics devote more time to learning about which journals their peers view as prestigious than to assessing journal preferences of practitioners. While researchers pursue the rewards associated with publication in top-ranked journals, some accounting academics and practitioners have expressed concerns regarding the relevance of accounting research (Jonsson 1998, O'Brian 1997) and suggest **a disconnect between accounting research and practice**...[T]he theoretical and statistical significance of many academically prestigious publications is often lost to practicing accountants.

One indication of **the remoteness of accountancy academia** from practice is the fact that many accounting qualifications do not demand an accountancy degree. If you can qualify as an accountant with a degree in philosophy or history, or with no degree at all, how relevant is an accountancy degree to the day-to-day practice of accountants?

7.3.1 Users of accounts

The objective of published financial statements is to satisfy the information needs of users. Some types of user will always need financial statements as their main source of information about a company. **Companies are normally required to file financial statements with the regulatory authorities** so that a certain amount of information is available to the general public. The government uses financial statements in order to assess taxation and to regulate the activities of businesses.

Financial reporting has evolved to meet the needs of investors in large public companies and their advisers. Yet **published financial statements have serious limitations**: they are based on historic information and they only reflect the financial effects of transactions and events. **Investors need to predict a company's future performance**, including changes in shareholder value. These are affected by the development of new products, the quality of management, the use of new technology and the economic and political environment.

Traditional financial statements are **only one of many sources of information used by investors**. Other sources include **market data, product information, quarterly earnings announcements, press conferences and other briefings given by the directors to institutional investors, analysts and financial journalists**.

Traditional ratio analysis is becoming outdated. The Association for Investment Management and Research (AIMR) has developed global investment performance standards. These are based on 'total return', which includes realised and unrealised gains and income and rates of return that are adjusted for daily-weighted cash flows. **Earnings per share and the price earnings ratio continue to be important, but analysts now calculate a range of other measures. These include cash flow per share, market value per share and 'consensus earnings per share', which predicts future performance.**

Free cash flow is a key performance measure used by analysts to value a company. Free cash flow is cash revenues less cash expenses, taxation paid, cash needed for working capital and cash required for routine capital expenditure. **This can be compared with the cost of capital employed to assess whether shareholder value has increased or decreased**. It can also be projected and discounted to provide an approximate market value.

When it comes to **users of accounts who are not practitioners**, the world of accounting theory may seem even more remote. Such users need to know what the figures mean, or more importantly, what they do not mean. Keynes once said that it is better to be vaguely right than precisely wrong. Arguably, historical cost is precisely wrong, while fair value has more chance of being vaguely right.

Not all users want or need precise information. Adherents of the efficient markets hypothesis argue that by the time financial reports are issued most of the important information contained in them has been factored into the share price.

7.3.2 Bridging the gap

The following are ways in which the gap between accounting theory and practice could be bridged:

(a) More consultation with practitioners, particularly from small and medium-sized entities in the standard-setting process

(b) Less jargon in accounting theory

(c) Better communication with non-specialist users

8 Management Commentary – a global Operating and Financial Review?

FAST FORWARD

Some of the limitations of financial statements may be addressed by a **management commentary.** The IASB has issued a practice statement on a **management commentary** to supplement and complement the financial statements.

8.1 Need for management commentary

In the UK, companies have been encouraged to produce an Operating and Financial Review, explaining the main factors underlying a company's financial position and performance, and analysing the main trends affecting this. A Reporting Statement on the OFR was issued in January 2006.

Financial statements alone are not considered sufficient without an **accompanying explanation of the performance**, eg highlighting a restructuring that has reduced profits or the cost of developing a new business channel in the current period which will generate profits in the future.

Perhaps more importantly a good management commentary not only talks about the past position and performance, but how this will translate **into future financial position** and performance.

The *Conceptual Framework for Financial Reporting* acknowledges, 'general purpose financial reports do not and cannot provide all of the information that existing and potential investors, lenders and other creditors need. Those users need to consider pertinent information from other sources, for example, general economic conditions and expectations, political events and political climate, and industry and company outlooks.' (Conceptual Framework: para. OB6)

Typically, larger companies are already making disclosures similar to a management commentary, eg as a 'Director's Report', but the aim of the IASB is **to define internationally what a management commentary** should contain. For example, a good commentary should be balanced and not just highlight the company's successes.

A management commentary would also address **risks and issues** facing the entity that may not be apparent from a review of the financial statements, and how they will be addressed

8.2 IFRS Practice Statement

In 2010, the IASB issued an IFRS Practice Statement *Management Commentary,* which is the international equivalent of the Operating and Financial Review.

The main objective of the Statement is that the IASB can **improve the quality of financial reports** by providing guidance 'for all jurisdictions, on order to promote comparability across entities that present management commentary and to improve entities' communications with their stakeholders'. In preparing this guidance, the team has reviewed existing requirements around the world, such as the OFR, Management's Discussion and Analysis (MD&A) in the USA and Canada, and the German accounting standard on Management Reporting.

8.2.1 Scope

The IASB has published a **Practice Statement rather than an IFRS** on management commentary. This 'provides a broad, non-binding framework for the presentation of management commentary that relates to financial statements that have been prepared in accordance with IFRSs'.

This guidance is designed for publicly traded entities, but it would **be left to regulators to decide** who would be required to publish management commentary (Management Commentary: para. IN 2).

This approach avoids the **adoption hurdle**, ie that the perceived cost of applying IFRSs might increase, which could otherwise dissuade jurisdictions/ countries not having adopted IFRSs from requiring its adoption, especially where requirements differ significantly from existing national requirements.

8.2.2 Definition of management commentary

The following preliminary definition is given in the Practice Statement:

Key term

Management commentary is a **narrative report** that provides a context within which to interpret the financial position, financial performance and cash flows of an entity. It also provides management with an opportunity to explain **its objectives and its strategies** for achieving those objectives. (Management Commentary: para. IN 3)

8.2.3 Principles for the preparation of a management commentary

When a management commentary relates to financial statements, then those financial statements should either be provided with the commentary or the commentary should clearly identify the financial statements to which it relates. The management commentary must be clearly distinguished from other information and must state to what extent it has followed the Practice Statement.

Management commentary should follow these principles (Management Commentary: para. 12 to 14):

(a) To provide **management's view** of the entity's performance, position and progress

(b) To **supplement and complement** information presented in the financial statements

(c) To include **forward-looking information**

(d) To include information that possesses the **qualitative characteristics** described in the *Conceptual Framework* (see Chapter 1)

8.2.4 Elements of management commentary

The Practice Statement says that to meet the objective of management commentary, an entity should include information that is essential to an understanding of (Management Commentary: para. 24):

(a) The **nature of the business**

(b) Management's **objectives and its strategies** for meeting those objectives

(c) The entity's most significant **resources, risks and relationships**

(d) The **results** of operations and **prospects**

(e) The critical **performance measures and indicators** that management uses to evaluate the entity's performance against stated objectives

The Practice Statement does not propose a fixed format as the nature of management commentary would vary between entities. It does not provide application guidance or illustrative examples, as this could be interpreted as a floor or ceiling for disclosures. Instead, the IASB anticipates that other parties will produce guidance (Management Commentary: para. IN 2.

However, the IASB ((Management Commentary: para. BC 48) has provided a table relating the five elements listed above to its assessments of the needs of the primary users of a management commentary (existing and potential investors, lenders and creditors).

Element	User needs
Nature of the business	The knowledge of the business in which an entity is engaged and the external environment in which it operates.
Objectives and strategies	To assess the strategies adopted by the entity and the likelihood that those strategies will be successful in meeting management's stated objectives.
Resources, risks and relationships	A basis for determining the resources available to the entity as well as obligations to transfer resources to others; the ability of the entity to generate long-term sustainable net inflows of resources; and the risks to which those resource-generating activities are exposed, both in the near term and in the long term.
Results and prospects	The ability to understand whether an entity has delivered results in line with expectations and, implicitly, how well management has understood the entity's market, executed its strategy and managed the entity's resources, risks and relationships.
Performance measures and indicators	The ability to focus on the critical performance measures and indicators that management uses to assess and manage the entity's performance against stated objectives and strategies.

8.2.5 Advantages and disadvantages of a compulsory management commentary

Advantages	Disadvantages
Entity • Promotes the entity, and attracts investors, lenders, customers and suppliers • Communicates management plans and outlook	**Entity** • Costs may outweigh benefits • Risk that investors may ignore the financial statements
Users • Financial statements not enough to make decisions (financial information only) • Financial statements backward looking (need forward looking information) • Highlights risks • Useful for comparability to other entities	**Users** • Subjective • Not normally audited • Could encourage companies to de-list (to avoid requirement to produce MC) • Different countries have different needs

Chapter Roundup

- Go back to your earlier studies and revise **IAS 1** and **IAS 8**. IAS 1 was revised in 2007 and 2011. The changes and new formats are given in this section.
- IAS 1 requires the presentation of items of other comprehensive income.
- An important aspect of reporting financial performance is **segment reporting**. This is covered by IFRS 8 *Operating segments,* which replaced IAS 14 *Segment reporting* in November 2006.
- **Reportable segments** are operating segments or aggregation of operating segments that meet specified criteria.
- IFRS 8 **disclosures** are of:
  - Operating segment profit or loss
  - Segment assets
  - Segment liabilities
  - Certain income and expense items
- Disclosures are also required about the **revenues derived from products or services** and about the **countries** in which revenues are earned or assets held, even if that information is not used by management in making decisions.
- **Earnings per share** is a measure of the amount of profits earned by a company for each ordinary share. Earnings are profits after tax and preferred dividends.
- **Basic EPS** is calculated by dividing the net profit or loss for the period attributable to ordinary shareholders by the weighted average number of ordinary shares outstanding during the period.
- You should know how to calculate **basic EPS** and how to deal with related complications (issue of shares for cash, bonus issue, share splits/reverse share splits, rights issues).
- **Diluted EPS** is calculated by adjusting the net profit attributable to ordinary shareholders and the weighted average number of shares outstanding for the effects of all dilutive potential ordinary shares.
- Keep the various **sources of financial information** in mind and the effects of insider dealing, the efficient market hypothesis and Stock Exchange regulations.
- Much of the material here on **ratios** should have been revision for you.
- Make sure that you can **define** all the ratios. Look out for variations in definitions of ratios which might appear in questions.
- Always remember that 'profit' and 'net assets' are fairly **arbitrary figures**, affected by different accounting policies and manipulation.
- Financial analysis is a vital tool for **auditors**.
- Accounting policies may be adopted for the purpose of **manipulation**.
- **Changes in accounting standards** can have a significant impact on the financial statements.
- You will probably be asked to **advise the directors** on the implication of a change in accounting standards, or on the effect of using the correct accounting treatment.
- Some of the limitations of financial statements may be addressed by a **management commentary.** The IASB has issued a practice statement on a **management commentary** to supplement and complement the financial statements.

Quick Quiz

1 The statement introduced by IAS 1 as revised in 2011 is:

A Statement of total recognised gains and losses
B Statement of profit or loss and other comprehensive income
C Statement of recognised income and expenses
D Statement of recognised gains and losses

2 What new financial statement name is introduced in the 2011 revision of IAS 1?

3 What is the full name for IAS 8? (**Fill in the blanks.**)

Accounting................, changes in accounting......................... and ....

4 All entities must disclose segment information. *True or false?*

5 Geographical and segment information is no longer required. *True or false?*

6 Which numerator is used to rank dilutive shares?

7 Why is the numerator adjusted for convertible bonds when calculating diluted EPS?

8 What are the main sources of financial information available to the external users?

9 What is the efficient market hypothesis?

10 Apart from ratio analysis, what other information might be helpful in interpreting a company's accounts?

11 In a period when profits are fluctuating, what effect does a company's level of gearing have on the profits available for ordinary shareholders?

12 The Management Commentary provides detailed disclosures. *True or False?*

Answers to Quick Quiz

1 The correct answer is B.

2 Statement of profit or loss and other comprehensive income.

3 Accounting **policies**, changes in accounting **estimates** and **errors**

4 False. Only entities whose equity or debt securities are publicly traded need disclose segment information.

5 False. Information about revenues from different countries must be disclosed unless it is not available and the cost to develop it would be excessive. It should always be disclosed if it is used by management in making operating decisions.

6 Net profit from continuing operations only

7 Because the issue of shares will affect earnings by the interest saving.

8 Published accounts and interim statement, filed documents, government statistics.

9 See Section 5.4

10
- Other comments in the accounts eg Directors' Report
- Age and nature of the assets
- Current and future market developments
- Recent acquisition or disposal of subsidiaries
- Notes to the accounts, auditors' report, after the reporting period events, etc.

11 Profits available for the shareholders will be highly volatile and some years there may not be an ordinary dividend paid.

12 False. It provides a disclosure framework only.

Now try the questions below from the Practice Question Bank

Number	Level	Marks	Time
Q15	Introductory	n/a	n/a

11 Related parties

Topic list	Syllabus reference
1 IAS 24 *Related party disclosures*	C9
2 Question	C9

Introduction

In general, P2 is not much concerned with disclosures. IAS 24 is an exception to this.

Study guide

		Intellectual level
C9	**Related parties**	
(a)	Determine the parties considered to be related to an entity	3
(b)	Identify the implications of related party relationships and the need for disclosure	3

Exam guide

This topic may come up as part of a scenario question.

1 IAS 24 *Related party disclosures* 6/11, 6/16

FAST FORWARD

IAS 24 is primarily a disclosure standard. It is concerned to improve the quality of information provided by published accounts and also to strengthen their stewardship roles.

In the absence of information to the contrary, it is assumed that a reporting entity has **independent discretionary power** over its resources and transactions and pursues its activities independently of the interests of its individual owners, managers and others. Transactions are presumed to have been undertaken on an **arm's length basis**, ie on terms such as could have obtained in a transaction with an external party, in which each side bargained knowledgeably and freely, unaffected by any relationship between them.

These assumptions may not be justified when **related party relationships** exist, because the requisite conditions for competitive, free market dealings may not be present. While the parties may endeavour to achieve arm's length bargaining the very nature of the relationship may preclude this occurring.

1.1 Objective

This is the related parties issue and IAS 24 tackles it by ensuring that financial statements contain the disclosures necessary to draw attention to the possibility that the reported financial position and results may have been affected by the existence of related parties and by material transactions with them. In other words, this is a standard which is primarily concerned with **disclosure** (IAS 24: para. 1).

1.2 Scope

The standard requires disclosure of related party transactions and outstanding balances in the **separate financial statements** of a parent, venturer or investor presented in accordance with IAS 27 as well as in consolidated financial statements.

An entity's financial statements disclose related party transactions and outstanding balances with other entities in a group. **Intragroup** transactions and balances are **eliminated** in the preparation of consolidated financial statements.

(IAS 24: para. 3)

1.3 Definitions

The following important definitions are given by the standard. Note that the definitions of **control** and **significant influence** are now the same as those given in IFRS 10, IAS 28 and IFRS 11.

Key terms

Related party. A related party is a person or entity that is related to the entity that is preparing its financial statements.

(a) A **person** or a close member of that person's family is **related** to a reporting entity if that person:

(i) Has control or joint control over the reporting entity;

(ii) Has significant influence over the reporting entity; or

(iii) Is a member of the key management personnel of the reporting entity or of a parent of the reporting entity.

(b) An **entity** is related to a reporting entity if any of the following conditions applies:

(i) The entity and the reporting entity are members of the same group (which means that each parent, subsidiary and fellow subsidiary is related to the others).

(ii) One entity is an associate or joint venture of the other entity (or an associate or joint venture of a member of a group of which the other entity is a member).

(iii) Both entities are joint ventures of the same third party.

(iv) One entity is a joint venture of a third entity and the other entity is an associate of the third entity.

(v) The entity is a post-employment defined benefit plan for the benefit of employees of either the reporting entity or an entity related to the reporting entity. If the reporting entity is itself such a plan, the sponsoring employers are also related to the reporting entity.

(vi) The entity is controlled or jointly controlled by a person identified in (a).

(vii) A person identified in (a)(i) has significant influence over the entity or is a member of the key management personnel of the entity (or of a parent of the entity).

(viii) The entity, or any member of a group of which it is a part, provides key management personnel services to the reporting entity or to the parent of the reporting entity.

Related party transaction. A transfer of resources, services or obligations between related parties, regardless of whether a price is charged.

Control is the power to govern the financial and operating policies of an entity so as to obtain benefits from its activities.

Significant influence is the power to participate in the financial and operating policy decisions of an entity, but is not control over these policies. Significant ownership may be gained by share ownership, statute or agreement.

Joint control is the contractually agreed sharing of control over an economic activity.

Key management personnel are those persons having authority and responsibility for planning, directing and controlling the activities of the entity, directly or indirectly, including any director (whether executive or otherwise) of that entity.

Close members of the family of an individual are those family members who may be expected to influence, or be influenced by, that individual in their dealings with the entity. They may include:

(a) The individual's domestic partner and children;
(b) Children of the domestic partner; and
(c) Dependants of the individual or the domestic partner. *(IAS 24: para. 9)*

The most important point to remember here is that, when considering each possible related party relationship, attention must be paid to the **substance of the relationship, not merely the legal form.**

IAS 24 lists the following which are **not necessarily related parties** (IAS 24: para. 11).

(a) **Two entities simply because they have a director or other key management in common** (notwithstanding the definition of related party above, although it is necessary to consider how that director would affect both entities)

(b) **Two venturers, simply because they share joint control over a joint venture**

(c) Certain other bodies, simply as a result of their **role in normal business dealings** with the entity:

 (i) Providers of finance
 (ii) Trade unions
 (iii) Public utilities
 (iv) Government departments and agencies

(d) **Any single customer, supplier, franchisor, distributor, or general agent** with whom the entity transacts a significant amount of business, simply by virtue of the resulting economic dependence.

1.4 Government-related entities

The disclosures listed above need not be made in respect of transactions with:

(a) A government that has control, joint control or significant influence over the reporting entity, and

(b) Another entity that is a related party because the same government has control, joint control or significant influence over both the reporting entity and the other entity.

Instead, the reporting entity should disclose:

(a) The name of the government and the nature of its relationship with the reporting entity

(b) Information in sufficient detail to enable users of the financial statements to understand the effect of related party transactions on those financial statements, including:

 (i) The nature and amount of each individually significant transaction, and

 (ii) Tor other transactions that are collectively significant, a qualitative or quantitative indication of their extent.

(IAS 24: paras. 24 to 26)

1.5 Disclosure

As noted above, IAS 24 is almost entirely concerned with disclosure and its provisions are meant to **supplement** those disclosure requirements required by national company legislation and other IFRSs (particularly IAS 1, IFRS 10, IFRS 11 and IFRS 12).

The standard lists some **examples** of transactions that are disclosed if they are with a related party (IAS 24: para. 21):

- Purchases or sales of goods (finished or unfinished)
- Purchases or sales of property and other assets
- Rendering or receiving of services
- Leases
- Transfer of research and development
- Transfers under licence agreements
- Provision of finance (including loans and equity contributions in cash or in kind)
- Provision of guarantees and collateral security
- Settlement of liabilities on behalf of the entity or by the entity on behalf of another party

Relationships between **parents and subsidiaries** must be **disclosed irrespective** of **whether** any **transactions** have **taken place between** the related parties. An entity must disclose the **name** of its **parent** and, if different, the **ultimate controlling party**. This will enable a reader of the financial statements to be able to form a view about the effects of a related party relationship on the reporting entity.

If neither the parent nor the ultimate controlling party produces financial statements available for public use, the name of the next most senior parent that does so shall also be disclosed.

An entity should disclose key management personnel compensation in total for various categories:

(a) Items of a similar nature may be **disclosed in aggregate unless** separate disclosure is necessary for an understanding of the effect on the financial statements.

(b) Disclosures that related party transactions were made on terms equivalent to those that prevail in arm's length transactions are made only if such disclosures can be substantiated.

1.6 Section summary

IAS 24 is primarily concerned with **disclosure**. You should learn the following:

- **Definitions**: these are very important
- Relationships covered
- Relationships that **may not** necessarily be between related parties
- **Disclosures**: again, very important, representing the whole purpose of the standard

Question — Related parties

Fancy Feet Co is a UK company which supplies handmade leather shoes to a chain of high street shoe shops. The company is also the sole importer of some famous high quality Greek stoneware which is supplied to an upmarket shop in London's West End.

Fancy Feet Co was set up 30 years ago by Georgios Kostades who left Greece when he fell out with the military government. The company is owned and run by Mr Kostades and his three children.

The shoes are purchased from a French company, the shares of which are owned by the Kostades Family Trust (Monaco).

Required

Identify the financial accounting issues arising out of the above scenario.

Answer

Issues

(a) The basis on which Fancy Feet trades with the Greek supplier and the French company owned by the Kostades family trust.

(b) Whether the overseas companies trade on commercial terms with the UK company or do the foreign entities control the UK company.

(c) Who owns the Greek company: is this a related party under the provisions of IAS 24?

(d) Should the nature of trade suggest a related party controls Fancy Feet Co? Detailed disclosures will be required in the accounts.

2 Question

Try this longer question on related parties.

Question — RP Group

Discuss whether the following events would require disclosure in the financial statements of the RP Group, a public limited company, under IAS 24 *Related party disclosures*.

The RP Group, merchant bankers, has a number of subsidiaries, associates and joint ventures in its group structure. During the financial year to 31 October 20X9 the following events occurred.

(a) The company agreed to finance a management buyout of a group company, AB, a limited company. In addition to providing loan finance, the company has retained a 25% equity holding in the company and has a main board director on the board of AB. RP received management fees, interest payments and dividends from AB.

(b) On 1 July 20X9, RP sold a wholly owned subsidiary, X, a limited company, to Z, a public limited company. During the year RP supplied X with second-hand office equipment and X leased its factory from RP. The transactions were all contracted for at market rates.

(c) The retirement benefit scheme of the group is managed by another merchant bank. An investment manager of the group retirement benefit scheme is also a non-executive director of the RP Group and received an annual fee for his services of $25,000 which is not material in the group context. The company pays $16m per annum into the scheme and occasionally transfers assets into the scheme. In 20X9, property, plant and equipment of $10m were transferred into the scheme and a recharge of administrative costs of $3m was made.

Answer

(a) IAS 24 does not require disclosure of transactions between companies and providers of finance in the ordinary course of business. As RP is a merchant bank, no disclosure is needed between RP and AB. However, RP owns 25% of the equity of AB and it would seem significant influence exists (IAS 28, **greater than 20% existing holding means significant influence is presumed**) and therefore AB could be an associate of RP. IAS 24 regards associates as related parties.

The decision as to associate status depends upon the ability of RP to exercise significant influence especially as the other 75% of votes are owned by the management of AB.

Merchant banks tend to regard companies which would qualify for associate status as trade investments since the relationship is designed to provide finance.

IAS 28 presumes that a party owning or able to exercise control over 20% of voting rights is a related party. So an investor with a 25% holding and a director on the board would be expected to have significant influence over operating and financial policies in such a way as to inhibit the pursuit of separate interests. If it can be shown that this is not the case, there is no related party relationship.

If it is decided that there is a related party situation then **all material transactions** should be disclosed including **management fees, interest, dividends and the terms of the loan**.

(b) **IAS 24 does *not* require intragroup transactions and balances eliminated** on **consolidation to be disclosed**. IAS 24 does not deal with the situation where an undertaking becomes, or ceases to be, a subsidiary during the year.

Best practice indicates that related party transactions should be disclosed for the period when X was not part of the group. Transactions between RP and X should be disclosed between 1 July 20X9 and 31 October 20X9 but transactions prior to 1 July will have been eliminated on consolidation.

There is no related party relationship between RP and Z since it is a normal business transaction unless either parties interests have been influenced or controlled in some way by the other party.

(c) **Employee retirement benefit schemes** of the reporting entity are included in the IAS 24 definition of **related parties**.

The contributions paid, the non current asset transfer ($10m) and the charge of administrative costs ($3m) must be disclosed.

The **pension investment manager** would **not normally** be **considered** a **related party. However,** the manager is **key management personnel** by virtue of his **non-executive directorship**.

Directors are deemed to be related parties by IAS 24, and the manager receives a $25,000 fee. IAS 24 requires the disclosure of **compensation paid to key management personnel** and the fee falls within the definition of compensation. Therefore, it must be disclosed.

Chapter Roundup

- **IAS 24** is primarily a disclosure standard. It is concerned to improve the quality of information provided by published accounts and also to strengthen their stewardship roles.

Quick Quiz

1 What is a related party transaction?

2 A managing director of a company is a related party. *True/False*?

Answers to Quick Quiz

1. A transfer of resources, services or obligations between related parties, regardless of whether a price is charged.
2. True. A member of the key management personnel of an entity is a related party of that entity.

Now try the question below from the Practice Question Bank

Number	Level	Marks	Time
Q16	Introductory	n/a	n/a

PART C

Group financial statements

12

Revision of basic groups

Topic list	Syllabus reference
1 IFRS 3: *Main points*	D1
2 IFRS 10 *Consolidated financial statements*	D1
3 IFRS 3, IFRS 13 and fair values	D1
4 IAS 28 *Investments in associates and joint ventures*	D1
5 IFRS 12 *Disclosure of interests in other entities*	D1

Introduction

Basic groups were covered in your earlier studies. In Paper P2, the emphasis is on the **more complex** aspects of consolidation. In this chapter, you will revise briefly the main principles of consolidation. If you have problems, then you should go back to your earlier study material and revise this topic more thoroughly.

Note. Throughout Part C, all undertakings are limited liability companies, unless otherwise stated. However, you should bear in mind that IFRS 10 includes unincorporated entities such as partnerships within the definition of subsidiary.

IAS 28 requires that **consolidated accounts** should be extended so that they include the share of earnings or losses of companies which are associated companies or joint ventures. You have covered associates in your earlier studies, but it is an important standard and so is covered in full again here.

Study guide

		Intellectual level
D1	**Group accounting including statement of cash flows**	
(a)	Apply the method of accounting for business combinations including complex group structures	3
(b)	Apply the principles relating to the cost of a business combination	3
(c)	Apply the recognition and measurement criteria for identifiable acquired assets and liabilities and goodwill, including step acquisitions	3
(d)	Apply and discuss the criteria used to identify a subsidiary and associate	3
(e)	Determine and apply appropriate procedures to be used in preparing group financial statements	3
(f)	Identify and outline: – The circumstances in which a group is required to prepare consolidated financial statements – The circumstances when a group may claim an exemption from the preparation of consolidated financial statements – Why directors may not wish to consolidate a subsidiary and where this is permitted	2
(g)	Apply the equity method of accounting for associates and joint ventures	3

Exam guide

You are unlikely to be examined just on the basic principles. However, you will gain marks for knowing the basic principles in a more complex consolidation.

1 IFRS 3: *Main points* 12/08, 6/11, 6/12

PER alert

One of the competences you need to fulfil Objective 10 of the Practical Experience Requirement (PER) is to record and understand financial transactions for single companies and combined entities. You can apply the knowledge you obtain from this chapter, on combined entities, to demonstrate this competence.

In traditional accounting terminology, a **group of companies** consists of a **parent company** and one or more **subsidiary companies** which are controlled by the parent company. We will be looking at six accounting standards in this and the next few chapters.

- IFRS 3 Business combinations (goodwill aspects are covered in an earlier chapter)
- IFRS 13 Fair value measurement
- IFRS 10 Consolidated financial statements
- IAS 28 Investments in associates and joint ventures
- IFRS 11 Joint arrangements
- IFRS 12 Disclosure of interests in other entities

You should have studied IFRS 3 *Business combinations* for Paper F7. Here is a re-cap.

1.1 Objective of IFRS 3

The objective of IFRS 3 is to improve the relevance, reliability and comparability of the information that a reporting entity provides in its financial statements about a business combination and its effects. To accomplish that, IFRS 3 establishes principles and requirements for how the acquirer:

(a) Recognises and measures in its financial statements the identifiable assets acquired, the liabilities assumed and any non-controlling interest in the acquiree

(b) Recognises and measures the goodwill acquired in the business combination or a gain from a bargain purchase

(c) Determines what information to disclose to enable users of the financial statements to evaluate the nature and financial effects of the business combination

(IFRS 3: para. 1)

1.2 Definitions

Exam focus point

All the definitions relating to group accounts are extremely important. You must **learn them** and **understand** their meaning and application.

FAST FORWARD

Go back to your earlier study material and practise more questions if you are unsure of basic consolidation techniques.

Definitions are very important when looking at group accounts.

Some of these definitions are from IAS 28 as well as IFRS 3 and IFRS 10. Some are new, and some you will have met before.

Key terms

Control. The power to govern the financial and operating policies of an entity so as to obtain benefits from its activities. *(IFRS 3: Appendix A, IFRS 10: Appendix A,)*

Subsidiary. An entity that is controlled by another entity (known as the parent). *(IFRS 10: Appendix A)*

Parent. An entity that has one or more subsidiaries. *(IFRS 10: Appendix A)*

Group. A parent and all its subsidiaries. *(IFRS 10: Appendix A)*

Associate. An entity, including an unincorporated entity such as a partnership, in which an investor has significant influence and which is neither a subsidiary nor an interest in a joint venture. *(IAS 28: para. 3)*

Significant influence is the power to participate in the financial and operating policy decisions of the investee but is not control or joint control over those policies. *(IAS 28: para. 3)*

Joint arrangement. An arrangement of which two or more parties have **joint control**. *(IAS 28: para. 3)*

Joint control. The **contractually agreed sharing of control** of an arrangement, which exists only when decisions about the relevant activities require the unanimous consent of the parties sharing control. *(IAS 28: para. 3)*

Joint venture. A joint arrangement whereby the parties that have joint control (the joint venturers) of the arrangement have **rights to the net assets** of the arrangement. *(IAS 28: para. 3, IFRS 11: Appendix A)*

Acquiree. The business or businesses that the **acquirer** obtains control of in a **business combination** *(IFRS 3: Appendix A)*

Acquirer. The entity that obtains control of the **acquiree** *(IFRS 3: Appendix A)*

Business combination. A transaction or other event in which an **acquirer** obtains control of one or more **businesses**. *(IFRS 3: Appendix A)*

Key terms cont'd

Contingent consideration. Usually, an obligation of the **acquirer** to transfer additional assets or **equity** *(IFRS 3: Appendix A)* **interests** to the former owners of an **acquiree** as part of the exchange for **control** of the **acquiree** if specified future events occur or conditions are met. *(IFRS 3: Appendix A)*

Equity interests. Broadly used in IFRS 3 to mean ownership interests.

Fair value. The price that would be received to sell an asset or paid to transfer a liability in an orderly transaction between market participants at the measurement date. *(IFRS 13: Appendix A)*

Non-controlling interest. The equity in a subsidiary not attributable, directly or indirectly, to a parent. *(IFRS 3: Appendix A)*

Before discussing IFRS 3 in detail, we can summarise the different types of investment *and* the required accounting for them as follows.

Investment	Criteria	Required treatment in group accounts
Subsidiary	Control	Full consolidation
Associate	Significant influence	Equity accounting
Joint venture	Contractual arrangement	Equity accounting
Investment which is none of the above	Asset held for accretion of wealth	As for single company accounts per IFRS 9

1.3 Identifying a business combination

IFRS 3 requires entities to determine whether a transaction or other event is a business combination by applying the definition in the IFRS.

1.4 The acquisition method

Entities must account for each business combination by applying the **acquisition method**. This requires:

(a) **Identifying the acquirer**. This is generally the party that obtains control.

(b) **Determining the acquisition date**. This is generally the date the consideration is legally transferred, but it may be another date if control is obtained on that date.

(c) Recognising and measuring the **identifiable assets acquired, the liabilities assumed** and any non-controlling interest in the acquiree. (See below.)

(d) Recognising and measuring goodwill or a gain from a bargain purchase. (See Chapter 3.)

The recognition and measurement of identifiable assets acquired and liabilities assumed other than non-controlling interest is dealt with in Section 3. Below we deal with the cost of the acquisition, the consideration transferred, the goodwill and the non-controlling interest.

(IFRS 3: paras. 4 and 5)

1.5 Acquisition-related costs

Under IFRS 3 **costs relating to the acquisition must be recognised as an expense** at the time of the acquisition. They are not regarded as an asset. (Costs of issuing debt or equity are to be accounted for under the rules of IFRS 9.)

(IFRS 3: para. 53)

1.6 Contingent consideration

FAST FORWARD

IFRS 3 **requires recognition of contingent consideration, measured at fair value, at the acquisition date**.

IFRS 3, Appendix Adefines contingent consideration as:

> Usually, an obligation of the acquirer to transfer additional assets or equity interests to the former owners of an acquiree as part of the exchange for control of the acquiree if specified future events occur or conditions are met. However, contingent consideration also may give the acquirer the right to the return of previously transferred consideration if specified conditions are met.

1.6.1 IFRS 3

IFRS 3 recognises that, by entering into an acquisition, the acquirer becomes obliged to make additional payments. Not recognising that obligation means that the consideration recognised at the acquisition date is not fairly stated.

IFRS 3 **requires recognition of contingent consideration, measured at fair value, at the acquisition date**. This is, arguably, consistent with how other forms of consideration are fair valued (IFRS 3: para. 39).

The acquirer may be required to pay contingent consideration in the form of equity or of a debt instrument or cash. Debt instruments are presented in accordance with IAS 32. Contingent consideration may occasionally be an asset, for example if the consideration has already been transferred and the acquirer has the right to the return of part of it, an asset may occasionally be recognised in respect of that right.

1.6.2 Post-acquisition changes in the fair value of the contingent consideration

The treatment depends on the circumstances (IFRS 3: para. 58):

(a) If the change in fair value is due to additional information obtained that affects the position at the acquisition date, goodwill should be re-measured.

(b) If the change is due to events which took place after the acquisition date, for example, meeting earnings targets:

- (i) Account for under IFRS 9 if the consideration is in the form of a financial instrument, for example loan notes.
- (ii) Account for under IAS 37 if the consideration is in the form of cash.
- (iii) An equity instrument is not re-measured.

1.7 Goodwill and the non-controlling interest 6/13

1.7.1 IFRS 3 methods – an introduction

IFRS 3 views the group as an economic entity. This means that it treats all providers of equity – including non-controlling interests – as shareholders in the group, even if they are not shareholders of the parent. Thus goodwill will arise on the non-controlling interest. We now need to consider how IFRS 3 sets out the calculation for goodwill.

1.7.2 IFRS 3 goodwill calculation

In words, IFRS 3 (revised) states:

> Consideration paid by parent + fair value of non-controlling interest – fair value of the subsidiary's net identifiable assets = consolidated goodwill

1.7.3 BPP proforma goodwill calculation

The proforma goodwill calculation should be set out like this:

	$	$
Consideration transferred		X
Non-controlling interests		X
Net assets acquired as represented by:		
Ordinary share capital	X	
Share premium	X	
Retained earnings on acquisition	X	
		(X)
Goodwill		X

1.7.4 Valuing non-controlling interest at acquisition

FAST FORWARD

The non-controlling interest may be valued **either at fair value or at the non-controlling interest's proportionate share of the acquiree's identifiable net assets.**

The non-controlling interest now forms part of the calculation of goodwill. The question now arises as to how it should be valued.

The 'economic entity' principle (see 1.7.1) suggests that the non-controlling interest should be valued at fair value. In fact, IFRS 3 gives a **choice**:

> For each business combination, the acquirer shall measure any non-controlling interest in the acquiree **either at fair value or at the non-controlling interest's proportionate share of the acquiree's identifiable net assets.** (IFRS 3: para. 19)

IFRS 3 revised suggests that the closest approximation to fair value will be the market price of the shares held by the non-controlling shareholders just before the acquisition by the parent.

Non-controlling interest at fair value will be different from non-controlling interest at proportionate share of the acquiree's net assets. The difference is goodwill attributable to non-controlling interest, which may be, but often is not, proportionate to goodwill attributable to the parent.

Exam focus point

The ACCA may refer to valuation at the non-controlling interest's proportionate share of the acquiree's identifiable net assets as the 'partial goodwill' method and to valuation at (full) fair value as the 'full goodwill' method.

1.7.5 Goodwill calculation: simple examples

Now we will look at two simple goodwill calculations: the revised IFRS 3 proportion of net assets method (proportion of net assets) and the revised IFRS 3 fair (or full) value method.

(a) **Revised IFRS 3 proportion of net assets method**

On 31 December 20X8, Penn acquired four million of the five million $1 ordinary shares of Sylvania, paying $10m in cash. On that date, the fair value of Sylvania's net assets was $7.5m.

It is the group's policy to value the non-controlling interest at its proportionate share of the fair value of the subsidiary's identifiable net assets.

Calculate goodwill on the acquisition.

Answer

	$'000
Consideration transferred	10,000
Non-controlling interest: 20% × $7.5m	1,500
	11,500
Net assets acquired	(7,500)
Goodwill	4,000

(b) **Revised IFRS 3 fair value method**

On 31 December 20X8, Penn acquired four million of the five million $1 ordinary shares of Sylvania, paying $10m in cash. On that date, the fair value of Sylvania's net assets was $7.5m.

It is the group's policy to value the non-controlling interest at fair value. The market price of the shares held by the non-controlling shareholders just before the acquisition was $2.00

Calculate goodwill on the acquisition.

Answer

	$'000
Consideration transferred	10,000
Non-controlling interest 1m × 2	2,000
	12,000
Net assets acquired	(7,500)
Goodwill	4,500

1.7.6 Non-controlling interest at the year end (fair value method)

Where the option is used to value non-controlling interest at fair value, this applies only to **non-controlling interest at acquisition**. At the year end, the non-controlling interest will have increased by its share of the subsidiary's post-acquisition retained earnings.

The non-controlling interest is measured at its fair value, measured on the basis of a quoted price in an active market for equity shares not held by the acquirer or, if this is not available, by using another valuation technique.

The workings will be the same as for the proportionate method.

This is illustrated in the following worked example.

1.7.7 Example: Goodwill and non-controlling interest

P acquired 75% of the shares in S on 1 January 2007 when S had retained earnings of $15,000. The market price of S's shares at the date of acquisition was $1.60. P values non-controlling interest at fair value at the date of acquisition. Goodwill is not impaired.

The statements of financial position of P and S at 31 December 20X7 were as follows.

	P	*S*
	$	$
Property, plant and equipment	60,000	50,000
Shares in S	68,000	–
	128,000	50,000
Current assets	52,000	35,000
	180,000	85,000
Share capital – $1 shares	100,000	50,000
Retained earnings	70,000	25,000
	170,000	75,000
Current liabilities	10,000	10,000
	180,000	85,000

Prepare the consolidated statement of financial position of the P Group.

Solution

P GROUP
CONSOLIDATED STATEMENT OF FINANCIAL POSITION

	$
Assets	
Property plant and equipment (60,000 + 50,000)	110,000
Goodwill (W1)	23,000
Current assets (52,000 + 35,000)	87,000
Total assets	220,000
Equity and liabilities	
Equity attributable to the owners of P	
Share capital	100,000
Retained earnings (W2)	77,500
	177,500
Non-controlling interest (W3)	22,500
Total equity	200,000
Current liabilities (10,000 + 10,000)	20,000
	220,000

Workings

1 *Goodwill*

	$
Consideration transferred	68,000
Non-controlling interest at acquisition (12,500 shares @ $1.60)	20,000
Net assets of S at acquisition (50,000 + 15,000)	(65,000)
Goodwill	23,000

2 *Retained earnings*

	P	*S*
	$	$
Per statement of financial position	70,000	25,000
Less pre- acquisition		(15,000)
		10,000
Group share of S (10,000 × 75%)	7,500	
Group retained earnings	77,500	

3 *Non-controlling interest at year end*

	$
NCI at acquisition (W1)	20,000
NCI share of S's post acquisition reserves (25% × 10,000(W2))	2,500
	22,500

1.7.8 Effect on non-controlling interest of fair value

You can see from the above example that the use of the fair value option increases goodwill and non-controlling interest by the same amount. That amount represents goodwill attributable to the shares held by non-controlling shareholders. It is not necessarily proportionate to the goodwill attributed to the parent. The parent may have paid more to acquire a controlling interest. If non-controlling interest was valued under the proportionate method (share of net assets), goodwill and non-controlling interest in the example above would be as follows.

W1 *Goodwill*

	$
Considered transferred	68,000
Non-controlling interest ((50,000 + 15,000) × 25%)	16,250
Net assets of S at acquisition (50,000 + 15,000)	(65,000)
	19,250

W3 *Non-controlling interest at year end*

	$
NCI at acquisition (W1)	16,250
NCI share of S's post acquisition retained earnings (25% × 10,000)	2,500
	18,750

Compare these with goodwill and non-controlling interest in the solution above and you will see that both have been reduced by $3,750 – the goodwill attributable to the non-controlling interest. So whether non-controlling interest is valued at share of net assets or at fair value, the statement of financial position will still balance.

1.7.9 Your P2 exam

The ACCA has stated that **both the 'partial goodwill' and the 'full goodwill' methods are examinable.** Specifically, the advice is as follows:

ACCA will require students to know both methods. The wording is as follows:

> *Full goodwill*
>
> 'It is the group policy to value the non-controlling interest at full (or fair) value.'
>
> *Partial goodwill*
>
> 'It is the group policy to value the non-controlling interest at its proportionate share of the (fair value of the) subsidiary's identifiable net assets.'

Questions can ask for both methods.

There are a number of ways of presenting the information to test the new method:

(i) As above, the subsidiary's share price just before the acquisition could be given and then used to value the non-controlling interest. It would then be a matter of multiplying the share price by the number of shares held by the non-controlling interests. (**Note**: the parent is likely to have paid more than the subsidiary's pre acquisition share price in order to gain control.)

(ii) The question could simply state that the directors valued the non-controlling interest at the date of acquisition at $2 million

(iii) An alternative approach would be to give (in the question) the value of the goodwill attributable to the non-controlling interest. In this case the NCI's goodwill would be added to the parent's goodwill (calculated by the traditional method) and to the carrying amount of the non-controlling interest itself.

1.8 Other aspects of group accounting

Note. Much of this will be revision from your earlier studies, but there are some significant changes to concepts and definitions introduced by IFRSs 10 and 11 and the revised IAS 28.

1.8.1 Investment in subsidiaries

The important point here is **control**. In most cases, this will involve the parent company owning a majority of the ordinary shares in the subsidiary (to which normal voting rights are attached). There are circumstances, however, when the parent may own only a minority of the voting power in the subsidiary, **but** the parent still has control.

IFRS 10 *Consolidated financial statements* has **control** as the key concept underlying the parent/subsidiary relationship but it has broadened the definition and clarified its application. This will be covered in more detail in Section 2 below.

IFRS 10 states that an investor **controls** an investee if and only if it has all of the following:

(i) **Power** over the investee

(ii) Exposure, or rights, to **variable returns** from its involvement with the investee (see Section 2), and

(iii) The **ability to use its power** over the investee to affect the amount of the investor's returns (see Section 2).

IFRS 10 paras. 10 to 12

Exam focus point

> You should learn the contents of the above paragraph as you may be asked to apply them in the exam.

Accounting treatment in group accounts

IFRS 10 requires a parent to present consolidated financial statements, in which the accounts of the parent and subsidiary (or subsidiaries) are combined and presented **as a single entity**. (IFRS 10: para. 4)

1.8.2 Investments in associates

This type of investment is something less than a subsidiary, but more than a simple investment (nor is it a joint venture). The key criterion here is **significant influence**. This is defined as the 'power to participate', but **not** to 'control' (which would make the investment a subsidiary).

Significant influence can be determined by the holding of voting rights (usually attached to shares) in the entity. IAS 28 *Investments in associates and joint ventures* states (IAS 28: para. 5) that if an investor holds **20% or more** of the voting power of the investee, it can be presumed that the investor has significant influence over the investee, **unless** it can be clearly shown that this is not the case.

Significant influence can be presumed **not** to exist if the investor holds **less than 20%** of the voting power of the investee, unless it can be demonstrated otherwise.

The **existence of significant influence** is evidenced in one or more of the following ways.

(a) Representation on the **board of directors** (or equivalent) of the investee
(b) Participation in the **policy making process**
(c) **Material transactions** between investor and investee
(d) Interchange of **management personnel**
(e) Provision of **essential technical information**

Accounting treatment in group accounts

IAS 28 (para. 16) requires the use of the **equity method** of accounting for investments in associates. This method will be explained in detail in Section 4.

1.8.3 Accounting for investments in joint arrangements

IFRS 11 *Joint arrangements* classes joint arrangements as either **joint operations** or **joint ventures** (IFRS 11: para. 6). The classification of a joint arrangement as a joint operation or a joint venture depends upon the rights and obligations of the parties to the arrangement.

The detail of how to distinguish between joint operations and joint ventures will be considered in Section 5.

Accounting treatment in group accounts

IFRS 11 requires that a joint operator recognises line-by-line the following in relation to its interest in a **joint operation**:

- Its assets, including its share of any jointly held assets
- Its liabilities, including its share of any jointly incurred liabilities
- Its revenue from the sale of its share of the output arising from the joint operation
- Its share of the revenue from the sale of the output by the joint operation, and
- Its expenses, including its share of any expenses incurred jointly

This treatment is applicable in both the separate and consolidated financial statements of the joint operator. (IFRS 11: para. 20)

In its consolidated financial statements, IFRS 11 requires that a joint venturer recognises its interest in a **joint venture** as an investment and accounts for that investment using the equity method in accordance with IAS 28 *Investments in associates and joint ventures* unless the entity is exempted from applying the equity method (see Section 4.2 which is also applicable to joint ventures) (IFRS 11: para. 24).

In its separate financial statements, a joint venturer should account for its interest in a joint venture in accordance with IAS 27 *Separate financial statements,* namely:

- At cost, or
- In accordance with IFRS 9 *Financial instruments,* or
- Using the equity method as described in IAS 28 *Investments in associates and joint ventures*

(IAS 27: para. 10)

1.8.4 Other investments

Investments which do not meet the definitions of any of the above should be accounted for according to IFRS 9 *Financial instruments.*

2 IFRS 10 *Consolidated financial statements* 12/12, 12/13, 12/14, 12/15

FAST FORWARD

IFRS 10 *Consolidated financial statements* requires a parent to present **consolidated** financial statements.

Goodwill should be calculated **after revaluing** the subsidiary company's assets.

If the subsidiary does not incorporate the revaluation in its own accounts, it should be done as a **consolidation adjustment**.

2.1 Introduction

Key point

Consolidated financial statements. The financial statements of a group presented as those of a single economic entity.

When a parent issues consolidated financial statements, it should consolidate **all subsidiaries**, both foreign and domestic. The first step in any consolidation is to identify the subsidiaries using the definition as set out in paragraph 1.8.1 above.

Exam focus point

You should make sure that you understand the various ways in which control can arise as this is something that you may be asked to discuss in the context of a scenario in the exam.

2.1.1 Power

Power is defined as **existing rights that give the current ability to direct the relevant activities of the investee**. There is no requirement for that power to have been exercised (IFRS 10: paras. 10 to 14).

Relevant activities may include:

- Selling and purchasing goods or services
- Managing financial assets
- Selecting, acquiring and disposing of assets
- Researching and developing new products and processes
- Determining a funding structure or obtaining funding

In some cases assessing power is straightforward, for example, where power is obtained directly and solely from having the majority of voting rights or potential voting rights, and as a result the ability to direct relevant activities.

In other cases, assessment is more complex and more than one factor must be considered. IFRS 10 gives the following examples of **rights**, other than voting or potential voting rights, which individually, or alone, can give an investor power (IFRS 10: para. B15).

- Rights to appoint, reassign or remove key management personnel who can direct the relevant activities
- Rights to appoint or remove another entity that directs the relevant activities
- Rights to direct the investee to enter into, or veto changes to transactions for the benefit of the investor
- Other rights, such as those specified in a management contract

IFRS 10 suggests that the **ability** rather than contractual right to achieve the above may also indicate that an investor has power over an investee.

An investor can have power over an investee even where other entities have significant influence or other ability to participate in the direction of relevant activities.

2.1.2 Returns

An investor must have exposure, or rights, to **variable returns** from its involvement with the investee in order to establish control.

This is the case where the investor's returns from its involvement have the potential to vary as a result of the investee's performance.

Returns may include (IFRS 10: paras. 15, B57):

- Dividends
- Remuneration for servicing an investee's assets or liabilities
- Fees and exposure to loss from providing credit support
- Returns as a result of achieving synergies or economies of scale through an investor combining use of their assets with use of the investee's assets

2.1.3 Link between power and returns

In order to establish control, an investor must be able to use its power to affect its returns from its involvement with the investee. This is the case even where the investor delegates its decision making powers to an agent (IFRS 10: paras. 17, B59).

2.2 Exemption from preparing group accounts

A parent **need not present** consolidated financial statements if and only if all of the following hold (IFRS 10: para. 4):

(a) The parent is itself a **wholly-owned subsidiary** or it is a **partially owned subsidiary** of another entity and its other owners, including those not otherwise entitled to vote, have been informed about, and do not object to, the parent not presenting consolidated financial statements.

(b) Its debt or equity instruments are **not publicly traded**.

(c) It is **not in the process of issuing securities** in public securities markets.

(d) The **ultimate or intermediate parent** publishes consolidated financial statements that comply with International Financial Reporting Standards.

A parent that does not present consolidated financial statements must comply with the IAS 27 rules on separate financial statements (discussed later in this section).

2.3 Potential voting rights

An entity may own share warrants, share call options, or other similar instruments that are **convertible into ordinary shares** in another entity. If these are exercised or converted they may give the entity voting power or reduce another party's voting power over the financial and operating policies of the other entity (potential voting rights). The **existence and effect** of potential voting rights, including potential voting rights held by another entity, should be considered when assessing whether an entity has control over another entity (and therefore has a subsidiary). Potential voting rights are considered only if the rights are **substantive** (meaning that the holder must have the practical ability to exercise the right).

In assessing whether potential voting rights give rise to control, the investor should consider the **purpose and design of the instrument**. This includes an assessment of the various terms and conditions of the instrument as well as the investor's apparent expectations, motives and reasons for agreeing to those terms and conditions.

(IFRS 10: paras. B47 to B50)

2.4 Exclusion of a subsidiary from consolidation

Where a parent controls one or more subsidiaries, IFRS 10 requires that consolidated financial statements are prepared to include **all subsidiaries, both foreign and domestic** other than (IFRS 10: para. 19):

- Those held for sale in accordance with IFRS 5
- Those held under such long-term restrictions that control cannot be operated

The rules on exclusion of subsidiaries from consolidation are necessarily strict, because this is a common method used by entities to manipulate their results. If a subsidiary which carries a large amount of debt can be excluded, then the gearing of the group as a whole will be improved. In other words, this is a way of taking debt **out of the consolidated statement of financial position.**

IFRS 10 is clear that a subsidiary should not be excluded from consolidation simply because it is loss making or its business activities are dissimilar from those of the group as a whole. IFRS 10 rejects the latter argument: exclusion on these grounds is not justified because better information can be provided about such subsidiaries by consolidating their results and then giving additional information about the different business activities of the subsidiary, eg under IFRS 8 *Operating segments*.

2.5 Different reporting dates

In most cases, all group companies will prepare accounts to the same reporting date. One or more subsidiaries may, however, prepare accounts to a different reporting date from the parent and the bulk of other subsidiaries in the group.

In such cases the subsidiary may prepare additional statements to the reporting date of the rest of the group, for consolidation purposes. If this is not possible, the subsidiary's accounts may still be used for the consolidation, **provided that** the gap between the reporting dates is **three months or less**.

Where a subsidiary's accounts are drawn up to a different accounting date, **adjustments should be made** for the effects of significant transactions or other events that occur between that date and the parent's reporting date.

(IFRS 10: para. B92, 93)

2.6 Uniform accounting policies

Consolidated financial statements should be prepared using **uniform accounting policies** for like transactions and other events in similar circumstances.

Adjustments must be made where members of a group use different accounting policies, so that their financial statements are suitable for consolidation.

(IFRS 10: para. B87)

2.7 Date of inclusion/exclusion

The results of subsidiary undertakings are included in the consolidated financial statements from:

(a) The date of 'acquisition', ie the **date on which the investor obtains control**, to
(b) The date of 'disposal', ie the **date when the investor loses control**

Once an investment is no longer a subsidiary, it should be treated as an associate under IAS 28 (if applicable) or as an investment under IFRS 9 (see Chapter 7).

(IFRS 10: para. 20, B88)

2.8 Accounting for subsidiaries, associates and joint ventures in the parent's separate financial statements

A parent company will usually produce its own single company financial statements. In these statements, governed by IAS 27 *Separate financial statements,* investments in subsidiaries, associates and joint ventures included in the consolidated financial statements should be **either:**

(a) Accounted for at **cost**, *or*
(b) In accordance with **IFRS 9** (see Chapter 7)
(c) Using the equity method as described in IAS 28 *Investments in associates and joint ventures*

The accounting option must be applied by category of investments.

Where subsidiaries are **classified as held for sale** in accordance with IFRS 5 they should be accounted for in accordance with IFRS 5 (see Chapter 15).

(IAS 27: para. 10)

2.8.1 Investment entities

An investment entity is defined as an entity that:

(a) Obtains funds from one or more investors for the purpose of providing those investors with investment management services

(b) Commits to its investors that its business purpose is to invest funds solely for returns from capital appreciation, investment income or both, and

(c) Measures and evaluates the performance of substantially all of its investments on a fair value basis

Investment entities therefore include private equity organisations, venture capital organisations, pension funds and other investment funds.

Prior to the introduction of guidance specific to investment entities, these entities were required to apply IFRS 10 and consolidate all subsidiaries which they controlled. Investors and other users of the accounts felt, however, that this did not result in useful information; the most useful and relevant information would be to recognise investments at fair value.

As a result**, since 2012, IFRS 10 has included a requirement that investment entities measure subsidiaries at fair value through profit or loss rather than consolidate them.**

This requirement applies only to the subsidiaries of an investment entity which do not provide services which relate to the investment entity's activities. Subsidiaries which provide investment-related services are consolidated as normal.

In January 2015, amendments to IFRS 10 further clarified the application of the investment entity exemption. These are effective from 1 January 2016:

(a) The exemption from preparing consolidated financial statements is still available to a parent even where the ultimate (or intermediate) parent is an investment entity and measures all of its subsidiaries at fair value rather than produce consolidated financial statements.

(b) The requirement to consolidate as normal a subsidiary that provides services to an investment entity only applies where:

(i) The subsidiary itself is not an investment entity, and

(ii) The subsidiary's main purpose is to provide services and activities that are related to the investment activities of the investment entity parent.

(IAS 27: paras. 27 to 33)

2.9 Disclosure

IFRS 12 *Disclosure of interests in other entities* was issued in 2011 as part of the 'package of five standards' relating to consolidation. It removes all disclosure requirements from other standards relating to group accounting and provides guidance applicable to consolidated financial statements.

The standard requires disclosure of:

(a) The significant judgements and assumptions made in determining the nature of an interest in another entity or arrangement, and in determining the type of joint arrangement in which an interest is held

(b) Information about interests in subsidiaries, associates, joint arrangements and structured entities that are not controlled by an investor

2.9.1 Disclosure of subsidiaries

The following disclosures are required in respect of subsidiaries (IFRS 12: paras. 10 to 19):

(a) The interest that non-controlling interests have in the group's activities and cash flows, including the name of relevant subsidiaries, their principal place of business, and the interest and voting rights of the non-controlling interests

(b) Nature and extent of significant restrictions on an investor's ability to use group assets and liabilities

(c) Nature of the risks associated with an entity's interests in consolidated structured entities, such as the provision of financial support

(d) Consequences of changes in ownership interest in subsidiary (whether control is lost or not)

2.9.2 Disclosure of associates and joint arrangements

The following disclosures are required in respect of associates and joint arrangements (IFRS 12: paras. 20 to 21A):

(a) Nature, extent and financial effects of an entity's interests in associates or joint arrangements, including name of the investee, principal place of business, the investor's interest in the investee, method of accounting for the investee and restrictions on the investee's ability to transfer funds to the investor

(b) Risks associated with an interest in an associate or joint venture

(c) Summarised financial information, with more detail required for joint ventures than for associates

2.10 Attribution of losses

Under IFRS 10, non-controlling interests can be negative. This is consistent with the idea that non-controlling interests are part of the equity of the group.

2.11 Revision: summary of techniques

The summary given below is very brief but it encompasses all the major, but basic, rules of consolidation for, first, the consolidated statement of financial position.

Knowledge brought forward from earlier studies

Summary of technique: consolidated statement of financial position

- **Net assets**: 100% P plus 100% S
- **Share capital**: P only
- **Reserves**: 100% P plus group share of post-acquisition retained reserves of S less consolidation adjustments
- **Non-controlling interest**: NCI at acquisition plus NCI share of S's post acquisition retained reserves

The next section is a recap of the techniques you should remember from your earlier studies. The P2 syllabus introduces a range of extra complications in consolidations, but the basics will always form part of any question.

Step 1 Read the question and draw up the group structure (W1), highlighting useful information:

- The percentage owned
- Acquisition date
- Pre-acquisition reserves

Step 2 Draw up a proforma taking into account the group structure identified:

- Leave out cost of investment
- Put in a line for goodwill
- Put in a line for investment in associate
- Remember to include non-controlling interests
- Leave lines in case of any additions

Step 3 Work methodically down the statement of financial position, transferring:

- Figures to proforma or workings
- 100% of all assets/liabilities controlled at the year end aggregated in brackets on face of proforma, ready for adjustments
- Cost of subsidiary/associate and reserves to group workings, setting them up as you work down the statement of financial position
- Share capital and share premium (parent only) to face of proforma answer
- Open up a (blank) working for non-controlling interests

Step 4 Read through the additional notes and attempt the adjustments showing workings for all calculations.

Do the double entry for the adjustments onto your proforma answer and onto your group workings (where the group workings are affected by one side of the double entry).

Examples:

Cancel any intragroup items eg current account balances, loans

Adjust for unrealised profits:

Unrealised profit on intragroup sales	X	
% held in inventories at year end	%	
= Provision for unrealised profit (PUP)	X	DR Retained earnings
(adjust in company **selling** goods)		CR Group inventories

Make fair value adjustments:

	Acq'n date	*Movement*	*Year end*
Inventories	X	(X)	X
Depreciable non-current assets	X	(X)	X
Non-depreciable non-current assets	X	(X)	X
Other fair value adjustments	X/(X)	(X)/X	X/(X)
	X	(X)	X
	This total appears in the goodwill working	*This total is used to adjust the subsidiary's reserves in the reserves working*	*The individual figures here are used to adjust the relevant balances on the consolidated statement of financial position*

Step 5 Complete goodwill calculation

Consideration transferred		X
Non-controlling interests (at % fair value (FV) of net assets or at 'full' FV)		X
Less net fair value of identifiable assets acquired and liabilities assumed:		
Share capital	X	
Share premium	X	
Retained earnings at acquisition	X	
Other reserves at acquisition	X	
Fair value adjustments at acquisition	X	
		(X)
		X
Less impairment losses on goodwill to date		(X)
		X

Step 6 Complete the consolidated retained earnings calculation:

	Parent	*Subsidiary*	*Assoc*
Per question	X	X	X
Adjustments	X/(X)	X/(X)	X/(X)
Fair value adjustments movement		X/(X)	X/(X)
Pre-acquisition retained earnings		(X)	(X)
Group share of post acq'n ret'd earnings:		Y	Z
Subsidiary (Y × %)	X		
Associate (Z × %)	X		
Less group share of impairment losses to date	(X)		
	X		

Note: Other reserves are treated in a similar way.

Step 7 Complete 'Investment in associate' calculation:

Cost of associate	X
Share of post-acquisition retained reserves (from reserves working Z × %)	X
Less group impairment losses on associate to date	(X)
	X

Complete the non-controlling interests calculation:

NCI at acquisition (from goodwill working)	X
NCI share of post acq'n reserves (from reserves working Y × NCI %)	X
Less NCI share of impairment losses (only if NCI at 'full' FV at acq'n)	(X)
	X

The technique for the preparation of a **consolidated statement of profit or loss and other comprehensive income** is given below.

Consolidated statement of profit or loss and comprehensive income

Overview

The statement of profit or loss and other comprehensive income shows a true and fair view of the group's activities since acquisition of any subsidiaries.

(a) The top part of the statement of profit or loss and other comprehensive income shows the income, expenses, profit and other comprehensive income controlled by the group.

(b) The reconciliation at the bottom of the statement of profit or loss and other comprehensive income shows the ownership of those profits and total comprehensive income.

Method

Step 1 Read the question and draw up the group structure and where subsidiaries/associates are acquired in the year identify the proportion to consolidate. A timeline may be useful.

Step 2 Draw up a pro-forma:

- Remember the non-controlling interests reconciliation at the foot of the statement.

Step 3 Work methodically down the statement of profit or loss and other comprehensive income, transferring figures to proforma or workings:

- 100% of all income/expenses (time apportioned × $^{x}/_{12}$ if appropriate) in brackets on face of proforma, ready for adjustments
- Exclude dividends receivable from subsidiary
- Subsidiary's profit for the year (PFY) and total comprehensive income (TCI) (for NCI) to face of proforma in brackets (or to a working if many adjustments).
- Associate's PFY and other comprehensive income (OCI) to face of proforma in brackets.

Step 4 Go through question, calculating the necessary adjustments showing workings for all calculations, transfer the numbers to your proforma and make the adjustments in the non-controlling interests working where the subsidiary's profit is affected.

Step 5 Calculate 'Share of profit of associate' and 'Share of other comprehensive income of associate' (where appropriate):

A's profit for the year (PFY) × Group %	X
Any group impairment loss recognised on the associate during the period	(X)
	X

Shown before group profit before tax.

A's other comprehensive income (OCI) × Group %	X

Both the associate's profit or loss and other comprehensive income are calculated based on after tax figures.

Step 6 Complete non-controlling interests in subsidiary's PFY and TCI calculation:

	PFY	*TCI (if req'd)*
PFY/TCI per question (time-apportioned × $^x/_{12}$ if appropriate)	X	X
Adjustments, eg PUP on sales made by S	(X)/X	(X)/X
Impairment losses (if NCI held at fair value)	(X)	(X)
	X	X
× NCI%	X	X

Now try the following question to refresh your memory on the topics listed above.

Exam focus point

> The consolidation questions in the Paper P2 exam are much more difficult than those in your earlier studies. The examiner will not bother to test basic consolidation techniques directly, although they may come up in a question: rather he will ask about one of the more complex areas which we will look at in the next few chapters.

Question — Groups revision: non-controlling interest at fair value

You are provided with the following statements of financial position (balance sheets) for Shark and Minnow.

STATEMENTS OF FINANCIAL POSITION AS AT 31 OCTOBER 20X0

	Shark		*Minnow*	
	$'000	$'000	$'000	$'000
Non-current assets, at net book value				
Plant		325		70
Fixtures		200		50
		525		120
Investment				
Shares in Minnow at cost		200		
Current assets				
Inventory at cost	220		70	
Receivables	145		105	
Bank	100		0	
		465		175
		1,190		295
Equity				
$1 Ordinary shares		700		170
Retained earnings		215		50
		915		220
Current liabilities				
Payables	275		55	
Bank overdraft	0		20	
		275		75
		1,190		295

The following information is also available.

(a) Shark purchased 70% of the issued ordinary share capital of Minnow four years ago, when the retained earnings of Minnow were $20,000. There has been no impairment of goodwill.

(b) For the purposes of the acquisition, plant in Minnow with a book value of $50,000 was revalued to its fair value of $60,000. The revaluation was not recorded in the accounts of Minnow. Depreciation is charged at 20% using the straight-line method.

(c) Shark sells goods to Minnow at a mark up of 25%. At 31 October 20X0, the inventories of Minnow included $45,000 of goods purchased from Shark.

(d) Minnow owes Shark $35,000 for goods purchased and Shark owes Minnow $15,000.

(e) It is the group's policy to value the non-controlling interest at fair value.

(f) The market price of the shares of the non-controlling shareholders just before the acquisition was $1.50.

Required

Prepare the consolidated statement of financial position of Shark as at 31 October 20X0.

Answer

SHARK

CONSOLIDATED STATEMENT OF FINANCIAL POSITION (BALANCE SHEET) AS AT 31 OCTOBER 20X0

	$'000	$'000
Non-current assets		
Plant (W4)	397	
Fixtures (200 + 50)	250	
		647
Intangible asset: goodwill (W1)		777
		724
Current assets		
Inventory (W5)	281	
Receivables (W6)	200	
Bank	100	
		581
		1,305
Capital and reserves		
Share capital		700
Retained earnings (W2)		222
		922
Non-controlling interests (W3)		83
		1,005
Current liabilities		
Payables (W7)	280	
Bank overdraft	20	
		300
		1,305

Workings

1 *Goodwill*

		Group
	$'000	$'000
Consideration transferred		200.0
FV NCI (30% × 170,000 × $1.50)		76.5
Net assets acquired		
Share capital	170	
Retained earnings	20	
Revaluation surplus (60 – 50)	10	
		200.0
Goodwill in parent		76.5m

2 *Retained earnings*

	Shark	*Minnow*
	$'000	$'000
Per question	215	50
Unrealised profit (W5)	(9)	
Excess dep'n on plant (W4)		(8)
At acquisition		(20)
		22
Share of Minnow's post-acquisition retained earnings (70% × 22)	16	
	222	

3 *Non-controlling interests*

	$'000
At acquisition (W1)	76.5
NCI share of post acqn. retained earnings (30% × 22)	6.6
	83.1

4 *Plant*

	$'000	$'000
Shark		325
Minnow		
Per question	70	
Revalued (60 – 50)	10	
Depreciation on revalued plant (10 × 20% × 4)	(8)	
		72
		397

5 *Inventory*

	$'000	$'000
Shark		220
Minnow	70	
Less PUP (45 × $^{25}/_{125}$)	(9)	
		61
		281

6 *Receivables*

	$'000	$'000
Shark		145
Less intragroup		35
		110
Minnow	105	
Less intragroup	15	
		90
		200

7 *Payables*

	$'000	$'000
Shark		275
Less intragroup		15
		260
Minnow	55	
Less intragroup	35	
		20
		280

3 IFRS 3, IFRS 13 and fair values

FAST FORWARD

Goodwill arising on consolidation is the difference between the purchase consideration and the fair value of the identifiable assets and liabilities acquired.

To understand the importance of fair values in the acquisition of a subsidiary consider again the definition of goodwill.

Key term

Goodwill. Any excess of the cost of the acquisition over the acquirer's interest in the fair value of the identifiable assets and liabilities acquired as at the date of the exchange transaction.

The **statement of financial position of a subsidiary company** at the date it is acquired may not be a guide to the fair value of its net assets. For example, the market value of a freehold building may have risen greatly since it was acquired, but it may appear in the statement of financial position at historical cost less accumulated depreciation.

3.1 What is fair value?

Fair value is defined as follows by IFRS 13 – it is an important definition.

Key term

> **Fair value**. The price that would be received to sell an asset or paid to transfer a liability in an orderly transaction between market participants at the measurement date. *(IFRS 13: Appendix A)*

We will look at the requirements of IFRS 3 and IFRS 13 regarding fair value in more detail below. First, let us look at some practical matters.

3.2 Fair value adjustment calculations

Until now we have calculated goodwill as the difference between the cost of the investment and the **book value** of net assets acquired by the group. If this calculation is to comply with the definition above we must ensure that the book value of the subsidiary's net assets is the same as their **fair value**.

There are two possible ways of achieving this.

(a) The **subsidiary company** might **incorporate any necessary revaluations** in its own books of account. In this case, we can proceed directly to the consolidation, taking asset values and reserves figures straight from the subsidiary company's statement of financial position.

(b) The **revaluations** may be made as a **consolidation adjustment without being incorporated** in the subsidiary company's books. In this case, we must make the necessary adjustments to the subsidiary's statement of financial position as a working. Only then can we proceed to the consolidation.

Note. Remember that when depreciating assets are revalued there may be a corresponding alteration in the amount of depreciation charged and accumulated.

3.3 Example: Fair value adjustments

P Co acquired 75% of the ordinary shares of S Co on 1 September 20X5. At that date the fair value of S Co's non-current assets was $23,000 greater than their net book value, and the balance of retained earnings was $21,000. The statements of financial position of both companies at 31 August 20X6 are given below. S Co has not incorporated any revaluation in its books of account.

P CO
STATEMENT OF FINANCIAL POSITION AS AT 31 AUGUST 20X6

	$	$
Assets		
Non-current assets		
Tangible assets	63,000	
Investment in S Co at cost	51,000	
		114,000
Current assets		82,000
Total assets		196,000
Equity and liabilities		
Equity		
Ordinary shares of $1 each	80,000	
Retained earnings	96,000	
		176,000
Current liabilities		20,000
Total equity and liabilities		196,000

S CO
STATEMENT OF FINANCIAL POSITION AS AT 31 AUGUST 20X6

	$	$
Assets		
Tangible non-current assets		28,000
Current assets		43,000
Total assets		71,000
Equity and liabilities		
Equity		
Ordinary shares of $1 each	20,000	
Retained earnings	41,000	
		61,000
Current liabilities		10,000
Total equity and liabilities		71,000

If S Co had revalued its non-current assets at 1 September 20X5, an addition of $3,000 would have been made to the depreciation charged to profit or loss for 20X5/X6. It is the group's policy to value the non-controlling interest at acquisition at its proportionate share of the fair value of the subsidiary's net assets.

Required

Prepare P Co's consolidated statement of financial position as at 31 August 20X6.

Solution

P CO CONSOLIDATED STATEMENT OF FINANCIAL POSITION AS AT 31 AUGUST 20X6

	$	$
Non-current assets		
Property, plant and equipment $(63,000 + 48,000*)	111,000	
Goodwill (W1)	3,000	
		114,000
Current assets		125,000
		239,000
Equity and liabilities		
Equity		
Ordinary shares of $1 each	80,000	
Retained earnings (W2)	108,750	
		188,750
Non-controlling interest (W3)		20,250
		209,000
Current liabilities		30,000
		239,000

* (28,000 + 23,000 – 3,000) = $48,000

Workings

1 *Goodwill*

	$	$
Consideration transferred		51,000
Non-controlling interest (64,000 × 25%)		16,000
		67,000
Net assets acquired as represented by		
Ordinary share capital	20,000	
Retained earnings	21,000	
Fair value adjustment	23,000	
		(64,000)
Goodwill		3,000

2 *Retained earnings*

	P Co	S Co
	$	$
Per question	96,000	41,000
Depreciation adjustment		(3,000)
Pre acquisition profits		(21,000)
Post acquisition S Co		17,000
Group share in S Co		
($17,000 × 75%)	12,750	
Group retained earnings	108,750	

3 *Non-controlling interest at reporting date*

	$
NCI at acquisition (W1)	16,000
NCI share of S's post-acquisition retained earnings (25% × 17,000)	4,250
	20,250

4 *Fair value adjustments*

	At acq'n date	*Movement*	*Year end*
	$	$	$
Property plant and equipment	23,000	(3,000)	20,000
	23,000	(3,000)	20,000
	↓	↓	↓
	Goodwill	Ret'd earnings	SOFP

Note: S Co has not incorporated the revaluation in its draft statement of financial position. Before beginning the consolidation workings we must therefore adjust for the fair value uplift at the acquisition date, the additional depreciation charge that must be reflected in the subsidiary's post acquisition retained earnings and the remaining uplift that must be reflected in the consolidated statement of financial position. The 'fair value table' working is an efficient way of dealing with this, even where there are several fair value adjustments.

Question

Fair value

An asset is recorded in S Co's books at its historical cost of $4,000. On 1 January 20X5 P Co bought 80% of S Co's equity. Its directors attributed a fair value of $3,000 to the asset as at that date. It had been depreciated for two years out of an expected life of four years on the straight line basis. There was no expected residual value. On 30 June 20X5 the asset was sold for $2,600. What is the profit or loss on disposal of this asset to be recorded in S Co's accounts and in P Co's consolidated accounts for the year ended 31 December 20X5?

Answer

S Co: NBV at disposal (at historical cost) = $4,000 × 1½/4 = $1,500

∴ Profit on disposal = $1,100 (depreciation charge for the year = $500)

P Co: NBV at disposal (at fair value) = $3,000 × 1½/2 = $2,250

∴ Profit on disposal for consolidation = $350 (depreciation for the year = $750)

The non-controlling interest would be credited with 20% of both items as part of the one line entry in the profit or loss statement.

3.4 IFRS 3 and IFRS 13: Fair values

FAST FORWARD

The accounting requirements and disclosures of the **fair value exercise** are covered by **IFRS 3**. **IFRS 13** *Fair value measurement* gives extensive guidance on how the fair value of assets and liabilities should be established.

IFRS 3 does not allow combinations to be accounted for as a **uniting of interests; all combinations must be treated as acquisitions.**

The general rule under the revised IFRS 3 is that the subsidiary's assets and liabilities **must be measured at fair value** except in **limited, stated cases**. The assets and liabilities must:

(a) Meet the definitions of assets and liabilities in the *Conceptual Framework*

(b) Be part of what the acquiree (or its former owners) exchanged in the business combination rather than the result of separate transactions

IFRS 13 *Fair value measurement* (see Chapter 7) provides extensive guidance on how the fair value of assets and liabilities should be established.

This standard requires that the following are considered in measuring fair value (IFRS 13: para. 23):

(a) The asset or liability being measured

(b) The principal market (ie that where the most activity takes place) or where there is no principal market, the most advantageous market (ie that in which the best price could be achieved) in which an orderly transaction would take place for the asset or liability

(c) The highest and best use of the asset or liability and whether it is used on a standalone basis or in conjunction with other assets or liabilities

(d) Assumptions that market participants would use when pricing the asset or liability

Having considered these factors, IFRS 13 provides a hierarchy of inputs for arriving at fair value. It requires that Level 1 inputs are used where possible (IFRS 13: para. 72):

Level 1 Quoted prices in active markets for identical assets that the entity can access at the measurement date

Level 2 Inputs other than quoted prices that are directly or indirectly observable for the asset

Level 3 Unobservable inputs for the asset

3.4.1 Examples of fair value and business combinations

For non-financial assets, fair value is decided based on the highest and best use of the asset as determined by a market participant. The following examples, adapted from the illustrative examples to IFRS 13, demonstrate what is meant by this.

Example: Land

Anscome Co has acquired land in a business combination. The land is currently developed for industrial use as a site for a factory. The current use of land is presumed to be its highest and best use unless market or other factors suggest a different use. Nearby sites have recently been developed for residential use as sites for high-rise apartment buildings. On the basis of that development and recent zoning and other changes to facilitate that development, Anscome determines that the land currently used as a site for a factory could be developed as a site for residential use (ie for high-rise apartment buildings) because market participants would take into account the potential to develop the site for residential use when pricing the land.

How would the highest and best use of the land be determined?

Solution

The highest and best use of the land would be determined by comparing both of the following:

(a) The value of the land as currently developed for industrial use (ie the land would be used in combination with other assets, such as the factory, or with other assets and liabilities).

(b) The value of the land as a vacant site for residential use, taking into account the costs of demolishing the factory and other costs (including the uncertainty about whether the entity would be able to convert the asset to the alternative use) necessary to convert the land to a vacant site (ie the land is to be used by market participants on a stand-alone basis).

The highest and best use of the land would be determined on the basis of the higher of those values.

Example: Research and development project

Searcher has a research and development (R & D) project in a business combination. Searcher does not intend to complete the project. If completed, the project would compete with one of its own projects (to provide the next generation of the entity's commercialised technology). Instead, the entity intends to hold (ie lock up) the project to prevent its competitors from obtaining access to the technology. In doing this the project is expected to provide defensive value, principally by improving the prospects for the entity's own competing technology.

If it could purchase the R & D project, Developer Co would continue to develop the project and that use would maximise the value of the group of assets or of assets and liabilities in which the project would be used (ie the asset would be used in combination with other assets or with other assets and liabilities). Developer Co does not have similar technology.

How would the fair value of the project be measured?

Solution

The fair value of the project would be measured on the basis of the price that would be received in a current transaction to sell the project, assuming that the R & D would be used with its complementary assets and the associated liabilities and that those assets and liabilities would be available to Developer Co.

Example: Decommissioning liability

Deacon assumes a decommissioning liability in a business combination. It is legally required to dismantle a power station at the end of its useful life, which is estimated to be twenty years.

How would the decommissioning liability be measured?

Solution

Because this is a business combination, Deacon must measure the liability at fair value in accordance with IFRS 13, rather than using the best estimate measurement required by IAS 37 *Provisions, contingent liabilities and contingent assets.*

Deacon will use the expected present value technique to measure the fair value of the decommissioning liability. If Deacon were contractually committed to transfer its decommissioning liability to a market participant, it would conclude that a market participant would use all of the following inputs, probability weighted as appropriate, when estimating the price it would expect to receive.

(a) Labour costs

(b) Allocated overhead costs

(c) The compensation that a market participant would generally receive for undertaking the activity, including profit on labour and overhead costs and the risk that the actual cash outflows might differ from those expected

(d) The effect of inflation

(e) The time value of money (risk-free rate)

(f) Non-performance risk, including Deacon's own credit risk

As an example of how the probability adjustment might work, Deacon values labour costs on the basis of current marketplace wages adjusted for expected future wage increases. It determines that there is a 20% probability that the wage bill will be $15 million, a 30% probability that it will be $25 million and a 50% probability that it will be $20 million. Expected cash flows will then be (20% × $15m) + (30% × $25m) + (50% × $20m) = $20.5m. The probability assessments will be developed on the basis of Deacon's knowledge of the market and experience of fulfilling obligations of this type.

3.4.2 Restructuring and future losses

An acquirer **should not recognise liabilities for future losses** or other costs expected to be incurred as a result of the business combination.

IFRS 3 explains (para. 23) that a plan to restructure a subsidiary following an acquisition is not a present obligation of the acquiree at the acquisition date. Neither does it meet the definition of a contingent liability. Therefore, an acquirer **should not recognise a liability for** such **a restructuring plan** as part of allocating the cost of the combination unless the subsidiary was already committed to the plan before the acquisition.

This **prevents creative accounting**. An acquirer cannot set up a provision for restructuring or future losses of a subsidiary and then release this to profit or loss in subsequent periods in order to reduce losses or smooth profits.

3.4.3 Intangible assets

The acquiree may have **intangible assets**, such as development expenditure. These can be recognised separately from goodwill only if they are **identifiable**. An intangible asset is identifiable only if it:

(a) Is **separable**, ie capable of being separated or divided from the entity and sold, transferred, or exchanged, either individually or together with a related contract, asset or liability, or

(b) Arises from **contractual or other legal rights**.

(IFRS 3: para. 29)

3.4.4 Contingent liabilities

Contingent liabilities of the acquiree are **recognised** if their **fair value can be measured reliably**. A **contingent liability** must be recognised even if the outflow is not probable, provided there is a present obligation.

This is a departure from the normal rules in IAS 37; contingent liabilities are not normally recognised, but only disclosed.

After their initial recognition, the acquirer should measure contingent liabilities that are recognised separately at the higher of:

(a) The amount that would be recognised in accordance with IAS 37

(b) The amount initially recognised

(IFRS 3: para. 56)

3.4.5 Other exceptions to the recognition or measurement principles

(a) **Deferred tax:** use IAS 12 values.

(b) **Employee benefits:** use IAS 19 values.

(c) **Indemnification assets:** measurement should be consistent with the measurement of the indemnified item, for example an employee benefit or a contingent liability.

(d) **Reacquired rights**: value on the basis of the remaining contractual term of the related contract regardless of whether market participants would consider potential contractual renewals in determining its fair value.

(e) **Share-based payment**: use IFRS 2 values.

(f) **Assets held for sale**: use IFRS 5 values.

Question

Fair values

Tyzo Co prepares accounts to 31 December. On 1 September 20X7 Tyzo Co acquired six million $1 shares in Kono Co at $2.00 per share. At that date Kono Co produced the following interim financial statements.

Non-current assets	$'000
Property, plant and equipment (Note 1)	16.0
Current assets	
Inventories (Note 2)	4.0
Receivables	2.9
Cash and cash equivalents	1.2
	8.1
Total assets	24.1
Equity and liabilities	
Equity	
Share capital ($1 shares)	8.0
Reserves	4.4
	12.4
Non-current liabilities	
Long-term loans	4.0
Current liabilities	
Trade payables	3.2
Provision for taxation	0.6
Bank overdraft	3.9
	(7.7)
Total equity and liabilities	24.1

Notes

(a) The following information relates to the property, plant and equipment of Kono Co at 1 September 20X7.

	$m
Gross replacement cost	28.4
Net replacement cost	16.6
Economic value	18.0
Net realisable value	8.0

The property, plant and equipment of Kono Co at 1 September 20X7 had a total purchase cost to Kono Co of $27.0 million. They were all being depreciated at 25 per cent per annum pro rata on that cost. This policy is also appropriate for the consolidated financial statements of Tyzo Co. No non-current assets of Kono Co which were included in the interim financial statements drawn up as at 1 September 20X7 were disposed of by Kono Co prior to 31 December 20X7. No non-current asset was fully depreciated by 31 December 20X7.

(b) The inventories of Kono Co which were shown in the interim financial statements are raw materials at cost to Kono Co of $4 million. They would have cost $4.2 million to replace at 1 September 20X7. Of the inventory of Kono Co in hand at 1 September 20X7, goods costing Kono Co $3.0 million were sold for $3.6 million between 1 September 20X7 and 31 December 20X7.

(c) On 1 September 20X7 Tyzo Co took a decision to rationalise the group so as to integrate Kono Co. The costs of the rationalisation were estimated to total $3.0 million and the process was due to start on 1 March 20X8. No provision for these costs has been made in any of the financial statements given above.

(d) It is the group's policy to value the non-controlling interests at its proportionate share of the fair value of the subsidiary's net assets.

Required

Compute the goodwill on consolidation of Kono Co that will be included in the consolidated financial statements of the Tyzo Co group for the year ended 31 December 20X7, explaining your treatment of the items mentioned above. You should refer to the provisions of relevant accounting standards.

Answer

Goodwill on consolidation of Kono Co

	$m	$m
Consideration ($2.00 × 6m)		12.0
Non-controlling interest (13.2m × 25%)		3.3
		15.3
Group share of fair value of net assets acquired		
Share capital	8.0	
Pre-acquisition reserves	4.4	
	$m	$m
Fair value adjustments		
Property, plant and equipment (16.6 – 16.0)	0.6	
Inventories (4.2 – 4.0)	0.2	
		(13.2)
Goodwill		2.1

Notes on treatment

(a) Share capital and pre-acquisition profits represent the book value of the net assets of Kono Co at the date of acquisition. Adjustments are then required to this book value in order to give the fair value of the net assets at the date of acquisition. For short-term monetary items, fair value is their carrying value on acquisition.

(b) IFRS 3 states that the fair value of property, plant and equipment should be measured by market value or, if information on a market price is not available (as is the case here), then by reference to depreciated replacement cost, reflecting normal business practice. The net replacement cost (ie $16.6m) represents the gross replacement cost less depreciation based on that amount, and so further adjustment for extra depreciation is unnecessary.

(c) IFRS 3 also states that raw materials should be valued at replacement cost. In this case that amount is $4.2m.

(d) The rationalisation costs cannot be reported in pre-acquisition results under IFRS 3 as they are not a liability of Kono Co at the acquisition date.

3.5 Goodwill arising on acquisition

Goodwill should be carried in the statement of financial position at **cost less any accumulated impairment losses** (IFRS 3: para. B63). The treatment of goodwill is covered in detail in Chapter 3.

3.6 Adjustments after the initial accounting is complete

Sometimes the fair values of the acquiree's identifiable assets, liabilities or contingent liabilities or the cost of the combination can only be measured **provisionally** by the **end of the period in which the combination takes place**. In this situation, the acquirer **should account for the combination using those provisional values**. The acquirer should **recognise any adjustments** to those provisional values as a result of completing the initial accounting (IFRS 3: para. 45):

(a) **Within twelve months** of the acquisition date, and
(b) **From** the acquisition date (ie, retrospectively)

This means that:

(a) The **carrying amount** of an item that is recognised or adjusted as a result of completing the initial accounting shall be calculated **as if its fair value** at the acquisition date **had been recognised from that date**.

(b) **Goodwill should be adjusted** from the acquisition date by an amount equal to the adjustment to the fair value of the item being recognised or adjusted.

Any further adjustments after the initial accounting is complete should be **recognised only to correct an error** in accordance with IAS 8 *Accounting policies, changes in accounting estimates and errors*. Any subsequent changes in estimates are dealt with in accordance with IAS 8 (ie, the effect is recognised in the current and future periods). IAS 8 requires an entity to account for an error correction retrospectively, and to present financial statements as if the error had never occurred by restating the comparative information for the prior period(s) in which the error occurred.

3.6.1 Reverse acquisitions

IFRS 3 also addresses a certain type of acquisition, known as a **reverse acquisition or takeover**. This is where Company A acquires ownership of Company B through a share exchange. (For example, a private entity may arrange to have itself 'acquired' by a smaller public entity as a means of obtaining a stock exchange listing.) The number of shares issued by Company A as consideration to the shareholders of Company B is so great that control of the combined entity after the transaction is with the shareholders of Company B.

In legal terms Company A may be regarded as the parent or continuing entity, but IFRS 3 states that, as it is the Company B shareholders who control the combined entity, **Company B should be treated as the acquirer**. Company B should apply the acquisition (or purchase) method to the assets and liabilities of Company A.

(IFRS 3: para. B15)

3.7 ED *Measuring quoted investments in subsidiaries, joint ventures and associates at fair value*

This exposure draft was published in September 2014, and contains proposals concerning the measurement of investments in subsidiaries, joint ventures and associates at fair value when those investments are quoted in an active market.

The proposed amendments are to IFRS 10 *Consolidated financial statements,* IFRS 12 *Disclosure of interests in other entities*, IAS 27 *Separate financial statements*, IAS 28 *Investments in associates and joint ventures*, IAS 36 *Impairment of assets* and IFRS 13 *Fair value measurement.*

Level 1 inputs in IFRS 13 should be prioritised even when those inputs do not correspond to the unit of account of the asset measured (the investment as a whole). The proposed amendments clarify that an entity should measure the fair value of quoted investments and quoted cash-generating units as **the product of the quoted price for the individual financial instruments that make up the investments held by the entity and the quantity of financial instruments.**

3.7.1 Specific amendments

The following IFRS/IAS would be amended.

(a) **IFRS 10 *Consolidated financial statements.*** When an investment entity has an investment in a subsidiary that is quoted in an active market, its fair value must be the product of the quoted price multiplied by the quantity of the financial instruments that make up the investment without adjustment.

(b) **IAS 27 *Separate financial statements.*** When an entity accounts for its investments in subsidiaries, joint ventures and associates at fair value and those investments are quoted in an active market, their fair value must be the product of the quoted price multiplied by the quantity of the financial instruments that make up the investments without adjustment.

(c) **IAS 28 *Investments in associates and joint ventures.*** As (a), above, when an entity measures its investments in associates or joint ventures at fair value and those investments are quoted in an active market.

(d) **IFRS 12 *Disclosure of interests in other entities.*** As (a), above.

(f) **IAS 36 *Impairment of assets.*** This proposed amendment is relevant to cash-generating units. When the cash-generating unit is an investment in a subsidiary, joint venture or associate that is quoted in an active market its fair value must be the product of the quoted price multiplied by the quantity of the financial instruments that make up the investment without adjustment.

(e) **IAS 13 *Fair value measurement.*** An illustrative example would be added showing the application of the exception in paragraph IFRS 13.48 to a group of financial assets and financial liabilities whose market risks are substantially the same and whose fair value measurement is categorised within Level 1 of the fair value hierarchy.

4 IAS 28 *Investments in associates and joint ventures*

12/14

FAST FORWARD

IAS 28 deals with accounting for associates and joint ventures. The definitions are important as they govern the accounting treatment, particularly '**significant influence**' and '**joint control**'.

IFRS 11 (see Chapter 13) and **IAS 28** require joint ventures to be accounted for using the equity method.

We looked at investments in associates briefly in Section 1. IAS 28 *Investments in associates and joint ventures* covers this type of investment. IAS 28 does not apply to investments in associates or joint ventures held by venture capital organisations, mutual funds, unit trusts, and similar entities. Those investments may be measured at fair value through profit or loss in accordance with IFRS 9.

In this section we will focus on **associates**. The criteria that exist to identify a **joint venture** will be covered in Chapter 13, although the method for accounting for a joint venture is identical to that used for associates.

Some of the important definitions in Section 1 are repeated here, with some additional important terms (IAS 28: para. 3).

Key terms

Associate. An entity, including an unincorporated entity such as a partnership, over which an investor has significant influence and which is neither a subsidiary nor a joint venture of the investor.

Significant influence is the power to participate in the financial and operating policy decisions of an economic activity but is not control or joint control over those policies.

Joint control is the contractually agreed sharing of control over an economic activity.

Equity method. A method of accounting whereby the investment is initially recorded at cost and adjusted thereafter for the post acquisition change in the investor's share of net assets of the investee. The profit or loss of the investor includes the investor's share of the profit or loss of the investee and the investor's other comprehensive income includes its share of the investee's other comprehensive income.

We have already looked at how the **status** of an investment in an associate should be determined. Go back to Section 2 to revise it. (Note that, as for an investment in a subsidiary, any **potential voting rights** should be taken into account in assessing whether the investor has **significant influence** over the investee.)

IAS 28 requires all investments in associates and joint ventures to be accounted for using the equity method, *unless* the investment is classified as 'held for sale' in accordance with IFRS 5 in which case it should be accounted for under IFRS 5 (see Chapter 15).

An investor is exempt from applying the equity method if:

(a) It is a parent exempt from preparing consolidated financial statements under IAS 27 or

(b) All of the following apply:

 (i) The investor is a **wholly-owned subsidiary** or it is a **partially owned subsidiary** of another entity and its other owners, including those not otherwise entitled to vote, have been informed about, and do not object to, the investor not applying the equity method

 (ii) Its securities are **not publicly traded**

 (iii) It is **not in the process of issuing securities** in public securities markets

 (iv) The **ultimate or intermediate parent** publishes consolidated financial statements that comply with International Financial Reporting Standards

IAS 28 **does not allow** an investment in an associate to be excluded from equity accounting when an investee operates under severe long-term restrictions that significantly impair its ability to transfer funds to the investor. Significant influence must be lost before the equity method ceases to be applicable.

The use of the equity method should be **discontinued** from the date that the investor **ceases to have significant influence**.

From that date, the investor shall account for the investment in accordance with IFRS 9 *Financial instruments*. The fair value of the retained interest must be regarded as its fair value on initial recognition as a financial asset under IFRS 9.

4.1 Separate financial statements of the investor

Note that in the separate financial statements of the investor, an interest in an associate is accounted for either:

- At cost, or
- In accordance with IFRS 9 *Financial instruments*, or
- Using the equity method as described in IAS 28 *Investments in associates and joint ventures*

(IAS 27: para. 10)

4.2 Application of the equity method: consolidated accounts

FAST FORWARD

The **equity method** should be applied in the consolidated accounts:

- **Statement of financial position**: investment in associate at cost plus (or minus) the group's share of the associate's post-acquisition profits (or losses).
- **Profit or loss (statement of profit or loss and other comprehensive income):** group share of associate's profit after tax.

- **Other comprehensive income (statement of profit or loss and other comprehensive income):** group share of associate's other comprehensive income after tax.

Many of the procedures required to apply the equity method are the same as are required for full consolidation. In particular, **fair value adjustments** are required and the group share of **intra-group unrealised profits** must be excluded.

4.2.1 Consolidated statement of profit or loss and other comprehensive income

The basic principle is that the investing company (X Co) should take account of its **share of the earnings** of the associate, Y Co, whether or not Y Co distributes the earnings as dividends. X Co achieves this by adding to consolidated profit the group's share of Y Co's profit after tax.

Notice the difference between this treatment and the **consolidation** of a subsidiary company's results. If Y Co were a subsidiary X Co would take credit for the whole of its sales revenue, cost of sales and so on and would then prepare a reconciliation at the end of the statement showing how much of the group profit and total comprehensive income is owned by non-controlling interests.

Under equity accounting, the associate's sales revenue, cost of sales and so on are **not amalgamated** with those of the group. Instead, the **group share** only of the associate's **profit after tax** and **other comprehensive income** for the year is included in the relevant sections of the statement of profit or loss and other comprehensive income.

4.2.2 Consolidated statement of financial position

A figure for **investment in associates** is shown which at the time of the acquisition must be stated at cost. This amount will increase (decrease) each year by the amount of the group's share of the associate's total comprehensive income retained for the year.

The group share of the associate's reserves are also included within the group reserves figure in the equity section of the consolidated statement of financial position.

4.2.3 Example: Associate

P Co, a company with subsidiaries, acquires 25,000 of the 100,000 $1 ordinary shares in A Co for $60,000 on 1 January 20X8. In the year to 31 December 20X8, A Co earns profits after tax of $24,000, from which it declares a dividend of $6,000.

How will A Co's results be accounted for in the individual and consolidated accounts of P Co for the year ended 31 December 20X8?

Solution

In the **individual accounts** of P Co, the investment will be recorded on 1 January 20X8 at cost. Unless there is an impairment in the value of the investment (see below), this amount will remain in the individual statement of financial position of P Co permanently. The only entry in P Co's statement of profit or loss and other comprehensive income will be to record dividends received. For the year ended 31 December 20X8, P Co will:

DEBIT	Cash	$1,500	
CREDIT	Income from shares in associated companies		$1,500

In the **consolidated accounts** of P Co equity accounting principles will be used to account for the investment in A Co. Consolidated profit after tax will include the group's share of A Co's profit after tax (25% × $24,000 = $6,000). To the extent that this has been distributed as dividend, it is already included in P Co's individual accounts and will automatically be brought into the consolidated results. That part of the group's profit share which has not been distributed as dividend ($4,500) will be brought into consolidation by the following adjustment.

DEBIT	Investment in associates	$4,500	
CREDIT	Income from shares in associates		$4,500

The asset 'Investment in associates' is then stated at $64,500, being cost plus the group share of post-acquisition retained profits.

4.3 Consolidated statement of profit or loss and other comprehensive income

The treatment of associates' profits in the following proforma should be studied carefully.

4.3.1 Pro-forma consolidated statement of profit or loss and other comprehensive income

The following is a **suggested layout** (for a statement of profit or loss and other comprehensive income) for a company having subsidiaries as well as associates.

	$'000
Sales revenue	1,400
Cost of sales	770
Gross profit	630
Distribution costs and administrative expenses	290
	340
Interest and similar income receivable	30
	370
Finance costs	(20)
	350
Share of profit (after tax) of associate	17
Profit before taxation	367
Income tax expense	
Parent company and subsidiaries	145
Profit for the year	222
Profit attributable to:	
Owners of the parent	200
Non-controlling interest	22
	222

4.4 Consolidated statement of financial position

As explained earlier, the consolidated statement of financial position will contain an **asset 'Investment in associated companies'**. The amount at which this asset is stated will be its original cost plus the group's share of the associate's **total comprehensive income earned since acquisition** which has not been distributed as dividends.

4.5 Other accounting considerations

The following points are also relevant and are similar to a parent-subsidiary consolidation situation (IAS 28: paras. 26 and 27).

(a) Use financial statements drawn up to the **same reporting date**.

(b) If this is impracticable, adjust the financial statements for **significant transactions/ events** in the intervening period. The difference between the reporting date of the associate and that of the investor must be no more than three months.

(c) Use **uniform accounting policies** for like transactions and events in similar circumstances, adjusting the associate's statements to reflect group policies if necessary.

(d) If an associate has **cumulative preferred shares** held by outside interests, calculate the share of the investor's profits/losses after adjusting for the preferred dividends (whether or not declared).

4.6 'Upstream' and 'downstream' transactions

A group (made up of a parent and its consolidated subsidiaries) may trade with its associates. This introduces the possibility of unrealised profits if goods sold within the group are still in inventories at the year end. This is similar to unrealised profits arising on trading between a parent and a subsidiary. The important thing to remember is that when an **associate** is involved, **only the group's share is eliminated**.'

The precise accounting entries depend on the direction of the transaction. 'Upstream' transactions are sales from an associate to the investor. 'Downstream' transactions are sales of assets from the investor to an associate.

The double entry is as follows, where A% is the parent's holding in the associate, and PUP is the provision for unrealised profit.

DEBIT	Retained earnings of parent	PUP × A%	
CREDIT	Group inventories		PUP × A%

For upstream transactions (associate sells to parent/subsidiary) where the parent holds the inventories.

OR

DEBIT	Retained earnings of parent /subsidiary	PUP × A%	
CREDIT	Investment in associate		PUP × A%

For downstream transactions, (parent/subsidiary sells to associate) where the associate holds the inventory.

(IAS 28: para. 28)

4.7 Example: Downstream transaction

A Co, a parent with subsidiaries, holds 25% of the equity shares in B Co. During the year, A Co makes sales of $1,000,000 to B Co at cost plus a 25% mark-up. At the year-end, B Co has all these goods still in inventories.

Solution

A Co has made an unrealised profit of $200,000 (1,000,000 × 25/125) on its sales to the associate. The group's share of this is 25%, ie $50,000. This must be eliminated.

The double entry is:

DEBIT	A: Retained earnings	$50,000	
CREDIT	Investment in associate (B)		$50,000

Because the sale was made to the associate, the group's share of the unsold inventories forms part of the investment in associate at the year end. If the sale had been from the associate B to A, ie an upstream transaction, the double entry would have been:

DEBIT	A: Retained earnings	$50,000	
CREDIT	A: Inventories		$50,000

If preparing the consolidated statement of profit or loss and other comprehensive income, you would add the $50,000 to cost of sales, as the **parent** made the sales in this example.

4.7.1 Associate's losses

When the equity method is being used and the investor's share of losses of the associate equals or exceeds its interest in the associate, the investor should **discontinue** including its share of further losses. The investment is reported at nil value. The interest in the associate is normally the carrying amount of the investment in the associate, but it also includes any other long-term interests, for example, preference shares or long term receivables or loans.

After the investor's interest is reduced to nil, **additional losses** should only be recognised where the investor has incurred obligations or made payments on behalf of the associate (for example, if it has guaranteed amounts owed to third parties by the associate).

Should the associate return to profit, the parent may resume recognising its share of profits only after they equal the share of losses not recognised.

(IAS 28: para. 38)

4.8 Impairment losses

IFRS 9 sets out a list of indications that a financial asset (including an associate) may have become impaired. Any impairment loss is recognised in accordance with IAS 36 *Impairment of assets* for each associate as a single asset. There is no separate testing for impairment of goodwill, as the goodwill that forms part of the carrying amount of an investment in an associate is not separately recognised. An impairment loss is not allocated to any asset, including goodwill, that forms part of the carrying amount of the investment in associate. Accordingly, any reversal of that impairment loss is recognised in accordance with IAS 36 to the extent that the recoverable amount of the investment subsequently increases.

(IAS 28: para. 39)

4.9 Non-controlling interest/associate held by a subsidiary

Where the investment in an associate is held by a subsidiary in which there are non-controlling interests, the non-controlling interest shown in the consolidated financial statements of the group should include the **non-controlling interest of the subsidiary's interest** in the results and net assets of the associated company.

This means that the group accounts must include the 'gross' share of net assets, pre-tax profits and tax, in accounting for the **non-controlling interest separately**. For example, we will suppose that P Co owns 60% of S Co which owns 25% of A Co, an associate of P Co. The relevant amounts for inclusion in the consolidated financial statements would be as follows.

CONSOLIDATED STATEMENT OF PROFIT OR LOSS AND OTHER COMPREHENSIVE INCOME
Operating profit (P 100% + S 100%)
Share of profit after tax of associate (A 25%)
Tax (P 100% + S 100%)
Non-controlling interest (S 40% + A 10%*)
Retained profits (P 100% + S 60% + A 15%)

CONSOLIDATED STATEMENT OF FINANCIAL POSITION
Investment in associate (figures based on 25% holding)
Non-controlling interest ((40% × shareholders' funds of S) + (10%* × post-acq'n retained earnings of A))
Unrealised reserves (15% × post-acquisition reserves of A)
Group retained earnings ((100% × P) + (60% × post-acquisition of S))
* 40% × 25% = 10%

4.10 Comprehensive question

The following question provides comprehensive revision of the topics covered up to this point in the chapter. It is written in the style of a P2 question, but only includes issues that you should remember from your earlier studies. It is important that you are confident about these techniques before moving on to the new and more complicated group accounting topics that are tested in Paper P2.

Otway, a public limited company, acquired a subsidiary, Holgarth, on 1 July 20X2 and an associate, Batterbee, on 1 July 20X5. The details of the acquisitions at the respective dates are as follows.

Investee	*Ordinary share capital of $1*	*Share premium*	*Reserves Retained earnings*	*Revaluation surplus*	*Fair value of net assets at acquisition*	*Cost of investment*	*Ordinary share capital acquired*
	$m	$m	$m	$m	$m	$m	$m
Holgarth	400	140	120	40	800	765	320
Batterbee	220	83	195	54	652	203	55

The draft financial statements for the year ended 30 June 20X6 are as follows.

STATEMENTS OF FINANCIAL POSITION AS AT 30 JUNE 20X6

	Otway	*Holgarth*	*Batterbee*
	$m	$m	$m
Non-current assets			
Property, plant and equipment	1,012	920	442
Intangible assets		350	27
Investment in Holgarth	765	–	–
Investment in Batterbee	203	–	–
	1,980	1,270	469
Current assets			
Inventories	620	1,460	214
Trade receivables	950	529	330
Cash and cash equivalents	900	510	45
	2,470	2,499	589
	4,450	3,769	1,058
Equity			
Share capital	1,000	400	220
Share premium	200	140	83
Retained earnings	1,128	809	263
Revaluation surplus	142	70	62
	2,470	1,419	628
Non-current liabilities			
Deferred tax liability	100	50	36
Current liabilities			
Trade and other payables	1,880	2,300	394
	4,450	3,769	1,058

STATEMENTS OF PROFIT OR LOSS AND OTHER COMPREHENSIVE INCOME FOR THE YEAR ENDED 30 JUNE 20X6

	Otway	*Holgarth*	*Batterbee*
	$m	$m	$m
Revenue	4,480	4,200	1,460
Cost of sales	(2,690)	(2,940)	(1,020)
Gross profit	1,790	1,260	440
Distribution costs and administrative expenses	(620)	(290)	(196)
Finance costs	(50)	(80)	(24)
Dividend income (from Holgarth and Batterbee)	260	–	–
Profit before tax	1,380	890	220
Income tax expense	(330)	(274)	(72)
PROFIT FOR THE YEAR c/f	1,050	616	148

		Otway	Holgarth	Batterbee
		$m	$m	$m
PROFIT FOR THE YEAR	b/f	1,050	616	148
Other comprehensive income that will not be reclassified to profit or loss				
Gain on revaluation of property		30	7	12
Income tax expense relating to other comp income		(9)	(2)	(4)
Other comprehensive income, net of tax		21	5	8
TOTAL COMPREHENSIVE INCOME FOR THE YEAR		1,071	621	156
Dividends paid in the year		250	300	80
Retained earnings brought forward		328	493	195

Additional information:

(a) Neither Holgarth nor Batterbee had any reserves other than retained earnings and share premium at the date of acquisition. Neither issued new shares since acquisition.

(b) The fair value difference on the subsidiary relates to property, plant and equipment being depreciated through cost of sales over a remaining useful life of 10 years from the acquisition date. The fair value difference on the associate relates to a piece of land (which has not been sold since acquisition).

(c) Group policy is to measure non-controlling interests at acquisition at fair value. The fair value of the non-controlling interests on 1 July 20X2 was calculated as $188m.

(d) Holgarth's intangible assets include $87 million of training and marketing expenditure incurred during the year ended 30 June 20X6. The directors of Holgarth believe that these should be capitalised as they relate to the start-up period of a new business venture in Scotland, and intend to amortise the balance over five years from 1 July 20X6.

(e) During the year ended 30 June 20X6 Holgarth sold goods to Otway for $1,300 million. The company makes a profit of 30% on the selling price. $140 million of these goods were held by Otway on 30 June 20X6 ($60 million on 30 June 20X5).

(f) Annual impairment tests have indicated impairment losses of $100m relating to the recognised goodwill of Holgarth including $25m in the current year. The Otway Group recognises impairment losses on goodwill in cost of sales. No impairment losses to date have been necessary for the investment in Batterbee.

Required

Prepare the statement of profit or loss and other comprehensive income for the year ended 30 June 20X6 for the Otway Group and a statement of financial position at that date.

Answer

OTWAY GROUP
CONSOLIDATED STATEMENT OF FINANCIAL POSITION AS AT 30 JUNE 20X6

	$m
Non-current assets	
Property, plant and equipment (1,012 + 920 + (W10) 60)	1,992
Goodwill (W2)	53
Other intangible assets (350 – (W9) 87)	263
Investment in associate (W3)	222
	2,530
Current assets	
Inventories (620 + 1,460 – (W8) 42)	2,038
Trade receivables (950 + 529)	1,479
Cash and cash equivalents (900 + 510)	1,410
	4,927
	7,457

	$m
Equity attributable to owners of the parent	
Share capital	1,000
Share premium	200
Retained earnings (W4)	1,481
Revaluation surplus (W5)	168
	2,849
Non-controlling interests (W6)	278
	3,127
Non-current liabilities	
Deferred tax liability (100 + 50)	150
Current liabilities	
Trade and other payables (1,880 + 2,300)	4,180
	7,457

OTWAY GROUP
CONSOLIDATED STATEMENT OF PROFIT OR LOSS AND OTHER COMPREHENSIVE INCOME
FOR THE YEAR ENDED 30 JUNE 20X6

	$m
Revenue (4,480 + 4,200 – (W8) 1,300)	7,380
Cost of sales (2,690 + 2,940 – (W8) 1,300 + (W8) 24 + (W10) 10 + 25)	(4,389)
Gross profit	2,991
Distribution costs and administrative expenses (620 + 290 + (W9) 87)	(997)
Finance costs (50 + 80)	(130)
Share of profit of associate (148 × 25%)	37
Profit before tax	1,901
Income tax expense (330 + 274)	(604)
PROFIT FOR THE YEAR	1,297
Other comprehensive income that will not be reclassified to profit or loss:	
Gain on revaluation of property (30 + 7)	37
Share of other comprehensive income of associate (8 × 25%)	2
Income tax expense relating to other comprehensive income (9 + 2)	(11)
Other comprehensive income for the year, net of tax	28
TOTAL COMPREHENSIVE INCOME FOR THE YEAR	1,325
Profit attributable to:	
Owners of the parent (1,297 – 94)	1,203
Non-controlling interests (W7)	94
	1,297
Total comprehensive income attributable to:	
Owners of the parent (1,325 – 95)	1,230
Non-controlling interests (W7)	95
	1,325

Workings

1 *Group structure*

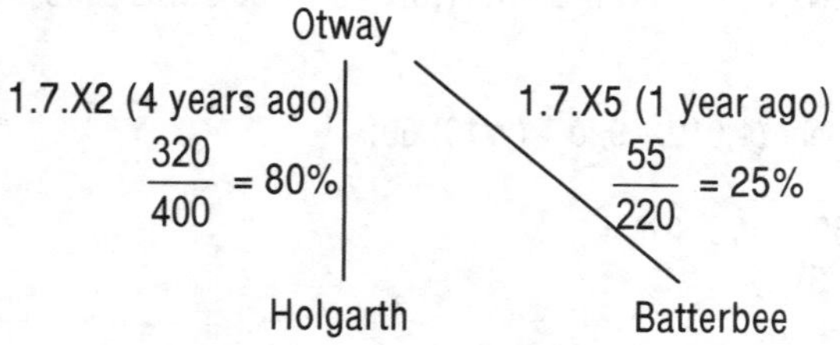

2 *Goodwill*

	Group	
	$m	$m
Consideration transferred		765
Fair value of non-controlling interests		188
Fair value of net assets acquired:		
Share capital	400	
Share premium	140	
Retained earnings at acq'n	120	
Revaluation surplus at acq'n	40	
∴ fair value adjustment	100	
Total FV of net assets		(800)
		153
Less cumulative impairment losses		(100)
		53

3 *Investment in associate*

	$m
Cost of associate	203
Share of post-acquisition retained reserves [(263 + 62 – 195 – 54) × 25%]	19
Less impairment losses on associate to date	(0)
	222

4 *Consolidated retained earnings c/f*

	Otway	*Holgarth*	*Batterbee*
	$m	$m	$m
Per question	1,128	809	263
PUP (W8)		(42)	
Start up costs (W9)		(87)	
Depreciation on FV adjustment (W10)		(40)	(0)
Less pre-acquisition		(120)	(195)
		520	68
Group share:			
Holgarth [520 × 80%]	416		
Batterbee [68 × 25%]	17		
Less impairment losses on goodwill:			
Holgarth [80% × 100] (W2)	(80)		
Less impairment losses on associate			
Batterbee	(0)		
	1,481		

5 *Consolidated revaluation surplus c/f*

	Otway	*Holgarth*	*Batterbee*
	$m	$m	$m
Per question	142	70	62
Less pre-acquisition		(40)	(54)
		30	8
Group share:			
Holgarth [30 × 80%]	24		
Batterbee [8 × 25%]	2		
	168		

6 *Non-controlling interests (statement of financial position)*

	$m
At acquisition (W2)	188
Share of post acquisition retained earnings [520 (W4) × 20%]	104
Share of post acquisition revaluation surplus [30 (W5) × 20%]	6
Less: impairment losses on goodwill [20% × 100] (W2)	(20)
	278

7 *Non-controlling interests (statement of profit or loss and other comprehensive income)*

	PFY	*TCI*
	$m	$m
Holgarth's PFY/TCI per question	616	621
Less impairment losses	(25)	(25)
Less PUP (W8)	(24)	(24)
Less start-up costs (W9)	(87)	(87)
Less FV depreciation (W10)	(10)	(10)
	470	475
× NCI share 20% =	94	95

8 *Intragroup trading*

Cancel intragroup sales and purchases:

DEBIT	Revenue	$1,300,000	
CREDIT	Cost of sales		$1,300,000

Unrealised profit (Holgarth to Otway):

	$m
In opening inventories (60 × 30%)	18
In closing inventories (140 × 30%)	42
Increase (to cost of sales)	24

9 *Start-up costs*

IAS 38 *Intangible assets* states that start-up, training and promotional costs should all be written off as an expense as incurred as no intangible asset is created that can be recognised (the benefits cannot be sufficiently distinguished from internally generated goodwill, which is not recognised).

10 *Fair value – Holgarth*

	At acquisition	*Additional depreciation**	*At year end*
	$m	$m	$m
Property, plant and equipment (800 – 400 – 140 –120 – 40)	100	(40)	60
	100	(40)	60

* Additional depreciation = $^{100}/_{10}$ = 10 per annum to cost of sales × 4 years = 40

4.11 ED Sale or contribution of assets between an investor and its associate or joint venture

In 2012, the IASB published an ED *Sale or contribution of assets between an investor and its associate or joint venture*. The ED proposes to **eliminate the inconsistency between IFRS 10, which requires full gain recognition, and IAS 28, which only allows gain recognition to the extent of the interest attributed to other shareholders**. The ED requires that:

(a) All gains and losses on non-monetary assets sold or contributed to an associate or joint venture which constitute a business would be fully recognised by the investor.

(b) Any gain or loss on assets sold or contributed that do not meet the definition of a business would be recognised only to the extent of the other investors' interest in the associate or joint venture.

The requirement of **full recognition** of gains or losses in transactions involving businesses would apply **regardless of the legal form of the transaction** in which such a business was transferred, for example through the sale of a group of assets and liabilities, through the sale and purchase of an investment in a subsidiary, or in some other manner. Existing guidance on 'linked transactions' in IFRS 10 would be explicitly extended to these types of transactions as well.

4.12 ED Equity method: share of other net asset changes

This Exposure Draft was published in November 2012. The objective of the proposed amendments is to provide **additional guidance** to IAS 28 on the **application of the equity method**. Specifically; the proposed amendments intend to specify the following.

(a) An investor should recognise, in the investor's equity, its share of the changes in the net assets of the investee that are not recognised in profit or loss or other comprehensive income (OCI) of the investee, and that are not distributions received ('other net asset changes').

(b) The investor must reclassify to profit or loss the cumulative amount of equity that the investor had previously recognised when the investor discontinues the use of the equity method.

(ED/2012/3: para. 10)

5 IFRS 12 *Disclosure of interests in other entities*

FAST FORWARD

IFRS 12 *Disclosure of interests in other entities* requires disclosure of a reporting entity's interests in other entities in order to help identify the profit or loss and cash flows available to the reporting entity and determine the value of a current or future investment in the reporting entity.

5.1 Objective

IFRS 12 was published in 2011. It is effective for annual accounting periods beginning on or after 1 January 2013, but earlier application is permitted.

The objective of the standard is to require entities to disclose information that enables the user of the financial statements to evaluate the nature of, and risks associated with, interests in other entities, and the effects of those interests on its financial position, financial performance and cash flows (IFRS 12: para. 1).

This is particularly relevant in light of the financial crisis and recent accounting scandals. The IASB believes that better information about interests in other entities is necessary to help users to identify the profit or loss and cash flows available to the reporting entity and to determine the value of a current or future investment in the reporting entity.

5.2 Scope

IFRS 12 covers disclosures for entities which have interests in (IFRS 12: para. 5):

- Subsidiaries
- Joint arrangements (ie joint operations and joint ventures, see Chapter 13)
- Associates, and
- Unconsolidated structured entities.

5.3 Structured entities

IFRS 12 defines a structured entity.

Key term

Structured entity. An entity that has been designed so that **voting or similar rights** are **not the dominant factor** in **deciding who controls** the entity, such as when any voting rights relate to administrative tasks only and the relevant activities are directed by means of contractual arrangements. *(IFRS 12: Appendix A)*

5.4 Main disclosures

The main disclosures required by IFRS 12 for an entity that has investments in other entities are as follows (IFRS 12: paras. 7 to 31).

(a) The **significant judgements and assumptions** made in determining whether the entity has control, joint control or significant influence of the other entities, and in determining the type of joint arrangement

(b) Information to understand the **composition of the group** and the interest that non-controlling interests have in the group's activities and cash flows

(c) The **nature, extent and financial effects** of interests in **joint arrangements and associates**, including the nature and effects of the entity's contractual relationship with other investors

(d) The **nature and extent** of interests in **unconsolidated** structured entities

(e) The nature and extent of **significant restrictions** on the entity's ability to **access or use assets and settle liabilities** of the group

(f) The nature of, and changes in, the **risks associated with the entity's interests** in consolidated structured entities, joint ventures, associates and unconsolidated structured entities (eg commitments and contingent liabilities)

(g) The **consequences of changes in the entity's ownership** interest in a subsidiary that do **not result in loss of control** (i.e. the effects on the equity attributable to owners of the parent)

(h) The **consequences of losing control** of a subsidiary during the reporting period (ie the gain or loss, and the portion of it that relates to measuring any remaining investment at fair value, and the line item(s) in profit or loss in which the gain or loss is recognised (if not presented separately)).

Chapter Roundup

- Go back to your earlier study material and practise more questions if you are unsure of basic consolidation techniques.
- **Definitions** are very important when looking at group accounts.
- Some of these definitions are from IAS 28 as well as IFRS 3 and IFRS 10. Some are new, and some you will have met before.
- IFRS 3 **requires recognition of contingent consideration, measured at fair value, at the acquisition date**.
- The non-controlling interest may be valued **either at fair value or at the non-controlling interest's proportionate share of the acquiree's identifiable net assets**.
- **IFRS 10 *Consolidated financial statements*** requires a parent to present **consolidated** financial statements.
- **Goodwill** should be calculated **after revaluing** the subsidiary company's assets.
- If the subsidiary does not incorporate the revaluation in its own accounts, it should be done as a **consolidation adjustment**.
- **Goodwill arising on consolidation** is the difference between the purchase consideration and the fair value of the identifiable assets and liabilities acquired.
- The accounting requirements and disclosures of the **fair value exercise** are covered by **IFRS 3. IFRS 13** *Fair value measurement* gives extensive guidance on how the fair value of assets and liabilities should be established.
- IFRS 3 does not allow combinations to be accounted for as a **uniting of interests; all combinations must be treated as acquisitions**.
- **IAS 28** deals with accounting for associates and joint ventures. The definitions are important as they govern the accounting treatment, particularly **'significant influence'** and **'joint control'**.
- **IFRS 11** (see Chapter 13) and **IAS 28** require joint ventures to be accounted for using the equity method.
- The **equity method** should be applied in the consolidated accounts:
  - **Statement of financial position**: investment in associate at cost plus (or minus) the group's share of the associate's post-acquisition profits (or losses).
  - **Profit or loss** (statement of profit or loss and other comprehensive income): group share of associate's profit after tax.
  - **Other comprehensive income** (statement of profit or loss and other comprehensive income): group share of associate's other comprehensive income after tax.
- **IFRS 12 *Disclosure of interests in other entities*** requires disclosure of a reporting entity's interests in other entities in order to help identify the profit or loss and cash flows available to the reporting entity and determine the value of a current or future investment in the reporting entity.

Quick Quiz

1 **Fill in the blanks** in the statements below, using the words in the box.

Per IFRS 10, A is a parent of B if:

(a) A holds (1) .... in B

(b) A can appoint, reassign or remove (2) ....

(c) A is exposed to (3) .... from its involvement with B

2 If a company holds 20% or more of the shares of another company, it has significant influence. *True or false*?

3 What is significant influence?

4 What is a non-controlling interest?

5 How is the non-controlling interest on acquisition to be valued?

6 How should an investment in a subsidiary be accounted for in the separate financial statements of the parent?

7 Describe the requirement of IFRS 3 in relation to the revaluation of a subsidiary company's assets.

8 Under IFRS 13 *Fair value measurement,* what is meant by Level 1 inputs?

9 Which party to a business combination is the acquirer?

10 An associate is a/an________________ in which a investor has a ________________, but which is not a subsidiary or a joint venture of the investor. *Complete the blanks.*

11 What is the effect of the equity method on the statement of profit or loss and other comprehensive income and the statement of financial position?

Answers to Quick Quiz

1 (a) A majority of the voting rights
(b) Key management personnel who can direct the relevant activities
(c) Variable returns

2 True.

3 The power to participate but not to control.

4 The part of the net profit or loss and the net assets attributable to interests not owned by the parent.

5 Either at fair value or at the non-controlling interest's proportionate share of the acquiree's identifiable net assets.

6 (a) At cost, or
(b) In accordance with IFRS 9 *Financial instruments*, or
(c) Using the equity method as described in IAS 28 *Investments in associates and joint ventures*

7 Fair value is not affected by the acquirer's intentions. Therefore, only intentions after acquisition are reflected in the statement of profit or loss and other comprehensive income after acquisition.

8 Quoted prices in active markets for identical assets that the entity can access at the measurement date.

9 The acquirer is the entity that obtains control of the other combining entities or businesses.

10 An associates is an **entity** in which an investor has a **significant influence**, but which is not a subsidiary or a joint venture of the investor.

11 (a) *Statement of profit or loss and other comprehensive income.* Investing entity includes its share of the earnings of the associate, by adding its share of profit after tax.

(b) *Statement of financial position.* Investment in associates is included in assets at cost. This will increase or decrease each year according to whether the associate makes a profit or loss.

Now try the question below from the Practice Question Bank

Number	Level	Marks	Time
Q17	Introductory	18	35 mins

13

Complex groups and joint arrangements

Topic list	Syllabus reference
1 Complex groups	D1
2 Consolidating sub-subsidiaries	D1
3 Direct holdings in sub-subsidiaries	D1
4 IFRS 11 *Joint arrangements*	D1

Introduction

This chapter introduces the first of several more complicated consolidation topics. The best way to tackle these questions is to be logical and to carry out the consolidation on a **step by step** basis.

In questions of this nature, it is very helpful to sketch a **diagram of the group structure**, as we have done. This clarifies the situation and it should point you in the right direction: always sketch the group structure as your first working and double check it against the information in the question.

In Chapter 12 you met the concept of the 'joint venture', a form of joint arrangement which is equity accounted under IAS 28. **IFRS 11** (Section 4) covers all types of **joint arrangements**. It establishes principles for how joint operations should be distinguished from joint ventures and how to account for each type of joint arrangement in individual accounts and in consolidated accounts.

Study guide

		Intellectual level
D1	**Group accounting including statement of cash flows**	
(a)	Apply the method of accounting for business combinations including complex group structures	3
(h)	Outline and apply the key definitions and accounting methods which relate to interests in joint arrangements	3

Exam guide

If the groups question does not involve an acquisition or disposal or a statement of cash flows, then it is likely to involve a complex group.

1 Complex groups

FAST FORWARD

When a holding company has **several subsidiaries**, the consolidated statement of financial position shows a single figure for non-controlling interests and for goodwill arising on consolidation. In cases where there are several subsidiary companies the technique is to open up a single non-controlling interest working and a single goodwill working.

1.1 Introduction

In this section we shall consider how the principles of statement of financial position consolidation may be applied to more complex structures of companies within a group.

(a) **Several subsidiary companies**

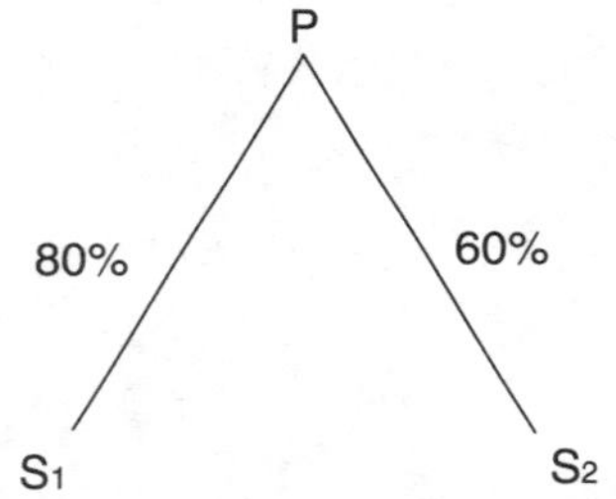

You have already seen this type of structure in your previous studies.

(b) **Sub-subsidiaries**

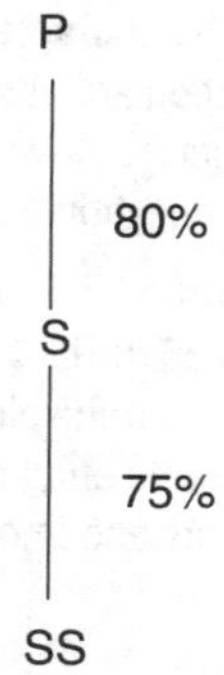

P holds a controlling interest in S which in turn holds a controlling interest in SS. SS is therefore a subsidiary of a subsidiary of P, in other words, a *sub-subsidiary* of P.

(c) **Direct holdings in sub-subsidiaries: 'D' shaped groups**

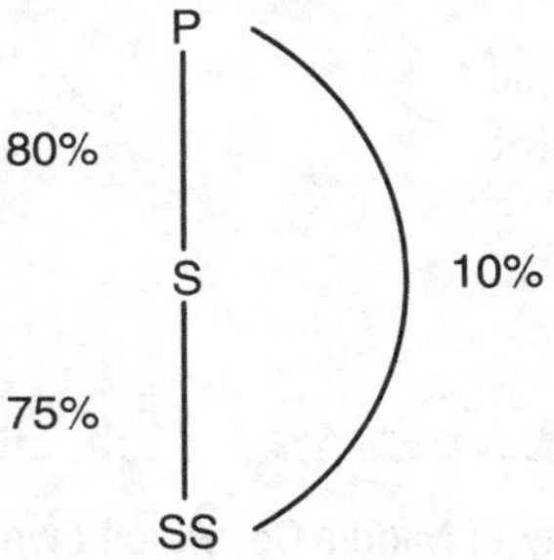

In this example, SS is a sub-subsidiary of P with additional shares held directly by P.

In practice, groups are usually larger, and therefore more complex, but the procedures for consolidation of large groups will not differ from those we shall now describe for smaller ones.

1.2 A parent company which has several subsidiaries

Where a company P has several subsidiaries S_1, S_2, S_3 and so on, the technique for consolidation is exactly as previously described. **Cancellation** is from the holding company, which has assets of investments in subsidiaries S_1, S_2, S_3, to each of the several subsidiaries.

The consolidated statement of financial position will show:

(a) A single figure for **non-controlling interest**, and
(b) A single figure for **goodwill** arising

A single working should be used for each of the constituents of the consolidated statement of financial position: one working for goodwill, one for non-controlling interest, one for retained earnings (reserves), and so on.

1.3 Sub-subsidiaries

A slightly different problem arises when there are sub-subsidiaries in the group, which is how should we **identify the non-controlling interest** in the retained earnings of the group? Suppose P owns 80% of the equity of S, and that S in turn owns 60% of the equity of SS.

It would appear that in this situation:

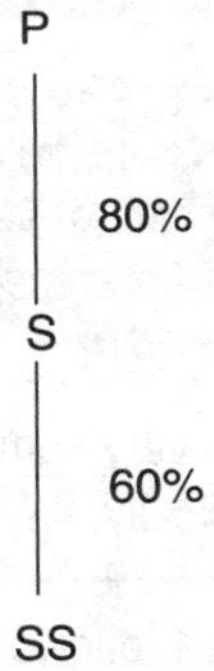

(a) P owns 80% of 60% = 48% of SS
(b) The non-controlling interest in S owns 20% of 60% = 12% of SS
(c) The non-controlling interest in SS itself owns the remaining 40% of the SS equity

SS is nevertheless a **sub-subsidiary** of P, because it is a subsidiary of S which in turn is a subsidiary of P. The chain of control thus makes SS a sub-subsidiary of P which owns only 48% of its equity.

The total non-controlling interest in SS may be checked by considering a **dividend** of $100 paid by SS where S then distributes its share of this dividend in full to its own shareholders.

		$
S will receive	$60	
P will receive	80% × $60 =	48
Leaving for the total NCI in SS		52
		100

Question

Effective interest

Top owns 60% of the equity of Middle Co, which owns 75% of the equity of Bottom Co. What is Top Co's effective holding in Bottom Co?

Answer

Top owns 60% of 75% of Bottom Co = 45%.

1.4 Date of effective control

The date the sub-subsidiary comes under the **control of the holding company** is either:

(a) The date P acquired S if S already holds shares in SS, or
(b) If S acquires shares in SS later, then that later date

You need to think about the dates of acquisition and the order in which the group is built up when you identify which balances to select as the **pre-acquisition** reserves of the sub-subsidiary.

Exam focus point

The examining team havestrongly indicated that fair value NCI will generally be tested with more difficult group topics. However, this chapter uses examples where the NCI is valued at its proportionate share of the subsidiary's identifiable net assets. Fair value NCI is shown as an alternative. This is to enable you to learn the new techniques. Fair value NCI is used in the questions in the exam question bank. You should keep an eye on *Student Accountant* magazine for articles giving further advice on this point.

2 Consolidating sub-subsidiaries

6/10, 12/12

FAST FORWARD

When dealing with **sub-subsidiaries,** you will need to calculate effective interest owned by the group and by the non-controlling interest. The date of acquisition is important when dealing with sub-subsidiaries. Remember that it is the post-acquisition reserves from a group perspective which are important.

Exam focus point

Don't panic when a question seems very complicated – sketch the group structure and analyse the information in the question methodically.

The basic consolidation method is as follows.

(a) **Net assets**: show what the group controls.

(b) **Equity (capital and reserves)**: show who owns the net assets included elsewhere in the statement of financial position. Reserves (retained earnings), therefore, are based on **effective holdings**.

The basic steps are exactly as you have seen in simpler group structures. As you will see in the examples in this chapter, there are some new complications to be aware of in the workings for **goodwill** and **non-controlling interests**.

2.1 Example: Subsidiary acquired first

The draft statements of financial position of P Co, S Co and SS Co on 30 June 20X7 were as follows.

	P Co	*S Co*	*SS Co*
Assets	$	$	$
Non-current assets			
Tangible assets	105,000	125,000	180,000
Investments, at cost			
80,000 shares in S Co	120,000	–	–
60,000 shares in SS Co	–	110,000	–
Current assets	80,000	70,000	60,000
	305,000	305,000	240,000
Equity and liabilities			
Equity			
Ordinary shares of $1 each	80,000	100,000	100,000
Retained earnings	195,000	170,000	115,000
	275,000	270,000	215,000
Payables	30,000	35,000	25,000
	305,000	305,000	240,000

P Co acquired its shares in S Co on 1 July 20X4 when the reserves of S Co stood at $40,000; and

S Co acquired its shares in SS Co on 1 July 20X5 when the reserves of SS Co stood at $50,000.

It is the group's policy to measure the non-controlling interest at acquisition at its proportionate share of the fair value of the subsidiary's net assets.

Required

Prepare the draft consolidated statement of financial position of P Group at 30 June 20X7.

Note. Assume no impairment of goodwill.

Solution

This is **two acquisitions** from the point of view of the P group. In 20X4, the group buys 80% of S. Then in 20X5 S (which is now part of the P group) buys 60% of SS.

P buys 80% of S, then S (80% of S from the group's point of view) buys 60% of SS.

Having calculated the non-controlling interest and the P group interest (see working 1 below), the workings can be constructed. You should, however, note the following.

(a) **Group structure working** (see working 1).

(b) **Goodwill working**: compare the costs of investments with the effective group interests acquired (80% of S Co and 48% of SS Co).

(c) **Retained earnings working**: bring in the share of S Co's and SS Co's post-acquisition retained earnings in the normal way.

(d) **Non-controlling interest working**: calculate non-controlling interests in the usual way, using a 20% NCI in S Co's post-acquisition retained earnings and a 52% non-controlling interests in SS Co's post acquisition retained earnings (52%). You will need to adjust this for the NCI share of S Co's cost of investment in SS Co.

1 *Group structure*

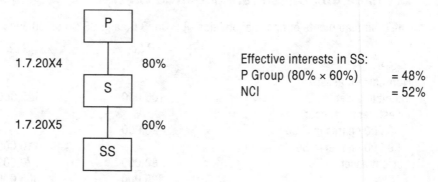

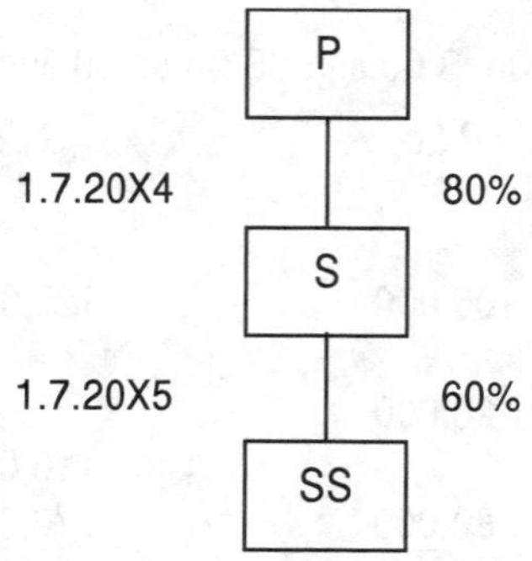

Effective interests in SS:

P Group (80% × 60%)	= 48%
NCI	= 52%

2 *Goodwill*

		P in S		*S in SS*
	$	$	$	$
Consideration transferred		120,000	(80% × 110,000)	88,000
Non-controlling interests	(20% × 140,000)	28,000	(52% × 150,000)	78,000
Fair value of identifiable NA acquired:				
Share capital	100,000		100,000	
Retained earnings	40,000		50,000	
		(140,000)		(150,000)
		8,000		16,000
			24,000	

3 *Retained earnings*

	P Co	*S Co*	*SS Co*
	$	$	$
Per question	195,000	170,000	115,000
Pre-acquisition		(40,000)	(50,000)
Post-acquisition		130,000	65,000
Group share:			
In S Co ($130,000 × 80%)	104,000		
In SS Co ($65,000 × 48%)	31,200		
Group retained earnings	330,200		

4 *Non-controlling interests*

	S	*SS*
	$	$
At acquisition (W2)	28,000	78,000
Share of post acquisition retained earnings ($130,000(W3) × 20%)/ ($65,000(W3) × 52%)	26,000	33,800
Less NCI in investment in SS $110,000 × 20%)	(22,000)	–
	32,000	111,800
	$ 143,800	

P CO
CONSOLIDATED STATEMENT OF FINANCIAL POSITION AT 30 JUNE 20X7

	$
Assets	
Non-current assets	
Tangible assets	410,000
Goodwill	24,000
Current assets	210,000
	644,000
Equity	
Ordinary shares of $1 each fully paid	80,000
Retained earnings	330,200
	410,200
Non-controlling interest	143,800
	554,000
Payables	90,000
	644,000

Note. The cost of the investment in SS Co must be split between the non-controlling interest and the goodwill workings to ensure that we have only P Co's share of the goodwill arising in the S Co subgroup appearing in the consolidated statement of financial position. This is done by taking the group share of the subsidiary's 'cost' in the goodwill working and by deducting the cost from the net assets allocated to the non-controlling interests.

2.2 Date of acquisition

Care must be taken when consolidating sub-subsidiaries, because (usually) either:

(a) The parent company acquired the subsidiary **before** the subsidiary bought the sub-subsidiary (as in the example above)

(b) The parent holding company acquired the subsidiary **after** the subsidiary bought the sub-subsidiary

Depending on whether (a) or (b) is the case, the retained earnings of the subsidiary at acquisition will be different.

The rule to remember here, when considering pre- and post-acquisition profits, is that we are only interested in the consolidated results of the **parent company**. We will use the example above to demonstrate the required approach.

2.3 Example: Sub-subsidiary acquired first

Again using the figures in Section 2.1, assume that:

(a) S Co purchased its holding in SS Co on 1 July 20X4
(b) P Co purchased its holding in S Co on 1 July 20X5

The retained earnings figures on the respective dates of acquisition are the same, but on the date P Co purchased its holding in S Co, the retained earnings of SS Co were $60,000.

It is the group's policy to measure the non-controlling interest at its proportionate share of the fair value of the subsidiary's net assets.

Solution

The point here is that SS Co only became part of the P group on 1 July 20X5, **not** on 1 July 20X4. This means that only the retained earnings of SS Co arising **after** 1 July 20X5 can be included in the post-acquisition reserves of P Co group. Goodwill arising on the acquisition will be calculated by comparing P's share of S's cost of the investment by S in SS to the effective group interests acquired represented by the share capital of SS and its retained earnings **at the date P acquired S** (here $60,000).

P CO
CONSOLIDATED STATEMENT OF FINANCIAL POSITION AS AT 30 JUNE 20X7

	$
Non-current assets	
Tangible	410,000
Goodwill (W2)	19,200
	429,200
Current assets	210,000
	639,200
Equity and liabilities	
Ordinary shares $1 each, fully paid	80,000
Retained earnings (W3)	325,400
	405,400
Non-controlling interest (W4)	143,800
	549,200
Payables	90,000
	639,200

Workings

1 *Group structure*

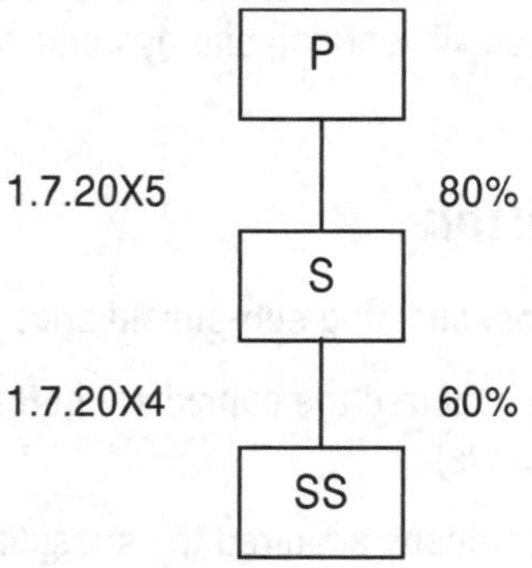

P owns an effective interest of 48% in SS. NCI in SS is 52%.

2 *Goodwill*

The working should be set out as:

	P in S		*S in SS*	
	$	$	$	$
Consideration transferred		120,000	(80% × 110,000)	88,000
Non-controlling interests	(20% × 140,000)	28,000	(52% × 160,000)	83,200
Fair value of identifiable NA acquired:				
Share capital	100,000		100,000	
Retained earnings	40,000		60,000	
		(140,000)		(160,000)
		8,000		11,200
			19,200	

> Retained earnings of SS are as at 1 July 20X5 when P got control of S

Note. Retained earnings of SS are as at 1 July 20X5 when P got control of S.

3 *Retained earnings*

	$
P Co (as above)	195,000
S Co (as above)	104,000
SS Co (115 – 60) × 48%	26,400
	325,400

4 *Non-controlling interests*

The cost of investment in SS is again deducted as the NCI is being calculated on the net assets that have been consolidated (see note above).

	S	*SS*
	$	$
At acquisition (W2)	28,000	83,200
Share of post-acquisition retained earnings (S Co as above)/ ((115 – 60) (W3) × 52%)	26,000	28,600
Less NCI in investment in SS $110,000 × 20%)	(22,000)	–
	32,000	111,800
	$ 143,800	

2.4 Example: Subsidiary acquired first: non-controlling interest at fair value

Exam focus point

The examiner has indicated that fair value NCI will be tested with more difficult group topics.

The draft statements of financial position of P Co, S Co and SS Co on 30 June 20X7 were as follows.

	P Co	*S Co*	*SS Co*
Assets	$	$	$
Non-current assets			
Tangible assets	105,000	125,000	180,000
Investments, at cost			
80,000 shares in S Co	120,000	–	–
60,000 shares in SS Co	–	110,000	–
Current assets	80,000	70,000	60,000
	305,000	305,000	240,000
Equity and liabilities			
Equity			
Ordinary shares of $1 each	80,000	100,000	100,000
Retained earnings	195,000	170,000	115,000
	275,000	270,000	215,000
Payables	30,000	35,000	25,000
	305,000	305,000	240,000

P Co acquired its shares in S Co on 1 July 20X4 when the reserves of S Co stood at $40,000; and

S Co acquired its shares in SS Co on 1 July 20X5 when the reserves of SS Co stood at $50,000.

It is the group's policy to measure the non-controlling interest at fair value at the date of acquisition. The fair value of the non-controlling interests in S on 1 July 20X4 was $29,000. The fair value of the 52% non-controlling interest on 1 July 20X5 was $80,000.

Required

Prepare the draft consolidated statement of financial position of P Group at 30 June 20X7.

Note. Assume no impairment of goodwill.

Solution

The group's policy on measurement of the non-controlling interest at acquisition does not change the steps we follow in the consolidation.

P CO
CONSOLIDATED STATEMENT OF FINANCIAL POSITION AT 30 JUNE 20X7

	$
Assets	
Non-current assets	
Tangible assets	410,000
Goodwill (W2)	27,000
Current assets	210,000
	647,000
Equity	
Ordinary shares of $1 each fully paid	80,000
Retained earnings (W3)	330,200
	410,200
Non-controlling interest (W4)	146,800
	557,000
Payables	90,000
	647,000

1 *Group structure*

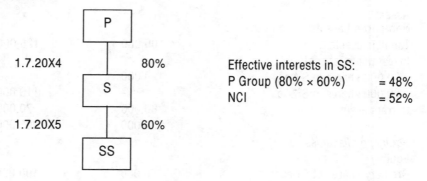

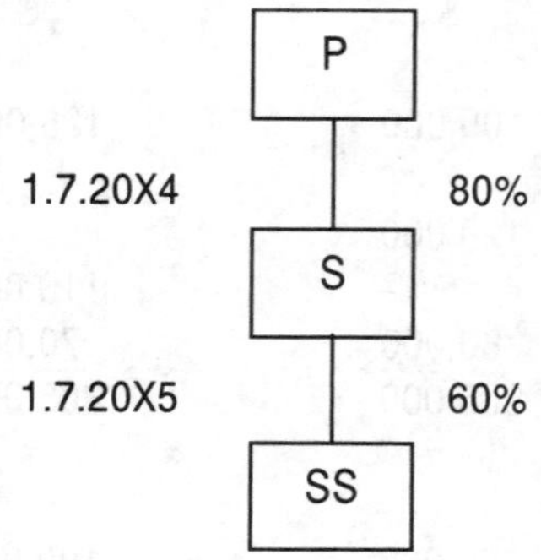

Effective interests in SS:
P Group (80% × 60%) = 48%
NCI = 52%

2 *Goodwill*

	P in S		*S in SS*	
	$	$	$	$
Consideration transferred		120,000	($110,000 × 80%)	88,000
Non-controlling interests (at FV)		29,000		80,000
Fair value of identifiable net assets acquired				
Share capital	100,000		100,000	
Retained earnings	40,000		50,000	
		(140,000)		(150,000)
		9,000		18,000

$27,000

3 *Retained earnings*

	P Co	*S Co*	*SS Co*
	$	$	$
Per question	195,000	170,000	115,000
Pre-acquisition		(40,000)	(50,000)
Post-acquisition		130,000	65,000
Group share:			
In S Co ($130,000 × 80%)	104,000		
In SS Co ($65,000 × 48%)	31,200		
Group retained earnings	330,200		

4 *Non-controlling interests*

The non-controlling interest working in this example has one extra step: adding on the non-controlling interest in goodwill as calculated in working 2. The cost of investment in SS is again deducted as the NCI is being calculated on the net assets that have been consolidated (see note above).

	S	*SS*
	$	$
At acquisition (W2)	29,000	80,000
Share of post acquisition retained earnings ($130,000(W3) × 20%)/ ($65,000(W3) × 52%)	26,000	33,800
Less NCI in investment in SS ($110,000 × 20%)	(22,000)	–
	33,000	113,800

$ 146,800

Question

Sub-subsidiary

The statements of financial position of Antelope Co, Yak Co and Zebra Co at 31 March 20X4 are summarised as follows.

	Antelope Co		*Yak Co*		*Zebra Co*	
	$	$	$	$	$	$
Assets						
Non-current assets						
Freehold property		100,000		100,000		–
Plant and machinery		210,000		80,000		3,000
		310,000		180,000		3,000
Investments in subsidiaries						
Shares, at cost	110,000		6,200			–
Loan account	–		3,800			–
Current accounts	10,000		12,200			–
		120,000		22,200		3,000
Current assets						
Inventories	170,000		20,500		15,000	
Receivables	140,000		50,000		1,000	
Cash at bank	60,000		16,500		4,000	
		370,000		87,000		20,000
		800,000		289,200		23,000
Equity and liabilities						
Equity						
Ordinary share capital	200,000		100,000		10,000	
Retained earnings	379,600		129,200		(1,000)	
		579,600		229,200		9,000

	Antelope Co		Yak Co		Zebra Co	
	$	$	$	$	$	$
Current liabilities						
Trade payables	160,400		40,200		800	
Due to Antelope Co	–		12,800		600	
Due to Yak Co	–				12,600	
Taxation	60,000		7,000		–	
			–		–	
		220,400		60,000		14,000
		800,000		289,200		23,000

Antelope Co acquired 75% of the shares of Yak Co in 20X1 when the credit balance on the retained earnings of that company was $40,000. No dividends have been paid since that date. Yak Co acquired 80% of the shares in Zebra Co in 20X3 when there was a debit balance on the retained earnings of that company of $3,000. Subsequently $500 was received by Zebra Co and credited to its retained earnings, representing the recovery of an irrecoverable debt written off before the acquisition of Zebra's shares by Yak Co. During the year to 31 March 20X4 Yak Co purchased inventory from Antelope Co for $20,000 which included a profit mark-up of $4,000 for Antelope Co. At 31 March 20X4 one half of this amount was still held in the inventories of Yak Co. Group accounting policies are to make a full allowance for unrealised intra-group profits.

It is the group's policy to measure the non-controlling interest at its proportionate share of the fair value of the subsidiary's net assets.

Prepare the draft consolidated statement of financial position of Antelope Co at 31 March 20X4. (Assume no impairment of goodwill.)

Answer

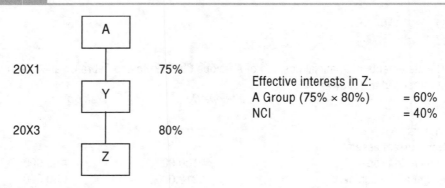

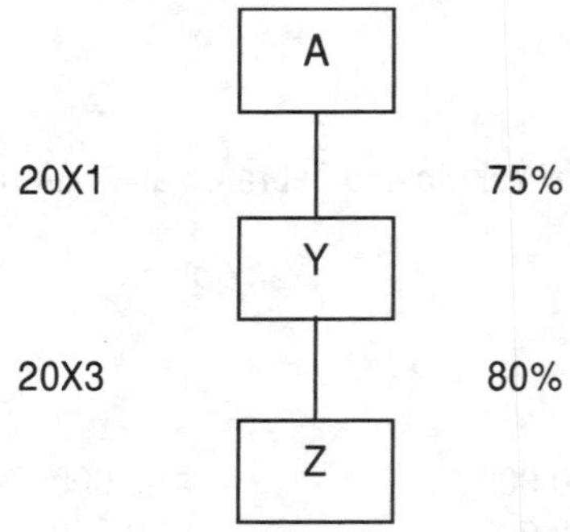

Effective interests in Z:

A Group (75% × 80%)	= 60%
NCI	= 40%

Workings

1 *Goodwill*

	A in Y		*Y in Z*	
	$	$	$	$
Consideration transferred		110,000	(75% × 6,200)	4,650
Non-controlling interests	(25% × 140,000)	35,000	(40% × 7,500)	3,000
Fair value of identifiable NA acquired:				
Share capital	100,000		10,000	
Retained earnings: ($3,000) + $500	40,000		(2,500)	
		(140,000)		(7,500)
		5,000		150
			$5,150	

2 *Retained earnings*

	Antelope	Yak	Zebra
	$	$	$
Per question	379,600	129,200	(1,000)
Adjustment irrecoverable recovery			(500)
Pre-acquisition profit/losses		(40,000)	3,000
Post-acquisition profits		89,200	1,500
Group share			
In Yak ($89,200 × 75%)	66,900		
In Zebra ($1,500 × 60%)	900		
Unrealised profit in inventories sitting in parent ($4,000) × ½)	(2,000)		
Group retained earnings	445,400		

3 *Non-controlling interests*

	Yak	Zebra
	$	$
NCI at acquisition (W1)	35,000	3,000
NCI in post acquisition retained earnings ($89,200 (W2) × 25%)/ ($1,500 (W2) × 40%)	22,300	600
Less NCI share of investment in Zebra ($6,200 × 25%)	(1,550)	–
	55,750	3,600
	59,350	

ANTELOPE CO
CONSOLIDATED STATEMENT OF FINANCIAL POSITION AS AT 31 MARCH 20X4

	$	$
Assets		
Non-current assets		
Freehold property		200,000
Plant and machinery		293,000
		493,000
Goodwill (W1)		5,150
		498,150
Current assets		
Inventories $(205,500 – 2,000)	203,500	
Receivables	191,000	
Cash at bank	80,500	
		475,000
		973,150
Equity and liabilities		
Equity		
Ordinary share capital		200,000
Retained earnings (W2)		445,400
Shareholders' funds		645,400
Non-controlling interests (W3)		59,350
		704,750
Current liabilities		
Trade payables	201,400	
Taxation	67,000	
		268,400
		973,150

2.5 Section summary

You should follow this **step by step approach** in all questions using the single-stage method. This applies to Section 3 below as well.

Step 1 Sketch the group **structure** and check it to the question.

Step 2 **Add details** to the sketch of dates of acquisition, holdings acquired (percentage and nominal values) and cost.

Step 3 Draw up a proforma **for the statement of financial position**.

Step 4 **Work** methodically down the statement of financial position, transferring figures to proforma or workings.

Step 5 Use the notes in the question to make adjustments such as eliminating intra-group balances and unrealised profits.

Step 6 **Goodwill working**. Compare consideration transferred with **effective** group interests acquired.

Step 7 **Reserves working**. Include the group share of subsidiary and sub-subsidiary post-acquisition retained earnings (effective holdings again).

Step 8 **Non-controlling interests working**: total NCI in subsidiary plus total NCI in sub-subsidiary.

Step 9 Prepare the **consolidated statement of financial position** (and statement of profit or loss and other comprehensive income if required).

3 Direct holdings in sub-subsidiaries 6/13

FAST FORWARD

'D shaped' groups are consolidated in the same way as a typical sub-subsidiary situation. It is the structure and non-controlling interest calculations that are important.

Consider the following structure, sometimes called a **'D-shaped' group**.

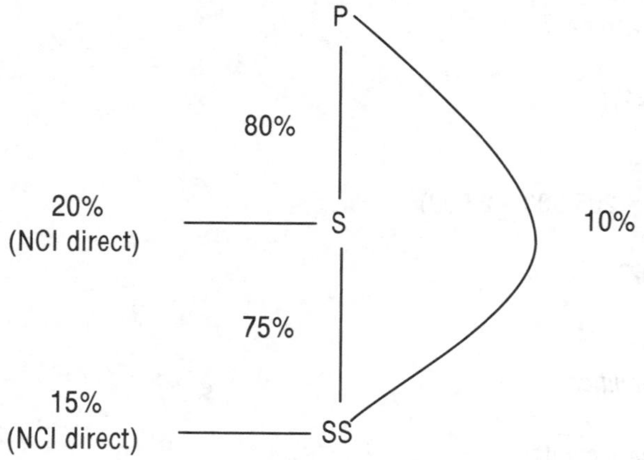

In the structure above, there is:

(a)	A **direct** non-controlling share in S of		20%
(b)	A **direct** non-controlling share in SS of	15%	
(c)	An **indirect** non-controlling share in SS of 20% × 75% =	15%	
			30%

The effective interest in SS is:

Group 80% × 75%	=	60% interest
Direct holding		10%
		70%
∴ NCI		30%
		100%

Having ascertained the structure and non-controlling interests, proceed as for a typical sub-subsidiary situation.

Question — 'D' shaped group

The draft statements of financial position of Hulk Co, Molehill Co and Pimple Co as at 31 May 20X5 are as follows.

	Hulk Co		*Molehill Co*		*Pimple Co*	
	$	$	$	$	$	$
Assets						
Non-current assets						
Tangible assets		90,000		60,000		60,000
Investments in subsidiaries(cost)						
Shares in Molehill Co	90,000		–		–	
Shares in Pimple Co	25,000		42,000		–	
		115,000		42,000		–
		205,000		102,000		60,000
Current assets		40,000		50,000		40,000
		245,000		152,000		100,000
Equity and liabilities						
Equity						
Ordinary shares $1	100,000		50,000		50,000	
Revaluation surplus	50,000		20,000			
Retained earnings	45,000		32,000		25,000	
		195,000		102,000		75,000
Non-current liabilities						
12% loan		–		10,000		–
		195,000		112,000		75,000
Current liabilities						
Payables		50,000		40,000		25,000
		245,000		152,000		100,000

(a) Hulk Co acquired 60% of the shares in Molehill on 1 January 20X3 when the balance on that company's retained earnings was $8,000 (credit) and there was no share premium account.

(b) Hulk acquired 20% of the shares of Pimple Co and Molehill acquired 60% of the shares of Pimple Co on 1 January 20X4 when that company's retained earnings stood at $15,000.

(c) There has been no payment of dividends by either Molehill or Pimple since they became subsidiaries.

(d) There was no impairment of goodwill.

(e) It is the group's policy to measure the non-controlling interest at acquisition at its proportionate share of the fair value of the subsidiary's net assets.

Required

Prepare the consolidated statement of financial position of Hulk Co as at 31 May 20X5.

Answer

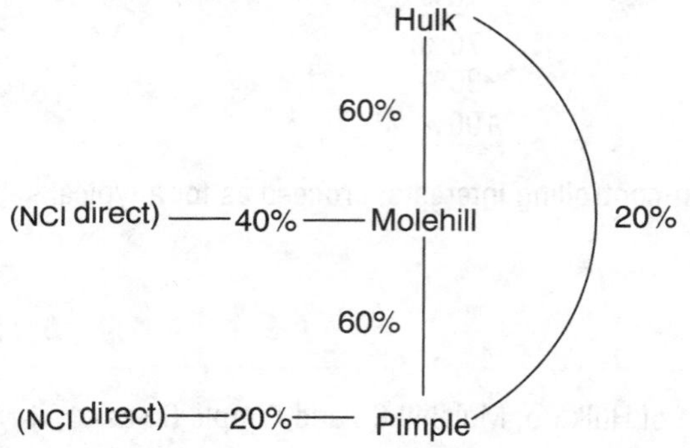

Effective interests in Pimple:
Hulk (60% × 60% + 20%) = 56%
∴ NCI = 44%

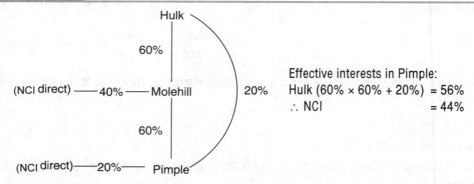

Note. Pimple comes into Hulk's control on 1 January 20X4. As the investments in Pimple by Hulk and Molehill both happened on the same date, only one goodwill calculation is needed in respect of Pimple.

The direct non-controlling interest in Molehill Co is		40%
The direct non-controlling interest in Pimple Co is	20%	
The indirect non-controlling interest in Pimple Co is (40% of 60%)	24%	
The total non-controlling interest in Pimple Co is		44%

The group share of Molehill Co is 60% and of Pimple Co is (100 – 44)% = 56%

Workings

1 *Goodwill*

	Hulk in Molehill		*Hulk and Molehill in Pimple*	
	$	$	$	$
Consideration transferred –direct		90,000		25,000
– indirect			(60% × 42,000)	25,200
Non-controlling interests ($58,000 × 40%)/ ($65,000 × 44%)		23,200		28,600
Fair value at NA acquired				
Share capital	50,000		50,000	
Retained earnings	8,000		15,000	
		(58,000)		(65,000)
		55,200		13,800

$69,000

2 *Retained earnings*

	Hulk	*Molehill*	*Pimple*
	$	$	$
Per question	45,000	32,000	25,000
Pre-acquisition profits		(8,000)	(15,000)
Post-acquisition retained earnings		24,000	10,000
Group share:			
In Molehill ($24,000 × 60%)	14,400		
In Pimple ($10,000 × 56%)	5,600		
Group retained earnings	65,000		

3 *Revaluation surplus*

	$
Hulk Co	50,000
Molehill Co: all post-acquisition ($20,000 × 60%)	12,000
	62,000

4 *Non-controlling interests*

	Molehill	Pimple
	$	$
NCI at acquisition (W1)	23,200	28,600
NCI in post acquisition retained earnings ($24,000 (W2) × 40%)/ ($10,000 (W2) × 44%)	9,600	4,400
NCI in post-acquisition revaluation surplus ($20,000 (W3) × 40%)	8,000	–
Less NCI share of investment in Pimple ($42,000 × 40%)	(16,800)	–
	24,000	33,000
	$57,000	

HULK CO
CONSOLIDATED STATEMENT OF FINANCIAL POSITION AS AT 31 MAY 20X8

	$	$
Assets		
Non-current assets		
Tangible assets	210,000	
Goodwill (W1)	69,000	
		279,000
Current assets		130,000
		409,000
Equity and liabilities		
Equity		
Ordinary shares $1	100,000	
Revaluation surplus (W3)	62,000	
Retained earnings (W2)	65,000	
Shareholders' funds	227,000	
Non-controlling interests (W4)	57,000	
		284,000
Non-current liabilities		
12% loan		10,000
		294,000
Current liabilities		
Payables		115,000
		409,000

4 IFRS 11 *Joint arrangements* 6/12, 12/14

FAST FORWARD

IFRS 11 classes joint arrangements as either **joint operations** or **joint ventures**.

The classification of a joint arrangement as a joint operation or a joint venture depends upon the **rights and obligations** of the parties to the arrangement.

Joint arrangements are often found when each party can **contribute in different ways** to the activity. For example, one party may provide finance, another purchases or manufactures goods, while a third offers its marketing skills.

IFRS 11 *Joint arrangements* covers all types of joint arrangements. It is not concerned with the accounts of the joint arrangement itself (if separate accounts are maintained), but rather **how the interest in a joint arrangement is accounted for by each** party.

4.1 Definitions

The IFRS begins by listing some important definitions.

Key terms

Joint arrangement. An arrangement of which two or more parties have joint control.

Joint control. The contractually agreed sharing of control of an arrangement, which exists only when decisions about the relevant activities require the unanimous consent of the parties sharing control.

Joint operation. A joint arrangement whereby the parties that have joint control of the arrangement have rights to the assets and obligations for the liabilities relating to the arrangement.

Joint venture. A joint arrangement whereby the parties that have joint control of the arrangement have rights to the net assets of the arrangement.

(IFRS 11: Appendix A)

4.2 Forms of joint arrangement

IFRS 11 classes joint arrangements as either joint operations or joint ventures. The classification of a joint arrangement as a joint operation or a joint venture depends upon the rights and obligations of the parties to the arrangement.

A **joint operation** is a joint arrangement whereby the parties that have joint control (the joint operators) have rights to the assets, and obligations for the liabilities, of that joint arrangement. A joint arrangement that is **not structured through a separate entity** is always a joint operation. (IFRS 11: para. 15)

A **joint venture** is a joint arrangement whereby the parties that have **joint control** (the joint venturers) of the arrangement have **rights to the net assets** of the arrangement. (IFRS 11: para. 16)

A **joint arrangement** that is structured through a **separate entity** may be either a joint operation or a joint venture. In order to ascertain the classification, the parties to the arrangement should assess the terms of the contractual arrangement together with any other facts or circumstances to assess whether they have:

- Rights to the assets, and obligations for the liabilities, in relation to the arrangement (indicating a joint operation)
- Rights to the net assets of the arrangement (indicating a joint venture)

Detailed guidance is provided in the appendices to IFRS 11 in order to help this assessment, giving consideration to, for example, the wording contained within contractual arrangements.

(IFRS 11: AG, para. B21)

IFRS 11 summarises the basic issues that underlie the classifications in the following diagram (IFRS 11: AG para. B21).

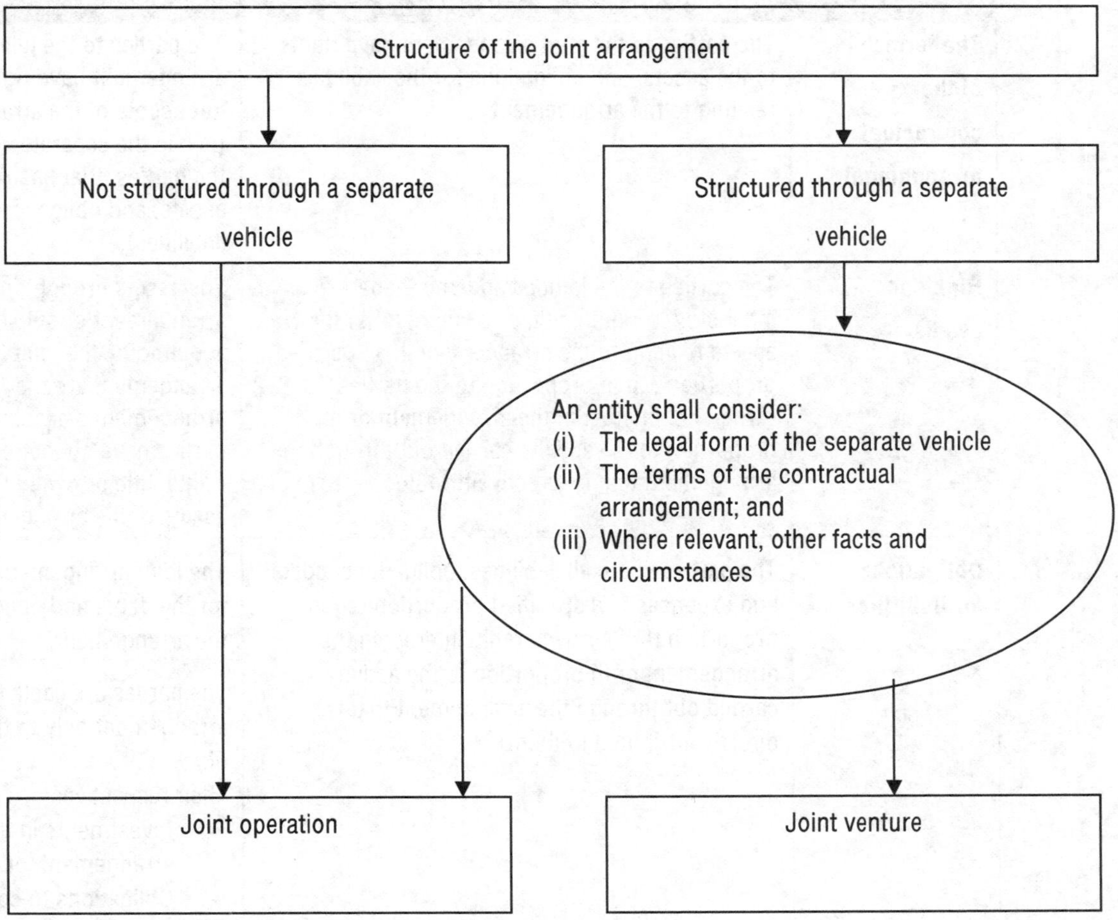

4.2.1 Contractual arrangement

The existence of a contractual agreement distinguishes a joint arrangement from an investment in an associate. **If there is no contractual arrangement, then a joint arrangement does not exist.**

Evidence of a contractual arrangement could be in one of several forms.

- **Contract** between the parties
- **Minutes** of discussion between the parties
- Incorporation in the **articles or by-laws** of the joint venture

The contractual arrangement is usually **in writing**, whatever its form, and it will deal with the following issues surrounding the joint venture.

- **Its activity, duration and reporting obligations**
- The appointment of its **board of directors** (or equivalent) and the **voting rights** of the parties
- **Capital contributions** to it by the parties
- How its output, income, expenses or results are **shared** between the parties

It is the contractual arrangement which establishes **joint control** over the joint venture, so that no single party can control the activity of the joint venture on its own. (IFRS 11: AG, para. B2, B4)

The terms of the contractual arrangement are key to deciding whether the arrangement is a joint venture or joint operation. IFRS 11 includes a table of issues to consider and explains the influence of a range of points that could be included in the contract (IFRS 11: AG, para. B27). The table is summarised below.

	Joint operation	Joint venture
The terms of the contractual arrangement	The parties to the joint arrangement have rights to the assets, and obligations for the liabilities, relating to the arrangement.	The parties to the joint arrangement have rights to the **net assets** of the arrangement (ie it is the separate vehicle, not the parties, that has rights to the assets, and obligations for the liabilities).
Rights to assets	The parties to the joint arrangement share all interests (eg rights, title or ownership) in the assets relating to the arrangement in a specified proportion (eg in proportion to the parties' ownership interest in the arrangement or in proportion to the activity carried out through the arrangement that is directly attributed to them).	The assets brought into the arrangement or subsequently acquired by the joint arrangement are the arrangement's assets. The parties have no interests (ie no rights, title or ownership) in the assets of the arrangement.
Obligations for liabilities	The parties share all liabilities, obligations, costs and expenses in a specified proportion (eg in proportion to their ownership interest in the arrangement or in proportion to the activity carried out through the arrangement that is directly attributed to them).	The joint arrangement is liable for the debts and obligations of the arrangement.
		The parties are liable to the arrangement only to the extent of: Their respective: • Investments in the arrangement, or • Obligations to contribute any unpaid or additional capital to the arrangement, or • Both
	The parties to the joint arrangement are liable for claims by third parties.	Creditors of the joint arrangement do not have rights of recourse against any party.
Revenues, expenses, profit or loss	The contractual arrangement establishes the allocation of revenues and expenses on the basis of the relative performance of each party to the joint arrangement. For example, the contractual arrangement might establish that revenues and expenses are allocated on the basis of the capacity that each party uses in a plant operated jointly.	The contractual arrangement establishes each party's share in the profit or loss relating to the activities of the arrangement.
Guarantees	The provision of guarantees to third parties, or the commitment by the parties to provide them, does not, by itself, determine that the joint arrangement is a joint operation.	

4.2.2 Section summary

- There are two **types of joint arrangement**: joint ventures and jointly controlled operations.
- A **contractual arrangement** must exist which establishes joint control.
- **Joint control** is important: one **operator** must not be able to govern the financial and operating policies of the joint venture.

Question

Joint arrangement

This question is based on Illustrative example 2 from IFRS 11 (IFRS 11: IE2).

Two real estate companies (the parties) set up a separate vehicle (Supermall) for the purpose of acquiring and operating a shopping centre. The contractual arrangement between the parties establishes joint control of the activities that are conducted in Supermall. The main feature of Supermall's legal form is that the entity, not the parties, has rights to the assets, and obligations for the liabilities, relating to the arrangement. These activities include the rental of the retail units, managing the car park, maintaining the centre and its equipment, such as lifts, and building the reputation and customer base for the centre as a whole.

The terms of the contractual arrangement are such that:

(a) Supermall owns the shopping centre. The contractual arrangement does not specify that the parties have rights to the shopping centre.

(b) The parties are not liable in respect of the debts, liabilities or obligations of Supermall. If Supermall is unable to pay any of its debts or other liabilities or to discharge its obligations to third parties, the liability of each party to any third party will be limited to the unpaid amount of that party's capital contribution.

(c) The parties have the right to sell or pledge their interests in Supermall.

(d) Each party receives a share of the income from operating the shopping centre (which is the rental income net of the operating costs) in accordance with its interest in Supermall.

Required

Explain how Supermall should be classified in accordance with IFRS 11 *Joint arrangements.*

Answer

Supermall has been set up as a **separate vehicle**. As such, it could be either a joint operation or joint venture, so other facts must be considered.

There are no facts that suggest that the two real estate companies have rights to substantially all the benefits of the assets of Supermall nor an obligation for its liabilities.

Each party's liability is limited to any unpaid capital contribution.

As a result, each party has an interest in the **net assets** of Supermall and should account for it as a **joint venture** using the **equity method**.

IFRS 11 contains many examples illustrating the principles of how to classify joint arrangements, you can find them at: www.iasb.org

4.3 Accounting treatment

FAST FORWARD

The accounting treatment of joint arrangements depends on whether the arrangement is a joint venture or joint operation.

4.3.1 Accounting for joint operations

IFRS 11 requires that a joint operator recognises line-by-line the following in relation to its interest in a joint operation (IFRS 11: paras. 20, 26):

(a) Its assets, including its share of any jointly held assets
(b) Its liabilities, including its share of any jointly incurred liabilities
(c) Its revenue from the sale of its share of the output arising from the joint operation
(d) Its share of the revenue from the sale of the output by the joint operation, and
(e) Its expenses, including its share of any expenses incurred jointly.

This treatment is applicable in both the separate and consolidated financial statements of the joint operator.

Question — **Joint operations**

Can you think of examples of situations where this type of arrangement might take place?

Answer

IFRS 1 gives examples in the oil, gas and mineral extraction industries. In such industries companies may, say, jointly control and operate on oil or gas pipeline. Each company transports its own products down the pipeline and pays an agreed proportion of the expenses of operating the pipeline (perhaps based on volume). In this case the parties have rights to assets (such as exploration permits and the oil or gas produced by the activities).

A further example is a property which is jointly controlled, each venturer taking a share of the rental income and bearing a portion of the expense.

Exam focus point

A joint operation was tested as part of the compulsory group case study question.

4.3.2 Joint ventures

FAST FORWARD

IFRS 11 and **IAS 28** require **joint ventures** to be accounted for using **the equity method.**

Prior to the set of group accounting standards issued in 2011, the old standard on joint ventures (IAS 31) permitted either equity accounting or proportionate consolidation to be used for joint ventures. The choice has now been removed. (Proportionate consolidation meant including the investor's share of the assets, liabilities, income and expenses of the joint venture, line by line.)

The rules for equity accounting are included in IAS 28 *Associates and joint ventures.* These have been covered in detail in Chapter 12.

4.3.3 Application of IAS 28 (2011) to joint ventures

The consolidated statement of financial position is prepared by (IAS 28: para. 27):

- Including the interest in the joint venture at cost plus share of post-acquisition total comprehensive income
- Including the group share of the post-acquisition total comprehensive income in group reserves

The consolidated statement of profit or loss and other comprehensive income will include:

- The group share of the joint venture's profit or loss
- The group share of the joint venture's other comprehensive income

The use of the equity method should be **discontinued** from the date on which the joint venturer ceases to have joint control over, or have significant influence on, a joint venture.

4.3.4 Transactions between a joint venturer and a joint venture

Upstream transactions

A joint venturer may **sell or contribute assets** to a joint venture so making a profit or loss. Any such gain or loss should, however, only be recognised to the extent that it reflects the substance of the transaction.

Therefore:

- Only the **gain** attributable to the interest of the other joint venturers should be recognised in the financial statements.
- The full amount of any **loss** should be recognised when the transaction shows evidence that the net realisable value of current assets is less than cost, or that there is an impairment loss.

Downstream transactions

When a joint venturer purchases assets from a joint venture, the joint venturer should not recognise its share of the profit made by the joint venture on the transaction in question until it resells the assets to an independent third party, ie until the profit is realised.

Losses should be treated in the same way, **except** losses should be recognised immediately if they represent a reduction in the net realisable value of current assets, or a permanent decline in the carrying amount of non-current assets.

(IAS 28: paras. 28 and 29)

4.3.5 Accounting for acquisition of an interest in a joint operation

IFRS 11 was amended in 2014 to address the issue of how to account for the acquisition of a joint operation. Guidance on this issue was not previously included in IFRS 11 and as a result divergence in practice has emerged:

- Some entities have applied the principles of IFRS 3 *Business combinations* and allocated consideration to the fair value of assets and liabilities acquired, recognising any excess as goodwill.
- Other entities have allocated consideration to assets and liabilities on the basis of their relative fair values, and so not recognised goodwill.

The amendment therefore clarifies that the principles of IFRS 3 must be applied on the acquisition of an interest in a joint operation where that joint operation constitutes a business as defined by IFRS 3. Therefore on the acquisition of a joint operation meeting the definition of a business, the joint operator must:

(a) Measure the identifiable assets and liabilities at fair value (or in accordance with IFRS 3)
(b) Recognise acquisition costs in accordance with IFRS 3
(c) Recognise goodwill for the excess consideration given
(d) Perform an impairment test for the cash-generating unit to which goodwill is allocated annually

The amendments are effective from 1 January 2016.

(IFRS 11: para. 21A, AG paras. 33A to D)

4.3.6 Section summary

- **Joint operations** are accounted for by including the investor's share of assets, liabilities, income and expenses as per the contractual arrangement
- **Joint ventures** are accounted for using the **equity method** as under IAS 28

Chapter Roundup

- When a holding company has **several subsidiaries**, the consolidated statement of financial position shows a single figure for non-controlling interests and for goodwill arising on consolidation. In cases where there are several subsidiary companies the technique is to open up a single non-controlling interest working and a single goodwill working.
- When dealing with **sub-subsidiaries,** you will need to calculate effective interest owned by the group and by the non-controlling interest. The date of acquisition is important when dealing with sub-subsidiaries. Remember that it is the post-acquisition reserves from a group perspective which are important.
- **'D shaped' groups** are consolidated in the same way as a typical sub-subsidiary situation. It is the structure and non-controlling interest calculations that are important.
- **IFRS 11** classes joint arrangements as either **joint operations** or **joint ventures**.
- The accounting treatment of **joint arrangements** depends on whether the arrangement is a joint venture or joint operation.
- **IFRS 11** and **IAS 28** require **joint ventures** to be accounted for using **the equity method.**

Quick Quiz

1. B Co owns 60% of the equity of C Co which owns 75% of the equity of D Co. What is the total non-controlling interest percentage ownership in D Co?
2. What is the basic consolidation method for sub-subsidiaries?
3. P Co owns 25% of R Co's equity and 75% of Q Co's equity. Q Co owns 40% of R Co's equity. What is the total non-controlling interest percentage ownership in R Co?
4. A joint venture is a joint arrangement whereby the parties that have_______________ of the arrangement have rights to the_____________ of the arrangement.
5. What forms of evidence of a contractual agreement might exist?
6. How should a venturer account for its share of a joint operation?
7. How should a venturer account for its share of a joint venture?
8. A joint arrangement that is structured through a separate vehicle will always be a joint venture. *True or false*?

Answers to Quick Quiz

1

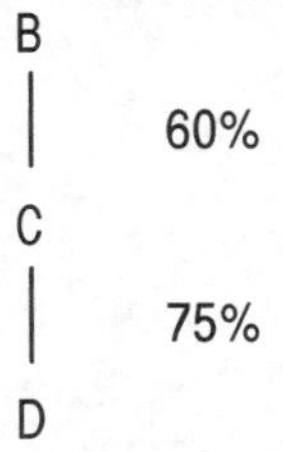

Non-controlling interest = 25% + (40% of 75%) = 55%

2
- Net assets: show what the group controls
- Equity (capital and reserves): show who owns the net assets

3

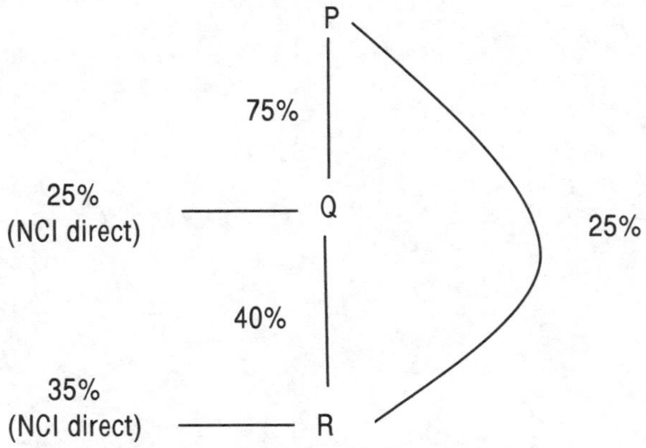

Total non-controlling interest in R is 35% + (25% × 40%) = 45%

4 A joint venture is a joint arrangement whereby the parties that have **joint control** of the arrangement have rights to the **net assets** of the arrangement.

5
- Contractual arrangement
- Joint control

6 (a) The assets it controls and the liabilities it incurs
(b) The expenses it incurs and the income it earns

7 A joint venture is accounted for using the equity method as required by IAS 28 *Associates and joint ventures.*

8 False. Joint arrangements that are structured through a separate vehicle may be either joint ventures or joint arrangements. The classification will depend on whether the venturer has rights to the **net assets** of the arrangement. This will depend on the terms of the contractual arrangements.

Now try the question below from the Practice Question Bank

Number	Level	Marks	Time
Q18	Examination	10	20 mins
Q19	Examination	18	35 mins
Q20	Examination	25	49 mins

14

Changes in group structures

Topic list	Syllabus reference
1 Business combinations achieved in stages	D1, D3
2 Acquisitions and disposals where control is retained	D1, D3
3 Disposals	D1, D3
4 Changes in direct ownership	D1, D3

Introduction

Complex consolidation issues are very likely to come up in this, the final stage of your studies on financial accounting. Your approach should be the same as for more simple consolidation questions: **methodical and logical**. If you understand the basic principles of consolidation, you should be able to tackle these complicated questions.

Purchase and sales within the group are dealt with in Section 4.

Study guide

		Intellectual level
D1	**Group accounting including statements of cash flows**	
(c)	Apply the recognition and measurement criteria for identifiable acquired assets and liabilities and goodwill including step acquisitions	3
D3	**Changes in group structure**	
(a)	Discuss the reasons behind a group reorganisation	3
(b)	Evaluate and assess the principal terms of a proposed group reorganisation	3

Exam guide

The examiner likes to test business combinations achieved in stages, sometimes called step or piecemeal acquisitions.

PER alert

One of the competences you need to fulfil Objective 10 of the Practical Experience Requirement (PER) is to prepare financial statements for single companies and combined entities. You can apply the knowledge you obtain from this Chapter, on combined entities, to demonstrate this competence.

1 Business combinations achieved in stages

12/07, 6/09, 12/09, 12/11, 6/12, 12/14, 6/15

FAST FORWARD

Transactions of the type described in this chapter can be very complicated and certainly look rather daunting. Remember and apply the **basic techniques** and you should find such questions easier than you expected.

Business combinations achieved in stages (piecemeal acquisitions) can lead to a company becoming an investment in equity instruments, an associate and then a subsidiary over time. Make sure you can deal with each of these situations.

Note. You may sometimes see the term 'trade investment' or just 'financial asset' instead of 'investment in equity instruments'. The main point to note is that the investment is not an associate or a subsidiary.

A parent company may acquire a controlling interest in the shares of a subsidiary as a result of **several successive share purchases**, rather than by purchasing the shares all on the same day. Business combinations achieved in stages may also be known as 'piecemeal acquisitions'.

1.1 Types of business combination achieved in stages

There are three possible types of business combinations achieved in stages:

(a) A previously held **interest**, say 10%, with **no significant influence** (accounted for under IFRS 9) is **increased to a controlling interest** of 50% or more.

(b) A **previously held equity interest**, say 35%, accounted for as an **associate** under IAS 28, is increased to a controlling interest of 50% or more.

(c) A **controlling interest** in a subsidiary is **increased**, say from 60% to 80%.

The first two transactions are treated in the same way, but the third is not. There is a reason for this.

1.2 General principle: 'Crossing an accounting boundary'

Under IFRS 3 *Business combinations,* a business combination occurs only when one entity **obtains control over another**, which is generally when 50% or more has been acquired. The Deloitte guide: *Business Combinations and Changes in Ownership interests* calls this '**crossing an accounting boundary**'.

When this happens, the original investment – whether an investment in equity instruments with no significant influence, or an associate – is treated as if it were **disposed of at fair value and re-acquired at fair value**. This **previously held interest** at fair value, together with any consideration transferred, is the **'cost' of the combination** used in calculating the goodwill.

If the 50% **boundary is not crossed**, as when the interest in a subsidiary is increased, the event is treated as a **transaction between owners.**

Whenever you cross the 50% boundary, you revalue, and a gain or loss is reported in profit or loss for the year. If you do not cross the 50% boundary, no gain or loss is reported; instead there is an adjustment to the parent's equity.

The following diagram, from the *Deloitte* guide may help you visualise the boundary:

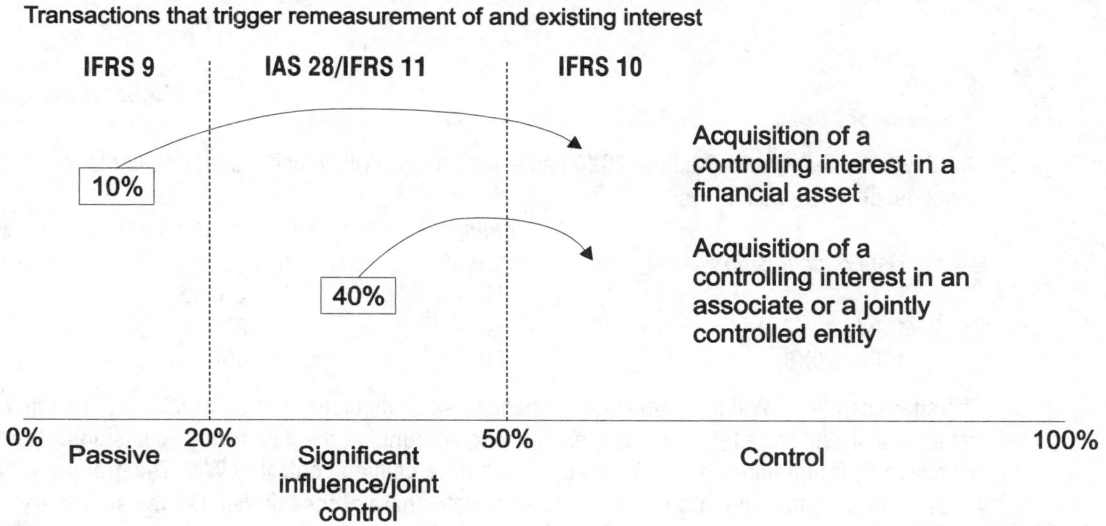

As you will see from the diagram, the third situation in Paragraph 1.1, where an interest in a subsidiary is increased from, say, 60% to 80%, does not involve crossing that all-important 50% threshold. Likewise, purchases of stakes of up to 50% do not involve crossing the boundary, and therefore do not trigger a calculation of goodwill. (Deloitte, 2008, Section 2.2)

Exam focus point

In an exam, if you get a question with a business combination achieved in stages, ignore all purchases made before control is achieved, that is purchases bringing the total holding to less than 50%.

1.3 Investment or associate becomes a subsidiary: calculation of goodwill

The previously held investment is re-measured to fair value, with any gain being reported in profit or loss, and the goodwill calculated as follows.

Consideration transferred	X
Non-controlling interest (at %FV of new assets or 'full' FV)	X
Fair value of acquirer's previously held equity interest	X
Less net fair value of identifiable assets acquired and liabilities assumed	(X)
	X

Point to note

> The gain or loss is recognised in **profit or loss** unless the equity interest previously held was an investment in equity instruments and an **irrevocable election** was made to hold the investment **at fair value through other comprehensive income**. In the latter case, in accordance with IFRS 9 (revised October 2010), the gain on derecognition of the investment is taken to other comprehensive income, or, in the SOFP, other components of equity.

1.3.1 Analogy: trading in a small car for a larger one

It may seem counter-intuitive that the previous investment is now part of the 'cost' for the purposes of calculating the goodwill. One way of looking at it is to imagine that you are part-exchanging a small car for a larger one. The value of the car you trade in is put towards the cost of the new vehicle, together with your cash (the 'consideration transferred'). Likewise, the company making the acquisition has part-exchanged its smaller investment – at fair value – for a larger one, and must naturally pay on top of that to obtain the larger investment.

This analogy is not exact, but may help.

Try the following question to get the hang of the calculation of goodwill and profit on de-recognition of the investment.

Question

Piecemeal acquisition 2

Good, whose year end is 30 June 20X9 has a subsidiary, Will, which it acquired in stages. The details of the acquisition are as follows.

Date of acquisition	*Holding acquired*	*Retained earnings at acquisition*	*Purchase consideration*
	%	$m	$m
1 July 20X7	20	270	120
1 July 20X8	60	450	480

The share capital of Will has remained unchanged since its incorporation at $300m. The fair values of the net assets of Will were the same as their carrying amounts at the date of the acquisition. Good did not have significant influence over Will at any time before gaining control of Will. The group policy is to measure non-controlling interest at its proportionate share of the fair value of the subsidiary's identifiable net assets.

Required

(a) Calculate the goodwill on the acquisition of Will that will appear in the consolidated statement of financial position at 30 June 20X9.

(b) Calculate the profit on the derecognition of any previously held investment in Will to be reported in group profit or loss for the year ended 30 June 20X9.

Answer

(a) *Goodwill (at date control obtained)*

	$m	$m
Consideration transferred		480
NCI (20% × 750)		150
Fair value of previously held equity interest ($480m × 20/60)		160
Fair value of identifiable assets acquired and liabilities assumed		
Share capital	300	
Retained earnings	450	
		(750)
		40

(b) *Profit on derecognition of investment*

	$m
Fair value at date control obtained (see part (a))	160
Cost	(120)
	40

In this short example, the figures for goodwill and profit on derecognition are the same. In the more complicated examples, such as the one in Paragraph 1.4 below, they may different because the investment (an investment in equity instruments) may be revalued before or after control was obtained.

1.4 Comprehensive example: Acquisition of a subsidiary in stages

Exam focus point

> The examiner has strongly indicated that he is more likely to test non-controlling interest at fair value in the group question in the exam. Accordingly, this example has fair value NCI. Additionally, the questions in the question bank at the end of this Study Text have fair value NCI.

Oscar acquired 25% of Tigger on 1 January 20X1 for $2,020,000 and exercised significant influence over the financial and operating policy decisions of Tigger. The fair value of Tigger's identifiable assets and liabilities at that date was equivalent to their book value, and Tigger's reserves stood at $5,800,000.

A further 35% stake in Tigger was acquired on 30 September 20X2 for $4,200,000 (paying a premium over Tigger's market share price to achieve control). The fair value of Tigger's identifiable assets and liabilities at that date was $9,200,000, and Tigger's reserves stood at $7,800,000.

At 30 September 20X2, Tigger's share price was $14.50.

Summarised statements of financial position of the two companies at 31 December 20X2 show:

	Oscar	*Tigger*
	$'000	$'000
Non-current assets		
Property, plant and equipment	38,650	7,600
Investment in Tigger (cost)	6,220	–
	44,870	7,600
Current assets	12,700	2,200
	57,570	9,800
Equity		
Share capital ($1 shares)	10,200	800
Reserves	39,920	7,900
	50,120	8,700
Liabilities	7,450	1,100
	57,570	9,800

Summarised statements of profit or loss and other comprehensive income for the year to 31 December 20X2:

	Oscar	*Tigger*
	$'000	$'000
Revenue	10,200	4,000
Cost of sales and expenses	(9,000)	(3,600)
Profit before tax	1,200	400
Income tax expense	(360)	(80)
Profit for the year	840	320
Other comprehensive income:		
Items that will not be reclassified to profit or loss:		
Gain on property valuation, net of tax	240	80
Other comprehensive income for the year, net of tax	240	80
Total comprehensive income for the year	1,080	400

The difference between the fair value of the identifiable assets and liabilities of Tigger and their book value relates to Tigger's brands. The brands were estimated to have an average remaining useful life of 5 years from 30 September 20X2.

Income and expenses are assumed to accrue evenly over the year. Neither company paid dividends during the year.

Oscar elected to measure non-controlling interests at the date of acquisition at fair value. No impairment losses on recognised goodwill have been necessary to date.

Required

Prepare the consolidated statement of financial position as at 31 December 20X2 and the consolidated statement of profit or loss and other comprehensive income of the Oscar Group for the year ended 31 December 20X2.

Solution

OSCAR GROUP

CONSOLIDATED STATEMENT OF FINANCIAL POSITION AS AT 31 DECEMBER 20X2

	$'000
Non-current assets	
Property, plant and equipment (38,650 + 7,600)	46,250
Goodwill (W2)	2,540
Other intangible assets (W6)	570
	49,360
Current assets (12,700 + 2,200)	14,900
	64,260
Equity attributable to owners of the parent	
Share capital	10,200
Reserves (W3)	40,842
	51,042
Non-controlling interests (W4)	4,668
	55,710
Liabilities (7,450 + 1,100)	8,550
	64,260

OSCAR GROUP
CONSOLIDATED STATEMENT OF PROFIT OR LOSS AND OTHER COMPREHENSIVE INCOME
FOR THE YEAR ENDED 31 DECEMBER 20X2

	$'000
Revenue (10,200 + (4,000 × 3/12))	11,200
Cost of sales and expenses (9,000 + (3,600 × 3/12) + (W5) 30)	(9,930)
Profit on derecognition of associate (W7)	380
Share of profit of associate (320 × 9/12 × 25%)	60
Profit before tax	1,710
Income tax expense (360 + (80 × 3/12))	(380)
Profit for the year	1,330
Other comprehensive income:	
Items that will not be reclassified to profit or loss:	
Gains on property revaluation, net of tax (240 + (80 × 3/12))	260
Share of gain on property revaluation of associate (80 × 9/12 × 25%)	15
Other comprehensive income for the year, net of tax	275
Total comprehensive income for the year	1,605
Profit attributable to:	
Owners of parent	1,310
Non-controlling interests (W5)	20
	1,330
Total comprehensive income attributable to:	
Owners of parent	1,577
Non-controlling interests (W5)	28
	1,605

Workings

1 *Group structure*

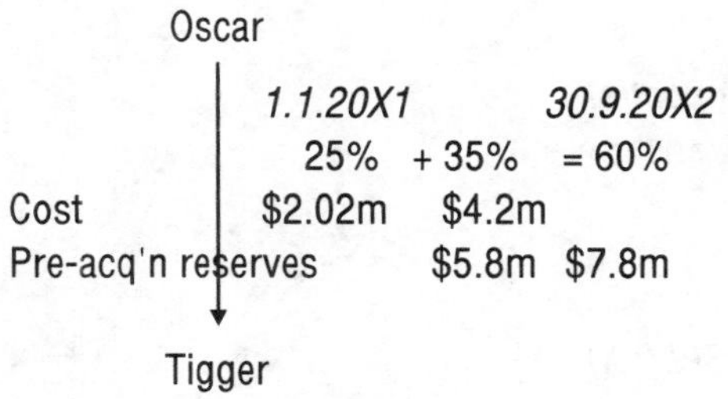

Timeline

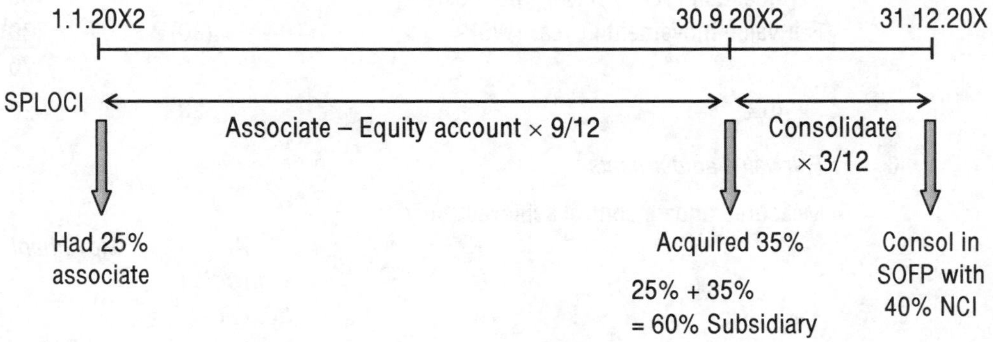

2 *Goodwill*

	$'000	$'000
Consideration transferred		4,200
Non-controlling interests (800,000 × 40% × $14.50)		4,640
FV of P's previously held equity interest *(800,000 × 25% × $14.50)*		*2,900*
Fair value of identifiable assets acq'd & liabilities assumed at acq'n:		
Share capital	800	
Reserves (W1)	7,800	
Fair value adjustments (W6)	600	
		(9,200)
		2,540

3 *Consolidated reserves*

	Oscar	*Tigger 25%*	*Tigger 60%*
	$'000	$'000	$'000
Per question/at date control obtained	39,920	7,800	7,900
Fair value movement (W6)			(30)
Profit on derecognition of investment (W7)	380		
Reserves at acquisition (W1)		(5,800)	(7,800)
		2,000	70
Group share of post-acquisition reserves:			
Tigger – 25% (2,000 × 25%)	500		
– 60% (70 × 60%)	42		
	40,842		

4 *Non-controlling interests (SOFP)*

	$'000
NCI at acquisition (W2)	4,640
NCI share of reserves post *control*:	
Tigger – 40% ((W3) 70 × 40%)	28
	4,668

5 *Non-controlling interests (SPLOCI)*

	PFY	*TCI*
	$'000	$'000
Per question (320 × 3/12)/(400 × 3/12)	80	100
Fair value movement in year (W6)	(30)	(30)
	50	70
× 40%	20	28

6 *Fair value adjustments*

Measured at date control achieved (only)

	At acquisition 30.9.20X2	*Movement*	*At year end 31.12.20X2*
	$'000	$'000	$'000
Brand (9,200 – (800 + 7,800))	600	(30)*	570
	↓ Goodwill (W2)	↓ Expenses /reserves (W3)	↓ Intangibles

* $600,000/5 years × 3/12

7 *Profit on derecognition of 25% associate*

	$'000
Fair value at date control obtained (800,000 x 25% x $14.50)	2,900
Carrying amount of associate (2,020 cost + (W3) 500)	(2,520)
	380

1.5 Section summary

Where control is **achieved in stages**:

- **Re-measure** any previously held equity interest to **fair value at the date control is achieved**
- Report any **gain in profit or loss** (unless an irrevocable election had been made to record gains in OCI)
- Where a **controlling interest is increased** treat as a transaction between owners and **adjust parent's equity**

2 Acquisitions and disposals where control is retained

6/14, 12/14, 6/15

FAST FORWARD

An **increase or decrease in controlling interest** where **control is retained** is accounted for under the revised IFRS 3 as a **transaction between owners.** The **difference between the consideration and the change in non-controlling interests** is shown as an **adjustment to parent's equity.**

Point to note

The non-controlling interest decreases with an acquisiton where control is retained and increases with a disposal where control is retained.

2.1 Increase in previously held controlling interest: adjustment to parent's equity

An example of this would be where an investment goes from a 60% subsidiary to an 80% subsidiary. This is in the right-hand third of the diagram in Section 1, repeated for your convenience here (Deloitte, 2008, Section 2.2).

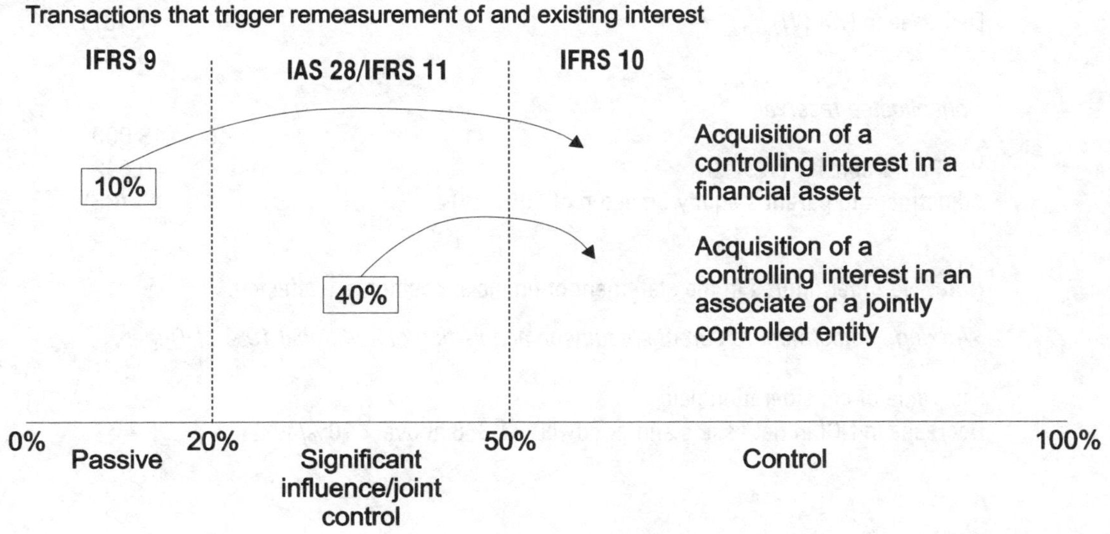

Where the controlling interest increases from 60% to 80%, the 50% threshold has not been crossed, so there is no re-measurement to fair value and no gain or loss to profit or loss for the year. The increase is treated as a **transaction between owners**. As with disposals, ownership has been **reallocated** between parent and non-controlling shareholders.

Accordingly the parent's equity is adjusted. The required adjustment is calculated by comparing the consideration paid with the decrease in non-controlling interest. (As the parent's share has increased, the NCI share has decreased.) The **calculation is as follows**.

	$
Fair value of consideration paid	(X)
Decrease in NCI in net assets at date of transaction	X
Decrease in NCI in goodwill at date of transaction*	X
Adjustment to parent's equity	(X)

***Note.** This line is only required where non-controlling interests are measured at fair value at the date of acquisition (ie where there is a decrease in the non-controlling interest share of goodwill already recognised).

If you are wondering why the increase in shareholding is treated as a transaction between owners, look back to Chapter 12, where we explained that the revised IFRS 3 views **the group as an economic entity**, and **views all providers of equity**, including non-controlling interests, as **owners of the group**.

You can practise this adjustment in the example below.

2.2 Example: Increase in previously held controlling interest: adjustment to parent's equity

The facts are the same as in Example 1.4 above. Show the consolidated current assets, non-controlling interests and reserves figures if Oscar acquired an **additional** 10% interest in Tigger on 31 December 20X2 for $1,200,000.

Solution

	$'000
Current assets (14,900 – 1,200)	13,700

Non-controlling interests

	$'000
NCI at acquisition: Para 1.4 (W4)	4,640
NCI share of reserves post control:	
Tigger – 40% (Para 1.4 (W3) 70 × 40%)	28
	4,668
Decrease in NCI (W)	(1,167)
	3,501

Consolidated reserves

	$'000
Per Paragraph 1.4 (W3)	40,842
Adjustment to parent's equity on acq'n of 10% (W)	(33)
	40,809

Note. No other figures in the statement of financial position are affected.

Working: adjustment to parent's equity on acquisition of additional 10% of Tigger

	$'000
Fair value of consideration paid	(1,200)
Decrease in NCI in net assets and goodwill* (4,668 above × 10%/40%)	1,167
	(33)

	$'000	$'000
DEBIT Non-controlling interests	1,167	
DEBIT Parent's equity (difference)	33	
CREDIT Cash		1,200

***Note.** An adjustment to the non-controlling interests in goodwill (ie a reallocation between the group and non-controlling interests) only occurs when it is group policy to measure NCI at fair value at the date of acquisition, which is the case here. In such cases, the NCI share of the goodwill is automatically included in the NCI figure used for the adjustment.

2.3 Disposals where control is retained

Control is retained where the disposal is from **subsidiary to subsidiary,** eg going from 80% to 60%. Again, the difference between the consideration and the change in non-controlling interests is shown as an adjustment to parent's equity. This is covered in Section 3 below.

2.4 Section summary

Where a **controlling interest is increased or decreased** treat as a transaction between owners and **adjust parent's equity**

3 Disposals 6/10, 6/14, 6/15, Sept/Dec 2016

FAST FORWARD

Disposals can drop a subsidiary holding to associate status, long-term investment status and to zero, or a parent might still retain a subsidiary with a reduced holding. Once again, you should be able to deal with all these situations. Remember particularly how to deal with **goodwill**.

Disposals of shares in a subsidiary may or may not result in a loss of control. If control is lost, then any remaining investment will need to be recategorised as an associate or an investment in equity instruments.

Point to note

Disposals are in many ways a mirror image of business combinations achieved in stages. The same principles underly both.

3.1 Types of disposal

3.1.1 Disposals where control is lost

There are three main kinds of disposals in which control is lost:

(a) Full disposal: all the holding is sold (say, 80% to nil)
(b) Subsidiary to associate (say, 80% to 30%)
(c) Subsidiary to trade investment (say, 80% to 10%)

In your exam, you are most likely to meet a partial disposal, either subsidiary to associate or subsidiary to trade investment.

3.1.2 Disposals where control is retained

There is only one kind of disposal where control is retained: **subsidiary to subsidiary**, for example an 80% holding to a 60% holding.

Disposals where control is lost are treated differently from disposals where control is retained. There is a reason for this.

3.2 General principle: 'crossing an accounting boundary'

Under IFRS 3 (revised) a gain on disposal occurs only when one entity loses control over another, which is generally when its holding is decreased to less than 50%. The Deloitte guide: *Business Combinations and Changes in Ownership Interests* calls this 'crossing an accounting boundary'.

On disposal of a controlling interest, any retained interest (an associate or trade investment) is measured at fair value on the date that control is lost. This fair value is used in the calculation of the gain or loss on disposal, and also becomes the carrying amount for subsequent accounting for the retained interest.

If the **50%** boundary is **not crossed**, as when the interest in a subsidiary is reduced, the event is treated as a **transaction between owners**.

Whenever you cross the 50% boundary, you revalue, and a gain or loss is reported in profit or loss for the year. If you do not cross the 50% boundary, no gain or loss is reported; instead there is an adjustment to the parent's equity.

The following diagram may help you visualise the boundary (Deloitte, 2008, 2.2):

Transactions that require remeasurement of a retained interest

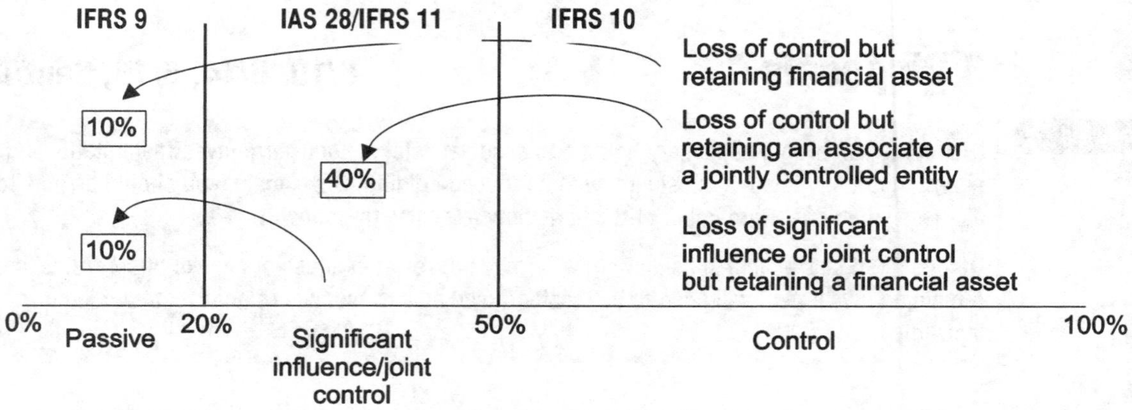

As you will see from the diagram, the situation in Paragraph 3.1.2, where an interest in a subsidiary is reduced from say 80% to 60%, does not involve crossing that all-important 50% threshold.

3.3 Effective date of disposal

The effective date of disposal is **when control passes**: the date for accounting for an undertaking ceasing to be a subsidiary undertaking is the date on which its former parent undertaking relinquishes its control over that undertaking. The consolidated statement of profit or loss and other comprehensive income should include the results of a subsidiary undertaking up to the date of its disposal. IAS 37 on provisions (Chapter 5) and IFRS 5 on disclosure of discontinued operations will have an impact here (see Chapter 15).

3.4 Control lost: calculation of group gain on disposal

A proforma calculation is shown below. This needs to be adapted for the circumstances in the question, in particular whether it is a full or partial disposal:

		$	$
Fair value of consideration received			X
Fair value of any investment retained			X
Less	share of consolidated carrying value at date control lost:		
	net assets	X	
	goodwill	X	
	less non-controlling interests	(X)	
			(X)
Group profit/(loss)			X/(X)

Following IAS 1, this gain may need to be disclosed separately if it is material.

3.4.1 Analogy: trading in a large car for a smaller one

It may seem counter-intuitive that the investment retained is now part of the 'proceeds' for the purposes of calculating the gain. One way of looking at it is to imagine that you are selling a larger car and putting part of the proceeds towards a smaller one. If the larger car you are selling cost you less than the smaller car and cash combined, you have made a profit. Likewise, the company making the disposal sold a larger stake to gain, at fair value, a smaller stake and some cash on top, which is the 'consideration received'.

This analogy is not exact, but may help.

3.5 Calculation of gain in parent's separate financial statements

This calculation is more straightforward: the proceeds are compared with the carrying value of the investment sold. The investment will be held at cost or at fair value if held as an investment in equity instruments:

	$
Fair value of consideration received	X
Less carrying value of investment disposed of	(X)
Profit/(loss) on disposal	X/(X)

The profit on disposal is generally taxable, and the **tax based on the parent's gain** rather than the group's will also need to be recognised in the consolidated financial statements.

3.6 Disposals where control is lost: accounting treatment

For a **full disposal**, apply the following treatment (IFRS 10: para. 25, B96).

(a) **Statement of profit or loss and other comprehensive income**

  (i) Consolidate results and non-controlling interest to the date of disposal.
  (ii) Show the group profit or loss on disposal.

(b) **Statement of financial position**

  There will be no non-controlling interest and no consolidation as there is no subsidiary at the date the statement of financial position is being prepared.

A full disposal is illustrated in requirement (a) of the Question Disposal later in this chapter.

For **partial disposals**, use the following treatments (IFRS 10: para. 25, B96).

(a) **Subsidiary to associate**

  (i) **Statement of profit or loss and other comprehensive income**

    (1) Treat the undertaking as a subsidiary up to the date of disposal, ie consolidate for the correct number of months and show the non-controlling interest in that amount.

    (2) Show the profit or loss on disposal.

    (3) Treat as an associate thereafter.

  (ii) **Statement of financial position**

    (1) The investment remaining is at its fair value at the date of disposal (to calculate the gain)

    (2) Equity account (as an associate) thereafter, using the fair value as the new 'cost'. (Post-'acquisition' retained earnings are added to this cost in future years to arrive at the carrying value of the investment in the associate in the statement of financial position.)

  A part disposal where a subsidiary becomes an associate is illustrated in requirement (c) of the Question 'Disposal', later in this chapter.

(b) **Subsidiary to trade investment/IEI**

(i) **Statement of profit or loss and other comprehensive income**

(1) Treat the undertaking as a subsidiary up to the date of disposal, ie consolidate.
(2) Show profit or loss on disposal.
(3) Show dividend income only thereafter.

(ii) **Statement of financial position**

(i) The investment remaining is at its fair value at the date of disposal (to calculate the gain).

(2) Thereafter, treat as an investment in equity instruments under IFRS 9.

A part disposal where a subsidiary becomes an investment in equity instruments is illustrated in requirement (d) of the Question 'Disposal', later in this chapter.

3.7 Disposals where control is retained

Control is retained where the disposal is from **subsidiary to subsidiary** (IFRS 10: para. 23). The accounting treatment is as follows.

3.7.1 Statement of profit or loss and other comprehensive income

(a) The subsidiary is **consolidated in full** for the whole period.

(b) The **non-controlling interest in the statement of profit or loss** will be based on percentage before and after disposal, ie time apportion.

(c) There is no profit or loss on disposal.

3.7.2 Statement of financial position

(a) The non-controlling interest in the statement of financial position is based on the year end percentage.

(b) The change (increase) in non-controlling interests is shown as an adjustment to the parent's equity.

(c) Goodwill on acquisition is unchanged in the consolidated statement of financial position.

3.7.3 Adjustment to the parent's equity

This reflects the fact that the non-controlling share has increased (as the parent's share has reduced). A subsidiary to subsidiary disposal is, in effect, **a transaction between owners**. Specifically, it is a reallocation of ownership between parent and non-controlling equity holders. **The goodwill is unchanged**, because it is a historical figure, unaffected by the reallocation. The adjustment to the parent's equity is calculated as follows.

	$
Fair value of consideration received	X
Increase in NCI in net assets at disposal	(X)
Increase in NCI in goodwill at disposal *	(X)
Adjustment to parent's equity	X

***Note.** This line is only required where non-controlling interests are measured at fair value at the date of acquisition (ie where there is an increase in the non-controlling interest share of goodwill already recognised).

If you are wondering why the decrease in shareholding is treated as a transaction between owners, look back to Chapter 12, where we explained that the revised IFRS 3 views **the group as an economic entity**, and views **all providers of equity**, including non-controlling interests, as **owners of the group**. Non-controlling shareholders are not outsiders, they are owners of the group just like the parent.

You can practise the adjustment to parent's equity in the example and in requirement (b) of the Question 'Disposal' below.

3.7.4 Gain in the parent's separate financial statements

This is calculated as for disposals where control is lost: see Paragraph 3.5 above.

3.8 Example: Partial disposals

Chalk Co bought 100% of the voting share capital of Cheese Co on its incorporation on 1 January 20X2 for $160,000. Cheese Co earned and retained $240,000 from that date until 31 December 20X7. At that date the statements of financial position of the company and the group were as follows.

	Chalk Co	*Cheese Co*	*Consolidated*
	$'000	$'000	$'000
Investment in Cheese	160	–	–
Other assets	1,000	500	1,500
	1,160	500	1,500
Share capital	400	160	400
Retained earnings	560	240	800
Current liabilities	200	100	300
	1,160	500	1,500

It is the group's policy to value the non-controlling interest at its proportionate share of the fair value of the subsidiary's identifiable net assets.

On 1 January 20X8 Chalk Co sold 40% of its shareholding in Cheese Co for $280,000. The profit on disposal (ignoring tax) in the financial statements of the parent company is calculated as follows.

	Chalk
	$'000
Fair value of consideration received	280
Carrying value of investment (40% × 160)	64
Profit on sale	216

We now move on to calculate the adjustment to equity for the group financial statements.

Because only 40% of the 100% subsidiary has been sold, leaving a 60% subsidiary, **control is retained**. This means that there is **no group profit on disposal in profit or loss for the year**. Instead, there is an **adjustment to the parent's equity**, which affects group retained earnings.

Point to note

Remember that, when control is retained, the disposal is just a transaction between owners. The non-controlling shareholders are owners of the group, just like the parent.

The adjustment to parent's equity is calculated as follows.

	$'000
Fair value of consideration received	280
Increase in non-controlling interest in net assets at the date of disposal (40% × 400)	160
Adjustment to parent's equity	120

This increases group retained earnings and does not go through group profit or loss for the year. (Note that there is no goodwill in this example, or non-controlling interest in goodwill, as the subsidiary was acquired on incorporation.)

Solution: Subsidiary status

The statements of financial position immediately after the sale will appear as follows.

	Chalk Co	*Cheese Co*	*Consolidated*
	$'000	$'000	$'000
Investment in Cheese (160-64)	96		
Other assets	1,280	500	1,780
	1,376	500	1,780
Share capital	400	160	400
Retained earnings*	776	240	920
Current liabilities	200	100	300
	1,376	500	1,620
Non-controlling interest			160
			1,780

*Chalk's retained earnings are $560,000 + $216,000 profit on disposal. Group retained earnings are increased by the adjustment above: $800,000 + $120,000 = $920,000.

Solution: Associate status

Using the above example, assume that Chalk Co sold 60% of its holding in Cheese Co for $440,000. The fair value of the 40% holding retained was $200,000. The gain or loss on disposal in the books of the parent company would be calculated as follows.

	Parent company
	$'000
Fair value of consideration received	440
Carrying value of investment (60% × 160)	(96)
Profit on sale	344

This time control is lost, so there will be a gain in group profit or loss, calculated as follows.

	$'000
Fair value of consideration received	440
Fair value of investment retained	200
Less Chalk's share of consolidated carrying value at date control lost 100% × 400	(400)
Group profit on sale	240

Note that there was no goodwill arising on the acquisition of Cheese, otherwise this too would be deducted in the calculation.

The statements of financial position would now appear as follows.

	Chalk Co	*Cheese Co*	*Consolidated*
	$'000	$'000	$'000
Investment in Cheese (Note 1)	64		200
Other assets	1,440	500	1,440
	1,504	500	1,640
Share capital	400	160	400
Retained earnings (Note 2)	904	240	1,040
Current liabilities	200	100	200
	1,504	500	1,640

Notes

1 The investment in Cheese is at fair value in the group SOFP. In fact it is equity accounted at fair value at date control lost plus share of post-'acquisition' retained earnings. But there are no retained earnings yet because control has only just been lost.

2 Group retained earnings are $800,000 (per question) plus group profit on the sale of $240,000, ie $1,040,000.

The following comprehensive question should help you get to grips with disposal problems. Try to complete the whole question without looking at the solution, and then check your answer very carefully. **Give yourself at least two hours**. This is a very difficult question.

Exam focus point

Questions may involve part-disposals leaving investments with both subsidiary and associate status. Disposals could well come up at P2, since you have not covered them before.

Question

Disposal

Smith Co bought 80% of the share capital of Jones Co for $324,000 on 1 October 20X5. At that date Jones Co's retained earnings balance stood at $180,000. The statements of financial position at 30 September 20X8 and the summarised statements of profit or loss to that date are given below. (There is no other comprehensive income.)

	Smith Co	*Jones Co*
	$'000	$'000
Non-current assets	360	270
Investment in Jones Co	324	–
Current assets	370	370
	1,054	640
Equity		
$1 ordinary shares	540	180
Retained earnings	414	360
Current liabilities	100	100
	1,054	640
Profit before tax	153	126
Tax	(45)	(36)
Profit for the year	108	90

No entries have been made in the accounts for any of the following transactions.

Assume that profits accrue evenly throughout the year.

It is the group's policy to value the non-controlling interest at its proportionate share of the fair value of the subsidiary's identifiable net assets.

Ignore taxation.

Required

Prepare the consolidated statement of financial position and statement of profit or loss at 30 September 20X8 in each of the following circumstances. (Assume no impairment of goodwill.)

(a) Smith Co sells its entire holding in Jones Co for $650,000 on 30 September 20X8.

(b) Smith Co sells one quarter of its holding in Jones Co for $160,000 on 30 June 20X8.

(c) Smith Co sells one half of its holding in Jones Co for $340,000 on 30 June 20X8, and the remaining holding (fair value $250,000) is to be dealt with as an associate.

(d) Smith Co sells one half of its holding in Jones Co for $340,000 on 30 June 20X8, and the remaining holding (fair value $250,000) is to be dealt with as an investment in equity instruments.

Answer

(a) *Complete disposal at year end (80% to 0%)*

CONSOLIDATED STATEMENT OF FINANCIAL POSITION AS AT 30 SEPTEMBER 20X8

	$'000
Non-current assets	360
Current assets (370 + 650)	1,020
	1,380
	$'000
Equity	
$1 ordinary shares	540
Retained earnings (W3)	740
Current liabilities	100
	1,380

CONSOLIDATED STATEMENT OF PROFIT OR LOSS FOR THE YEAR ENDED 30 SEPTEMBER 20X8

	$'000
Profit before tax (153 + 126)	279
Profit on disposal (W2)	182
Tax (45 + 36)	(81)
	380
Profit attributable to:	
Owners of the parent	362
Non-controlling interest (20% × 90)	18
	380

Workings

1 *Timeline*

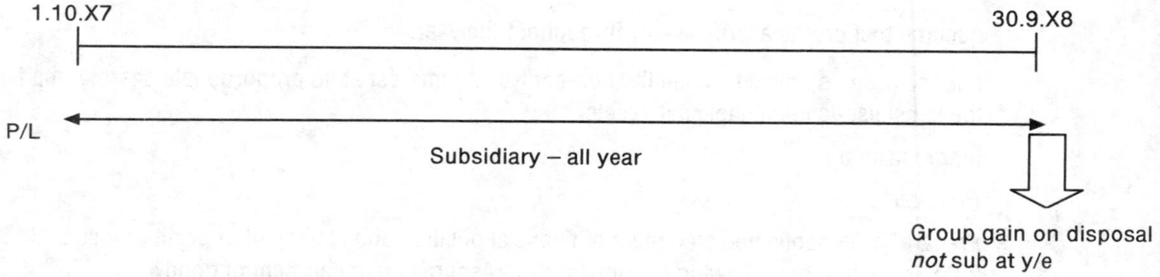

2 *Profit on disposal of Jones Co*

	$'000	$'000
Fair value of consideration received		650
Less share of consolidated carrying value when control lost:		
net assets	540	
goodwill	36	
non-controlling interest: 20% × 540	(108)	
		(468)
		182

Note: goodwill

	$'000
Consideration transferred	324
NCI (20% × 360)	72
Acquired: (180 + 180)	(360)
	36

3 *Retained earnings carried forward*

	Smith	Jones
	$'000	$'000
Per question/date of disposal	414	360
Add group gain on disposal (W2)	182	–
Reserves at acquisition	–	(180)
		180
Share of post-acq'n reserves up to the disposal (80% × 180)	144	
	740	

(b) *Partial disposal: subsidiary to subsidiary (80% to 60%)*

CONSOLIDATED STATEMENT OF FINANCIAL POSITION AS AT 30 SEPTEMBER 20X8

	$'000
Non-current assets (360 + 270)	630
Goodwill (part (a))	36
Current assets (370 + 160 + 370)	900
	1,566
Equity	
$1 ordinary shares	540
Retained earnings (W2)	610
	1,150
Non-controlling interest (W4)	216
Current liabilities (100 + 100)	200
	1,566

CONSOLIDATED STATEMENT OF PROFIT OR LOSS FOR THE YEAR ENDED 30 SEPTEMBER 20X8

	$'000	$'000
Profit before tax (153 +126)		279
Tax (45 + 36)		(81)
Profit for the period		198
Profit attributable to:		
Owners of the parent		175.5
Non-controlling interest		
20% × 90 × 9/12	13.5	
40% × 90 × 3/12	9.0	
		22.5
		198.0

Workings

1 *Timeline*

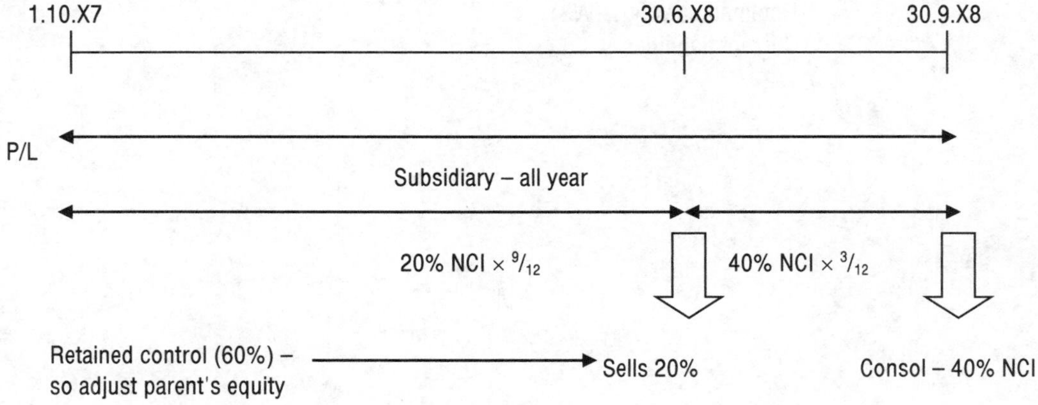

2 *Adjustment to parent's equity on disposal of 20% of Jones*

	$'000	$'000
Fair value of consideration received		160.0
Less increase in NCI in net assets at disposal		
20% × (540 – (3/12 × 90))		(103.5)
		56.5

3 *Group retained earnings*

	Smith	*Jones 80%*	*Jones 60% retained*
	$'000	$'000	$'000
Per question/at date of disposal (360 – (90 × 3/12))	414.0	337.5	360.0
Adjustment to parent's equity on disposal (W2)	56.5		
Retained earnings at acquisition		(180.0)	(337.5)
		157.5	22.5
Jones: share of post acq'n. earnings (157.5 × 80%)	126.0		
Jones: share of post acq'n. earnings (22.5 × 60%)	13.5		
	610.0		

4 *Non-controlling interests (SOFP)*

	$'000	$'000
NCI at acquisition (part (a) – goodwill)	72.0	
NCI share of post acq'n reserves (W3) (157.5 × 20%)	31.5	
	103.5	
(22.5 × 40%)	9.0	
		112.5
Increase in NCI (W3)		103.5
		216.0

(c) *Partial disposal: subsidiary to associate (80% to 40%)*

CONSOLIDATED STATEMENT OF FINANCIAL POSITION AS AT 30 SEPTEMBER 20X8

	$'000
Non-current assets	360
Investment in associate (W4)	259
Current assets (370 + 340)	710
	1,329
Equity	
$1 ordinary shares	540
Retained earnings (W3)	689
Current liabilities	100
	1,329

CONSOLIDATED STATEMENT OF PROFIT OR LOSS FOR THE YEAR ENDED 30 SEPTEMBER 20X8

	$'000
Profit before tax (153 + 9/12 × 126)	247.5
Profit on disposal (W2)	140.0
Share of profit of associate (90 × 3/12 × 40%)	9.0
Tax 45 + (9/12 × 36)	(72.0)
Profit for the period	324.5
Profit attributable to:	
Owners of the parent	311.0
Non-controlling interest (20% × 90 × 9/12)	13.5
	324.5

Workings

1 *Timeline*

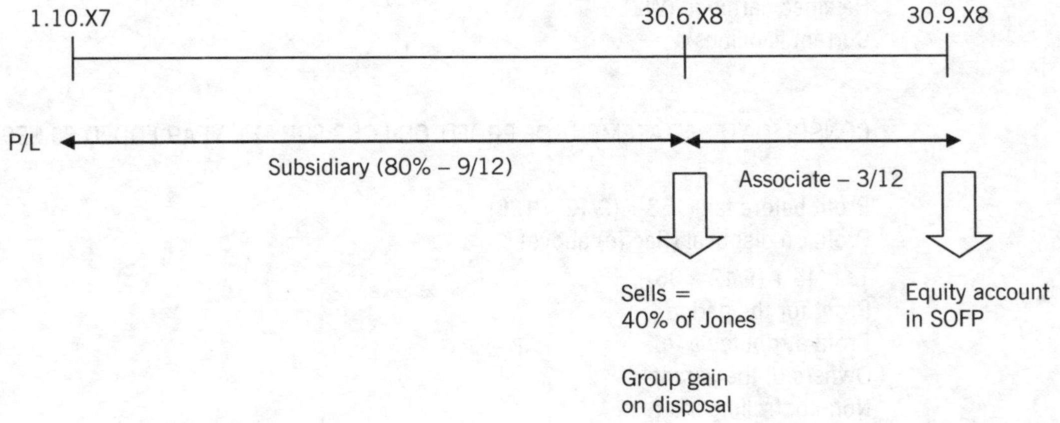

2 *Profit on disposal in Smith Co*

	$'000	$'000
Fair value of consideration received		340
Fair value of 40% investment retained		250
Less share of consolidated carrying value when control lost		
540 – (90 × 3/12)	517.5	
Goodwill (part (a))	36.0	
Less NCI 20% × ((540 – (90 × 3/12))	(103.5)	
		(450)
		140

3 *Group retained earnings*

	Smith	*Jones 80%(sub)*	*Jones 40% retained (assoc.)*
	$'000	$'000	$'000
Per question/at date of disposal (360 – (90 × 3/12))	414	337.5	360
Group profit on disposal (W2)	140		
Retained earnings at acquisition/date control lost		(180)	(337.5)
		157.5	22.5
Jones: share of post acqn. earnings (157.5 × 80%)	126		
Jones: share of post acqn. earnings (22.5 × 40%)	9		
	689		

4 *Investment in associate*

	$'000
Fair value at date control lost (new 'cost')	250
Share of post 'acq'n' retained reserves (90 × 3/12 × 40%) (or from W3)	9
	259

(d) *Partial disposal: subsidiary to investment in equity instruments (80% to 40%)*

CONSOLIDATED STATEMENT OF FINANCIAL POSITION AS AT 30 SEPTEMBER 20X8

	$'000
Non-current assets	360
Investment	250
Current assets (370 + 340)	710
	1,320
Equity	
$1 ordinary shares	540
Retained earnings (W2)	680
Current liabilities	100
	1,320

CONSOLIDATED STATEMENT OF PROFIT OR LOSS FOR THE YEAR ENDED 30 SEPTEMBER 20X8

	$'000
Profit before tax (153 + (9/12 × 126)	247.5
Profit on disposal (See (c) above)	140.0
Tax (45 + (9/12 × 36))	(72.0)
Profit for the period	315.5
Profit attributable to:	
Owners of the parent	302.0
Non-controlling interest	13.5
	315.5

Workings

1 *Timeline*

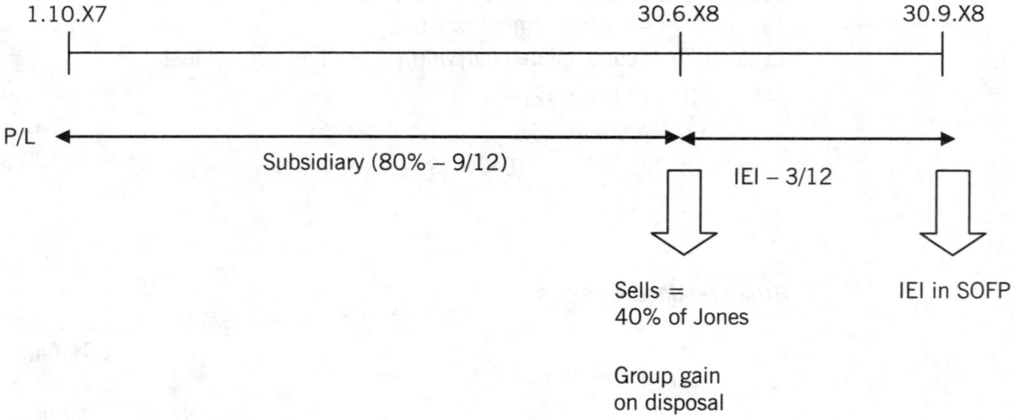

2 *Retained earnings*

	Smith $'000	*Jones* $'000
Per question/at date of disposal (360 – (90 × 3/12))	414	337.5
Group profit on disposal (see (c) above)	140	
Retained earnings at acquisition		(180.0)
		157.5
Jones: share of post acq'n. earnings (157.5 × 80%)	126	
	680	

3.9 Section summary

Disposals occur frequently in Paper P2 consolidation questions.

- The effective date of disposal is when **control passes**
- Treatment of **goodwill** is according to IFRS 3
- Disposals may be **full** or **partial**, to subsidiary, associate or investment status
  - **if control is lost,** the interest retained is **fair valued** and becomes part of the calculation of the gain on disposal
  - **if control is retained**, the change in non-controlling interests is shown as **an adjustment to parent's equity**
- **Gain or loss** on disposal is calculated for the parent company and the group

4 Changes in direct ownership 12/11

FAST FORWARD

Changes in direct ownership (ie internal group reorganisations) can take many forms. Apart from divisionalisation, all other internal reorganisations will not affect the consolidated financial statements, but they will affect the accounts of individual companies within the group.

Groups will reorganise on occasions for a variety of reasons.

(a) A group may want to float a business to **reduce the gearing** of the group. The holding company will initially transfer the business into a separate company.

(b) Companies may be transferred to another business during a **divisionalisation** process.

(c) The group may 'reverse' into another company to obtain a **stock exchange quotation**.

(d) Internal reorganisations may create efficiencies of group structure for **tax purposes**.

Such reorganisations involve a restructuring of the relationships within a group. Companies may be transferred to another business during a divisionalisation process. There is generally no effect on the consolidated financial statements, **provided that** no non-controlling interests are affected, because such reorganisations are only internal. The impact on the individual companies within the group, however, can be substantial. A variety of different transactions are described here, **only involving 100% subsidiaries**.

4.1 New top parent company

A new top holding company might be needed as a vehicle for flotation or to improve the co-ordination of a diverse business. The new company, P, will issue its own shares to the holders of the shares in S.

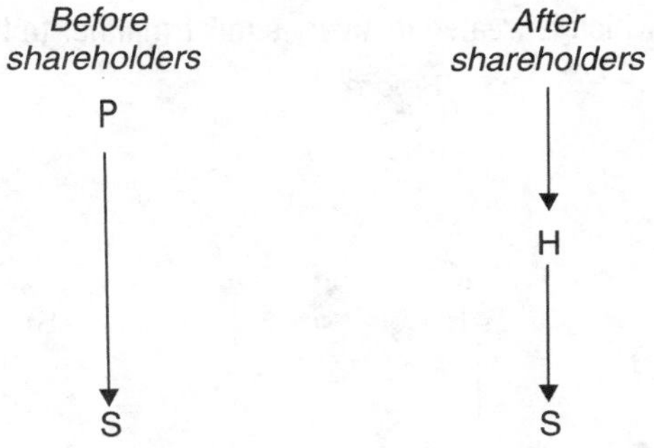

4.2 Subsidiary moved up

This transaction is shown in the diagram below. It might be carried out to allow S_1 to be **sold** while S_2 is retained, or to **split diverse businesses**.

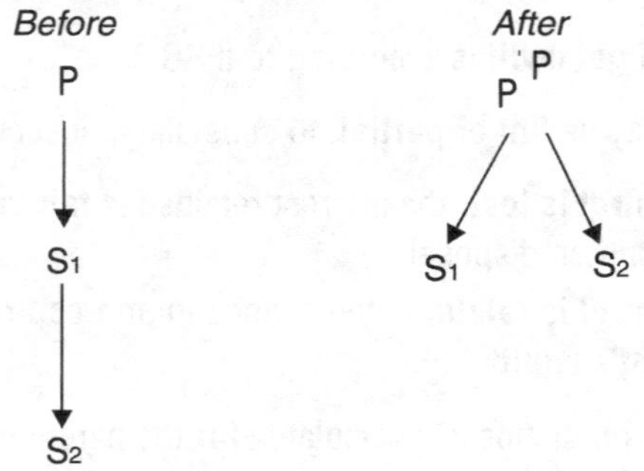

S_1 could transfer its investment in S_2 to P as a dividend *in specie* or by P paying cash. A share for share exchange is not possible because an allotment by P to S_1 is void. A **dividend in specie** is simply a dividend paid other than in cash.

S_1 must have sufficient **distributable profits** for a dividend *in specie*. If the investment in S_2 has been revalued then that can be treated as a realised profit for the purposes of determining the legality of the distribution. For example, suppose the statement of financial position of S_1 is as follows.

	$m
Investment in S_2 (cost $100m)	900
Other net assets	100
	1,000
Share capital	100
Revaluation surplus	800
Retained earnings	100
	1,000

It appears that S_1 cannot make a distribution of more than $100m. If, however, S_1 makes a distribution in kind of its investment in S_2, then the **revaluation surplus** can be treated as realised.

It is not clear how P should account for the transaction. The carrying value to S_2 might be used, but there may be **no legal rule**. P will need to write down its investment in S_1 at the same time. A transfer for cash is probably easiest, but there are still legal pitfalls as to what is distributable, depending on how the transfer is recorded.

There will be **no effect** on the group financial statements as the group has stayed the same: it has made no acquisitions or disposals.

4.3 Subsidiary moved along

This is a transaction which is treated in a very similar manner to that described above.

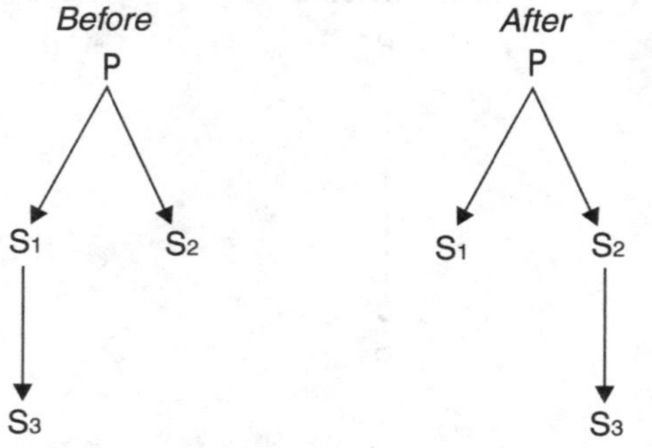

The problem of an effective distribution does not arise here because the holding company did not buy the subsidiary. There may be problems with **financial assistance** if S_2 pays less than the fair value to purchase S_3 as a prelude to S_1 leaving the group.

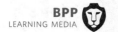

4.4 Subsidiary moved down

This situation could arise if H is in one country and S_1 and S_2 are in another. A **tax group** can be formed out of such a restructuring.

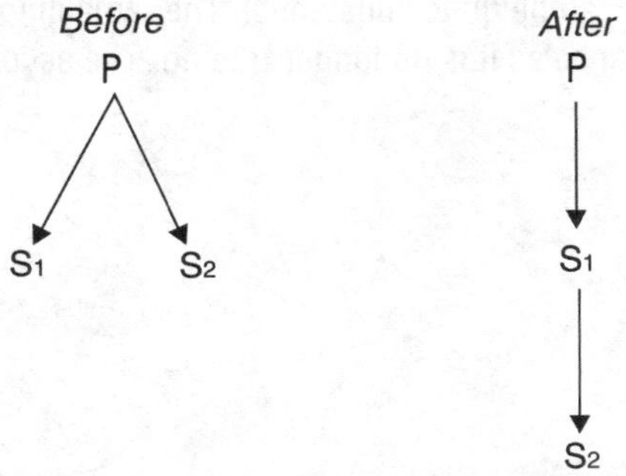

If S_1 paid cash for S_2, the transaction would be straightforward (as described above). It is unclear whether H should recognise a gain or loss on the sale if S_2 is sold for more or less than carrying value. S_1 would only be deemed to have made a distribution (avoiding any advance tax payable) only if the **price was excessive**.

A share for share exchange accounted for as a uniting of interests may obtain partial relief against the need to create a **share premium account**. A share premium account must be set up with a 'minimum premium value'. This is the amount by which the book value of the shares (or lower cost) exceeds the nominal value of the shares issued. This preserves the book value of the investment.

4.5 Example: Minimum premium value

Hop Co has two 100% subsidiaries, Skip and Jump. The statements of financial position at 31 December 20X5 are as follows.

	Hop Co	*Skip Co*	*Jump Co*	*Group*
	$'000	$'000	$'000	$'000
Investment in Skip Co	1,000			
Investment in Jump Co	500			
Net assets	1,500	1,375	1,500	4,375
	3,000	1,375	1,500	4,375
Share capital	2,500	1,000	500	2,500
Retained earnings	500	375	1,000	1,875
	3,000	1,375	1,500	4,375

Hop Co wants to transfer Jump Co to Skip Co.

Solution

Skip Co issues 250,000 $1 shares in exchange for Hop Co's investment in Jump Co. The minimum premium value is $500,000 (carrying value) – $250,000 = $250,000. The statements of financial position are now as follows.

	Hop Co	*Skip Co*	*Jump Co*	*Group*
	$'000	$'000	$'000	$'000
Investment in Skip	1,500			
Investment in Jump		500		
Net assets	1,500	1,375	1,500	4,375
	3,000	1,875	1,500	4,375
Share capital	2,500	1,250	500	2,500
Share premium		250		
Retained earnings	500	375	1,000	1,875
	3,000	1,875	1,500	4,375

4.6 Divisionalisation

This type of transaction involves the **transfer of businesses** from subsidiaries into just one company. The businesses will all be similar and this is a means of rationalising and streamlining. The savings in administration costs can be quite substantial. The remaining shell company will leave the cash it was paid on an intragroup balance as it is no longer trading. The accounting treatment is generally straightforward.

Chapter Roundup

- Transactions of the type described in this chapter can be very **complicated** and certainly look rather daunting. Remember and apply the basic techniques and you should find such questions easier than you expected.
- **Business combinations achieved in stages** (piecemeal acquisitions) can lead to a company becoming an investment in equity instrument, an associate and then a subsidiary over time. Make sure you can deal with each of these situations.
- An **increase or decrease in controlling interest** where **control is retained** is accounted for under the revised IFRS 3 as a **transaction between owners.** The **difference between the consideration and the change in non-controlling interests** is shown as an **adjustment to parent's equity.**
- **Disposals** can drop a subsidiary holding to associate status, long-term investment status and to zero, or a parent might still retain a subsidiary with a reduced holding. Once again, you should be able to deal with all these situations. Remember particularly how to deal with **goodwill**.
- **Disposals of shares** in a subsidiary may or may not result in a loss of control. If control is lost, then any remaining investment will need to be recategorised as an associate or an investment in equity instruments.
- **Changes in direct ownership** (ie internal group reorganisations) can take many forms. Apart from divisionalisation, all other internal reorganisations will not affect the consolidated financial statements, but they will affect the accounts of individual companies within the group.

Quick Quiz

1 Control is always lost when there is a disposal. *True or false?*

2 Why is the fair value of the interest retained used in the calculation of a gain on disposal where control is lost?

3 When is the effective date of disposal of shares in an investment?

4 Subside owns 60% of Diary at 31 December 20X8. On 1 July 20X9, it buys a further 20% of Diary. How should this transaction be treated in the group financial statements at 31 December 20X9.

5 Ditch had a 75% subsidiary, Dodge, at 30 June 20X8. On 1 January 20X9, it sold two-thirds of this investment, leaving it with a 25% holding, over which it retained significant influence. How will the remaining investment in Dodge appear in the group financial statements for the year ended 30 June 20X9?

Answers to Quick Quiz

1 False. Control may be retained if the disposal is from subsidiary to subsidiary, even though the parent owns less and the non-controlling interest owns more.

2 It may be viewed as part of the consideration received.

3 When control passes

4 As a transaction between owners, with an adjustment to the parent's equity to reflect the difference between the consideration paid and the decrease in non-controlling interest.

5 At its fair value at the date of disposal plus a 25% share of the profits accrued between the date of disposal and the year end, less any impairment at the year end.

Now try the questions below from the Practice Question Bank

Number	Level	Marks	Time
Q21	Examination	22	43 mins

15

Continuing and discontinued interests

Topic list	Syllabus reference
1 IFRS 5 *Non-current assets held for sale and discontinued operations*	C2, D2
2 Classification of assets held for sale	C2, D2
3 Measurement of assets held for sale	C2, D2
4 Presenting discontinued operations	C2, D2

Introduction

Separate analysis of discontinued operations and of non-current assets held for sale allows the user of the accounts to make more accurate assessments of a company's prospects in the future, because it excludes these items.

Study guide

		Intellectual level
C2	**Non-current assets**	
(b)	Apply and discuss the treatment of non-current assets held for sale	3
D2	**Continuing and discontinued interests**	
(a)	Prepare group financial statements where activities have been classified as discontinued or have been acquired or disposed in the period	3
(b)	Apply and discuss the treatment of a subsidiary which has been acquired exclusively with a view to subsequent disposal	3

Exam guide

IFRS 5 was tested in December 2007.

1 IFRS 5 *Non-current assets held for sale and discontinued operations* 12/07, 6/10, 12/12, 6/13, 6/14

Background

FAST FORWARD

IFRS 5 requires assets 'held for sale' to be presented separately in the statement of financial position.

The results of discontinued operations should be presented separately in the statement of profit or loss and other comprehensive income.

PER alert

One of the competences you need to fulfil Objective 10 of the Practical Experience Requirement (PER) is to compile financial statements and accounts in line with appropriate standards and guidelines. This includes situations where an operation has been discontinued and therefore not to present separately would give a misleading impression of future performance.

IFRS 5 requires assets and groups of assets that are 'held for sale' to be presented separately in the statement of financial position and the results of discontinued operations to be presented separately in the statement of profit or loss and other comprehensive income. This is required so that users of financial statements will be better able to make projections about the financial position, profits and cash flows of the entity (IFRS 5: para. 1).

Key term

Disposal group: a group of assets to be disposed of, by sale or otherwise, together as a group in a single transaction, and liabilities directly associated with those assets that will be transferred in the transaction. (In practice, a disposal group could be a subsidiary, a cash-generating unit or a single operation within an entity.) (*IFRS 5: Appendix A*)

IFRS 5 does not apply to certain assets covered by other accounting standards (IFRS 5: para. 5):

(a) Deferred tax assets (IAS 12)
(b) Assets arising from employee benefits (IAS 19)
(c) Financial assets (IFRS 9)
(d) Investment properties accounted for in accordance with the fair value model (IAS 40)
(e) Agricultural and biological assets measured at fair value less estimated point of sale costs (IAS 41)
(f) Insurance contracts (IFRS 4)

2 Classification of assets held for sale 6/14

A non-current asset (or disposal group) should be classified as **held for sale** if its carrying amount will be recovered **principally through a sale transaction** rather than **through continuing use** (IFRS 5: para. 6). A number of detailed criteria must be met (IFRS 5: para. 7):

(a) The asset must be **available for immediate sale** in its present condition.
(b) Its sale must be **highly probable** (ie, significantly more likely than not).

For the sale to be highly probable, the following must apply (IFRS 5: para. 8).

(a) Management must be **committed** to a plan to sell the asset.

(b) There must be an active programme to **locate a buyer**.

(c) The asset must be marketed for sale at a **price that is reasonable** in relation to its current fair value.

(d) The sale should be expected to take place **within one year** from the date of classification.

(e) It is unlikely that significant changes to the plan will be made or that the plan will be withdrawn.

An asset (or disposal group) can still be classified as held for sale, even if the sale has not actually taken place within one year. However, the delay must have been **caused by events or circumstances beyond the entity's control** and there must be sufficient evidence that the entity is still committed to sell the asset or disposal group. Otherwise the entity must cease to classify the asset as held for sale. (IFRS 5: para. 9)

If an entity acquires a disposal group (eg, a subsidiary) exclusively with a view to its subsequent disposal it can classify the asset as held for sale only if the sale is expected to take place within one year and it is highly probable that all the other criteria will be met within a short time (normally three months).

An asset that is to be **abandoned** should not be classified as held for sale. This is because its carrying amount will be recovered principally through continuing use. However, a disposal group to be abandoned may meet the definition of a discontinued operation and therefore separate disclosure may be required (see below). (IFRS 5: para. 11)

Question — Held for sale?

On 1 December 20X3, a company became committed to a plan to sell a manufacturing facility and has already found a potential buyer. The company does not intend to discontinue the operations currently carried out in the facility. At 31 December 20X3 there is a backlog of uncompleted customer orders. The subsidiary will not be able to transfer the facility to the buyer until after it ceases to operate the facility and has eliminated the backlog of uncompleted customer orders. This is not expected to occur until spring 20X4.

Required

Can the manufacturing facility be classified as 'held for sale' at 31 December 20X3?

Answer

The facility will not be transferred until the backlog of orders is completed; this demonstrates that the facility is not available for immediate sale in its present condition. The facility cannot be classified as 'held for sale' at 31 December 20X3. It must be treated in the same way as other items of property, plant and equipment: it should continue to be depreciated and should not be separately disclosed.

3 Measurement of assets held for sale 12/13

Key terms

Fair value: the price that would be received to sell an asset or paid to transfer a liability in an orderly transaction between market participants at the measurement date.

Costs to sell: the incremental costs directly attributable to the disposal of an asset (or disposal group), excluding finance costs and income tax expense.

Recoverable amount: the higher of an asset's fair value less costs to sell and its value in use.

Value in use: the present value of estimated future cash flows expected to arise from the continuing use of an asset and from its disposal at the end of its useful life. *(IFRS 5: Appendix A)*

A non-current asset (or disposal group) that is held for sale should be measured at the **lower of** its **carrying amount** and **fair value less costs to sell**. Fair value less costs to sell is equivalent to net realisable value (IFRS 5: para. 15) .

A non-current asset (or disposal group) classified as held for distribution to owners should be measured at at the **lower of its carrying amount** and **fair value less costs to distribute** (IFRS 5: para. 15A).

An impairment loss should be recognised where fair value less costs to sell is lower than carrying amount. Note that this is an exception to the normal rule. IAS 36 *Impairment of assets* requires an entity to recognise an impairment loss only where an asset's recoverable amount is lower than its carrying value. Recoverable amount is defined as the higher of net realisable value and value in use. IAS 36 does not apply to assets held for sale (IFRS 5: para. 20.

Non-current assets held for sale **should not be depreciated**, even if they are still being used by the entity (IFRS 5: para. 25).

A non-current asset (or disposal group) that is **no longer classified as held for sale** (for example, because the sale has not taken place within one year) is measured at the **lower of** (IFRS 5: para. 27):

(a) Its **carrying amount** before it was classified as held for sale, adjusted for any depreciation that would have been charged had the asset not been held for sale

(b) Its **recoverable amount** at the date of the decision not to sell

4 Presenting discontinued operations

Key terms

Discontinued operation: a component of an entity that has either been disposed of, or is classified as held for sale, and:

(a) Represents a separate major line of business or geographical area of operations

(b) Is part of a single co-ordinated plan to dispose of a separate major line of business or geographical area of operations, or

(c) Is a subsidiary acquired exclusively with a view to resale

Component of an entity: operations and cash flows that can be clearly distinguished, operationally and for financial reporting purposes, from the rest of the entity. *(IFRS 5: Appendix A)*

An entity should **present and disclose information** that enables users of the financial statements to evaluate the financial effects of **discontinued operations** and disposals of non-current assets or disposal groups.

An entity should disclose a **single amount** in the **statement of profit or loss and other comprehensive income** comprising the total of:

(a) The **post-tax profit or loss** of discontinued operations and

(b) The post-tax gain or loss recognised on the **measurement to fair value less costs to sell** or on the disposal of the assets or disposal group(s) constituting the discontinued operation.

An entity should also disclose an **analysis** of the above single amount into:

(a) The revenue, expenses and pre-tax profit or loss of discontinued operations

(b) The related income tax expense

(c) The gain or loss recognised on the measurement to fair value less costs to sell or on the disposal of the assets or the discontinued operation

(d) The related income tax expense

This may be presented either in the statement of profit or loss and other comprehensive income or in the notes. If it is presented in the statement of profit or loss and other comprehensive income it should be presented in a section identified as relating to discontinued operations, ie separately from continuing operations. This analysis is not required where the discontinued operation is a newly acquired subsidiary that has been classified as held for sale.

An entity should disclose the **net cash flows** attributable to the operating, investing and financing activities of discontinued operations. These disclosures may be presented either on the face of the statement of cash flows or in the notes.

Gains and losses on the remeasurement of a disposal group that is not a discontinued operation but is held for sale should be included in profit or loss from continuing operations.

(IFRS 5: para. 32)

4.1 Illustration

The following illustration is taken from the implementation guidance to IFRS 5 (IG, Example 11). Profit for the year from discontinued operations would be analysed in the notes.

XYZ GROUP
STATEMENT OF PROFIT OR LOSS AND OTHER COMPREHENSIVE INCOME
FOR THE YEAR ENDED 31 DECEMBER 20X2

	20X2	*20X1*
Continuing operations	$'000	$'000
Revenue	X	X
Cost of sales	(X)	(X)
Gross profit	X	X
Other income	X	X
Distribution costs	(X)	(X)
Administrative expenses	(X)	(X)
Other expenses	(X)	(X)
Finance costs	(X)	(X)
Share of profit of associates	X	X
Profit before tax	X	X
Income tax expense	(X)	(X)
Profit for the year from continuing operations	X	X
Discontinued operations		
Profit for the year from discontinued operations	X	X
Profit for the year	X	X
Period attributable to:		
Owners of the parent	X	X
Non-controlling interest	X	X
	X	X

An alternative to this presentation would be to analyse the profit from discontinued operations in a separate column in the statement of profit or loss and other comprehensive income.

Question — Treatment of closure

On 20 October 20X3 the directors of a parent company made a public announcement of plans to close a steel works. The closure means that the group will no longer carry out this type of operation, which until recently has represented about 10% of its total turnover. The works will be gradually shut down over a period of several months, with complete closure expected in July 20X4. At 31 December output had been significantly reduced and some redundancies had already taken place. The cash flows, revenues and expenses relating to the steel works can be clearly distinguished from those of the subsidiary's other operations.

Required

How should the closure be treated in the financial statements for the year ended 31 December 20X3?

Answer

Because the steel works is being closed, rather than sold, it cannot be classified as 'held for sale'. In addition, the steel works is not a discontinued operation. Although at 31 December 20X3 the group was firmly committed to the closure, this has not yet taken place and therefore the steel works must be included in continuing operations. Information about the planned closure could be disclosed in the notes to the financial statements.

4.2 Presentation of a non-current asset or disposal group classified as held for sale

Non-current assets and disposal groups classified as held for sale should be **presented separately** from other assets in the statement of financial position. The liabilities of a disposal group should be presented separately from other liabilities in the statement of financial position.

(a) Assets and liabilities held for sale **should not be offset**.

(b) The **major classes** of assets and liabilities held for sale should be **separately disclosed** either in the statement of financial position or in the notes.

4.3 Additional disclosures

In the period in which a non-current asset (or disposal group) has been either classified as held for sale or sold the following should be disclosed.

(a) A **description** of the non-current asset (or disposal group)

(b) A description of the **facts and circumstances** of the disposal

(c) Any **gain or loss** recognised when the item was classified as held for sale

(d) If applicable, the **segment** in which the non-current asset (or disposal group) is presented in accordance with IFRS 8 *Operating segments*

Where an asset previously classified as held for sale is **no longer held for sale**, the entity should disclose a description of the facts and circumstances leading to the decision and its effect on results.

(IFRS 5: paras. 38 to 40)

Chapter Roundup

- **IFRS 5** requires assets 'held for sale' to be presented separately in the statement of financial position.
- The results of discontinued operations should be presented separately in the statement of profit or loss and other comprehensive income.

Quick Quiz

1. For a non-current asset to be held for sale, a buyer must already have been found. True or false?
2. An asset held for sale should be measured at the lower of.......................... and .... *(Fill in the blanks.)*

Answers to Quick Quiz

1 False. There must be an **active programme** to locate a buyer.

2 The lower of **its carrying amount** and **fair value less costs to sell.**

Now try the questions below from the Practice Question Bank

Number	Level	Marks	Time
Q22	Examination	25	49 mins

16

Foreign currency transactions and entities

Topic list	Syllabus reference
1 Foreign currency translation	D4
2 IAS 21: *Individual company stage*	D4
3 IAS 21: *Consolidated financial statements stage*	D4

Introduction

Many of the largest companies in any country, while based there, have subsidiaries and other interests all over the world: they are truly **global companies** and so foreign currency consolidations take place frequently in practice.

Study guide

		Intellectual level
D4	**Foreign transactions and entities**	
(a)	Outline and apply the translation of foreign currency amounts and transactions into the functional currency and the presentation currency	3
(b)	Account for the consolidation of foreign operations and their disposal	3

Exam guide

Foreign currency consolidation questions are likely to appear frequently in Paper P2. Students have always found such questions difficult but, as with most financial accounting topics, you only need to adopt a **logical approach** and to **practise plenty of questions**.

1 Foreign currency translation 12/12

FAST FORWARD

Questions on foreign currency translation have always been popular with examiners. In general, you are required to prepare **consolidated accounts** for a group which includes a foreign subsidiary.

If a company trades overseas, it will buy or sell assets in foreign currencies. For example, an Indian company might buy materials from Canada, and pay for them in US dollars, and then sell its finished goods in Germany, receiving payment in Euros, or perhaps in some other currency. If the company owes money in a foreign currency at the end of the accounting year, or holds assets which were bought in a foreign currency, those liabilities or assets must be translated into the local currency (in this Text $), in order to be shown in the books of account.

A company might have a subsidiary abroad (ie a foreign entity that it owns), and the subsidiary will trade in its own local currency. The subsidiary will keep books of account and prepare its annual accounts in its own currency. However, at the year end, the holding company must 'consolidate' the results of the overseas subsidiary into its group accounts, so that somehow, the assets and liabilities and the annual profits of the subsidiary must be translated from the foreign currency into $.

If foreign currency exchange rates remained constant, there would be no accounting problem. As you will be aware, however, foreign exchange rates are continually changing, and it is not inconceivable for example, that the rate of exchange between the Polish zlotych and sterling might be Z6.2 to £1 at the start of the accounting year, and Z5.6 to £1 at the end of the year (in this example, a 10% increase in the relative strength of the zlotych).

There are two distinct types of foreign currency transaction, conversion and translation.

1.1 Conversion gains and losses

Conversion is the process of exchanging amounts of one foreign currency for another. For example, suppose a local company buys a large consignment of goods from a supplier in Germany. The order is placed on 1 May and the agreed price is €124,250. At the time of delivery the rate of foreign exchange was €3.50 to $1. The local company would record the amount owed in its books as follows.

DEBIT	Inventory account (124,250 ÷ 3.5)	$35,500	
CREDIT	Payables account		$35,500

When the local company comes to pay the supplier, it needs to obtain some foreign currency. By this time, however, if the rate of exchange has altered to €3.55 to $1, the cost of raising €124,250 would be (÷ 3.55) $35,000. The company would need to spend only $35,000 to settle a debt for inventories 'costing' $35,500. Since it would be administratively difficult to alter the value of the inventories in the company's books of account, it is more appropriate to record a profit on conversion of $500.

DEBIT	Payables account	$35,500	
CREDIT	Cash		$35,000
CREDIT	Profit on conversion		$500

Profits (or losses) on conversion would be included in profit or loss for the year in which conversion (whether payment or receipt) takes place.

Suppose that another home company sells goods to a Chinese company, and it is agreed that payment should be made in Chinese Yuan at a price of Y116,000. We will further assume that the exchange rate at the time of sale is Y10.75 to $1, but when the debt is eventually paid, the rate has altered to Y10.8 to $1. The company would record the sale as follows.

DEBIT	Receivables account (116,000 ÷ 10.75)	$10,800	
CREDIT	Sales account		$10,800

When the Y116,000 are paid, the local company will convert them into $, to obtain (÷ 10.8) $10,750. In this example, there has been a loss on conversion of $50 which will be written off to profit of loss for the year:

DEBIT	Cash	$10,750	
DEBIT	Loss on conversion	$50	
CREDIT	Receivables account		$10,800

There are **no accounting difficulties** concerned with foreign currency conversion gains or losses, and the procedures described above are uncontroversial.

1.2 Translation

Foreign currency translation, as distinct from conversion, does not involve the act of exchanging one currency for another. **Translation is required at the end of an accounting period when a company still holds assets or liabilities in its statement of financial position which were obtained or incurred in a foreign currency.**

These assets or liabilities might consist of any of the following:

(a) An individual home company holding individual **assets** or **liabilities** originating in a foreign currency 'deal'.

(b) An individual home company with a separate **branch** of the business operating abroad which keeps its own books of account in the local currency.

(c) A home company which wishes to consolidate the **results of a foreign subsidiary**.

There has been great **uncertainty** about the method which should be used to translate the following:

- Value of assets and liabilities from a foreign currency into $ for the year end statement of financial position
- Profits of an independent foreign branch or subsidiary into $ for the annual statement of profit or loss and other comprehensive income

Suppose, for example, that a Belgian subsidiary purchases a piece of property for €2,100,000 on 31 December 20X7. The rate of exchange at this time was €70 to $1. During 20X8, the subsidiary charged depreciation on the building of €16,800, so that at 31 December 20X8, the subsidiary recorded the asset as follows.

	€
Property at cost	2,100,000
Less accumulated depreciation	16,800
Net book value	2,083,200

At this date, the rate of exchange has changed to €60 to $1.

The local holding company must translate the asset's value into $, but there is a **choice of exchange rates**.

(a) Should the rate of exchange for translation be the rate which existed at the date of purchase, which would give a net book value of 2,083,200 ÷ 70 = $29,760?

(b) Should the rate of exchange for translation be the rate existing at the end of 20X8 (the closing rate of €60 to $1)? This would give a net book value of $34,720.

Similarly, should depreciation be charged to group profit or loss at the rate of €70 to $1 (the historical rate), €60 to $1 (the closing rate), or at an average rate for the year (say, €64 to $1)?

1.3 Consolidated accounts

If a parent has a subsidiary whose accounts are presented in a foreign currency, those accounts must be translated into the local currency before they can be included in the consolidated financial statements.

- Should the subsidiary's accounts be translated as if the subsidiary is an extension of the parent?
- Or should they be translated as if the subsidiary is a separate business?

As we will see in more detail later in the chapter, the translation rules will depend on which currency has most impact on the subsidiary. If this is the same as the parent's currency, the rules will follow those used in the financial statements of a single company (covered in Section 2 below).

Where a foreign operation is mainly exposed to a different currency and is effectively a separate business, the **closing rate** is used for most items in the statement of financial position **Exchange differences** are recognised in **other comprehensive income**.

We will look at the consolidation of foreign subsidiaries in much more detail in Section 3 of this chapter.

2 IAS 21: Individual company stage 6/14

The questions discussed above are addressed by IAS 21 *The effects of changes in foreign exchange rates.* We will examine those matters which affect single company accounts here.

2.1 Definitions

These are some of the definitions given by IAS 21.

Key terms

Foreign currency. A currency other than the functional currency of the entity.

Functional currency. The currency of the primary economic environment in which the entity operates.

Presentation currency. The currency in which the financial statements are presented.

Exchange rate. The ratio of exchange for two currencies.

Exchange difference. The difference resulting from translating a given number of units of one currency into another currency at different exchange rates.

Closing rate. The spot exchange rate at the year end date.

Spot exchange rate. The exchange rate for immediate delivery.

Monetary items. Units of currency held and assets and liabilities to be received or paid in a fixed or determinable number of units of currency. *(IAS 21: para. 8)*

Each entity – whether an individual company, a parent of a group, or an operation within a group (such as a subsidiary, associate or branch) – should determine its **functional currency** and **measure its results and financial position in that currency**.

For most individual companies the functional currency will be the currency of the country in which they are located and in which they carry out most of their transactions. Determining the functional currency is much more likely to be an issue where an entity operates as part of a group. IAS 21 contains detailed guidance on how to determine an entity's functional currency and we will look at this in more detail in Section 3.

An entity can present its financial statements in any currency (or currencies) it chooses. IAS 21 deals with the situation in which financial statements are presented in a currency other than the functional currency.

Again, this is unlikely to be an issue for most individual companies. Their presentation currency will normally be the same as their functional currency (the currency of the country in which they operate). A company's presentation currency may be different from its functional currency if it operates within a group and we will look at this in Section 3.

2.2 Foreign currency transactions: initial recognition

IAS 21 states that a foreign currency transaction should be recorded, on initial recognition in the functional currency, by applying the exchange rate between the reporting currency and the foreign currency **at the date of the transaction** to the foreign currency amount (IAS 21: para. 21) .

An **average rate** for a period may be used if exchange rates do not fluctuate significantly.

2.3 Reporting at subsequent year ends

The following rules apply at each subsequent year end (IAS 21: para. 23).

(a) Report foreign currency **monetary items** using the **closing rate**

(b) Report **non-monetary items** (eg non-current assets, inventories) which are carried at **historical cost** in a foreign currency using the **exchange rate at the date of the transaction** (historical rate)

(c) Report **non-monetary items** which are carried at **fair value** in a foreign currency using the exchange rates that existed **when the values were measured.**

2.4 Recognition of exchange differences

Exchange differences occur when there is a **change in the exchange rate** between the transaction date and the date of settlement of monetary items arising from a foreign currency transaction.

Exchange differences arising on the settlement of monetary items (receivables, payables, loans, cash in a foreign currency) or on translating an entity's monetary items at rates different from those at which they were translated initially, or reported in previous financial statements, should be **recognised in profit or loss** in the period in which they arise.

There are two situations to consider:

(a) The transaction is **settled in the same period** as that in which it occurred: all the exchange difference is recognised in that period.

(b) The transaction is **settled in a subsequent accounting period**: the exchange difference recognised in each intervening period up to the period of settlement is determined by the change in exchange rates during that period.

In other words, where a monetary item has not been settled at the end of a period, it should be **restated using the closing exchange rate** and any gain or loss taken to profit or loss (IAS 21: para. 32).

Question — Entries

White Cliffs Co, whose year end is 31 December, buys some goods from Rinka SA of France on 30 September. The invoice value is €40,000 and is due for settlement in equal instalments on 30 November and 31 January. The exchange rate moved as follows.

	€= $1
30 September	1.60
30 November	1.80
31 December	1.90
31 January	1.85

Required

State the accounting entries in the books of White Cliffs Co.

Answer

The purchase will be recorded in the books of White Cliffs Co using the rate of exchange ruling on 30 September.

DEBIT	Purchases	$25,000	
CREDIT	Trade payables		$25,000

Being the $ cost of goods purchased for €40,000 (€40,000 ÷ €1.60/$1)

On 30 November, White Cliffs must pay €20,000. This will cost €20,000 ÷ €1.80/$1 = $11,111 and the company has therefore made an exchange gain of $12,500 – $11,111 = $1,389.

DEBIT	Trade payables	$12,500	
CREDIT	Exchange gains: I & E account		$1,389
CREDIT	Cash		$11,111

On 31 December, the year end, the outstanding liability will be recalculated using the rate applicable to that date: €20,000 ÷ €1.90/$1 = $10,526. A further exchange gain of $1,974 has been made and will be recorded as follows.

DEBIT	Trade payables	$1,974	
CREDIT	Exchange gains: I & E account		$1,974

The total exchange gain of $3,363 will be included in the operating profit for the year ending 31 December.

On 31 January, White Cliffs must pay the second instalment of €20,000. This will cost them $10,811 (€20,000 ÷ €1.85/$1).

DEBIT	Trade payables	$10,526	
	Exchange losses: I & E account	$285	
CREDIT	Cash		$10,811

When a gain or loss on a non-monetary item is recognised **in other comprehensive income** (for example, where property is revalued), any **related exchange differences** should also be **recognised in other comprehensive income.**

3 IAS 21: *Consolidated financial statements stage*

6/08, 6/11, 6/14, 12/15

3.1 Definitions

The following definitions are relevant here.

Key terms

Foreign operation. A subsidiary, associate, joint venture or branch of a reporting entity, the activities of which are based or conducted in a country or currency other than those of the reporting entity.

Net investment in a foreign operation. The amount of the reporting entity's interest in the net assets of that operation. *(IAS 21: para. 8)*

3.2 Determining functional currency

FAST FORWARD

You may have to make the decision yourself as to whether the subsidiary has the same functional currency as the parent or a different functional currency from the parent. This determines whether the subsidiary is treated as an **extension of the parent** or as a **net investment.**

A holding or parent company with foreign operations must **translate the financial statements** of those operations into its own reporting currency before they can be consolidated into the group accounts. There are two methods: **the method used depends** upon **whether** the foreign operation has the **same functional currency as the parent**.

IAS 21 states that an entity should consider the following factors in determining its functional currency:

(a) The currency that mainly **influences sales prices** for goods and services (often the currency in which prices are denominated and settled)

(b) The currency of the **country whose competitive forces and regulations** mainly determine the sales prices of its goods and services

(c) The currency that mainly **influences labour, material and other costs** of providing goods or services (often the currency in which prices are denominated and settled)

Sometimes the functional currency of an entity is not immediately obvious. Management must then exercise judgement and may also need to consider:

(a) The currency in which **funds from financing activities** (raising loans and issuing equity) are generated

(b) The currency in which **receipts from operating activities** are usually retained

Where a parent has a foreign operation a number of factors are considered:

(a) Whether the activities of the foreign operation are carried out as an **extension of the parent**, rather than being carried out with a **significant degree of autonomy**.

(b) Whether **transactions with the parent** are a high or a low proportion of the foreign operation's activities.

(c) Whether **cash flows** from the activities of the foreign operation **directly affect the cash flows of the parent** and are readily available for remittance to it.

(d) Whether the activities of the foreign operation are **financed from its own cash flows** or by **borrowing from the parent**.

Exam focus point

A question involving foreign currency is almost certain, in P2, to consist of a foreign operation consolidation.

To sum up: in order to determine the functional currency of a foreign operation it is necessary to consider the **relationship** between the foreign operation and its parent:

- If the foreign operation carries out its business as though it were an **extension of the parent's operations**, it almost certainly has the **same functional currency** as the parent.
- If the foreign operation is **semi-autonomous** it almost certainly has **a different functional currency** from the parent.

The translation method used has to reflect the economic reality of the relationship between the reporting entity (the parent) and the foreign operation.

(IAS 21: paras. 9 to 11)

3.2.1 Same functional currency as the reporting entity

In this situation, the foreign operation normally carries on its business as though it were an **extension of the reporting entity's operations.** For example, it may only sell goods imported from, and remit the proceeds directly to, the reporting entity.

Any **movement in the exchange rate** between the reporting currency and the foreign operation's currency will have an **immediate impact** on the reporting entity's cash flows from the foreign operations. In other words, changes in the exchange rate affect the **individual monetary items** held by the foreign operation, *not* the reporting entity's net investment in that operation.

(IAS 21: para. 11)

3.2.2 Different functional currency from the reporting entity

In this situation, although the reporting entity may be able to exercise control, the foreign operation normally operates in a **semi-autonomous** way. It accumulates cash and other monetary items, generates income and incurs expenses, and may also arrange borrowings, all **in its own local currency**.

A change in the exchange rate will produce **little or no direct effect on the present and future cash flows** from operations of either the foreign operation or the reporting entity. Rather, the change in exchange rate affects the reporting entity's **net investment** in the foreign operation, not the individual monetary and non-monetary items held by the foreign operation. (IAS 21: para. 15)

Exam focus point

Where the foreign operation's functional currency is different from the parent's, the financial statements need to be translated before consolidation.

3.3 Accounting treatment: Different functional currency from the reporting entity

The financial statements of the foreign operation must be translated to the functional currency of the parent. Different procedures must be followed here, because the functional currency of the parent is the **presentation currency** of the foreign operation (IAS 21: para. 29).

(a) The **assets and liabilities** shown in the foreign operation's statement of financial position are translated at the **closing rate** at the year end, regardless of the date on which those items originated. The balancing figure in the translated statement of financial position represents the reporting entity's net investment in the foreign operation.

(b) Amounts in the **statement of profit or loss and other comprehensive income** should be translated at the rate ruling at the date of the transaction (an **average rate** will usually be used for practical purposes).

(c) **Exchange differences** arising from the re-translation at the end of each year of the parent's net investment should be **recognised in other comprehensive income**, not through the profit or loss for the year, until the disposal of the net investment. On disposal, the gains or losses recognised to date will be reclassified to profit or loss.

3.4 Example: Different functional currency from the reporting entity

A dollar-based company, Stone Co, set up a foreign subsidiary on 30 June 20X7. Stone subscribed €24,000 for share capital when the exchange rate was €2 = $1. The subsidiary, Brick Inc, borrowed €72,000 and bought a non-monetary asset for €96,000. Stone Co prepared its accounts on 31 December 20X7 and by that time the exchange rate had moved to €3 = $1. As a result of highly unusual circumstances, Brick Inc sold its asset early in 20X8 for €96,000. It repaid its loan and was liquidated. Stone's capital of €24,000 was repaid in February 20X8 when the exchange rate was €3 = $1.

Required

Account for the above transactions as if the entity has a different functional currency from the parent.

Solution

From the above it can be seen that Stone Co will record its initial investment at $12,000 which is the starting cost of its shares. The statement of financial position of Brick Inc at 31 December 20X7 is summarised below.

	€'000
Non-monetary asset	96
Share capital	24
Loan	72
	96

This may be translated as follows.

	$'000
Non-monetary asset (€3 = $1)	32
Share capital and reserves (retained earnings) (balancing figure)	8
Loan (€3 = $1)	24
	32
Exchange gain/(loss) for 20X7	(4)

The exchange gain and loss are the differences between the value of the original investment ($12,000) and the total of share capital and reserves (retained earnings) as disclosed by the above statements of financial position.

On liquidation, Stone Co will receive $8,000 (€24,000 converted at €3 = $1). No gain or loss will arise in 20X8.

3.5 Some practical points

The following points apply.

(a) For consolidation purposes calculations are simpler if a subsidiary's share capital is translated at the **historical rate** (the rate when the investing company acquired its interest) and post-acquisition reserves are found as a balancing figure.

(b) IAS 21 requires that the accumulated exchange differences should be shown as a separate component of equity (IAS 21: para. 41) but for exam purposes these can be merged with retained earnings.

You must be able to calculate **exchange differences**.

FAST FORWARD

Practising examination questions is the best way of learning this topic.

3.6 Summary of method

A summary of the translation method is given below, which shows the main steps to follow in the consolidation process.

Exam focus point

You should learn this summary.

	Translation
Step 1 Translate the **closing statement of financial position** (assets/equity) and use this for preparing the consolidated statement of financial position in the normal way.	Use the **closing rate** at the year end for all items (see note to step 4).
Step 2 Translate the **statement of profit or loss and other comprehensive income**. (In all cases, dividends should be translated at the rate ruling when the dividend was paid.)	Use the **average rate** for the year for all items (but see comment on dividends). The figures obtained can then be used in preparing the consolidated statement of profit or loss and other comprehensive income but the statement of profit or loss and other comprehensive income cannot be completed until the exchange difference has been calculated.
Step 3 Translate the **shareholders' funds** (net assets) at the beginning of the year.	Use the **closing rate** at the beginning of the year (the opening rate for the current year).
Step 4 Calculate the **total exchange difference** for the year as follows. $ Closing net assets at closing rate (Step 1) X Less opening net assets at opening rate (Step 3) X X Less retained profit as translated (Step 2 less any dividends) X Exchange differences X It may be necessary to adjust for any profits or losses taken direct to reserves during the year.	This stage will be **unnecessary** if you are only required to prepare the statement of financial position. If you are asked to state the total exchange differences or are asked to prepare a statement of profit or loss and other comprehensive income, where the exchange difference will be shown. For **exam purposes** you can translate the closing shareholders' funds as follows. (a) Share capital + pre-acquisition reserves at historical rate. (b) Post-acquisition reserves as a balancing figure.

Question

Consolidated financial statements

The abridged statements of financial position and statement of profit or loss and other comprehensive incomes of Darius Co and its foreign subsidiary, Xerxes Inc, appear below.

DRAFT STATEMENT OF FINANCIAL POSITION AS AT 31 DECEMBER 20X9

	Darius Co	Xerxes Inc
	$	€
Assets		
Non-current assets		
Plant at cost	600	500
Less depreciation	(250)	(200)
	350	300
Investment in Xerxes		
100 €1 shares	25	–
	375	300
Current assets		
Inventories	225	200
Receivables	150	100
	375	300
	750	600
Equity and liabilities		
Equity		
Ordinary $1/€1 shares	300	100
Retained earnings	300	280
	600	380
Long-term loans	50	110
Current liabilities	100	110
	750	600

STATEMENTS OF PROFIT OR LOSS AND OTHER COMPREHENSIVE INCOME FOR THE YEAR ENDED 31 DECEMBER 20X9

	Darius Co	Xerxes Inc
	$	€
Profit before tax	200	160
Tax	100	80
Profit after tax, retained	100	80

The following further information is given.

(a) Darius Co has had its interest in Xerxes Inc since the incorporation of the company. Neither company paid dividends during the year to 31 December 20X9 and neither company had any other comprehensive income in their separate financial statements.

(b) Depreciation is 8% per annum on cost.

(c) There have been no loan repayments or movements in non-current assets during the year. The opening inventory of Xerxes Inc was €120. Assume that inventory turnover times are very short.

(d) Exchange rates:
€ 4 to $1 when Xerxes Inc was incorporated
€ 2.5 to $1 when Xerxes Inc acquired its non-current assets
€ 2 to $1 on 31 December 20X8
€ 1.6 to $1 average rate of exchange year ending 31 December 20X9
€ 1 to $1 on 31 December 20X9.

Required

Prepare the summarised consolidated financial statements of Darius Co.

Answer

Step 1 The statement of financial position of Xerxes Inc at 31 December 20X9, other than share capital and retained earnings, should be translated at €1 = $1.

SUMMARISED STATEMENT OF FINANCIAL POSITION AT 31 DECEMBER 20X9

	$
Non-current assets (NBV)	300
Current assets	
Inventories	200
Receivables	100
	300
	600
Non-current liabilities	110
Current liabilities	110

∴ Shareholders' funds = 600 – 110 – 110 = $380

Since Darius Co acquired the whole of the issued share capital on incorporation, the post-acquisition retained earnings including exchange differences will be the value of shareholders' funds arrived at above, less the original cost to Darius Co of $25.
Post-acquisition retained earnings = $380 – $25 = $355.

SUMMARISED CONSOLIDATED STATEMENT OF FINANCIAL POSITION AS AT 31 DECEMBER 20X9

		$
Assets		
Non-current assets (NBV)	$(350 + 300)	650
Current assets		
Inventories	$(225 + 200)	425
Receivables	$(150 + 100)	250
		675
		1,325
Equity and liabilities		
Equity		
Ordinary $1 shares (Darius only)		300
Retained earnings	$(300 + 355)	655
		955
Non-current liabilities: loans	$(50 + 110)	160
Current liabilities	$(100 + 110)	210
		1,325

Note. It is quite unnecessary to know the amount of the exchange differences when preparing the consolidated statement of financial position.

Step 2 The statement of profit or loss and other comprehensive income should be translated at average rate (€1.6 = $1).

XERXES INC
SUMMARISED STATEMENT OF PROFIT OR LOSS AND OTHER COMPREHENSIVE INCOME FOR THE YEAR ENDED 31 DECEMBER 20X9

	$
Profit before tax	100
Tax	50
Profit after tax	50

SUMMARISED CONSOLIDATED STATEMENT OF PROFIT OR LOSS AND OTHER COMPREHENSIVE INCOME FOR THE YEAR ENDED 31 DECEMBER 20X9

		$
Profit before tax	$(200 + 100)	300
Tax	$(100 + 50)	150
Profit after tax	$(100 + 50)	150

The statement of profit or loss and other comprehensive income cannot be completed until the exchange difference has been calculated.

Step 3 The equity interest at the beginning of the year can be found as follows.

	€
Equity value at 31 December 20X9	380
Retained profit for year	80
Equity value at 31 December 20X8	300
Translated at €2 = $1, this gives	$150

Step 4 The exchange difference can now be calculated and the statement of profit or loss and other comprehensive income completed.

	$
Equity interest at 31 December 20X9 (stage 1)	380
Equity interest at 1 January 20X9 (stage 3)	150
	230
Less retained profit (stage 2)	50
Exchange gain	180

SUMMARISED CONSOLIDATED STATEMENT OF PROFIT OR LOSS AND OTHER COMPREHENSIVE INCOME FOR THE YEAR ENDED 31 DECEMBER 20X9

		$
Profit before tax	$(200 + 100)	300
Tax	$(100 + 50)	150
Profit after tax	$(100 + 50)	150
Other comprehensive income (items that may be re-classified to profit or loss*)		
Exchange difference on translating foreign operations		180
Total comprehensive income		330

*See Chapter 10 for an explanation of this caption.

CONSOLIDATED STATEMENT OF CHANGES IN EQUITY (EXTRACT FOR RESERVES) FOR THE YEAR ENDED 31 DECEMBER 20X9

	$
Consolidated reserves at 31 December 20X8	325
Total comprehensive income	330
Consolidated reserves at 31 December 20X9	655

(**Note.** The post-acquisition reserves of Xerxes Inc at the beginning of the year must have been $150 – $25 = $125 and the reserves of Darius Co must have been $300 – $100 = $200. The consolidated reserves must therefore have been $325.)

3.7 Analysis of exchange differences

The exchange differences in the above exercise could be reconciled by splitting them into their component parts.

Exam focus point

> Such a split is not required by IAS 21, nor is it required in your exam, but it may help your understanding of the subject.

The exchange difference consists of those exchange gains/losses arising from:

- Translating **income/expense items** at the exchange rates at the date of transactions, whereas **assets/liabilities** are translated at the closing rate.
- Translating the **opening net investment** (opening net assets) in the foreign entity at a closing rate different from the closing rate at which it was previously reported.

This can be demonstrated using the above question.

Using the opening statement of financial position and translating at €2 = $1 and €1 = $1 gives the following.

	€2 = $1	€1 = $1	Difference
	$	$	$
Non-current assets at NBV	170	340	170
Inventories	60	120	60
Net current monetary liabilities	(25)	(50)	(25)
	205	410	205
Equity	150	300	150
Loans	55	110	55
	205	410	205

Translating the statement of profit or loss and other comprehensive income using €1.60 = $1 and €1 = $1 gives the following results.

	€1.60 = $1	€1 = $1	Difference
	$	$	$
Profit before tax, depreciation and increase in inventory values	75	120	45
Increase in inventory values	50	80	30
	125	200	75
Depreciation	(25)	(40)	(15)
	100	160	60
Tax	(50)	(80)	(30)
Profit after tax, retained	50	80	30

The overall position is then:

	$	$
Gain on non-current assets ($170 – $15)		155
Loss on loan		(55)
Gain on inventories ($60 + $30)	90	
Loss on net monetary current assets/ Liabilities (all other differences) ($45 – $30 – $25)	(10)	
		80
Net exchange gain: as above		180

3.8 Non-controlling interests

In problems involving non-controlling interest the following points should be noted.

(a) The figure for **non-controlling interest in the statement of financial position** will be calculated using the method seen in earlier chapters and including the appropriate proportion of the translated share capital and reserves of the subsidiary.

(b) The **non-controlling interest in the reconciliation following the statement of profit or loss and other comprehensive income** will be the appropriate proportion of dollar profits and other comprehensive income. The non-controlling interest in other comprehensive income will include their share of exchange differences on translating the subsidiary but will exclude exchange differences arising on retranslating goodwill (see below) if the group measures non-controlling interests at acquisition using the proportionate method.

3.9 Goodwill and fair value adjustments

Goodwill and fair value adjustments arising on the acquisition of a foreign operation should be treated as assets and liabilities of the acquired entity. This means that they should be expressed in the functional currency of the foreign operation and translated at the **closing rate**.

Here is a layout for calculating goodwill and the exchange gain or loss. The parent holds 90% of the shares. NCI is valued as the proportionate share of the fair value of the subsidiary's identifiable net assets.

Goodwill

	F'000	F'000	*Rate*	$'000
Consideration transferred (12,000 × 6)		72,000		
Non-controlling interest		6,600		
66,000 × 10%		78,600		
Less				
Less share capital	40,000			
Pre acquisition retained earnings	26,000			
		(66,000)		
At 1.4.X1		12,600	6*	2,100
Foreign exchange gain		–	Balance	420
At 31.3.X7		12,600	5**	2,520

* Historic rate

** Closing rate

3.10 Example: including goodwill and non-controlling interests

Henley acquired 70% of Saar a foreign company for Units 4,500 on 31 December 20X4 when the retained reserves of Saar were Units 1,125. No impairment losses had been necessary up to 31 December 20X7. Neither company paid or declared dividends during the year.

Group policy is to measure non-controlling interests at acquisition at their proportionate share of the fair value of the identifiable net assets.

Exchange rates	Units to $1
31 December 20X4	4.5
31 December 20X6	4.3
31 December 20X7	4
Average exchange rate for year ended 31 December 20X7	3.8

Required

Prepare the consolidated statement of profit or loss and other comprehensive income, statement of financial position and statement of changes in equity (attributable to equity holders of the parent *only*) for the Henley Group for the year ended 31 December 20X7.

Note. In the exam you would expect the question to show the separate financial statements of the parent and the subsidiary. These have been included alongside the solution below, to make it easier to illustrate the methods being used.

Solution

Statement of financial position

In questions asking for a full set of financial statements including a foreign subsidiary, it is always best to start with the statement of financial position. The starting point, as always, is to draw up the group structure:

Group structure

Henley

31.12.X4 | 70%

Pre-acquisition ret'd reserves 1,125 Units

Saar

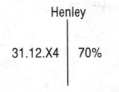

The following table includes:

- The separate statements of financial position of Henley and Saar, each in their own currency (these would normally be given within the question information)
- A column showing the exchange rates chosen to translate Saar's balances into $
- A column showing the translated statement of financial position of Saar
- A final column showing the consolidated statement of financial position for the Saar Group (consolidation workings are shown below the table)

STATEMENTS OF FINANCIAL POSITION AT 31 DECEMBER 20X7

	Henley	*Saar*	*Rate*	*Saar*	*Consol*
	$	Units		$	$
Property, plant and equipment	4,500	4,000	4	1,000	5,500
Goodwill (W1)					534
Investment in Saar	1,000				
Current assets	2,400	3,000	4	750	3,150
	7,900	7,000		1,750	9,184
Share capital	2,000	2,250	4.5	500	2,000
Pre-acquisition reserves		1,125	4.5	250	
				750	
Post-acquisition reserves (W2)	4,400	2,825	β	800	5,019
	6,400	6,200		1,550	7,019
Non-controlling interest					465
					7,484
Loans	1,500	800	4	200	1,700
	7,900	7,000		1,750	9,184

Workings

1 *Goodwill*

	Units	*Units*	Rate	$
Consideration transferred		4,500	4.5	1,000
Non-controlling interests (30% × 3,375)		1,012	4.5	225
Share capital	2,250			
Retained reserves	1,125			
		(3,375)	4.5	(750)
		2,137	4.5	475
Exchange gain 20X5-20X6 b/d		–	β	22
At 31.12.X6		2,137	4.3	497
Exchange gain 20X7		–	β	37
At 31.12.X7		2,137	4	534

Note. Goodwill is initially measured in the **subsidiary's currency**, then retranslated at each year end so that we can identify the cumulative exchange differences. In the consolidated statement of financial position these are taken to reserves (see working 2)

2 *Retained reserves carried forward*

	$
Henley	4,400
Saar (800(W2) × 70%)	560
Goodwill – exchange gain ((W1): (22 + 37) × 70%	41
	5,001

Note. The post-acquisition reserves of Saar have been taken from the translated statement of financial position of Saar, where it was calculated as a balancing figure.

3 *Non-controlling interests (SOFP)*

	$
NCI at acquisition (W1)	225
Add: NCI share of post-acquisition retained reserves of Saar ((W2) 800 + (22 + 37) × 30%)	258
	483

Statement of profit or loss and other comprehensive income

Again this has been laid out with the separate statements for the parent and subsidiary alongside the solution. The following table includes:

- The separate statements of profit or loss and other comprehensive income of Henley and Saar, each in their own currency (these would normally be given within the question information)
- A column showing the exchange rates chosen to translate Saar's balances into $
- A column showing the translated statement of profit or loss and other comprehensive income of Saar
- A final column showing the consolidated statement of profit or loss and other comprehensive income for the Saar Group (consolidation workings are shown below the table)

STATEMENTS OF PROFIT OR LOSS AND OTHER COMPREHENSIVE INCOME
FOR THE YEAR ENDED 31 DECEMBER 20X7

	Henley $	*Saar* Units	*Rate*	*Saar* $	*Consol* $
Revenue	12,000	5,700	3.8	1,500	13,500
Cost of sales	(7,000)	(2,470)	3.8	(650)	(7,650)
Gross profit	5,000	3,230		850	5,850
Operating expenses	(3,025)	(570)	3.8	150	(3,175)
Profit before tax	1,975	2,660		700	2,675
Income tax expense	(500)	(760)	3.8	(200)	(700)
Profit for the year	1,475	1,900		500	1,975
Other comprehensive income:					
Exchange difference on translating foreign operations (W4)					87
Total comprehensive income for the year					2,062
Profit attributable to:					
Equity holders of the parent					1,825
Non-controlling interests (500 (from Saar's translated profit) × 30%)					150
					1,975
Total comprehensive income attributable to:					
Owners of the parent (2,062 – 165)					1,897
Non-controlling interests ((500 (Saar's translated profit) + 50 (W4)) × 30%)					165
					2,062

Note. *(i)* It is worth noticing that you can translate the subsidiary's figures, complete the consolidation as far as the profit for the year and complete the reconciliation of profit showing amounts attributable to the owners of the parent and to the non-controlling interest **before calculating the exchange difference**.

Note. *(ii)* The **total** exchange differences arising are shown as other comprehensive income in the consolidated statement of financial position, but the non-controlling interest only includes the NCI share of the exchange difference on retranslating Saar's net assets. This is because there is no NCI in goodwill in this example as the group uses the proportionate method to measure non-controlling interests at acquisition.

Workings (continued)

4 *Exchange differences in period (gross)*

	$	$
On translation of net assets		
Closing NA @ CR (6,200 @ 4)	1,550	
Opening NA @ OR ((Units 6,200 –1,900) @ 4.3)	1,000	
	550	
Less retained profit as translated	(500)	
		50
On goodwill (W1)		37
		87

Note. The closing net asset figure is taken from Saar's local currency statement of financial position and translated at the year end rate. The opening net asset figure is calculated by deducting Saar's profit for the year to work back to the opening figure, then translating it at the prior year's closing rate.

Statement of changes in equity

CONSOLIDATED STATEMENT OF CHANGES IN EQUITY (ATTRIBUTABLE TO EQUITY HOLDERS OF THE PARENT) FOR THE YEAR ENDED 31 DECEMBER 20X7

	$
Balance at 31 December 20X6 (2,000 + (W5) 3,122)	5,122
Total comprehensive income for the year	1,897
Balance at 31 December 20X7 (per SOFP)	7,019

Note: If a question like this appears in the exam, notice that once you have completed the other requirements, you can take the year end figure for equity from the consolidated statement of financial position, and the total comprehensive income for the year from the statement of profit or loss and other comprehensive income. At that point you could fill in a balancing figure for the brought forward balance. It can also be calculated by adding the parent's share capital to the brought forward group retained reserves (see working below).

5 *Retained reserves brought forward*

	$	$
Henley per question (4,400 – 1,475)		2,925
Saar NA b/d (W4)	1,000	
NA at acquisition (see Saar's translated SOFP)	(750)	
	250	
Saar – Group share (250 × 70%)		175
Exchange gain on goodwill b/d (W1)		22
		3,122

3.11 Further matters relating to foreign operations

3.11.1 Consolidation procedures

Follow normal consolidation procedures, except that where an exchange difference arises on **long – or short-term intra-group monetary items**, these cannot be offset against other intra-group balances. This is because these are commitments to convert one currency into another, thus exposing the reporting entity to a gain or loss through currency fluctuations.

If the foreign operation's **reporting date** is different from that of the parent, it is acceptable to use the accounts made up to that date for consolidation, as long as adjustments are made for any significant changes in rates in the interim.

3.11.2 Disposal of foreign entity

When a parent disposes of a foreign entity, the cumulative amount of deemed exchange differences relating to that foreign entity should be **recognised as an income or expense** in the same period in which the gain or loss on disposal is recognised. Effectively, this means that these exchange differences are recognised once by taking them to reserves and then are recognised for a second time ('recycled') by transferring them to profit or loss on disposal of the foreign operation (IAS 21: para. 48).

3.11.3 In the parent's accounts

In the parent company's own accounts, exchange differences arising on a **monetary item** that is effectively part of the parent's net investment in the foreign entity should be recognised **in profit or loss** in the separate financial statements of the reporting entity or the individual financial statements of the foreign operation, as appropriate (IAS 21: para. 34).

3.12 Change in functional currency

The functional currency of an entity can be changed only if there is a change to the underlying transactions, events and conditions that are relevant to the entity. For example, an entity's functional currency may change if there is a change in the currency that mainly influences the sales price of goods and services.

Where there is a change in an entity's functional currency, the entity translates all items into the new functional currency **prospectively** (ie, from the date of the change) using the exchange rate at the date of the change.

(IAS 21: para. 13, 35)

3.12.1 Tax effects of exchange differences

IAS 12 *Income taxes* should be applied when there are tax effects arising from gains or losses on foreign currency transactions and exchange differences arising on the translation of the financial statements of foreign operations. (IAS 21: paras. 28, 29)

3.12.2 Foreign associated undertakings

Foreign associates will be companies with substantial autonomy from the group and so their **functional currency will be different** from that of the parent.

3.13 Section summary

- Where the functional currency of a foreign operation is **different** from that of the parent/reporting entity, they need to be translated before consolidation
  - Operation is semi-autonomous
  - Translate assets and liabilities at **closing rate**
  - Translate statement of profit or loss and other comprehensive income at **average rate**
  - Exchange differences through **reserves/equity**

Chapter Roundup

- Questions on foreign currency translation have always been popular with examiners. In general, you are required to prepare **consolidated accounts** for a group which includes a foreign subsidiary.
- You may have to make the decision yourself as to whether the subsidiary has the same functional currency as the parent or a different functional currency from the parent. This determines whether the subsidiary is treated as an **extension of the parent** or as a **net investment**.
- **Practising** examination questions is the best way of learning this topic.

Quick Quiz

1 What is the difference between conversion and translation?

2 Define 'monetary' items according to IAS 21.

3 How should foreign currency transactions be recognised initially in an individual enterprise's accounts?

4 What factors must management take into account when determining the functional currency of a foreign operation?

5 How should goodwill and fair value adjustments be treated on consolidation of a foreign operation?

6 When can an entity's functional currency be changed?

Answers to Quick Quiz

1 (a) Conversion is the process of exchanging one currency for another.
  (b) Translation is the restatement of the value of one currency in another currency.

2 Money held and assets and liabilities to be received or paid in fixed or determinable amounts of money.

3 Use the exchange rate at the date of the transaction. An average rate for a period can be used if the exchange rates did not fluctuate significantly.

4 See Section 3.2

5 Treat as assets/liabilities of the foreign operation and translate at the closing rate.

6 Only if there is a change to the underlying transactions relevant to the entity.

Now try the question below from the Practice Question Bank

Number	Level	Marks	Time
Q23	Examination	18	35 mins

Group statements of cash flows

17

Topic list	Syllabus reference
1 Cash flows	D1
2 IAS 7 *Statement of cash flows: Single company*	D1
3 Consolidated statements of cash flows	D1

Introduction

A statement of cash flows is an additional primary statement of **great value** to users of financial statements for the extra information it provides.

You should be familiar with the basic principles, techniques and definitions relating to statements of cash flows from your earlier studies. This chapter develops the principles and preparation techniques to include **consolidated financial statements**.

Study guide

		Intellectual level
D1	**Group accounting including statements of cash flows**	
(j)	Prepare and discuss group statements of cash flows	3

Exam guide

A group statement of cash flows could well appear in the case study question in compulsory Section A of the paper as it did in the Pilot Paper.

1 Cash flows 12/13

FAST FORWARD

Statements of cash flows are a useful addition to the financial statements of companies because it is recognised that accounting profit is not the only indicator of a company's performance.

Statements of cash flows concentrate on the sources and uses of cash and are a useful indicator of a company's **liquidity and solvency**.

Cash flows are much easier to understand as a concept than accounting profits. The main advantages of using cash flow accounting (including both historical and forecast cash flows) are as follows:

(a) **Survival** of a company depends on its ability to generate cash. Cash flow accounting directs attention towards this critical issue.

(b) Cash flow is more **comprehensive** than 'profit' which is dependent on accounting conventions and concepts.

(c) Creditors (long- and short-term) are more interested in an entity's **ability to repay** them than in its profitability. Whereas 'profits' might indicate that cash is likely to be available, cash flow accounting is more direct with its message.

(d) Cash flow reporting provides a better means of **comparing** the results of different companies than traditional profit reporting.

(e) Cash flow reporting satisfies the **needs of all users** better.

   (i) For **management**. It provides the sort of information on which decisions should be taken (in management accounting, 'relevant costs' to a decision are future cash flows). Traditional profit accounting does not help with decision-making.

   (ii) For **shareholders and auditors**. Cash flow accounting can provide a satisfactory basis for stewardship accounting.

   (iii) For **creditors and employees**. Their information needs will be better served by cash flow accounting.

(f) **Cash flow forecasts** are easier to prepare, as well as more useful, than profit forecasts.

(g) Cash flow accounts can be **audited more easily** than accounts based on the accruals concept.

(h) The accruals concept is confusing, and cash flows are more **easily understood**.

(i) Cash flow accounting can be both **retrospective**, and also include a **forecast** for the future. This is of great information value to all users of accounting information.

(j) Forecasts can subsequently be monitored by the use of **variance statements** which compare actual cash flows against the forecast.

Looking at the same question from a different angle, readers of accounts can be **misled** by the profit figure.

(a) Shareholders might believe that if a company makes a profit after tax of, say $100,000 then this is the amount which it could afford to pay as a **dividend**. Unless the company has sufficient cash available to stay in business and also to pay a dividend, the shareholders' expectations would be wrong.

(b) Employees might believe that if a company makes profits, it can afford to pay **higher wages** next year. This opinion may not be correct: the ability to pay wages depends on the availability of cash.

(c) Creditors might consider that a profitable company is a **going concern**.

   (i) If a company builds up large amounts of **unsold inventories** of goods, their cost would not be chargeable against profits, but cash would have been used up in making them, thus weakening the company's liquid resources.

   (ii) A company might capitalise large **development costs**, having spent considerable amounts of money on R & D, but only charge small amounts against current profits. As a result, the company might show reasonable profits, but get into severe difficulties with its liquidity position.

(d) Management might suppose that if their company makes a historical cost profit, and reinvests some of those profits, then the company must be **expanding**. This is not the case: in a period of inflation, a company might have a historical cost profit but a current cost accounting loss, which means that the operating capability of the firm will be declining.

(e) **Survival** of a business entity depends not so much on profits as on its ability to pay its debts when they fall due. Such payments might include 'profit or loss' items such as material purchases, wages, interest and taxation etc, but also capital payments for new non-current assets and the repayment of loan capital when this falls due (eg on the redemption of debentures).

2 IAS 7 *Statement of cash flows: Single company*

FAST FORWARD

You need to be aware of the **format** of the statement as laid out in **IAS 7**. Setting out the format is an essential first stage in preparing the statement, so this format must be learnt.

The aim of IAS 7 is to provide information to users of financial statements about the cash flows of an entity's **ability to generate cash and cash equivalents**, as well as indicating the cash needs of the entity. The statement of cash flows provides **historical** information about cash and cash equivalents, classifying cash flows between operating, investing and financing activities.

2.1 Scope

A statement of cash flows should be presented as an **integral part** of an entity's financial statements. All types of entity can provide useful information about cash flows as the need for cash is universal, whatever the nature of their revenue-producing activities. Therefore **all entities are required by the standard to produce a statement of cash flows**. (IAS 7: para. 1)

2.2 Benefits of cash flow information

The use of statements of cash flows is very much **in conjunction** with the rest of the financial statements. Users can gain further appreciation of the change in net assets, of the entity's financial position (liquidity and solvency) and the entity's ability to adapt to changing circumstances by affecting the amount and timing of cash flows. Statements of cash flows **enhance comparability** as they are not affected by differing accounting policies used for the same type of transactions or events.

Cash flow information of a historical nature can be used as an indicator of the amount, timing and certainty of future cash flows. Past forecast cash flow information can be **checked for accuracy** as actual figures emerge. The relationship between profit and cash flows can be analysed as can changes in prices over time.

2.3 Definitions

The standard gives the following definitions, the most important of which are **cash** and **cash equivalents**.

Key terms

Cash comprises cash on hand and demand deposits.

Cash equivalents are short-term, highly liquid investments that are readily convertible to known amounts of cash and which are subject to an insignificant risk of changes in value.

Cash flows are inflows and outflows of cash and cash equivalents.

Operating activities are the principal revenue-producing activities of the entity and other activities that are not investing or financing activities.

Investing activities are the acquisition and disposal of long-term assets and other investments not included in cash equivalents.

Financing activities are activities that result in changes in the size and composition of the equity capital and borrowings of the entity. *(IAS 7: para. 6)*

2.4 Cash and cash equivalents

The standard expands on the definition of cash equivalents: they are not held for investment or other long-term purposes, but rather to meet short-term cash commitments. To fulfil the above definition, an investment's **maturity date should normally be three months from its acquisition date**. It would usually be the case then that equity investments (ie shares in other companies) are **not** cash equivalents. An exception would be where preferred shares were acquired with a very close maturity date.

Loans and other borrowings from banks are classified as investing activities. In some countries, however, **bank overdrafts** are repayable on demand and are treated as part of an entity's total cash management system. In these circumstances an overdrawn balance will be included in cash and cash equivalents. Such banking arrangements are characterised by a balance which fluctuates between overdrawn and credit.

Movements between different types of cash and cash equivalent are not included in cash flows. The investment of surplus cash in cash equivalents is part of cash management, not part of operating, investing or financing activities. (IAS 7: paras. 7 to 9)

2.5 Presentation of a statement of cash flows

IAS 7 requires statements of cash flows to report cash flows during the period classified by **operating, investing and financing activities**. (IAS 7: para. 10)

The manner of presentation of cash flows from operating, investing and financing activities **depends on the nature of the entity**. By classifying cash flows between different activities in this way users can see the impact on cash and cash equivalents of each one, and their relationships with each other. We can look at each in more detail.

2.5.1 Operating activities

This is perhaps the key part of the statement of cash flows because it shows whether, and to what extent, companies can **generate cash from their operations**. It is these operating cash flows which must, in the end pay for all cash outflows relating to other activities, ie paying loan interest, dividends and so on.

Most of the components of cash flows from operating activities will be those items which **determine the net profit or loss of the entity**, ie they relate to the main revenue-producing activities of the entity. The standard gives the following as examples of cash flows from operating activities (IAS 7: para. 14).

- Cash receipts from the sale of goods and the rendering of services
- Cash receipts from royalties, fees, commissions and other revenue
- Cash payments to suppliers for goods and services

- Cash payments to and on behalf of employees
- Cash payments/refunds of income taxes unless they can be specifically identified with financing or investing activities
- Cash receipts and payments from contracts held for dealing or trading purposes

Certain items may be included in the net profit or loss for the period which do *not* relate to operational cash flows, for example the profit or loss on the sale of a piece of plant will be included in net profit or loss, but the cash flows will be classed as **financing**.

2.5.2 Investing activities

The cash flows classified under this heading show the extent of new investment in **assets which will generate future profit and cash flows**. The standard gives the following examples of cash flows arising from investing activities (IAS 7: para. 16).

- Cash payments to acquire property, plant and equipment, intangibles and other long-term assets, including those relating to capitalised development costs and self-constructed property, plant and equipment
- Cash receipts from sales of property, plant and equipment, intangibles and other long-term assets
- Cash payments to acquire shares or debentures of other entities
- Cash receipts from sales of shares or debentures of other entities
- Cash advances and loans made to other parties
- Cash receipts from the repayment of advances and loans made to other parties
- Cash payments for or receipts from futures/forward/option/swap contracts except where the contracts are held for dealing purposes, or the payments/receipts are classified as financing activities

2.5.3 Financing activities

This section of the statement of cash flows shows the share of cash which the entity's capital providers have claimed during the period. This is an indicator of **likely future interest and dividend payments**. The standard gives the following examples of cash flows which might arise under these headings (IAS 7: para. 17):

- Cash proceeds from issuing shares
- Cash payments to owners to acquire or redeem the entity's shares
- Cash proceeds from issuing debentures, loans, notes, bonds, mortgages and other short or long-term borrowings
- Cash repayments of amounts borrowed
- Cash payments by a lessee for the reduction of the outstanding liability relating to a lease

2.6 Reporting cash flows from operating activities

The standard offers a choice of method for this part of the statement of cash flows (IAS 7: para. 18).

(a) **Direct method:** disclose major classes of gross cash receipts and gross cash payments.

(b) **Indirect method**: net profit or loss is adjusted for the effects of transactions of a non-cash nature, any deferrals or accruals of past or future operating cash receipts or payments, and items of income or expense associated with investing or financing cash flows.

The **direct method is the preferred method** because it discloses information, not available elsewhere in the financial statements, which could be of use in estimating future cash flows. The example below shows both methods (IAS 7: para. 19).

2.6.1 Using the direct method

There are different ways in which the **information about gross cash receipts and payments** can be obtained. The most obvious way is simply to extract the information from the accounting records. This may be a laborious task, however, and the indirect method below may be easier.

2.6.2 Using the indirect method

This method is undoubtedly **easier** from the point of view of the preparer of the statement of cash flows. The net profit or loss for the period is adjusted for the following (IAS 7: para. 20).

(a) Changes during the period in inventories, operating receivables and payables
(b) Non-cash items, eg depreciation, provisions, profits/losses on the sales of assets
(c) Other items, the cash flows from which should be classified under investing or financing activities

A **proforma** of such a calculation is as follows and this method may be more common in the exam. This has been adapted from IAS 7: Illustrative Examples, para. 3.

	$
Profit before taxation (statement of profit or loss and other comprehensive income)	X
Add depreciation	X
Loss (profit) on sale of non-current assets	X
(Increase)/decrease in inventories	(X)/X
(Increase)/decrease in receivables	(X)/X
Increase/(decrease) in payables	X/(X)
Cash generated from operations	X
Interest (paid)/received	(X)
Income taxes paid	(X)
Net cash flows from operating activities	X

It is important to understand why **certain items are added and others subtracted.** Note the following points.

(a) Depreciation is not a cash expense, but is deducted in arriving at the profit figure in the statement of comprehensive income. It makes sense, therefore, to eliminate it by adding it back.

(b) By the same logic, a loss on a disposal of a non-current asset (arising through underprovision of depreciation) needs to be added back and a profit deducted.

(c) An increase in inventories means less cash – you have spent cash on buying inventory.

(d) An increase in receivables means the company's credit customers have not paid as much, and therefore there is less cash.

(e) If we pay off payables, causing the figure to decrease, again we have less cash.

2.6.3 Indirect versus direct **12/10**

The direct method is encouraged where the necessary information is not too costly to obtain, but IAS 7 does not require it, and **favours the indirect method**. In practice, therefore, the direct method is rarely used. It is not obvious that IAS 7 is right in favouring the indirect method. It could be argued that companies ought to monitor their cash flows carefully enough on an ongoing basis to be able to use the direct method at minimal extra cost.

Exam focus point

In December 2010 students were asked to discuss the ethical implications of favouring the indirect method over the direct method.

2.7 Interest and dividends

Cash flows from interest and dividends received and paid should each be **disclosed separately**. Each should be classified in a consistent manner from period to period as either operating, investing or financing activities.

Dividends paid by the entity can be classified in **one of two ways**:

(a) As a **financing cash flow**, showing the cost of obtaining financial resources.

(b) As a component of **cash flows from operating activities** so that users can assess the entity's ability to pay dividends out of operating cash flows.

(IAS 7: para. 31)

2.8 Taxes on income

Cash flows arising from taxes on income should be **separately disclosed** and should be classified as cash flows from operating activities **unless** they can be specifically identified with financing and investing activities.

Taxation cash flows are often **difficult to match** to the originating underlying transaction, so most of the time all tax cash flows are classified as arising from operating activities.

(IAS 7: para. 35)

2.9 Components of cash and cash equivalents

The components of cash and cash equivalents should be disclosed and a **reconciliation** should be presented, showing the amounts in the statement of cash flows reconciled with the equivalent items reported in the statement of financial position.

It is also necessary to disclose the **accounting policy** used in deciding the items included in cash and cash equivalents, in accordance with IAS 1, but also because of the wide range of cash management practices worldwide.

(IAS 7: para. 45)

2.10 Other disclosures

All entities should disclose, together with a **commentary by management**, any other information likely to be of importance (IAS 7: paras. 48 to 50).

(a) Restrictions on the use of or access to any part of cash equivalents.

(b) The amount of undrawn borrowing facilities which are available.

(c) Cash flows which increased operating capacity compared to cash flows which merely maintained operating capacity.

2.11 Example of a statement of cash flows

In the next section we will look at the procedures for preparing a statement of cash flows. First, look at this **example**, adapted from the example given in the standard.

2.11.1 Direct method

STATEMENT OF CASH FLOWS (DIRECT METHOD)
YEAR ENDED 20X7

	$m	$m
Cash flows from operating activities		
Cash receipts from customers	30,150	
Cash paid to suppliers and employees	(27,600)	
Cash generated from operations	2,550	
Interest paid	(270)	
Income taxes paid	(900)	
Net cash from operating activities c/fwd		1,380
Net cash from operating activities b/fwd		1,380
Cash flows from investing activities		
Purchase of property, plant and equipment	(900)	
Proceeds from sale of equipment	20	
Interest received	200	
Dividends received	200	
Net cash used in investing activities		(480)
Cash flows from financing activities		
Proceeds from issuance of share capital	250	
Proceeds from long-term borrowings	250	
Payment of lease liabilities	(90)	
Dividends paid*	(1,200)	
Net cash used in financing activities		(790)
Net increase in cash and cash equivalents		110
Cash and cash equivalents at beginning of period (Note)		120
Cash and cash equivalents at end of period (Note)		230

* This could also be shown as an operating cash flow

2.11.2 Indirect method

STATEMENT OF CASH FLOWS (INDIRECT METHOD)
YEAR ENDED 20X7

	$m	$m
Cash flows from operating activities		
Profit before taxation	3,390	
Adjustments for:		
Depreciation	450	
Investment income	(500)	
Interest expense	400	
	3,740	
Increase in trade and other receivables	(500)	
Decrease in inventories	1,050	
Decrease in trade payables	(1,740)	
Cash generated from operations	2,550	
Interest paid	(270)	
Income taxes paid	(900)	
Net cash from operating activities		1,380
Cash flows from investing activities		
Purchase of property, plant and equipment	(900)	
Proceeds from sale of equipment	20	
Interest received	200	
Dividends received	200	
Net cash used in investing activities		(480)
Cash flows from financing activities		
Proceeds from issue of share capital	250	
Proceeds from long-term borrowings	250	
Payment of lease liabilities	(90)	
Dividends paid*	(1,200)	
Net cash used in financing activities		(790)
Net increase in cash and cash equivalents c/f		110
		$m
Net increase in cash and cash equivalents b/f		110
Cash and cash equivalents at beginning of period (Note)		120
Cash and cash equivalents at end of period (Note)		230

* This could also be shown as an operating cash flow

	20X7	*20X6*
	$m	$m
Cash on hand and balances with banks	40	25
Short-term investments	190	95
Cash and cash equivalents	230	120

2.12 Criticisms of IAS 7

The main disadvantages of cash accounting are essentially the advantages of accruals accounting (proper matching of related items). There is also the practical problem that few businesses keep historical cash flow information in the form needed to prepare a historical statement of cash flows and so extra record keeping is likely to be necessary.

The inclusion of **cash equivalents** has been criticised because it does not reflect the way in which businesses are managed: in particular, the requirement that to be a cash equivalent an investment has to be within three months of maturity is considered **unrealistic**.

The management of assets similar to cash (ie 'cash equivalents') is not distinguished from other investment decisions.

Further issues have been identified by the IASB include the following.

(a) **Volatility of cash flows.** Under accruals accounting, by contrast, uneven inflows and outflows are assigned to the period in which they are earned or incurred.

(b) **Exclusion of non-cash transactions,** such as the acquisition of assets under leases and goods and services acquired in exchange for shares. While it may be possible to modify the cash flow statement to include such transactions, that undermine the purpose of the statement. It would also be difficult to determine which non-cash transactions should be included and which should not.

(c) **There are many variants of 'free cash flow'.** It would probably be difficult to obtain agreement on what is the single measure that should be prescribed by an accounting standard. It would seem likely that no single measure would be the best for all purposes.

These deficiencies have led the IASB to consider better disclosures as part of their Disclosure Initiative project.

2.13 Amendments to IAS 7 under the IASB's Disclosure Initiative

An overview of the IASB's disclosure initiative is given in Chapter 19 on current developments. In January 2016, the IASB published amendments to IAS 7 intended to improve information provided to users of financial statements **about an entity's financing activities.** They are effective for annual periods beginning on or after 1 January 2017.

2.13.1 Improved information about an entity's financing activities, excluding equity items

The objective of the amendments is that IAS 7 should provide disclosures that enable users of financial statements to evaluate changes in liabilities arising from financing activities (IAS 7: Para. 44A).

To achieve this objective, entities reporting cash flows under IAS 7 must **disclose the following changes in liabilities arising from financing activities** (IAS 7: Para. 44B):

(a) Changes from financing cash flows
(b) Changes arising from obtaining or losing control of subsidiaries or other businesses
(c) The effect of changes in foreign exchange rates;
(d) Changes in fair values, and
(e) Other changes.

Liabilities arising from financing activities are defined by the IASB as liabilities 'for which cash flows were, or future cash flows will be, classified in the statement of cash flows as cash flows from financing activities'. If financial assets meet the same definition, then the new disclosure requirements will also relate to financial assets (IAS 7: Para. 44C).

One way (IAS 7: Para. 44C). to fulfil the new disclosure requirement is to provide a **reconciliation of cash flows arising from financing activities** (as reported in the statement of cash flows excluding contributed equity) **to the corresponding liabilities in the opening and closing statement of financial position.**

The reconciliation could include:

(a) Opening balances in the statement of financial position
(b) Movements in the period
(c) Closing balances in the statement of financial position

However, this reconciliation is not obligatory, as was proposed in the 2014 ED on the subject.

Lastly, the amendments state that changes in liabilities arising from financing activities must **be disclosed separately from changes in other assets and liabilities** (IAS 7: Para. 44E).

2.14 Section summary

FAST FORWARD

Remember the **step-by-step preparation procedure** and use it for all the questions you practise.

Remember the steps involved in preparation of a statement of cash flows.

Step 1 Set out the proforma leaving plenty of space.

Step 2 Complete the reconciliation of operating profit to net cash from operating activities, as far as possible.

Step 3 Calculate the following where appropriate.

- Tax paid
- Dividends paid
- Purchase and sale of non-current assets
- Issues of shares
- Repayment of loans

Step 4 Work out the profit if not already given using: opening and closing balances, tax charge and dividends.

Step 5 Complete the note of gross cash flows. Alternatively the information may go straight into the statement.

Step 6 Slot the figures into the statement and any notes required.

Question — Single company

Kane Co's statement of profit or loss and other comprehensive income for the year ended 31 December 20X8 and statements of financial position at 31 December 20X7 and 31 December 20X8 were as follows.

KANE CO
STATEMENT OF PROFIT OR LOSS AND OTHER COMPREHENSIVE INCOME FOR THE YEAR ENDED 31 DECEMBER 20X8

	$'000	$'000
Sales		720
Raw materials consumed	70	
Staff costs	94	
Depreciation	118	
Loss on disposal of long-term asset	18	
		300
		420
Interest payable		28
Profit before tax		392
Income tax expense		124
Profit for the year		268

KANE CO
STATEMENT OF FINANCIAL POSITION AS AT 31 DECEMBER

	20X8		*20X7*	
	$'000	$'000	$'000	$'000
Assets				
Property, plant and equipment				
Cost	1,596		1,560	
Depreciation	318		224	
		1,278		1,336
Current assets				
Inventory	24		20	
Trade receivables	76		58	
Bank	48		56	
		148		134
Total assets		1,426		1,470
Equity and liabilities				
Equity				
Share capital	360		340	
Share premium	36		24	
Retained earnings	686		490	
		1,082		854
Non-current liabilities				
Long-term loans		200		500
Current liabilities				
Trade payables	42		30	
Taxation	102		86	
		144		116
		1,426		1,470

During the year, the company paid $90,000 for a new piece of machinery.

Required

Prepare a statement of cash flows for Kane Co for the year ended 31 December 20X8 in accordance with the requirements of IAS 7, using the indirect method.

Answer

KANE CO
STATEMENT OF CASH FLOWS FOR THE YEAR ENDED 31 DECEMBER 20X8

	$'000	$'000
Net cash flow from operating activities		
Operating profit	420	
Depreciation charges	118	
Loss on sale of property, plant and equipment	18	
Increase in inventories (W4)	(4)	
Increase in receivables (W4)	(18)	
Increase in payables(W4)	12	
Cash generated from operations	546	
Interest paid	(28)	
Dividends paid (W2)	(72)	
Tax paid (W3)	(108)	
Net cash flow from operating activities		338

	$'000	$'000
Cash flows from investing activities		
Payments to acquire tangible non-current assets	(90)	
Receipts from sales of tangible non-current assets (W1)	12	
Net cash outflow from investing activities		(78)
Cash flows from financing activities		
Issues of share capital (W2)	32	
Long-term loans repaid (W3)	(300)	
Net cash flows from financing		(268)
Decrease in cash and cash equivalents		(8)
Cash and cash equivalents at 1.1.X8		56
Cash and cash equivalents at 31.12.X8		48

1 *Assets*

	PPE
	$'000
b/d	1,336
Depreciation (non-cash)	(118)
Disposals* (NBV)	(30)
Cash paid (given in question but working shown for clarity)	**90** β
c/d	1,278

**Property, plant and equipment disposals*

	$'000
Non-current asset cost c/d	1,560
Purchases	90
Disposals (balancing figure)	(54)
Non-current asset cost c/d	1,596

	$'000
Non-current asset depreciation b/d	224
Depreciation charge for year	118
Depreciation on disposals (balancing figure)	(24)
Non-current asset depreciation c/d	318
NBV of disposals (54 – 24)	30
Net loss reported	(18)
Proceeds of disposals	12

2 *Equity*

	Share capital (incl premium)	*Retained earnings*
	$'000	$'000
b/d (340 + 24)	364	490
Profit for the year		268
Acquisition of subsidiary		
Cash received/(paid) β	**32**	**(72)**
c/d (360 + 36)	396	686

3 *Liabilities*

	Long-term borrowings	*Tax payable*
	$'000	$'000
b/d	500	86
P/L		124
Cash (paid)/rec'd β	**(300)**	**(108)**
c/d	200	102

4 *Working capital changes*

	Inventories	*Trade receivables*	*Trade payables*
	$m	$m	$m
b/d	20	58	30
∴ **Increase**	**4** β	**18** β	**12** β
c/d	24	76	42

3 Consolidated statements of cash flows

Pilot paper, 12/08, 12/10, 12/13, 6/16

FAST FORWARD

Consolidated cash flows should not present a great problem if you understand how to deal with acquisitions and disposals of subsidiaries, non-controlling interest and dividends.

Consolidated statements of cash flows follow the same principles as for single company statements, with some additional complications.

Cash flows that are **internal to the group** should be eliminated in the preparation of a consolidated statement of cash flows. Where a subsidiary undertaking **joins or leaves** a group during a financial year the cash flows of the group should include the cash flows of the subsidiary undertaking concerned for the same period as that for which the group's statement of profit or loss and other comprehensive income includes the results of the subsidiary undertaking.

3.1 Acquisitions and disposals of subsidiaries and other business units

An entity should present separately the aggregate cash flows arising from acquisitions and from disposals of subsidiaries or other business units and classify them as **investing activities**.

Disclosure is required of the following, in aggregate, in respect of both acquisitions and disposals of subsidiaries or other business units during the period.

- Total purchase/disposal consideration
- Portion of purchase/disposal consideration discharged by means of cash/cash equivalents
- Amount of cash/cash equivalents in the subsidiary or business unit disposed of
- Amount of assets and liabilities other than cash/cash equivalents in the subsidiary or business unit acquired or disposed of, summarised by major category

The amounts shown in the statements of cash flows for purchase or disposal of subsidiaries or business units will be the amounts paid or received **net** of cash/cash equivalents acquired or disposed of.

(IAS 7: para 39 – 40, 42):

3.2 Consolidation adjustments and non-controlling interest

The group statement of cash flows should only deal with flows of cash and cash equivalents external to the group, so all intra-group cash flows should be eliminated. **Dividends paid to non-controlling interest** should be included under the heading 'cash flow from financing' and disclosed separately.

3.3 Example: Non-controlling interest

The following are extracts of the consolidated results for Jarvis Co for the year ended 31 December 20X8.

CONSOLIDATED STATEMENT OF PROFIT OR LOSS AND OTHER COMPREHENSIVE INCOME (EXTRACT)

	$'000
Group profit before tax	90
Income tax expense	(30)
Profit for the year	60
Profit attributable to:	
Owners of the parent	45
Non-controlling interest	15
	60

CONSOLIDATED STATEMENT OF FINANCIAL POSITION (EXTRACT)

	20X7	*20X8*
	$'000	$'000
Non-controlling interest	300	306

Calculate the dividends paid to the non-controlling interest during the year

Solution

The non-controlling interest share of profit after tax represents retained profit plus dividends paid.

Dividends paid to non-controlling interests

	$'000
b/d	300
TCI attributable to NCI	15
	315
Dividends paid to NCI (balancing figure)	(9)
c/d	306

Points to note:

(a) In this example, there is no 'other comprehensive income' so the total comprehensive income (TCI) here is equal to the profit for the year.

(b) On the statement of financial position, the NCI balance includes the NCI share of **retained earnings** (ie **after** deduction of dividends). Dividends are not deducted in the statement of profit or loss and other comprehensive income so the NCI share of total comprehensive income is stated **before** deduction of dividends. Therefore the balancing figure in this working must be the dividends paid to the NCI.

3.4 Associates and joint ventures

An entity which that reports its interest in an associate or a joint venture using the equity method includes in its statement of cash flows the cash flows in respect of its investments in the associate or joint venture, and distributions and other payments or receipts between it and the associate or joint venture.

Dividends should be included in **operating or investing cash flows.**

3.5 Example: Associate

The following are extracts of the consolidated results of Pripon Co for the year ended 31 December 20X8.

CONSOLIDATED STATEMENT OF PROFIT OR LOSS AND OTHER COMPREHENSIVE INCOME (EXTRACT)

	$'000
Group profit before tax	150
Share of associate's profit after tax (60 – 30)	30
	180
Tax (group)	75
Profit after tax	105

CONSOLIDATED STATEMENT OF FINANCIAL POSITION (EXTRACTS)

	20X7	*20X8*
	$'000	$'000
Investment in associate	264	276

Calculate the dividend received from the associate.

Solution

Investment in associate

	$'000
b/d	264
Share of profit after tax (60 – 30)	30
Dividend received (**β**)	**(18)**
c/d	276

Note. In the statement of financial position, the investment in associate balance includes the group share of the associate's **retained earnings** (ie **after** deduction of dividends). Dividends are not deducted in the statement of comprehensive income so the group share of the associate's profit and other comprehensive income (if any) is stated **before** deduction of dividends. Therefore the balancing figure in this working must be the dividends received from the associate.

3.6 Lease transactions

When rentals under a right-of-use asset lease are paid, the **interest and capital elements are split out** and included under the net cash from operations (interest paid)' and 'financing activities' headings respectively.

Exam focus point

> Various complications may arise in a consolidated statement of cash flows in the exam, the most important of which are covered above. The question, given below, is comprehensive. You may also have a written element. The Pilot Paper asked for the preparation of a consolidated statement of cash flows and a report on the usefulness of group statements of cash flows, generally and specifically to the entity in the question. In December 2010 students were asked whether it was acceptable for the proceeds of a loan to be classified as operating cash flow.

3.7 Section summary

The preparation of consolidated statements of cash flows will, in many respects, be the same as those for single companies, with the following **additional complications**.

- Acquisitions and disposals of subsidiary undertaking
- Cancellation of intra-group transactions
- Non-controlling interest
- Associates and joint ventures
- Leases

Question — Consolidated cash flow 1

Topiary Co is a 40 year old company producing garden statues carved from marble. 22 years ago it acquired a 100% interest in a marble importing company, Hardstuff Co. In 20W9 it acquired a 40% interest in a competitor, Landscapes Co and on 1 January 20X7 it acquired a 75% interest in Garden Furniture Designs. The draft consolidated accounts for the Topiary Group are as follows.

DRAFT CONSOLIDATED STATEMENT OF PROFIT OR LOSS AND OTHER COMPREHENSIVE INCOME FOR THE YEAR ENDED 31 DECEMBER 20X7

		$'000	$'000
Operating profit			4,455
Share of profit after tax of associate			1,050
Income from long-term investment			465
Interest payable			(450)
Profit before taxation			5,520
Tax on profit			
Income tax		1,173	
Deferred taxation		312	
			(1,485)
Profit for the year			4,035
Attributable to:	owners of the parent		3,735
	non-controlling interest		300
			4,035

DRAFT CONSOLIDATED STATEMENT OF FINANCIAL POSITION
AS AT 31 DECEMBER

	20X6		20X7	
	$'000	$'000	$'000	$'000
Assets				
Non-current assets				
Tangible assets				
Buildings at net book value		6,600		6,225
Machinery: cost	4,200		9,000	
aggregate depreciation	(3,300)		(3,600)	
net book value		900		5,400
		7,500		11,625
Goodwill				300
Investments in associates		3,000		3,300
Long-term investments		1,230		1,230
		11,730		16,455
Current assets				
Inventories	3,000		5,925	
Receivables	3,825		5,550	
Cash	5,460		13,545	
		12,285		25,020
		24,015		41,475
Equity and liabilities				
Equity				
Share capital: 25c shares	6,000		11,820	
Share premium account	6,285		8,649	
Retained earnings	7,500		10,335	
	19,785		30,804	
Non-controlling interest	–		345	
Total equity c/f		19,785		31,149
Total equity b/f		19,785		31,149
Non-current liabilities				
Obligations under leases	510		2,130	
Loans	1,500		4,380	
Deferred tax	39		90	
		2,049		6,600
Current liabilities				
Trade payables	840		1,500	
Obligations under leases	600		720	
Income tax	651		1,386	
Accrued interest and finance charges	90		120	
		2,181		3,726
		24,015		41,475

Note

1 There had been no acquisitions or disposals of buildings during the year.

Machinery costing $1.5m was sold for $1.5m resulting in a profit of $300,000. New machinery was acquired in 20X7 including additions of $2.55m acquired under leases.

2 *Information relating to the acquisition of Garden Furniture Designs*

	$'000
Machinery	495
Inventories	96
Trade receivables	84
Cash	336
Trade payables	(204)
Income tax	(51)
	756
Non-controlling interest	(189)
	567
Goodwill	300
	867
2,640,000 shares issued as part consideration	825
Balance of consideration paid in cash	42
	867

3 Loans were issued at a discount in 20X7 and the carrying amount of the loans at 31 December 20X7 included $120,000 representing the finance cost attributable to the discount and allocated in respect of the current reporting period.

Required

Prepare a consolidated statement of cash flows for the Topiary Group for the year ended 31 December 20X7 as required by IAS 7, using the indirect method. There is no need to provide notes to the statement of cash flows.

Answer

TOPIARY CO
CONSOLIDATED STATEMENT OF CASH FLOWS
FOR THE YEAR ENDED 31 DECEMBER 20X7

	$'000	$'000
Cash flows from operating activities		
Net profit before tax	5,520	
Adjustments for:		
Depreciation (W1)	975	
Profit on sale of plant	(300)	
Share of associate's profits	(1,050)	
Investment income	(465)	
Interest payable	450	
Operating profit before working capital changes	5,130	
Increase in trade and other receivables (W4)	(1,641)	
Increase in inventories (W4)	(2,829)	
Increase in trade payables (W4)	456	
Cash generated from operations	1,116	
Interest paid (W5)	(300)	
Income taxes paid (W3)	(750)	
Net cash from operating activities		66
Cash flows from investing activities		
Purchase of subsidiary undertaking (W6)	294	
Purchase of property, plant and equipment (W1)	(3,255)	
Proceeds from sale of plant	1,500	
Dividends from investment	465	
Dividends from associate (W1)	750	
Dividends paid to non-controlling interest (W2)	(144)	
Net cash used in investing activities		(390)
Cash flows from financing activities		
Issue of ordinary share capital (W2)	7,359	
Issue of loan notes (W3)	2,760	
Capital payments under leases (W3)	(810)	
Dividends paid (W2)	(900)	
Net cash flows from financing activities		8,409
Net increase in cash and cash equivalents		8,085
Cash and cash equivalents at 1.1.X7		5,460
Cash and cash equivalents at 31.12.X7		13,545

Workings

1 *Assets*

	Buildings $'000	Plant and machinery $'000	Goodwill $'000	Associate $'000	Long-term investment $'000
b/d	6,600	900	-	3,000	1,230
P/L				1,050	
Dep'n*/ Amort'n/			- β		
Impairment	**(375) β**	(600)			
Acquisition of sub/assoc	-	495	300		
Non-cash additions (W3)	-	2,550	-		
Disposals	-	(1,200)	-		
Cash paid/(rec'd) β	-	**3,255 β**	-	(750) β	
c/d	6,225	5,400	300	3,300	1,230

** Depreciation charges*

	$'000
Accumulated depreciation b/d	3,300
Depreciation on disposal (1,500 – 1,200*)	(300)
Depreciation charge (balancing figure)	600
Accumulated depreciation c/d	3,600

*Disposal	$'000
Proceeds	1,500
Net book value (balancing figure)	(1,200)
Profit on disposal	300

Freehold buildings ($6,600,000 – $6,225,000) = $375,000

Total depreciation charge: ($375,000 + $600,000) = $975,000

Note. The share of the associate's profit, recognised in the consolidated statement of profit or loss and other comprehensive income, is not a cash item so is added back on the face of the statement of cash flows in the section that calculates the cash generated from operations. The **dividend received** from the associate is the cash item and appears in the investing activities section.

2 *Equity*

	Share capital $'000	Share premium $'000	Retained earnings $'000	NCI $'000
b/d	6,000	6,285	7,500	-
P/L			3,735	300
Acquisition of subsidiary	660	165		189
Cash (paid)/rec'd β	**5160**	**2,199**	**(900)**	**(144)**
c/d	11.820	8,649	10,335	345

3 *Liabilities*

	Loans	Lease	Tax payable
	$'000	$'000	$'000
		(600 + 510)	(651 + 39)
b/d	1,500	1,110	690
P/L	(W5)120		(1,173 + 312) 1,485
New lease commitment (machinery)		2,550	
Acquisition of subsidiary			51
Cash (paid)/rec'd β	**2,760**	**(810)**	**(750)**
c/d			
	4,380	2,850	1,476
		(720 + 2.130)	(1,386 + 90)

4 *Working capital changes*

	Inventories	Receivables	Payables
	$'000	$'000	$'000
Balance b/d	3,000	3,825	840
Acquisition of subsidiary	96	84	204
	3,096	3,909	1,044
Increase/(decrease) (balancing figure)	**2,829**	**1,641**	**456**
Balance c/d	5,925	5,550	1,500

5 *Interest*

	$'000
Balance b/d	90
SPLOCI (450 – 120) (excluding the discount credited to the carrying value of loans)	330
Interest paid in cash (balancing figure)	(300)
Balance c/d	120

6 *Purchase of subsidiary*

	$'000
Cash received on acquisition of subsidiary	336
Less cash consideration	(42)
Cash inflow	294

Note. Only the **cash** consideration is included in the figure reported in the statement of cash flows. The **shares** issued as part of the consideration are reflected in the share capital working (W2) above.

Question — Consolidated cash flow 2

The following are extracts from the financial statements of Tastydesserts and one of its wholly owned subsidiaries, Custardpowders, the shares in which were acquired on 31 October 20X2.

STATEMENTS OF FINANCIAL POSITION

	Tastydesserts and subsidiaries		*Custardpowders*
	31 December 20X2	*31 December 20X1*	*31 October 20X2*
	$'000	$'000	$'000
Non-current assets			
Property, plant & equipment	4,764	3,685	694
Goodwill	42		
Investment in associates	2,195	2,175	–
	7,001	5,860	694
Current assets			
Inventories	1,735	1,388	306
Receivables	2,658	2,436	185
Bank balances and cash	43	77	7
	4,436	3,901	498
	11,437	9,761	1,192
Equity			
Share capital	4,896	4,776	400
Share premium	216		
Retained earnings	2,540	2,063	644
	7,652	6,839	1,044
Non-current liabilities			
Loans	1,348	653	–
Deferred tax	111	180	–
	1,459	833	–
Current liabilities			
Payables	1,915	1,546	148
Bank overdrafts	176	343	
Current tax payable	235	200	–
	2,326	2,089	148
	11,437	9,761	1,192

CONSOLIDATED STATEMENT OF PROFIT OR LOSS AND OTHER COMPREHENSIVE INCOME FOR THE YEAR ENDED 31 DECEMBER 20X2

	$'000
Profit before interest and tax	546
Finance costs	–
Share of profit of associates	120
Profit before tax	666
Income tax expense	126
PROFIT/TOTAL COMPREHENSIVE INCOME FOR THE YEAR	540
Attributable to:	
Owners of the parent	540
Non-controlling interests	0
	540

The following information is also given:

(a) The consolidated figures at 31 December 20X2 include Custardpowders.

(b) The amount of depreciation on property, plant and equipment during the year was $78,000. There were no disposals.

(c) The cost on 31 October 20X2 of the shares in Custardpowders was $1,086,000 comprising the issue of $695,000 unsecured loan stock at par, 120,000 ordinary shares of $1 each at a value of 280c and $55,000 in cash.

(d) No write down of goodwill was required during the period.

(e) Total dividends paid by Tastydesserts (parent) during the period amounted to $63,000.

Required

Prepare a statement of cash flows for Tastydesserts and subsidiaries for the year ended 31 December 20X2 using the indirect method.

Notes to the statement of cash flows are not required.

Answer

TASTYDESSERTS
STATEMENT OF CASH FLOWS FOR THE YEAR ENDED 31 DECEMBER 20X2

	$'000	$'000
Cash flows from operating activities		
Profit before taxation	666	
Adjustments for:		
Depreciation	78	
Share of profit of associates	(120)	
Interest expense	–	
	624	
Increase in receivables (W4)	(37)	
Increase in inventories (W4)	(41)	
Increase in payables (W4)	221	
Cash generated from operations	767	
Interest paid	–	
Income taxes paid (W3)	(160)	
Net cash from operating activities		607
Cash flows from investing activities		
Acquisition of subsidiary Custardpowders net of cash acquired (W5)	(48)	
Purchase of property, plant and equipment (W1)	(463)	
Dividends received from associates (W1)	100	
Net cash used in investing activities		(411)
Cash flows from financing activities		
Dividends paid	(63)	
Net cash used in financing activities		(63)
Net increase in cash and cash equivalents		133
Cash and cash equivalents at beginning of year		(266)
Cash and cash equivalents at end of year		(133)

Workings

1 *Assets*

	Property, plant and equipment	*Goodwill*	*Associate*
	$'000	$'000	$'000
b/d	3,685	-	2,175
P/L			120
Depreciation/ Impairment	(78)	- β	
Acquisition of sub/assoc	694	42 (W5)	
Cash paid/(rec'd) β	**463**	-	**(100)**
c/d	4,764	42	2,195

Note. The share of the associate's profit, recognised in the consolidated statement of profit or loss and other comprehensive income, is not a cash item so is added back on the face of the statement of cash flows in the section that calculates the cash generated from operations. The **dividend received** from the associate is the cash item and appears in the investing activities section.

2 *Equity*

	Share capital	*Share premium*	*Retained earnings*
	$'000	$'000	$'000
b/d	4,776	-	2,063
P/L			540
Acquisition of subsidiary	120	216	
Cash (paid)/rec'd β	-	-	**(63)***
c/d	4,896	216	2,540

*Dividend paid is given in question but working shown for clarity.

3 *Liabilities*

	Loans	*Tax payable*
	$'000	$'000
		(200 + 180)
b/d	653	380
P/L		126
Acquisition of subsidiary	695	-
Cash (paid)/rec'd	-	**(160) β**
c/d	1,348	346
		(235 + 111)

4 *Working capital changes*

	Inventories	*Receivables*	*Payables*
	$'000	$'000	$'000
Balance b/d	1,388	2,436	1,546
Acquisition of subsidiary	306	185	148
	1,694	2,621	1,694
Increase/(decrease) (balancing figure)	**41**	**37**	**221**
Balance c/d	1,735	2,658	1,915

5 *Purchase of subsidiary*

	$'000
Cash received on acquisition of subsidiary	7
Less cash consideration	(55)
Cash outflow	(48)

Note. Only the **cash** consideration is included in the figure reported in the statement of cash flows. The **shares** issued as part of the consideration are reflected in the share capital working (W2) above.

Goodwill on acquisition (to show no impairment):

	$'000
Consideration: 55 + 695 (W3) + 120 (W2) + 216	1,086
Non-controlling interest	-
Net assets acquired	(1,044)
Goodwill	42

Chapter Roundup

- **Statements of cash flows** are a useful addition to the financial statements of companies because it is recognised that accounting profit is not the only indicator of a company's performance.
- Statements of cash flows concentrate on the sources and uses of cash and are a useful indicator of a company's **liquidity and solvency**.
- You need to be aware of the **format** of the statement as laid out in **IAS 7**. Setting out the format is an essential first stage in preparing the statement, so this format must be learnt.
- Remember the **step-by-step preparation procedure** and use it for all the questions you practise.
- **Consolidated cash flows** should not present a great problem if you understand how to deal with acquisitions and disposals of subsidiaries, non-controlling interest and dividends.

Quick Quiz

1 What is the objective of IAS 7?

2 What are the benefits of cash flow information according to IAS 7?

3 What are the standard headings required by IAS 7 to be included in a statement of cash flows?

4 What is the 'indirect method' of preparing a statement of cash flows?

5 How should an acquisition or disposal of a subsidiary be shown in the statement of cash flows?

Answers to Quick Quiz

1 To provide users of financial statements with information about the entity's ability to generate cash and cash equivalents, and the entity's cash needs

2 See Paragraph 2.2

3 Operating, investing and financing activities.

4 The net profit or loss for the period is adjusted for non-cash items; changes in inventories, receivables and payables from operations; and other items resulting from investing or financing activities.

5 Cash flows from acquisitions and disposal are disclosed separately under investing activities.

Now try the question below from the Practice Question Bank

Number	Level	Marks	Time
Q24	Examination	25	49 mins

PART D

Developments in reporting

18

Environmental and social reporting

Topic list	Syllabus reference
1 Environmental reporting	A3, H1
2 Sustainability	A3
3 Social responsibility	A3
4 Human resource accounting	A3
5 Integrated reporting	A3, H1

Introduction

Environmental issues are very topical. Just because these topics are discursive does not mean that you can 'waffle'. Environmental reporting also comes under current developments as this is an area that is changing.

Study guide

		Intellectual level
A3	**Social responsibility**	
(a)	Discuss the increased demand for transparency in corporate reports and the emergence of non-financial reporting standards	3
(b)	Discuss the progress towards a framework for environmental and sustainability reporting/integrated reporting	3
H1	**Environmental and social reporting**	
(a)	Appraise the impact of environmental, social and ethical factors on performance measurement	3
(b)	Evaluate current reporting requirements in the area including the development of Integrated Reporting	3
(c)	Discuss why entities might include disclosures relating to the environment and society	3

Exam guide

This topic could be tested as a current issue, or as an aspect of the limitations of conventional financial statements, or alternatively in the context of provisions, covered in Chapter 5.

Environmental reporting may be tested under the broader heading of social responsibilities.

1 Environmental reporting 12/07

FAST FORWARD

Although not compulsory, **environmental reports** are becoming increasingly important. You should distinguish:

- Items that **affect the financial statements** (eg IAS 37)
- Items that **affect the environmental report**

At the end of the 1980s there were perhaps only two or three companies in the world issuing environmental reports. Now most listed companies produce them. Worldwide there are around 20 award schemes for environmental reporting, notably the ACCA's. This section looks at environmental reporting mainly under three headings:

- The effect of environmental matters on management information and accounting
- External reporting and auditing
- Possible future developments

Let us consider the major areas of impact on (any) accountant's job caused by consideration of environmental matters.

(a) **Management accountant**

(i) Investment appraisal: evaluation of environmental costs and benefits
(ii) Incorporating new costs, capital expenditure and so on, into budgets and business plans
(iii) Undertake cost/benefit analysis of any environmental improvements

(b) **Financial accountant**

(i) The effect of revenue costs: site clean up costs, waste disposal or waste treatment costs and so on, which will affect the statement of profit or loss and other comprehensive income

(ii) Gauging impacts on the statement of financial position, particularly liabilities, contingencies, provisions **and** valuation of assets.

(iii) The effect of environmental matters, and particularly potential liabilities, on a company's relationship with bankers, insurers and major shareholders (institutional shareholders)

(iv) Environmental performance evaluation in annual reports

(c) **Project accountant**

(i) Environmental audit of proposed takeovers, mergers and other planning matters
(ii) Investment appraisal

(d) **Internal auditor**: environmental audit

(e) **Systems accountant**: effect on, and required changes to management and financial information systems

1.1 What is environmental accounting?

The following list encompasses the major aspects of environmental accounting.

(a) Recognising and seeking to mitigate the negative environmental effects of conventional accounting practice.

(b) Separately **identifying environmentally related costs and revenues** within the conventional accounting systems.

(c) Devising new forms of financial and non-financial accounting systems, information systems and control systems to **encourage more environmentally benign management decisions**.

(d) Developing new forms of **performance measurement**, reporting and appraisal for both internal and external purposes.

(e) Identifying, examining and seeking to **rectify** areas in which conventional (financial) criteria and environmental criteria are in **conflict**.

(f) Experimenting with ways in which, **sustainability** may be assessed and incorporated into organisational orthodoxy.'

(Gray, 1993)

The whole environmental agenda is **constantly changing** and businesses therefore need to monitor the situation closely. Most businesses, certainly those in the UK, have generally ignored environmental matters in the past. How long will they be able to do so?

1.2 Management information and accounting

The means of codifying a company's attitude towards the environment is often the creation of a published **environmental policy document** or charter. This may be internally generated or it may be adopted from a standard environmental charter, such as the **CERES Principles** (CERES, 1989.)

The CERES Principles

We adopt, support and will implement the principles of:

1 Protection of the biosphere
2 Sustainable use of natural resources
3 Reduction and disposal of waste
4 Wise use of energy
5 Risk reduction
6 Marketing of safe products and services
7 Damage compensation
8 Disclosure
9 Environmental directors and managers
10 Assessment and annual audit

The problem here, as with other similar principles or charters, is that the commitment required from companies is generally too high and the fear exists that the principles may have legal status which could have a severe effect on a company's liability. Other documents available which are similar to the *CERES Principles* are:

- The International Chamber of Commerce Business Charter for Sustainable Developments
- The Chemical Industries Association Responsible Care Programme
- The Confederation of British Industry Agenda for Voluntary Action
- Friends of the Earth Environmental Charter for Local Government

Adopting such a charter is one thing; implementing and monitoring it are more important and generally more difficult to achieve.

1.3 Environmental audit

Environmental auditing is exactly what it says: auditing a business to assess its impact on the environment, or as the CBI expressed it 'the systematic examination of the interactions between any business operation and its surroundings'.

The audit will cover a range of areas and will involve the performance of different types of testing. The scope of the audit must be determined and this will depend on each individual organisation. There are, however, some aspects of the approach to environmental auditing which are worth mentioning.

(a) **Environmental Impact Assessments (EIAs)** are required, under EU directive, for all major projects which require planning permission and have a material effect on the environment. The EIA process can be incorporated into any environmental auditing strategy.

(b) **Environmental surveys** are a good way of starting the audit process, by looking at the organisation as a whole in environmental terms. This helps to identify areas for further development, problems, potential hazards and so forth.

(c) **Environmental SWOT analysis**. A 'strengths, weaknesses, opportunities, threats' analysis is useful as the environmental audit strategy is being developed. This can only be done later in the process, when the organisation has been examined in much more detail.

(d) **Environmental Quality Management (EQM).** This is seen as part of TQM (Total Quality Management) and it should be built in to an environmental management system. Such a strategy has been adopted by companies such as IBM, Dow Chemicals and by the Rhone-Poulenc Environmental Index which has indices for levels of water, air and other waste products.

(e) **Eco-audit**. The European Commission has adopted a proposal for a regulation for a voluntary community environmental auditing scheme, known as the eco-audit scheme. The scheme aims to promote improvements in company environmental performance and to provide the public with information about these improvements. Once registered, a company will have to comply with certain on-going obligations involving disclosure and audit.

(f) **Eco-labelling**. Developed in Germany, this voluntary scheme will indicate those EC products which meet the highest environmental standards, probably as the result of an EQM system. It is suggested that eco-audit **must** come before an eco-label can be given.

(g) **BS 7750 Environmental Management Systems**. BS 7750 also ties in with eco-audits and eco-labelling and with the quality BSI standard BS 5750. Achieving BS 7750 is likely to be a first step in the eco-audit process.

(h) **Supplier audits**, to ensure that goods and services bought in by an organisation meet the standards applied by that organisation.

Case Study

In June 1999 BP Amoco commissioned KPMG to conduct an independent audit of its greenhouse gas emissions in the first ever environmental audit.

1.4 Financial reporting

There are **no disclosure requirements relating to environmental matters under IFRSs**, so any disclosures tend to be **voluntary** unless environmental matters happen to fall under standard accounting principles (eg recognising liabilities).

(a) In most cases disclosure is descriptive and unquantified.

(b) There is little motivation to produce environmental information and many reasons for not doing so, including secrecy.

(c) The main factor seems to be apathy on the part of businesses but more particularly on the part of shareholders and investors. The information is not demanded, so it is not provided.

Environmental matters may be reported in the accounts of companies in the following areas:

- Contingent liabilities
- Exceptional charges
- Operating and financial review comments
- Profit and capital expenditure forecasts

The voluntary approach contrasts with the position in the United States, where the SEC/FASB accounting standards are obligatory.

While nothing is compulsory, there are a number of **published guidelines** and **codes of practice**, including:

- The Confederation of British Industry's guideline *Introducing Environmental Reporting*
- The ACCA's *Guide to Environment and Energy Reporting*
- The Coalition of Environmentally Responsible Economies (CERES) formats for environmental reports
- The Friends of the Earth *Environmental Charter for Local Government*
- The Eco Management and Audit Scheme Code of Practice

1.5 Example: Environmental liabilities

You have met IAS 37 *Provisions, contingent liabilities and contingent assets* in your earlier studies. IAS 37 deals with the issue of whether environmental liabilities should be provided for. The example below is taken from an article by Alan Pizzey which appeared in a past edition of *CIMA Student*. Study the example and attempt the question which follows it.

MegaBux Co is a multinational holding company. During the year a number of situations have arisen and the board is to meet soon to determine an appropriate treatment.

Site A
This site is occupied by a small refinery. The site and some adjacent land has been contaminated by chemical spillages. The cost of remedying the contamination is $20m, but under local laws there is no requirement to clean up the site.

Site B
Similar contamination has arisen but the local government, and a neighbouring land owner, require the contamination to be remedied soon. The cost of cleaning up the site is $15m, but an extra $5m could be spent to raise the standard of the operation in line with undertakings given to the local community ten years ago.

Solution

Site A
The mere existence of contamination does not establish an obligation on the part of the company and without an obligation there is no need for a provision.

Site B
An obligation does exist which the local government and a neighbour can prove in court. At least $15m must be provided, but there may be a constructive obligation, wider than a legal obligation, to spend an extra $5m to raise the standard of rectification. Concern for its long term reputation may influence the company to honour its undertaking given to the local community.

Question — Contamination

Site C
Considerable contamination needs to be remedied, but the managing director is arguing that no provision is required this year since the amount concerned cannot be estimated with accuracy.

Site D
Spillage of chemicals has reduced the value of the site from $25m, its book value, to $10m, its current realisable value. By spending $5m on rectification, the site value will be increased to $20m. The spillage has seeped into a local river and fines of $3m are now payable.

Answer

Site C
While the exact amount of the expenditure may not be known with certainty, it should be possible to arrive at a realistic and prudent estimate. It is not acceptable to omit a liability on the grounds that its amount is not known with certainty – this would be a distortion.

Site D
The fines of $3m are a current cost to be charged to profit or loss. The spillage has impaired the value of the site, which must be written down to its new market value of $20m after rectification. The cost of the write-down ($5m) and the cost of the rectification ($5m) are charged to profit or loss. The site is now carried in the books at its recoverable amount.

1.6 The environmental report and the exam

You may be asked in the exam to interpret an environmental report, though not to prepare one. Your report should distinguish between:

(a) Transactions that affect the financial statements, for example provisions that need to be made under IAS 37

(b) Information to be disclosed elsewhere, for example in the operating and financial review, or in a separate environmental report

Exam focus point

Have a go at the question Glowball in the Exam Question Bank. This distinguishes between environmental matters that affect the financial statements and those which do not, but are nevertheless important. You are more likely to get part of a question on this topic than a full question.

er unit 'produced').

2 Sustainability

2.1 What is sustainability?

Pressure is mounting for companies to **widen** their **scope for corporate public accountability**. Many companies are responding by measuring and disclosing their social impacts.

Examples of social measures include: philanthropic donations, employee satisfaction levels and remuneration issues, community support, and stakeholder consultation information.

The next step beyond environmental and social reporting is sustainability reporting which includes the economic element of sustainability (such as wages, taxes and core financial statistics) and involves integrating environmental, social and economic performance data and measures.

2.2 The Global Reporting Initiative (GRI)

FAST FORWARD

The Global Reporting Initiative arose from the need to **address the failure of the current governance structures to respond to changes in the global economy**.

It is 'a long-term, multi-stakeholder, international undertaking whose mission is to develop and disseminate globally applicable Sustainability Reporting Guidelines for voluntary use by organisations reporting on the economic, environmental and social dimensions of their activities, products and services'.

2.3 GRI Guidelines

The GRI published revised Sustainability Reporting Guidelines ('G3') in 2006. In 2011 the GRI launched G3.1, an update with expanded guidance for reporting on human rights (application of risk assessments, grievance remediation), local community impacts and gender (return and retention rates after employee leave, equal remuneration).

The Guidelines set out the framework of a sustainability report. It consists of five sections (GRI, 2011):

GRI Report content		Detail of GRI requirements
1	*Strategy and Analysis*	Provides a high-level, strategic view of the organisation's relationship to sustainability in order to provide context for subsequent and more detailed reporting, including a statement from the CEO.
2	*Organisational Profile*	The organisation's structure including brands, location of operations, geographical markets served and size of operations.
3	*Report Parameters*	The reporting period, materiality, report boundaries (eg countries),

		data measurement techniques and a GRI Content Index.
4	*Governance, Commitments and Engagement*	Governance structure of the organisation, commitments to external initiatives and how the organisation engages the stakeholders in its business.
5	*Management Approach and Performance Indicators*	Organised by economic, environmental, and social categories. Each category includes a Disclosure on Management Approach and a corresponding set of Core and Additional Performance Indicators.

2.4 Indicators in the GRI framework

GRI structures key performance indicators according to a hierarchy of category, aspect and indicator. Indicators are grouped in terms of the three dimensions of the conventional definition of sustainability – economic, environmental, and social.

	CATEGORY	ASPECT
Economic	Economic	Economic performance Market presence Indirect economic impacts
Environmental	Environmental	Materials Energy Water Biodiversity Emissions, effluents, and waste Products and services Compliance Transport Overall
Social	Labour Practices and Decent Work	Employment Labour/management relations Occupational health and safety Training and education Diversity and equal opportunity
	Human Rights	Investment and procurement practices Non-discrimination Freedom of association and collective bargaining Child labour Forced and compulsory labour Security practices Indigenous rights
	Society	Community Corruption Public policy Anti-competitive behaviour Compliance
	Product Responsibility	Customer health and safety Product and service labelling Marketing communications Customer privacy Compliance

2.5 Influence of GRI

There is a trend to report on broader sustainability issues and to include **social and economic information** alongside environmental disclosures.

An increasing number of companies, including BT, Vauxhall Motors Ltd, British Airways and Shell are following the GRI guidelines to some extent in their reporting.

2.6 Example: BT

BT's Social and Environmental Report for the year ended 31 March 2004 complies with the Global Reporting Initiative Guidelines. To give an overview of the company's social and environmental performance, the report selects 11 non-financial key performance indicators. This performance relates to the 2004 financial year, compared with 2003. (BT, 2004)

(a) Customer dissatisfaction down 22%

(b) Broadband now available to more than 85% of all UK homes and businesses, up from 67%

(c) People Satisfaction Index increased from 67% to 71%

(d) Increase in the percentage of ethnic minority employees from 8.6% to 8.9% and disabled employees from 2.0% to 2.1%, though the percentage of women declined from 23.6% to 22.7%

(e) Global Warming CO_2 emissions now 42% lower than 1996

(f) Waste to landfill down 10,201 tonnes to 79,677 tonnes, percentage of total waste recycled up from 25% to 26%

(g) Health & Safety significant incident rate down from 113 to 87 per 10,000 full-time employees

(h) Percentage of suppliers stating they have a good working relationship with BT is 94%

(i) Ethical trading risk assessment questionnaires completed by 242 suppliers and 13 on-site assessments undertaken

(j) Awareness of our Statement of Business Practice in the UK up 1% to 84%

(k) Direct community investment of £5.6 million plus £12.4 million in further funding and support in mind.

Question — **Indicators**

Compare this brief summary with the table above, ticking off performance indicators. If you have time, look for further details and developments on www.globalreporting.org.

3 Social responsibility

FAST FORWARD

The **stakeholder** view holds that there are many groups in society with an interest in the organisation's activities. Some firms have objectives for these issues. Some argue, however, that a business's only objective should be to make money: the State, representing the public interest, can levy taxes to spend on socially desirable projects or can regulate organisational activities.

Not only does the environment have a significant influence on the structure and behaviour of organisations, but also organisations have some influence on their environment.

Since organisations have an effect on their environment, it is arguable that they should act in a way which shows **social awareness and responsibility**.

> 'A society, awakened and vocal with respect to the urgency of social problems, is asking the managers of all kinds of organisations, particularly those at the top, what they are doing to discharge their social responsibilities and why they are not doing more.'
>
> *Koontz, O'Donnell and Weihrich*

Social responsibility is expected from all types of organisation.

(a) **Local government** is expected to provide services to the local community, and to preserve or improve the character of that community, but at an acceptable cost to the ratepayers.

(b) **Businesses** are expected to provide goods and services, which reflect the needs of users and society as a whole. These needs may not be in harmony – arguably, the development of the Concorde aeroplane and supersonic passenger travel did not contribute to the public interest, and caused considerable inconvenience to residents near airports who suffer from excessive aircraft noise. A business should also be expected to anticipate the future needs of society; examples of socially useful products might be energy-saving devices and alternative sources of power.

(c) **Pollution control** is a particularly important example of social responsibility by industrial organisations, and some progress has been made in the development of commercial processes for re-cycling waste material. British Coal attempts to restore the environment by planting on old slag heaps.

(d) **Universities and schools** are expected to produce students whose abilities and qualifications will prove beneficial to society. A currently popular view of education is that greater emphasis should be placed on vocational training for students.

(e) In some cases, **legislation** may be required to enforce social need, for example to regulate the materials used to make crash helmets for motor cyclists, or to regulate safety standards in motor cars and furniture. Ideally, however, organisations should avoid the need for legislation by taking **earlier self-regulating action**.

3.1 Social responsibility and businesses

Arguably, institutions like hospitals, schools and so forth exist because health care and education are seen to be desirable social objectives by government at large, if they can be afforded.

However, where does this leave businesses? How far is it reasonable, or even appropriate, for businesses to exercise 'social responsibility' by giving to charities, voluntarily imposing strict environmental objectives on themselves and so forth?

One school of thought would argue that **the management of a business has only one social responsibility, which is to maximise wealth for its shareholders**. There are two reasons to support this argument:

(a) If the business is owned by the shareholders the assets of the company are, ultimately, the shareholders' property. Management has no moral right to dispose of business assets (like cash) on non-business objectives, as this has the effect of reducing the return available to shareholders. The shareholders might, for example, disagree with management's choice of beneficiary. Anyhow, it is for the shareholders to determine how their money should be spent.

(b) A second justification for this view is that management's job is to maximise wealth, as this is the best way that society can benefit from a business's activities.

   (i) Maximising wealth has the effect of increasing the tax revenues available to the State to disburse on socially desirable objectives.

   (ii) Maximising wealth for the few is sometimes held to have a 'trickle down' effect on the disadvantaged members of society.

   (iii) Many company shares are owned by pension funds, whose ultimate beneficiaries may not be the wealthy anyway.

This argument rests on certain assumptions.

(a) The first assumption is, in effect, the opposite of the stakeholder view. In other words, it is held that the **rights** of legal ownership are paramount over all other **interests** in a business: while other stakeholders have an interest, they have few legal or moral rights over the wealth created.

(b) The second assumption is that a business's **only** relationship with the wider social environment is an economic one. After all, that is what businesses exist for, and any other activities are the role of the State.

(c) The defining purpose of business organisations is the maximisation of the wealth of their owners.

Henry Mintzberg (in *Power In and Around Organisations*) suggests that simply viewing organisations as vehicles for shareholder investment is inadequate (Mintzberg, 1983).

(a) In practice, he says, organisations are rarely controlled effectively by shareholders. Most shareholders are passive investors.

(b) Large corporations can manipulate markets. Social responsibility, forced or voluntary, is a way of recognising this.

(c) Moreover, businesses do receive a lot of government support. The public pays for roads, infrastructure, education and health, all of which benefits businesses. Although businesses pay tax, the public ultimately pays, perhaps through higher prices.

(d) Strategic decisions by businesses always have wider social consequences. In other words, says Mintzberg, the firm produces two outputs: **goods and services** and the **social consequences of its activities** (eg pollution).

3.1.1 Externalities

If it is accepted that businesses do not bear the total social cost of their activities, then the exercise of social responsibility is a way of compensating for this.

An example is given by the environment. Industrial pollution is injurious to health: if someone is made ill by industrial pollution, then arguably the polluter should pay the sick person, as damages or in compensation, in the same way as if the business's builders had accidentally bulldozed somebody's house.

In practice, of course, while it is relatively easy to identify statistical relationships between pollution levels and certain illnesses, mapping out the chain of cause and effect from an individual's wheezing cough to the dust particles emitted by Factory X, as opposed to Factory Y, is quite a different matter.

Of course, it could be argued that these external costs are met out of general taxation: but this has the effect of spreading the cost amongst other individuals and businesses. Moreover, the tax revenue may be spent on curing the disease, rather than stopping it at its source. Pollution control equipment may be the fairest way of dealing with this problem. Thus advocates of social responsibility in business would argue that business's responsibilities then do not rest with paying taxes.

However, is there any justification for social responsibility outside remedying the effects of a business's direct activities? For example, should businesses give to charity or sponsor the arts? There are several reasons why they should.

(a) If the **stakeholder concept** of a business is held, then the public is a stakeholder in the business. A business only succeeds because it is part of a wider society. Giving to charity is one way of encouraging a relationship.

(b) Charitable donations and artistic sponsorship are a useful medium of **public relations** and can reflect well on the business. It can be regarded, then, as another form of promotion, which like advertising, serves to enhance consumer awareness of the business, while not encouraging the sale of a particular brand.

The arguments for and against social responsibility of business are complex ones. However, ultimately they can be traced to different assumptions about society and the relationships between the individuals and organisations within it.

Question **Ethics**

The Heritage Carpet Company is a London-based retailer which imports carpets from Turkey, Iran and India. The company was founded by two Europeans who travelled independently through these countries in the 1970s. The company is the sole customer for carpets made in a number of villages in each of the source countries. The carpets are hand woven. Indeed, they are so finely woven that the process requires that children be used to do the weaving, thanks to their small fingers. The company believes that it is preserving a 'craft', and the directors believe that this is a justifiable social objective. Recently a UK television company has reported unfavourably on child exploitation in the carpet weaving industry. There were reports of children working twelve hour shifts in poorly lit sheds and cramped conditions, with consequent deterioration in eyesight, muscular disorders and a complete absence of education. The examples cited bear no relation to the Heritage Carpet Company's suppliers although children are used in the labour force, but there has been a spate of media attention. The regions in which the Heritage Carpet Company's supplier villages are found are soon expected to enjoy rapid economic growth.

What boundary management issues are raised for the Heritage Carpet Company?

Answer

Many. This is a case partly about boundary management and partly about enlightened self-interest and business ethics. The adverse publicity, although not about the Heritage Carpet Company's own suppliers, could rebound badly. Potential customers might be put off. Economic growth in the area may also mean that parents will prefer to send their children to school. The Heritage Carpet Company as well as promoting itself as preserving a craft could reinvest some of its profits in the villages (eg by funding a school), or by enforcing limits on the hours children worked. It could also pay a decent wage. It could advertise this in a 'code of ethics' so that customers are reassured that the children are not simply being exploited. Alternatively, it could not import child-made carpets at all. (This policy, however, would be unlikely to help communities in which child labour is an economic necessity. Children already living on the margins of subsistence might end up even more exploited, in begging or prostitution.)

Question — More ethics

(a) Identify some common barriers to the successful adoption of ethical standards in business practice.

(b) Explain the practical steps that organisations can take towards creating an ethical framework for corporate governance.

Answer

(a) **Problems with ethical framework**

Over the past few years the topic of business ethics has been examined and debated by many writers and academics. Although many organisation world-wide have adopted or redefined their business with ethics in mind, there are many people both in business and who study the area who see many barriers to businesses implementing an ethical framework.

What constitutes ethics?

Defining 'what we mean by ethics' is for the most part easy to understand (inappropriate gifts, accepting money, environmental protection are all ethical issues). More **contentious issues** are topics such as workplace safety, product safety standards, advertising content and whistle-blowing which are areas where some businesses have been considered less ethical.

Necessity for action

Actions speak **louder than words.** Ethics are guidelines or rules of conduct by which we aim to live by. It is the actual conduct of the people in the organisation that, collectively, determines the organisation's standards – in other words it is not what the organisations 'says', but rather what it 'does' which is the real issue. It is no good having a code of ethics that is communicated to the outside world, but is ignored and treated with disdain by those inside the organisation.

Varying cultures

Globalisation and the resultant need to operate within different ethical frameworks has **undermined the idea** that ethical guidance can be defined in simple absolute terms. It may be culturally acceptable to promote by merit in one country, or by seniority in another. Paying customs officials may be acceptable in some cultures, but taboo in others.

Ethical versus commercial interests

Ethical and commercial interests have, it is argued, always diverged to some extent. Some organisations have seen for example the issues of **'being seen to be ethical'** as a good business move. However this viewpoint is pragmatic rather than idealistic; being ethical is seen as a means towards the end of gaining a better reputation and hence increasing sales.

Policies of others

Modern commercialism places great demands on everyone in organisations to succeed and provide the necessary revenues for the future growth and survival of the business. Acting with social responsibility can be hard, as not everyone plays by the same rules.

(b) **Need for practical steps**

If organisations are to **achieve a more ethical stance** they **need to put into place a range of practical steps** that will achieve this. Developing an ethical culture within the business will require the organisation to communicate to its workforce the 'rules' on what is considered to be ethical and is not. Two approaches have been identified to the management of ethics in organisations.

Rules-based approach

This is primarily designed to ensure that the organisation acts within the letter of the law, and that violations are **prevented, detected and punished**. This is very much the case in the US, where legal compliance is very much part of the business environment. The problem here is that legislation alone will not have the desired effect, particularly for those businesses who operate internationally and therefore may not be subject to equivalent legislation in other jurisdictions.

Integrity-based programmes

Here the concern is not for any legal control, but with developing an **organisational culture**. The task of ethics management is to define and give life to an organisation's **defining values** and to create an environment that supports ethical behaviour and to instil a sense of **shared accountability** among all employees. Integrity-based programmes require not just words or statements, but on seeing and doing and action. The purpose with this approach is not to exact revenge through legal compliance but to develop within the workforce a **culture of ethics** that has **value and meaning** for those in it.

The integrity-based approach encompasses all aspects of the business – **behavioural assumptions** of what is right or is wrong; staffing, education and training, audits and activities that promote a social responsibility across the workforce.

Organisations can also take further steps to reinforce their values by adopting **ethical committees** who are appointed to rule on misconduct and to develop ethical standards for the business.

Kohlberg's framework

Kohlberg's ethical framework demonstrates how individuals advance through different levels of moral development, their advance relating to how their **moral reasoning develops**. Kohlberg's framework goes from individuals who see ethical decisions solely in terms of the good or bad consequences for themselves through to individuals who choose to follow universal ethical principles, even if these conflict with the values of the organisation for which they are working.

The importance of different components of an organisation's ethical framework can indicate the level of moral reasoning that staff are in effect expected to employ.

Pre-conventional reasoning

A rules-based framework that sets out **expected behaviour** in detail and has strong provisions for punishing breaches implies that staff are at the lowest stage of development – they define right or wrong solely in terms of expected rewards or punishments. An emphasis on bureaucratic controls, including the reporting of all problems that occur with staff, would be designed to prevent 'You scratch my back, I scratch yours' behaviour that is also part of moral reasoning at this level.

Conventional reasoning

An emphasis on a **strong ethical culture** would indicate staff are expected to adopt the intermediate stage of Kohlberg's framework. **Peer pressure**, also the concepts that managers should set an **example**, are features of this sort of ethical approach; if also the organisation appears to be responding to **pressures from outside** to behave ethically, this suggests higher level reasoning within this stage.

Post-conventional reasoning

An ethical approach based on staff using post-conventional reasoning would be likely to emphasise adherence to an ethical code. A detailed code based on rights and values of society would imply ethical reasoning based on the idea of the organisation **enforcing a social contract**. Higher-level reasoning would be expected if the code was framed in terms of more abstract principles such as justice or equality.

Question — Social responsibility

Mineral, a public limited company, has prepared its financial statements for the year ended 31 October 20X3. The following information relates to those financial statements.

	20X3	*20X2*
	$m	$m
Group revenue	250	201
Gross profit	45	35
Profit before interest and tax	10	9
Profit before tax	12	8
Profit for the year	5	4
Non-current assets	42	36
Current assets	55	43
Current liabilities	25	24
Non-current liabilities – long-term loans	13	9
Equity	59	46

The company expects to achieve growth in retained earnings of about 20% in the year to 31 October 20X4. Thereafter retained earnings are expected to accelerate to produce growth of between 20% and 25%. The growth will be generated by the introduction of new products and business efficiencies in manufacturing and in the company's infrastructure.

Mineral manufactures products from aluminium and other metals and is one of the largest producers in the world. Production for 20X3 increased by 18% through the acquisition of a competitor company, increased production at three of its plants and through the regeneration of old plants. There has been a recent growth in the consumption of its products because of the substitution of aluminium for heavier metals in motor vehicle manufacture. Cost reductions continued as a business focus in 20X3 and Mineral has implemented a cost reduction programme to be achieved by 20X6. Targets for each operation have been set.

Mineral's directors feel that its pricing strategy will help it compensate for increased competition in the sector. The company recently reduced the price of its products to the motor vehicle industry. This strategy is expected to increase demand and the usage of aluminium in the industry. However, in spite of the environmental benefits, certain car manufacturers have formed a cartel to prevent the increased usage of aluminium in car production.

In the period 20X3 to 20X5, Mineral expects to spend around $40 million on research and development and investment in non-current assets. The focus of the investments will be on enlarging the production capabilities. An important research and development project will be the joint project with a global car manufacturer to develop a new aluminium alloy car body.

In January 20X3, Mineral commenced a programme of acquisition of its own ordinary shares for cancellation. At 31 October 20X3, Mineral had purchased and cancelled five million ordinary shares of $1. In addition, a subsidiary of Mineral had $4 million of convertible redeemable loan notes outstanding. The loan notes mature on 15 June 20X6 and are convertible into ordinary shares at the option of the holder. The competitive environment requires Mineral to provide medium and long term financing to its customers in connection with the sale of its products. Generally the financing is placed with third party lenders but due to the higher risks associated with such financing, the amount of the financing expected to be provided by Mineral itself is likely to increase.

The directors of Mineral have attempted to minimise the financial risk to which the group is exposed. The company operates in the global market place with the inherent financial risk that this entails. The management have performed a sensitivity analysis assuming a 10% adverse movement in foreign exchange rates and interest rates applied to hedging contracts and other exposures. The analysis indicated that such market movement would not have a material effect on the company's financial position.

Mineral has a reputation for responsible corporate behaviour and sees the work force as the key factor in the profitable growth of the business. During the year the company made progress towards the aim of linking environmental performance with financial performance by reporting the relationship between the eco-productivity index for basic production, and water and energy costs used in basic production. A feature of this index is that it can be segregated at site and divisional level and can be used in the internal management decision-making process.

The directors of Mineral are increasingly seeing their shareholder base widen with the result that investors are more demanding and sophisticated. As a result, the directors are uncertain as to the nature of the information which would provide clear and credible explanations of corporate activity. They wish their annual report to meet market expectations. They have heard that many companies deal with three key elements of corporate activity, namely reporting business performance, the analysis of the financial position, and the nature of corporate citizenship, and have asked your firm's advice in drawing up the annual report.

Required

Draft a report to the directors of Mineral setting out the nature of information which could be disclosed in annual reports in order that there might be better assessment of the performance of the company.

Candidates should use the information in the question and produce their report under the headings:

(a) Reporting business performance
(b) Analysis of financial position
(c) The nature of corporate citizenship

Note. Use your knowledge of ratios from your F7 studies, but build on it.

Answer

REPORT

To: The Directors, Mineral
From: Accountant
Date: 12 November 20X3

Information to improve assessment of corporate performance

In addition to the main financial statements, annual reports need to contain information about **key elements of corporate activity**. This report focuses on three main areas:

- Reporting business performance
- Analysis of the financial position
- Nature of corporate citizenship

(a) **Reporting business performance**

A report on business performance may include a ratio analysis, with a year on year comparison. The ratios commonly selected are those concerned with **profitability and liquidity:**

Profitability

	20X3	*20X2*
Return on capital employed	$\frac{10}{59+13}$ = 13.9%	$\frac{9}{46+9}$ = 16.4%
$\frac{\text{Gross profit}}{\text{Sales}}$	$\frac{45}{250}$ = 18%	$\frac{35}{201}$ = 17.4%
$\frac{\text{PBIT}}{\text{Sales}}$	$\frac{10}{250}$ × 100% = 4%	$\frac{9}{201}$ × 100% = 4.5%

	20X3	*20X2*
Long- and short-term liquidity		
$\frac{\text{Current assets}}{\text{Current liabilities}}$	$\frac{55}{25}$ = 2.2	$\frac{43}{24}$ = 1.8
$\frac{\text{Long-term liabilities}}{\text{Equity}}$	$\frac{13}{59}$ × 100% = 22%	$\frac{9}{46}$ × 100% = 19.6%

These ratios raise a number of questions.

Use of ratios

(i) **Gross profit margin** has **risen**, while **operating profit margin** and **return on capital employed** have **fallen**. Possible problems with **control of overheads?**

(ii) **Short-term liquidity** has **improved**, but **gearing** has **deteriorated**. Is the company using long-term loans to finance expansion? The company has **expanded**, both in revenue and non-current assets.

(iii) **Standard ratios** are a useful tool, but must be discussed in relation to the **specific circumstances of the company**.

(1) The **impact of the increase in production** through the **acquisition** of the **competitor company** and the **regeneration** of **old plants** needs to be taken into account when considering revenue and non-current asset ratios and other comments in the report.

(2) When considering profit ratios, the **effectiveness of the cost control programme** might be assessed.

(iv) As well as **year on year comparison**, a report on business performance might usefully **compare actual performance against targets**. To enhance the usefulness of the information, the targets should be industry specific, measurable and realistic.

(1) The targets set for growth in retained earnings are 20% for 20X2 and between 20% to 25% thereafter. Reporting on actual performance would be informative.

(2) An objective is to generate the growth by the introduction of new products and improved efficiency. The actual performance in these areas might also be worthy of comment.

(v) The discussion of **business performance** also takes into consideration the **risks** that the business faces. In the context of Mineral, such a discussion would cover:

(1) The proposed $40m **expenditure on research and development and investment in non-current assets.** Are the directors justified in assuming the **predicted growth** in **retained earnings** that this **large expenditure** is meant to bring about?

(2) The **joint project** to develop a new aluminium car body will be very lucrative if successful, but is the risk v return decision appropriate?

(3) The company's pricing strategy and projected increase in demand should be discussed.

(vi) **Knowledge management** is also an important issue where new processes and products are being developed.

(vii) As modern investors become more sophisticated, they are also likely to want to learn about the company's **strategic objectives** including the maintenance and development of **income and profit streams**, future projects and capital expenditure projects.

(b) **Analysis of the financial position**

(i) Annual reports should contain a review of the company's **financing arrangements** and **financial position** as well as a review of its **operating activities**.

(ii) In the case of Mineral plc, such a review is likely to note that:

(1) **Gearing has increased, but it is still low**, so the expenditure on research and development could be financed by borrowing, if not by retained earnings.

(2) Of the long-term loans of $13m, debentures of $4m could be converted into shares or redeemed.

(3) Should the debentures be **converted**, the **existing shareholders' interest will be diluted**, and they should be made aware of this.

(4) Current assets are comfortably in excess of current liabilities (by $30m), so the company should have little problem in redeeming the debentures.

(iii) The report will need to disclose information about the **treasury management policies** of the company. This would cover such issues as the potential adverse movement in **foreign exchange risk** and details of the use of **financial instruments** for **hedging**.

(iv) **Currency risk and interest rate risk** need to be **managed and minimised**, and the report needs to disclose the **company's approach** for dealing with this.

(v) **Credit risk** is also an **important issue**, particularly as the company operates in the **global market place**.

(vi) A **statement of cash flows** will be provided as part of the financial statements, but the annual report should also indicate the **maturity profile of borrowings**.

(vii) Finally, the financial analysis might benefit from the use of techniques such as **SWOT analysis,** covering **potential liquidity problems** and **market growth**. Reference would be made to the **cartel** of car manufacturers aiming to prevent the increased use of aluminium in the car industry.

(c) **Nature of corporate citizenship**

(i) Increasingly businesses are expected to be **socially responsible as well as profitable**.

(ii) **Strategic decisions** by businesses, particularly global businesses nearly always have wider **social consequences**. It could be argued, as Henry Mintzberg does, that a company produces two outputs:

(1) Goods and services
(2) The social consequences of its activities, such as pollution

(iii) One **major development** in the area of corporate citizenship is the **environmental report**.

(1) This is not a legal requirement, but a large number of UK FTSE 100 companies produce them.

(2) Worldwide there are around 20 award schemes for environmental reporting, notably the ACCA's.

(iv) Mineral shows that it is responsible with regard to the environment by disclosing the following information.

(1) The use of the **eco-productivity index** in the financial performance of sites and divisions. This **links environmental and financial performance**

(2) The **regeneration of old plants**

(3) The development of **eco-friendly cars**. Particularly impressive, if successful, is the project to develop a new aluminium alloy car body. Aluminium is rust-free, and it is also lighter, which would reduce fuel consumption.

(v) Another environmental issue which the company could consider is **emission levels** from factories. Many companies now **include details** of this in their **environmental report**.

(vi) The other main aspect of corporate citizenship where Mineral plc scores highly is in its **treatment of its workforce**. The company sees the workforce as the **key factor** in the **growth** of its business. The car industry had a reputation in the past for **restrictive practices,** and the annual report could usefully discuss the extent to which these have been eliminated.

(vii) **Employees** of a businesses are **stakeholders** in that business, along with shareholders and customers. A company wishing to demonstrate good corporate citizenship will therefore be concerned with **employee welfare**. Accordingly, the annual report might usefully contain information on details of **working hours**, **industrial accidents** and **sickness of employees**.

(viii) In conclusion, it can be seen that the annual report can, and should go **far beyond the financial statements** and traditional ratio analysis.

4 Human resource accounting

FAST FORWARD

Human resource accounting is an approach which regards **people as assets.**

4.1 Introduction

Human resource accounting has at its core the principle that **employees are assets.** Competitive advantage is largely gained by **effective use of people**.

4.2 Implications of regarding people as organisational assets

(a) **People are a resource** which needs to be carefully and efficiently managed with overriding concern for organisational objectives.

(b) The organisation needs to **protect its investment** by retaining, safeguarding and developing its human assets.

(c) **Deterioration in the attitudes and motivation** of employees, increases in labour turnover (followed by costs of hiring and training replacements) are **costs to the company** – even though a 'liquidation' of human assets, brought about by certain managerial styles, may produce short-term increases in profit.

(d) A concept developed some time ago was that of **human asset accounting** (the inclusion of human assets in the financial reporting system of the organisation).

Case Study

There are difficulties in isolating and measuring human resources, and it is also hard to forecast the time period (and area of business) over which benefits will be received from expenditure on human assets. *Texas Instruments* uses a system which identifies potential replacement costs for groups of people, taking into account the learning time required by the replacement, and the individual's salary during that period.

4.3 Intellectual assets

FAST FORWARD

There are **problems in putting a value on people** which traditional accounting has yet to overcome.

Because of the difficulties found in both theory and practice, the concept of **human assets was broadened and became intellectual assets**. Intellectual assets, or 'intellectual capital' as they are sometimes called can be divided into three main types.

(a) **External assets.** These include the reputation of brands and franchises and the strength of customer relationships.

(b) **Internal assets.** These include patents, trademarks and information held in customer databases.

(c) **Competencies.** These reflect the capabilities and skills of individuals.

'Intellectual assets' thus includes 'human assets'.

The value of intellectual assets will continue to rise and will represent an increasing proportion of the value of most companies. Whether or not traditional accounting will be able to measure them, remains to be seen.

5 Integrated reporting 6/15, 6/16

Exam focus point

The role of integrated reporting in communicating strategy is a new addition to the P2 syllabus. It is important that you are familiar with integrated reporting as exam questions may require an explanation of how it can be used by a company featured in the question. You may also be required to comment on the implications of introducing integrated reporting.

In June 2015, candidates were asked to discuss the principles and key components of the integrated reporting framework, which would have been quite straightforward for those who had learnt it. In June 2016, as a Part (b) to the group cash flow question in Section A, candidates where asked whether the statement of cash flow provided stakeholders with useful information, and whether this information would be improved by the entity introducing an Integrated Report.

Next time, application to a scenario could be tested.

FAST FORWARD

Integrated reporting is concerned with conveying a wider message on organisational performance. It is fundamentally concerned with reporting on the value created by the organisation's resources. Resources are referred to as 'capitals', value is created or lost when capitals interact with one another. It is intended that integrated reporting should lead to a holistic view when assessing organisational performance.

5.1 Rise of integrated reporting

In recent years there has been increasing demand for the senior management in large organisations to provide greater detail on how they use the resources at their disposal to create value. Traditional corporate reporting which focuses on financial performance is said to only tell part of the story.

5.2 Wider performance appraisal

Integrated reporting is concerned with conveying a wider message on an entity's performance. It is not solely centred on profit or the organisation's financial position but details how its activities interact to create value over the short, medium and long term.

5.3 Value creation

In December 2013, the International Integrated Reporting Council published the *International <IR> Framework* (International Integrated Reporting Framework). The Framework refers to an organisation's resources as 'capitals'. Capitals are used to assess value creation. Increases or decreases in these capitals indicate the level of value created or lost over a period. Capitals cover various types of resources found in a standard organisation. These may include financial capitals, such as the entity's financial reserves through to its intellectual capital which is concerned with intellectual property and staff knowledge (IIRC, 2013).

5.4 Types of capital

The integrated reporting framework classifies the capitals as (IIRC, 2013, Section 2):

Capital	Comment
Financial capital	The pool of funds that is: • Available to an organisation for use in the production of goods or the provision of services • Obtained through financing, such as debt, equity or grants, or generated

Capital	Comment
	through operations or investments
Manufactured capital	Manufactured physical objects (as distinct from natural physical objects) that are available to an organisation for use in the production of goods or the provision of services, including: • Buildings • Equipment Infrastructure (such as roads, ports, bridges and waste and water treatment plants) Manufactured capital is often created by other organisations, but includes assets manufactured by the reporting organisation for sale or when they are retained for its own use.
Intellectual capital	Organisational knowledge-based intangibles, including: • Intellectual property, such as patents, copyrights, software, rights and Licences • 'Organisational capital' such as tacit knowledge, systems, procedures and protocols
Human capital	People's competencies, capabilities and experience, and their motivations to innovate, including their: • Alignment with and support for an organisations governance framework, risk management approach and ethical values • Ability to understand, develop and implement an organisation's strategy • Loyalties and motivations for improving processes, goods and services, including their ability to lead, manage and collaborate
Natural	Input to goods and services and what activities impact: • Water, land, minerals and forests • Biodiversity and eco-system health
Social and relationship capital	The institutions and the relationships within and between communities, groups of stakeholders and other networks, and the ability to share information to enhance individual and collective well-being. Social and relationship capital includes: • Shared norms and common values and behaviours • Key stakeholder relationships and the trust and willingness to engage that an organisation developed and strives to build and protect with external stakeholders • Intangibles associated with the brand and reputation that an organisation has developed • An organisations social licence to operate

Source: *The International Integrated Reporting Framework*, www.theiirc.org

PER alert

One of the competences you need to fulfil Objective 3 of the Practical Experience Requirement (PER) is to raise awareness of non-financial risk. Loyalty is a non-financial risk, but if not managed properly, it could turn into a financial risk.

5.5 Interaction of capitals

Capitals continually interact with one another, an increase in one will result in a decrease another. For example, a decision to purchase a new IT system would improve an entity's 'manufactured' capital while decreasing its financial capital in the form of its cash reserves.

At present adopting integrated reporting is voluntary, as a result organisations are free to report only on those 'capitals' felt to be most relevant in communicating performance.

5.6 Short term v long term

Integrated reporting forces management to balance the organisation's short term objectives against its longer term plans. Business decisions which are solely dedicated to the pursuit of increasing profit (financial capital) at the expense of building good relations with key stakeholders such as customers (social capital) is likely to hinder value creation in the longer term. It is thought that by producing a holistic view of organisational performance that this will lead to improved management decision making, ensuring that decisions are not taken in isolation.

5.7 Monetary values

Integrated reporting is not aimed at attaching a monetary value to every aspect of the organisations operations. It is fundamentally concerned with evaluating value creation through the communication of qualitative and quantitative performance measures. Key performance indicators are effective in communicating performance.

For example when providing detail on customer satisfaction this can be communicated as the number of customers retained compared to the previous year. Best practice in integrated reporting requires organisations to report on both positive and negative movements in 'capital' to avoid only providing half the story.

5.8 Materiality

When preparing an integrated report management should disclose matters which are likely to impact on an organisations ability to create value. The inclusion of both internal and external threats regarded as being materially important are evaluated and quantified. This provides users with an indication of how management intend to combat risks should they materialise.

5.9 Implications of introducing integrated reporting

Implications	Comment
IT costs	The introduction of integrated reporting will most likely require significant upgrades to be made to the organisation's IT and information system infrastructure. Such developments will be needed to capture KPI data. Due to the broad range of business activities reported on using integrated reporting (customer, supplier relations, finance and human resources) it is highly likely the costs of improving the infrastructure will be significant.
Time/ staff costs	The process of gathering and collating the data for inclusion in the report is likely to require a significant amount of staff time. This may serve to decrease staff morale if they are expected to undertake this work in addition to existing duties. This may require additional staff to be employed.
Consultancy costs	Organisations producing their first integrated report may seek external guidance from an organisation which provides specialist consultancy on integrated reporting. Consultancy fees are likely to be significant.
Disclosure	There is a danger that organisations may volunteer more information about their operational performance than intended. Disclosure of planned

	strategies and key performance measures are likely to be picked up by competitors.

Case Study

The Association of Chartered Certified Accountants (ACCA)

The ACCA produced its first integrated report in 2011/2012. The intentions of the report are made clear at the outset, 'we are aiming to tell a clear and coherent story about the ACCA's strategic performance and future prospects. Most importantly, we are using this report to explain how we create value for our stakeholders – primarily our members – and the place we occupy in society'.

Key elements from the ACCA's integrated report

Mission

The ACCA's mission to 'be the global leader in the profession', this is set out alongside its core values early in the report. This acts as a source of reference, putting into context how the ACCA has performed against its goals.

Key achievements

As illustrated by the following extract, the ACCA published its key achievements over the period in pursuit of its objectives. These are measured through the use of a number of key performance indicators. The commentary gives some detail as to the targets achieved and those not met.

Our 2015 strategic objective	How we measure this	The target we set ourselves for 2011-12	What was delivered in 2011-12	The target we have set ourselves for 2012-13
To be the leading global professional accountancy body in reputation, influence and size	Number of members	154,700	**Not achieved**: we had 154,337 members at 31.03.12	To have 162,015 members
To have sustainable growth	Gross operating surplus	£15.83m	**Achieved**: £20.147m	£11.92m
To have accountancy qualifications that are required by employers	% of members retained	98.3%	**Achieved**: 98.5%	98.5%

Stakeholders

The ACCA acknowledges its obligations to its key stakeholders. The report highlights how it engages with a number of groups including, members, students and employers.

Strategic focus and risk

The report places a strong focus on the steps the ACCA has taking to achieve its vision up to 2015. Consideration is given to the organisations three strategic priorities over the period 2011/2012. Factors likely to impact on its ability to achieve its objectives are covered in a section designated to risk management.

Value creation

In addition to the traditional reporting of financial performance the report also details those 'capitals' regarded as being important in creating value over the long term. One capital mentioned focuses on the role of people in the organisation.

The ACCA regard having the right people with the right skills and capability as being critical in being able to deliver its strategy. Over the year the ACCA enhanced its people capital through investments in staff development and training programmes.

Source: ACCA, 2012

The ACCA's first *integrated* report can be found at www.accaglobal.com under 'Annual Report 2011-12'

Chapter Roundup

- Although not compulsory, **environmental reports** are becoming increasingly important. You should distinguish
  - Items that **affect the financial statements** (eg IAS 37)
  - Items that **affect the environmental report**
- The Global Reporting Initiative arose from the need to **address the failure of the current governance structures to respond to changes in the global economy**.
- The **stakeholder** view holds that there are many groups in society with an interest in the organisation's activities. Some firms have objectives for these issues. Some argue, however, that a business's only objective should be to make money: the State, representing the public interest, can levy taxes to spend on socially desirable projects or can regulate organisational activities.
- **Human resource accounting** is an approach which regards **people as assets**.
- There are **problems in putting a value on people** which traditional accounting has yet to overcome.
- **Integrated reporting** is concerned with conveying a wider message on organisational performance. It is fundamentally concerned with reporting on the value created by the organisation's resources. Resources are referred to as 'capitals'. Value is created or lost when capitals interact with one another. It is intended that integrated reporting should lead to a holistic view when assessing organisational performance.

Quick Quiz

1. Give an example of an environmental audit.
2. Name four areas of company accounts where environmental matters may be reported.
3. If a site is contaminated, a provision must be made. *True or False*?
4. What objectives might a company have in relation to wider society?
5. To whom might management have responsibilities, and what are some of these responsibilities?
6. Why does Mintzberg say that the profit motive is not enough?
7. What is the basic principle of human resource accounting?
8. Give three examples of intellectual assets.

Answers to Quick Quiz

1 In 1999 KPMG conducted an audit of the greenhouse gas emissions of BP Amoco.

2 Contingent liabilities
Exceptional charges
Operating and financial review comments
Profit and capital expenditure forecasts

3 False. An obligation must be established.

4 Protection of the environment, support for good causes, a responsible attitude to product safety.

5 Managers of businesses are responsible to the owners for economic performance and to wider society for the externalities related to their business operations.

6 Large businesses are rarely controlled by their shareholders; they receive a lot of support from public funds; and their activities have wider consequences.

7 Employees are assets.

8 External assets
Internal assets
Competencies

Now try the question below from the Practice Question Bank

Number	Level	Marks	Time
Q25	Introductory	n/a	n/a

19

Current developments

Topic list	Syllabus reference
1 Current issues in corporate reporting	F2, H3
2 Conceptual framework ED and other recent documents	F2
3 Other current issues and debates	F2
4 Managing the change to IFRS	F2
5 Progress towards global harmonisation	F2
6 Benefits of and barriers to global harmonisation	F2
7 IASB Work Plan	F2

Introduction

This chapter deals with a number of current issues and developments. Sections 1 to 3 highlight the latest developments. These are mainly dealt with within the relevant chapters elsewhere in this Study Text.

You should be familiar with the accounting standards covered in Part B. If you are in a hurry or revising, go straight to the sections highlighted in this chapter as current issues.

Study guide

		Intellectual level
B1	**The applications, strength and weaknesses of an accounting framework**	
(a)	Evaluate the valuation models adopted by standard setters	3
F1	**The effect of changes in accounting standards on accounting systems**	
(a)	Apply and discuss the accounting implications of the first time adoption of a body of new accounting standards	3
F2	**Proposed changes to accounting standards**	
(a)	Identify the issues and deficiencies which have led to a proposed change to an accounting standard	2
H2	**Convergence between national and international reporting standards**	
(a)	Evaluate the implications, nationally and globally, of convergence with International Financial Reporting Standards	3
(b)	Discuss the influence of national regulators on international financial reporting	3
H3	**Current reporting issues**	
(a)	Discuss current issues in corporate reporting	3

Exam guide

Current issues may come up in the context of a question requiring advice. For example, in the scenario question involving groups, perhaps you might have to explain the difference that the proposed changes will make.

Current issues are summarised here, but discussed in detail in the context of the topic to which they relate.

Revenue recognition and leasing are very topical.

1 Current issues in corporate reporting 6/08 – 12/16

FAST FORWARD

You should know which are the **current issues** and concentrate your studying on these.

Exam focus point

The P2 examining team have given the following guidance on current issues:

'The IASB's work programme will be the basis for many of the current issue discursive questions asked in the paper. However the work programme will not be the exclusive source of questions.'

The June 2014 paper had a question on the debt/equity distinction.

1.1 Hot topics

The IASB Work Plan, as at November 2016 is reproduced in Section 7. Below are the examinable current issues, with an indication of where to find them. Most are dealt with in the chapters on the individual topic.

ED *Conceptual Framework for Financial Reporting*	Chapter 1
IFRS 16 *Leases*	Chapter 8
IFRS 15 *Revenue from contracts with customers*	Chapter 1
IFRS 9 *Financial instruments* (final July 2014 version)	Chapter 7

7 ED *Measuring quoted investments in subsidiaries, joint ventures and associates at fair value*	Chapter 12
ED *Classification of liabilities – proposed amendments to IAS 1*	Chapter 10
ED *Conceptual Framework for Financial Reporting*	Chapter 1
ED Practice Statement: Application of Materiality in Financial Statements	Chapter 10
Disclosure initiative	Chapter 10, 17, Section 3 of this chapter
Annual Improvements to IFRS	Section 2 of this chapter
2015 Amendments to the IFRS for SMEs	Chapter 21

Exam focus point

Keep your eye out for articles on these topics in *Student Accountant*, a good indication that the topic will be examined. The examining team have emphasised that current issues are not confined to the EDs in the examinable documents, but cover other matters such as alternative performance measures, debt versus equity (see Section 3).

2 Conceptual Framework ED and other recent documents

FAST FORWARD

The most important current issue is the ED on the *Conceptual Framework* but **IFRS 15** and the **final version of IFRS 9,** although published in 2014, are still very topical. Summaries are given here, but you should refer to the relevant topic chapters for full coverage.

2.1 IFRS 16 *Leases*

IFRS 16 was published in January 2016 after many years of debate. It is covered in detail in Chapter 8. The key principle of IFRS 16 is that **all leases must be reported in the statement of financial position.**

- There are exceptions for leases of low value assets and leases of under twelve months.
- A lessee measures a **right-of-use asset** similarly to other non-financial assets, such as PPE, requiring **depreciation** of the right-of-use asset.
- A lessee must measure the **lease liability** similarly to other lease liabilities and recognise **interest** on the liability.
- Lease assets and liabilities are initially measured on a **present value** basis.
- Requirements for **lessors** are essentially **unchanged.**
- There are **extensive disclosure requirements** for both lessees and lessors.

(IFRS 16: paras. IN 10 to IN 14)

Exam focus point

IFRS 16 interacts with another important recent standard, IFRS 15 *Revenue* in the context of a sale and leaseback, so you can expect a question on this in the near future.

IFRS 16 is covered in full in Chapter 8 of this Study Text.

2.2 IFRS 15 *Revenue from contracts with customers*

IFRS 15 was published in 2014. It aims to give clarity and consistency to an issue that had been the subject of a number of contradictory or vague rules. The core principle of the IFRS is that an entity should:

> 'recognise revenue to depict the transfer of promised goods or services to customers in an amount that reflects the consideration to which the entity expects to be entitled in exchange for those goods or services'.

IFRS 15 details a five step process for revenue recognition:

Step 1 – identify the contract with a customer

Step 2 – identify the performance obligations in the contract

Step 3 – determine the transaction price

Step 4 – allocate the transaction price to performance obligations

Step 5 – recognise revenue when performance obligations are satisfied

(IFRS 15: para. IN 7)

IFRS 15 is covered in full in Chapter 1 of this Study Text.

Exam focus point

The examining team have emphasised the importance of revenue in the light of IFRS 15, so a question is very likely indeed. It was examined as a current issue in the second half of 2015, but will likely be examined as a mainstream issue in the future.

2.3 IFRS 9 *Financial instruments*

The IASB has completed its work on IFRS 9 *Financial instruments,* which comes into effect on 1 January 2018, and is examinable from September 2015. The main features are:

(a) **Classification and measurement.** IFRS 9 introduces a logical approach for the classification of financial assets, which is driven by cash flow characteristics and the business model in which an asset is held. This replaces the rules-based approach of IAS 39.

(b) **A new impairment model.** The IAS 39 impairment rules were criticised during the financial crisis for a delayed recognition of credit losses on loans and other financial instruments. IFRS 9 brings in expected-loss impairment model that will require more timely recognition of expected credit losses. Specifically, IFRS 9 requires entities to account for expected credit losses from when financial instruments are first recognised and to recognise full lifetime expected losses on a more timely basis.

(c) **Hedge accounting.** IFRS 9 introduces significant reforms to hedge accounting, with a new model that aligns the accounting treatment with risk management activities, enabling entities to better reflect these activities in their financial statements. These changes are expected to provide users of the financial with better information about risk management and the effect of hedge accounting on the financial statements.

(d) **Own credit.** Under IFRS 9, gains caused by the deterioration of an entity's own credit risk on liabilities elected to be measured at fair value are no longer recognised in profit or loss. This removes the volatility in profit or loss, and apparent anomaly that a deterioration increases reported profit.

IFRS 9 is covered in full in Chapter 7 of this Study Text.

Exam focus point

IFRS 9 is very topical and ripe for examination.

2.4 ED *Conceptual Framework for Financial Reporting*

This ED was published in May 2015, following a 2013 Discussion Paper, which in turn resulted from a project lasting several years. The project was designed to **fill gaps, update, and clarify**. Many believed that the existing guidance on recognition of assets and liabilities needed updating, and there is minimal guidance in the current *Framework* on measurement. Key changes proposed are as follows.

Chapter 1 *Objective:* Stewardship has been added to the objective of general purpose financial reporting.

Chapter 2 *Qualitative characteristics:* There is now an explicit reference to substance over form and prudence has been reinstated as a component of neutrality.

Chapter 3 *Reporting entity:* This chapter defines reporting entity, which may be one legal entity or more or a portion of a legal entity. It also provides guidance for determining boundaries of reporting entities.

Chapter 4 *Elements:* This chapter refines the definitions of assets and liabilities, defines income as an increase in assets or decrease in liabilities and defines expense as a decrease in assets or increase in liabilities.

Chapter 5 *Recognition and derecognition:* For recognition, this chapter removes the probability threshold and adds factors to consider in deciding whether to recognise an asset or liability. For the first time there is guidance on derecognition: full derecognition, partial derecognition, and continued recognition

Chapter 6 *Measurement:* the chapter stipulates a mixed measurement model of both historical cost and current value measures

Chapter 7 *Presentation and disclosure:* profit or loss is the primary performance indicator. There is some discussion of other comprehensive income (OCI), which notes that its use should be limited

Chapter 8 *Concepts of capital maintenance:* Carried forward from Chapter 4 of the current *Framework* with only minor changes to terminology.

The *Conceptual Framework* and this ED are covered in full in Chapter 1 of this Study Text.

2.5 ED *Classification of liabilities – proposed amendments to IAS 1*

In February 2015, the IASB published an ED *Classification of liabilities – proposed amendments to IAS 1.* The proposed amendments aim at a more general approach to the classification of liabilities under IAS 1 **based on the contractual arrangements** in place at the reporting date. They address three main topics:

(a) Replacing 'discretion' in paragraph 73 of the IAS 1 with 'right' to align it with the requirements of paragraph 69(d) of the standard

(b) Making it explicit in paragraphs 69(d) and 73 of IAS 1 that only rights in place at the reporting date should affect this classification of a liability

(c) Deleting 'unconditional' from paragraph 69(d) of the Standard so that 'an unconditional right' is replaced by 'a right'

The IASB also proposes making clear the link between the settlement of the liability and the outflow of resources from the entity by adding that settlement 'refers to the transfer to the counterparty of cash, equity instruments, other assets or services' to paragraph 69 of IAS 1.

The IASB further proposes that guidance in IAS 1should be reorganised so that similar examples are grouped together.

Finally, the IASB proposes that retrospective application should be required and that early application should be permitted.

The ED is covered in more detail in Chapter 10 of this Study Text in the context of IAS 1.

2.6 Amendment *Recognition of deferred tax assets for unrealised losses*

This amendment was published in January 2016. It considers the question of whether an unrealised loss on a debt instrument measured at fair value gives rise to a deductible temporary difference when the holder expects to recover the carrying amount of the asset by holding it to maturity and collecting all the contractual cash flows.

The amendment is covered in more detail in Chapter 6 of this Study Text in the context of IAS 12.

2.7 ED *Measuring quoted investments in subsidiaries, joint ventures and associates at fair value*

This exposure draft was published in September 2014, and contains proposals concerning the measurement of investments in subsidiaries, joint ventures and associates at fair value when those investments are quoted in an active market.

The proposed amendments are to IFRS 10 *Consolidated financial statements,* IFRS 12 *Disclosure of interests in other entities,* IAS 27 *Separate financial statements,* IAS 28 *Investments in associates and joint ventures,* IAS 36 *Impairment of assets* and IFRS 12 *Fair value measurement..*

The proposed amendments clarify that an entity should measure the fair value of quoted investments and quoted cash-generating units as **the product of the quoted price for the individual financial instruments that make up the investments held by the entity and the quantity of financial instruments.**

The ED is covered in more detail in Chapter 12 of this Study Text in the context of group financial statements and fair value.

2.8 Amendment to IFRS 2*Classification and measurement of share-based payment transactions*

This amendment was issued in June 2016. It addresses the three following issues (IFRS 2: paras 33A to 33D).

(a) Accounting for cash-settled share-based payment transactions that include a performance condition

(b) Classification of share-based payment transactions with net settlement features

(c) Accounting for modifications of share-based payment transactions from cash-settled to equity-settled.

The amendment is covered in more detail in Chapter 9 of this Study Text in the context of IFRS 2.

2.9 Initial comprehensive review of the *IFRS for SMEs*

In 2015, the IASB completed its comprehensive review of the *IFRS for SMEs.* The most significant amendments are as follows:

(a) SMEs are now permitted to use a revaluation model for property, plant and equipment.

(b) The main recognition and measurement requirements for deferred income tax are aligned with full IFRS.

The changes are incorporated in the coverage of the *IFRS for SMEs* in Chapter 21 of the Study Text.

2.10 Improvements to IFRS 2014 to 2016 Cycle

The *Annual Improvements to IFRSs 2014 to 2016 Cycle* was issued in November 2015. Below is a summary of its main changes.

2.10.1 IFRS 1 *First-time adoption of International Financial Reporting Standards*

This amendment removes the short-term exemptions in paragraphs E3–E7 of IFRS 1, because they have now served their intended purpose.

2.10.2 IFRS 12 *Disclosure of interests in other entities*

The purpose of this amendment is to clarify the scope of the standard by specifying that most of the disclosure requirements in the standard apply to an entity's interests that are classified as held for sale, as held for distribution or as discontinued operations in accordance with IFRS 5 *Non-current assets held for sale and discontinued operations.*

2.10.3 Amendment to IAS 28 *Investments in associates and joint ventures*

This amendment clarifies that the election to measure at fair value through profit or loss an investment in an associate or a joint venture that is held by an entity that is a venture capital organisation, or other qualifying entity, is available on initial recognition for each investment in an associate or joint venture. This applies on an investment-by-investment basis.

3 Other current issues and debates

FAST FORWARD

Other current issues highlighted by the examining team are:

- Disclosure initiative
- Profit or loss versus other comprehensive income
- Equity accounting
- Debt versus equity
- Additional performance measures

3.1 Disclosure initiative

3.1.1 Overview

The IASB's disclosure initiative is a broad-based undertaking exploring how disclosures in IFRS financial reporting can be improved. It is made up of a number of projects, the second of which was completed in January 2016.

The disclosure initiative was formally begun in 2012. Subsequently IASB undertook a constituent survey on disclosure and held a disclosure forum designed to bring together securities regulators, auditors, investors and preparers. This led to issued Feedback Statement Discussion Forum – Financial Reporting Disclosure in May 2013, which outlined the IASB's intention to consider a number of further initiatives, including short-term and research projects.

The disclosure initiative is intended to **complement the work being done on the *Conceptual Framework* project** (covered in Chapter 1).

3.1.2 Current status of projects

Two projects, the amendments to IAS 1 and IAS 7 are complete, one, a draft Practice Statement on materiality is at the ED stage and the remainder at the research stage.

3.1.3 Disclosure initiative: Amendments to IAS 1

This is a narrow scope project which aims to ensure that entities are able to use judgement when presenting their financial reports as the wording of some of the requirements in IAS 1 had in some cases been read to prevent the use of judgement. The final Standard *Disclosure Initiative (Amendments to IAS 1)* was published in 2014, and is effective for annual periods beginning on or after 1 January 2016 with earlier application permitted.

The following amendments are made.

(a) **Materiality.** Information should not be obscured by aggregating or by providing immaterial information. Materiality considerations apply to the all parts of the financial statements. Materiality considerations still apply, even when a standard requires a specific disclosure. (IAS 1: paras. 35, 55A)

(b) **Statement of financial position and statement of profit or loss and other comprehensive income.** The list of line items to be presented in these statements can be disaggregated and aggregated as relevant and additional guidance on subtotals in these statements. An entity's share of other comprehensive income of equity-accounted associates and joint ventures should be presented in aggregate as single line items based on whether or not it will subsequently be reclassified to profit or loss. (IAS 1: para. 55)

(c) **Notes.** Additional examples have been added of possible ways of ordering the notes to clarify that understandability and comparability should be considered when determining the order of the notes and to demonstrate that the notes need not be presented in the order so far listed in paragraph 114 of IAS 1. The IASB also removed guidance and examples with regard to the identification of significant accounting policies that were perceived as being potentially unhelpful.

This topic is covered in more detail in the context of IAS 1 in Chapter 10.

3.1.4 Draft Practice Statement: Application of Materiality to Financial Statements

This Draft Practice Statement was issued as part of the Disclosure Initiative in October 2015. The statement is divided into the following three key areas (ED/2015/8: Para. IN4):

(a) Characteristics of

(b) How to apply the concept of materiality when making decisions about presenting and disclosing information in the financial statements

(c) How to assess **whether omissions and misstatements of information are material** to the financial statements.

This topic is covered in more detail in the context of IAS 1 in Chapter 10.

3.1.5 Disclosure initiative: amendments to IAS 7

In January 2016, the IASB published amendments to IAS 7 intended to improve information provided to users of financial statements **about an entity's financing activities**. The amendments require disclosure of **changes in liabilities arising from financing activities** and recommend a reconciliation of liabilities relating to financing activities.

This topic is covered in more detail in the context of IAS 7 in Chapter 17.

3.1.6 Disclosure initiative: other projects

The following disclosure initiative projects are at the pre-exposure-draft or research stage.

(a) **Amendments to IAS 8 *Accounting Policies, Changes in Accounting Estimates and Errors.*** These amendments would clarify the definitions of a change in accounting policy and a change in accounting estimate. An ED is expected in early 2016.

(b) **Materiality project.** The IASB is considering how materiality is applied in practice in IFRS financial statements. The IASB has tentatively decided to provide guidance on the application of materiality, which will take the form of a Practice Statement. In April 2015 the IASB tentatively decided that the Principles of Disclosure Discussion Paper should include a discussion on whether the definition of materiality should be changed and whether IAS 1 *Presentation of financial statements* should include additional guidance that clarifies the key characteristics of materiality.

(c) **Principles of disclosure.** This project aims to identify and develop a set of principles for disclosure in IFRS that could form the basis of a Standards-level project. The focus is on reviewing the general requirements in IAS 1 *Presentation of financial statements,* and considering how it may be revised.

(d) **Standards level review of disclosures.** The IASB will review disclosures in existing Standards to identify targeted improvements and to develop a drafting guide. This project will be informed by the principles being developed in the Principles of Disclosure (PoD) project.

3.2 Profit or loss versus other comprehensive income

3.2.1 The classification issue

The statement of profit or loss and other comprehensive income aims to present the financial performance of an entity to a wide variety of users in a way that is understandable and comparable for the purpose of assessing the net cash inflows of the entity. The manner in which the information in the statement is classified and aggregated plays a key role in fulfilling this aim.

Since the 2011 revision of IAS 1, entities have been required to show separately in other comprehensive income those items that may be reclassified to profit or loss (recycled) and those which may never be reclassified (together with the related tax effects).

There has been di**sagreement as to which items should appear in profit or loss, and which in other comprehensive income** (OCI). The issue of **reclassification** has also been **controversial**.

3.2.2 Profit or loss items

Generally, changes resulting from or related to an entity's **primary performance or main revenue-producing activities** are reported in profit or loss. Examples include sales revenue, administration expenses and gains on disposal of property, plant and equipment. Reclassification adjustments, that is when items are recycled from other comprehensive income, are also included.

Investors tend to focus on profit or loss rather than OCI, and many accounting ratios are calculated using profit or loss for the year, rather than total comprehensive income.

3.2.3 Other comprehensive income

Generally, these are items of income and expense arising from other, **non-primary or non-revenue producing activities** of the company that are not reported in profit or loss **as required or permitted by other IFRS.**

3.2.4 Profit or loss v OCI ≠ realised v unrealised

A common misconception in considering the classification of items is that profit or loss is for realised gains and losses and OCI for unrealised. However, this distinction is itself controversial and therefore of limited use in determining the P/L versus OCI classification.

3.2.5 OCI as the 'dumping ground'

It could be argued that OCI is defined in opposition to profit or loss, that is items that are not profit or loss, or even that it has been used as a 'dumping ground' for items that entities do not wish to report in profit or loss. Reclassification from OCI has been said to compromise the reliability of both profit or loss and OCI.

3.2.6 Approach in Conceptual Framework

Part of the problem is conceptual – the current *Conceptual Framework* does not contain principles to determine:

(a) What items are recognised in **profit or loss**
(b) What items are recognised in **other comprehensive income**
(c) Whether, and when, items can be **recycled** from other comprehensive income to profit or loss

In response, a 2013 Discussion Paper proposed that the *Conceptual Framework* should:

(a) Require a **profit or loss total or subtotal** that also **results, or could result**, in some items of income or **expense being recycled.**

(b) **Limit the use of OCI** (only to income and expenses resulting from remeasurements of assets and liabilities).

This approach was carried forward into the 2015 Exposure Draft.

The Discussion Paper proposed a **narrow and broad approach** to what should be included in other comprehensive income, but the IASB has not yet decided which approach it will use.

(a) **Narrow approach.** Other comprehensive income would only **include bridging items and mismatched remeasurements**.

Bridging items are items of income or expense which represent the difference between measurement used in determining profit or loss and remeasurement used in the statement of financial position. An example would be investments in equity instruments with changes in fair value recorded in other comprehensive income. Such items would have to be **recycled as a consequence of the measurement basis presented in profit or loss.**

Mismatched remeasurements represent the effects of part of a linked set of assets, liabilities or past or planned transactions. It represents their effect so incompletely that, in the opinion of the IASB, the item provides little relevant information about the return that the entity has made on its economic resources in the period. An example would be a cash flow hedge, where fair value gains and losses are accumulated in other comprehensive income until the hedged transaction affects profit or loss. These amounts should **be recycled when the item can be presented with the matched item.**

(b) **Broad approach.** In addition to the narrow approach, this would also include transitory remeasurements. **Transitory remeasurements** are remeasurements of long-term assets and liabilities that are likely to reverse or significantly change over time. These items would be shown in OCI - for example, the remeasurement of a net defined pension benefit liability or asset. The IASB would **decide in each IFRS whether a transitory remeasurement should be subsequently recycled.**

The ED on the *Conceptual Framework* does not provide any guidance as to which of the above approaches it recommends.

(The *Conceptual Framework* and the related ED is covered in full in Chapter 1.)

3.3 Equity accounting

Equity accounting has been used in recent years to account for associates and joint ventures (see Chapter 12), but it was originally used to account for subsidiaries as an alternative to consolidation, at a time when acquisition accounting was considered inappropriate because it showed assets and liabilities not owned by the reporting entity. Its use has been **called into question in recent years**, because it does not apply IFRS 3 consolidation principles consistently.

There are two main recent developments.

3.3.1 Separate financial statements of the investor

The option to apply the equity method in separate financial statements had been removed in the 2003 revision of IAS 27 *Consolidated and separate financial statements* as the IASB noted at that time that the information provided by the equity method is reflected in the investor's economic entity financial statements and that there was no need to provide the same information in the separate financial statements. The decision was carried forward to IAS 27 *Separate financial statements* in 2011. However, the IASB reconsidered this decision in the light of feedback and reinstated the option in a 2014 amendment to IAS 27.

Accordingly, investments in subsidiaries, associates and joint ventures in the separate financial statements of the parent is should be:

(a) Accounted for at **cost, or**
(b) In accordance with **IFRS 9, or**
(c) Using the equity method as described in IAS 28 *Investments in associates and joint ventures*

(IAS 27: para. 10)

The amendments also clarify that when a parent ceases to be an investment entity, or becomes an investment entity, it must account for the change from the date when the change in status occurred.

3.3.2 ED *Equity method: share of other net asset changes*

This Exposure Draft was published in 2012. The objective of the proposed amendments is to provide additional guidance to IAS 28 on the application of the equity method. Specifically; the proposed amendments intend to specify the following.

(a) An investor should recognise, in the investor's equity, its share of the changes in the net assets of the investee that are not recognised in profit or loss or other comprehensive income (OCI) of the investee, and that are not distributions received ('other net asset changes').
(b) The investor must reclassify to profit or loss the cumulative amount of equity that the investor had previously recognised when the investor discontinues the use of the equity method.

These amendments have by no means resolved all the uncertainties about the method, and it is still perceived to **lack a clear conceptual basis.**

(ED/2012/3: para. 10)

3.4 Debt versus equity — 12/13, 6/14, Sept/Dec 2016

3.4.1 Classification differences

It is not always easy to **distinguish between debt and equity in an entity's** statement of financial position, partly because many financial instruments have elements of both. IAS 32 *Financial instruments: presentation* brings clarity and consistency to this matter, so that the **classification is based on principles** rather than driven by perceptions of users.

IAS 32 defines an **equity instrument** as: 'any contract that evidences a residual interest in the assets of an entity after deducting all of its liabilities' (IAS 32: para. 11). It must first be **established that an instrument is not a financial liability,** before it can be classified as equity.

A key feature of the **IAS 32 definition of a financial liability** is that it **is a contractual obligation to deliver cash or another financial asset to another entity** (IAS 32: para. 11). The contractual obligation may arise from a requirement to make payments of principal, interest or dividends. The contractual obligation may be explicit, but it may be implied indirectly in the terms of the contract. An example of a debt instrument is a bond which requires the issuer to make interest payments and redeem the bond for cash.

A financial instrument is an **equity instrument** only if there is no obligation to deliver cash or other financial assets to another entity and if the instrument will or may be settled in the issuer's own equity instruments. An example of an equity instrument is **ordinary shares, on which dividends are payable at the discretion of the issuer.** A less obvious example is preference shares required to be converted into a fixed number of ordinary shares on a fixed date or on the occurrence of an event which is certain to occur.

An instrument may be classified as an equity instrument if it contains a **contingent settlement provision** requiring settlement in cash or a variable number of the entity's own shares **only on the occurrence of an event which is very unlikely to occur** – such a provision is **not considered to be genuine.** If the **contingent payment condition** is **beyond the control of** both the entity and the holder of the instrument, then the instrument is classified as a **financial liability**.

A **contract resulting in the receipt or delivery of an entity's own shares is not automatically an equity instrument.** The classification depends on the so-called **'fixed test'** in IAS 32. A contract which will be settled by the entity receiving or delivering a **fixed number of its own equity instruments in exchange for a fixed amount of cash is an equity instrument**. The reasoning behind this is that by fixing upfront the number of shares to be received or delivered on settlement of the instrument in question, the holder is exposed to the upside and downside risk of movements in the entity's share price.

In contrast, if the **amount of cash or own equity shares to be delivered or received is variable,** then the contract is a **financial liability or asset.** The reasoning behind this is that using a variable number of own equity instruments to settle a contract can be similar to using own shares as 'currency' to settle what in substance is a financial liability. Such a contract does not evidence a residual interest in the entity's net assets. Equity classification is therefore inappropriate.

IAS 32 gives two **examples** of contracts where the number of own equity instruments to be received or delivered varies so that their fair value equals the amount of the contractual right or obligation.

(a) A contract to deliver a variable number of own equity instruments equal in value to a fixed monetary amount on the settlement date is classified as a financial liability.

(b) A contract to deliver as many of the entity's own equity instruments as are equal in value to the value of 100 ounces of a commodity results in liability classification of the instrument.

(IAS 32: para. AG 27)

There are **other factors** which might result in an instrument being **classified as debt.**

(1) Dividends are non-discretionary.

(2) Redemption is at the option of the instrument holder.

(3) The instrument has a limited life.

(4) Redemption is triggered by a future uncertain event which is beyond the control of both the issuer and the holder of the instrument.

Other factors which might result in an instrument being **classified as equity** include the following.

(a) Dividends are discretionary.
(b) The shares are non-redeemable.
(c) There is no liquidation date.

(IAS 32: para. AG 16C)

3.4.2 Significance of the classification

The distinction between debt and equity is very important, since the classification of a financial instrument as either debt or equity **can have a significant impact on the entity's reported earnings and gearing ratio**, which in turn can affect debt covenants. Companies may wish to classify a financial instrument as **equity,** in order to give a **favourable impression of gearing,** but this may in turn have a **negative effect** on the perceptions of existing shareholders if it is seen **as diluting existing equity interests.**

The distinction is also relevant in the context of a **business combination** where an entity **issues financial instruments as part consideration, or to raise funds to settle a business combination in cash.** Management is often called upon to **evaluate different financing options**, and in order to do so must **understand the classification rules and their potential effects**. For example, **classification as a liability** generally means that **payments are treated as interest** and charged to profit or loss, and this may, in turn, **affect the entity's ability to pay dividends** on equity shares.

3.5 Additional performance measures

The problem of presenting financial performance was discussed in Section 3.1 above, in the context of the profit or loss/OCI distinction. Another topical issue is the use of **additional performance measures.** These can take the form of additional key performance indicators or providing more information on the individual items within the financial statements.

Users have driven the demand for additional performance measures (APMs) because financial statements, prepared in accordance with applicable financial reporting standards, have been restricted in the amount of information that can be provided.

3.5.1 Purpose and common types of APMs

Preparers of financial statements may wish to report **'sustainable' earnings**. This means, in effect, that certain items of income and expense are excluded because they are considered irrelevant as regards their impact on future years' performance. Examples of such items include fair value gains or losses on financial instruments.

Common APMs include the following:

(a) **Normalised profit.** This may be defined in various ways, but principally means profit per IFRS (or other applicable standards) excluding non-recurring items such as disposals of business, and other items such as amortisation of intangibles.

(b) **EBIT.** This means earnings before interest and tax.

(c) **EBITDA.** This stands for earnings before interest, tax and amortisation.

(d) **Net financial debt.** This is gross financial debt less cash and cash equivalents and other financial assets, and is a useful indicator of an entity's ability to meet its financial obligations.

In general, APMs are any measures of financial performance not specifically defined by the applicable financial reporting framework.

3.5.2 Potential problems with APMS

The **problematic nature** of some APMs may be seen in the case of EBITDA. This is a proxy for operating cash flows, although it is not the same. It takes operating profit and strips out depreciation, amortisation and (normally) any separately-disclosed items such as exceptional items.

EBITDA is not a cash flow ratio as such, but it is a widely used, and sometimes misused, approximation. Particular reservations include:

(a) EBITDA is not a cash flow measure and, while it excludes certain subjective accounting practices, it is still subject to accounting manipulation in a way that cash flows would not be. Examples would include revenue recognition practice and items that have some unusual aspects but are not disclosed separately and, therefore, not added back.

(b) EBITDA is not a sustainable figure as there is no charge for capital replacement such as depreciation in traditional profit measures or CAPEX (capital expenditure) as in free cash flow.

More generally, APMs are sometimes used by issuers to present an **overly favourable picture** of an entity's financial performance by stripping out the negative aspects.

3.5.3 ESMA guidance

While both the IASB and the UK Financial Reporting Council have acknowledged the usefulness of APMs, guidance is needed in order to ensure that users have the information they need to judge them appropriately. The European Securities and Markets Authority (ESMA) has begun a consultation process and developed some **draft guidelines** in this area, published in 2015. Key points from these guidelines are as follows.

(a) Preparers must provide a definition of the APM used and the basis of its calculation.

(b) The definition and calculation of the APM must be consistent over time.

(c) Preparers must show comparatives for the APM.

(d) If an APM is discontinued, an explanation must be given as to why it is no longer used, and a reason given for any replacement APM.

(e) APMs must be reconciled to the financial statements.

(ESMA, 2015)

Because the aim of the above guidelines is consistency, the APMs should not change much between accounting periods and so the **cost of compliance** with these guidelines should **not be prohibitive**. The costs will, it is hoped, be outweighed by the benefits of greater transparency.

4 Managing the change to IFRS 6/08, 6/11, 6/16

4.1 IFRS 1 *First-time Adoption of International Financial Reporting Standards*

FAST FORWARD

IFRS 1 gives guidance to entities applying IFRS for the first time.

The adoption of a new body of accounting standards will inevitably have a significant effect on the accounting treatments used by an entity and on the related **systems and procedures**. In 2005 many countries adopted IFRS for the first time and over the next few years other countries are likely to do the same. In addition, many Alternative Investment Market (AIM) companies and public sector companies adopted IFRS for the first time for accounting periods ending in 2009 and 2010, and US companies are likely to move increasingly to IFRS.

IFRS 1 *First-time adoption of International Financial Reporting Standards* was issued to ensure that an entity's first IFRS financial statements contain high quality information that:

(a) Is transparent for users and comparable over all periods presented
(b) Provides a suitable starting point for accounting under IFRSs
(c) Can be generated at a cost that does not exceed the benefits to users

(IFRS 1: para. 1)

4.1.1 General principles

An entity applies IFRS 1 in its first IFRS financial statements.

An entity's first IFRS financial statements are the first annual financial statements in which the entity adopts IFRS by an **explicit and unreserved statement of compliance** with IFRS.

Any other financial statements (including fully compliant financial statements that did not state so) are not the first set of financial statements under IFRS.

(IFRS 1: para. IN 4)

4.1.2 Opening IFRS statement of financial position

An entity **prepares and presents** an **opening IFRS statement of financial position** at the date of transition to IFRS as a starting point for IFRS accounting (IFRS 1: para. IN 4).

Generally, this will be the beginning of the **earliest comparative period shown** (ie full retrospective application). Given that the entity is applying a change in accounting policy on adoption of IFRS, IAS 1 *Presentation of Financial Statements* (para. 40A) requires the presentation of **at least three statements of financial position** (and two of each of the other statements). (IFRS 1: para. 21)

Illustration: Opening IFRS SOFP

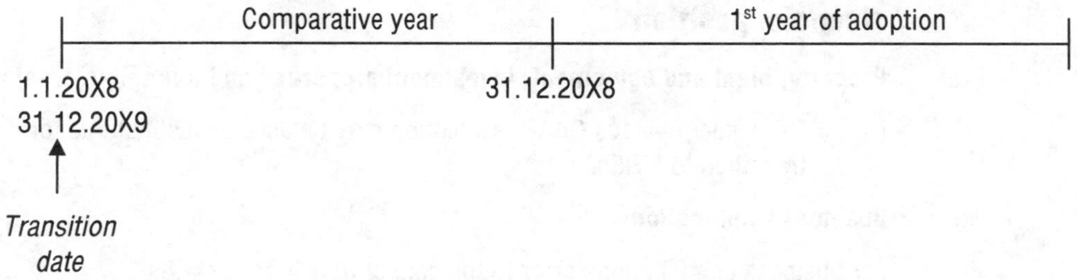

Preparation of an opening IFRS statement of financial position typically involves adjusting the amounts reported at the same date under previous GAAP.

All adjustments are recognised **directly in retained earnings** (or, if appropriate, another category of equity) not in profit or loss.

4.1.3 Estimates

Estimates in the opening IFRS statement of financial position must be consistent with estimates **made at the same date under previous GAAP** even if further information is now available (in order to comply with IAS 10). (IFRS 1: para. IG 3)

4.1.4 Transition process

(a) **Accounting policies**

The entity should select accounting policies that comply with IFRSs effective **at the end of the first IFRS reporting period**.

These accounting policies are used in the opening IFRS statement of financial position and throughout all periods presented. The entity does not apply different versions of IFRS effective at earlier dates.

(b) **Derecognition of assets and liabilities**

Previous GAAP statement of financial position may contain items that do not qualify for recognition under IFRS.

For example, IFRS does not permit capitalisation of research, staff training and relocation costs.

(c) **Recognition of new assets and liabilities**

New assets and liabilities may need to be recognised.

For example, deferred tax balances and certain provisions such as environmental and decommissioning costs.

(d) **Reclassification of assets and liabilities**

For example, compound financial instruments need to be split into their liability and equity components.

(e) **Measurement**

Value at which asset or liability is measured may differ under IFRS.

For example, discounting of deferred tax assets/liabilities not allowed under IFRS.

(IFRS 1: para. 10)

4.1.5 Main exemptions from applying IFRS in the opening IFRS statement of financial position

(a) **Property, plant and equipment, investment properties and intangible assets**

(i) Fair value/previous GAAP revaluation may be used as a substitute for cost at date of transition to IFRSs.

(b) **Business combinations**

For business combinations **prior** to the date of transition to IFRSs:

(i) The same classification (acquisition or uniting of interests) is retained as under previous GAAP.

(ii) For items requiring a cost measure for IFRSs, the carrying value **at the date of the business combination** is treated as deemed cost and IFRS rules are applied from thereon.

(iii) Items requiring a fair value measure for IFRSs are revalued at the date of transition to IFRSs.

(iv) The carrying value of goodwill at the date of transition to IFRSs is the amount as reported under previous GAAP.

(c) **Employee benefits**

Unrecognised actuarial gains and losses can be deemed zero at the date of transition to IFRSs. IAS 19 is applied from then on.

(d) **Cumulative translation differences on foreign operations**

Translation differences (which must be disclosed in a separate translation reserve under IFRS) may be deemed zero at the date of transition to IFRS. IAS 21 is applied from then on.

(e) **Adoption of IFRS by subsidiaries, associates and joint ventures**

If a subsidiary, associate or joint venture adopts IFRS later than its parent, it measures its assets and liabilities:

Either: At the amount that would be included in the parent's financial statements, based on the parent's date of transition

Or: At the amount based on the subsidiary (associate or joint venture)'s date of transition.

(IFRS 1: Appendix B)

Disclosure

(a) A **reconciliation of previous GAAP equity** to IFRSs is required at the date of transition to IFRSs and for the most recent financial statements presented under previous GAAP.

(b) A **reconciliation of profit** for the most recent financial statements presented under previous GAAP.

(IFRS 1: para. 24)

FAST FORWARD

The **change to IFRS** must be carefully managed.

4.2 Practical issues

The implementation of the change to IFRS is likely to entail careful management in most companies. Here are some of the **change management considerations** that should be addressed.

(a) **Accurate assessment of the task involved**. Underestimation or wishful thinking may hamper the effectiveness of the conversion and may ultimately prove inefficient.

(b) **Proper planning**. This should take place at the overall project level, but a **detailed** task **analysis** could be drawn up to **control work performed**.

(c) **Human resource management**. The project must be properly structured and staffed.

(d) **Training**. Where there are **skills gaps**, remedial training should be provided.

(e) **Monitoring and accountability**. A relaxed 'it will be alright on the night' attitude could spell danger. Implementation **progress** should be **monitored** and **regular meetings** set up so that participants can **personally account for what they are doing** as well as **flag up any problems** as early as possible. **Project drift should be avoided**.

(f) **Achieving milestones**. Successful completion of key steps and tasks should be appropriately acknowledged, ie what managers call 'celebrating success', so as to **sustain motivation and performance**.

(g) **Physical resourcing**. The need for IT **equipment** and **office space** should be properly assessed.

(h) **Process review**. Care should be taken not to perceive the change as a one-off quick fix. Any change in **future systems** and processes should be assessed and properly implemented.

(i) **Follow-up procedures**. As with general good management practice, the **follow up procedures** should be planned in to **make sure that the changes stick** and that any further changes are identified and addressed.

4.2.1 Financial reporting infrastructure

As well as sound management judgement, implementation of IFRS requires a sound financial reporting infrastructure. Key aspects of this include the following:

(a) A **robust regulatory framework**. For IFRS to be successful, they must be rigorously enforced.

(b) **Trained and qualified staff**. Many preparers of financial statements will have been trained in local GAAP and not be familiar with the principles underlying IFRS, let alone the detail. Some professional bodies provide conversion qualifications – for example, the ACCA's Diploma in International Financial Reporting – but the availability of such qualifications and courses may vary from country to country.

(c) **Availability and transparency of market information**. This is particularly important in the determination of fair values, which are such a key component of many IFRSs.

(d) **High standards of corporate governance and audit**. This is all the more important in the transition period, especially where there is resistance to change.

Overall, there are significant advantages to the widespread adoption of IFRS, but if the transition is to go well, there must be a realistic assessment of potential challenges.

4.3 Other implementation challenges

4.3.1 More detailed rules

Implementation of International Financial Reporting Standards entails **a great deal of work** for many companies, particularly those in countries where local GAAP has not been so onerous. For example, many jurisdictions will not have had such detailed rules about recognition, measurement and presentation of financial instruments, and many will have had no rules at all about share-based payment.

A challenge for preparers of financial statements is also **a challenge for users**. When financial statements become far more complex under IFRS than they were under local GAAP, users may find them hard to understand, and consequently of little relevance.

4.3.2 Presentation

Many developed countries have legislation requiring set formats and layouts for financial statements. For example, in the UK there is the Companies Act 2006. IFRS demands that presentation is in accordance with IAS 1 *Presentation of financial statements,* but this standard allows alternative forms of presentation. In choosing between alternatives, **countries tend to adopt the format that is closest to local GAAP**, even if this is not necessarily the best format. For example, UK companies are likely to adopt the two-statement format for the statement of profit or loss and other comprehensive income, because this is closest to the old profit and loss account and statement of total recognised gains and losses.

4.3.3 Concepts and interpretation

Although later IAS and IFRS are based to an extent on the IASB *Conceptual Framework,* there is **no consistent set of principles** underlying them. The *Conceptual Framework* itself is being revised, and there is controversy over the direction the revision should take. Consequently, preparers of accounts are likely to think in terms of the conceptual frameworks – if any – that they have used in developing local GAAP, and these may be different from that of the IASB. German accounts, for example, have traditionally been aimed at the tax authorities.

Where IFRS themselves give clear guidance, this may not matter, but where there is uncertainty, preparers of accounts will fall back on their traditional conceptual thinking.

4.3.4 Choice of accounting treatment

Although many so-called 'allowed alternatives' have been eliminated from IFRS in recent years, choice of treatment remains. For example, IAS 16 *Property, plant and equipment* gives a choice of either the cost model or the revaluation model for a class of property, plant or equipment.

It could be argued that choice is a good thing, as companies should be able to select the treatment that most fairly reflects the underlying reality. However, in the context of change to IFRS, there is a danger that companies **will choose the alternative that closely matches the approach followed under local GAAP, or the one that is easier to implement**, regardless of whether this is the best choice.

4.3.5 Inconsistency in recognition or measurement methods

As well as the broader choice of which accounting model to adopt (cost or revaluation, and so on), IFRS allows further choice on recognition and measurement within a particular reporting standard. In countries where local GAAP is not very developed on this matter, preparers of accounts might well **choose the least complex option**, or the option that does not involve making a decision, rather than the correct one.

4.3.6 Timing and exemptions taken

IFRSs have provision for early adoption, and this can affect comparability, although impact of a new standard must be disclosed under IAS 8 *Accounting policies, changes in accounting estimates and errors.* Further, IFRS 1 *First time adoption of International Financial Reporting Standards* permits a number of exemptions during the periods of transition to IFRS. This gives scope for manipulation, if **exemptions are 'cherry-picked'** to produce a favourable picture.

4.3.7 Subjectivity

The extent of the impact will vary, depending on how developed local GAAP was before the transition. However, in general it is likely that **management judgement will have a greater impact** on financial statements prepared under IFRS than under local GAAP. The main reasons for this are as follows:

(a) The **volume** of rules and number of areas addressed by IFRS is likely to be greater than that under local GAAP

(b) Many issues are perhaps **addressed for the first time**, for example share-based payment

(c) IFRSs are likely to be **more complex** than local standards

(d) IFRSs allow **choice** in many cases, which leads to subjectivity

(e) Selection of **valuation method** (see above)

5 Progress towards global harmonisation

ST FORWARD

Close co-ordination between IASB due process and due process of national standard-setters is important to the success of the IASB's mandate. This area is constantly changing.

You should be able to discuss **progress towards harmonisation, barriers to harmonisation** and the **advantages** of harmonisation.

5.1 Integration with national standard setters

The IASB is exploring ways of further integrating its due process with that of national standard-setters. This integration may grow as the relationship between IASB and national standard-setters evolves. In particular, the IASB is exploring the following procedure for projects that have international implications:

(a) IASB and national standard-setters would **co-ordinate their work plans** so that when the IASB starts a project, national standard-setters would also add it to their own work plans so that they can play a full part in developing international consensus. Similarly, where national standard-setters start projects, the IASB would consider whether it needs to develop a new Standard or review its existing Standards. Over a reasonable period, the IASB and national standard-setters should aim to review all standards where significant differences currently exist, giving priority to the areas where the differences are greatest.

(b) National standards-setters would **not be required to vote for IASB's preferred solution** in their national standards, since each country remains free to adopt IASB standards with amendments or to adopt other standards. However, the existence of an international consensus is clearly one factor that members of national standard-setters would consider when they decide how to vote on national standards.

(c) The **IASB would continue to publish its own Exposure Drafts** and other documents for public comment.

(d) **National standard-setters would publish their own exposure document at approximately the same time** as IASB Exposure Drafts and would seek specific comments on any significant divergences between the two exposure documents. In some instances, national standard-setters may include in their exposure documents specific comments on issues of particular relevance to their country or include more detailed guidance than is included in the corresponding IASB document.

(e) **National standard-setters would follow their own full due process,** which they would ideally choose to integrate with the IASB's due process. This integration would avoid unnecessary delays in completing standards and would also minimise the likelihood of unnecessary differences between the standards that result.

5.2 IASB liaison members

Seven of the full-time members of the IASB have formal liaison responsibilities with national standard-setters in order to promote the convergence of national accounting standards and IAS/IFRS. The IASB envisages a partnership between the IASB and these national standard-setters as they work together to achieve convergence of accounting standards worldwide.

The countries with these formal liaison relationships are Australia and New Zealand, Canada, France, Germany, Japan, UK and the USA. In addition, the Technical Expert Group of the European Financial Reporting Advisory Group (EFRAG) has the same rights as those bodies formally designated as liaison standard-setters. However, the concept of liaison with accounting standard-setters is broader than this. Members of the IASB are assigned to liaison not only with formally designated liaison standard-setters and EFRAG, but also with other accounting standard-setters throughout the world and many countries are also represented on the IFRS Advisory Council.

5.3 Worldwide effect of IFRS and the IASB

The IASB, and before it the IASC, has now been in existence for more than 30 years, therefore it is worth looking at the effect it has had in that time.

5.3.1 Europe

As far as Europe is concerned, the consolidated financial statements of many of Europe's top multinationals are already prepared in conformity with national requirements, EC directives and IFRS. These developments have been given added impetus by the internationalisation of capital markets. As discussed, IFRS has been implemented in the EU since 2005 for listed companies, and there is an established 'endorsement' process for the adoption of new standards.

5.3.2 Japan

The IASB and the Accounting Standards Board of Japan (ASBJ) have been working together to achieve convergence of IFRSs and Japanese Generally Accepted Accounting Principles (GAAP) since 2005. This work was formalised in 2007 with the Tokyo Agreement. Since 2010, certain qualifying listed companies in Japan have been allowed to use IFRSs as designated by the Financial Services Agency of Japan (FSA) in their consolidated financial statements, in lieu of Japanese GAAP.

IFRSs may not be used in statutory separate financial statements.

Although Japan has considered potential mandatory adoption of IFRS by public companies for some time, a decision is yet to be made. Currently, Japan is promoting greater use of IFRSs based on voluntary adoption. For example, the ASBJ is considering approving 'endorsed IFRS' which would be available for voluntary adoption by Japanese companies.

5.3.3 America

In America, the Securities and Exchange Commission (SEC) agreed in 1993 to permit but not require foreign issuers (of shares, etc) to follow IAS/IFRS treatments on certain issues, including cash flow statements under IAS 7. The overall effect is that, where an IAS/IFRS treatment differs from US GAAP, these treatments are acceptable. Domestic issuers are required to apply US GAAP. The SEC is now supporting the IASB because it wants to attract foreign listings and, as discussed, the FASB is engaged in a long-term convergence project with the IASB. In certain countries, the application of IFRS is **mandatory** for all domestic listed companies. The following provides an example of some of the countries, but the list is not exhaustive: Barbados, Cyprus, Georgia, Jamaica, Jordan, Kenya, Kuwait, Malawi, Mauritius, Nepal, Peru, Serbia and Trinidad and Tobago.

5.3.4 Other

Countries that implemented IFRS for the 2005 European ruling in respect of the consolidated financial statements of public listed companies include Austria, Belgium, Czech Republic, Denmark, Estonia, Finland, France, Germany, Greece, Hungary, Iceland, Ireland, Italy, Liechtenstein, Lithuania, Luxembourg, the Netherlands, Norway, Poland, Portugal, Slovenia, Slovak Republic, Spain, Sweden and the United Kingdom.

Many non-European counties also require their listed companies to adopt IFRS. These include Australia, Bahamas, Bahrain, Chile, Costa Rica, Egypt, Hong Kong, Kenya, Kuwait, Mauritius, New Zealand, and South Africa.

There are some countries where the implementation of IFRS is **not mandatory but discretionary**. These include Aruba, Bermuda, Bolivia, Botswana, Cayman Islands, Dominica, El Salvador, Gibraltar, Japan, Laos, Lesotho, Swaziland, Switzerland, Turkey, Uganda, Zambia and Zimbabwe.

However, there are several countries where the **use of IFRS is not currently permitted**. The following are some of the countries, but the list is not exhaustive: Cuba, Indonesia, Iran, Senegal, Thailand, Tunisia and Vietnam.

5.4 Harmonisation in Europe

The objective of the European Commission (EC) is to build a fully integrated, globally competitive market. A key element of this is the harmonisation of company law across the member states. In line with this, the **EC aims to establish a level playing field for financial reporting**, supported by an effective enforcement regime. The commission is uniquely the only organisation whose accounting standards are legally enforceable, in the form of directives which must be included in the national legislation of member states. However, the directives have been criticised as they might become constraints on the application of worldwide standards, and may bring accounting standardisation and harmonisation into the political arena.

5.4.1 The EC regulation

FAST FORWARD

The EC has required that **since 2005** consolidated accounts of all listed companies should **comply with IFRS.**

The EC adopted a regulation under which from 2005 consolidated financial statements of listed companies were required to comply with IFRS. The implications of this measure are far reaching. However, member states currently have the discretion to extend the implementation of IFRS to include non-listed companies. In the UK, for example, unlisted companies may report their consolidated financial statements under IFRS or UK GAAP. Small companies may choose to report under UK GAAP, with many taking advantage of the reduced disclosure requirements of the FRSSE (Financial Reporting Standard for Smaller Entities).

In 2009 the IASB issued the *IFRS for SMEs* (Small and medium-sized entities) and this was an important step toward the introduction of IFRS for all companies.

Many commentators believe that in the light of the EC's commitment to IFRS it is only a matter of time before national standard-setting bodies are, in effect, replaced by the IASB, with national standards falling into disuse. However, the IASB will continue to need input and expertise from valued national standard-setters.

5.5 IFRS in the USA

FAST FORWARD

Convergence between IFRS and US GAAP is **one of the bigger issues** in the global implementation of IFRS.

5.5.1 Progress

Convergence between IFRS and US GAAP is **one of the bigger issues** in the global implementation of IFRS. At present, all US entities must file accounts prepared under US GAAP. However, in 2002 the IASB and its US equivalent, the FASB (Financial Accounting Standards Board) agreed to harmonise their work plans, and to work towards reducing the differences between IFRS and US GAAP.

In **2008 the Securities and Exchange Commission (SEC) issued a 'roadmap'** for the use of IFRS, proposing the eventual mandatory use of IFRS for all US public companies by 2014. At present, only overseas issuers of securities are allowed to file accounts under IFRS (without having to provide a reconciliation to US GAAP).

The SEC's 'roadmap' allowed some companies the option of using IFRS from 2010. It envisaged phasing in IFRS by requiring companies to file accounts under both IFRS and US GAAP for the two years 2012-2014, after which accounts would be prepared under IFRS alone.

This has **not played out in practice** and the pace of convergence has slowed over the past few years. The **SEC's draft strategic plan for 2014-2018** states within its objectives:

> 'Due to the increasingly global nature of the capital markets, the agency will work to promote higher quality financial reporting worldwide and will consider, among other things, whether a single set of high-quality global accounting standards is achievable.'

which appears to be a **step backwards from its previous roadmap**. However, 2014 saw the publication of **IFRS 15** *Revenue from contracts with customers*, which is the **result of an IASB/FASB collaboration.**

5.5.2 Rules-based versus principles-based approach

US GAAP is an example of a rules-based approach. It consists of a large number of specific accounting standards, and each standard contains a large number of rules (as well as exceptions to the rules), attempting to prescribe treatments for every possible situation that might arise. However, in 2002 the incoming chairman of the **FASB** signalled his support for a **shift to a principles-based approach**:

> 'I understand the US environment where there has been such a proliferation of rules. I like the principles-based approach but some people have exaggerated the differences. You are always going to have rules but the question is: 'Where do I start?' You can never have a rule for everything and at that point you have to go back to principles.'

Bob Hertz, FASB Chairman (*Financial Times, 27 May 2002*)

A principles-based approach, such as that used in developing IFRSs, is one where the individual standards can be clearly seen to be applications of the approach to accounting adopted by the standards as a whole. Thus each individual IAS/IFRS applies the IASB *Conceptual Framework*, and each Standard is an individual reflection of the whole. Specificity at the level of detail is sacrificed for clarity in terms of the overall approach.

Accountants working under **IFRS** are required to use **more professional judgement** than under a rules-based approach. There may not be a specific rule that applies to the event that they need to report, so they need to use judgement in applying the principles contained in the relevant IFRS. It is the view of the IASB that this will result in better quality financial reporting. Accounts will have to be **true to the overall principles of IFRS**, rather than to an individual rule that may not be appropriate for the event being reported, and which may therefore result in an accounting treatment that is not true to the intentions of IFRS as a whole.

5.6 UK Accounting Standards Board convergence approach

The convergence process between UK GAAP and IFRS began in 2003 but was subsequently paused. During that time, UK standards did not keep pace with business changes and with evolving types of transaction, particularly with regard to financial instruments.

5.6.1 Five standards

UK GAAP

A new financial reporting framework came into effect on 1 January 2015 in the UK and Ireland. The UK's Financial Reporting Council (FRC) published four standards, forming the basis of the new regime.

- **FRS 100** *Application of Financial Reporting Requirements* which sets out the overall reporting framework
- **FRS 101** *Reduced Disclosure Framework* which permits disclosure exemptions from the requirements of EU-adopted IFRSs for certain qualifying entities
- **FRS 102** *The Financial Reporting Standard applicable in the UK and Republic of Ireland* which ultimately replaces all existing FRSs, SSAPs and UITF Abstracts

- **FRS 103** *Insurance contracts* which consolidates existing financial reporting requirements for insurance contracts

In March 2015 these were followed by **FRS 104** *Interim financial reporting.* This is intended for use in the preparation of interim financial reports for entities that apply FRS 102 but may also be used as a basis for preparing interim reports by those entities applying FRS 101 *Reduced Disclosure Framework*. The Standard is based on IAS 34 *Interim Financial Reporting*, with certain adaptations. It replaces the existing Accounting Standards Board (ASB) Statement *Half-yearly Financial Reports*.

July 2015 changes

In July 2015, the UK Financial Reporting Council issued **amended versions of FRS 100, FRS 101 and FRS 102.** At the same time it issued **FRS 105** *The Financial Reporting Standard applicable to the Micro-entities Regime*. The changes were largely made in response to the implementation of the new EU Accounting Directive, which was incorporated into UK Company Law in April 2015, but it also incorporate other clarifications and simplifications.

5.6.2 Purpose

The aim is to make financial reporting more relevant to the needs of eligible companies. FRS 102 has 35 chapters **based mainly on the IFRS for SMEs with some cross-reference to full IFRS.** The **disclosure requirements are less than for full IFRS**. Some of **the key changes that will impact UK** companies on moving to FRS 102 are:

(a) New requirements for **financial instruments,** bringing all derivatives on balance sheet measured at fair value through profit or loss.

(b) **More intangible assets to be recognised separately** from goodwill when there is a business combination.

(c) **Useful life of goodwill and intangible assets not to exceed five years** when no reliable estimate can be made.

(d) **Merger accounting** only permitted in **limited** cases.

The new standards are **mandatory for accounting periods beginning on or after 1 January 2015.**

5.6.3 Micro-entities

In 2015, the FRC issued FRS 105 *The Financial Reporting Standard applicable to the Micro-entities Regime*.

6 Benefits of and barriers to global harmonisation

FAST FORWARD

Harmonisation in accounting is likely to come from international accounting standards, but not in the near future. There are enormous difficulties to overcome, both technical and political.

6.1 Benefits of harmonisation

The benefits of harmonisation will be based on the benefits to users and preparers of accounts, as follows:

(a) **Investors,** both individual and corporate, would gain confidence by being able to **evaluate the comparable financial results** of different companies internationally as well as nationally when making investment decisions.

(b) **Multinational companies** would benefit from harmonisation for many reasons including the following:

   (i) Better access would be gained to foreign investor funds.

   (ii) Management control would be improved, because harmonisation would aid internal communication of financial information.

   (iii) Appraisal of foreign entities for take-overs and mergers would be more straightforward.

   (iv) It would be easier to comply with the reporting requirements of overseas stock exchanges.

   (v) Preparation of group accounts would be less complex.

   (vi) A reduction in audit costs might be achieved.

   (vii) Transfer of accounting staff across national borders would be simpler.

(c) **Governments of developing countries would save time and money** if they could adopt international standards and, if these were used internally, governments of developing countries could attempt to control the activities of foreign multinational companies in their own country. These companies could not 'hide' behind foreign accounting practices which may be difficult to understand.

(d) **Tax authorities.** It would be easier to calculate the tax liability of investors, including multinationals who receive income from overseas sources.

(e) **Regional economic groups usually promote trade** within a specific geographical region. This would be **aided by common accounting practices** within the region.

(f) **Large international accounting firms would** benefit as accounting and auditing would be more straightforward if similar accounting practices existed throughout the world.

6.2 Barriers to harmonisation

There are undoubtedly many barriers to international harmonisation: if there were not then greater progress would probably have been made by now. The main problems are as follows:

(a) **Different purposes of financial reporting.** In some countries the purpose is solely for tax assessment, while in others it is for investor decision-making.

(b) **Different legal systems.** These prevent the development of certain accounting practices and restrict the options available.

(c) **Different user groups.** Countries have different ideas about who the relevant user groups of financial reporting are and their respective importance. In the USA, investor and creditor groups are given prominence, while in Europe employees enjoy a higher profile.

(d) **Needs of developing countries.** Developing countries are obviously behind in the standard-setting process and they need to first develop the basic standards and principles already in place in most developed countries.

(e) **Nationalism** is demonstrated in an unwillingness to accept another country's standard.

(f) **Cultural differences** result in objectives for financial reporting and accounting systems differing from country to country.

(g) **Unique circumstances.** Some countries may be experiencing unusual circumstances which affect all aspects of everyday life and impinge on the ability of companies to produce proper reports, for example hyperinflation, civil war, currency restriction and so on.

(h) **The lack of strong accountancy bodies**. Many countries do not have strong independent accountancy or business bodies which would support better standards and greater harmonisation.

7 IASB Work Plan

Below is the latest available (November 2016) version of the IASB Work Plan. Not all the topics are examinable but all examinable aspects are covered in this Text.

Work plan—projected targets as at November 2016

	Current activity	Next major milestone		
		Within 3 months	Within 6 months	After 6 months
Research projects				
Disclosure Initiative: Principles of Disclosure	Drafting		Publish DP	
Primary Financial Statements	Analysis	Decide Project Scope		
Business Combinations under Common Control	Analysis			Publish DP
Dynamic Risk Management	Analysis			Publish DP
Financial Instruments with Characteristics of Equity	Analysis			Publish DP
Goodwill and Impairment	Analysis			Decide Project Direction
Discount rates	Analysis		Publish Research Summary	
Share-based Payment	Drafting	Publish Research Summary		
Standard-setting and related projects				
Conceptual Framework	Analysis			Publish Conceptual Framework
Disclosure Initiative: Materiality Practice Statement	Analysis	Decide Project Direction		Publish Practice Statement
Insurance Contracts	Drafting		Issue IFRS Standard(expected Marcy	
Rate-regulated Activities	Analysis			Publish DP

Source: IASB, 2016

Chapter Roundup

- You should know which are the **current issues** and concentrate your studying on these.
- The most important current issue is the ED on the *Conceptual Framework* but **IFRS 15** and the **final version of IFRS 9,** although published in 2014, are still very topical. Summaries are given here, but you should refer to the relevant topic chapters for full coverage.
- **Other current issues** highlighted by the examining team are:
  - Disclosure initiative
  - Profit or loss versus other comprehensive income
  - Equity accounting
  - Debt versus equity
  - Additional performance measures
- IFRS 1 gives guidance to entities applying IFRS for the first time.
- The **change to IFRS** must be carefully managed.
- **Close co-ordination** between IASB due process and due process of national standard-setters is important to the success of the IASB's mandate. This area is constantly changing.
- You should be able to discuss **progress towards harmonisation, barriers to harmonisation** and the **advantages** of harmonisation.
- The EC has required that **since 2005** consolidated accounts of all listed companies should **comply with IFRS.**
- Convergence between IFRS and US GAAP is **one of the bigger issues** in the global implementation of IFRS.
- **Harmonisation** in accounting is likely to come from international accounting standards, but not in the near future. There are enormous difficulties to overcome, both technical and political.

Quick Quiz

1. Which preparers and users of accounts can be expected to benefit from global harmonisation of accounting?
2. How many IFRSs are in existence at the moment?
3. What is the latest examinable IFRS?
4. What was the SEC 'Roadmap'?
5. Which standard has undergone major revisions?

Answers to Quick Quiz

1 Investors, multinational companies, governments of developing countries, the authorities (overseas income), regional economic groups, large international accounting firms

2 15

3 IFRS 16 *Leases*, published in January 2016.

4 An agreement allowing some companies the option of using IFRS from 2010. It envisaged phasing in IFRS by requiring companies to file accounts under both IFRS and US GAAP for the two years 2012-2014, after which accounts would be prepared under IFRS alone.

5 IFRS 9, published in 2014 in its final form after several years' work.

Now try the question below from the Practice Question Bank

Number	Level	Marks	Time
Q28	Introductory	n/a	n/a
Q29	Examination	25	49 mins

Reporting for specialised entities

20

Topic list	Syllabus reference
1 Specialised entities and the exam	E1
2 The not-for-profit sector: Primary aims	E1
3 The not-for-profit sector: Regulatory framework	E1
4 The not-for-profit sector: Performance measurement	E1
5 IAS 41 *Agriculture*	E1
6 Entity reconstructions	E2

Introduction

Concentrate on Sections 1, 5 and 6 – these are the most important for your exam.

You should be aware that not-for-profit entities and smaller entities may have different accounting needs from the larger profit-making entities that you are used to. This chapter gives you the background you need to set you thinking about whether a one-size-fits-all set of standards is adequate.

We also include a couple of standards relating to specialist businesses. IAS 41 *Agriculture was* re-added to the examinable documents for exams from December 2014 onwards.

Entity reconstructions are a kind of specialised entity, where the normal rules do not apply because the business is not a going concern.

Study guide

		Intellectual level
E1	**Financial reporting in specialised, not-for-profit and public sector entities**	
(a)	Apply knowledge from the syllabus to straightforward transactions and events arising in specialised, not-for-profit and public sector entities	3
E2	**Entity reconstructions**	
(a)	Identify when a party may no longer be viewed as a going concern, or uncertainty exists surrounding the going concern status	2
(b)	Identify and outline the circumstances in which a reconstruction would be an appropriate alternative to a company liquidation	2
(c)	Outline the appropriate accounting treatment required relating to reconstructions	2

Exam guide

The examiner has stated specifically that specialised entities will be tested in terms of **current IFRS**.

This could be tested in essay form, or you could be given a scenario of a not-for-profit entity and have to apply your knowledge from the rest of the syllabus to it. The examiner has said that he will give you the information you need for a question on specialised entities.

E2 (a) specifically includes IAS 41 *Agriculture.*

1 Specialised entities and the exam 12/07 – 12/16

FAST FORWARD

Questions on specialist entities will be set in terms of **current IFRS**.

1.1 Examiner's approach

The P2 examiner has stated explicitly that questions on specialist entities will be set in terms of current accounting standards. So do not be alarmed if the setting for a question is a club, or a local council rather than a company. The principles will be the same.

1.2 Typical specialist entity questions

Below are some typical questions. The examiner is simply testing whether you are flexible enough to apply your knowledge and understanding of accounting standards in a fresh context.

1.2.1 An agricultural college

An agricultural college is not the kind of setting you are used to encountering in your accountancy studies. It doesn't manufacture or trade in goods. But there are issues that it will have in common with companies that do.

Question **Agricultural college**

Swindale Agricultural College derives its income from a variety of sources. It receives a grant from Central Government, further subsidies from the European Union and money from the local Council Tax. In addition, students pay fees.

The Diploma in Agriculture course lasts nine months – from October till the end of June. The College's accounting year end is 31 December 20X8. Students pay $3,000 subsidised tuition fees. As at 1 October

20X8, twenty students have enrolled, each paying a non-refundable deposit of $1,200. The balance of $1,800 per student is to be paid in nine monthly instalments of $200.

The College Bursar argues that because the deposit is non-refundable, the fee income should be recognised on a cash receipt basis.

Required

Advise the College Bursar on the correct accounting treatment for the fee income. Show the journal entries for this treatment.

Answer

This question deals with revenue recognition, specifically in the context of the provision of a service.

Total fee income from students for this course (deposits and instalments) will be:

(20 × $1,200) + (20 × $200 × 9) = $60,000

Currently it is proposed to recognise revenue on the basis of cash received, which, as at 31 December 20X8, is the deposit plus three monthly instalments:

(20 × $1,200) + (20 × $200 × 3) = $36,000

This is wrong, as it does not take account of the amount of performance obligation that has been satisfied. As at 31 December 20X8, only one third of the course (three out of nine months) has been delivered, so only one third of the total fee income should be recognised. Income recognised should be $20,000.

There is an element of deferred consideration. As this is over months, rather than years, it will not be necessary to discount to arrive at the fair value of the consideration. But it must be recognised as the performance obligations are satisfied. The deposits received of $24,000 (20 × $1,200) but not yet recognised as revenue at the year end are to be regarded as deferred income. These deposits are non-refundable, but they create an obligation to complete the contract. Accordingly they should be a liability in the statement of financial position.

The journal entries are as follows:

DEBIT	Cash	$36,000	
CREDIT	Fee income (recognised)		$20,000
CREDIT	Deferred income (received in advance of delivery of services)		$16,000

Note that one third of the deposit ($24,000 ÷ $8,000) has been recognised in the period, which is correct, because one third of the course has been delivered.

1.2.2 A football club

This question, from a past exam paper was specifically mentioned by the examiner as being the sort of setting that could be tested. Note the advice given at the end of the question: you do not need any specialist knowledge of the football club finance sector to answer this question.

Question

Football club

Seejoy is a famous football club but has significant cash flow problems. The directors and shareholders wish to take steps to improve the club's financial position. The following proposals had been drafted in an attempt to improve the cash flow of the club. However, the directors need advice upon their implications.

(a) **Player registrations**

The club capitalises the unconditional amounts (transfer fees) paid to acquire players.

The club proposes to amortise the cost of the transfer fees over ten years instead of the current practice which is to amortise the cost over the duration of the player's contract. The club has sold most of its valuable players during the current financial year but still has two valuable players under contract.

Player	*Transfer fee capitalised*	*Amortisation to 31 December 20X6*	*Contract commenced*	*Contract expires*
	$m	$m		
A Steel	20	4	1 January 20X6	31 December 20Y0
R Aldo	15	10	1 January 20X5	31 December 20X7

If Seejoy win the national football league, then a further $5 million will be payable to the two players' former clubs. Seejoy are currently performing very poorly in the league.

(b) **Issue of bond**

The club proposes to issue a 7% bond with a face value of $50 million on 1 January 20X7 at a discount of 5% that will be secured on income from future ticket sales and corporate hospitality receipts, which are approximately $20 million per annum. Under the agreement the club cannot use the first $6 million received from corporate hospitality sales and reserved tickets (season tickets) as this will be used to repay the bond. The money from the bond will be used to pay for ground improvements and to pay wages to players.

The bond will be repayable, both capital and interest, over 15 years with the first payment of $6 million due on 31 December 20X7. It has an effective interest rate of 7.7%. There will be no active market for the bond and the company does not wish to use valuation models to value the bond.

(c) **Player trading**

Another proposal is for the club to sell its two valuable players, Aldo and Steel. It is thought that it will receive a total of $16 million for both players. The players are to be offered for sale at the end of the current football season on 1 May 20X7.

Required

Discuss how the above proposals would be dealt with in the financial statement of Seejoy for the year ending 31 December 20X6, setting out their accounting treatment and appropriateness in helping the football club's cash flow problems.

(Candidates do not need knowledge of the football finance sector to answer this question.)

Answer

(a) **Player registrations**

The player registrations are **capitalised** by the club as intangible non-current assets under IAS 38 *Intangible assets*. This is an **acceptable** accounting treatment; the transfer fees classify as assets as it is probable that expected future benefits will flow to the club as a result of the contracts and the cost can be measured reliably at the amount of the transfer fees actually paid.

According to IAS 38, intangible non-current assets which are capitalised should be **amortised over their useful life**. Therefore, on the face of it, claiming a useful life of 10 years might be acceptable. However IAS 38 recommends that amortisation reflects the useful life of the assets and the pattern of economic benefits. Therefore, the proposal to amortise the transfer fees over a period of **ten years is not acceptable as the contracts are only for five years and three years**.

In terms of **cash flow** this proposal regarding the amortisation would have **no effect** at all. It would simply be a bookkeeping entry which would reduce the amortisation charge to profit or loss.

The potential payment to the two players' former clubs of $5 million would **not** appear to be **probable** due to the current form of the club. Therefore, under IAS 37 *Provisions, contingent liabilities and contingent assets no provision* would be recognised for this amount. However, the possible payment does fall within the IAS 37 definition of a contingent liability which is a possible obligation arising out of past events whose existence will be confirmed only by the occurrence or non-occurrence of one or more uncertain future events not wholly within the control of the entity. Therefore, as a contingent liability the amount and details would be **disclosed** in the notes to the financial statements.

(b) **Issue of bond**

What the club is proposing here is known as **securitisation**. This particular type of securitisation is often called 'future flow' securitisation. In some forms of securitisation a special purpose vehicle is set up to administer the income stream or assets involved in which case there is potentially an off balance sheet effect. However, in this case there is **no special purpose vehicle** and therefore the only accounting issue is how the bond is to be treated under IFRS 9 *Financial instruments*.

The bond will be recorded as a **financial liability** and will either be classified as a financial liability at fair value through profit or loss or as a financial liability measured at amortised cost. To be a financial liability at fair value through profit or loss the bond must either be held for trading or be part of a group of financial assets, financial liabilities, or both, that are managed on a fair value basis. It is unlikely that this is the case, therefore the bond will be **classified as measured at amortised cost**.

The bond will be **initially recognised at its fair value** which is the price that would be paid to transfer a liability in an orderly transaction between market participants at the measurement date.

Fair value at inception will normally be the amount of the consideration received for the instrument. Subsequent to initial recognition the instrument will be measured using amortised cost or fair value. In this case the club does not wish to use the valuation model, therefore the bond will be measured at amortised cost.

When the bond is issued on 1 January 20X7 it will be measured at the value of the consideration received of $47.5 million ($50m × 95%).

At 31 December 20X7 the valuation will be:

	$m
Initial value	47.5
Interest at 7.7%	3.7
Cash paid	(6.0)
Value on SOFP	45.2

In terms of cash flow the issue of the bond will **bring $47.5 million into the club**. The bond is effectively secured on the income stream of the future corporate hospitality sales and season tickets receipts and due to this security the coupon rate of interest is lower than the market rates. The money is to be used to improve the grounds which is an appropriate use of long-term funds. However, the proposal to pay the **short term costs of the players' wages** out of these long term funds is a **misuse of long-term capital** which is likely to lead to future liquidity problems.

(c) **Player trading**

In accounting terms there is no issue to deal with at 31 December 20X6 as the potential sale of the players will not fall to be classified as 'held for sale' non-current assets under IFRS 5 *Non-current assets held for sale and discontinued operations*. In order for these players to classify as held for sale they would need to be available for immediate sale which they are not.

However, the club must consider carrying out an **impairment review** of these assets at 31 December 20X6. If the players are sold for the anticipated figure of $16 million then the following loss will be incurred:

	$m
Carrying value at 1 May 20X7	
A Steel ($20m – ($4m + 4/12 × $4m)	14.7
R Aldo ($15m – ($10 + 4/12 × $5)	3.3
	18.0
Potential sales value	16.0
Potential loss	2.0

This potential loss of $2 million on the sale of these players may be evidence of impairment and a review should be carried out at 31 December 20X6 and the **players' value written down to recoverable amount** if necessary.

In terms of cash flow, the sale of the players would **provide much needed cash**. However, as the club is performing poorly currently the sale of the two best players **may lead to even worse performance** which is likely to have a detrimental affect on ticket sales and the liquidity of the club in future.

1.3 Other possibilities

Another recent exam question was set in the entertainment industry. The possibilities are wide ranging, and you need to apply common sense. Suppose, for example, you got a property dealer, who was trying to classify his properties as investment properties? This would not be permitted, because the properties are for sale and not for investment potential.

1.4 Section summary

Questions on specialised entities will be set in terms of **current IFRS**.

- You will not need specialist knowledge, beyond a common sense awareness that different organisations do things in different ways
- Any required specialist information (unlikely) will be given to you
- Any setting, type of company or organisation could come up

2 The not-for-profit sector: Primary aims

FAST FORWARD

The not-for-profit sector includes **public sector entities** and **private** not-for-profit entities such as charities.

Not-for-profit entities have **different goals** from profit making entities, but they still need to be **properly managed** and their accounts need to present the information fairly.

What organisations do we have in mind when we refer to **not-for-profit and public sector entities**? These are the most obvious examples:

(a) Central government departments and agencies
(b) Local or federal government departments
(c) Publicly-funded bodies providing healthcare (in the UK this would be the NHS) and social housing
(d) Further and higher education institutions
(e) Charitable bodies

The first four are **public sector entities**. Charities are **private** not-for-profit entities.

Not-for-profit entities have different goals and purposes to profit-making entities and are responsible to different stakeholders. However, they are dealing in very large sums of money and it is important that they are properly managed and that their accounts present fairly the results of their operations.

Until recently, **public sector** accounts were prepared on a **cash basis**. A transition is still in progress which will get them operating on an **accruals basis**, in line with normal practice in the private sector.

2.1 Conceptual framework for not-for profit entities

The International Federation of Accountants (IFAC) published Phase 1 of a *Public Sector Conceptual Framework* in 2014. It has eight chapters as follows:

(1) Role and authority of the Conceptual Framework
(2) Objectives and users of general purpose financial reporting
(3) Qualitative characteristics
(4) Reporting entity
(5) Elements in financial statements
(6) Recognition in financial statements
(7) Measurement of assets and liabilities in financial statements
(8) Presentation in general purpose financial reports

(IFAC, 2014)

In preparing the conceptual framework IFAC had to bear in mind that not-for profit entities have different objectives, different operating environments and other different characteristics to private sector businesses.

Some of the issues that arise in considering financial reporting by not-for-profit entities are:

- Insufficient emphasis on accountability/stewardship
- A need to broaden the definition of users and user groups
- The emphasis on future cash flows is inappropriate to not-for-profit entities
- Insufficient emphasis on budgeting

2.2 Accountability/stewardship

Not-for-profit entities are not reporting to shareholders, but it is very important that they can account for funds received and show how they have been spent. In some cases, resources may be contributed for specific purposes and management is required to show that they have been utilised for that purpose. Perhaps most importantly, taxpayers are entitled to see how the government is spending their money.

2.3 Users and user groups

The primary user group for not-for-profit entities is providers of funds. In the case of public bodies, such as government departments, this primary group will consist of taxpayers. In the case of private bodies such as charities it will be financial supporters, and also potential future financial supporters. There is also a case for saying that a second primary user group should be recognised, being the recipients of the goods and services provided by the not-for-profit entity.

2.4 Cash flow focus

The financial statements of not-for-profit entities need to provide information which will enable users to assess an entity's ability to generate net cash inflows. Not-for-profit entities need to generate cash flows, but other aspects are generally more significant – for instance, the resources the entity has available to deliver future goods and services, the cost and effectiveness of those it has delivered in the past and the degree to which it is meeting its objectives.

2.5 Budgeting

Another issue is whether financial reporting should include forecast information. For not-for-profit entities, budgets and variance analyses are more important. In some cases, funding is supplied on the basis of a formal, published budget.

3 The not-for-profit sector: Regulatory framework

FAST FORWARD

> The **IASB** and the **FASB** are working on a **framework** for reporting, which includes not-for-profit entities.
>
> The International Public Sector Accounting Standards Board (IPSAB) is developing a set of **International Public Sector Accounting Standards** based on IFRS.

Regulation of public not-for-profit entities, principally local and national governments and governmental agencies, is by the International Public Sector Accounting Standards Board (IPSAB), which comes under the International Federation of Accountants (IFAC).

3.1 International public sector accounting standards

The IPSASB is developing a set of International Public Sector Accounting Standards (IPSASs), based on IFRSs. To date 21 IPSASs have been issued.

Exam focus point

> You don't need to know these – skim over for background only.

1 Presentation of financial statements
2 Statements of cash flows
3 Net surplus or deficit for the period, fundamental errors and changes in accounting policies
4 The effect of changes in foreign exchange rates
5 Borrowing costs
6 Consolidated financial statements and accounting for controlled entities
7 Accounting for investments in associates
8 Financial reporting of Interests in joint ventures
9 Revenue from exchange transactions
10 Financial reporting in hyperinflationary economies
11 Construction contracts
12 Inventories
13 Leases
14 Events after the reporting date
15 Financial instruments: disclosure and presentation
16 Investment property
17 Property, plant and equipment
18 Segment reporting
19 Provisions, contingent liabilities and contingent assets
20 Related party disclosures
21 Impairment of non-cash-generating assets

You are not required to remember this list of IPSASs, or know any of their detailed provisions, but you can see that they closely mirror the IAS/IFRSs and each one is based on the relevant International Financial Reporting Standard.

The IPSASs are all based on the accrual method of accounting and one of the aims of the IPSAB is to move public sector organisations from the cash to the accruals basis of accounting.

3.2 Characteristics of not-for-profit entities

As part of its preliminary report on the new *Conceptual Framework*, the IASB sets out some of the characteristics of not-for-profit entities as follows.

3.2.1 Private sector

Not-for-profit entities in the private sector have the following characteristics:

(a) Their objective is to provide goods and services to various recipients and not to make a profit.

(b) They are generally characterised by the absence of defined ownership interests (shares) that can be sold, transferred or redeemed.

(c) They may have a wide group of stakeholders to consider (including the public at large in some cases).

(d) Their revenues generally arise from contributions (donations or membership dues) rather than sales.

(e) Their capital assets are typically acquired and held to deliver services without the intention of earning a return on them.

3.2.2 Public sector

Nor-for-profit entities in the public sector have similar key characteristics to those in the private sector. They are typically established by legislation and:

(a) Their objective is to provide goods and services to various recipients or to develop or implement policy on behalf of governments and not to make a profit.

(b) They are characterised by the absence of defined ownership interests that can be sold, transferred or redeemed.

(c) They typically have a wide group of stakeholders to consider (including the public at large).

(d) Their revenues are generally derived from taxes or other similar contributions obtained through the exercise of coercive powers.

(e) Their capital assets are typically acquired and held to deliver services without the intention of earning a return on them.

3.3 Not-for-profit entities – specific issues

While the general trend is to get not-for-profit entities producing accounts which are based as far as possible on the provisions of IFRS and which are generally comparable to those produced for profit-making entities, there are two issues which have yet to be resolved.

3.3.1 Cost of transition

While there has been a general assumption that for public sector entities the move to the accruals basis will result in more relevant and better quality financial reporting, no actual cost-benefit analysis has been undertaken on this.

One of the arguments in favour of the adoption of the accruals basis is that it will be possible to compare the cost of providing a service against the same cost in the private sector. It will then be possible to see how goods and services can be most cheaply sourced.

However, it is questionable whether governments get a good deal anyway when they involve themselves with the private sector and the move to accruals accounting has not gained universal acceptance. The governments of Germany, Italy and Holland have so far made no plans for the transition and the governments of China, Japan, Malaysia and Singapore have decided against it. The main issue is the huge cost involved in terms of the number of qualified accountants required. For developing countries this cost is considered to be prohibitive.

3.3.2 Definition of a liability

The *Conceptual Framework* defines a liability as 'a present obligation of the entity arising from past events, the settlement of which is expected to result in an outflow from the entity of resources embodying economic benefits'. A liability is recognised when the amount of the outflow can be reliably measured.

(IFAC, 2014: para. 5.14)

Public benefit entities are subject to a commitment to provide public benefits, but there is an issue to be resolved over whether this commitment meets the definition of a liability. In this situation there has been no 'exchange'. The entity has not received any goods or services for which it is required to make 'settlement'. A distinction can be drawn between 'general commitments to provide public benefits' and 'specific commitments to provide public benefits'. The specific commitment can be regarded as a 'present obligation', but it can be argued that the obligation only arises when the entity formally undertakes to provide something such as a non-performance-related grant. (If the grant were performance-related, the entity would be able to withdraw from the agreement if the performance targets were not reached.)

There is also the issue of 'reliable measurement'. Governments in particular often find themselves funding projects which go a long way over budget, suggesting that reliable measurement was not obtained at the outset.

This issue is still being debated by the IPSAB. It is of major importance in the financial reporting of the social policies of governments.

3.4 Charities

Charities are regulated by accounting standards, charity law, relevant company law and best practice. This will vary from country to country. Here we are taking the UK as a typical example.

3.4.1 Statement of financial activities

In addition to a statement of financial position, charities also produce a Statement of Financial Activities (SOFA), an Annual Report to the Charity Commission and sometimes an income and expenditure account. The Statement of Financial Activities is the primary statement showing the results of the charity's activities for the period.

The SOFA shows Incoming resources, Resources expended, and the resultant Net movement in funds. Under incoming resources, income from all sources of funds are listed. These can include:

- Subscription or membership fees
- Public donations
- Donations from patrons
- Government grants
- Income from sale of goods
- Investment income
- Publication sales
- Royalties

The resources expended will show the amount spent directly in furtherance of the Charity's objects. It will also show items which form part of any statement of profit or loss and other comprehensive income, such as salaries, depreciation, travelling and entertaining, audit and other professional fees. These items can be very substantial.

Charities, especially the larger charities, now operate very much in the way that profit-making entities do. They run high-profile campaigns which cost money and they employ professional people who have to be paid. At the same time, their stakeholders will want to see that most of their donation is not going on running the business, rather than achieving the aims for which funds were donated.

One of the problems charities experience is that, even although the accruals basis is being applied, they will still have income and expenditure recognised in different periods, due to the difficulty of correlating them. The extreme example is a campaign to persuade people to leave money to the charity in their will. The costs will have to be recognised, but there is no way to predict when the income will arise.

4 The not-for-profit sector: Performance measurement

Not-for-profit and public sector entities produce financial statements in the same way as profit-making entities do but, while they are expected to remain solvent, their performance cannot be measured simply by the bottom line.

A public sector entity is not expected to show a profit or to underspend its budget. In practice, central government and local government departments know that if they underspend the budget, next year's allocation will be correspondingly reduced. This leads to a rash of digging up the roads and other expenditure just before the end of the financial year as councils strive to spend any remaining funds.

Private and public sector entities are judged principally on the basis of what they have achieved, not how much or how little they have spent in achieving it. So how is performance measured?

4.1 Public sector entities

These will have performance measures laid down by government. The emphasis is on economy, efficiency and effectiveness. Departments and local councils have to show how they have spent public money and what level of service they have achieved. Performance measurement will be based on Key Performance Indicators (KPIs).

Examples of these for a local council could be:

- Number of homeless people rehoused
- % of rubbish collections made on time
- Number of children in care adopted

Public sector entities use the services of outside contractors for a variety of functions. They then have to be able to show that they have obtained the best possible value for what they have spent on outside services. This principle is usually referred to as Value For Money (VFM). In the UK, local authorities are required to report under a system known as Best Value. They have to show that they applied 'fair competition' in awarding contracts.

Best Value is based on the principle of the 'four Cs':

1. **Challenging** why, how and by whom a service is provided
2. **Comparing** performance against other local authorities
3. **Consulting** service users, the local community etc
4. Using fair **Competition** to secure efficient and effective services

4.2 Charities

While charities must demonstrate that they have made proper use of whatever funds they have received, their stakeholders will be more interested in what they have achieved in terms of their stated mission. People who donate money to a relief fund for earthquake victims will want to know what help has been given to survivors, before enquiring how well the organisation has managed its funds. Although it must be said that any mismanagement of funds by a charity is taken very seriously by the donating public.

Some charities produce 'impact reports' which highlight what the charity set out to achieve, what it has achieved and what it has yet to do. Stakeholders should know what the organisation is aiming to achieve and how it is succeeding. Each charity will have its own performance indicators which enable it to measure this.

Question — Definite variables

Choose a charity with which you are familiar and produce a possible set of performance indicators for it.

5 IAS 41 *Agriculture*

The importance of the agricultural sector in a country's economy will vary. It is reasonable to assume, however, that although agriculture is important in first world countries, it is likely to be of greater significance to **developing countries** in terms of the proportion of Gross Domestic Product it represents.

Exam focus point

This topic was reintroduced into the syllabus for exams from December 2014. **Question 3** is a likely place to find it, although, in line with other specialised entity standards, the question is likely to include more than one IFRS.

The main reason for developing a standard on agriculture is the same reason that any standard is developed, ie because there is great **diversity in practice in accounting** for agriculture at both a transnational and national level. Accounting guidelines have been piecemeal, developed as required to tackle specific issues in specific countries.

Question — Agriculture

If you work in agriculture, or if agriculture is important in your country, you may like to investigate the accounting treatment of items such as forestry activity or livestock activity in your country. Are there differences within your own country? How do these practices compare with other countries?

Perhaps more interestingly, it is quite difficult to apply **traditional accounting methods** to agricultural activities, which explains why agriculture is excluded from many IASs.

(a) When and how do you account for the **critical events** associated with biological transformation (growth, procreation, production and degeneration), which alter the substance of biological assets?

(b) **Statement of financial position classification** is made difficult by the variety and characteristics of the living assets of agriculture.

(c) The nature of the management of agricultural activities also causes problems, particularly determination of the **unit of measurement**, ie whether biological assets are a perpetual group of assets or a number of limited life assets.

A standard would improve and harmonise practice in accounting for agriculture, which demonstrates fundamental **differences in its nature and characteristics** to other business activities.

5.1 Definitions

FAST FORWARD

IAS 41 *Agriculture* is now examinable.

The following definitions are used in IAS 41 (you should be familiar with the definitions of fair value and carrying amount by now).

Key terms

Agricultural activity is the management by an entity of the biological transformation of biological assets for sale, into agricultural produce or into additional biological assets.

Agricultural produce is the harvested product of an entity's biological assets.

A **biological asset** is a living animal or plant.

Biological transformation comprises the processes of growth, degeneration, production and procreation that cause qualitative and quantitative changes in a biological asset.

A **group of biological assets** is an aggregation of similar living animals or plants.

Harvest is the detachment of produce from a biological asset or the cessation of a biological asset's life processes

Fair value is the price that would be received to sell an asset or paid to transfer a liability in an orderly transaction between market participants at the measurement date. *(IFRS 13: Appendix A)*

Carrying amount is the amount at which an asset is recognised in the statement of financial position. *(IAS 41: para. 5)*

Note the key parts of the definition of **agriculture**.

(a) **Biological**: agriculture relates to 'life phenomena', living animals and plants with an innate capacity of biological transformation which are dependent upon a combination of natural resources (sunlight, water, etc).

(b) **Transformation**: agriculture involves physical transformation, whereby animals and plants undergo a change in biological quantity (fat cover, density, etc) and/or quantity (progeny, live weight etc) over time, which is measured and monitored (increasingly objectively) as part of management control.

(c) **Management**: biological transformation is managed.

(i) Conditions are stabilised or enhanced.

(ii) The transparency of the relationship between inputs and outputs is determined by the degree of control (intensive versus extensive).

(iii) It is different from exploitation through extraction, where no attempt is made to facilitate the transformation.

(iv) Biological assets are managed in groups of plant or animal classes, using individual assets to ensure the sustainability of the group.

(v) Sustainability of an agricultural activity is a function of quality and quantity.

(d) **Produce**: agricultural produce is diverse and may require further processing before ultimate consumption.

Question — Accounting issues

Before we look at the way the standard tackles accounting for agriculture, can you think of some of the main accounting issues, given some of the things we have looked at so far?

Answer

The standard lists the following.

(a) Biological assets meet the definition and recognition criteria of tangible assets (see IAS 16).

(b) Biological transformation is the source of sector uniqueness and significant events within agricultural activities.

(c) Biological transformations are critical events separable from the transactions entered into to facilitate them.

(d) In agricultural activities there is a general lack of clarity in the relationship between inputs and outputs which increases the complexity of the allocation process, ie between joint costs and joint products.

(e) A consistent basis of management must be applied to all outcomes to produce meaningful representations of current period performance, because of the range of outcomes and lack of traceability. This means that both biological assets and agricultural produce should be measured using the same basis.

(f) Active and efficient markets for both biological assets and agricultural produce increases the reliability of measures of net market value and existing use value respectively.

(g) Using the class or collective of biological assets as a unit of measurement has implications for: measurement (the class is more reliable than the individual, future benefits not confined to immediately available uses, values are normally expressed in the collective); for classification (a collective is a regenerative perpetual asset, even though individual members have a limited life); and for going concern (sustainability is an important indicator of going concern).

(h) Different agricultural activities have different risk and reward characteristics and will therefore be reported under different segments (see IFRS 8).

5.2 Scope

The standard applies to the three elements that form part of, or result from, agricultural activity (IAS 41: paras. 1 and 2).

- Biological assets
- Agricultural produce at the point of harvest
- Government grants

The standard does not apply to agricultural land (IASs 16 and 40), right-of-use assets arising from a lease of land for agricultural activity (see IFRS 16 *Leases)* or intangible assets related to agricultural activity (IAS 38). After harvest, IAS 2 is applied.

5.3 Biological assets

We have seen the definition given above. Biological assets are the core income-producing assets of agricultural activities, held for their transformative capabilities. Biological transformation leads to various different outcomes (IAS 41: para. 7).

- **Asset changes:**
  - Growth: increase in quantity and or quality
  - Degeneration: decrease in quantity and/or quality
- **Creation of new assets:**
  - Production: producing separable non-living products
  - Procreation: producing separable living animals

We can distinguish between the importance of these by saying that asset changes are **critical to the flow of future economic benefits** both in and beyond the current period, but the relative importance of new asset creation will depend on the purpose of the agricultural activity.

The IAS distinguishes therefore between two broad categories of agricultural production system (IAS 41: para. 43).

(a) **Consumable**: animals/plants themselves are harvested
(b) **Bearer**: animals/plants bear produce for harvest

A few further points are made.

(a) Biological assets are usually managed in groups of animal or plant classes, with characteristics (eg male/female ratio) which allow **sustainability in perpetuity**.

(b) **Land often forms an integral part** of the activity itself in pastoral and other land-based agricultural activities.

The Standard then goes on to look at the principal issues in accounting for biological assets.

5.3.1 Bearer biological assets

Plant-based bearer biological assets include trees grown in plantations, such as grape vines, rubber trees and oil palms. These plants are used solely to grow produce crops over several periods and are not in themselves consumed. When no longer productive they are usually scrapped.

It was decided that fair value was not an appropriate measurement for these assets as, once they reach maturity, the only economic benefit they produce comes from the agricultural produce they create. In this respect, they are similar to assets in a manufacturing activity.

Consequently, these assets were removed from the scope of IAS 41 and should be accounted for under IAS 16 *Property, Plant and Equipment*. They are measured at accumulated costs until maturity and are then subject to depreciation and impairment charges. The IAS 16 revaluation model could also be applied. Agricultural produce from these plants continues to be recognised under IAS 41.

5.3.2 Recognition of biological assets

The recognition criteria are very **similar to those for other assets**, in that animals or plants should be recognised as assets in the following circumstances.

(a) The entity **controls** the asset as a result of past events
(b) It is probable that the **future economic benefits** associated with the asset will flow to the entity
(c) The fair value or cost of the asset to the entity can be **measured reliably**

(IAS 41: para. 10)

The significant physical attributes of biological assets can be measured using various methods (which are used by markets to measure value) and generally indicate the source of future economic benefits. The **certainty** of the flow of rewards can be determined by formal ownership records, eg land title, branding. The availability of both cost and value for biological assets indicates the reliability aspect of the measurement criteria is fulfilled.

5.3.3 Measurement of biological assets

The IAS requires that at each year end **all biological assets should be measured at fair value** less estimated point-of-sale costs (IAS 41: para. 13).

The IAS allows an alternative method of valuation, if a fair value cannot be determined because market-determined prices or values are not available. Then the biological asset can be measured at cost less accumulated depreciation and impairment losses (IAS 41: para. 30).

This alternative basis is only allowed on **initial recognition.**

The **measurement basis** used to depict the fair value of a biological asset will differ depending on the existence of an active market, market efficiency and the use made of the asset.

In summary, it is felt that **fair value**, when compared to historical cost, has greater relevance, reliability, comparability and understandability as a measure of future economic benefits.

5.3.4 Measuring fair value

IFRS 13 (para. 16) requires the fair value of a biological asset to be determined by reference to the **principal market** for the asset. This may or may not be the most favourable market.

An active and efficient market may not be available for a class of biological assets in a specific location, or there may be imperfections in the market.

5.3.5 Recognition

This is an important principle, whereby the change in the carrying amount for a group of biological assets should be allocated between:

(a) The change attributable to **differences in fair value,** and
(b) The **physical change** in biological assets held

The total change in carrying value between the beginning and end of the period thus consists of two components. Although the separation of these two components might appear impractical, the Standard states that separate disclosure of each is **fundamental to appraising current period performance and future prospects**. This is because they will not be reported in the same way in the financial statements.

(a) The change in carrying amount attributable to the **physical change in biological assets** must be recognised as income or expense and described as the change in biological assets. This allows management's performance to be evaluated in relation to the production from, and maintenance and renewal of, biological assets. This is the 'operating' part of the change in carrying amount.

(b) The change in carrying amount attributable to **differences in fair value** should be recognised in the statement of non-owner movements in equity and presented in equity under the heading of surplus/(deficit) on fair valuation of biological assets. This is the 'holding' part of the change in carrying amount.

(IAS 41: para. 51)

In the **statement of financial position** the biological assets must be shown at fair value, incorporating the consequences of all biological transformations. These assets, with their differing risk and return characteristics, should be identified clearly.

The recommended **method of separating the above components** is to calculate the change attributable to the differences in fair value by restating biological assets on hand at the opening reporting date using end of period fair values and comparing this with the closing carrying amount. The biological assets on hand at the beginning and end of the period will then be expressed in a common measurement unit, ie period-end fair value. This allows the relative significance of sales, disposals, purchases, additions and biological transformations to be evaluated in relation to the overall change in substance of the biological assets held during the period.

There are **exceptions to this approach** in certain situations. For example, in some agricultural systems the predominant activity has a production cycle of less than a year (eg broiler chickens, mushroom growing, cereal crops). In such cases the total change in carrying amount is reported in the statement of comprehensive income as a single item of income or expense.

Any other events giving rise to a change in biological assets of such a **size, nature or incidence** that their disclosure is relevant to explain the entity's performance (as defined in IAS 8 para. 3) should be included in the change in biological assets recognised as income or expense. They should, however, be shown as a statement of financial position item in the reconciliation required to determine the change attributable to biological transformation.

(IAS 41: para. 50)

5.3.6 Presentation and disclosure

In the statement of financial position biological assets should be classified as a separate class of assets falling under neither current nor non-current classifications. This reflects the view of such assets as having an unlimited life on a collective basis; it is the total exposure of the entity to this type of asset that is important.

Biological assets should also be **sub-classified** (either in the statement of financial position or as a note to the accounts).

(IAS 41: para. 43)

(a) Class of animal or plant
(b) Nature of activities (consumable or bearer)
(c) Maturity or immaturity for intended purpose

Where activities are **consumable**, the maturity criterion will be attainment of harvestable specifications, whereas in **bearer** activities, it will be attainment of sufficient maturity to sustain economic harvests.

(IAS 41: para. 45)

In the **statement of profit or loss and other comprehensive income**, entities with significant agricultural activity are encouraged to provide an analysis of the income and expenses used in determining profit from operating activities based on the nature of income and expenses (ie rather than the cost of sales method).

5.4 Agricultural produce

This was defined in the key terms above. It is **recognised at the point of harvest** (eg detachment from the biological asset). Agricultural produce is either incapable of biological process or such processes remain dormant (eg stored grain). **Recognition ends** once the produce enters trading activities or production processes within integrated agribusinesses, although processing activities that are incidental to agricultural activities and that do not materially alter the form of the produce (eg drying or cleaning) are not counted as processing. Following harvest, the provisions of IAS 2 apply. (IAS 41: para. 2)

5.4.1 Measurement and presentation

Following the treatment of biological assets above, the IAS states (IAS 41: para. 12) that agricultural produce should be **measured at each year end at fair value** less estimated point-of-sale costs, to the extent that it is sourced from an entity's biological assets, which are also valued at fair value. This is logical when you consider that, until harvest, the agricultural produce was valued at fair value anyway as part of the biological asset.

The **change in the carrying amount** of the agricultural produce held at year end should be recognised as **income or expense** in profit or loss. This will be rare as such produce is usually sold or processed within a short time, so that produce held over two balance sheet dates is being held for a specific management purpose and the consequences of that should be reflected in the current period.

Agricultural produce that is harvested for **trading or processing activities** within integrated agricultural/ agribusiness operations should be measured at **fair value** at the date of harvest and this amount is deemed cost for application of IAS 2 to consequential inventories (IAS 41: para. 13).

Presentation in the statement of financial position

Agricultural produce should be classified as inventory in the statement of financial position and disclosed separately either in the statement of financial position or in the notes (IAS 41: para. 13).

5.5 Government grants

An unconditional government grant related to a biological asset measured at its fair value less estimated point-of-sale costs should be recognised as income when, and only when, the grant becomes receivable (IAS 41: para. 34).

If a government grant requires an entity not to engage in specified agricultural activity (eg the EU's set aside grant), an entity should only recognise the grant as income when, and only when, the conditions are met (IAS 41: para. 35).

IAS 20 does not apply to a government grant on biological assets measured at fair value less estimated point-of-sale costs. However if a biological asset is measured at cost less accumulated depreciation and accumulated impairment losses then IAS 20 does apply (IAS 41: para. 37).

5.6 Section summary

In relation to agriculture you should be able to discuss:

- Accounting for **biological assets**
- **Transformation** and changes in substance
- **Unit of measurement** and changes in the carrying amount

6 Entity reconstructions

Note. Group reorganisations are covered in Chapter 14.

FAST FORWARD

- You need to identify when an entity may no longer be viewed as a **going concern** and why a reconstruction might be an appropriate alternative to a liquidation.
- You will not need to suggest a scheme of **reconstruction**, but you will need an outline of the accounting treatment.

6.1 Background

Most of a Study Text on financial accounting is inevitably concerned with profitable, even expanding businesses. It must of course be recognised that some companies fail. From a theoretical discounted cash flow viewpoint, a company should be wound up if the expected return on its value in liquidation is less than that required. In practice (and in law), a company is regarded as **insolvent** if it is unable to pay its debts.

This terms needs some qualification. It is not uncommon, for example, to find a company that continues to trade and pays its creditors on time despite the fact that its liabilities exceed its assets. On the other hand, a company may be unable to meet its current liabilities although it has substantial sums locked up in assets which cannot be liquidated sufficiently quickly.

The procedures and options open to a failing company will depend on the degree of financial difficulties it faces. If the outlook is hopeless, liquidation may be the only feasible solution. However, many firms in serious financial positions can be revived to the benefit of creditors, members and society. When considering any scheme of arrangement it is important to remember that the **protection of creditors** is usually of paramount importance. The position of the shareholders and in particular, the protection of class rights, must be considered but the creditors come first.

Exam focus point

This section considers some possibilities, but local legislation will govern these situations. In an exam, simply follow the instructions in the question.

6.2 Going concern

Key term

Going concern. The entity is normally viewed as a going concern, that is, as continuing in operation for the foreseeable future. It is assumed that the entity has neither the intention nor the necessity of liquidation or of curtailing materially the scale of its operations.

(Conceptual Framework, Chapter 4: para. 4.1)

It is generally assumed that the entity has no intention to liquidate or curtail major operations. If it did, then the financial statements would be prepared on a **different (disclosed) basis**. Indications that an entity may no longer be a going concern include the following (from International Standard on Auditing, ISA 570 *Going concern*):

(a) **Financial indicators**, eg recurring operating losses, net liability or net current liability position, negative cash flow from operating activities, adverse key financial ratios, inability to obtain financing for essential new product development or other essential investments, default on loan or similar agreements, arrear as in dividends, denial of usual trade credit from suppliers, restructuring of debt, non-compliance with statutory capital requirements, need to seek new sources or methods of financing or to dispose of substantial assets.

(b) **Operating matters**, eg loss of key management without replacement, loss of a major market, key customers, licence, or principal suppliers, labour difficulties, shortages of important supplies or the emergence of a highly successful competitor.

(c) **Other matters**, eg pending legal or regulatory proceedings against the entity, changes in law or regulations that may adversely affect the entity; or uninsured or underinsured catastrophe such as a drought, earthquake or flood.

6.3 Internal reconstructions

A company may be able to enter into **any type of scheme** regarding either its creditors or its shareholders as long as the scheme does not conflict with general law or any particular statutory provision.

For a reconstruction of this type to be considered worthwhile in the first place, the business must have some **future** otherwise it might be better for the creditors if the company went into liquidation.

In any **scaling down of claims** from creditors and loan stock holders, two conditions should be met.

(a) A reasonable chance of successful operations
(b) Fairness to parties

6.3.1 First example: Reconstruction scheme

Boswell Co has been making losses over the last few years. Its statement of financial position at 31 December 20X1 showed the following.

	$		$
Ordinary capital	50,000	Plant	40,000
Retained earnings	(70,000)	Inventory	10,000
Loan stock (secured)	50,000	Receivables	20,000
Payables	40,000		
	70,000		70,000

On liquidation, the assets would realise the following.

	$
Plant	15,000
Inventory	6,000
Receivables	18,000
	39,000

If the company continued to trade for the next four years, profits after charging $10,000 per annum depreciation on the plant would be as follows.

	$
20X2	2,000
20X3	10,000
20X4	13,000
20X5	14,000
	39,000

Assuming that there would be no surplus cash to repay the creditors and loan stock holders until after four years and that inventory and receivables could then be realised at their book values, you are required to prepare a reconstruction scheme. Ignore taxation.

Solution

If liquidation took place now only $39,000 would be raised which would be given to the loan stock holders leaving them with a deficiency of $11,000. There would be nothing for the creditors and shareholders. However, if trading continues for the next four years and estimated results are achieved, the cash available would be as follows.

	$
Profits	39,000
Depreciation	40,000
Inventory and receivables: full value	30,000
	109,000

$90,000 would enable the loan stock holders and creditors to be paid in full leaving $19,000 available for the ordinary shareholders.

Everyone will be better off if the company is allowed to continue trading. However, the loan stock holders probably have the right to appoint a receiver and would insist on some compensation for not enforcing their right. The creditors might also expect something for having to wait four years before receiving some payment.

There is no unique solution to such a question but one that might be acceptable would be for the loan stock holders and creditors to waive the amounts owed to them in exchange for ordinary shares, so that they will have full participation in the future profitability of the company. Terms of such an exchange might be as follows.

(a) 37,500 $1 ordinary shares to the loan stock holders (3 $1 ordinary shares for every $4 of loan stock)

(b) 20,000 $1 ordinary shares to the creditors (1 $1 ordinary share for every $2 due)

(c) 12,500 $1 ordinary shares to the old ordinary shareholders (1 $1 ordinary share for every 4 of the old $1 ordinary shares)

The creditors might prefer to receive loan stock as they would then have a legal right to repayment of nominal capital and could also insist on payment of interest.

The reconstructed statement of financial position of Boswell Co at 31 December 20X1 would then be as follows.

	$		$
Ordinary capital	70,000	Plant	40,000
		Inventory	10,000
		Receivables	20,000
	70,000		70,000

6.3.2 Accounting procedures for internal reconstructions

The normal procedure to undertake an internal reconstruction scheme are as follows:

Step 1 Open a reorganisation account.

Step 2 Transfer in all shares/loan stock to be replaced.

Step 3 Put through all asset write-downs/revaluations and expenses of the scheme.

Step 4 Issue new shares/loan stock from this account.

Step 5 Transfer the balance to a capital reserve (or write off against, eg a share premium account, if it is a debit balance).

In practice, schemes of reduction of capital can be very complex, but they must be fair to all parties concerned. Where arrears of dividend on cumulative preferred shares are involved, an arrangement must be found to compensate the shareholders for giving up their rights to the arrears, for example by issuing them with fixed interest loan stock.

6.4 External reconstructions

A court may make orders for the transfer of all the company's assets and liabilities and for its **dissolution**. Such a scheme might provide for the formation of a new company to take over the undertaking of the old company, or an amalgamation, to acquire the undertakings of a number of companies, the members and creditors of which accept shares or loan stock in the new company in exchange for their former rights.

6.4.1 Second example: Reconstruction scheme

Extracts from the statement of financial position of Brave World Co are as follows.

	Debit	*Credit*
	$	$
Ordinary $1 shares, fully paid		70,000
Payables		32,100
Inventory	29,000	
Receivables	16,000	
Cash	100	
Patents	30,000	
Preliminary expenses	2,000	
Retained earnings	25,000	
	102,100	102,100

A scheme of reconstruction was agreed by the shareholders and creditors of the company.

(a) The company to go into voluntary liquidation and a new company, New Brave World Co, to be formed with an authorised share capital of $50,000 which will take over the assets and liabilities of the old company.

(b) The inventory, receivables and cash of the old company to be taken over at book value. The patents are subject to adjustment.

(c) Creditors are to receive settlement as follows.

		$
(i)	Preferential creditors to be paid in full	2,100
(ii)	$20,000 of unsecured creditors to be discharged for a cash compensation of 80c in the $	20,000
(iii)	$10,000 of unsecured creditors to accept $12,000 6% loan stock in the new company	10,000
	Book value	32,100

(d) 50,000 $1 ordinary shares in New Brave World Co to be issued, 50c already paid up to shareholders in the old company and 50c payable on application and allotment to make the shares fully paid up.

(e) Costs of liquidation amounting to $1,000 will be paid by the new company as part of the purchase consideration.

Required

Prepare the statement of financial position of the new company.

Solution

NEW BRAVE WORLD CO STATEMENT OF FINANCIAL POSITION

	$		$
Authorised, issued and fully paid		Inventories	29,000
ordinary share capital		Receivables	16,000
50,000 shares of $1 each	50,000	Cash (W3)	6,000
6% loan stock	12,000	Patents, at cost (W2)	11,000
	62,000		62,000

Workings

1 *Purchase consideration*

	$
Cash	
To pay off creditors ($2,100 + 80% of $20,000)	18,100
Liquidation expenses	1,000
	19,100
Loan stock	12,000
Paid up part of new shares	25,000
	56,100

2 *Assets*

	$
Inventories	29,000
Receivables	16,000
Cash	100
	45,100
Patents at cost (balance)	11,000
	56,100

3 *Cash balance*

	$
Cash from shareholders	25,000
Cash acquired from old company	100
	25,100
Less cash payments in purchase consideration	19,100
Cash balance held	6,000

6.5 Transfer of assets to a new company

Another form of reconstruction is by means of **voluntary liquidation** whereby the liquidator transfers the assets of the company to a new company in exchange for shares or other securities in the new company. The old company may be able to retain certain of its assets, usually cash, and make a distribution to the shareholders of the old company who still have an interest in the undertaking through their shareholding in the new company. There may be various rules governing the protection of non-controlling shareholders.

Such a procedure would be applied to the company which is proposed to be or is in course of being wound up voluntarily. A company in liquidation must dispose of its assets (other than cash) by sale in order to pay its debts and distribute any surplus to its members. The special feature of this kind of reconstruction is that the business or property of Company P is transferred to Company Q in **exchange for shares** of the latter company which are allotted direct or distributed by the liquidator to members of Company P. Obviously the creditors of Company P will have to be paid cash.

Finding the cash to pay creditors and to buy out shareholders who object to the scheme is often the major drawback to a scheme of this kind. It is unlikely to be used much because the same result can be more satisfactorily achieved by a **takeover**: Company Q simply acquires the share capital of Company P, which becomes its subsidiary, and the assets and liabilities are transferred from the subsidiary to the new holding company. In this situation usually no cash has to be found (although obviously there is no guarantee of success).

The **advantage** of transferring a business from one company to another (with the same shareholders in the end) is that by this means the business may be moved away from a company with a tangled history to a new company which makes a fresh start. As explained above this procedure can also be used to effect a merger of two companies each with an existing business.

6.5.1 Accounting procedures for a transfer to a new company

The basic procedure when transferring the undertaking to a new company is as follows.

(a) To close off the ledger accounts in the books of the old company.
(b) To open up the ledger accounts in the books of the new company.

The basic procedure is as follows.

Step 1 Open a **realisation account** and transfer in all the assets and liabilities to be taken over by the new company at book value.

Step 2 Open a **sundry members account** with columns for ordinary and preference shareholders. Transfer in the share capital, reserve balances, assets written off and gains and losses on realisation.

Step 3 With the **purchase consideration** for the members:

DEBIT	Sundry members a/c	
CREDIT		Realisation a/c

Take any profit or loss on realisation to the sundry members account (ordinary).

Step 4 In the new company, open a **purchase of business account**:

CREDIT it with assets taken over
(DEBIT asset accounts)

DEBIT it with liabilities taken over
(CREDIT liabilities a/cs)

DEBIT it with the purchase consideration
(CREDIT shares, loan stock etc)

Any balance is goodwill or a gain on a bargain purchase.

Chapter Roundup

- Questions on specialist entities will be set in terms of **current IFRS**.
- The not-for-profit sector includes **public sector entities** and **private** not-for-profit entities such as charities.
- Not-for-profit entities have **different goals** from profit making entities, but they still need to be **properly managed** and their accounts need to present the information fairly.
- The **IASB** and the **FASB** are working on a **framework** for reporting, which includes not-for-profit entities.
- The International Public Sector Accounting Standards Board (IPSAB) is developing a set of **International Public Sector Accounting Standards** based on IFRS.
- IAS 41 *Agriculture* is now examinable.
- You need to identify when an entity may no longer be viewed as a **going concern** and why a reconstruction might be an appropriate alternative to a liquidation.
- You will not need to suggest a scheme of **reconstruction**, but you will need an outline of the accounting treatment.

Quick Quiz

1 Charities are public sector entities. *True or false?*

2 Why do not-for-profit entities need to keep accounts if they are not reporting to shareholders?

3 Are there any special IFRSs for the public sector?

4 IAS 41 has abolished the concept of cost for measurement purposes.

True ☐

False ☐

5 What are steps 1 and 2 in the normal procedure for accounting for internal reconstructions?

Answers to Quick Quiz

1 False. Charities are private not-for-profit profit entities.

2 They often deal in large sums of money.

3 Yes, the IPSASB is developing a set of International Public Sector Accounting Standards.

4 False. Cost is still allowed if fair value is not available at initial recognition.

5 Step 1: Open a reorganisation account
Step 2: Transfer all shares/loan stock to be replaced.

Now try the questions below from the Practice Question Bank

Number	Level	Marks	Time
Q26	Introductory	n/a	n/a

21

Reporting for small and medium-sized entities

Topic list	Syllabus reference
1 Background	C11
2 Application of IFRS to smaller entities	C11
3 *IFRS for Small and Medium-Sized Entities*	C11
4 Consequences, good and bad	C11

Introduction

Concentrate on Section 1 – this is the most important for your exam.

You should be aware that smaller entities may have different accounting needs from the larger entities, but IFRS are generally designed for larger ones. This chapter gives you the background you need to set you thinking about whether a one-size-fits-all set of standards is adequate.

Study guide

		Intellectual level
C11	**Reporting requirements of small and medium entities (SMEs)**	
(a)	Discuss the accounting treatments not allowable under the IFRS for SMEs including the revaluation model for certain assets and proportionate consolidation	3
(b)	Discuss and apply the simplifications introduced by the IFRS for SMEs including accounting for goodwill and intangible assets, financial instruments, defined benefit schemes, exchange differences and associates and joint ventures	3

Exam guide

This topic has a separate syllabus section, indicating that the examiner regards it as important and topical.

1 Background 12/10

FAST FORWARD

IFRSs are designed for entities quoted on the world's capital markets. However, most **entities are small or medium sized**.

1.1 Scope of IFRS

Any limitation of the applicability of a specific IFRS is made clear within that standard. IFRSs are **not intended to be applied to immaterial items, nor are they retrospective**. Each individual IFRS lays out its scope at the beginning of the standard.

1.2 Application

Within each individual country **local regulations** govern, to a greater or lesser degree, the issue of financial statements. These local regulations include accounting standards issued by the national regulatory bodies and/or professional accountancy bodies in the country concerned.

The IFRSs **concentrate on essentials** and are designed not to be too complex, otherwise they would be impossible to apply on a worldwide basis.

IFRSs do not override local regulations on financial statements. Accounting bodies that are members of the IASB should simply disclose the fact where IFRSs are complied with in all material respects. Members of the IASB in individual countries will attempt to persuade local authorities, where current regulations deviate from IFRSs, that the benefits of harmonisation make local change worthwhile.

2 Application of IFRS to smaller entities 12/10

FAST FORWARD

Various approaches were proposed to deal with the so-called **Big GAAP/Little GAAP divide**.

2.1 Big GAAP/little GAAP divide

In most countries the majority of companies or other types of entity are **very small**. They are generally owned and managed by one person or a family. The owners have invested their own money in the business and there are no outside shareholders to protect.

Large entities, by contrast, particularly companies listed on a stock exchange, may have shareholders who have invested their money, possibly through a pension fund, with no knowledge whatever of the company. These shareholders need protection and the regulations for such companies need to be more stringent.

It could therefore be argued that company accounts should be of two types.

(a) 'Simple' ones for small companies with fewer regulations and disclosure requirements
(b) 'Complicated' ones for larger companies with extensive and detailed requirements

This is sometimes called the **big GAAP/little GAAP divide**.

2.2 Possible solutions

There are two approaches to overcoming the big GAAP/little GAAP divide:

1 Differential reporting, ie producing new reduced standards specifically for smaller companies, such as the UK FRSSE or the IFRS for SMEs (see below.)

2 Providing exemptions for smaller companies from some of the requirements of existing standards.

2.3 Differential reporting

A one-size-fits-all framework does not generate relevant, and useful information, even if this information is reliable:

(a) The costs may not be justified for the more limited needs of users of SME accounts.

(b) The purpose of the financial statements and the use to which they are put will not be the same as for listed companies.

Differential reporting overcomes this by tailoring the reporting requirements to the entity. The main characteristic that distinguishes SMEs from other entities is the degree of public accountability. For example, a listed company or a public utility, or a company such as a bank, which holds assets in a fiduciary capacity might be regarded as publicly accountable. Despite the name SME, size is not the only or even the main criterion. (This was the position the IASB adopted – see below.)

Differential reporting may have drawbacks in terms of reducing comparability between small and larger company accounts.

Furthermore, problems may arise where entities no longer meet the criteria to be classified as small.

2.4 Exemptions from IFRS

Some IFRSs do not have any bearing on small company accounts, for example, a company with equity not quoted on a stock exchange has no need to comply with IAS 33 *Earnings per share*. Also an entity with a small local market, may find IFRS 8 *Operating segments* to be superfluous.

Other standards always have an impact. In particular, almost all small companies will be affected by the IFRSs on:

- Property, plant and equipment
- Inventories
- Presentation of financial statements
- Events occurring after the reporting period
- Taxes on income
- Revenue
- Provisions and contingencies

Does this mean that companies below a certain size should be exempt from other IFRSs? An alternative approach would be to reduce the exposure of small companies to IFRSs on a **standard by standard basis**. For those 'core' standards listed above, small companies would be required to follow all or most of their provisions. For more complicated standards, small companies would face nothing but very brief general obligations.

It is difficult to see how the IASB could impose any kind of specific size limits to define small companies if such an approach were adopted. Instead, it might specify that size limits which are already given in national legislation or standards could be adopted for the purpose.

To a certain extent (see IAS 33 and IFRS 8 above) partial exemption already applies. Indeed, an IFRS for Small and Medium-sized Entities that applies some but not all of the requirements of existing IFRS achieves this aim.

2.4.1 Cost of compliance

If the cost of compliance exceeds the benefits to users, an entity may decide not to follow an IFRS. This applies to all reporting entities, not just smaller ones. However, smaller entities are more likely to make use of this exception.

For example, impairment reviews can be time-consuming and a smaller entity may not have sufficient staff to spare to carry out these reviews.

2.4.2 Materiality

Another point to note is that IFRSs apply to **material** items. In the case of smaller entities, the amount that is material may be very small in monetary terms. However, the effect of not reporting that item may be material in that it would mislead users of the financial statements. A case in point is IAS 24 *Related Party Disclosures*. Smaller entities may well rely on trade with relatives of the directors/shareholders and this needs to be disclosed.

3 International Financial Reporting Standard for Small and Medium-sized Entities 12/10

FAST FORWARD

Published in 2009 and revised in 2015, the *IFRS for Small and Medium-sized Entities* aims to simplify financial reporting for SMEs by omitting irrelevant topics, reducing guidance and disclosure and eliminating choice. It also simplifies some of the recognition and measurement principles.

The *IFRS for Small and Medium-Sized Entities* (IFRS for SMEs) was published in 2009 and revised in 2015. It is only 230 pages, and has simplifications that reflect the needs of users of SMEs' financial statements and cost-benefit considerations. It is designed to facilitate financial reporting by small and medium-sized entities in a number of ways:

(a) It provides significantly less guidance than full IFRS.

(b) Many of the principles for recognising and measuring assets, liabilities, income and expenses in full IFRSs are simplified.

(c) Where full IFRSs allow accounting policy choices, the IFRS for SMEs allows only the easier option.

(d) Topics not relevant to SMEs are omitted.

(e) Significantly fewer disclosures are required.

(f) The standard has been written in clear language that can easily be translated.

3.1 Scope

The IFRS is suitable for all entities except those whose securities are publicly traded and financial institutions such as banks and insurance companies. It is the first set of international accounting requirements developed specifically for small and medium-sized entities (SMEs). Although it has been prepared on a similar basis to IFRS, it is a stand-alone product and will be updated on its own timescale.

The IFRS will be revised only once every three years. It is hoped that this will further reduce the reporting burden for SMEs.

There are no quantitative thresholds for qualification as a SME; instead, the scope of the IFRS is determined by a test of public accountability. As with full IFRS, it is up to legislative and regulatory authorities and standard setters in individual jurisdictions to decide who is permitted or required to use the IFRS for SMEs.

(IFRS for SMEs: paras. 1 to 3)

3.2 Effective date

The IFRS for SMEs does not contain an effective date; this is determined in each jurisdiction. The IFRS will be revised only once every three years. It is hoped that this will further reduce the reporting burden for SMEs. (IFRS for SMEs: paras. P16 and P17)

3.3 Accounting policies

For situations where the IFRS for SMEs does not provide specific guidance, it provides a hierarchy for determining a suitable accounting policy. An SME must consider, in descending order:

- The guidance in the IFRS for SMEs on similar and related issues.
- The definitions, recognition criteria and measurement concepts in Section 2 *Concepts and Pervasive Principles* of the standard.

The entity also has the option of considering the requirements and guidance in full IFRS dealing with similar topics. However, it is under no obligation to do this, or to consider the pronouncements of other standard setters.

(IFRS for SMEs: paras. P16 and P17)

3.4 Overlap with full IFRS

In the following areas, the recognition and measurement guidance in the IFRS for SMEs is like that in the full IFRS.

- Provisions and contingencies
- Hyperinflation accounting
- Events after the end of the reporting period
- Taxation (since the 2015 revisions)
- Property, plant and equipment (since the 2015 revisions)

3.5 Omitted topics

The IFRS for SMEs does not address the following topics that are covered in full IFRS.

- Earnings per share
- Interim financial reporting
- Segment reporting
- Classification for non-current assets (or disposal groups) as held for sale

3.6 Examples of options in full IFRS not included in the IFRS for SMEs

- Choice between cost and fair value models for investment property (measurement depends on the circumstances)
- Options for government grants

3.7 Initial comprehensive review of the *IFRS for SMEs*

In May 2015, the IASB completed its comprehensive review of the *IFRS for SMEs*. The most significant amendments are as follows:

(a) SMEs are now permitted to use a revaluation model for property, plant and equipment (IFRS for SMEs: Section 29).

(b) The main recognition and measurement requirements for deferred income tax are aligned with full IFRS. (IFRS for SMEs: para. 17.15B)

These revisions are taken into account in the table below.

3.8 Principal recognition and measurement simplifications

Area	IFRS for SMEs	Full IFRSs
Presentation & disclosure	**Combined** statement of profit or loss and other comprehensive income and statement of changes in equity **permitted** (where no OCI nor equity movements other than profit or loss, dividends and/or prior period adjustments) **Segment disclosures** and **earnings per share not required**. Other disclosures reduced by 90% versus full IFRSs.	**Not permitted** **Required** (as full IFRSs apply only to publicly quoted companies)
Revenue	*Goods*: when significant **risks and rewards of ownership transferred** (and no continuing managerial involvement nor effective control) *Services:* **stage of completion.**	When **performance obligation** satisfied (IFRS 15 five step approach).
Financial instruments	**Amortised cost** • All 'basic' financial instruments other than those publicly traded or whose fair value can be measured reliably. **Cost** • Unquoted investments in equity instruments (where FV not reliably measurable) **Fair value through profit or loss** • All other financial instruments SMEs can also choose to use the IFRS 9 rules (limiting disclosures to those required for SMEs).	**Amortised cost** • *Financial assets:* business model is held to collect cash flows • *Financial liabilities*: all others not held at fair value through profit or loss **Cost** Also the case **Fair value through profit or loss** • *Financial assets:* all others • *Financial liabilities:* held for trading or part of group evaluated on FV basis

Area	IFRS for SMEs	Full IFRSs
		Fair value through OCI • *Investments in equity instruments* which are investments in equity instruments not held for trading and irrevocable election made at inception • *Financial assets* where business model is held to collect contractual cash flows and to sell financial assets
Investment property	**Fair value through profit or loss** (where fair value can be measured without undue cost or effort, otherwise as PPE under cost-depreciation-impairment model)	**Fair value** model, **or** **Cost** model (accounting policy choice)
Intangible assets	All intangibles (including goodwill) are **amortised.** Useful life cannot exceed 10 years if cannot be established reliably. Revaluation model **not permitted.** All internally generated research and development expenditure is **expensed.**	Only a**mortised if finite useful life** No specific limit Revaluations **permitted** where active market **Capitalised** when the 'PIRATE' criteria met
Separate financial statements of investor	Investments in subsidiaries, associates and joint ventures can be held at **cost** (less any impairment) or **fair value through profit or loss.**	**Cost** *or* **under IFRS 9** (fair value through **profit or loss**, or fair value through **other comprehensive income** if an election was made on purchase)
Consolidated and separate financial statements	Investments in associates and joint ventures can **remain at that same value** or be **equity accounted.** Only **partial goodwill** allowed, ie non-controlling interests cannot be measured at full fair value. It is **amortised** as for intangible assets. Exchange differences on translating a foreign operation are recognised in **other comprehensive income** and **not subsequently reclassified** to profit or loss.	**Associates and joint ventures** equity accounted. Choice of **full or partial goodwill** method. Compulsory **annual test for impairment**, not amortised. Recognised in **other comprehensive income** and **reclassified to profit or loss** on disposal of the foreign operation.
Government grants	No specified future performance conditions: → recognise as **income** when the grant is receivable. Otherwise: → recognise as **income** when performance conditions met.	**Grants relating to income** recognised in P/L **over period** to match to related costs **Grants relating to assets either**: – presented as **deferred income**; *or* – **deducted** in arriving at the carrying amount of the asset.
Borrowing costs	**Expensed** when incurred	**Capitalised** (when relate to an asset being constructed).

Area	IFRS for SMEs	Full IFRSs
Impairment of assets	Impairment test (carrying amount vs recoverable amount) only required where there are **indicators of impairment** (except for **inventories** which are tested **annually**). Impairment losses are charged to **profit or loss**. Non-current assets **held for sale** tested for impairment in the same way as other assets.	**Annual tests for:** • indefinite life intangibles • intangibles not yet available for use • goodwill Impairment losses charged 1st to OCI re any rev'n surplus on revalued assets Non-current assets held for sale held under IFRS 5 rules.
Employee benefits	Actuarial gains and losses can be recognised immediately in **profit or loss** *or* **other comprehensive income**. Actual return on plan assets recognised in **profit or loss**. **Simplified calculation** of defined benefit obligations permitted.	Remeasurements in **other comprehensive income** only. Projected unit credit method must be used.

(Adapted and updated from PriceWaterhouseCoopers, 2009)

4 Consequences, good and bad 12/10

FAST FORWARD

There is **no perfect solution** to the Big GAAP/Little GAAP divide. It remains to be seen how well the *IFRS for SMEs will* work in practice.

4.1 Likely effect

Because there is no supporting guidance in the IFRS for SMEs, it is likely that differences will arise from full IFRS, even where the principles are the same. Most of the exemptions in the IFRS for SMEs are on grounds of cost or undue effort. However, despite the practical advantages of a simpler reporting framework, there will be costs involved for those moving to IFRS – even a simplified IFRS – for the first time.

4.2 Advantages and disadvantages of the IFRS for SMEs

4.2.1 Advantages

(a) It is virtually a '**one stop shop**'.
(b) It is **structured according to topics**, which should make it practical to use.
(c) It is written in an **accessible style**.
(d) There is **considerable reduction in disclosure requirements**.
(e) Guidance **not relevant** to private entities is **excluded**.

4.2.2 Disadvantages

(a) It does **not** focus on the **smallest companies**.

(b) The scope extends to 'non-publicly accountable' entities. Potentially, the **scope is too wide**.

(c) The standard will be **onerous** for **small companies**.

(d) **Further simplifications** could be made. These might include:

  (i) Amortisation for goodwill and intangibles

  (ii) No requirement to value intangibles separately from goodwill on a business combination

  (iii) No recognition of deferred tax

  (iv) No measurement rules for equity-settled share-based payment

  (v) No requirement for consolidated accounts (as for EU small and medium-sized entities currently)

  (vi) Fair value measurement when readily determinable without undue cost or effort.

Chapter Roundup

- IFRSs are designed for entities quoted on the world's capital markets. However, **most entities are small or medium sized**.
- Various approaches were proposed to deal with the so-called **Big GAAP/Little GAAP divide**.
- Published in July 2009, the *IFRS for Small and Medium-sized Entities* aims to simplify financial reporting for SMEs by omitting irrelevant topics, reducing guidance and disclosure and eliminating choice. It also simplifies some of the recognition and measurement principles.
- There is **no perfect solution** to the Big GAAP/Little GAAP divide. It remains to be seen how well the *IFRS for SMEs* will work in practice.

Quick Quiz

1 What is differential financial reporting?

2 The treatment of provisions is simpler in the *IFRS for SMEs* than in IAS 37. *True or false?*

3 The financial instruments categories 'held-to-maturity' and 'available-for-sale' are not included in the *IFRS for SMEs. True or false?*

4 Proportionate consolidation of investments in jointly controlled entities is allowed in:

A IAS 28 only
B IAS 28 and the *IFRS for SMEs*
C The *IFRS for SMEs* only
D It is not allowed anywhere

Answers to Quick Quiz

1 Producing new reduced standards specifically for smaller companies.

2 False. Provisions are one area in which the recognition and measurement guidance in the *IFRS for SMEs* is like that in the full IFRS.

3 True, and once IFRS 9 is in force they will no longer be available in full IFRS.

4 D. It is not allowed at all. IAS 28 was revised to reflect this, but the *IFRS for SMEs* was there first.

Now try the questions below from the Practice Question Bank

Number	Level	Marks	Time
Q27	Examination	25	49 mins
Q29	Examination	25	49 mins
Q30	Examination	50	98 mins

Practice question and answer bank

1 Conceptual Framework

(a) Explain the main purposes of the International Accounting Standards Board's *Conceptual Framework for Financial Reporting.*

(b) Identify any four user groups of financial statements and explain what information they are likely to want from them.

2 Fundamental principles

Fundamental principles require that a member of a professional accountancy body should behave with integrity in all professional, business and financial relationships and should strive for objectivity in all professional and business judgements. Objectivity can only be assured if the member is and is seen to be independent. Conflicts of interest have an important bearing on independence and hence also on the public's perception of the integrity, objectivity and independence of the accounting profession.

The following scenario is an example of press reports in recent years which deal with issues of objectivity and independence within a multinational firm of accountants:

'A partner in the firm was told by the regulatory body that he must resign because he was in breach of the regulatory body's independence rules, as his brother-in-law was financial controller of an audit client. He was told that the alternative was that he could move his home and place of work at least 400 miles from the offices of the client, even though he was not the reporting partner. This made his job untenable. The regulatory body was seen as 'taking its rules to absurd lengths' by the accounting firm. Shortly after this comment, the multinational firm announced proposals to split the firm into three areas between audit, tax and business advisory services; management consultancy; and investment advisory services'.

Required

Discuss the impact that the above events may have on the public perception of the integrity, objectivity and independence of the multinational firm of accountants.

3 Tree

You are the accountant of Tree, a listed limited liability company that prepares consolidated financial statements. Your Managing Director, who is not an accountant, has recently attended a seminar at which key financial reporting issues were discussed. She remembers being told the following.

- Financial statements of an entity should reflect the substance of its transactions;
- Revenue from the contracts with customers should only be recognised when certain conditions have been satisfied. Transfer of legal title to the goods is not necessarily sufficient for an entity to recognise revenue from their 'sale'.

The year-end of Tree is 31 August. In the year to 31 August 20X1, the company entered into the following transactions.

Transaction 1

On 1 March 20X1, Tree sold a property to a bank for $5 million. The market value of the property at the date of the sale was $10 million. Tree continues to occupy the property rent-free. Tree has the option to buy the property back from the bank at the end of every month from 31 March 20X1 until 28 February 20X6. Tree has not yet exercised this option. The repurchase price will be $5 million plus $50,000 for every complete month that has elapsed from the date of sale to the date of repurchase. The bank cannot require Tree to repurchase the property and the facility lapses after 28 February 20X6. The directors of Tree expect property prices to rise at around 5% each year for the foreseeable future.

Transaction 2

On 1 September 20X0, Tree sold one of its branches to Vehicle for $8 million. The net assets of the branch in the financial statements of Tree immediately before the sale were $7 million. Vehicle is a subsidiary of a bank and was specifically incorporated to carry out the purchase – it has no other business operations. Vehicle received the $8 million to finance this project from its parent in the form of a loan.

Tree continues to control the operations of the branch and receives an annual operating fee from Vehicle. The annual fee is the operating profit of the branch for the 12 months to the previous 31 August less the interest payable on the loan taken out by Vehicle for the 12 months to the previous 31 August. If this amount is negative, then Tree must pay the negative amount to Vehicle.

Any payments to or by Tree must be made by 30 September following the end of the relevant period. In the year to 31 August 20X1, the branch made an operating profit of $2,000,000. Interest payable by Vehicle on the loan for this period was $800,000.

Required

(a) Explain the conditions that need to be satisfied before revenue can be recognised. You should support your answer with reference to International Financial Reporting Standards as appropriate.

(b) Explain how the transactions described above will be dealt with in the consolidated financial statements (statement of financial position and statements of profit or loss and other comprehensive income) of Tree for the year ended 31 August 20X1.

4 Camel Telecom **49 mins**

Camel Telecom operates in the telecommunications industry under the name Mobistar which it developed itself. Camel has entered into a number of transactions relating to non-current assets on which it would like accounting advice.

(a) Camel won the government contest to be awarded a licence to operate 3.5G services. Only 4 such licences were available in the country. Under the terms of the agreement, Camel can operate 3.5G mobile phone services for a period of 10 years from the commencement of the licence which was 1 July 20X7. During that period Camel can sell the licence on if it chooses to another operator meeting certain government criteria, and sharing any profits made equally with the government.

Camel paid $344m for the licence on 1 July 20X7. Its market value was estimated at $370m at that date.

Due to lower take up than expected of 3.5G services, the fair value of the licence was valued at $335m at the company's year end 30 June 20X8, by Valyou, a professional services firm. **(6 marks)**

(b) In September 20X7, Camel has purchased a plot of land on which it intends to build its new head office and service centre in 2 years' time. In the meantime the land is rented out to a local farm. The land cost $10.4m. It has been valued at the year end by Valyou and has a value of $10.6m as farmland and $14.3m as land for development. Planning permission is in process at the year end, but Camel's lawyer expects it to be granted by mid 20X9. **(4 marks)**

(c) Camel purchased a number of hilltop sites a number of years ago on which (after receiving planning permission), it erects mobile phone transmitter masts.

Because of the prime location of the sites, their market value has increased substantially since the original purchase. Camel is also able to lease part of the sites to other mobile communication companies. **(4 marks)**

(d) During the year, Camel did a deal with a mobile operator in another country whereby Camel sold its fixed line ADSL business to another company Purple for an agreed market value of $320m and in return acquired Purple's mobile phone business in the other country. Camel paid $980m to Purple in addition to the legal transfer of its fixed line ADSL business. Purple did not make any payment other than the transfer of its mobile business.

Under the terms of the agreement, the mobile phone business will remain under the name Purple for up to 1 year, after Camel time intends to re-brand the business under its own national and international mobile brand Mobistar. **(5 marks)**

(e) An embarrassing incident occurred in February 20X8 where a laptop containing details of all of Camel's national customers and the expiry date of their contracts was stolen. The details subsequently fell into the hands of competitors who have been contacting Camel's clients when their Mobistar contracts are up for renewal.

As a result of this Camel has realised that the value of the client details is significant and propose to recognise a value determined by Valyou in its financial statements. This valuation of $44m takes into account business expected to be lost as a result of the incident. **(4 marks)**

Required

Discuss, with suitable computations, how the above transactions should be accounted for in the financial statements of the Camel Telecom Group under IFRSs for the year ended 30 June 20X8.

All amounts are considered material to the group financial statements.

Professional marks for clarity and expression **(2 marks)**

(Total = 25 marks)

5 Acquirer **49 mins**

Acquirer is an entity that regularly purchases new subsidiaries. On 30 June 20X0, the entity acquired all the equity shares of Prospects for a cash payment of $260 million. The net assets of Prospects on 30 June 20X0 were $180 million and no fair value adjustments were necessary upon consolidation of Prospects for the first time.

On 31 December 20X0, Acquirer carried out a review of the goodwill on consolidation of Prospects for evidence of impairment. The review was carried out despite the fact that there were no obvious indications of adverse trading conditions for Prospects. The review involved allocating the net asset of Prospects into three cash-generating units and computing the value in use of each unit. The carrying values of the individual units before any impairment adjustments are given below.

	Unit A	*Unit B*	*Unit C*
	$ million	$ million	$ million
Patents	5		
Property, plant and equipment	60	30	40
Net current assets	20	25	20
	85	55	60
Value in use of unit	72	60	65

It was not possible to meaningfully allocate the goodwill on consolidation to the individual cash-generating units, but all other net assets of Prospects are allocated in the table shown above. The patents of Prospects have no ascertainable market value but all the current assets have a market value that is above carrying value. The value in use of Prospects as a single cash-generating unit at 31 December 20X1 is £205 million.

Required

(a) Explain what is meant by a cash-generating unit. **(5 marks)**

(b) Explain why it was necessary to review the goodwill on consolidation of Prospects for impairment at 31 December 20X0. **(3 marks)**

(c) Explain briefly the purpose of an impairment review and why the net assets of Prospects were allocated into cash-generating units as part of the review of goodwill for impairment. **(5 marks)**

(d) Demonstrate how the impairment loss in unit A will affect the carrying value of the net assets of unit A in the consolidated financial statements of Acquirer. **(5 marks)**

(e) Explain and calculate the effect of the impairment review on the carrying value of the goodwill on consolidation of Prospects at 31 December 20X0. **(7 marks)**

(Total = 25 marks)

6 Investor **49 mins**

Investor is a listed company with a number of subsidiaries located throughout the United Kingdom. Investor currently appraises investment opportunities using a cost of capital of 10 per cent.

On 1 April 20X9 Investor purchased 80 per cent of the equity share capital of Cornwall for a total cash price of $60m. Half the price was payable on 1 April 20X9; the balance was payable on 1 April 20Y1. The net identifiable assets that were actually included in the statement of financial position of Cornwall had a carrying value totalling $55m at 1 April 20X9. With the exception of the pension provision (see below), you discover that the fair values of the net identifiable assets of Cornwall at 1 April 20X9 are the same as their carrying values. When performing the fair-value exercise at 1 April 20X9, you discover that Cornwall has a defined-benefit pension scheme that was actuarially valued three years ago and found to be in deficit. As a result of that valuation, a provision of $6m has been built up in the statement of financial position. The fair-value exercise indicates that on 1 April 20X9, the pension scheme was in deficit by $11m. This information became available on 31 July 20X9.

Assume that today's date is 31 October 20X9. You are in the process of preparing the consolidated financial statements of the group for the year ended 30 September 20X9. Intangible assets are normally written off on a pro-rata basis over twenty years. Your financial director is concerned that profits for the year will be lower than originally anticipated. She is therefore wondering about changing the accounting policy used by the group, so that all intangible assets are treated as having an indefinite useful life.

Required

(a) Calculate the value of goodwill on acquisition of Cornwall in the consolidated accounts of Investor for the year ended 30 September 20X9. You should fully explain and justify all parts of the calculation. **(10 marks)**

(b) Write a memorandum to your financial director.

  (i) Evaluate the policy of writing off all intangible assets over twenty years

  (ii) Explain whether it is ever permissible to select a longer write-off period for intangible assets, and describe the future implications of selecting such a period **(10 marks)**

(c) Cornwall has purchased some valuable brands, which are included in the statement of financial position. Explain the justification for including purchased brands in the statement of financial position and how non-purchased brands should be treated. **(5 marks)**

(Total = 25 marks)

7 Radost **23 mins**

Radost, a public limited company, has a defined benefit pension plan for its staff. Staff are eligible for an annual pension between the date of their retirement and the date of their death equal to:

$$\text{Annual pension} = \frac{\text{Final salary per year}}{50} \times \text{years' service.}$$

You are given the following data relating to the year ended 31 December 20X3:

(a) Yield on high quality corporate bonds: 10% pa.

(b) Contributions paid by Radost to pension plan: $12 million

(c) Pensions paid to former employees: $8 million

(d) Current service cost was $3.75 million

(e) After consultation with employees, an amendment was agreed to the terms of the plan, reducing the benefits payable. The amendment takes effect from 31 December 20X3 and the actuary has calculated that the resulting reduction in the pension obligation is $6 million.

(f) NPV of the pension obligation at:

1.1.X3 – $45 million
31.12.X3 – $44 million (as given by the actuary, after adjusting for the plan amendment)

(g) Fair value of the plan assets, as valued by the actuary:

1.1.X3 – $52 million
31.12.X3 – $64.17 million

Required

(a) Produce the notes to the statement of financial position and statement of profit or loss and other comprehensive income in accordance with IAS 19. **(8 marks)**

(b) Explain why the pension plan assets are recognised in the financial statements of Radost, even though they are held in a separate legal trust for Radost's employees. **(4 marks)**

Notes:

1 Work to the nearest $1,000 throughout.

2 You should assume contributions and benefits were paid on the last day of the year.

(Total = 12 marks)

8 Clean — 49 mins

Clean prepares its financial statements in accordance with International Accounting Standards. On 25 June 20X0, Clean made a public announcement of a decision to reduce the level of emissions of harmful chemicals from its factories. The average useful lives of the factories on 30 June 20X0 (the accounting reference date) was 20 years. The depreciation of the factories is computed on a straight-line basis and charged to cost of sales. The directors formulated the proposals for emission reduction following agreement in principle earlier in the year.

The directors prepared detailed estimates of the costs of their proposals and these showed that the following expenditure would be required.

- $30 million on 30 June 20X1
- $30 million on 30 June 20X2
- $40 million on 30 June 20X3

All estimates were for the actual anticipated cash payments. No contracts were entered into until after 1 July 20X0. The estimate proved accurate as far as the expenditure due on 30 June 20X1 was concerned. When the directors decided to proceed with this project, they used discounted cash flow techniques to appraise the proposed investment. The annual discount rate they used was 8%. The entity has a reputation of fulfilling its financial commitments after it has publicly announced them. Clean included a provision for the expected costs of its proposal in its financial statements for the year ended 30 June 20X0.

Required

(a) Explain why there was a need for an accounting standard dealing with provisions, and summarise the criteria that need to be satisfied before a provision is recognised. **(10 marks)**

(b) Explain the decision of the directors of Clean to recognise the provision in the statement of financial position at 30 June 20X0. **(5 marks)**

(c) Compute the appropriate provision in the statements of financial position in respect of the proposed expenditure at 30 June 20X0 AND 30 June 20X1. **(4 marks)**

(d) Compute the two components of the charge to profit or loss in respect of the proposal for the year ended 30 June 20X1. You should explain how each component arises and identify where in the statements of profit or loss and other comprehensive income each component is reported. **(6 marks)**

(Total = 25 marks)

9 DT Group

49 mins

(a) IAS 12 *Income taxes* focuses on the statement of financial position in accounting for deferred taxation, which is calculated on the basis of temporary differences. The methods used in IAS 12 can lead to accumulation of large tax assets or liabilities over a prolonged period and this could be remedied by discounting these assets or liabilities. There is currently international disagreement over the discounting of deferred tax balances.

Required

(i) Explain what the terms 'focus on the statement of financial position' and 'temporary differences' mean in relation to deferred taxation. **(6 marks)**

(ii) Discuss the arguments for and against discounting long-term deferred tax balances. **(6 marks)**

(b) DT, a public limited company, has decided to adopt the provisions of IFRSs for the first time in its financial statements for the year ending 30 November 20X1. The amounts of deferred tax provided as set out in the notes of the group financial statements for the year ending 30 November 20X0 were as follows:

	$m
Tax depreciation in excess of accounting depreciation	38
Other temporary differences	11
Liabilities for health care benefits	(12)
Losses available for offset against future taxable profits	(34)
	3

The following notes are relevant to the calculation of the deferred tax liability as at 30 November 20X1:

(i) DT acquired a 100% holding in a foreign company on 30 November 20X1. The subsidiary does not plan to pay any dividends for the financial year to 30 November 20X1 or in the foreseeable future. The carrying amount in DT's consolidated financial statements of its investment in the subsidiary at 30 November 20X1 is made up as follows:

	$m
Carrying value of net assets acquired excluding deferred tax	76
Goodwill (before deferred tax and impairment losses)	14
Carrying amount/cost of investment	90

The tax base of the net assets of the subsidiary at acquisition was $60m. No deduction is available in the subsidiary's tax jurisdiction for the cost of the goodwill.

Immediately after acquisition on 30 November 20X1, DT had supplied the subsidiary with inventories amounting to $30m at a profit of 20% on selling price. The inventories had not been sold by the year end and the tax rate applied to the subsidiary's profit is 25%. There was no significant difference between the fair values and carrying values on the acquisition of the subsidiary.

(ii) The carrying amount of the property, plant and equipment (excluding that of the subsidiary) is $2,600m and their tax base is $1,920m. Tax arising on the revaluation of properties of $140m, if disposed of at their revalued amounts, is the same at 30 November 20X1 as at the beginning of the year. The revaluation of the properties is included in the carrying amount above.

Other taxable temporary differences (excluding the subsidiary) amount to $90m as at 30 November 20X1.

(iii) The liability for health care benefits in the statement of financial position had risen to $100m as at 30 November 20X1 and the tax base is zero. Health care benefits are deductible for tax purposes when payments are made to retirees. No payments were made during the year to 30 November 20X1.

(iv) DT Group incurred $300m of tax losses in 20X0. Under the tax law of the country, tax losses can be carried forward for three years only. The taxable profits for the years ending 30 November were anticipated to be as follows:

20X1	20X2	20X3
$m	$m	$m
110	100	130

The auditors are unsure about the availability of taxable profits in 20X3 as the amount is based upon the projected acquisition of a profitable company. It is anticipated that there will be no future reversals of existing taxable temporary differences until after 30 November 20X3.

(v) Income tax of $165m on a property disposed of in 20X0 becomes payable on 30 November 20X4 under the deferral relief provisions of the tax laws of the country. There had been no sales or revaluations of property during the year to 30 November 20X1.

(vi) Income tax is assumed to be 30% for the foreseeable future in DT's jurisdiction and the company wishes to discount any deferred tax liabilities at a rate of 4% if allowed by IAS 12.

(vii) There are no other temporary differences other than those set out above. The directors of DT have calculated the opening balance of deferred tax using IAS 12 to be $280m.

Required

Calculate the liability for deferred tax required by the DT Group at 30 November 20X1 and the deferred tax expense in profit or loss for the year ending 30 November 20X1 using IAS 12, commenting on the effect that the application of IAS 12 will have on the financial statements of the DT Group. **(13 marks)**

(Total = 25 marks)

10 PQR **20 mins**

PQR has the following financial instruments in its financial statements for the year ended 31 December 20X5:

(a) An investment in the debentures of STU, nominal value $40,000, purchased on their issue on 1 January 20X5 at a discount of $6,000 and carrying a 4% coupon. PQR plans to hold these until their redemption on 31 December 20X8. The internal rate of return of the debentures is 8.6%.

(b) A foreign currency forward contract purchased to hedge the commitment to purchase a machine in foreign currency six months after the year end.

(c) 100,000 redeemable preference shares issued in 20X0 at $1 per share with an annual dividend payment of 6 cents per share, redeemable in 20X8 at their nominal value.

Required

Advise the directors (insofar as the information permits) about the accounting for the financial instruments stating the effect of each on the gearing of the company. Your answer should be accompanied by calculations where appropriate.

(Total = 10 marks)

11 Hedging

A company owns 100,000 barrels of crude oil which were purchased on 1 July 20X2 at a cost of $26.00 per barrel.

In order to hedge the fluctuation in the market value of the oil the company signs a futures contract on the same date to deliver 100,000 barrels of oil on 31 March 20X3 at a futures price of $27.50 per barrel.

Due to unexpected increased production by OPEC, the market price of oil on 31 December 20X2 slumped to $22.50 per barrel and the futures price for delivery on 31 March 20X3 was $23.25 per barrel at that date.

Required

Explain the impact of the transactions on the financial statements of the company for the year ended 31 December 20X2.

12 Sirus (June 2008 Q3) **49 mins**

Sirus is a large national public limited company (plc). The directors' service agreements require each director to purchase 'B' ordinary shares on becoming a director and this capital is returned to the director on leaving the company. Any decision to pay a dividend on the 'B' shares must be approved in a general meeting by a majority of all of the shareholders in the company. Directors are the only holders of 'B' shares.

Sirus would like advice on how to account under International Financial Reporting Standards (IFRSs) for the following events in its financial statements for the year ended 30 April 20X8.

(a) The capital subscribed to Sirus by the directors and shareholders is shown as follows in the statement of financial position as at 30 April 20X8:

Equity

	$m
Ordinary 'A' shares	100
Ordinary 'B' shares	20
Retained earnings	30
Total equity	150

On 30 April 20X8 the directors had recommended that $3 million of the profits should be paid to the holders of the ordinary 'B' shares, in addition to the $10 million paid to directors under their employment contracts. The payment of $3 million had not been approved in a general meeting. The directors would like advice as to whether the capital subscribed by the directors (the ordinary 'B' shares) is equity or a liability and how to treat the payments out of profits to them. **(6 marks)**

(b) When a director retires, amounts become payable to the director as a form of retirement benefit as an annuity. These amounts are not based on salaries paid to the director under an employment contract. Sirus has contractual or constructive obligations to make payments to former directors as at 30 April 20X8 as follows.

(i) Certain former directors are paid a fixed annual amount for a fixed term beginning on the first anniversary of the director's retirement. If the director dies, an amount representing the present value of the future payment is paid to the director's estate.

(ii) In the case of other former directors, they are paid a fixed annual amount which ceases on death.

The rights to the annuities are determined by the length of service of the former directors and are set out in the former directors' service contracts. **(6 marks)**

(c) On 1 May 20X7 Sirus acquired another company, Marne plc. The directors of Marne, who were the only shareholders, were offered an increased profit share in the enlarged business for a period of two years after the date of acquisition as an incentive to accept the purchase offer. After this period, normal remuneration levels will be resumed. Sirus estimated that this would cost them $5 million at 30 April 20X8, and a further $6 million at 30 April 20X9. These amounts will be paid in cash shortly after the respective year ends. **(5 marks)**

(d) Sirus raised a loan with a bank of $2 million on 1 May 20X7. The market interest rate of 8% per annum is to be paid annually in arrears and the principal is to be repaid in 10 years time. The terms of the loan allow Sirus to redeem the loan after seven years by paying the interest to be charged over the seven year period, plus a penalty of $200,000 and the principal of $2 million. The effective interest rate of the repayment option is 9.1%. The directors of Sirus are currently restructuring the funding of the company and are in initial discussions with the bank about the possibility of repaying the loan within the next financial year. Sirus is uncertain about the accounting treatment for the current loan agreement and whether the loan can be shown as a current liability because of the discussions with the bank. **(6 marks)**

Appropriateness of the format and presentation of the report and quality of discussion **(2 marks)**

Required

Draft a report to the directors of Sirus which discusses the principles and nature of the accounting treatment of the above elements under International Financial Reporting Standards in the financial statements for the year ended 30 April 20X8.

(Total = 25 marks)

13 Eastway

(a) A contract is, or contains, a lease if the contract conveys the right to control the use of an identified asset for a period of time in exchange for consideration (IFRS 16: para.9).

Explain what is meant by 'control' in this context.

(b) Propfield Co, a property company, owns Eastway, a large shopping centre with a 30 units which it rents out to retailers.

Sellerwell Co enters into a contract with Propfield Co giving Sellerwell the right to use Unit 21 of Eastway for a four-year period.

The contract gives Propfield the right to require Sellerwell to move to another retail unit. However, if it does so, Propfield must pay for Sellerwell's relocation costs and provide Sellerwell with a retail unit of similar quality and specifications to Unit 21. The only reason Propfield would benefit economically from relocating Sellerwell is if a major new tenant were to decide to occupy a large amount of retail space at a rate high enough to cover the costs of relocating Sellerwell and other tenants in the retail space. While this scenario is possible, at inception of the contract, it is thought to be unlikely to occur.

Sellerwell must, under the contract, use Unit 21 to operate its well-known retail brand to sell its goods during the hours that the shopping centre is open. Sellerwell makes all of the decisions about how the retail unit is used. For example, Sellerwell decides on the mix of goods sold from the unit, the pricing of the goods sold and the quantities of inventory held. Sellerwell also controls physical access to the unit throughout the four-year period of use.

The contract requires Sellerwell to make fixed payments to Propfield, as well as variable payments that are a percentage of sales from Unit 21.

As part of the contract, Propfield provides marketing, cleaning and security services.

Required

Determine whether the contract between Propfield and Sellerwell contains a lease.

14 Vident (June 2005 Q2) 49 mins

The directors of Vident, a public limited company, are reviewing the impact of IFRS 2 *Share-based payment* on the financial statements for the year ended 31 May 20X5 as they will adopt the IFRS. However, the directors of Vident are unhappy about having to apply the standard and have put forward the following arguments as to why they should not recognise an expense for share-based payments.

(i) They feel that share options have no cost to their company and, therefore, there should be no expense charged in profit and loss.

(ii) They do not feel that the expense arising from share options under IFRS 2 actually meets the definition of an expense under the *Conceptual Framework* document.

(iii) The directors are worried about the dual impact of the IFRS on earnings per share, as an expense is shown in the income statement and the impact of share options is recognised in the diluted earnings per share calculation.

(iv) They feel that accounting for share-based payment may have an adverse effect on their company and may discourage it from introducing new share option plans.

The following share option schemes were in existence at 31 May 20X5:

Director's name	*Grant date*	*Options granted*	*Fair value of options at grant date* $	*Exercise price* $	*Performance conditions*	*Vesting date*	*Exercise date*
J. Van Heflin	1 June 20X3	20,000	5	4·50	A	6/20X5	6/20X6
R. Ashworth	1 June 20X4	50,000	6	6	B	6/20X7	6/20X8

The price of the company's shares at 31 May 20X5 is $12 per share and at 31 May 20X4 was $12·50 per share.

The performance conditions which apply to the exercise of executive share options are as follows:

Performance Condition A

The share options do not vest if the growth in the company's earnings per share (EPS) for the year is less than 4%.

The rate of growth of EPS was 4·5% (20X3), 4·1% (20X4), 4·2% (20X5). The directors must still work for the company on the vesting date.

Performance Condition B

The share options do not vest until the share price has increased from its value of $12·50 at the grant date (1 June 20X4) to above $13·50. The director must still work for the company on the vesting date.

No directors have left the company since the issue of the share options and none are expected to leave before June 20X7. The shares vest and can be exercised on the first day of the due month.

The directors are uncertain about the deferred tax implications of adopting IFRS 2. Vident operates in a country where a tax allowance will not arise until the options are exercised and the tax allowance will be based on the option's intrinsic value at the exercise date.

Assume a tax rate of 30%.

Required

Draft a report to the directors of Vident setting out:

(a) The reasons why share-based payments should be recognised in financial statements and why the directors' arguments are unacceptable **(9 marks)**

(b) A discussion (with suitable calculations) as to how the directors' share options would be accounted for in the financial statements for the year ended 31 May 20X5 including the adjustment to opening balances **(9 marks)**

(c) The deferred tax implications (with suitable calculations) for the company which arise from the recognition of a remuneration expense for the directors' share options **(7 marks)**

(Total = 25 marks)

15 Grow by acquisition

Expand is a large group that seeks to grow by acquisition. The directors of Expand have identified two potential target entities (A and B) and obtained copies of their financial statements. Extracts from these financial statements, together with notes providing additional information, are given below.

STATEMENTS OF PROFIT OR LOSS AND OTHER COMPREHENSIVE INCOME
YEAR ENDED 31 DECEMBER 20X1

	A	*B*
	$'000	$'000
Revenue	68,000	66,000
Cost of sales	(42,000)	(45,950)
Gross profit	26,000	20,050
Other operating expenses	(18,000)	(14,000)
Profit from operations	8,000	6,050
Finance cost	(3,000)	(4,000)
Profit before tax	5,000	2,050
Income tax expense	(1,500)	(1,000)
Profit for the year	3,500	1,050
Other comprehensive income (items that will not be reclassified to profit or loss) Surplus on revaluation of properties	NIL	6,000
Total comprehensive income	3,500	7,050

STATEMENTS OF CHANGES IN EQUITY
YEAR ENDED 31 DECEMBER 20X1

	A	*B*
	$'000	$'000
Balance at 1 January 20X1	22,000	16,000
Total comprehensive income for the year	3,500	7,050
Dividends paid	(2,000)	(1,000)
Balance at 31 December 20X1	23,500	22,050

STATEMENTS OF FINANCIAL POSITION AT 31 DECEMBER 20X1

	A		*B*	
	$'000	$'000	$'000	$'000
Non-current assets				
Property, plant and equipment	32,000		35,050	
		32,000		35,050
Current assets				
Inventories	6,000		7,000	
Trade receivables	12,000		10,000	
		18,000		17,000
		50,000		52,050
Equity				
Issued capital ($1 shares)		16,000		12,000
Revaluation reserve		Nil		5,000
Retained earnings		7,500		5,050
		23,500		22,050
Non-current liabilities				
Interest bearing borrowings		16,000		18,000
Current liabilities				
Trade payables	5,000		5,000	
Income tax	1,500		1,000	
Short-term borrowings	4,000		6,000	
		10,500		12,000
		50,000		52,050

Notes

1 *Sale by A to X*

On 31 December 20X1, A supplied goods, at the normal selling price of $2.4 million, to another entity, X. A's normal selling price is at a mark-up of 60% on cost. X paid for the goods in cash on the same day. The terms of the selling agreement were that A repurchase these goods on 30 June 20X2 for $2.5 million. A has accounted for the transaction as a sale.

2 *Revaluation of non-current assets by B*

B revalued its non-current assets for the first time on 1 January 20X1. The non-current assets of A are very similar in age and type to the non-current assets of B. However, A has a policy of maintaining all its non-current assets at depreciated historical cost. Both entities charge depreciation of non-current assets to cost of sales. B has transferred the excess depreciation on the revalued assets from the revaluation reserve to retained earnings as permitted in IAS 16 – *Property, plant and equipment.*

Expand uses ratio analysis to appraise potential investment opportunities. It is normal practice to base the appraisal on four key ratios.

- Return on capital employed
- Gross profit margin
- Turnover of capital employed
- Leverage

For the purposes of the ratio analysis, Expand computes:

(i) Capital employed as capital and reserves plus borrowings

(ii) Borrowings as interest–bearing borrowings plus short-term borrowings

Your assistant has computed the four key ratios for the two entities from the financial statements provided and the results are summarised below.

Ratio	*A*	*B*
Return on capital employed	18.4%	13.1%
Gross profit margin	38.2%	30.4%
Turnover of capital employed	1.6	1.4
Leverage	46.0%	52.1%

Your assistant has informed you that, on the basis of the ratios calculated, the performance of A is superior to that of B in all respects. Therefore, Expand should carry out a more detailed review of A with a view to making a bid to acquire it. However, you are unsure whether this is necessarily the correct conclusion given the information provided in Notes 1 and 2.

Required

(a) Explain and compute the adjustments that would be appropriate in respect of Notes 1 and 2 so as to make the financial statements of A and B comparable for analysis.

(b) Recalculate the four key ratios mentioned in the question for both A and B after making the adjustments you have recommended in your answer to part (a). You should provide appropriate workings to support your calculations.

(c) In the light of the work that you have carried out in answer to parts (a) and (b), evaluate your assistant's conclusion that a more detailed review of A should be carried out, with a view to making a bid to acquire it.

16 Ace

On 1 April 20X1, Ace Co owned 75% of the equity share capital of Deuce Co and 80% of the equity share capital of Trey Co. On 1 April 20X2, Ace Co purchased the remaining 25% of the equity shares of Deuce Co. In the two years ended 31 March 20X3, the following transactions occurred between the three companies:

(a) On 30 June 20X1 Ace Co manufactured a machine for use by Deuce Co. The cost of manufacture was $20,000. The machine was delivered to Deuce Co for an invoiced price of $25,000. Deuce Co paid the invoice on 31 August 20X1. Deuce Co depreciated the machine over its anticipated useful life of five years, charging a full year's depreciation in the year of purchase.

(b) On 30 September 20X2, Deuce Co sold some goods to Trey Co at an invoiced price of $15,000. Trey Co paid the invoice on 30 November 20X2. The goods had cost Deuce Co $12,000 to manufacture. By 31 March 20X3, Trey Co had sold all the goods outside the group.

(c) For each of the two years ended 31 March 20X3, Ace Co provided management services to Deuce Co and Trey Co. Ace Co did not charge for these services in the year ended 31 March 20X2 but in the year ended 31 March 20X3 decided to impose a charge of $10,000 per annum to Trey Co. The amount of $10,000 is due to be paid by Trey Co on 31 May 20X3.

Required

Summarise the related party disclosures which will be required in respect of transactions (a) to (c) above for both of the years ended 31 March 20X2 and 31 March 20X3 in the financial statements of Ace Co, Deuce Co and Trey Co.

Note. You may assume that Ace Co presents consolidated financial statements for both of the years dealt with in the question.

17 Highland **35 mins**

Highland owns two subsidiaries acquired as follows:

1 July 20X1 80% of Aviemore for $5 million when the book value of the net assets of Aviemore was $4 million.

30 November 20X7 65% of Buchan for $2.6 million when the book value of the net assets of Buchan was $3.35 million.

The companies' statements of profit or loss and other comprehensive income for the year ended 31 March 20X8 were:

	Highland	*Aviemore*	*Buchan*
	$'000	$'000	$'000
Revenue	5,000	3,000	2,910
Cost of sales	(3,000)	(2,300)	(2,820)
Gross profit	2,000	700	90
Administrative expenses	(1,000)	(500)	(150)
Other income	230	–	–
Finance costs		(50)	(210)
Profit/(loss) before tax	1,230	150	(270)
Income tax expense	(300)	(50)	–
PROFIT/(LOSS) FOR THE YEAR	930	100	(270)
Other comprehensive income that will not be reclassified to profit or loss, net of tax	130	40	120
TOTAL COMPREHENSIVE INCOME FOR THE YEAR	1,060	140	(150)
Dividends paid during the year	200	50	–

Additional information

(a) On 1 April 20X7, Buchan issued $2.1 million 10% loan stock to Highland. Interest is payable twice yearly on 1 October and 1 April. Highland has accounted for the interest received on 1 October 20X7 only.

(b) On 1 July 20X7, Aviemore sold a freehold property to Highland for $800,000 (land element – $300,000). The property originally cost $900,000 (land element – $100,000) on 1 July 20W7. The property's total useful life was 50 years on 1 July 20W7 and there has been no change in the useful life since. Aviemore has credited the profit on disposal to 'Administrative expenses'.

(c) The property, plant and equipment of Buchan on 30 November 20X7 was valued at $500,000 (book value $350,000) and was acquired in April 20X7. The property, plant and equipment has a total useful life of ten years. Buchan has not adjusted its accounting records to reflect fair values. The group accounting policy to measure non-controlling interests at the proportionate share of the fair value of net identifiable assets at acquisition.

(d) All companies use the straight-line method of depreciation and charge a full year's depreciation in the year of acquisition and none in the year of disposal. Depreciation on fair value adjustments is time apportioned from the date of acquisition.

(e) Highland charges Aviemore an annual fee of $85,000 for management services and this has been included in 'Other income'.

(f) Highland has accounted for its dividend received from Aviemore in 'Other income'.

(g) Impairment tests conducted at the year end revealed recoverable amounts of $7,040,000 for Aviemore and $3,700,000 for Buchan versus book values of net assets of $4,450,000 and $3,300,000 in the separate financial statements of Aviemore and Buchan respectively (adjusted for the effects of group fair value adjustments). No impairment losses had previously been recognised.

Required

Prepare the consolidated statements of profit or loss and other comprehensive income for Highland for the year ended 31 March 20X8.

(Total = 18 marks)

18 Armoury — 20 mins

Bayonet, a public limited company, purchased 6m shares in Rifle, a public limited company, on 1 January 20X5 for $10m. Rifle had purchased 4m shares in Pistol, a public limited company for $9m on 31 December 20X2 when its retained earnings stood at $5m. The balances on retained earnings of the acquired companies were $8m and $6.5m respectively at 1 January 20X5. The fair value of the identifiable assets and liabilities of Rifle and Pistol was equivalent to their book values at the acquisition dates.

The statements of financial position of the three companies as at 31 December 20X9 are as follows:

	Bayonet	*Rifle*	*Pistol*
	$'000	$'000	$'000
Non-current assets			
Property, plant and equipment	14,500	12,140	17,500
Investment in Rifle	10,000		
Investment in Pistol	–	9,000	–
	24,500	21,140	17,500
Current assets			
Inventories	6,300	2,100	450
Trade receivables	4,900	2,000	2,320
Cash	500	1,440	515
	11,700	5,540	3,285
	36,200	26,680	20,785
Equity			
50c ordinary shares	5,000	4,000	2,500
Retained earnings	25,500	20,400	16,300
	30,500	24,400	18,800
Current liabilities	5,700	2,280	1,985
	36,200	26,680	20,785

Group policy is to value non-controlling interests at fair value at acquisition. The fair value of the non-controlling interests in Rifle was calculated as $3,230,000 on 1 January 20X5. The fair value of the 40% non-controlling interests in Pistol on 1 January 20X5 was $4.6m.

Impairment tests in current and previous years did not reveal any impairment losses.

Required

Prepare the consolidated statement of financial position of Bayonet as at 31 December 20X9.

(Total = 10 marks)

19 Murder, Mystery and Suspense — 35 mins

On 1 January 20X3 Murder, a public limited company acquired 60% of Mystery, a public limited company. On 30 July 20X1 Murder acquired 10% of Suspense, a public limited company, and on the same day Mystery acquired 80% of Suspense.

The statements of financial position of the three companies as at 31 December 20X7 are as follows:

	Murder	*Mystery*	*Suspense*
	$'m	$'m	$'m
Non-current assets			
Property, plant and equipment	2,458	1,410	870
Investment in Mystery	900		
Investment in Suspense	27	240	–
	3,385	1,650	870
Current assets			
Inventories	450	200	260
Trade receivables	610	365	139
Cash	240	95	116
	1,300	660	515
	4,685	2,310	1,385
Equity			
Ordinary share capital	500	200	100
Share premium	250	120	50
Retained earnings	2,805	1,572	850
	3,555	1,892	1,000
Current liabilities			
Trade payables	1,130	418	385
	4,685	2,310	1,385

During the year, Mystery sold goods to Suspense of $260m including a mark-up of 25%. All of these goods remain in inventories at the year end.

The retained earnings of the three companies at the acquisition dates was:

	30.7.X1	*1.1.X3*
	$'m	$'m
Murder	1,610	1,860
Mystery	700	950
Suspense	40	100

The book values of the identifiable net assets at the acquisition date are equivalent to their fair values. The fair value of Murder's 10% holding in Suspense on 1 January 20X3 was $50m.

Murder and Mystery hold their investments in subsidiaries at cost in their separate financial statements. It is group policy to value the non-controlling interests at fair value at acquisition. The directors valued the non-controlling interests in Mystery at $536m and Suspense at $210m on 1 January 20X3.

No impairment losses have been necessary in the consolidated financial statements to date.

Required

Prepare the consolidated statement of financial position of Murder group as at 31 December 20X7.

(Total = 18 marks)

20 Burley (December 2009 Q3) — 49 mins

Burley, a public limited company, operates in the energy industry. It has entered into several arrangements with other entities as follows.

(a) Burley and Slite, a public limited company, jointly control an oilfield. Burley has a 60% interest and Slite a 40% interest and the companies are entitled to extract oil in these proportions. An agreement was signed on 1 December 20X8, which allowed for the net cash settlement of any over/under extraction by one company. The net cash settlement would be at the market price of oil at the date of settlement. Both parties have used this method of settlement before. 200,000 barrels of oil were produced up to 1 October 20X9 but none were produced after this up to 30 November 20X9 due to production difficulties. The oil was all sold to third parties at $100 per barrel. Burley has extracted 10,000 barrels more than the company's quota and Slite has under extracted by the same amount. The market price of oil at the year end of 30 November 20X9 was $105 per barrel. The excess oil extracted by Burley was settled on 12 December 20X9 under the terms of the agreement at $95 per barrel.

Burley had purchased oil from another supplier because of the production difficulties at $98 per barrel and has oil inventory of 5,000 barrels at the year end, purchased from this source. Slite had no inventory of oil. Neither company had oil inventory at 1 December 20X8. Selling costs are $2 per barrel.

Burley wishes to know how to account for the recognition of revenue, the excess oil extracted and the oil inventory at the year end. **(9 marks)**

(b) Burley also entered into an agreement with Jorge, a public limited company, on 1 December 20X8. Each of the companies holds one half of the equity in an entity, Wells, a public limited company, which operates offshore oil rigs. The contractual arrangement between Burley and Jorge establishes joint control of the activities that are conducted in Wells. The main feature of Wells's legal form is that Wells, not Burley or Jorge, has rights to the assets, and obligations for the liabilities, relating to the arrangement.

The terms of the contractual arrangement are such that:

(i) Wells owns the oil rigs. The contractual arrangement does not specify that Burley and Jorge have rights to the oil rigs.

(ii) Burley and Jorge are not liable in respect of the debts, liabilities or obligations of Wells. If Wells is unable to pay any of its debts or other liabilities or to discharge its obligations to third parties, the liability of each party to any third party will be limited to the unpaid amount of that party's capital contribution.

(iii) Burley and Jorge have the right to sell or pledge their interests in Wells

(iv) Each party receives a share of the income from operating the oil rig in accordance with its interest in Wells.

Burley wants to account for the interest in Wells by using the equity method, and wishes for advice on the matter.

The oilrigs of Wells started operating on 1 December 20W8, ie ten years before the agreement was signed, and are measured under the cost model. The useful life of the rigs is 40 years. The initial cost of the rigs was $240 million, which included decommissioning costs (discounted) of $20 million. At 1 December 20X8, the carrying amount of the decommissioning liability has grown to $32.6 million, but the net present value of decommissioning liability has decreased to $18.5 million as a result of the increase in the risk-adjusted discount rate from 5% to 7%. Burley is unsure how to account for the oilrigs in the financial statements of Wells for the year ended 30 November 20X9.

Burley owns a 10% interest in a pipeline, which is used to transport the oil from the offshore oilrig to a refinery on the land. Burley has joint control over the pipeline and has to pay its share of the maintenance costs. Burley has the right to use 10% of the capacity of the pipeline. Burley wishes to show the pipeline as an investment in its financial statements to 30 November 20X9.

(10 marks)

(c) Burley has purchased a transferable interest in an oil exploration licence. Initial surveys of the region designated for exploration indicate that there are substantial oil deposits present, but further surveys will be required in order to establish the nature and extent of the deposits. Burley also has to determine whether the extraction of the oil is commercially viable. Past experience has shown that the licence can increase substantially in value if further information becomes available as to the viability of the extraction of the oil. Burley wishes to capitalise the cost of the licence but is unsure as to whether the accounting policy is compliant with International Financial Reporting Standards. **(4 marks)**

Required

Discuss with suitable computations where necessary, how the above arrangements and events would be accounted for in the financial statements of Burley.

Professional marks will be awarded in this question for clarity and expression. **(2 marks)**

(Total = 25 marks)

21 Holmes & Deakin — 43 mins

Holmes, a public limited company, has owned 85% of the ordinary share capital of Deakin, a public limited company, for some years. The shares were bought for $255m and Deakin's reserves at the time of purchase were $20m.

On 28 February 20X3 Holmes sold 40m of the Deakin shares for $160m. The only entry made in respect of this transaction has been the receipt of the cash, which was credited to the 'investment in subsidiary' account. No dividends were paid by either entity in the period.

The following draft summarised financial statements are available:

STATEMENTS OF PROFIT OR LOSS AND OTHER COMPREHENSIVE INCOME
FOR THE YEAR TO 31 MAY 20X3

	Holmes	*Deakin*
	$m	$m
Profit before tax	130	60
Income tax expense	(40)	(20)
PROFIT FOR THE YEAR	90	40
Other comprehensive income, net of tax	20	10
TOTAL COMPREHENSIVE INCOME FOR THE YEAR	110	50

STATEMENTS OF FINANCIAL POSITION AS AT 31 MAY 20X3

	$m	$m
Non-current assets		
Property, plant and equipment	535	178
Investment in Deakin	95	–
	630	178
Current assets		
Inventories	320	190
Trade receivables	250	175
Cash	80	89
	650	454
	1,280	632
Equity		
Share capital $1 ordinary shares	500	200
Reserves	310	170
	810	370
Current liabilities		
Trade payables	295	171
Income tax payable	80	60
Provisions	95	31
	470	262
	1,280	632

No impairment losses have been necessary in the group financial statements to date.

Assume that the gain as calculated in the parent's separate financial statements will be subject to corporate income tax at a rate of 30% and that profit and other comprehensive income accrue evenly throughout the year.

Holmes elected to measure the non-controlling interests in Deakin at fair value at the date of acquisition. The fair value of the non-controlling interests in Deakin was $45m at the date of acquisition. No control premium was paid on acquisition.

Required

Prepare:

(a) The statement of profit or loss and other comprehensive income and a statement of changes in equity (total) of Holmes for the year ended 31 May 20X3 **(5 marks)**

(b) The consolidated statement of profit or loss and other comprehensive income of Holmes for the same period **(6 marks)**

(c) A consolidated statement of financial position as at 31 May 20X3 **(9 marks)**

(d) A consolidated statement of changes in equity (total) for the year ended 31 May 20X3 **(2 marks)**

(Total = 22 marks)

22 Ghorse **49 mins**

12/07, amended

Ghorse, a public limited company, operates in the fashion sector and had undertaken a group re-organisation during the current financial year to 30 September 20X7. As a result the following events occurred.

(a) Ghorse identified two manufacturing units, Cee and Gee, which it had decided to dispose of in a single transaction. These units comprised non-current assets only. One of the units, Cee, had been impaired prior to the financial year end on 30 September 20X7 and it had been written down to its recoverable amount of $35 million. The criteria in IFRS 5 *Non-current assets held for sale and discontinued operations*, for classification as held for sale had been met for Cee and Gee at 30 September 20X7. The following information related to the assets of the cash generating units at 30 September 20X7:

	Depreciated historical cost	*Fair value less costs of disposal and recoverable amount*	*Carrying value under IFRS*
	$m	$m	$m
Cee	50	35	35
Gee	70	90	70
	120	125	105

The fair value less costs of disposal had risen at the year end to $40 million for Cee and $95 million for Gee. The increase in the fair value less costs of disposal had not been taken into account by Ghorse. **(7 marks)**

(b) As a consequence of the re-organisation, and a change in government legislation, the tax authorities have allowed a revaluation of the non-current assets of the holding company for tax purposes to market value at 31 October 20X7. There has been no change in the carrying values of the non-current assets in the financial statements. The tax base and the carrying values after the revaluation are as follows:

	Carrying amount at 31 October 20X7	*Tax base at 31 October 20X7 after revaluation*	*Tax base at 31 October 20X7 before revaluation*
	$m	$m	$m
Property	50	65	48
Vehicles	30	35	28

Other taxable temporary differences amounted to $5 million at 31 October 20X7. Assume income tax is paid at 30%. The deferred tax provision at 31 October 20X7 had been calculated using the tax values before revaluation. **(6 marks)**

(c) A subsidiary company had purchased computerised equipment for $4 million on 31 October 20X6 to improve the manufacturing process. Whilst re-organising the group, Ghorse had discovered that the manufacturer of the computerised equipment was now selling the same system for $2.5 million. The projected cash flows from the equipment are:

		Cash flows
		$
Year ended 31 October	20X8	1.3
	20X9	2.2
	20Y0	2.3

The residual value of the equipment is assumed to be zero. The company uses a discount rate of 10%. The directors think that the fair value less costs of disposal of the equipment is $2 million. The directors of Ghorse propose to write down the non-current asset to the new selling price of $2.5 million. The company's policy is to depreciate its computer equipment by 25% per annum on the straight line basis. **(6marks)**

(d) The manufacturing property of the group, other than the head office, was held on an operating lease over eight years in accordance with IAS 17, the predecessor of IFRS 16 *Leases*. On re-organisation on 31 October 20X7, the lease has been renegotiated and is held for twelve years at a rent of $5 million per annum paid in arrears. IFRS 16 has also come into force The fair value of the property is $35 million and its remaining economic life is thirteen years. The lease relates to the buildings and not the land. The factor to be used for an annuity at 10% for 12 years is 6.8137. **(4 marks)**

The directors are worried about the impact that the above changes will have on the value of its non-current assets and its key performance indicator which is 'Return on Capital Employed' (ROCE). ROCE is defined as operating profit before interest and tax divided by share capital, other reserves and retained earnings. The directors have calculated ROCE as $30 million divided by $220 million, ie 13.6% before any adjustments required by the above.

Formation of opinion on impact on ROCE. **(2 marks)**

Required

Discuss the accounting treatment of the above transactions and the impact that the resulting adjustments to the financial statements would have on ROCE.

Note. Your answer should include appropriate calculations where necessary and a discussion of the accounting principles involved.

(Total = 25 marks)

23 Harvard **35 mins**

The draft financial statements of Harvard, a public limited company, and its subsidiary, Krakow sp. z o.o. are set out below.

STATEMENTS OF FINANCIAL POSITION AT 31 DECEMBER 20X5	*Harvard*	*Krakow*
	$'000	PLN'000
Non-current assets		
Property, plant and equipment	2,870	4,860
Investment in Krakow	840	–
	3,710	4,860
Current assets		
Inventories	1,990	8,316
Trade receivables	1,630	4,572
Cash	240	2,016
	3,860	14,904
	7,570	19,764
Equity		
Share capital ($1/PLN1)	118	1,348
Retained reserves	502	14,060
	620	15,408
Non-current liabilities		
Loans	1,920	–
Current liabilities		
Trade payables	5,030	4,356
	7,570	19,764

STATEMENTS OF PROFIT OR LOSS AND COMPREHENSIVE INCOME FOR THE YEAR ENDED 31 DECEMBER 20X5		
Revenue	40,425	97,125
Cost of sales	(35,500)	(77,550)
Gross profit	4,925	19,575
Distribution and administrative expenses	(4,400)	(5,850)
Investment income	720	–
Profit before tax	1,245	13,725
Income tax expense	(300)	(4,725)
PROFIT/TOTAL COMPREHENSIVE INCOME FOR THE YEAR	945	9,000
Dividends paid during the period	700	3,744

The following additional information is given:

(a) *Exchange rates*

	Zloty (PLN) to $
31 December 20X2	4.40
31 December 20X3	4.16
31 December 20X4	4.00
15 May 20X5	3.90
31 December 20X5	3.60
Average for 20X5	3.75

(b) Harvard acquired 1,011,000 shares in Krakow for $840,000 on 31 December 20X2 when Krakow's retained reserves stood at PLN 2,876,000. Krakow operates as an autonomous subsidiary. Its functional currency is the Polish zloty.

The fair value of the identifiable net assets of Krakow were equivalent to their book values at the acquisition date. Group policy is to measure non-controlling interests at fair value at the acquisition date. The fair value of the non-controlling interests in Krakow was measured at $270,000 on 31 December 20X2.

(c) Krakow paid an interim dividend of PLN 3,744,000 on 15 May 20X5. No other dividends were paid or declared in the period.

(d) No impairment losses were necessary in the consolidated financial statements by 31 December 20X5.

Required

(a) Prepare the consolidated statement of financial position at 31 December 20X5. **(6 marks)**

(b) Prepare the consolidated statements of profit or loss and other comprehensive income and an extract from the statement of changes in equity for retained reserves for the year ended 31 December 20X5. **(12 marks)**

Ignore deferred tax on translation differences.

(Total = 18 marks)

24 Porter **49 mins**

The following consolidated financial statements relate to Porter, a public limited company:

PORTER GROUP: STATEMENT OF FINANCIAL POSITION AS AT 31 MAY 20X6

	20X6	*20X5*
	$'m	$'m
Non-current assets		
Property, plant and equipment	958	812
Goodwill	15	10
Investment in associate	48	39
	1,021	861
Current assets		
Inventories	154	168
Trade receivables	132	112
Financial assets at fair value through profit or loss	16	0
Cash and cash equivalents	158	48
	460	328
	1,481	1,189
Equity attributable to owners of the parent		
Share capital ($1 ordinary shares)	332	300
Share premium account	212	172
Retained earnings	188	165
Revaluation surplus	101	54
	833	691
Non-controlling interests	84	28
	917	719
Non-current liabilities		
Long-term borrowings	380	320
Deferred tax liability	38	26
	418	346
Current liabilities		
Trade and other payables	110	98
Interest payable	8	4
Current tax payable	28	22
	146	124
	1,481	1,189

PORTER GROUP: STATEMENT OF PROFIT OR LOSS AND OTHER COMPREHENSIVE INCOME FOR THE YEAR ENDED 31 MAY 20X6

	$'m
Revenue	956
Cost of sales	(634)
Gross profit	322
Other income	6
Distribution costs	(97)
Administrative expenses	(115)
Finance costs	(16)
Share of profit of associate	12
Profit before tax	112
Income tax expense	(34)
PROFIT FOR THE YEAR	78
Other comprehensive income:	
Items that will not be reclassified to profit or loss:	
Gains on property revaluation	58
Share of gain on property revaluation of associate	8
Income tax relating to items that will not be reclassified	(17)
Other comprehensive income for the year, net of tax	49
TOTAL COMPREHENSIVE INCOME FOR THE YEAR	127
Profit attributable to:	
Owners of the parent	68
Non-controlling interests	10
	78
Total comprehensive income attributable to:	
Owners of the parent	115
Non-controlling interests	12
	127

The following information relates to the consolidated financial statements of Porter:

1 During the period, Porter acquired 60% of a subsidiary. The purchase was effected by issuing shares of Porter on a 1 for 2 basis, at their market value on that date of $2.25 per share, plus $26m in cash.

A statement of financial position of the subsidiary, prepared at the acquisition date for consolidation purposes showed the following position:

	$'m
Property, plant and equipment	92
Inventories	20
Trade receivables	16
Cash and cash equivalents	8
	136
Share capital ($1 shares)	80
Reserves	40
	120
Trade payables	12
Income taxes payable	4
	136

An impairment test conducted at the year end, resulted in a write-down of goodwill relating to another wholly owned subsidiary. This was charged to cost of sales.

Group policy is to value non-controlling interests at the date of acquisition at the proportionate share of the fair value of the acquiree's identifiable assets acquired and liabilities assumed.

2 Depreciation charged to the consolidated profit or loss amounted to $44m. There were no disposals of property, plant and equipment during the year.

3 Other income represents gains on financial assets at fair value through profit or loss. The financial assets are investments in quoted shares. They were purchased shortly before the year end with surplus cash, and were designated at fair through profit loss as they are expected to be sold after the year end. No dividends have yet been received.

4 Included in 'trade and other payables' is the $ equivalent of an invoice for 102m shillings for some equipment purchased from a foreign supplier. The asset was invoiced on 5 March 20X6, but had not been paid for at the year end, 31 May 20X6.

Exchange gains or losses on the transaction have been included in administrative expenses. Relevant exchange rates were as follows:

	Shillings to $1
5 March 20X6	6.8
31 May 20X6	6.0

5 Movement on retained earnings was as follows:

	$'m
At 31 May 20X5	165
Total comprehensive income	68
Dividends paid	(45)
At 31 May 20X6	188

Required

Prepare a consolidated statement of cash flows for Porter for the year ended 31 May 20X6 in accordance with IAS 7 *Statements of cash flows*, using the indirect method.

Notes to the statement of cash flows are not required.

(Total = 25 marks)

25 German competitor

You are the chief accountant of Tone plc, a UK company. The managing director has provided you with the financial statements of Tone plc's main competitor, Hilde GmbH, a German company. He finds difficulty in reviewing these statements in their non-UK format, presented below.

HILDE GmbH

STATEMENT OF FINANCIAL POSITION AS AT 31 MARCH 20X5 (in € million)

	31.3.X5	*31.3.X4*		*31.3.X5*	*31.3.X4*
ASSETS			CAPITAL AND LIABILITIES		
Tangible non-current assets			Capital and reserves		
Land	1,000	750	Share capital	850	750
Buildings	750	500	Share premium	100	–
Plant	200	150	Legal reserve	200	200
	1,950	1,400	Profit & loss b/fwd	590	300
			Profit & loss for year	185	290
Current assets			NET WORTH	1,925	1,540
Inventory	150	120			
Trade receivables	180	100	Payables		
Cash	20	200	Trade payables	170	150
	350	420	Taxation	180	150
			Other payables	75	50
Prepayments and accrued income				425	350
Prepayments	50	70			
	2,350	1,890		2,350	1,890

HILDE GmbH
STATEMENT OF PROFIT OR LOSS AND OTHER COMPREHENSIVE INCOME
FOR THE YEAR ENDED 31 MARCH 20X5 (in € million)

	20X5	*20X4*
EXPENSES		
Operating expenses:		
Purchase of raw materials	740	400
Variation in inventories thereof	90	40
Taxation	190	125
Wages	500	285
Valuation adjustment on non-current assets: depreciation	200	150
Valuation adjustment on current assets: amounts written off	30	20
Other operating expenses	50	40
Total operating expenses	1,800	1,060
Financial expenses		
Interest	100	50
Total financial expenses	100	50
TOTAL EXPENSES	1,900	1,110
Balance: PROFIT	185	290
SUM TOTAL	2,085	1,400

	20X5	*20X4*
INCOME		
Operating income:		
Sale of goods produced	1,890	1,270
Variation in inventory of finished goods and WIP	120	80
Other operating income	75	50
Total operating income	2,085	1,400
TOTAL INCOME	2,085	1,400
	2,085	1,400

Required

Prepare a report for the managing director:

(a) Analysing the performance of Hilde GmbH using the financial statements provided.

(b) Explaining why a direct comparison of the results of Tone plc and Hilde GmbH may be misleading.

26 Public sector organisations

The laws, regulations and guidelines relating to public sector accounts are rather different from those which apply to private sector organisations. As far as public sector organisations are concerned:

(a) State why these differences exist

(b) Explain the main differences

(c) Outline the consequences for public sector accounts

(d) State how the business aims and objectives would differ between:

(i) A stock market quoted clothes retailer

(ii) A state-funded hospital run as a not-for-profit organisation

(e) Biltshire Health Authority is considering adopting IFRS in place of cash accounting. Briefly explain the potential effect of the change in respect of:

(i) Provisions

(ii) Leases

27 Small and medium-sized entities — 49 mins

In July 2009, the IASB issued its *IFRS for SMEs*. The aim of the standard is to provide a simplified, self-contained set of accounting principles for companies which are not publicly accountable. The IFRS reduces the volume of accounting guidance applicable to SMEs by more than 90% when compared to a full set of IFRSs.

Required

(a) Discuss the advantages and disadvantages of SMEs following a separate *IFRS for SMEs* as opposed to full IFRSs. **(10 marks)**

The *IFRS for SMEs* removes choices of accounting treatment, eliminates topics that are not generally relevant to SMEs, simplifies methods for recognition and measurement and reduces the disclosure requirements of full IFRSs.

Required

(b) Give some examples from full IFRSs with choice or complex recognition and measurement requirements. Explain how the *IFRS for SME* removes this choice or simplifies the recognition and measurement requirements. **(13 marks)**

Appropriateness and quality of discussion **(2 marks)**

(Total = 25 marks)

28 Peter Holdings

Peter Holdings is a large investment conglomerate.

Required

Explain how divisional performance should be measured in the interest of the group's shareholders.

29 Planet — 49 mins

Planet has provided the following draft consolidated statement of financial position as at 30 November 20X2.

PLANET
GROUP STATEMENT OF FINANCIAL POSITION AS AT 30 NOVEMBER 20X2

	$'000
Non-current assets	
Property, plant and equipment	76,240
Intangible assets	10,360
	86,600
Net current assets	55,800
Total assets less current liabilities	142,400
Equity	
Share capital	32,200
Share premium account	10,000
Retained earnings	54,800
	97,000
Non-controlling interest	18,200
Non-current liabilities	
Long-term borrowings	25,400
Provisions	1,800
	142,400

The group accountant has asked your advice on several matters. These issues are set out below and have not been dealt with in the draft group financial statements.

(i) Planet purchased a wholly owned subsidiary company, Moon, on 1 December 20X0. The purchase consideration was based on the performance of the subsidiary. The vendors commenced a legal action on 31 March 20X2 over the amount of the purchase consideration. An amount had been paid to the vendors and included in the calculation of goodwill but the vendors disputed the amount of this payment. On 30 November 20X2 the court ruled that Planet should pay an additional $16 million to the vendors. The directors do not know how to treat the additional purchase consideration and have not accounted for the item.

Note. Ignore the effect of the time value of money.

(ii) Planet has corporate offices under a lease. A requirement of the lease for the buildings is that the asset is returned in good condition. The lease was signed in the current year and lasts for six years. Planet intends to refurbish the building in six years' time at a cost of $12 million in order to meet the requirements of the lease. This amount includes the renovation of the exterior of the building and is based on current price levels. Currently there is evidence that due to exceptionally severe weather damage the company will have to spend $2.4 million in the next year on having the exterior of the building renovated. The company feels that this expenditure will reduce the refurbishment cost at the end of the lease by an equivalent amount. There is no provision for the above expenditure in the financial statements.

An 80% owned subsidiary company, Galaxy, has a leasehold property (depreciated historical cost $16 million). It has been modified to include a swimming pool for the employees. Under the terms of the lease, the property must be restored to its original state when the lease expires in ten years' time or earlier termination. The present value of the costs of reinstatement are likely to be $4 million and the directors wish to provide for $400,000 per annum for ten years. The lease was signed and operated from 1 December 20X1. The directors estimate that the lease has a recoverable value of $19 million at 30 November 20X2 and have not provided for any of the above amounts.

Additionally, Planet owns buildings at a carrying value of $40 million which will require repair expenditure of approximately $12 million over the next five years. There is no provision for this amount in the financial statements. Depreciation is charged on owned buildings at 5% per annum and on leasehold buildings at 10% per annum on the straight line basis.

(iii) On 1 December 20X1, Planet entered into an agreement with a wholly owned overseas subsidiary, Dimanche, to purchase components at a value of 4.2 million krona on which Dimanche made a profit of 20% on selling price. The goods were to be delivered on 31 January 20X2 with the payment due on 31 March 20X2. Planet took out a foreign currency contract on 1 December 20X0 to buy 4.2 million krona on 31 March 20X1 at the forward rate of $1 = 1.4 krona.

At 30 November 20X2, Planet had two-thirds of the components in inventory. The spot rates were as follows.

$1 equivalent	
1 December 20X1	1.3 krona
31 January 20X2	1.46 krona
31 March 20X2	1.45 krona
30 November 20X2	1.35 krona

The initial purchase of the inventory had been recorded on receipt at the forward rate and the forward rate had been used for the year end valuation of inventory. The directors are unsure as to how to treat the items above both for accounting and disclosure purposes but they have heard that the simplest method is to translate the asset and liability at the forward rate and they wish to use this method.

(iv) Galaxy has developed a database during the year to 30 November 20X2 and it is included in intangible non-current assets at a cost of $6 million. The asset comprises the internal and external costs of developing the database. The database is used to produce a technical computing manual which is used by the whole group and sold to other parties. It has quickly become a market leader in this field. Any costs of maintaining the database and the computing manual are written off as incurred. Sales of the manual are expected to general net revenue of $4m. The computing manual requires substantial revision every four years.

Required

(a) Explain how the above four issues should be dealt with in the consolidated financial statements of Planet. Show the accounting entries that need to be made. **(19 marks)**

(b) Prepare a revised group statement of financial position at 30 November 20X2 taking into account the four issues discussed in part (a). **(6 marks)**

(Total = 25 marks)

30 Jay

98 mins

(a) Jay, a public limited company, has acquired the following shareholdings in Gee and Hem, both public limited companies.

Date of Acquisition	*Holding acquired*	*Fair value of net assets*	*Purchase consideration*
Gee		$m	$m
1 June 20X3	30%	40	15
1 June 20X4	50%	50	30
Hem			
1 June 20X4	25%	32	12

The following statements of financial position relate to Jay, Gee and Hem at 31 May 20X5.

	Jay	*Gee*	*Hem*
	$m	$m	$m
Property, plant and equipment	300	40	30
Investment in Gee	52		
Investment in Hem	22		
Current assets	100	20	15
Total assets	474	60	45
Share capital of $1	100	10	6
Share premium account	50	20	14
Revaluation surplus	15		
Retained earnings	139	16	10
Total equity	304	46	30
Non-current liabilities	60	4	3
Current liabilities	110	10	12
Total equity and liabilities	474	60	45

The following information is relevant to the preparation of the group financial statements of the Jay Group.

(i) Gee and Hem have not issued any new share capital since the acquisition of the shareholdings by Jay. The excess of the fair value of the net assets of Gee and Hem over their carrying amounts at the dates of acquisition is due to an increase in the value of Gee's non-depreciable land of $10 million at 1 June 20X3 and a further increase of $4 million at 1 June 20X4, and Hem's non-depreciable land of $6 million at 1 June 20X4. There has been no change in the value of non-depreciable land since 1 June 20X4. Before obtaining control of Gee, Jay did not have significant influence over Gee but has significant influence over Hem. Jay has accounted for the investment in Gee at fair value with changes being recorded in profit or loss. The market price of the shares of Gee at 31 May 20X5 had risen to $6.50 per share as there was speculation regarding a takeover bid.

(ii) On 1 June 20X4, Jay sold goods costing $13 million to Gee for $19 million. Gee has used the goods in constructing a machine which began service on 1 December 20X4. Additionally, on 31 May 20X5, Jay purchased a portfolio of investments from Hem at a cost of $10 million on which Hem had made a profit of $2 million. These investments have been incorrectly included in Jay's statement of financial position under the heading 'Investment in Hem'.

(iii) Jay sold some machinery with a carrying value of $5 million on 28 February 20X5 for $8 million. The terms of the contract, which was legally binding from 28 February 20X5, was that the purchaser would pay a non-refundable initial deposit of $2 million followed by two instalments of $3·5 million (including total interest of $1 million) payable on 31 May 20X5 and 20X6. The purchaser was in financial difficulties at the year end and subsequently went into liquidation on 10 June 20X5. No payment is expected from the liquidator. The deposit had been received on 28 February 20X5 but the first instalment was not received. The terms of the agreement were such that Jay maintained title to the machinery until the first instalment was paid. The machinery was still physically held by Jay and the machinery had been treated as sold in the financial statements. The amount outstanding of $6 million is included in current assets and no interest has been accrued in the financial statements.

(iv) Group policy on depreciation of plant and equipment is that depreciation of 10% is charged on a reducing balance basis.

(v) There are no intra-group amounts outstanding at 31 May 20X5.

(vi) It is the group's policy to value the non-controlling interest on acquisition at fair value. The fair value at the non-controlling interest in Gee on 1 July 20X4 was $12m.

Required

Prepare the consolidated statement of financial position of the Jay Group as at 31 May 20X5 in accordance with International Financial Reporting Standards.

(Candidates should calculate figures to one decimal place of $ million.) **(35 marks)**

(b) In the year ended 31 May 20X6 Jay purchased goods from a foreign supplier for 8 million euros on 28 February 20X6. At 31 May 20X6, the trade payable was still outstanding and the goods were still held by Jay. Similarly Jay has sold goods to a foreign customer for 4 million euros on 28 February 20X6 and it received payment for the goods in euros on 31 May 20X6. Additionally Jay had purchased an investment property on 1 June 20X5 for 28 million euros. At 31 May 20X6, the investment property had a fair value of 24 million euros. The company uses the fair value model in accounting for investment properties.

Jay would like advice on how to treat this transaction in the financial statements for the year ended 31 May 20X6. Its functional and presentation currency is the dollar.

Exchange rates	*Euro: $*	*Average rate (Euro: $) for year to*
1 June 20X5	1.4	
28 February 20X6	1.6	
31 May 20X6	1.3	1.5

(8 marks)

(c) Jay has a reputation for responsible corporate behaviour and sees the workforce as the key factor in the profitable growth of the business. The company is also keen to provide detailed disclosures relating to environmental matters and sustainability.

Discuss what matters should be disclosed in Jay's annual report in relation to the nature of corporate citizenship, in order that there might be a better assessment of the performance of the company. **(7 marks)**

(Total = 50 marks)

1 Conceptual Framework

(a) The stated **purposes** of the *Conceptual Framework* are as follows.

(i) To assist the Board in the development of future IFRSs and in its review of existing IFRSs.

(ii) To assist the Board in promoting harmonisation of regulations, accounting standards and procedures by reducing the number of alternative accounting treatment permitted by IFRSs.

(iii) To assist national standard-setting bodies in developing national standards.

(iv) To assist preparers of financial statements in applying IFRSs and in dealing with topics that have yet to form the subject of an IFRS.

(v) To assist auditors in forming an opinion on whether financial statements comply with IFRSs.

(vi) To assist users of financial statements in interpreting the information contained in financial statements prepared in compliance with IFRSs.

(vii) To provide those who are interested in the work of the IASB with information about its approach to the formulation of IFRSs.

(b) The people who might be **interested** in financial information about the company may be classified as follows.

(i) **Shareholders in the company**. They will be interested in the company's profitability and its ability to pay dividends. They will also be interested in the company's long term prospects.

(ii) **Managers of the company**. These are people appointed by the company's owners to supervise the day-to-day activities of the company. They need information about the company's financial situation as it is currently and as it is expected to be in the future. This is to enable them to manage the business efficiently and to take effective control and planning decisions.

(iii) **Trade contacts**, including suppliers who provide goods to the company on credit and customers who purchase the goods or services provided by the company. Suppliers will want to know about the company's ability to pay its debts; customers need to know that the company is a secure source of supply and is in no danger of having to close down.

(iv) **Providers of finance to the company.** These might include a bank which permits the company to operate an overdraft, or provides longer-term finance by granting a loan. The bank will want to ensure that the company is able to keep up with interest payments, and eventually to repay the amounts advanced.

(v) **The taxation authorities**, who will want to know about business profits in order to assess the tax payable by the company on its profits and any sales taxes.

(vi) **Employees of the company**. These should have a right to information about the company's financial situation, because their future careers and the size of their wages and salaries depend on it.

2 Fundamental principles

Tutorial note. Don't let this scenario panic you in the long list of details it gives you. Deal with each point as it arises. Also, don't be afraid to draw a conclusion about the facts given to you, but remember to back your opinions up with justification. Consider what the fundamental principles and general guidance of the ACCA say, but also think about practical issues, such as ease of modern communication. Deal with the two issues raised in the scenario (the individual partner issue and the firm split) separately, there is no need to assume any connection between them. However, you may feel there is a point to be made about the juxtaposition of the two events.

Independence

It is important that auditors are, and are seen to be, independent. **Independence** is at the heart of the auditing profession as auditors claim to give an **impartial, objective** opinion on the truth and fairness of the financial statements.

Objectivity

A **family relationship** between an auditor and the client **can substantially affect the objectivity** of the audit, so auditors are advised not to build close personal relationships with audit clients and should not audit a company where family are employed in a capacity which is sensitive to the accounts, for example, in the finance department, although this is **not prohibited by law**.

In this instance, the **partner was not the reporting partner** for the audit client in which his brother-in-law was a financial controller. According to generally accepted ethical practice then, the firm appeared to be independent of the audit client if the related partner did not have anything to do with the audit.

Resolution?

The regulatory body required the audit partner to move 400 miles. This presumably implies that the partner was requested to change offices within the firm by which he was employed. Given current levels of computer networking and other **communications** common in business, this would appear to be an **arbitrary distinction**, as a partner in an office 400 miles away could have similar access and influence over a single audit carried out by the firm as a partner in the locality.

Independence in appearance

However, in this situation, the regulatory body appear to be concerned about the appearance of independence. They appear to be concerned that the public will not perceive the distinction between a partner and a partner who reports on a specific engagement. This may or may not be fair. Arguably, it is only in publicising the problem that the public are likely to have a perception at all.

Also, given the comments made about modern communications above, the public are unlikely to be convinced that moving a member of staff to a different office will solve this independence problem, if they perceive that there is one.

Split of audit firm

The decision of the firm to split into three divisions could **enhance the public perception of the independence of the audit department**. While there might be **underlying scepticism** relating to the reasons behind the split (which could merely be for marketing purposes or to enable non-audit divisions to raise capital more easily), the **underlying benefit for objectivity still exists**.

However, some audit clients will be unhappy with the move of the firm as it will entail their appointing several different service providers to gain the services they previously got from the one audit firm.

3 Tree

(a) IFRS 15 *Revenue from contracts with customers* states the following:

Revenue is recognised when (or as) a performance obligation is satisfied. The entity satisfies a performance obligation by transferring **control** of a promised good or service to the customer. A performance obligation can be satisfied **at a point in time**, such as when goods are delivered to the customer, or **over time**. An obligation satisfied **over time** will meet one of the following criteria:

- The customer simultaneously receives and consumes the benefits as the performance takes place.
- The entity's performance creates or enhances an asset that the customer controls as the asset is created or enhanced.
- The entity's performance does not create an asset with an alternative use to the entity and the entity has an enforceable right to payment for performance completed to date.

The amount of revenue recognised is the amount allocated to that performance obligation. An entity must be able to **reasonably measure** the outcome of a performance obligation before the related revenue can be recognised. In some circumstances, such as in the early stages of a contract, it may not be possible to reasonably measure the outcome of a performance obligation, but the entity expects to recover the costs incurred. In these circumstances, revenue is recognised only to the extent of costs incurred.

(b) **Transaction 1**

Tree has the option to repurchase the property but cannot be required to do so. This is a call option in which the repurchase price is equal to or above the original selling price, so it should be accounted for as a financing arrangement.

Tree has not transferred control of the property to the bank as it still has the right to exercise this option, so no performance obligation has been satisfied which could justify the recognition of revenue.

The transaction is essentially a **loan secured on the property**, rather than an outright sale. The $50,000 payable for each month that the bank holds the property is **interest** on the loan.

The property **remains in the consolidated statement of financial position** at its cost or market value (depending on the accounting policy adopted by Tree). The **loan** of $5 million and **accrued interest** of $300,000 (6 × 50,000) are reported under **non-current liabilities**. Interest of $300,000 is recognised in consolidated profit or loss.

Transaction 2

The key issue is whether Tree **has transferred control** of the branch.

Tree **continues to control the operations** of the branch and the amount that it receives from Vehicle is the operating profit of the branch less the interest payable on the loan. Tree also suffers the effect of any operating losses made by the branch. Therefore, the **position is essentially the same as before** the 'sale' and Tree has not satisfied any performance obligation in return for the consideration of $8 million.

Although Vehicle is not a subsidiary of Tree plc as defined by IFRS 10 *Consolidated financial statements,* it is a special purpose entity (**quasi-subsidiary**). It gives rise to benefits for Tree that are in substance no different from those that would arise if it were a subsidiary. Its assets, liabilities, income and expenses **must be included** in the consolidated financial statements.

The assets and liabilities of Vehicle are included in the consolidated statement of financial position at $7 million (their original value to the group). The loan of $8 million is recognised as a non-current liability. The profit on disposal of $1 million and the operating fee of $1,200,000 are cancelled as intra-group transactions. The operating profit of $2,000,000 is included in consolidated profit or loss as is the loan interest of $800,000.

4 Camel Telecom

(a) The licence is an intangible asset accounted for under IAS 38 *Intangible assets*.

Given that the market value on the date of acquisition was more than the amount paid by Camel, a government grant has been given.

This means that the asset is normally initially recognised at its market value of $370m, showing the difference between the market value and amount paid ($26m) as deferred income. Alternatively the asset can be recognised at its cost of $344m.

Given that it has a limited rather than indefinite useful life it will be amortised over the 10 year licence period to a zero residual value. Any deferred income will be amortised as a credit to profit or loss over the same period and disclosed divided between its current and non-current portions in the statement of financial position.

Either way the annual effect on profit or loss is a charge of $34.4m (either $344m/10 or $370m/10 less a credit of $26m/10).

The lower take up of 3.5G services is an impairment indicator and so an impairment test must be undertaken at the year end. However, after taking into account amortisation for the period, the net book value of the asset at the year end is $309.6m ($344m – $34.4m) or $333m ($370m – $37m) if initially measured at fair value due to the grant). Therefore the asset is not impaired.

The asset cannot be revalued upwards to $335m because IAS 38 requires an active market to exist for revaluation of intangible assets and, despite the fact that the licence can be sold, there is no active market in these four licences due to their nature. An active market is defined as a market in which transactions for the particular asset take place with sufficient frequency and volume to provide pricing information on an ongoing basis. This is not the case as there are only four licences.

(b) Camel's intention is to use the land for its new head office. Therefore it does not meet the definition of investment property under IAS 40 *Investment Property*:

'property held to earn rentals or for capital appreciation or both, **rather than for**:

- Use in the production or supply of goods or services or for administrative purposes, or
- Sale in the ordinary course of business.'

This is confirmed by IAS 40 para 9(c). Therefore the land is held under IAS 16 *Property, Plant and Equipment* and is initially recorded at its cost of $10.4m. Being land, ordinarily it would not be depreciated.

The land can either be held under the cost model or revaluation model depending on Camel's accounting policy which applies to **all** of its land as a class.

If revalued, the fair value measurement of the land should take into account a market participant's ability to generate economic benefits by using the asset in its **highest and best use** or by selling it to another market participant that would use the asset in its highest and best use. The highest and best use of an asset takes into account the use that is physically possible, **legally permissible** and financially feasible. At the current year end, as planning permission has not been granted, use for development is not legally permissible so the value of $14.3m cannot be used. If Camel's policy is to revalue its land, it can be revalued to $10.6m at the year end, ie its value as farmland. The gain of $0.2m ($10.6m – $10.4m) would be reported in other comprehensive income.

(c) The land is also used for the supply or services and therefore meets the definition of property, plant and equipment. However, if the portion leased to other parties is separate and could be sold separately, that portion could be treated separately as investment property.

Camel therefore has the option of using the cost model (for both property, plant and equipment and investment property portions) or the revaluation model (for the property, plant and equipment portion) or the fair value model (for the investment property portion). This depends on Camel's underlying accounting policy.

Given that the sites have increased substantially in value, this would result in gains in other comprehensive income (for the property, plant and equipment portion) or profit or loss (for the investment property portion) if the revaluation/fair value models are used for the property, plant and equipment/investment property portions respectively. Any rental income is credited to profit or loss (assuming that they are operating leases under IFRS 16 *Leases* as it applies to lessors).

Any portion of land held under the fair value model is not depreciated, whereas any other scenario is theoretically subject to depreciation, but as land generally has an unlimited useful life, no depreciation would ordinarily be necessary.

(d) An exchange transaction has occurred here. Under IAS 16 *Property, plant and equipment* and IAS 38 *Intangible assets* which cover exchanges of tangible and intangible assets, the cost of the new asset is measured at fair value, unless the transaction lacks commercial substance, which does not appear to be the case here, as the assets given up relate to different products to those acquired, ie landline vs mobile businesses.

The best indication of the fair value of the assets acquired is the fair value of the non-monetary assets given up ($320m) plus the monetary consideration of $980m. A gain or loss is therefore reported in Camel's financial statements on derecognition of its fixed line ADSL business comparing the selling price ($320m) with net book value.

Part of the $980m paid to Purple includes the value of the Purple brand (ie its customer base and their loyalty and the brand recognition in the market). The brand must be given up after 1 year it will have no value to Camel in that country at that time. However, during the period of re-branding from Purple to Mobistar, the brand still has a value

Consequently a fair value should be attributed to the brand during the acquisition accounting and the brand should be amortised to a residual value of zero over the next year.

(e) The Mobistar brand is internally generated as it developed the brand itself. Therefore, under IAS 38 *Intangible assets*, the brand cannot be recognised in the financial statements of Camel as its value is deemed not to be able to be measured on a reliable basis.

Camel should analyse further the impact of the stolen customer details. An impairment test may be necessary on Camel's national business if customers are leaving beyond what had been expected in normal market conditions. Further, a provision may be necessary for a fine over the loss of private data under national law since the event occurred before the year end, which would be considered the obligating event for fines under IAS 37 *Provisions, contingent liabilities and contingent assets*. Disclosure would also need to be made of the nature of the incident/provision and uncertainty over the amount of any fine accrued.

5 Acquirer

Top tips. This question tests students' ability to apply the principles of IFRS 3 and IAS 36. In Part (d) you should have computed the value in use of the relevant net assets. This involved allocating assets into cash generating units. In Part (e) you needed to allocate this impairment loss by computing the carrying value of the goodwill and therefore of the total carrying value of the individual subsidiary. The whole impairment loss was allocated to goodwill. Remember that the impairment review has to be done in two stages.

(a) To determine whether impairment of a non-current asset has occurred, it is necessary to compare the carrying amount of the asset with its **recoverable amount**. The recoverable amount is the **higher of fair value less costs to sell and value in use**. It is not always easy to estimate value in use. In particular, it is not always practicable to identify cash flows arising from an individual non-current asset. If this is the case, value in use should be calculated at the level of **cash generating units**.

A **cash generating unit** is defined as a group of assets, liabilities and associated goodwill that generates income that is **largely independent of the reporting entity's other income streams**. The assets and liabilities include those already involved in generating the income and an appropriate portion of those used to generate more than one income stream.

(b) IAS 36 *Impairment of assets* requires that there should be some indication of impairment of a non-current asset before an impairment review is carried out. However, IFRS 3 *Business combinations* sets out different requirements for the special case of goodwill.

IFRS 3 states that goodwill resulting from a business combination should be recognised in the statement of financial position and measured at cost. Goodwill is **not amortised**. Instead, it should be **reviewed for impairment annually** and written down to its recoverable amount where necessary. Where goodwill is acquired in a business combination during the current annual period, it should be tested for impairment before the end of the current annual period. Prospects was acquired on 30 June 20X0, so the impairment review should be carried out by 31 December 20X0.

(c) An impairment review involves a **comparison of the carrying value of a non-current asset or goodwill with its recoverable amount**. To the extent that the carrying amount exceeds the recoverable amount, the non-current asset or goodwill is impaired and needs to be written down.

Recoverable amount is the higher of fair value less costs to sell and value in use. Generally, recoverable amount is taken to be **value in use**. This is because fair value less costs to sell may be difficult to determine, and may in any case be very low, because the asset is only of use in the business rather than of value in the open market. This means that an impairment review usually involves computing value in use, particularly in the case of goodwill.

It is not always easy to estimate value in use. In particular, it is not always practicable to identify cash flows arising from an individual non-current asset. This is certainly true of goodwill, which cannot generate cash flows in isolation from other assets. If this is the case, value in use should be calculated at the level of **cash generating units**. A cash generating unit is the smallest grouping of assets that can be said to generate cash flows that are independent of those generated by other units. To calculate value in use, we therefore need to **identify the cash generating units and the cash flows attributable to them.**

(d) The value in use of the assets of Unit A is $72m, which is less than the carrying value of $85m. There is therefore an **impairment loss of $13m**. This must be allocated as follows.

(i) To any **assets** which have suffered **obvious impairment**. We are not given any indication that there are any such assets here.

(ii) To **goodwill** in the unit. We are not told that there is any.

(iii) To **other assets** in the unit, ie the patents of $5 and tangible non-current assets of $60m.

(iv) Therefore the $13m is written off in proportion against patents (5/65 × $13m = $1m) and tangible non-current assets (60/65 × $13m = $12m).

(e) The goodwill on consolidation is:

	$m
Cost of investment	260
Net assets acquired	180
	80

This goodwill cannot be allocated to individual units, so the impairment review must be carried out in two stages:

Stage 1: Review individual units for impairment.

It is clear that the assets of unit A have suffered impairment, since the value in use of $72m is less than the carrying value of $85m. The assets of unit A must therefore be written down to $72m.

Stage 2: Compare the adjusted carrying value of the net assets of Prospects, including goodwill, with the value in use of the whole business.

The carrying value is as follows.

	$m
Goodwill	80
Unit A	72
Unit B	55
Unit C	60
Total	267

The value in use of the whole business is $205m, so an additional impairment loss of $267m – $205m = $62m must be provided for. This is allocated first to goodwill, reducing the goodwill to $80m – $62m = $18m.

6 Investor

(a) The recognition and measurement of goodwill on acquisition is governed by IFRS 3. Where the purchase price is paid in instalments, the cost of the investment is calculated on a discounted cash basis and the fair value is based on present values.

Goodwill arising on acquisitions

	$m	$m
Cost of Cornwall $\left(30m + \frac{30m}{1.10^2}\right)$		54.793
Net assets	55	
Add back pension provision	6	
Deduct pension scheme deficit	(11)	
	50	
Fair value of assets acquired (80% × $50m)		40.000
Goodwill		14.793

Goodwill recognised in a business acquisition is not amortised, but reviewed for impairment annually.

(b) **MEMORANDUM**

To: The financial director
From: The accountant
Subject: Intangible assets

1 Introduction

1.1 It is group policy to write off all intangible assets over twenty years. This complies with the requirements of IAS 38.

1.2 However it is possible to select a longer period.

2 Determining the useful life of an intangible asset

2.1 IAS 38 states that an entity should assess the useful life of its intangible assets. Assets with a finite useful life are amortised over that useful life.

2.2 The useful life of an intangible asset depends on many factors. For example, many computer related assets have short lives because they are susceptible to technological obsolescence. Where an asset arises from contractual or legal rights, the period of the rights normally determines the useful life. However, some types of asset, such as brand names, may have very long lives or indefinite lives.

2.3 An intangible asset has an indefinite useful life when there is **no foreseeable limit** to the period over which the asset is expected to generate net cash inflows for the entity.

2.4 IAS 38 allows intangible assets to be treated as having indefinite lives. An intangible asset with an indefinite life is not amortised.

2.5 However, it is clearly not appropriate to treat assets as having an indefinite useful life unless this can be demonstrated to be the case. IAS 38 requires that the useful life of an asset should be realistic; it is not acceptable to select a useful life simply on the basis of practical simplicity or expediency.

2.6 Therefore, it is possible to avoid amortising intangible assets in theory; but the intangible assets needs to be able to be continually measured, so that impairment reviews can be carried out.

3 Future implications

3.1 Where an intangible asset is assessed as having an indefinite useful life, IAS 38 requires an impairment review to be carried out annually. In addition, the useful life of the asset should be reviewed each period to determine whether events and circumstances continue to support this assessment.

3.2 If an asset is assessed as having a finite useful life, then an impairment review is only required if there are indications that the carrying value is not recoverable.

3.3 Therefore adopting your proposals would mean carrying out an annual impairment review, which could be costly both in time and staff.

(c) **Arguments for capitalisation**

(i) The statement of financial position reflects commercial reality if brands are included, provided they meet fully the IAS 38 definition of a purchased intangible asset.

(ii) IAS 38 does not permit non purchased or internally generated brands to be recognised. This may be unfair since predator entities could acquire entities with valuable brand names at less than true value.

(iii) Many entities would argue that the inclusion of non-purchased brands might provide valuable information to users. However, the difficulties associated with revaluation and assigning an appropriate amortisation period may negate these benefits.

7 Radost

(a) **Notes to the statement of profit or loss and other comprehensive income**

Defined benefit expense recognised in profit or loss

	$'m
Current service cost	3.75
Past service cost – plan amendment	(6.00)
Net interest income (from SOFP: 4.5 – 5.2)	(0.70)
Profit or loss expense/(credit)	(2.95)

Other comprehensive income (items that will not be reclassified to profit or loss): Remeasurements of defined benefit plans

	$'m
Actuarial gain/(loss) on defined benefit obligation	(4.75)
Return on plan assets (excluding amounts included in net interest)	2.97
	(1.78)

Notes to the statement of financial position

Net defined benefit asset recognised in the statement of financial position

	$'m
Fair value of plan assets	64.17
Present value of defined benefit obligation	(44.00)
Net asset	20.17

Changes in the present value of the defined benefit obligation

	$'m
Opening defined benefit obligation	45.00
Interest on obligation (45 × 10%)	4.50
Current service cost	3.75
Past service cost	(6.00)
Benefits paid	(8.00)
Loss on remeasurement recognised in OCI (balancing figure)	4.75
Closing defined benefit obligation – per actuary	44.00

Changes in the fair value of plan assets

	$'m
Opening fair value of plan assets	52.00
Interest on plan assets (52 × 10%)	5.20
Contributions	12.00
Benefits paid	(8.00)
Gain on remeasurement recognised in OCI (balancing figure)	2.97
Closing fair value of plan assets – per actuary	64.17

(b) Legally the assets of the Radost pension plan do not belong to Radost once the contributions are made. This is because to meet the definition of plan assets of a post-employment benefit plan under IAS 19 *Employee Benefits* they must be held by an entity/fund that is legally separate from the reporting entity. This provides the employees with a measure of protection should the entity go bankrupt or should the directors fraudulently attempt to plunder the assets of the pension plan. Nevertheless, the substance of the arrangement is that the assets are held exclusively to pay the company's future defined benefit obligation and it is therefore logical that they should be shown in the company's statement of financial position reducing that liability. In the case of plan assets that exceed the value of the associated obligation (as in Radost's case), a net asset would normally be recognised in the company's statement of financial position on the grounds that the definition of an asset ('a resource controlled by the entity as a result of past events and from which future economic benefits are expected to flow to the entity') is met. In this case the 'benefits' are reduced future contributions as the plan is in surplus.

8 Clean

(a) **Why there was a need for an accounting standard dealing with provisions**

IAS 37 *Provisions, contingent liabilities and contingent assets* was issued to prevent entities from using provisions for creative accounting. It was common for entities to recognise material provisions for items such as future losses, restructuring costs or even expected future expenditure on repairs and maintenance of assets. These could be combined in one large provision (sometimes known as the 'big bath'). Although these provisions reduced profits in the period in which they were recognised (and were often separately disclosed on grounds of materiality), they were then released to enhance profits in subsequent periods. To make matters worse, provisions were often recognised where there was no firm commitment to incur expenditure. For example, an entity might set up a provision for restructuring costs and then withdraw from the plan, leaving the provision available for profit smoothing.

The criteria that need to be satisfied before a provision is recognised

IAS 37 states that a provision should not be recognised unless:

- An entity has a present obligation to transfer economic benefits as a result of a past transaction or event; and
- It is probable that a transfer of economic benefits will be required to settle the obligation; and
- A reliable estimate can be made of the amount of the obligation.

An obligation can be legal or constructive. An entity has a constructive obligation if:

- It has indicated to other parties that it will accept certain responsibilities (by an established pattern of past practice or published policies); and
- As a result, it has created a valid expectation on the part of those other parties that it will discharge those responsibilities.

(b) Two of the three conditions in IAS 37 are very clearly met. Clean will **incur expenditure** (transfer of economic benefits is virtually certain) and the directors have prepared **detailed estimates** of the amount.

Although Clean is not legally obliged to carry out the project, it appears that it has a **constructive obligation** to do so. IAS 37 states that an entity has a constructive obligation if both of the following apply.

(i) It has **indicated to other parties** that it will accept certain responsibilities (by an **established pattern** of past practice or published policies).

(ii) As a result, it has created a **valid expectation** on the part of those other parties that it will discharge those responsibilities.

Clean has a reputation of fulfilling its financial commitments once they have been publicly announced. Therefore the obligating event is the announcement of the proposal on 25 June 20X0, the obligation exists at 30 June 20X0 (the year-end) and Clean is **required to recognise a provision.**

(c) **Provision at 30 June 20X0:**

		$'000
Expenditure on:		
30 June 20X1	30,000 × 0.926	27,780
30 June 20X2	30,000 × 0.857	25,710
30 June 20X3	40,000 × 0.794	31,760
		85,250

Provision at 30 June 20X1:

		$'000
Expenditure on:		
30 June 20X2	30,000 × 0.926	27,780
30 June 20X3	40,000 × 0.857	34,280
		62,060

(d) The charge to profit or loss for the year ended 30 June 20X1 consists of:

(i) Depreciation (85,250,000 ÷ 20) — $ 4,262,500

This is reported in cost of sales.

The provision of $85,250,000 also represents an **asset** as it gives rise to future economic benefits (it enhances the performance of the factories). This is **capitalised and depreciated over 20 years** (the average useful life of the factories).

(ii) Unwinding of the discount (see working) — $ 6,810,000

This is reported as a **finance cost**.

Working

	$'000
Provision at 1 July 20X0	85,250
Expenditure on 30 June 20X1	(30,000)
Unwinding of discount (balancing figure)	6,810
Provision at 30 June 20X1	62,060

Alternative calculation

	$'000
Expenditure on:	
30 June 20X1 (30,000 – 27,780)	2,220
30 June 20X2 (27,780 – 25,710)	2,070
30 June 20X3 (34,280 – 31,760)	2,520
	6,810

9 DT Group

(a) (i) IAS 12 focuses on the statement of financial position in accounting for deferred taxation. It is based on the principle that a deferred tax liability or asset should be recognised if the recovery of the carrying amount of the asset or the settlement of the liability will result in higher or lower tax payments in the future than would be the case if that recovery or settlement were to have no tax consequences. Future tax consequences of past events determine the deferred tax liabilities or assets. (IAS 12 gives certain exceptions to this general rule, eg deferred tax is not provided on goodwill.) The calculation of deferred tax balances is determined by looking at the difference between the tax base of an asset and its statement of financial position carrying value. Thus the calculation is focused on the statement of financial position.

Differences between the carrying amount of the asset and liability and its tax base are called 'temporary differences'. The word 'temporary' is used because it is a fundamental proposition in the IAS framework that an enterprise will realise its assets and settle its liabilities over time at which point the tax consequences will crystallise.

The objective of the temporary difference approach is to recognise the future tax consequences inherent in the carrying amounts of assets and liabilities in the statement of financial position. The approach looks at the tax payable if the assets and liabilities were realised for the pre tax amounts recorded in the statement of financial position. The presumption is that there will be recovery of statement of financial position items out of future revenues and tax needs to be provided in relation to such a recovery. This involves looking at temporary differences between the carrying values of the assets and liabilities and the tax base of the elements. The standard recognises two types of temporary differences, which are described as 'taxable' and 'deductible' temporary differences.

(ii) By definition, deferred tax involves the postponement of the tax liability and it is possible, therefore, to regard the deferred liability as equivalent to an interest free loan from the tax authorities. Thus it could be argued that it is appropriate to reflect this benefit of postponement by discounting the liability and recording a lower tax charge. This discount is then amortised over the period of deferment. The purpose of discounting is to measure future cash flows at their present value and, therefore, deferred tax balances can only be discounted if they can be viewed as future cash flows that are not already measured at their present value.

Some temporary differences clearly represent future tax cash flows. For example, where there is an accrual for an expense that is to be paid in the future and tax relief will only be given when the expense is paid. Some expenses are already measured on a discounted basis (eg retirement benefits), and it is not appropriate to discount the resulting deferred tax. However, there is controversy over whether it is valid to discount deferred tax when tax cash flows have already occurred as in the case of accelerated tax depreciation. It is argued that this temporary difference does not give rise to a future cash flow and there is no basis for discounting. An alternative view is that accelerated tax depreciation is a liability that will be repaid in the form of higher tax assessments in the future. It can be argued that there are two cash flows, with the second cash flow occurring on the reversal of the temporary difference, as the tax payment will be higher.

Discounting, however, makes the deferred tax computation more difficult to calculate and more subjective. Also there will be an additional cost in scheduling and calculating deferred taxation, as well as the problem of the determination of the discount rate. IAS 12 specifically prohibits discounting.

(b) **Calculation of deferred tax liability**

			Carrying amount	*Tax base*	*Temporary differences*
			$m	$m	$m
Goodwill (note 1)			14	–	–
Subsidiary (note 1)			76	60	16
Inventories (note 2)			24	30	(6)
Property, plant and equipment (note 3)			2,600	1,920	680
Other temporary differences					90
Liability for health care benefits			(100)	0	(100)
Unrelieved tax losses (note 4)					(100)
Property sold – tax due 30.11.20X4 (165/30%)					550
Temporary differences					1,130
Deferred tax liability (680 + 90 + 550)	1,320	at 30%			396
Deferred tax liability	16	at 25%			4
Deferred tax asset	(200)	at 30%			(60)
Deferred tax asset	(6)	at 25%			(1.5)
	1,130				338.5

Deferred tax liability b/d (given)	280
Deferred tax attributable to subsidiary to goodwill (76 – 60) × 25%	4
∴ Deferred tax expense for the year charged to P/L (balance)	54.5
Deferred tax liability c/d (from above)	338.5

Notes

1 As no deduction is available for the cost of goodwill in the subsidiary's tax jurisdiction, then the tax base of goodwill is zero. Paragraph 15(a) of IAS 12, states that DT Group should not recognise a deferred tax liability of the temporary difference associated in B's jurisdiction with the goodwill. Goodwill will be increased by the amount of the deferred tax liability of the subsidiary ie $4 million.

2 Unrealised group profit eliminated on consolidation are provided for at the receiving company's rate of tax (ie at 25%).

3 The tax that would arise if the properties were disposed of at their revalued amounts which was provided at the beginning of the year will be included in the temporary difference arising on the property, plant and equipment at 30 November 20X1.

4 DT Group has unrelieved tax losses of $300m. This will be available for offset against current year's profits ($110m) and against profits for the year ending 30 November 20X2 ($100m). Because of the uncertainty about the availability of taxable profits in 20X3, no deferred tax asset can be recognised for any losses which may be offset against this amount. Therefore, a deferred tax asset may be recognised for the losses to be offset against taxable profits in 20X2. That is $100m × 30% ie $30m.

Comment

The deferred tax liability of DT Group will rise in total by $335.5 million ($338.5m – $3m), thus reducing net assets, distributable profits, and post-tax earnings. The profit for the year will be reduced by $54.5 million which would probably be substantially more under IAS 12 than the old method of accounting for deferred tax. A prior period adjustment will occur of $280m – $3m as IAS are being applied for the first time (IFRS 1) ie $277m. The borrowing position of the company may be affected and the directors may decide to cut dividend payments. However, the amount of any unprovided deferred tax may have been disclosed under the previous GAAP standard used. IAS 12 brings this liability into the statement of financial position but if the bulk of the liability had already been disclosed the impact on the share price should be minimal.

10 PQR

Investment in debentures

Given that these debentures are planned to be held until redemption, under IFRS 9 *Financial instruments* they would be held at amortised cost, on the assumption that:

(a) The objective of the business model within which the asset is held is to hold assets in order to collect contractual cash flows, and

(b) The contractual terms of the financial asset give rise on specified dates to cash flows that are solely payments of principal and interest on the principal outstanding.

This means that they are initially shown at their cost (including any transaction costs) and their value increased over time to the redemption value by applying a constant effective interest rate which takes into account not only the annual income due from the coupon, but also amortisation of the redemption premium. Their value is reduced by distributions received, ie the coupon.

Consequently the amortised cost valuation of these debentures at the year end would be:

Cost (40,000 – 6,000)	34,000	
Effective interest at 8.6%	2,924	shown as finance income
Coupon received (4% × 40,000)	(1,600)	Debited to cash
	35,324	

The debentures are an asset belonging to the equity holders and so as the increase in value is recognised until redemption, the equity of the business will increase, marginally reducing gearing.

Forward contract

Providing the forward meets the following criteria it qualifies for hedge accounting:

(a) the hedging relationship consists only of **eligible hedging instruments** and **eligible hedged items**.

(b) it was **designated at its inception** as a hedge with full **documentation** of how this hedge fits into the company's strategy.

(c) the hedging relationship meets all of the following **hedge effectiveness requirements**:

  (i) there is an **economic relationship** between the hedged item and the hedging instrument, i.e. the hedging instrument and the hedged item have values that generally move in the opposite direction because of the same risk, which is the hedged risk;

  (ii) the **effect of credit risk does not dominate the value changes** that result from that economic relationship, i.e. the gain or loss from credit risk does not frustrate the effect of changes in the underlyings on the value of the hedging instrument or the hedged item, even if those changes were significant; and

  (iii) the **hedge ratio of the hedging relationship** (quantity of hedging instrument vs quantity of hedged item) is the **same** as that resulting from the quantity of the hedged item that the entity **actually hedges** and the quantity of the hedging instrument that the entity **actually uses to** hedge that quantity of hedged item.

A foreign currency forward contract can be argued to be either a hedge of the future cash flow or a hedge of the fair value of the machine to be purchased. IFRS 9 *Financial Instruments* therefore allows foreign currency hedges of firm commitments to be classed as either a cash flow hedge or a fair value hedge.

If the contract is classed as a cash flow hedge, given that the machine is not yet recognised in the books, any gain or loss on the hedging instrument is split into two components:

- The effective portion of the hedge (which matches the change in expected cash flow) is recognised initially in other comprehensive income (and in the cash flow hedge reserve). It is transferred out of the cash flow hedge reserve when the asset is recognised (adjusting the asset base and future depreciation). This applies the accruals concept.
- The ineffective portion of the hedge is recognised in profit or loss immediately as it has not hedged anything.

If the contract is classed as a fair value hedge, all gains and losses on the hedging instrument must be recognised immediately in profit or loss. However, in order to match those against the asset hedged, the gain or loss on the fair value of the asset hedged is also recognised in profit or loss (and as an asset or liability in the statement of financial position). This is arguably less transparent as it results in part of the asset value (the change in fair value) being recognised in the statement of financial position until the purchase actually occurs – consequently, IFRS 9 allows the option to treat foreign currency forward contracts as a cash flow hedge.

Gearing will be different depending on whether the forward contract is accounted for as a cash flow hedge or a fair value hedge (and whether a gain or loss on the hedging instrument occurs). Gearing will be less volatile if a fair value hedge is used as the change in fair value of the hedged asset is also recognised offsetting gains or losses on the hedging instrument, whereas this is not the case until the asset is purchased (and recognised) for the cash flow hedge.

Redeemable preference shares

Redeemable preference shares, although called shares, are not, in substance, equity, they are a debt instrument, ie a loan made to the company which receives interest and is paid back at a later date.

Consequently, IAS 32 requires them to be classed as such, ie as a non-current liability in the statement of financial position. The 'dividends' paid will be shown in profit or loss as finance costs and accrued at the end of the year if outstanding, whether declared or not.

The shares are consequently a financial liability held at amortised cost. In this case, given that the shares are issued and redeemed at the same value, the effective interest rate and nominal coupon rate will be the same (6%) and each year $6,000 will be shown as a finance cost in profit or loss and the balance outstanding under non-current liabilities at each year end will be $100,000 as follows:

	$	
Cash received/ b/d value	100,000	
Effective interest at 6%	6,000	shown as finance cost
Coupon paid (6% × 100,000)	(6,000)	credited to cash
	100,000	

In the financial statements for the year ending 31 December 20X7, the shares will need to be reclassified as a current liability given that they will be repaid within one year.

Given that these shares are classed as a financial liability, gearing will be higher (as they are treated as debt) than if they were ordinary shares (which would be treated as equity).

11 Hedging

The futures contract was entered into to protect the company from a fall in oil prices and hedge the value of the inventories. It is therefore a fair value hedge.

The inventories are recorded at their cost of $2,600,000 (100,000 barrels at $26.00) on 1 July 20X2.

The futures contract has a zero value at the date it is entered into and so no entry is made in the financial statements.

Tutorial note: however, the existence of the contract and associated risk would be disclosed from that date in accordance with IFRS 7 (detail outside the scope of the syllabus).

At the year end the inventories must be shown at the lower of cost and net realisable value. Hence they will be shown at $2,250,000 (100,000 barrels at $22.50) and a loss of $350,000 recognised in profit or loss.

However, a gain has been made on the futures contract:

	$
The company has a contract to sell on 31 March 20X3 at $27.50	2,750,000
A contract entered into at the year end would sell at $23.25 on 31 March 20X3	2,325,000
Gain (= the value the contract could be sold on for to a third party)	425,000

The gain on the futures contract is also recognised in profit or loss:

DEBIT	Future contract asset	$425,000	
CREDIT	Profit or loss		$425,000

The net effect on profit or loss is a gain of $75,000 ($425,000 less $350,000) whereas without the hedging contract the whole loss of $350,000 would have been the only impact on profit or loss.

Note

If the inventories had gained in value, this gain would also be recognised in profit or loss as hedge accounting is being applied (normally gains on inventories are not recognised until sale). A loss would have occurred on the futures contract, which would also be recognised in profit or loss.

12 Sirus

Marking scheme

		Marks
(a)	Definition of financial liability and equity	3
	Principle in IAS 32	1
	Discussion	2
(b)	IAS 19	1
	Financial liability	2
	Provision	1
	Build up over service period	1
	Recalculate annually	1
(c)	Purchase method	1
	Cost of business combinations	1
	Future payment	1
	Remuneration versus cost of acquisition	2
(d)	Not exercised	2
	Expected exercise	1
	IFRS 9	1
	Current v non-current	2
Communication in report		2
	Maximum	25

Report

To: The Directors, Sirus
From: Accountant
Date: 15 June 20X8

Accounting treatment of items in the financial statements

(a) **Directors' ordinary 'B' shares**

The capital of Sirus must be shown **either as a liability or as equity**. The criteria for distinguishing between financial liabilities and equity are found in IAS 32 *Financial instruments: presentation.* Equity and liabilities must be classified **according to their substance, not just their legal form,**

A **financial liability** is defined as any liability that is:

(i) A contractual obligation:

– To deliver cash or another financial asset to another entity, or
– To exchange financial instruments with another entity under conditions that are potentially unfavourable; or

(ii) A contract that will or may be settled in the entity's own equity instruments.

An **equity instrument** is any contract that evidences a **residual interest** in the assets of an entity after deducting all of its liabilities

The **ordinary 'B' shares,** the capital subscribed by the directors must, according to the directors' service agreements, be returned to any director on leaving the company. There is thus a **contractual obligation** to deliver cash. The redemption **is not discretionary,** and Sirus has no right to avoid it. The mandatory nature of the repayment makes this capital a **liability** (if it were discretionary, it would be equity). On initial recognition, that is when the 'B' shares are purchased, the financial liability must be stated at the **present value of the amount due on redemption,** discounted over the life of the service contract. In subsequent periods, the financial liability may be carried at fair value through profit or loss, or at amortised cost under IFRS 9.

In contrast, the **payment of $3 million** to holders of 'B' shares, is discretionary in that it must be approved in a general meeting by a majority of all shareholders. This approval may be refused, and so it would not be correct to show the $3 million as a liability in the statement of financial position at 30 April 20X8. Instead, it should be recognised when approved. The dividend when recognised will be treated as **interest expense**. This is because IAS 32 (para 35-36) requires the treatment of dividends to follow the treatment of the instrument, ie because the instrument is treated as a liability, the dividends are treated as an expense.

(b) **Directors' retirement benefits**

These are unfunded defined benefit plans, which are likely to be governed by IAS 19 *Employee benefits,* but IAS 32 and IFRS 9 on financial instruments, and IAS 37 *Provisions, contingent liabilities and contingent assets* also apply.

Sirus has contractual or constructive obligations to make payments to former directors. The treatment and applicable standard depends on the obligation.

(i) **Fixed annuity with payment to director's estate on death**. This **meets the definition of a financial liability under IAS 32**, because there is a contractual obligation to deliver cash or a financial asset. The firm does not have the option to withhold the payment. The rights to these annuities are earned over the directors' period of service, so it follows that the costs should also be recognised over this service period.

(ii) **Fixed annuity ceasing on death**
The timing of the death is clearly uncertain, which means that the annuities have a **contingent element** with a mortality risk to be calculated by an actuary. It meets the definition of an insurance contract, which is outside the scope of IFRS 9, as are employers' obligations under IAS 19. However, insofar as there is a constructive obligation, these annuities fall within the scope of IAS 37, because these are liabilities of uncertain timing or amount. The amount of the obligation should be measured in a manner similar to a warranty provision: that is the **probability of the future cash outflow** of the present obligation should be measured for the class of all such obligations. An estimate of the costs should include any liability for post retirement payments that directors have earned so far. The liability should **be built up over the service period** and will in practice be calculated on an actuarial basis as under IAS 19 *Employee benefits*. If the effect is material, the liability will be discounted. It should be **re-calculated every year** to take account of directors joining or leaving, or any other changes.

(c) **Acquisition of Marne**

An increased profit share is payable to the directors of Marne if the purchase offer is accepted. The question arises of whether this additional payment constitutes **remuneration or consideration** for the business acquired. Because the payment is for two years only, after which time remuneration falls back to normal levels, the payment should be seen as part of the **purchase consideration.**

The second issue is the treatment of this consideration. IFRS 3 (revised January 2008) *Business combinations* requires that an acquirer must be identified for all business combinations. In this case Sirus is the acquirer. The cost of the combination must be measured as the sum of the fair values, at the date of exchange, of assets given or liabilities assumed in exchange for control.

IFRS 3 recognises that, by entering into an acquisition, the acquirer becomes obliged to make additional payments. Not recognising that obligation means that the consideration recognised at the acquisition date is not fairly stated.

The revised IFRS 3 **requires recognition of contingent consideration, measured at fair value, at the acquisition date.** This is, arguably, consistent with how other forms of consideration are fair valued.

The acquirer may be required to pay contingent consideration in the form of equity or of a debt instrument or cash. In this case, it is in the form of cash, or increased remuneration.

Accordingly, the **cost of the combination must include the full $11m,** measured at net present value at 1 May 20X7. The payment of $5 million would be discounted for one year and the payment of $6 million for two years.

(d) **Repayment of bank loan**

The bank loan is to be repaid in ten years' time, but the terms of the loan state that Sirus can pay it off in seven years. The issue arises as to **whether the early repayment option is likely to be exercised.**

If, when the loan was taken out on 1 May 20X7 the option **of early repayment was not expected to be exercised, t**hen at 30 April 20X8 the normal terms apply. The loan would be stated at $2 million in the statement of financial position, and the effective interest would be 8% × $2 million = $160,000, the interest paid.

If at 1 May 20X7 it was expected that the **early repayment option would be exercised**, then the **effective interest rate would be 9.1%,** and the effective interest 9.1% × $2 million = $182,000. The cash paid would still be $160,000, and the difference of $22,000 would be added to the carrying amount of the financial liability in the statement of financial position, giving $2,022,000.

IFRS 9 *Financial instruments requires* that the carrying amount of a financial asset or liability should be adjusted to reflect actual cash flows or revised estimates of cash flows. This means that, even if it was thought at the outset that early repayment would not take place, if **expectations then change, the carrying amount must be revised** to reflect future estimated cash flows using the effective interest rate.

The directors of Sirus are currently in discussion with the bank regarding repayment in the next financial year. However, these discussions do not create a legal obligation to repay the loan in twelve months, and Sirus has an unconditional right to defer settlement for longer than twelve months. Accordingly, **it would not be correct to show the loan as a current liability on the basis of the discussions with the bank.**

I hope that this report is helpful to you.

Signed, Accountant

13 Eastway

(a) The right to control the use of an identified asset depends on the lessee having:

(i) The right to obtain substantially all of the economic benefits from use of the identified asset; and

(ii) The right to direct the use of the identified asset (IFRS 16: para. B9). This arises if either:

(1) The customer has the right to direct how and for what purpose the asset is used during the whole of its period of use, or

(2) The relevant decisions about use are pre-determined and the customer can operate the asset without the supplier having the right to change those operating instructions.

A lessee does not control the use of an identified asset if the lessor can substitute the underlying asset for another asset during the lease term and would benefit economically from doing so. (IFRS 16: para B14)

(b) The contract contains a lease of retail space. Sellerwell has the right to use Unit 21 for four years.

Unit 21 is an identified asset. It is explicitly specified in the contract. While Propfield has the right to substitute the retail unit, Propfield could benefit economically from substituting it only in specific circumstances. Propfield's substitution right is not substantive because, at inception of the contract, those circumstances are not considered likely to occur.

Sellerwell has the right to control the use of Unit 21 throughout the four-year period of use because:

(i) Sellerwell has the right to obtain substantially all of the economic benefits from use of Unit 21 over the four-year period of use. Sellerwell has exclusive use of Unit 21 throughout the period of use. Although a portion of the cash flows derived from sales from Unit 21 will flow from Sellerwell to Propfield, this represents consideration that Sellerwell pays Propfield for the right to use the retail unit. It does not prevent Sellerwell from having the right to obtain substantially all of the economic benefits from use of Unit 21.

(ii) Sellerwell has the right to direct the use of Unit 21 because the conditions in paragraph IFRS 16B24(a) exist. The contractual restrictions on the goods that can be sold from Unit 21, and when Unit 21 is open, define the scope of Sellerwell's right to use Unit 21. Within the scope of its right of use defined in the contract, Sellerwell makes the relevant decisions about how and for what purpose Retail Unit A is used by being able to decide, for example, the mix of products that will be sold in the retail unit and the sale price for those products. Sellerwell has the right to change these decisions during the five-year period of use.

Although marketing, cleaning and security are essential to the efficient use of Unit 21, Propfield's decisions in this regard do not give it the right to direct how and for what purpose Unit 21 is used. Consequently, Propfield does not control the use of Unit 21 during the period of use and Propfield's decisions do not affect Sellerwell's control of the use of Unit 21.

14 Vident

Marking scheme

			Marks
(a)	Discussion		9
(b)	Computation and discussion		9
(c)	Computation and discussion		7
		Available/Maximum	25

REPORT

To:	Directors of Vident	From:
Subject:	IFRS 2 Share based payment	Date: 20X5

As requested, this report explains why share based payments should be recognised in the financial statements. It also explains how the directors' share options should be accounted for in the financial statements for the year ended 31 May 20X5.

(a) **Why share based payments should be recognised in the financial statements**

IFRS 2 *Share based payment* applies to **all share option schemes granted after 7 November 2002**. The directors have put forward several arguments for not recognising the expense of remunerating directors in this way.

Share options have no cost to the company

When shares are **issued for cash** or in a business acquisition, **an accounting entry is needed** to **recognise the receipt of cash** (or other resources) as consideration for the issue. Share options (the right to receive shares in future) **are also issued in consideration for resources**: services rendered by directors or employees. These resources are **consumed by the company** and it would be **inconsistent not to recognise an expense**.

Share issues do not meet the definition of an expense in the IASB Conceptual Framework

The *Framework* defines an expense as a **decrease in economic benefits** in the form of **outflows of assets** or **incurrences of liabilities**. It is not immediately obvious that employee services meet the definition of an asset and therefore **it can be argued that consumption of those services does not meet the definition of an expense**. However, share options **are issued for consideration in the**

form of employee services so that **arguably there is an asset**, although it is **consumed at the same time that it is received**. Therefore the recognition of an expense relating to share based payment is **consistent with the *Conceptual Framework***.

The expense relating to share options is already recognised in the diluted earnings per share calculation

It can be argued that to recognise an expense in profit or loss **would have the effect of distorting diluted earnings per share** as diluted earnings per share would then **take the expense into account twice**. This is not a valid argument. There are **two events** involved: **issuing the options**; and **consuming the resources** (the directors' services) received as consideration. The diluted earnings per share calculation **only reflects the issue of the options**; there is **no adjustment to basic earnings.** Recognising an expense reflects the consumption of services. There is **no 'double counting'**.

Accounting for share based payment may discourage the company from introducing new share option plans

This is quite **possibly true**. Accounting for share based payment **reduces earnings**. However, it **improves the information provided** in the financial statements, as these now make users aware of the **true economic consequences** of issuing share options as remuneration. The economic consequences are the reason why share option schemes may be discontinued. IFRS 2 simply **enables management and shareholders** to **reach an informed decision** on the best method of remuneration.

(b) **Accounting for share options in the financial statements for the year ended 31 May 20X5**

The basic principle of accounting for share options is that **an expense is recognised** for the **services rendered** by the directors and a **corresponding amount is credited to equity**. The transaction is **measured at the fair value of the options granted at the grant date** and fair value is taken to be the **market price**. Where (as is usual) options vest only after staff have completed a specified period of service, the expense is **allocated to accounting periods over this period of service.**

Options granted to J. Van Heflin on 1 June 20X3

The **performance conditions have been met** and the director is **still working for the company** at 31 May 20X5. As the **number of shares** that will vest is **fixed**, the expense is **allocated on a straight line basis to the two years ended 31 May 20X5.**

Options granted to R. Ashworth on 1 June 20X4

The **performance conditions** (the increase in the share price to $13.50) **have not yet been met.** However, such 'market conditions' need not be considered as they are already factored into the fair value of the share options. In terms of the period of service condition, the director is **still working for the company** and **must work for the company for three years** before the options vest, so the **expense is recognised**. Again, the **number of shares is fixed**, so the expense is **allocated on a straight line basis over the three years to 31 May 20X7.** The expense to be recognised is calculated as follows:

	At 1 June 20X4	*Year ended 31 May 20X5*
	$	$
J. Van Heflin (20,000 × $5 × ½)	50,000	50,000
R. Ashworth (50,000 × $6 × 1/3)		100,000
	50,000	150,000

At 1 June 20X4 the **opening balance of retained earnings is reduced by $50,000** and a **separate component of equity is increased by $50,000.**

An **expense of $150,000 is recognised** in profit or loss for the year ended 31 May 20X5. **Equity** (the same separate component as before) is **credited with $150,000.**

(c) **Deferred tax implications of the recognition of an expense for directors' share options**

The company will **recognise an expense** for the consumption of employee services given in consideration for share options granted, **but will not receive a tax deduction until the share ptions are actually exercised.** Therefore a **temporary difference arises** and IAS 12 *Income taxes* requires the recognition of deferred tax.

A **deferred tax asset** (a deductible temporary difference) results from the **difference** between the **tax base of the services received** (a tax deduction in future periods) and the **carrying value of zero**. IAS 12 requires the **measurement** of the deductible temporary difference to be based on the **intrinsic value of the options at the year end**. This is the **difference** between the **fair value of the share** and the **exercise price of the option.**

If the amount of the **estimated future tax deduction exceeds the amount of the related cumulative remuneration expense**, the tax deduction relates not only to the remuneration expense, but to equity. If this is the case, the **excess should be recognised directly in equity**.

At 1 June 20X4

Deferred tax asset:

	$
Fair value (20,000 × $12.50 × 1/2)	125,000
Exercise price of option (20,000 × $4.50 × ½)	(45,000)
Intrinsic value (estimated tax deduction)	80,000
Tax at 30%	24,000

The cumulative remuneration expense is $50,000, which is less than the estimated tax deduction. Therefore:

- A deferred tax asset of $24,000 is recognised in the opening statement of financial position.
- Opening retained earnings are increased by $15,000 (50,000 × 30%).
- The excess of $9,000 (30,000 × 30%) goes to equity.

The comparative is re-stated for the options granted on 1 June 20X3.

Year to 31 May 20X5

Deferred tax asset:

	$
Fair value:	
(20,000 × $12)	240,000
(50,000 × $12 × 1/3)	200,000
	440,000
Exercise price of options	
(20,000 × $4.50)	(90,000)
(50,000 × $6 × 1/3)	(100,000)
Intrinsic value (estimated tax deduction)	250,000
Tax at 30%	75,000
Less previously recognised	(24,000)
	51,000

The cumulative remuneration expense is $200,000, which is less than the estimated tax deduction. Therefore:

- A deferred tax asset of $75,000 is recognised in the statement of financial position at 31 May 20X5.
- There is potential deferred tax income of $51,000 for the year ended 31 May 20X5.
- Of this, $6,000 (50,000 × 30% – 9,000) goes directly to equity.
- The remainder ($45,000) is recognised in profit or loss for the year.

I hope that the above explanations and advice are helpful. Please do not hesitate to contact me should you require any further assistance.

15 Grow by acquisition

(a) **Note 1**

The substance of this transaction is that X has made a loan of $2.4m to A. All aspects of the 'sale' should be eliminated, as follows.

(i) Reduce revenue by $2,400,000.
(ii) Reduce cost of sales by $2,400,000 × 100/160 = $1,500,000.
(iii) Reduce gross profit by ($2,400,000 – $1,500,000) = $900,000.
(iv) Increase loans by $2,400,000.

Note 2

To be comparable, the non-current assets of A and B should either both be shown at cost or both at a revalued amount, with the revaluation done on the same basis. It is not feasible to 'revalue' A's non-current assets for purposes of comparison. However, B's non-current assets can be shown at cost by reversing out the revaluation, as follows.

(i) Reduce non-current assets by $5,000,000.
(ii) Reduce the revaluation reserve to nil.
(iii) Reduce cost of sales by $1,000,000. This is the excess depreciation no longer required.
(iv) Increase gross profit by $1,000,000.

Summary

A

Item	*Per original f/s*	*Adjustment*	*New figure*
	$'000	$'000	$'000
Revenue	68,000	(2,400)	65,600
Cost of sales	42,000	(1,500)	40,500
Gross profit	26,000	(900)	25,100
Profit from operations	8,000	(900)	7,100
Inventory	6,000	1,500	7,500
Short term borrowing	–	2,400	2,400
Total borrowings (4,000 + 16,000)	20,000	2,400	22,400
Shareholders' funds	23,500	(900)	22,600

B

Item	*Per original f/s*	*Adjustment*	*New figure*
Non-current assets	35,050	(5,000)	30,050
Revaluation reserve	5,000	(5,000)	Nil
Cost of sales	45,950	(1,000)	44,950
Gross profit	20,050	1,000	21,050
Profit from operations	6,050	1,000	7,050
Shareholders' funds	22,050	(5,000)	17,050

(b) All monetary amounts in $'000

Ratio	*A*		*B*	
Return on capital employed	$\frac{7,100}{22,600 + 22,400}$	= 15.8%	$\frac{7,050}{17,050 + 6,000 + 18,000}$	= 17.2%
Gross profit margin	$\frac{25,100}{65,600}$	= 38.3%	$\frac{21,050}{66,000}$	= 31.9%
Turnover of capital employed	$\frac{65,600}{45,000}$	= 1.5	$\frac{66,000}{41,050}$	= 1.6
Leverage	$\frac{22,400}{45,000}$	= 49.8%	$\frac{24,000}{41,050}$	= 58.5%

BPP note. The effective loan of $2.4m could arguably be excluded from borrowings as it is short term.

(c) The adjustments carried out to make the financial statements of the two entities comparable make it **far less easy to decide** which entity to target. The ratios are now far more similar. **A** has a **higher gross profit and gross profit margin**. However, the **return on capital employed is lower**. The main reason for this is that A's other operating expenses are higher than B's. The revenue figures are now nearly identical due to the elimination of the 'sale' from the accounts of A. The asset turnover ratios, both before and after adjustments, do not show significant differences.

Where **A** has an **advantage** over B is in **the leverage ratio**. Leverage of both entities has increased, but more so in the case of B. Whether this influences the directors' decision depends on whether they intend to change the financial structure of the company.

Overall it would appear that **B** would be a **better investment**. However, there is not a great deal to choose between the two entities, and this exercise shows the importance of adjusting financial statements to achieve uniform accounting policies when making this kind of decision. It is notable that the 'sale' by A was **incorrectly** accounted for, while B's revaluation is **permissible**.

16 Ace

Year ended 31 March 20X2

Relationship

Ace Co has a 75% subsidiary (Deuce Co) and an 80% subsidiary (Trey Co).

Ace is a related party of Deuce and Trey and *vice versa.*

Deuce and Trey are also related parties because they are subject to 'common control'. Any transactions between Ace, Deuce and Trey need not be disclosed in Ace's *consolidated* accounts as they are eliminated.

Disclosures

Ace Co

- Intragroup sale of machine for $25,000 at profit of $5,000. No balances outstanding.
- Management services provided to Deuce (nil charge) and Trey (nil charge)

No disclosure is required in the group accounts of Ace of these items as they are eliminated.

Deuce

- Parent (and ultimate controlling party) is Ace Co
- Machine purchased from parent $25,000 (original cost $20,000) and depreciation charge $5,000. No amounts outstanding at year end.
- Purchase of management services from Ace (nil charge)

Trey

- Parent (and ultimate controlling party) is Ace Co
- Purchase of management services from Ace (nil charge)

For all transactions the nature of the related party relationship (ie parent, subsidiary, fellow subsidiary) should be disclosed.

Year ended 31 March 20X3

Relationship

Ace Co has a 100% subsidiary (Deuce Co) and an 80% subsidiary (Trey Co).

Ace is a related party of Deuce and Trey and *vice versa.* Deuce and Trey are related because they remain under common control. Any transactions between Ace, Deuce and Trey need not be disclosed in Ace's *consolidated* accounts as they are eliminated.

Disclosures

Ace Co

- Management services provided to Deuce (nil charge) and Trey ($10,000 outstanding)

No disclosure is required in the group accounts of Ace of these items as they are eliminated.

Deuce

- Parent (and ultimate controlling party) is Ace Co

Disclosures of intragroup transactions is still required even though Deuce is a wholly-owned subsidiary:

- Sale of inventories to Trey for $15,000 (original cost $12,000) all sold on, no amounts outstanding at year end
- Purchase of management services from Ace (nil charge)

Trey

- Parent (and ultimate controlling party) is Ace Co
- Purchase of inventories from Deuce $15,000 (original cost $12,000) all sold, no amounts outstanding at year end
- Purchase of management services from Ace costing $10,000. All outstanding at year end

For all transactions the nature of the related party relationship (ie parent, subsidiary, fellow subsidiary) should be disclosed.

17 Highland

HIGHLAND GROUP
CONSOLIDATED STATEMENT OF PROFIT OR LOSS AND OTHER COMPREHENSIVE INCOME
FOR THE YEAR ENDED 31 MARCH 20X8

	$'000
Revenue (5,000 + 3,000 + (2,910 × $^4/_{12}$))	8,970
Cost of sales (3,000 + 2,300 + (2,820 × $^4/_{12}$))	(6,240)
Gross profit	2,730
Administrative expenses (1,000 + 500 + (150 × $^4/_{12}$) + (W4) 63.5 + (W5) 5 – (W6) 85 + (W8) 65)	(1,599)
Finance income* (230 + (W3) 35 – (W6) 85 – (W6) 40)	140
Finance costs (50 + (210 × $^4/_{12}$) – (W3) 70)	(50)
Profit before tax	1,221
Income tax expense (300 + 50)	(350)
PROFIT FOR THE YEAR	871
Other comprehensive income, net of tax (130 + 40 + (120 × $^4/_{12}$))	210
TOTAL COMPREHENSIVE INCOME FOR THE YEAR	1,081
Profit attributable to:	
Owners of the parent (871 + 26)	897
Non-controlling interests (W2)	(26)
	871
Total comprehensive income attributable to:	
Owners of the parent (1,081 + 4)	1,085
Non-controlling interests (W2)	(4)
	1,081

* *Other income becomes finance income as only interest income from Buchan remains*

Workings

1 *Group structure*

Highland

Aviemore 80%

Buchan 65% (owned for 4 months)

2 *Non-controlling interests*

	\$'000 *Aviemore*	\$'000 *Buchan*	\$'000 *Aviemore*	\$'000 *Buchan*
Profit/(loss) for the year (B: 270 loss × $\frac{4}{12}$)	100	(90)		
Total comp income for the year (B: 150 loss × $\frac{4}{12}$)			140	(50)
Unrealised profit on disposal (W4)	(63.5)		(63.5)	
FV depreciation (W5)		(5)		(5)
	36.5	(95)	76.5	(55)
NCI share (20%/35%/20%/35%)	7.3 DR	(33.3) CR	15.3 DR	(19.3) CR
	(26.0) CR		(4.0) CR	

Hence, rounding to nearest \$'000, NCI *increases* profit/total comprehensive income attributable to owners of the parent.

3 *Interest income/payable*

	\$'000	
Interest income: \$2,100,000 × 10% × 6/12	105	recorded on 1 October 20X7
× 6/12	105	to be recorded
	210	

Pre-acquisition: 210 × 8/12 = 140 → Genuine finance income

Post-acquisition: (210 × 4/12) = 70 → Cancel on consolidation:
DR Finance income 70
CR Finance costs 70

Overall adjustment to interest income:

	\$'000
Interest income from Buchan not yet recorded (210 × 6/12)	105
Less: post acquisition intragroup element (210 × 4/12)	(70)
	35

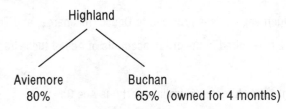

4 *Unrealised profit on disposal of freehold property*

		$'000	$'000
Land	Proceeds	300	
	Net book value	(100)	
	Profit on disposal (in Aviemore)		200
Buildings	Proceeds (800 – 300)	500	
	Net book value (800 × $^{40}/_{50}$)	(640)	
	Loss on disposal (in Aviemore)		(140)
Proportion of loss depreciated (1/40)			3.5
			63.5

5 *Fair value depreciation*

	At acquisition	*Additional depreciation**	*At year end*
	$'000	$'000	$'000
Property, plant and equipment (500 – 350)	150	(5)	145
	150	(5)	145

* Additional depreciation = $^{150}/_{10}$ = 15 per annum × $\frac{4}{12}$ = $5,000

6 *Intragroup cancellations*

Cancel management services:

DEBIT Other income	$85,000	
CREDIT Administrative expenses		$85,000

Cancel dividend income from Aviemore:

DEBIT Other income (50 × 80%)	$40,000	
CREDIT Aviemore's retained earnings		$40,000

7 *Goodwill*

	Aviemore		*Buchan*	
	$'000	$'000	$'000	$'000
Consideration transferred		5,000		2,600
Non-controlling interests	(4,000 × 80%)	800	(3,500 × 35%)	1,225
FV net assets at acq'n:				
Net book value per Q	4,000		3,350	
Fair value adjustment (W5)	–		150	
		(4,000)		(3,500)
		1,800		325

8 *Impairment losses*

	Aviemore	*Buchan*
	$'000	$'000
Goodwill (W7)	1,800	325
'Notional' goodwill (× 100%/80%) (× 100%/65%)	2,250	500
Net assets at 31 March 20X7	4,450	3,300
	6,700	3,800
Recoverable amount	7,040	3,700
Impairment loss	0	100
Allocated to:		
'Notional' goodwill	–	100
Other assets	–	–
	0	100
Recognised impairment loss:		
Recognised goodwill (100 × 65%)	–	65
Other assets (100%)	–	–

18 Armoury

BAYONET GROUP
CONSOLIDATED STATEMENT OF FINANCIAL POSITION AS AT 31 DECEMBER 20X9

	$'000
Non-current assets	
Property, plant and equipment (14,500 + 12,140 + 17,500)	44,140
Goodwill (W2)	3,580
	47,720
Current assets	
Inventories (6,300 + 2,100 + 450)	8,850
Trade receivables (4,900 + 2,000 + 2,320)	9,220
Cash (500 + 1,440 + 515)	2,455
	20,525
	68,245
Equity attributable to owners of the parent	
Share capital – 50c ordinary shares	5,000
Retained earnings (W3)	40,680
	45,680
Non-controlling interests (W4)	12,600
	58,280
Current liabilities (5,700 + 2,280 + 1,985)	9,965
	68,245

Workings

1 *Group structure*

	B	
1.1.X5	↓	$\frac{6,000}{8,000}$ = 75% ∴ NCI: 25%
	R	
31.12.X2	↓	$\frac{4,000}{5,000}$ = 80%
	P	Effective interest in P (75% × 80%) 60%
		∴ NCI 40%
		100%

2 *Goodwill*

	Rifle		*Pistol*	
	$'000	$'000	$'000	$'000
Consideration transferred		10,000	(9,000 × 75%)	6,750
Non-controlling interests (at 'full' fair value)		3,230		4,600
Fair value of identifiable net assets at acq'n:				
Share capital	4,000		2,500	
Pre-acquisition retained earnings	8,000		6,500	
		(12,000)		(9,000)
		1,230		2,350
			3,580	

3 *Retained earnings*

	Bayonet	*Rifle*	*Pistol*
	$'000	$'000	$'000
Per question	25,500	20,400	16,300
Retained earnings at acquisition		(8,000)	(6,500)
		12,400	9,800
Group share of post acquisition ret'd earnings:			
Rifle (12,400 × 75%)	9,300		
Pistol (9,800 × 60%)	5,880		
	40,680		

4 *Non-controlling interests*

	Rifle	*Pistol*
	$'000	$'000
NCI at acquisition (W2)	3,230	4,600
NCI share of post acquisition ret'd earnings:		
Rifle ((W3) 12,400 × 25%)	3,100	
Pistol ((W3) 9,800 × 40%)		3,920
Less NCI share of investment in Pistol (9,000 × 25%)	(2,250)	
	4,080	8,520
	12,600	

19 Murder, Mystery and Suspense

MURDER GROUP
CONSOLIDATED STATEMENT OF FINANCIAL POSITION AS AT 31 DECEMBER 20X7

	$'m
Non-current assets	
Property, plant and equipment (2,458 + 1,410 + 870)	4,738
Goodwill (W2)	320
	5,058
Current assets	
Inventories (450 + 200 + 260 – (W5) 52)	858
Trade receivables (610 + 365 + 139)	1,114
Cash (240 + 95 + 116)	451
	2,423
	7,481
Equity attributable to owners of the parent	
Ordinary share capital	500
Share premium	250
Retained earnings (W3)	3,605
	4,355
Non-controlling interests (W4)	1,193
	5,548
Current liabilities	
Trade payables (1,130 + 418 + 385)	1,933
	7,481

Workings

1 *Group structure*

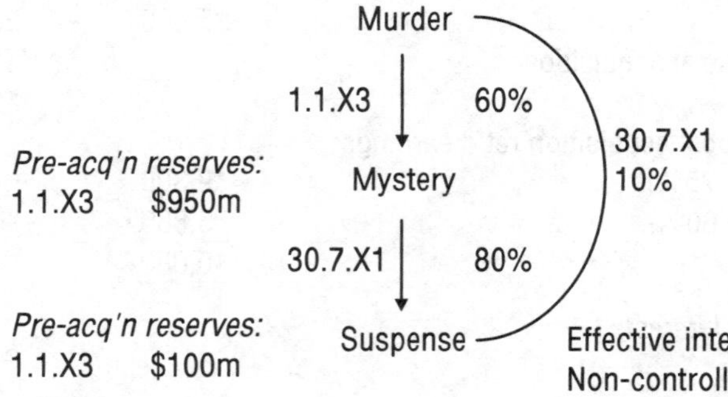

Effective interest (60% × 80%) + 10%	58%
Non-controlling interests	42%
	100%

2 Goodwill (including step acquisition of Suspense)

	Murder in Mystery		*Murder in Suspense*	
	$'m	$'m	$'m	$'m
Consideration transferred		900	(240 x 60%)	144
Fair value of non-controlling interests		536		210
Fair value of 10% equity interest in Suspense				50
Fair value of identifiable net assets at acq'n:				
Share capital	200		100	
Share premium	120		50	
Pre-acquisition retained earnings (1.1.X3)	950		100	
		(1,270)		(250)
		166		154
			320	

3 *Retained earnings*

	Murder	Mystery	Suspense
	$'m	$'m	$'m
Per question	2,805	1,572	850
P/L gain on investment in Suspense (50 – 27)	23		
Less unrealised profit (W5)		(52)	
Retained earnings at acq'n (W2)		(950)	(100)
		570	750
Group share of post acq'n ret'd earnings:			
Mystery (570 × 60%)	342		
Suspense (750 × 58%)	435		
Group share of impairment losses to date	(0)		
	3,605		

4 *Non-controlling interests*

	Mystery	Suspense
	$'m	$'m
NCI at acquisition (W2)	536	210
NCI share of post acq'n ret'd earnings:		
Mystery (570 × 40%)	228	
Suspense (750 × 42%)		315
Less NCI share of investment in Suspense (240 × 40%)	(96)	
	668	525
	1,193	

5 *Unrealised profit on inventories*

Mark-up = $260m × $\frac{25}{125}$ = 52m

20 Burley

Marking scheme

		Marks
(a)	Revenue recognition	3
	Inventory	3
	Events after reporting period	3
		9
(b)	Jointly controlled	3
	Accounting for entity	2
	Decommissioning	5
		10
(c)	Asset definition/IAS 38/IAS 36	4
	Professional marks	2
		25

(a) Revenue from the sale of goods should only be recognised when **all the following conditions** are satisfied.

(i) The entity has transferred the **significant risks and rewards** of ownership of the goods to the buyer

(ii) The entity has **no continuing managerial involvement** to the degree usually associated with ownership, and no longer has effective control over the goods sold

(iii) The amount of revenue can be **measured reliably**

(iv) It is probable that the **economic benefits** associated with the transaction will flow to the enterprise

(v) The **costs incurred** in respect of the transaction can be measured reliably

The transfer of risks and rewards can only be decided by examining each transaction. In the case of the oil sold to third parties, all the revenue should be recognised as all the criteria have been met.

IFRS 15 *Revenue from contracts with customers* requires revenue to be recognised when (or as) a performance obligation is satisfied i.e. when an entity transfers a promised good or service to a customer. The good or service is considered transferred when (or as) the customer obtains control of that good or service (ie the ability to direct the use of, and obtain substantially all of the remaining benefits from, the asset).

The sale of oil results in satisfaction of an obligation at a point in time. To determine the point in time when a customer obtains control of a promised asset and an entity satisfies a performance obligation, the entity would consider indicators of the transfer of control that include, but are not limited to, the following.

(i) The entity has a **present right to payment** for the asset.
(ii) The customer has **legal title** to the asset.
(iii) The entity has **transferred physical possession** of the asset.
(iv) The customer has the **significant risks and rewards of ownership** of the asset.
(v) The customer has **accepted** the asset.

These criteria need to be assessed on a transaction by transaction basis. In the case of the oil sold to third parties, revenue should be recognised as the performance obligation is the delivery of the oil to the customers which took place prior to the year end. Control has been transferred as the customers can now obtain the benefits of the oil either through use or resale.

Revenue up to 1 October 20X9

The arrangement between Burley and Slite is a **joint arrangement** under IFRS 11 *Joint arrangements*, since both entities jointly control an asset – the oilfield. However, the arrangement is not structured as a separate entity, so it is a **joint operation not a joint venture.** This means that **each company accounts for its share of revenue** in respect of oil produced up to 1 October 20X9, calculated, using the selling price to third parties of $100 per barrel, as:

Burley: 60%
Slite: 40%

Excess oil extracted

Burley has over-extracted and Slite under-extracted by 10,000 barrels of oil. The **substance** of the transaction is that **Burley has purchased the oil from Slite** at the point of production at the market value ruling at that point, namely $100 per barrel. Burley should therefore **recognise a purchase** from Slite in the amount of 10,000 × $100 = $1m.

The accounting entries would be:

DEBIT	Purchases	$1m	
CREDIT	Slite – financial liability		$1m

The **amount payable to Slite at the year-end** will **change with the movement in the price of oil** and therefore the financial liability recorded at the year-end should reflect the best estimate of the cash payable. By the year end the price of oil has risen to $105 per barrel, so the financial liability will be 10,000 × $105 = $1,050,000, an **increase of $50,000**. The accounting entries to reflect this increase in liability and expense to profit or loss at the year-end will be:

DEBIT	Expense (P/L)	$50,000	
CREDIT	Slite – financial liability		$50,000

After the year end the price of oil changes again, and the transaction is settled at $95 per barrel. The cash paid by Burley to Slite on 12 December 20X9 is 10,000 × $95 = $950,000. This means that a **gain arises after the year-end** of $1,050,000 - $950,000 = $100,000. This gain will be **taken to profit or loss** in the **following accounting period**:

DEBIT	Slite – financial liability	$100,000	
CREDIT	Profit or loss		$100,000

The gain arising is an **event after the reporting period.** These are defined by IAS 10 *Events after the reporting period* as events, both favourable and unfavourable, that occur between the end of the reporting period and the date that the financial statements are authorised for issue.

The question arises of whether this is an **adjusting or non-adjusting** event. An adjusting event is an event after the reporting period that provides further evidence of conditions that existed at the end of the reporting period. A non-adjusting event is an event after the reporting period that is indicative of a **condition that arose after the end of the reporting period.** The price of oil changes frequently in response to a number of factors, reflecting events that arose after the year end. It would therefore not be appropriate to adjust the financial statements in response to the decline in the price of oil. The gain is therefore a **non-adjusting** event after the reporting period.

Inventory

IAS 2 *Inventories* requires that inventories should be stated at the **lower of cost and net realisable value.** Net realisable value (NRV) is the estimated selling price in the ordinary course of business less the estimated cost of completion and the estimated costs of making the sale.

In estimating NRV, entities must use reliable evidence of the **market price** available at the time. Such evidence includes any movements in price that reflect conditions at the year end, including prices recorded after the year end to the extent that they confirm these conditions. In the case of Burley, the appropriate market price to use is that recorded at the year end, namely **$105 per barrel**, since the decline to $95 results from conditions arising after the year end. Selling costs are $2 per barrel, so the amount to be used for NRV in valuing the inventory is $105 – $2 = $103 per barrel.

Net realisable value, in this instance, is higher than cost, which was $98 per barrel. The inventory should be stated at the lower of the two, that is at $98 per barrel, giving a total inventory value of $98 × 5,000 = $490,000. No loss is recorded as no write-down to NRV has been made.

(b) **Arrangement with Jorge**

Burley wishes to account for its arrangement with Jorge using the equity method. It can only do so if the arrangement meets the criteria in IFRS 11 *Joint arrangements* for a **joint venture.**

A **joint arrangement** is an arrangement, as here, of which two or more parties have joint control. A **joint venture** is a joint arrangement whereby the parties that have control of the arrangement have **rights to the net assets** of the arrangement.

Wells is a **separate vehicle**. As such, it could be either a joint operation or joint venture, so other facts must be considered.

There are no facts that suggest that Burley and Jorge have rights to substantially all the benefits of the assets of Wells nor an obligation for its liabilities.

Each party's liability is limited to any unpaid capital contribution.

As a result, each party has an interest in the **net assets** of Wells and should account for it as a **joint venture** using the **equity method.**

Decommissioning costs

Decommissioning costs are not payable until some future date, therefore the **amount of costs** that will be incurred is generally **uncertain**. IAS 16 *Property, plant and equipment* requires that management should record **its best estimate** of the entity's obligations. Since the cash flows are delayed, **discounting is used.** The estimate of the amount payable is discounted to the date of initial recognition and the discounted amount is capitalised. A corresponding credit is recorded in provisions. Changes in the liability and resulting from changes in the discount rate adjust the cost of the related asset in the current period.

The decommissioning costs of Wells are accounted for as follows:

	$m
Cost ten years ago	240.0
Depreciation: 240 ×10/40	(60.0)
Decrease in decommissioning costs: 32.6 – 18.5	(14.1)
Carrying value at 1 December 20X8	165.9
Less depreciation: 165.9 ÷ 30 years	(5.5)
Carrying amount at 30 November 20X9	160.4

The provision as restated at 1 December 20X8 would be increased at 30 November 20X9 by the unwinding of the discount of the new rate of 7%.

	$m
Decommissioning liability: 32.6 – 14.1	18.5
Finance costs: 18.5 × 7%	1.3
Decommissioning liability at 30 November 20X9	19.8

Pipeline

Since Burley has joint control over the pipeline, even though its interest is only 10%, it would not be appropriate to show the pipeline as an investment. This is a **joint arrangement** under IFRS 11.

The pipeline is a **jointly controlled asset,** and it is **not structured through a separate vehicle.** Accordingly, the arrangement is a **joint operation.**

IFRS 11 *Joint arrangements* requires that a joint operator **recognises line-by-line the following** in relation to its interest in a joint operation:

(i) Its **assets**, including its share of any jointly held assets
(ii) Its **liabilities**, including its share of any jointly incurred liabilities
(iii) Its **revenue** from the sale of its share of the output arising from the joint operation
(iv) Its **share of the revenue from the sale of the output** by the joint operation, and
(v) Its **expenses**, including its share of any expenses incurred jointly.

This treatment is applicable in both the separate and consolidated financial statements of the joint operator.

(c) **Intangible asset**

The relevant standard here is IAS 38 *Intangible assets.* An intangible asset may be recognised if it meets the **identifiability criteria** in IAS 38, if it is probable that **future economic benefits** attributable to the asset will flow to the entity and if its **fair value can be measured reliably.** For an intangible asset to be identifiable, the asset must be separable, or it must arise from contractual or other legal rights.

It appears that these **criteria have been met.** The licence has been acquired separately, and its value can be measured reliably at the purchase price.

Burley does not yet know if the extraction of oil is commercially viable, and does not know for sure whether oil will be discovered in the region. If, on further exploration, some or all activities must be discontinued, then the licence must be **tested for impairment** following IAS 36 *Impairment of assets.* (IAS 36 has a number of impairment indicators, both internal and external.)

It is possible that the licence may **increase in value** if commercial viability is proven. However, IAS 38 does not allow revaluation unless there is an **active market** for the asset.

21 Holmes & Deakin

(a) HOLMES
STATEMENT OF PROFIT OR LOSS AND OTHER COMPREHENSIVE INCOME
FOR THE YEAR ENDED 31 MAY 20X3

	$'000
Profit before gain on disposal of shares in subsidiary	130
Gain on disposal of shares in subsidiary (W5)	100
Profit before tax	230
Income tax expense (40 + (W5) 30)	(70)
PROFIT FOR THE YEAR	160
Other comprehensive income, net of tax	20
TOTAL COMPREHENSIVE INCOME FOR THE YEAR	180

Statement of changes in equity (Total)	$m
Balance at 1 June 20X2 (810 – 110)	700
Total comprehensive income for the year	180
Balance at 31 May 20X3	880

(b) HOLMES GROUP
CONSOLIDATED STATEMENT OF PROFIT OR LOSS AND OTHER COMPREHENSIVE INCOME FOR THE YEAR ENDED 31 MAY 20X3

	$m
Profit before tax (130 + 60)	190
Income tax expense (40 + 20)	(60)
PROFIT/ FOR THE YEAR	130
Other comprehensive income, net of tax (20 + 10)	30
TOTAL COMPREHENSIVE INCOME FOR THE YEAR	160
Profit attributable to:	
Owners of the parent	122
Non-controlling interests $[(40 \times \frac{9}{12} \times 15\%) + (40 \times \frac{3}{12} \times 35\%)]$	8
	130
Total comprehensive income attributable to:	
Owners of the parent	150
Non-controlling interests $[(50 \times \frac{9}{12} \times 15\%) + (50 \times \frac{3}{12} \times 35\%)]$	10
	160

(c) HOLMES GROUP
CONSOLIDATED STATEMENT OF FINANCIAL POSITION AS AT 31 MAY 20X3

	$m
Non-current assets	
Property, plant and equipment (535 + 178)	713
Goodwill (W2)	80
	793
Current assets	
Inventories (320 + 190)	510
Trade receivables (250 + 175)	425
Cash (80 + 89)	169
	1,104
	1,897

Equity attributable to owners of the parent	
Share capital $1 ordinary shares	500
Reserves (W3)	477.5
	977.5
Non-controlling interests (W4)	157.5
	1,135.0
Current liabilities	
Trade payables (295 + 171)	466
Income tax payable (80 + 60 + (W5) 30)	170
Provisions (95 + 31)	126
	762
	1,897

(d) STATEMENT OF CHANGES IN EQUITY (TOTAL COLUMN)

	Group	*NCI*	*Total*
	$m	$m	$m
Balance at 1 June 20X2 (500 + (W7) 285)/ (45 + ((W7) 100 × 15%))	785	60	845
Adjustment to parent's equity on sale of non-controlling interests ((W6) 72.5 – (W5) 30)	42.5		42.5
Increase in non-controlling interests ((W6) 71.5 + 16)		87.5	87.5
Total comprehensive income for the year	150	10	160.0
Balance at 31 May 20X3 (from SOFP)	977.5	157.5	1,135.0

Shown for clarity (not required) (refers to the NCI and Total columns)

Workings

1 *Timeline*

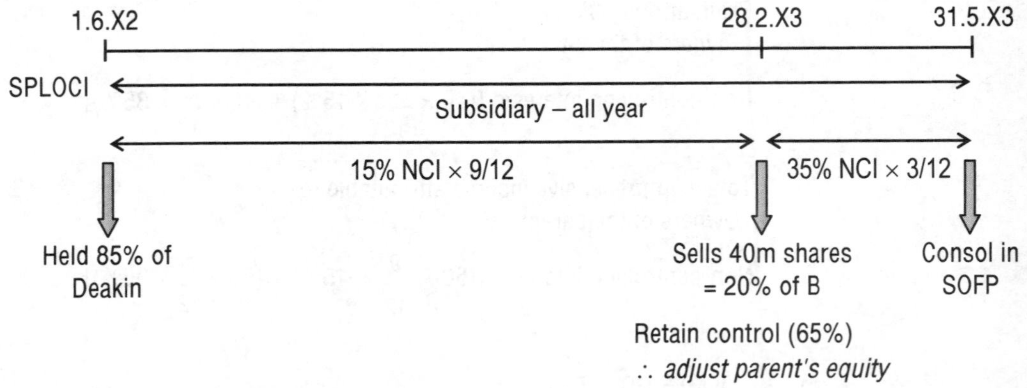

2 *Goodwill*

	$m	$m
Consideration transferred		255
Non-controlling interests (at fair value)		45
Fair value of identifiable net assets at acquisition:		
Share capital	200	
Pre-acquisition reserves	20	
		(220)
		80

3 *Group reserves at 31 May 20X3*

	Holmes	Deakin 85%	Deakin 65% ret'd
	$m	$m	$m
Per question/at date of disposal (170 – (50 × $\frac{3}{12}$))	310	157.5	170
Adjustment to parent's equity on disposal (W6)	72.5		
Tax on parent's gain (W5)	(30)*		
Reserves at acquisition (W2)/date of disposal (as above)		(20)	(157.5)
		137.5	12.5
Group share of post acquisition reserves:			
Deakin – 85% (137.5 × 85%)	116.9		
Deakin – 65% (12.5 × 65%)	8.1		
	477.5		

* Tax recognised directly in reserves in the consolidated financial statements as the item it relates to is recognised in reserves (matching concept and IAS 12 para 61A(b)).

4 *Non-controlling interests (SOFP)*

	$m
NCI at acquisition (W2)	45
NCI share of post acquisition reserves:	
Deakin (137.5 × 15%)	20.6
	65.6
Deakin (12.5 × 35%)	4.4
Increase in NCI (W6)	87.5
	157.5

5 *Gain on disposal of shares in parent's separate financial statements*

	$m
Fair value of consideration received	160
Less original cost of shares (255 × 20%/85%)	(60)
Parent gain	100
Less tax on parent's gain (30%)	(30)
	70

6 *Adjustment to parent's equity on disposal of shares in group financial statements*

	$m
Fair value of consideration received	160.0
Increase in NCI in net assets and goodwill at disposal ((W4) 65.6 × 20%/15%)	(87.5)
	72.5

OR (as a double entry):

	$m	$m
DEBIT Cash	160	
CREDIT Non-controlling interests ((W4) 65.6 × 20%/15%)		87.5
CREDIT Parent's equity (balancing figure)		72.5

7 *Reserves brought forward*

	Holmes	Deakin
	$m	$m
Per question (31.5.X3)	310	170
Less comprehensive income for the year	(110)	(50)
Reserves at acquisition		(20)
		100
Group share of post acquisition reserves:		
Deakin (100 × 85%)	85	
	285	

22 Ghorse

Text reference. Group re-organisations are covered in Chapter 14; deferred tax in Chapter 6; impairment in Chapter 3 and leases in Chapter 8.

Top tips. This is a 'mixed bag' question, dealing with a group re-organisation, deferred tax and revaluation, impairment and re-classification of a lease. These are all linked in with a calculation of the effect on return on capital employed. In Part (a) there is no need to spend time giving the IFRS 5 criteria for classification as held for sale, since we are told in the question that these criteria have been met.

Easy marks. None of this question is easy except for the calculation of ROCE; however, because it split equally across four topics, it is a good question to do. Do the parts you feel sure about, but have a go at all parts as the first few marks are the easiest to pick up.

Examiner's comments. Part (a) of the question was not well answered as many candidates did not realise that there was a disposal group as the two manufacturing units were being sold in a single transaction. Part (b) was quite well answered although many did not realise that the resultant balance was a deferred tax asset with the recognition issues that this represents. In Part (c), many candidates calculated the 'value in use' of the equipment but failed to apply the principles which often had correctly been described earlier in the answer. The answers to Part (d) were quite good but several candidates then could not outline the accounting treatment of a lease. The adjustments to ROCE were poorly done; in fact many candidates did not even attempt this part of the question. The issues required a degree of thought and understanding of the impact on the financial statements of the adjustments and ROCE. For example there were instances (deferred tax) where profit before tax was not affected but the capital employed was affected. The professional marks were awarded for analysing the impact of the information, drawing conclusions and considering the implications for ROCE.

Marking scheme

		Marks
(a)	Discontinuance	7
(b)	Deferred tax asset	6
(c)	Impairment	6
(d)	Lease	4
	Formation of opinion of impact on ROCE	2
	Maximum	25

(a) The criteria in IFRS 5 *Non-current assets held for sale and discontinued operations* have been met for Cee and Gee. As the assets are to be disposed of in a single transaction, Cee and Gee together are deemed to be a **disposal group** under IFRS 5.

The disposal group as a whole is **measured on the basis required for non-current assets held for sale**. Any impairment loss reduces the carrying amount of the non-current assets in the disposal group, the loss being allocated in the order required by IAS 36 *Impairment of assets.* Before the manufacturing units are classified as held for sale, impairment is tested for on an individual cash generating unit basis. Once classified as held for sale, the impairment testing is done on a **disposal group basis.**

A disposal group that is held for sale should be measured at the **lower of** its **carrying amount** and **fair value less costs to sell**. Immediately before classification of a disposal group as held for sale, the entity must recognise impairment in accordance with applicable IFRS. Any impairment loss is generally recognised in profit or loss, but if the asset has been measured at a revalued amount under IAS 16 *Property, plant and equipment* or IAS 38 *Intangible assets,* the impairment will be treated as a revaluation decrease. **Once** the disposal group has been **classified as held for sale**, any **impairment loss** will be based on the **difference between the adjusted carrying amounts and the fair value less cost to sell**. The impairment loss (if any) will be **recognised in profit or loss**.

A **subsequent increase** in fair value less costs to sell may be **recognised** in profit or loss **only to the extent of any impairment previously recognised**. To summarise:

Step 1 Calculate carrying value under the individual standard, here given as $105m.

Step 2 Classified as held for sale. Compare the carrying amount ($105m) with fair value less costs to sell ($125m). Measure at the lower of carrying value and fair value less costs to sell, here $105m.

Step 3 Determine fair value less costs to sell at the year-end (see below) and compare with carrying value of $105m.

Ghorse has not taken account of the increase in fair value less cost to sell, but only part of this increase can be recognised, calculated as follows.

	$m
Fair value less costs to sell: Cee	40
Fair value less costs to sell: Gee	95
	135
Carrying value	(105)
Increase	30

Impairment previously recognised in Cee: $15m ($50m – $35m)

Step 4 The change in fair value less cost to sell is recognised but the gain recognised cannot exceed any impairment losses to date. Here the gain recognised is $50m – $35m = $15m

Therefore **carrying value can increase** by $15m to $120m as loss reversals are limited to impairment losses previously recognised (under IFRS 5 or IAS 36).

These adjustments **will affect ROCE**.

(b) IAS 12 *Income taxes* requires that deferred tax liabilities must be recognised for all taxable temporary differences. Deferred tax assets should be recognised for deductible temporary differences but only to the extent that taxable profits will be available against which the deductible temporary differences may be utilised.

The differences between the carrying amounts and the tax base represent temporary differences. These **temporary differences are revised** in the light of the revaluation for tax purposes to market value permitted by the government.

Deferred tax liability before revaluation

	Carrying amount	*Tax base*	*Temporary difference*
	$m	$m	$m
Property	50	48	2
Vehicles	30	28	2
			4
Other temporary differences			5
			9

Provision: 30% × $9m = $2.7m

Deferred tax asset after revaluation

	Carrying amount	*Tax base*	*Temporary difference*
	$m	$m	$m
Property	50	65	15
Vehicles	30	35	5
Other temporary differences			(5)
			15

Deferred tax asset: $15m × 30% = $4.5m

This will have a **considerable impact on ROCE**. While the release of the provision of $2.7m and the creation of the asset of $4.5m will not affect the numerator, profit before interest and tax (although it will affect profit or loss for the year), it will **significantly affect the capital employed figure**.

(c) IAS 36 *Impairment of assets* requires that no asset should be carried at more than its recoverable amount. At each reporting date, Ghorse must **review all assets for indications of impairment,** that is indications that the carrying value may be higher than the recoverable amount. Such indications include fall in the market value of an asset or adverse changes in the technological, economic or legal environment of the business. (IAS 36 has an extensive list of criteria.) If **impairment is indicated**, then the asset's **recoverable amount** must be calculated. The manufacturer has reduced the selling price, but this does not automatically mean that the asset is impaired.

The **recoverable amount** is defined as the **higher of the asset's fair value less disposal of disposal and its value in use.** If the recoverable amount is less than the carrying amount, then the resulting impairment loss should be charged to profit or loss as an expense.

Value in use is the discounted present value of estimated future cash flows expected to arise from the continuing use of an asset and from its disposal at the end of its useful life. The value in use of the equipment is calculated as follows:

Year ended 31 October	*Cash flows*	*Discounted (10%)*
	$m	$m
20X8	1.3	1.2
20X9	2.2	1.8
20Y0	2.3	1.7
Value in use		4.7

The fair value less disposal costs of the asset is estimated at $2m. The recoverable amount must be the value in use of $4.7m, as this is higher. **Since the recoverable amount is higher than the carrying value of $3m, the asset is not impaired.** Consequently there will be no effect on ROCE.

(d) The manufacturing property was held under an operating lease. IAS 17 *Leases* required that operating lease payments are charged to profit or loss over the term of the lease, generally on straight line basis.

The renegotiation of the lease means that its **terms have changed significantly**. In addition, **IFRS 16** now requires that **all leases of more than twelve months** (other than leases of low-value assets) must be **recognised in the statement of financial position.**

Since the IFRS 16 is now in force, it will be shown in the statement of financial position. The entity must measure the lease liability at **present value of the remaining lease payments ($(5 × 6.8137)m = $34.1m)**, ie at $34.1m. The entity must also **recognise a right-of-use asset of $34.1m.**

However, since both assets and liabilities would increase, this reclassification would **not affect ROCE.**

Recalculation of ROCE

	$m
Profit before interest and tax	30.0
Add increase in value of disposal group	15.0
	45.0
Capital employed	220.0
Add increase in value of disposal group	15.0
Add release of deferred tax provision and deferred tax asset: 4.5 + 2.7	7.2
	242.2

∴ ROCE is 45/242.2 = 13.6%

The directors were concerned that the above changes would adversely affect ROCE. In fact, the effect has been favourable, as **ROCE has risen from 13.6% to 18.6%,** so the **directors' fears were misplaced.**

23 Harvard

(a) HARVARD GROUP
CONSOLIDATED STATEMENT OF FINANCIAL POSITION AT 31 DECEMBER 20X5

	$'000
Non-current assets	
Property, plant and equipment (2,870 + (W2) 1,350)	4,220.0
Goodwill (W4)	183.3
	4,403.3
Current assets	
Inventories (1,990 + (W2) 2,310)	4,300.0
Trade receivables (1,630 + (W2) 1,270)	2,900.0
Cash at bank and in hand (240 + (W2) 560)	800.0
	8,000.0
	12,403.3
Equity attributable to owners of the parent	
Share capital ($1)	118.0
Retained reserves (W5)	3,017.0
	3,135.0
Non-controlling interests (W6)	1,108.3
	4,243.3
Non-current liabilities	
Loans	1,920
Current liabilities	
Trade payables (5,030 + (W2) 1,210)	6,240
	12,403.3

(b) CONSOLIDATED STATEMENT OF PROFIT OR LOSS AND OTHER COMPREHENSIVE INCOME FOR YEAR ENDED 31 DECEMBER 20X5

	$'000
Revenue (40,425 + (W3) 25,900)	66,325
Cost of sales (35,500 + (W3) 20,680)	(56,180)
Gross profit	10,145
Distribution and administrative expenses (4,400 + (W3) 1,560)	(5,960)
Profit before tax	4,185
Income tax expense (300 + (W3) 1,260)	(1,560)
PROFIT FOR THE YEAR	2,625
Other comprehensive income:	
Items that may be reclassified to profit or loss:	
Exchange differences on translating foreign operations (W7)	320.3
Other comprehensive income for the year	320.3
TOTAL COMPREHENSIVE INCOME FOR THE YEAR	2,945.3
Profit attributable to:	
Owners of the parent (2,625 – 600)	2,025
Non-controlling interests ((W3) 2,400 × 25%)	600
	2,625
Total comprehensive income attributable to:	
Owners of the parent (2,945.3 – 680.1)	2,265.2
Non-controlling interests [((W3) 2,400 + (W7) 320.3) × 25%]	680.1
	2,945.3

STATEMENT OF CHANGES IN EQUITY
FOR THE YEAR ENDED 31 DECEMBER 20X5 (EXTRACT)

	$'000 *Retained reserves*
Balance at 1 January 20X5 (W5)	1,451.8
Dividends	(700)
Total comprehensive income for the year (per SPLOCI)	2,265.2
Balance at 31 December 20X5 (W5)	3,017.0

Workings

1 *Group structure*

Harvard

31.12.X2 | 1,011 / 1,348 = 75%

Pre-acq'n ret'd reserves = PLN 2,876,000

Krakow

2 *Translation of Krakow – statement of financial position*

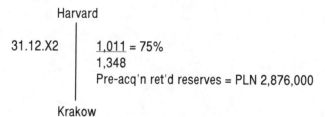

	PLN '000	Rate	$'000
Property, plant and equipment	4,860	3.6	1,350
Inventories	8,316	3.6	2,310
Trade receivables	4,572	3.6	1,270
Cash	2,016	3.6	560
	19,764		5,490

	PLN '000	Rate	$'000
Share capital	1,348	4.4	306.4
Retained reserves			
– pre-acquisition	2,876	4.4	653.6
– post-acquisition (14,060 – 2,876)	11,184	β	3,320
	15,408		4,280
Trade payables	4,356	3.6	1,210
	19,764		5,490

3 *Translation of Krakow – statement of profit or loss and other comprehensive income*

	PLN '000	Rate	$'000
Revenue	97,125	3.75	25,900
Cost of sales	(77,550)	3.75	(20,680)
Gross profit	19,575		5,220
Distribution and administrative expenses	(5,850)	3.75	(1,560)
Profit before tax	13,725		3,660
Income tax expense	(4,725)	3.75	(1,260)
Profit for the year	9,000		2,400

4 *Goodwill*

	PLN '000	PLN '000	Rate	$'000
Consideration transferred (840 × 4.4)		3,696		840
Non-controlling interests (at FV: 270 × 4.4)		1,188		270
Less share of net assets at acquisition:			4.4	
Share capital	1,348			
Retained reserves	2,876			
		(4,224)		(960)
Goodwill at acquisition		660		150
Exchange gain 20X3 – 20X4		–	ß	15
Goodwill at 31 December 20X4		660	4.0	165
Exchange gain 20X5		–	ß	18.3
Goodwill at year end		660	3.6	183.3

5 *Proof of retained reserves*

		$'000
(i)	At 31 December 20X5	
	Harvard	502
	Add group share of post-acquisition retained reserves of Krakow ((W2) 3,320 × 75%)	2,490
	Group share of impairment losses to date	(0)
	Group share of exchange differences on goodwill ((W4) 15 + 18.3) × 75%)	25.0
		3,017.0

		$'000
(ii)	At 31 December 20X4	
	Harvard (502 – (945 – 700))	257
	Add group share of post-acquisition retained reserves of Krakow * ((PLN15,408 – 9,000 + 3,744)/4) – (PLN (W2) (1,348 + 2,876)/4.4) × 75%)	1,183.5
	Group share of impairment losses to 31.12.X4	(0)
	Group share of exchange differences on goodwill ((W4) 15 × 75%)	11.3
		1,451.8

* **Note.** This is calculated by comparing the net assets at the two dates.

6 *Non-controlling interests*

	$'000
NCI at acquisition (W4)	270
Add NCI share of post-acquisition retained reserves of Krakow ((W2) 3,320 × 25%)	830
NCI share of impairment losses to date	(0)
NCI share of exchange differences on goodwill (((W4) 15 + 18.3) × 25%)	8.3
	1,108.3

7 *Exchange differences arising during the year*

	SPLOCI $'000
On translation of net assets of Krakow:	
Closing NA at CR (W2)	4,280
Opening NA @ OR [(15,408 – 9,000 + 3,744)/4.0]	(2,538)
	1,742
Less retained profit as translated ((W3) 2,400 – 3,744/3.90)	(1,440)
	302
On goodwill (W4)	18.3
	320.3

24 Porter

PORTER GROUP

STATEMENT OF CASH FLOWS FOR THE YEAR ENDED 31 MAY 20X6

	$'m	$'m
Cash flows from operating activities		
Profit before taxation	112	
Adjustments for:		
Depreciation	44	
Impairment losses on goodwill (W1)	3	
Foreign exchange loss (W7)	2	
Investment income – share of profit of associate	(12)	
Investment income – gains on financial assets at fair value through profit or loss	(6)	
Interest expense	16	
	159	
Increase in trade receivables (W4)	(4)	
Decrease in inventories (W4)	34	
Decrease in trade payables (W4)	(17)	
Cash generated from operations	172	
Interest paid (W5)	(12)	
Income taxes paid (W3)	(37)	
Net cash from operating activities		123
Cash flows from investing activities		
Acquisition of subsidiary, net of cash acquired (W6)	(18)	
Purchase of property, plant and equipment (W1)	(25)	
Purchase of financial assets (W1)	(10)	
Dividend received from associate (W1)	11	
Net cash used in investing activities		(42)

	$'m	$'m
Cash flows from financing activities		
Proceeds from issuance of share capital (W2)	18	
Proceeds from long-term borrowings (W3)	60	
Dividend paid	(45)	
Dividends paid to non-controlling interests (W2)	(4)	
Net cash from financing activities		29
Net increase in cash and cash equivalents		110
Cash and cash equivalents at the beginning of the year		48
Cash and cash equivalents at the end of the year		158

Workings

1 Assets

	Property, plant and equipment	*Goodwill*	*Associate*	*Financial asset*
	$m	$m	$m	$m
b/d	812	10	39	–
P/L			12	6
OCI	58		8	
Depreciation/ Impairment	(44)	(3) β		
Acquisition of sub/assoc	92	8 (W6)		
Additions on credit (W7)	15			
Cash paid/(rec'd) β	**25**	–	**(11)**	**10**
c/d	958	15	48	16

Note. The share of the associate's profit, recognised in the consolidated statement of profit or loss and other comprehensive income, is not a cash item so is added back on the face of the statement of cash flows in the section that calculates the cash generated from operations. The **dividend received** from the associate is the cash item and appears in the investing activities section.

2 *Equity*

	Share capital	*Share premium*	*Retained earnings*	*Non-controlling interest*
	$m	$m	$m	$m
b/d	300	172	165	28
TCI			68	12
Acquisition of subsidiary	24	30		48 (W6)
Cash (paid)/rec'd β	**8**	**10**	**(45)***	**(4)***
c/d	332	212	188	84

*80 × 60%/2 SC, 80 × 60%/2 × 1.25 SP

**Dividend paid is given in question but working shown for clarity.

3 *Liabilities*

	Loans	*Tax payable*
	$m	$m (22 + 26)
b/d	320	48
P/L		34
OCI		17
Acquisition of subsidiary		4
Cash (paid)/rec'd	**60**	**(37) β**
c/d	380	66 (28 + 38)

4 *Working capital changes*

	Inventories	*Receivables*	*Payables*
	$m	$m	$m
Balance b/d	168	112	98
PPE payable (W7)			17
Acquisition of subsidiary	20	16	12
	188	128	127
Increase/(decrease) (balancing figure)	**(34)**	**4**	**(17)**
Balance c/d	154	132	110

5 Interest paid

	$m
Balance b/d	4
Profit or loss	16
∴ **Interest paid β**	**(12)**
Balance c/d	8

6 Purchase of subsidiary

	$m
Cash received on acquisition of subsidiary	8
Less cash consideration	(26)
Cash outflow	18

Note. Only the **cash** consideration is included in the figure reported in the statement of cash flows. The **shares** issued as part of the consideration are reflected in the share capital working (W2) above.

Goodwill on acquisition (to calculate impairment):

	$m
Consideration: 26 + (80 × 60%/2 × 2.25)	80
Non-controlling interest: 120 × 40%	48
Net assets acquired	(120)
Goodwill	8

7 *Foreign currency transaction*

Transactions recorded on:			$m	$m
(1)	5 March	DEBIT Property, plant and equipment (102m/6.8)	15	
		CREDIT Payables		15
(2)	31 May	Payable = 102m/6.0 = $17m		
		DEBIT P/L (Admin expenses)	2	
		CREDIT Payables (17 – 15)		2

25 German competitor

Tutorial note. You do not need to know about German accounting practice to answer this question, just a basic knowledge of the differences between the European and UK models and your common sense! Think of this as an interpretation of accounts questions.

To: Managing Director
From: An Accountant
Date: xx.xx.xx
Re: *Hilde GmbH*

(a) *Analysis of performance plus commentary (€ million)*

Statement of profit or loss and other comprehensive income	*20X4*	*20X5*	*% Increase (decrease)*
Sales	1,270	1,890	49
Cost of sales			
Material purchased	400	740	
De-stocking of materials	40	90	
Material cost	440	830	89
Labour cost	285	500	75
Depreciation	150	200	33
Current assets written off	20	30	50
Other operating expenses	40	50	25
Finished goods inventory increase	(80)	(120)	50
	855	1,490	
Operating profit before other income	415	400	(4)
Profit rate on revenue	32%	21%	
Other operating income	50	75	50

Cash flows

	€ million
Share capital issued	200
Increased payables	75
Increased accruals	20
Profit ploughed back (185 + 200)	385
	680
These flows were used to finance:	
Purchases of plant (550 + 200)	750
Net inventory	30
More credit to customers	80
	860
Difference: reduction in cash reserves	180

Other relevant performance measures

	20X4	*20X5*
Receivables turnover $= \frac{\text{Trade receivables}}{\text{Sales}} \times 365$	$\frac{100}{1,270} \times 365$ = 29 days	$\frac{180}{1,890} \times 365$ = 35 days
Current ratio $= \frac{\text{Current assets}}{\text{Current liabilities}}$	$\frac{420 + 70}{350}$ = 1.4	$\frac{350 + 50}{425}$ = 0.94
Quick ratio $= \frac{\text{Current assets} - \text{Inventory}}{\text{Current liabilities}}$	$\frac{100 + 200 + 70}{350}$ = 1.06	$\frac{180 + 20 + 50}{425}$ = 0.59

Commentary

(i) Material costs and labour costs have risen at an alarming rate in 20X5 and to a certain extent other costs have also increased substantially. These increases are far greater than the increase in revenue. A lack of co-ordination of production to sales has created a substantial build up of finished goods in inventory.

(ii) Interest costs and other operating income have both increased substantially, but because debt and investments (respectively) are not shown on the statement of financial position it is not possible to judge why these rises have taken place. One possibility is that the increases in the value of land and buildings represent additions which are being rented out.

(iii) Payables have increased only slightly considering the increases in purchases during the year. This may indicate that the company's trade payables are taking a very firm line with the company and thus the trade payables balance is being held firm.

(iv) Although shares were issued during the year, at a premium of 100%, the fact that appropriations are not disclosed in the statement of profit or loss and other comprehensive income makes it very difficult to determine what type of dividend policy the company is following, and hence what kind of return shareholders have received over the two years.

(v) The length of credit period given to customers has increased (if all sales are on credit). While trading conditions may make this slip in credit control a necessity, it is regrettable that the company cannot obtain the same more relaxed terms from its suppliers; this would balance out working capital requirements, at least to some extent.

(vi) The inventory situation is what has changed most dramatically between 20X4 and 20X5. The rise in position statement inventories of € 30m may appear moderate, but it represents a rise of € 120m in finished goods and a fall of € 90 m in raw materials. It may be the case that the company is manufacturing less and buying in more finished goods, but the increase in labour costs would tend to negate this. It seems more likely that the company has greatly over-estimated the level of sales for 20X5, and has therefore ended 20X5 with an anomalous inventory position.

(vii) The cash levels held by the business, while perhaps on the high side at the beginning of the year, now appear far too low. The company is verging on an overdraft situation, in spite of receiving cash from a share issue during the year. The working capital situation, and in particular the inventory levels, must be resolved in order to recover the liquidity position of the business. If not, then there will be some difficulty in paying suppliers and taxes in the near future.

(b) A direct comparison of the results of Tone and Hilde GmbH may be misleading for the following reasons.

(i) It is unlikely that the two companies follow the same, or even similar, accounting policies, for example on inventory valuation, depreciation, valuation of land and buildings etc. Also, the general approach to receivables recoverability may be more or less prudent in the UK than under Tone's approach. These policies would have to be investigated to discover whether comparison is really feasible.

(ii) Hilde GmbH's payables are not split between short and long term, ie those due within one year and in more than one year (if any). Gearing ratios cannot be calculated, and the current and quick ratios calculated in (a) are of limited value.

(iii) There may be local or country-specific types of relationships between customers and suppliers which are different from the UK methods of doing business.

(iv) There is an interest charge shown in the statement of profit or loss and other comprehensive income but the statement of financial position shows no separate disclosure of loans. The explanation may be that an interest charge is payable on the share capital in place of dividends.

(v) A legal reserve is shown. There is no indication of what type of reserve this may be comparable with (if any) in UK financial statements.

(vi) The statement of profit or loss and other comprehensive income does not show a figure of gross profit making it difficult to compare margins.

(vii) The expenses include valuation adjustments for depreciation and current assets. It is not clear how these arise. They may simply comprise the normal depreciation charge and, say, a provision against doubtful receivables and obsolete inventory. It is true of many of the statement of profit or loss and other comprehensive income figures, that a lack of knowledge about how, say, 'cost of sales' is computed, prevents comparison with UK accounts.

26 Public sector organisations

(a) The principal reason for the differences stem from the different way in which the organisations receive their funding and how they are controlled.

In the private sector capital funds are generally provided by means of the issue of shares or by the owners. From the point of view of the company, accounts are necessary initially to report to the shareholders or owners. Since shareholders will be interested in comparing investment prospects of different companies it is necessary that accounts are prepared using standard accounting principles.

Private sector accounts are also used by potential lenders and creditors to determine the credit worthiness of companies so the accounts need to be prepared in such a way that this can be determined.

In the private sector, revenue income is derived from the customers but this does not result in any accounting obligation because customers are free to use other suppliers if the service provided is unsatisfactory.

In the public sector, the sources of funds both capital and revenue are ultimately from the public in the form of taxation, council tax and charges for services. These are controlled by central government and local authorities. Since there is no choice on behalf of the providers of these funds the function of the accounts is rather different to those of the private sector and more rigorously controlled.

(b) The main differences between laws, regulations and guidelines are as follows.

(i) **Laws.** In the private sector the accounts are governed by statute. These specify the items which must be included in the accounts and the general format. The purpose of the provisions in these Acts is to ensure the accounts give a 'true and fair' view of the financial position and performance of the company for the shareholders, lenders and creditors.

In the public sector there are separate laws for each service requiring them to produce accounts. Some of these services, such as health care, are funded by central government and in these cases the laws generally state simply that accounts must be prepared. The relevant government department is responsible for the format in which the accounts are to be prepared for the purpose of reporting to Government.

In the case of local authorities, funds come from central government in the form of the revenue support grant, from the local population in the form of local taxes and from the users of services in the form of charges. The laws relating to the accounts of local authorities require the accounts to be prepared in such a way as to account to each of these groups.

(ii) **Regulations.** Although the laws indicate the general way in which accounts are to be prepared, not all eventualities can be covered and there is much room for variation in the way particular financial transactions can be accounted for. As a consequence of this, International Financial Reporting Standards have been produced by the accounting profession specifying in more detail how items are to be treated in the accounts with a view to producing accounts which are more comparable and reliable.

However, these standards are written primarily with the private sector in mind and under certain circumstances the requirements of central government regarding the accounts in some public sector organisations will override these.

(iii) **Guidelines.** In the public sector the purpose of the accounts is to report to central government, local taxpayers and users of the services. As a consequence it is often necessary that the accounts be produced in a particular format to provide the necessary information, or to include details of particular aspects of the financial transactions. Consequently, Government has considerable powers under the law to issue detailed guidelines on how the accounts are to be prepared. An example of this is the Manual of Accounts produced by the Department of Health. This gives the precise format of the accounts together with great detail of accounting procedures to be adopted. In some cases these powers have been delegated to Standard Setting bodies, for example for local authority accounts.

(c) The consequences for the public accounts in the public sector is that, although the accounts are produced using generally the same principles as the private sector, their details are often quite different depending on the bodies to be reported to.

In central government departments, such as the Health Service, the accounts are produced fundamentally to account to Government for the funds voted to the Health Service. Consequently they are produced in an absolutely prescribed form so that they can be easily consolidated. The reporting to the general public on the use of funds is a secondary consideration as it is assumed that parliament are responsible for the use of the funds on behalf of the taxpayers.

In case of local government, the annual report which they are required to produce includes comparative statistics and information about the council's policies which are intended to inform the general public about the activities of the council. This is necessary because the council which is responsible for the expenditure is elected by the residents of the area.

(d) **Stock market quoted clothes retailer**

The main objective of a stock market quoted company will generally be to maximise profit, net assets and share price for the shareholders.

Individual companies may have slightly different objectives depending on who their shareholders are, for example maintaining a constant dividend payment if their main shareholders are looking for income.

Consequently, main objectives of management will be:

- Revenue maximisation (at the right price)
- Maintaining or increasing market share
- Product innovation to attract new customers and retain existing ones
- Cost minimisation, eg purchasing fabric at the best price for the quality required
- Profit maximisation and growth.

Public companies may also have secondary aims imposed by government or by their stakeholders, such as producing their goods ethically (eg paying decent wages where clothes are made in developing countries) or minimising the negative effects of their activities on the environment (the so called 'carbon footprint').

State-funded not-for-profit hospital

A state-funded hospital will presumably have a fixed income or grant from the government, or at least a budget that must be adhered to.

The primary objective of a hospital will therefore be to treat the maximum number of patients without exceeding the funds available.

This will require similar budgeting skills to a profit-oriented organisation to ensure that funds are used in the most efficient way, but a hospital will also have other social considerations:

- The need to prioritise treatment to those most in need
- To minimise waiting lists for treatment
- The need to set aside funds to cover an unexpected public health crisis.

The 'three Es' (Economy, Efficiency and Effectiveness) would be relevant objectives here, which would provide a good basis for assessment.

(e) (i) **Provisions.** Under full cash accounting, provisions are generally not recognised. When transitioning to accrual accounting, entities need to consider what particular organisational activities may give rise to provisions.

(ii) **Leases.** Currently many leases in the public sector are accounted for as operating leases. Under cash accounting the treatment is similar to the accruals accounting treatment of operating leases. If IFRS 16 is adopted in the public sector, more leases will appear on the statement of financial position.

27 Small and medium-sized entities

(a) **Advantages**

Although International Financial Reporting Standards (IFRSs) issued by the International Accounting Standards Board (IASB) were originally designed to be suitable for all types of entity, in recent years IFRSs have come increasingly complex. They are now designed primarily to meet the information needs of **institutional investors in large listed entities**.

Shareholders of SMEs are often also directors. Therefore, through managing the company and maintaining the financial records, they are already aware of the company's financial performance and position and so do not need the level of detail in financial statements required by external institutional investors of larger companies.

The main external **users of SMEs tend to be lenders, trade suppliers and the tax authorities**. They have **different needs** from institutional investors and are more likely to focus on shorter-term cash flows, liquidity and solvency.

Full IFRSs cover a wide range of issues, contain a sizeable amount of implementation guidance and include disclosure requirements appropriate for public companies. This can make them **too complex for users of SMEs to understand**.

Many SMEs feel that following full IFRSs places an unacceptable burden on preparers of SME accounts – a burden that has been growing as IFRSs become more detailed and more countries adopt them. The **cost of following full IFRSs often appears to outweigh the benefits**.

The **disclosure** requirements of full IFRSs are very **extensive** and as such, can result in **information overload** for the users of SME accounts, reducing the understandability of financial statements.

Some IFRSs still offer **choice of accounting treatments**, leading to **lack of comparability** between different companies adopting different accounting standards.

Disadvantages

If SMEs follow their own simplified IFRSs, their accounts are **no longer be comparable** with larger companies following full IFRSs or with SMEs choosing to follow full IFRSs. This may make it harder to attract investors.

The changeover from full IFRSs to the simplified *IFRS for SMEs*, will require training and possible changes in systems. This will place both a **time and cost** burden on the company.

Full IFRSs are now well established and respected and act as a form of **quality control** on financial statements which comply with them. It could be argued therefore that financial statements which no longer comply with full IFRSs will **lose their credibility**. This is often called the 'Big GAAP, Little GAAP divide'.

The *IFRS for SMEs* **reduce disclosures** required by full IFRSs substantially. Omission of certain key information might actually make the financial statements **harder to understand**.

Conclusion

The IASB believes that the advantages for SMEs of having a separate simplified set of IFRSs outweigh the disadvantages. They believe that both preparers and users of SME accounts will benefit.

(b) **Examples of full IFRSs with choice**

(i) Under IAS 40 *Investment property*, either the cost model or fair value model (through profit or loss) are permitted. The *IFRS for SMEs* requires the fair value model (through profit or loss) to be used as long as fair value can be measure without undue cost or effort. This promotes consistency in the treatment of investment properties between SMEs financial statements.

(ii) IAS 38 *Intangible assets* allows either the cost model or revaluation model (where there is an active market). The *IFRS for SMEs* does not permit the revaluation model to be used. This eliminates the use of other comprehensive income, simplifying financial reporting and the need for costly revaluations.

(iii) IFRS 3 *Business combinations* allows an entity to adopt the full or partial goodwill method in its consolidated financial statements. The *IFRS for SMEs* only allows the partial goodwill method, ie excluding non-controlling interests in goodwill. This avoids the need for SMEs to determine the fair value of the non-controlling interests not purchased when undertaking a business combination.

The *IFRS for SMEs* does not eliminate choice completely but disallows the third of the above options. It is one of the rare uses of other comprehensive income under the *IFRS for SMEs*.

Examples of IFRSs with complex recognition and measurement requirements

(iv) IAS 38 *Intangible assets* requires internally generated assets to be capitalised if certain criteria (proving future economic benefits) are met. In reality, it is an onerous exercise to test these criteria for each type of internally generated asset and leads to inconsistency with some items being expensed and some capitalised.

The *IFRS for SMEs* removes these capitalisation criteria and requires all internally generated research and development expenditure to be expensed through profit or loss.

(v) IFRS 3 *Business combinations* requires goodwill to be tested annually for impairment. In reality, it is very difficult to ascertain the recoverable amount for goodwill so instead the assets of the business need to be combined into cash-generating units or even a group of cash-generating units in order to determine any impairment loss. The impairment then needs to be allocated to goodwill and the other individual assets. This is a complex exercise.

The *IFRS for SMEs* requires goodwill to be amortised instead. This is a much simpler approach and the *IFRS for SMEs* specifies that if an entity is unable to make a reliable estimate of the useful life, it is presumed to be ten years, simplifying things even further.

(vi) IAS 20 *Accounting for government grants and disclosure of government assistance* requires grants to be recognised only when it is reasonably certain that the entity will comply with the conditions attached to the grant and the grants will be received. Grants relating to income are recognised in profit or loss over the period the related costs are recognised in profit or loss. Grants relating to assets are either netted off the cost of the asset (reducing depreciation by the amount of the grant over the asset's useful life) or presented as deferred income (and released to profit or loss as income over the useful life of the asset).

The *IFRS for SMEs* simplifies this and specifies that where there are no specified future performance conditions, the grant should be recognised as income when it is receivable. Otherwise, it should be recognised as income when the performance conditions are met. This is more consistent with the IASB *Framework's* definition of income than the IAS 20 approach.

(vii) IAS 23 *Borrowing costs* requires borrowing costs to be capitalised for qualifying assets for the period of construction. This involves a complex calculation particularly where funds are borrowed generally as a weighted average rate on loans outstanding has to be calculated in order to determine the amount of interest to be capitalised.

The *IFRS for SMEs* requires borrowing costs to be expensed, removing the need for such a complex calculation.

(viii) IAS 36 *Impairment of assets* requires annual impairment tests for indefinite life intangibles, intangibles not yet available for use and goodwill. This is a complex, time-consuming and expensive test.

The *IFRS for SMEs* only requires impairment tests where there are indicators of impairment.

The full IFRS requires impairment losses to be charged firstly to other comprehensive income for revalued assets then to profit or loss. The *IFRS for SMEs* requires all impairment losses to be recognised in profit or loss, given that tangible and intangible assets cannot be revalued under the *IFRS for SMEs*.

28 Peter Holdings

Divisional performance should be measured, in the interests of the group's shareholders, in such a way as to indicate what sort of return each subsidiary is making on the **shareholder's investment**. Shareholders themselves are likely to be interested in the performance of the group as a whole, measured in terms of return on shareholders' capital, earnings per share, dividend yield, and growth in earnings and dividends. These performance ratios cannot be used for subsidiaries in the group, and so an alternative measure has to be selected, which compares the return from the subsidiary with the value of the investment in the subsidiary.

Two performance measures could be used. Both would provide a suitable indication of performance from the point of view of the group's shareholders.

(a) Return on capital employed, which from the shareholders' point of view would be:

$$\frac{\text{Profit after interest}}{\text{Net assets at current valuation minus non-current liabilities (eg long-term borrowings)}}$$

(b) Alternatively, residual income could be used. This might be:

	Profit after debt interest
Minus	A notional interest charge on the value of assets financed by shareholders' capital
Equals	Residual income.

Residual income might be measured instead as:

	Profit before interest (controllable by the subsidiary's management)
Minus	A notional interest charge on the controllable investments of the subsidiary
Equals	Residual income.

Each subsidiary would be able to increase its residual income if it earned an incremental profit in excess of the notional interest charges on its incremental investments – ie in effect, if it added to the value of the group's equity.

29 Planet

Top tip. A typical multi-standard question, requiring advice to a client.

(a) (i) **Additional purchase consideration**

The company should **recognise a liability of $16 million and additional goodwill of $16 million**. Although IFRS 3 *Business combinations* sets a time limit for recognition of fair value adjustments this applies only to the acquired assets and liabilities. There is **no time limit** for the recognition of **goodwill relating to contingent consideration**.

The accounting entries required are:

		$'000	$'000
DEBIT	Intangible assets (goodwill)	16,000	
CREDIT	Current liabilities		16,000

(ii) **Buildings**

In each case the main issue is whether Planet should recognise a provision for future repair and refurbishment expenditure.

Lease

IAS 37 *Provisions, contingent liabilities and contingent assets* states that a provision should only be recognised if there is **a present obligation resulting from a past event.** The terms of the lease contract mean that Planet has an obligation to incur expenditure in order to return the buildings to the lessee in good condition. The past obligating event appears to be the signing of the lease.

However, **future repairs and maintenance costs** relate to the future operation of the business. They are **not present obligations** resulting from past events. If IAS 37 is interpreted strictly, no provision should be recognised. The repair costs should either be charged as operating expenses in the period in which they occur or capitalised as assets.

Despite this, there is a strong case for recognising a provision for at least some of the expenditure. A lessee may be required to incur periodic charges to **make good dilapidations** or other damage occurring during the rental period. These liabilities **may be recognised, provided that the event giving rise to the obligation** under the lease **has occurred**. Damage to the building has occurred because of the severe weather and therefore a provision should be recognised for the $2.4 million needed to rectify this damage.

Whether any further amounts should be provided depends on the event that gives rise to the present obligation. It is possible to argue that the obligating event is the occurrence of specific damage to the building, but the cost of repairing actual dilapidation to the building during the year would be **difficult to estimate accurately**. It could also be argued that the obligating event is the passage of time, because some expenditure would be necessary if the lease were terminated immediately. Therefore a further $1,600,000 should be provided ($12 million less $2.4 million divided by six). The total provision is $4 million.

The accounting entries required are:

		$'000	$'000
DEBIT	Retained earnings	4,000	
CREDIT	Provisions		4,000

Leasehold property

In this case the company has a present obligation to incur expenditure as a result of a past event (the creation of the swimming pool). Under IAS 37 **a provision should be recognised for the full restoration cost** of $4 million. It is not possible to build up the provision over ten years as the directors propose.

Because the swimming pool represents access to future economic benefits, the future cost also represents an **asset** and this **should be recognised**. The asset will be depreciated at 10% per annum.

The carrying value of the leased building is $19.6 million ($16 million + $4 million – $400,000). This is above the recoverable amount of $19 million and therefore an impairment loss of $600,000 should be recognised.

The accounting entries required are:

		$'000	$'000
DEBIT	Non-current assets	4,000	
CREDIT	Provisions		4,000
DEBIT	Retained earnings (group retained profits)	320	
DEBIT	Non-controlling interest	80	
CREDIT	Depreciation (4,000 × 10%)		400
DEBIT	Retained earnings (group retained profits)	480	
DEBIT	Non-controlling interest	120	
CREDIT	Non-current assets		600

Owned buildings

Future repair expenditure does **not** represent a **present obligation** of the company because there has been **no past obligating event**. The repairs relate to the future operations of the company and in theory the expenditure **could be avoided** by selling the buildings. Under IAS 37 no provision can be recognised.

Any loss in service potential of the asset should be reflected in the depreciation charge. If the repairs are necessary to restore the service potential of the asset the expenditure should be capitalised.

(iii) **Agreement with subsidiary**

This has several implications for the financial statements. Because two thirds of the inventory remains unsold, the **unrealised intra-group profit** of \$400,000 (2/3 × 4.2 million krona ÷ 1.4 × 20%) **must be eliminated.**

The accounting entries required are:

		\$'000	\$'000
DEBIT	Retained earnings (group retained profit)	400	
CREDIT	Inventory		400

In addition, because Planet is a listed company it must comply with the requirements of IAS 32 *Financial instruments: disclosure and presentation* and IFRS 9 *Financial instruments.* The **forward contract is a derivative financial instrument**. By entering into the contract the company has fixed the price of the inventory and has avoided the effect of changes in the exchange rate. **No exchange gain or loss is recognised** on the transaction. The company is required to **disclose its accounting policy** in respect of hedge accounting, which is to translate its foreign currency assets and liabilities at the forward rate at the date of delivery. It is also required to disclose certain information about the contract, including details of any gains and losses carried forward in the statement of financial position at the year end and the extent to which these are expected to be recognised in the profit or loss in the next accounting period.

Because Planet entered into the contract without incurring any costs, the **book value** and the **fair value** of the forward contract were nil at its inception date. The cost of the inventory to the company was \$3 million (4.2 million ÷ 1.4) but by 31 March 20X0 (the settlement date), exchange rates had moved so that the company would only have paid \$2,896,552 for the inventory at the spot rate of 1.45. Therefore the company has made a **loss** of \$103,448. **One third** of this (\$34,482) relates to the **inventory sold** and has effectively been **recognised in the profit or loss for the year**. The **remainder** (\$68,966) is **carried forward in the value of inventory** and will be recognised in the profit or loss in the next accounting period. There is an argument for **reducing this figure by 20%** as this is the amount of the intra-company profit which is eliminated on consolidation. The amount of the loss to be disclosed is therefore \$55,173.

(iv) **Database**

The issue here is whether the cost of developing the database can be capitalised as an intangible asset. IAS 38 *Intangible assets* **prohibits the recognition** of internally generated brands, mastheads, publishing titles, customer lists and items similar in substance as assets. It could be argued that the database is similar to these items.

However, the expenditure has resulted in a new product which is now generating income for the group. IAS 38 **permits the capitalisation of development costs**, provided that the project meets **certain criteria**. The company must be able to demonstrate the technical feasibility of completing the asset, and the intention and ability to complete the asset and to use or sell it. The company must also be able to demonstrate that the asset will generate probable future economic benefits and that adequate technical, financial and other resources are available to complete the development. It must be possible to measure the expenditure attributable to the asset reliably.

Although the cost of the database is \$6 million, sales of the manual are only expected to generate net revenue of \$4 million. Therefore \$4 million is **the amount of the future economic benefits that will flow to the company** and this is the amount that should be recognised as an intangible asset. Because the manual will require substantial revision every four years the development costs should be **amortised over this period**.

The accounting entries required are:

		$'000	$'000
DEBIT	Retained earnings	1,600	
DEBIT	Non-controlling interest	400	
CREDIT	Intangible assets (6,000 – 4,000)		2,000
To write down the development costs to $4,000			

		$'000	$'000
DEBIT	Retained earnings	800	
DEBIT	Non-controlling interest	200	
CREDIT	Intangible assets		1,000
To amortise the asset over four years (4,000 ÷ 4)			

(b) PLANET

REVISED GROUP STATEMENT OF FINANCIAL POSITION AT 30 NOVEMBER 20X2

	$'000
Non-current assets	
Property, plant and equipment (76,240 + 4,000 – 600 – 400)	79,240
Intangible assets (10,360 + 16,000 – 2,000 – 1,000)	23,360
	102,600
Net current assets (55,800 – 16,000 – 400)	39,400
Total assets less current liabilities	142,000
Equity attributable to owners of the parent	
Share capital	32,200
Share premium	10,000
Retained earnings (W)	47,200
	89,400
Non-controlling interest (18,200 – 80 – 120 – 400 – 200)	17,400
	106,800
Non-current liabilities:	
Long term borrowings	25,400
Provisions (1,800 + 4,000 + 4,000)	9,800
	142,000

Working: retained earnings

	$'000
Draft	54,800
Provision for repairs (lease)	(4,000)
Additional depreciation (leased property)	(320)
Impairment loss (leased property)	(480)
Unrealised profit (intra-company sales)	(400)
Impairment loss (database)	(1,600)
Amortisation of development expenditure (database)	(800)
	47,200

30 Jay

Top tips. In this question, candidates had to account for the step-by-step acquisition, inter-company sales, an associate, and an impairment test. Additionally, there were some revenue recognition issues to be dealt with. Part (b) deals with foreign currency transactions. Part (c), on corporate citizenship, is the kind of question you can expect to find regularly as part of question 1.

Marking scheme

		Marks
(a)	Property, plant and equipment	4
	Goodwill	5
	Associate	4
	Investment	1
	Current assets	1
	Share capital	1
	Revaluation surplus	2
	Retained earnings	7
	Non-controlling interest	6
	Non-current liabilities	4
	Current liabilities	
(b)	Inventory, goods sold	8
(c)	Corporate citizenship:	
	Corporate governance	2
	Ethics	2
	Employee reports	2
	Environment	1
	Maximum	50

(a) JAY GROUP
CONSOLIDATED STATEMENT OF FINANCIAL POSITION AT 31 MAY 20X5

	$m
Assets	
Property, plant and equipment (W9) 300 + 40 + 14 + (5 – 0.1) – 5.7 (W9)	353.2
Goodwill (W2)	10.0
Investment in associate (W3)	13.0
Investment (10 – 0.5) (W6)	9.5
Current assets (120 – 6) (W7)	114.0
	499.7
Equity and liabilities	
Share capital	100.0
Share premium	50.0
Revaluation surplus (W8)	15.0
Retained earnings (W4)	136.7
	301.7
Non-controlling interest (W5)	14.0
	315.7
Non-current liabilities	64.0
Current liabilities	120.0
	499.7

Workings

1 *Group structure*

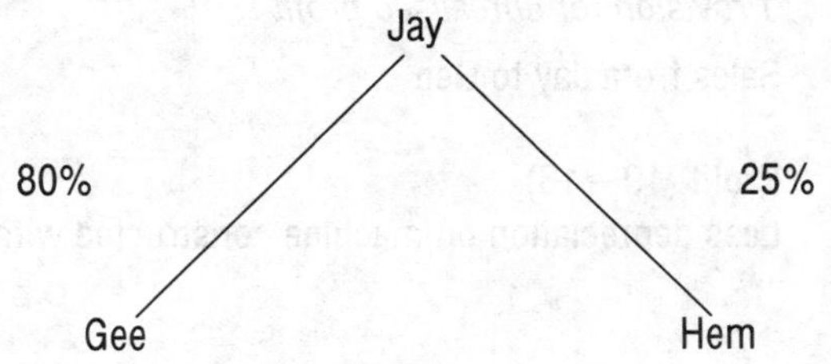

2 *Goodwill: Gee (on acquiring control)*

	$m
Consideration transferred	30
Non-controlling interests	12
Fair value of previously held equity interest ($30m consideration transferred × 30%/50%)	18
Fair value of identifiable net assets at acq'n	(50)
	10

3 *Investment in associate*

	$m
Cost of investment	12
Share of profit for year ended 31 May 20X5 (W5)	1
	13

4 *Retained earnings*

	Jay	*Gee*	*Hem*
	$m	$m	$m
Per question	139.00	16	10
PUP on machinery (W6)	(5.70)		
PUP on investment (associate) (W6)	(0.5)		
Impairment loss on receivable	(1.10)		
Pre-acquisition (NA excl FV adjustments, SC and SP):			
50 – 14 – 10 – 20		(6)	
32 – 6 – 6 – 14			(6)
		10	4
Group share			
Gee: 80% × 10	8.0		
Hem: 25% × 4	1		
Less fair value gain recognised in Jay's separate FS since Gee has been a sub *:	(4.0)		
	136.7		

* Fair value gain in Jay's separate FS since Gee has been a sub (from 1 June 20X4)	$m
Fair value of 80% at 31 May 20X5	52
Less fair value of 50% at 1 June 20X4	(30)
Less fair value of 30% at 1 June 20X4 (30 × 30%/50%)	(18)
Fair value gain since 1 June 20X4	4

Tutorial note. There is no gain or loss on derecognition of the 30% financial asset at 1 June 20X4 because the financial asset is already stated at fair value.

5 *Non-controlling interests*

	$m
NCI at acquisition (date of control ie1 June 20X4)	12
NCI share of post-acquisition retained earnings ((W4) 10 × 20%)	2
	14

6 *Provision for unrealised profit*

Sales from Jay to Gee

	$m
Profit (19 – 13)	6.0
Less depreciation on machine constructed with goods: (6 × 10% × 6/12)	(0.3)
	5.7

Sale of investments from Hem to Jay

	$m
Group share of profit (25% × 2)	0.5

7 *Impairment of receivable*

	$m
Cost of machinery	8.0
Less deposit received	(2.0)
Bad debt written off	6.0
Less net book value of machine (included in tangible assets) (W9)	(4.9)
Impairment loss deducted from retained earnings	1.1

8 *Revaluation surplus*

	$m
Jay	15.00
Gee: at date control acquired (80% × 14 – 14)	0.00
	15.00

9 *Property, plant and equipment*

	$m	$m
Jay		300.0
Gee		40.0
Fair value adjustment (land)		14.0
Machine		
Cost	5.0	
Less depreciation (3/12 × 10% × 5)	(0.1)	
		4.9
Provision for unrealised profit (W6)		(5.7)
		353.2

Note that Jay has retained title to the machinery because the first instalment has not been paid.

(b) The initial transaction of the purchase of goods from the foreign supplier would be **recorded in the ledger accounts at $5 million (€8/1.6)**. Therefore both the purchase and the payables balance would be recorded at this amount. At the **year end** the payables balance is **restated to the closing rate** but the **inventories remain at $5 million**. Therefore the payable is restated to $6.2 million (€8m/1.3) and an **exchange loss** is taken to profit or loss of $1.2 million ($6.2 – 5m).

On the **sale**, the original transaction is recorded at $2.5 million (€4m/1.6) as both a sale and a receivable. When payment is made the amount actually received is $3.1 million (€4m/1.3) and an **exchange gain** is recognised in profit or loss of $0.6 million ($3.1 – 2.5m).

When the investment property was first purchased it should have been recognised in the statement of financial position at $20 million (€28m/1.4). At the year end the investment property has fallen in value to €24 million and the exchange rate has changed to 1.3. Therefore at 31 May 20X6 the property would be valued at $18.5 million (€24m/1.3).

The **fall in value** of $1.5 million ($20 – 18.5m) is recognised in **profit or loss**. The loss is a mixture of a fall in value of the property and a gain due to the exchange rate movement. However, as the investment property is a **non-monetary asset the foreign currency element is not recognised separately**.

(c) **Nature of corporate citizenship**

Increasingly businesses are expected to be **socially responsible as well as profitable**. Strategic decisions by businesses, particularly global businesses nearly always have wider social consequences. It could be argued, as Henry Mintzburg does, that a company produces two outputs: goods and services, and the social consequences of its activities, such as pollution.

One major development in the area of corporate citizenship is the **environmental report.** While this is not a legal requirement, a large number of major companies produce them. Worldwide there are around 20 award schemes for environmental reporting, notably the ACCA's.

Jay might be advised to adopt the guidelines on sustainability given in the **Global Reporting Initiative**. These guidelines cover a number of areas (economic, environmental and social). The GRI specifies key performance indicators for each area. For environmental reporting, the indicators are:

(i) Energy
(ii) Water
(iii) Biodiversity
(iv) Emissions
(v) Energy and waste
(vi) Products and services
(vii) Compliance
(viii) Transport

Another environmental issue which the company could consider is **emission levels** from factories. Many companies now include details of this in their environmental report.

The other main aspect of corporate citizenship where Jay scores highly is in its **treatment of its workforce.** The company sees the workforce as the key factor in the growth of its business. The car industry had a reputation in the past for **restrictive practices,** and the annual report could usefully discuss the extent to which these have been eliminated.

Employees of a businesses are **stakeholders** in that business, along with shareholders and customers. A company wishing to demonstrate good corporate citizenship will therefore be concerned with **employee welfare**. Accordingly, the annual report might usefully contain information on details of working hours, industrial accidents and sickness of employees.

In conclusion, it can be seen that the annual report can, and should go **far beyond the financial statements** and traditional ratio analysis.

Mathematical tables

Present value table

Present value of £1 = $(1+r)^{-n}$ where r = interest rate, n = number of periods until payment or receipt.

Periods (n)	Discount rates (r) 1%	2%	3%	4%	5%	6%	7%	8%	9%	10%
1	0.990	0.980	0.971	0.962	0.952	0.943	0.935	0.926	0.917	0.909
2	0.980	0.961	0.943	0.925	0.907	0.890	0.873	0.857	0.842	0.826
3	0.971	0.942	0.915	0.889	0.864	0.840	0.816	0.794	0.772	0.751
4	0.961	0.924	0.888	0.855	0.823	0.792	0.763	0.735	0.708	0.683
5	0.951	0.906	0.863	0.822	0.784	0.747	0.713	0.681	0.650	0.621
6	0.942	0.888	0.837	0.790	0.746	0.705	0.666	0.630	0.596	0.564
7	0.933	0.871	0.813	0.760	0.711	0.665	0.623	0.583	0.547	0.513
8	0.923	0.853	0.789	0.731	0.677	0.627	0.582	0.540	0.502	0.467
9	0.914	0.837	0.766	0.703	0.645	0.592	0.544	0.500	0.460	0.424
10	0.905	0.820	0.744	0.676	0.614	0.558	0.508	0.463	0.422	0.386
11	0.896	0.804	0.722	0.650	0.585	0.527	0.475	0.429	0.388	0.350
12	0.887	0.788	0.701	0.625	0.557	0.497	0.444	0.397	0.356	0.319
13	0.879	0.773	0.681	0.601	0.530	0.469	0.415	0.368	0.326	0.290
14	0.870	0.758	0.661	0.577	0.505	0.442	0.388	0.340	0.299	0.263
15	0.861	0.743	0.642	0.555	0.481	0.417	0.362	0.315	0.275	0.239
16	0.853	0.728	0.623	0.534	0.458	0.394	0.339	0.292	0.252	0.218
17	0.844	0.714	0.605	0.513	0.436	0.371	0.317	0.270	0.231	0.198
18	0.836	0.700	0.587	0.494	0.416	0.350	0.296	0.250	0.212	0.180
19	0.828	0.686	0.570	0.475	0.396	0.331	0.277	0.232	0.194	0.164
20	0.820	0.673	0.554	0.456	0.377	0.312	0.258	0.215	0.178	0.149

Periods (n)	Discount rates (r) 11%	12%	13%	14%	15%	16%	17%	18%	19%	20%
1	0.901	0.893	0.885	0.877	0.870	0.862	0.855	0.847	0.840	0.833
2	0.812	0.797	0.783	0.769	0.756	0.743	0.731	0.718	0.706	0.694
3	0.731	0.712	0.693	0.675	0.658	0.641	0.624	0.609	0.593	0.579
4	0.659	0.636	0.613	0.592	0.572	0.552	0.534	0.516	0.499	0.482
5	0.593	0.567	0.543	0.519	0.497	0.476	0.456	0.437	0.419	0.402
6	0.535	0.507	0.480	0.456	0.432	0.410	0.390	0.370	0.352	0.335
7	0.482	0.452	0.425	0.400	0.376	0.354	0.333	0.314	0.296	0.279
8	0.434	0.404	0.376	0.351	0.327	0.305	0.285	0.266	0.249	0.233
9	0.391	0.361	0.333	0.308	0.284	0.263	0.243	0.225	0.209	0.194
10	0.352	0.322	0.295	0.270	0.247	0.227	0.208	0.191	0.176	0.162
11	0.317	0.287	0.261	0.237	0.215	0.195	0.178	0.162	0.148	0.135
12	0.286	0.257	0.231	0.208	0.187	0.168	0.152	0.137	0.124	0.112
13	0.258	0.229	0.204	0.182	0.163	0.145	0.130	0.116	0.104	0.093
14	0.232	0.205	0.181	0.160	0.141	0.125	0.111	0.099	0.088	0.078
15	0.209	0.183	0.160	0.140	0.123	0.108	0.095	0.084	0.074	0.065
16	0.188	0.163	0.141	0.123	0.107	0.093	0.081	0.071	0.062	0.054
17	0.170	0.146	0.125	0.108	0.093	0.080	0.069	0.060	0.052	0.045
18	0.153	0.130	0.111	0.095	0.081	0.069	0.059	0.051	0.044	0.038
19	0.138	0.116	0.098	0.083	0.070	0.060	0.051	0.043	0.037	0.031
20	0.124	0.104	0.087	0.073	0.061	0.051	0.043	0.037	0.031	0.026

Cumulative present value table

This table shows the present value of £1 per annum, receivable or payable at the end of each year for *n* years.

Periods	Discount rates (r)									
(n)	1%	2%	3%	4%	5%	6%	7%	8%	9%	10%
1	0.990	0.980	0.971	0.962	0.952	0.943	0.935	0.926	0.917	0.909
2	1.970	1.942	1.913	1.886	1.859	1.833	1.808	1.783	1.759	1.736
3	2.941	2.884	2.829	2.775	2.723	2.673	2.624	2.577	2.531	2.487
4	3.902	3.808	3.717	3.630	3.546	3.465	3.387	3.312	3.240	3.170
5	4.853	4.713	4.580	4.452	4.329	4.212	4.100	3.993	3.890	3.791
6	5.795	5.601	5.417	5.242	5.076	4.917	4.767	4.623	4.486	4.355
7	6.728	6.472	6.230	6.002	5.786	5.582	5.389	5.206	5.033	4.868
8	7.652	7.325	7.020	6.733	6.463	6.210	5.971	5.747	5.535	5.335
9	8.566	8.162	7.786	7.435	7.108	6.802	6.515	6.247	5.995	5.759
10	9.471	8.983	8.530	8.111	7.722	7.360	7.024	6.710	6.418	6.145
11	10.37	9.787	9.253	8.760	8.306	7.887	7.499	7.139	6.805	6.495
12	11.26	10.58	9.954	9.385	8.863	8.384	7.943	7.536	7.161	6.814
13	12.13	11.35	10.63	9.986	9.394	8.853	8.358	7.904	7.487	7.103
14	13.00	12.11	11.30	10.56	9.899	9.295	8.745	8.244	7.786	7.367
15	13.87	12.85	11.94	11.12	10.38	9.712	9.108	8.559	8.061	7.606
16	14.718	13.578	12.561	11.652	10.838	10.106	9.447	8.851	8.313	7.824
17	15.562	14.292	13.166	12.166	11.274	10.477	9.763	9.122	8.544	8.022
18	16.398	14.992	13.754	12.659	11.690	10.828	10.059	9.372	8.756	8.201
19	17.226	15.678	14.324	13.134	12.085	11.158	10.336	9.604	8.950	8.365
20	18.046	16.351	14.877	13.590	12.462	11.470	10.594	9.818	9.129	8.514

Periods	Discount rates (r)									
(n)	11%	12%	13%	14%	15%	16%	17%	18%	19%	20%
1	0.901	0.893	0.885	0.877	0.870	0.862	0.855	0.847	0.840	0.833
2	1.713	1.690	1.668	1.647	1.626	1.605	1.585	1.566	1.547	1.528
3	2.444	2.402	2.361	2.322	2.283	2.246	2.210	2.174	2.140	2.106
4	3.102	3.037	2.974	2.914	2.855	2.798	2.743	2.690	2.639	2.589
5	3.696	3.605	3.517	3.433	3.352	3.274	3.199	3.127	3.058	2.991
6	4.231	4.111	3.998	3.889	3.784	3.685	3.589	3.498	3.410	3.326
7	4.712	4.564	4.423	4.288	4.160	4.039	3.922	3.812	3.706	3.605
8	5.146	4.968	4.799	4.639	4.487	4.344	4.207	4.078	3.954	3.837
9	5.537	5.328	5.132	4.946	4.772	4.607	4.451	4.303	4.163	4.031
10	5.889	5.650	5.426	5.216	5.019	4.833	4.659	4.494	4.339	4.192
11	6.207	5.938	5.687	5.453	5.234	5.029	4.836	4.656	4.486	4.327
12	6.492	6.194	5.918	5.660	5.421	5.197	4.988	4.793	4.611	4.439
13	6.750	6.424	6.122	5.842	5.583	5.342	5.118	4.910	4.715	4.533
14	6.982	6.628	6.302	6.002	5.724	5.468	5.229	5.008	4.802	4.611
15	7.191	6.811	6.462	6.142	5.847	5.575	5.324	5.092	4.876	4.675
16	7.379	6.974	6.604	6.265	5.954	5.668	5.405	5.162	4.938	4.730
17	7.549	7.120	6.729	6.373	6.047	5.749	5.475	5.222	4.990	4.775
18	7.702	7.250	6.840	6.467	6.128	5.818	5.534	5.273	5.033	4.812
19	7.839	7.366	6.938	6.550	6.198	5.877	5.584	5.316	5.070	4.843
20	7.963	7.469	7.025	6.623	6.259	5.929	5.628	5.353	5.101	4.870

Index

Note: **Key Terms** and their page references are given in **bold**.

Bibliography

Bibliography

ACCA (2012). ACCA Annual Report, 2011-12. Available from: http://www.accaglobal.com/content/dam/acca/global/pdf-agm/ar2011-12.pdf [Accessed on 24 November 2016].

Accounting Standards Board (1999) *Statement of Principles for Financial Reporting,* [Online] Available from: https://www.frc.org.uk/Our-Work/Publications/ASB/Statement-Statement-of-Principles-for-Financial-Re.pdf [Accessed on 14 November 2016].

Association of Chartered Certified Accountants(2016) ACCA Code of Ethics and Conduct. [Online] London, AAT. Available from: http://www.accaglobal.com/ubcs/en/member/professional-standards/ethics/code-ethics-conduct.html [Accessed 14 November 2016].

BT (2004) Social and Environmental Report (2004). British Telecommunications plc. Available from http://aeca.es/old/comisiones/rsc/biblioteca_memorias_rsc/informes_empresas_extranjeras_2/bt_2004_report.pdf [Accessed on 24 November 2016].

Deloitte (2008) Business Combinations and Changes in Ownership interests (2008). Available from: http://www.iasplus.com/en-gb/publications/global/guides/pub2690/at_download/file/ [Accessed on 22 November 2016].

CERES (1989). The CERES Principles (1989). Available from: https://www.ceres.org/about-us/our-history/ceres-principles [Accessed on 24 November 2016].

ESMA (2015). ESMA Guidelines on Alternative Performance Measures (2015). Available from: https://www.esma.europa.eu/press-news/esma-news/esma-publishes-final-guidelines-alternative-performance-measures [Accessed on 28 November 2016].

FASB (1985) Statement of Financial Accounting Concepts No. 6 [Online] Available from: www.fasb.org/resources/ccurl/792/293/CON6.pdf [Accessed on 14 November 2016].

Gray, R (1993) *Accounting for the Environment* , Gray, R., Bebbington, J., Walters, D. Markus Wiener Publishers

GRI (2011). Sustainability Reporting Guidelines, Global Reporting Initiative (2011).). Available from https://www.globalreporting.org/resourcelibrary/G3.1-Guidelines-Incl-Technical-Protocol.pdf [Accessed on 24 November 2016].

IASB (2016). International Accounting Standards Board. Work Plan as at 18 November 2016. Available from: http://eifrs.ifrs.org [Accessed 22 November 2016]. Available from: http://www.ifrs.org/current-projects/iasb-projects/pages/iasb-work-plan.aspx [Accessed 28 November 2016].

IFAC (2014). Conceptual Framework for General Purpose Financial Reporting by Public Sector Entities, International Federation of Accountants (2014). Available from: https://www.ifac.org/publications-resources/conceptual-framework-general-purpose-financial-reporting-public-sector-enti-8 [Accessed 28 November 2016].

IIRC (2013). Integrated Reporting <IE>Framework (2013). Available from:

http://www.iasplus.com/en-gb/publications/global/guides/pub2690/at_download/file/ [Accessed on 24 November 2016].

International Accounting Standards Board. (2010) Conceptual Framework for Financial Reporting. In International Financial Reporting Standards (2010). Available from: http://eifrs.ifrs.org [Accessed 22 November 2016].

International Accounting Standards Board. (1989) Framework for the Preparation and Presentation of Financial Statements. In International Financial Reporting Standards (1989). Available from: http://eifrs.ifrs.org [Accessed 22 November 2016].

International Accounting Standards Board. (2007) IAS 1 Presentation of financial statements. In International Financial Reporting Standards (2007). Available from: http://eifrs.ifrs.org [Accessed 22 November 2016]. Available from: http://eifrs.ifrs.org [Accessed 22 November 2016].

International Accounting Standards Board. (2003) IAS 2 Inventories. In International Financial Reporting Standards (2003). Available from: http://eifrs.ifrs.org [Accessed 22 November 2016].

International Accounting Standards Board. (1992) IAS 7 Statement of cash flows. In International Financial Reporting Standards (1992). Available from: http://eifrs.ifrs.org [Accessed 22 November 2016].

International Accounting Standards Board. (2005) IAS 8 Accounting policies, changes in accounting estimates and errors. In International Financial Reporting Standards (2005). Available from: http://eifrs.ifrs.org [Accessed 22 November 2016].

International Accounting Standards Board. (2003) IAS 10 Events after the reporting period. In International Financial Reporting Standards (2003). Available from: http://eifrs.ifrs.org [Accessed 22 November 2016].

International Accounting Standards Board. (1996) IAS 12 Income taxes. In International Financial Reporting Standards (1996). Available from: http://eifrs.ifrs.org [Accessed 22 November 2016].

International Accounting Standards Board. (1996) IAS 16 Property, plant and equipment. In International Financial Reporting Standards (1996). Available from: http://eifrs.ifrs.org [Accessed 22 November 2016].

International Accounting Standards Board. (2003) IAS 17 Leases. In International Financial Reporting Standards (2003). Available from: http://eifrs.ifrs.org [Accessed 22 November 2016].

International Accounting Standards Board. (1995) IAS 18 Revenue. In International Financial Reporting Standards (1995). Available from: http://eifrs.ifrs.org [Accessed 22 November 2016].

International Accounting Standards Board. (2011) IAS 19 Employee benefits. In International Financial Reporting Standards (2011). Available from: http://eifrs.ifrs.org [Accessed 22 November 2016].

International Accounting Standards Board. (1995) IAS 20 Accounting for government grants and disclosure of government assistance. In International Financial Reporting Standards (1995). Available from: http://eifrs.ifrs.org [Accessed 22 November 2016]. Available from: http://eifrs.ifrs.org [Accessed 22 November 2016].

International Accounting Standards Board. (2003) IAS 21 The effects of changes in foreign exchange rates. In International Financial Reporting Standards (2003). Available from: http://eifrs.ifrs.org [Accessed 22 November 2016].

International Accounting Standards Board. (1993) IAS 23 Borrowing costs. In International Financial Reporting Standards (2003). Available from: http://eifrs.ifrs.org [Accessed 22 November 2016].

International Accounting Standards Board. (2003) IAS 24 Related party disclosures. In International Financial Reporting Standards (2003).

International Accounting Standards Board. (2003) IAS 24 Related party disclosures. In International Financial Reporting Standards (2003). Available from: http://eifrs.ifrs.org [Accessed 22 November 2016].

International Accounting Standards Board. (2003) IAS 27 Separate financial statements. In International Financial Reporting Standards (2014). Available from: http://eifrs.ifrs.org [Accessed 22 November 2016].

International Accounting Standards Board. (2011) IAS 28 Investments in associates and joint ventures. In International Financial Reporting Standards (2011). Available from: http://eifrs.ifrs.org [Accessed 22 November 2016].

International Accounting Standards Board. (2003) IAS 32 Financial instruments: presentation. In International Financial Reporting Standards (2003). Available from: http://eifrs.ifrs.org [Accessed 22 November 2016].

International Accounting Standards Board. (2003) IAS 33 Earnings per share. In International Financial Reporting Standards (2003). Available from: http://eifrs.ifrs.org [Accessed 22 November 2016].

International Accounting Standards Board. (1998) IAS 34 Interim financial reporting. In International Financial Reporting Standards (1998). Available from: http://eifrs.ifrs.org [Accessed 22 November 2016].

International Accounting Standards Board. (2004) IAS 36 Impairment of assets. In International Financial Reporting Standards (2004). Available from: http://eifrs.ifrs.org [Accessed 22 November 2016].

International Accounting Standards Board. (1998) IAS 37 Provisions, contingent liabilities and contingent assets. In International Financial Reporting Standards (1998). Available from: http://eifrs.ifrs.org [Accessed 22 November 2016]. Available from: http://eifrs.ifrs.org [Accessed 22 November 2016].

International Accounting Standards Board. (1998) IAS 38 Intangible assets. In International Financial Reporting Standards (1998). Available from: http://eifrs.ifrs.org [Accessed 22 November 2016].

International Accounting Standards Board. (2009) IAS 39 Financial instruments: recognition and measurement. In International Financial Reporting Standards (2009). Available from: http://eifrs.ifrs.org [Accessed 22 November 2016].

International Accounting Standards Board. (2003) IAS 40 Investment property. In International Financial Reporting Standards (2003). Available from: http://eifrs.ifrs.org [Accessed 22 November 2016].

International Accounting Standards Board. (2001) IAS 41 Agriculture. In International Financial Reporting Standards (2001). Available from: http://eifrs.ifrs.org [Accessed 22 November 2016].

International Accounting Standards Board. (2003) IFRS 1 First-time adoption of International Financial Reporting Standards (2003). Available from: http://eifrs.ifrs.org [Accessed 22 November 2016].

International Accounting Standards Board. (2004) IFRS 2 Share-based payment. In International Financial Reporting Standards (2004). Available from: http://eifrs.ifrs.org [Accessed 22 November 2016].

International Accounting Standards Board. (2008) IFRS 3 Business combinations. In International Financial Reporting Standards (2008). Available from: http://eifrs.ifrs.org [Accessed 22 November 2016].

International Accounting Standards Board. (2004) IFRS 5 Non-current assets held for sale and discontinued operations. In International Financial Reporting Standards (2004). Available from: http://eifrs.ifrs.org [Accessed 22 November 2016]. Available from: http://eifrs.ifrs.org [Accessed 22 November 2016].

International Accounting Standards Board. (2005) IFRS 7 Financial instruments: disclosures. In International Financial Reporting Standards (2005). Available from: http://eifrs.ifrs.org [Accessed 22 November 2016].

International Accounting Standards Board. (2006) IFRS 8 Operating segments. In International Financial Reporting Standards (2006). Available from: http://eifrs.ifrs.org [Accessed 22 November 2016].

International Accounting Standards Board. (2014) IFRS 9 Financial instruments. In International Financial Reporting Standards (2014). Available from: http://eifrs.ifrs.org [Accessed 22 November 2016].

International Accounting Standards Board. (2011) IFRS 10 Consolidated financial statements. In International Financial Reporting Standards (2011). Available from: http://eifrs.ifrs.org [Accessed 22 November 2016].

International Accounting Standards Board. (2011) IFRS 11 Joint arrangements. In International Financial Reporting Standards (2011). Available from: http://eifrs.ifrs.org [Accessed 22 November 2016].

International Accounting Standards Board. (2011) IFRS 12 Disclosure of interests in other entities. In International Financial Reporting Standards (2011). Available from: http://eifrs.ifrs.org [Accessed 22 November 2016].

International Accounting Standards Board. (2011) IFRS 13 Fair value measurement. In International Financial Reporting Standards (2011). Available from: http://eifrs.ifrs.org [Accessed 22 November 2016].

International Accounting Standards Board. (2014) IFRS 15 Revenue from contracts with customers. In International Financial Reporting Standards (2014). Available from: http://eifrs.ifrs.org [Accessed 22 November 2016].

International Accounting Standards Board. (2016) IFRS 16 Leases. In International Financial Reporting Standards (2016). Available from: http://eifrs.ifrs.org [Accessed 22 November 2016].

International Accounting Standards Board. (2015) Available from: http://eifrs.ifrs.org [Accessed 22 November 2016]. IFRS for Small and Medium-sized Entities. In International Financial Reporting Standards (2015).

International Accounting Standards Board. (2010) Practice Statement: Management Commentary. In International Financial Reporting Standards (2010). Available from: http://eifrs.ifrs.org [Accessed 22 November 2016].

International Accounting Standards Board. (2014) Exposure Draft: ED Equity method: share of other net asset changes. In International Financial Reporting Standards (2012). Available from: http://eifrs.ifrs.org [Accessed 28 November 2016].

International Accounting Standards Board. (2014) Exposure Draft: Measuring quoted investments in subsidiaries, joint ventures and associates at fair value. In International Financial Reporting Standards (2014). Available from: http://eifrs.ifrs.org [Accessed 22 November 2016].

International Accounting Standards Board. (2015) Exposure Draft: Classification of liabilities – proposed amendments to IAS 1. In International Financial Reporting Standards (2015). Available from: http://eifrs.ifrs.org [Accessed 22 November 2016].

International Accounting Standards Board. (2015) Exposure Draft: Conceptual Framework for Financial Reporting. In International Financial Reporting Standards (2015).

International Accounting Standards Board. (2015) IFRS Practice Statement: Application of Materiality in Financial Statements (2015). Available from: http://eifrs.ifrs.org [Accessed 22 November 2016].

EYGM (2014) IASB and FASB issue new revenue recognition standard — IFRS 15, [Online] Available from: http://www.ey.com/Publication/vwLUAssets/EY-Devel80-Revenue-May2014/%24FILE/EY-Devel80-Revenue-May2014.pdf [Accessed on 14 November 2016].

EYGM (2015) Applying IFRS: IASB issues the Conceptual Framework exposure draft, [Online] Available from:
http://www.ey.com/Publication/vwLUAssets/Applying_IFRS:_IASB_issues_the_Conceptual_Framework_exposure_draft./%24File/Applying-Framework-June2015.pdf [Accessed on 14 November 2016].

Hampden-Turner, C. (1990) *Corporate Culture.* London, Economist Books.

Mintzberg, H. (1983) *Power in and around Organisations.* New Jersey, Prentice Hall.

PriceWaterhouseCoopers (2009) Similarities and differences A comparison of 'full IFRS' and IFRS for SMEs (2009). Available from: https://www.pwc.no/no/ifrs/publikasjoner/similarities-and-differences-a-comparison-of-ifrs-for-smes-and-full-ifrs.pdf [Accessed 29 November 2016].

Walton, C. (1977) *The Ethics of Corporate Conduct.* Oxford, Prentice-Hall, Inc.

Review Form – Paper P2 Corporate Reporting (International and UK) (01/17)

Please help us to ensure that the ACCA learning materials we produce remain as accurate and user-friendly as possible. We cannot promise to answer every submission we receive, but we do promise that it will be read and taken into account when we update this Study Text.

Name: ______________________ **Address:** ______________________

____

____

How have you used this Study Text?
(Tick one box only)

- ☐ On its own (book only)
- ☐ On a BPP in-centre course ______________
- ☐ On a BPP online course
- ☐ On a course with another college
- ☐ Other ______________

Why did you decide to purchase this Study Text? *(Tick one box only)*

- ☐ Have used BPP Study Texts in the past
- ☐ Recommendation by friend/colleague
- ☐ Recommendation by a lecturer at college
- ☐ Saw information on BPP website
- ☐ Saw advertising
- ☐ Other ______________

During the past six months do you recall seeing/receiving any of the following?
(Tick as many boxes as are relevant)

- ☐ Our advertisement in *ACCA Student Accountant*
- ☐ Our advertisement in *Pass*
- ☐ Our advertisement in *PQ*
- ☐ Our brochure with a letter through the post
- ☐ Our website www.bpp.com

Which (if any) aspects of our advertising do you find useful?
(Tick as many boxes as are relevant)

- ☐ Prices and publication dates of new editions
- ☐ Information on Study Text content
- ☐ Facility to order books off-the-page
- ☐ None of the above

Which BPP products have you used?

Study Text	☑	*Passcards*	☐	*Other*	☐
Kit	☐	*i-Pass*	☐		

Your ratings, comments and suggestions would be appreciated on the following areas.

	Very useful	*Useful*	*Not useful*
Introductory section	☐	☐	☐
Chapter introductions	☐	☐	☐
Key terms	☐	☐	☐
Quality of explanations	☐	☐	☐
Case studies and other examples	☐	☐	☐
Exam focus points	☐	☐	☐
Questions and answers in each chapter	☐	☐	☐
Fast forwards and chapter roundups	☐	☐	☐
Quick quizzes	☐	☐	☐
Question Bank	☐	☐	☐
Answer Bank	☐	☐	☐
Index	☐	☐	☐

Overall opinion of this Study Text *Excellent* ☐ *Good* ☐ *Adeqate* ☐ *Poor* ☐

Do you intend to continue using BPP products? *Yes* ☐ *No* ☐

On the reverse of this page is space for you to write your comments about our Study Text. We welcome your feedback.

The author of this edition can be emailed at: accaqueries@bpp.com

Please return this form to: Head of ACCA & FIA Programmes, BPP Learning Media Ltd, FREEPOST, London, W12 8AA

TELL US WHAT YOU THINK

Please note any further comments and suggestions/errors below. For example, was the text accurate, readable, concise, user-friendly and comprehensive?